ROME, CHINA, AND THE BARBARIANS

This book addresses a largely untouched historical problem: the fourth to fifth centuries AD witnessed remarkably similar patterns of foreign invasion, conquest, and political fragmentation in Rome and China. Yet while the Western Roman Empire was never reestablished, China was reunified at the end of the sixth century. Following a comparative discussion of earlier historiographical and ethnographic traditions in the classical Greco-Roman and Chinese worlds, the book turns to the late antique/early medieval period, when the Western Roman Empire "fell" and China was reconstituted as a united empire after centuries of foreign conquest and political division. Analyzing the discourse of ethnic identity in the historical texts of this later period, with original translations by the author, the book explores the extent to which notions of Self and Other, of "barbarian" and "civilized," help us understand both the transformation of the Roman world as well as the restoration of a unified imperial China.

RANDOLPH B. FORD currently teaches Roman history at the State University of New York at Albany. He has previously taught Roman history, Rome–China comparative history, and Latin language at the University of Notre Dame. He obtained his doctorate at New York University's Institute for the Study of the Ancient World, and his research has concentrated on comparative approaches to the study of the Greco-Roman world and ancient China.

ROME, CHINA, AND THE BARBARIANS

Ethnographic Traditions and the Transformation of Empires

RANDOLPH B. FORD

State University of New York, Albany

CAMBRIDGE
UNIVERSITY PRESS

CAMBRIDGE
UNIVERSITY PRESS

University Printing House, Cambridge CB2 8BS, United Kingdom

One Liberty Plaza, 20th Floor, New York, NY 10006, USA

477 Williamstown Road, Port Melbourne, VIC 3207, Australia

314–321, 3rd Floor, Plot 3, Splendor Forum, Jasola District Centre, New Delhi – 110025, India

79 Anson Road, #06–04/06, Singapore 079906

Cambridge University Press is part of the University of Cambridge.

It furthers the University's mission by disseminating knowledge in the pursuit of education, learning, and research at the highest international levels of excellence.

www.cambridge.org
Information on this title: www.cambridge.org/9781108473958
DOI: 10.1017/9781108564090

© Randolph B. Ford 2020

First published 2020

Printed in the United Kingdom by TJ International Ltd, Padstow Cornwall

A catalogue record for this publication is available from the British Library.

Library of Congress Cataloging-in-Publication Data
NAMES: Ford, Randolph B., 1976– author.
TITLE: Rome, China, and the barbarians : ethnographic traditions and the transformation of empires / Randolph B. Ford, State University of New York, Albany.
DESCRIPTION: Cambridge, United Kingdom ; New York : Cambridge University Press, [2020] | Includes bibliographical references and index.
IDENTIFIERS: LCCN 2019046110 (print) | LCCN 2019046111 (ebook) | ISBN 9781108473958 (hardback) | ISBN 9781108463010 (paperback) | ISBN 9781108564090 (epub)
SUBJECTS: LCSH: History, Ancient–Historiography. | Imperialism–History. | China–Ethnic relations–History–To 1500. | National characteristics, Chinese–History–To 1500. | China–History–221 B.C.–960 A.D. | Rome–History–Empire, 30 B.C.–476 A.D. | Rome–History–Germanic Invasions, 3rd-6th centuries. | Group identity–Rome–History. | National characteristics, Roman.
CLASSIFICATION: LCC D56 .F65 2020 (print) | LCC D56 (ebook) | DDC 931/.04–dc23
LC record available at https://lccn.loc.gov/2019046110
LC ebook record available at https://lccn.loc.gov/2019046111

ISBN 978-1-108-47395-8 Hardback

In loving memory of Mary Burch Tracy Ford

Contents

Maps

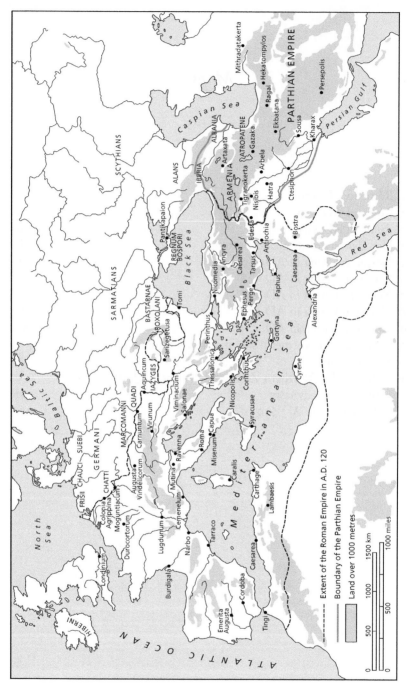

Map 1   Rome in AD 120

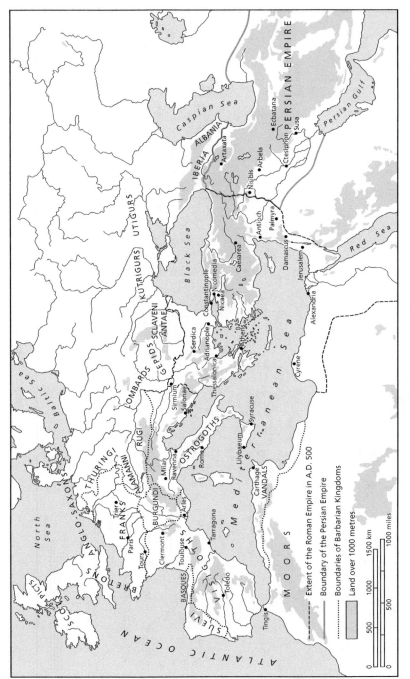

Map 2   Rome in AD 500

ATLANTIC OCEAN

North Sea

Baltic Sea

SCOTS

PICTS

BRETONS

ANGLO-SAXONS

THURINGI

FRANKS
Paris
Tours
Clermont
Trier
ALAMANNI
BURGUNDI
Arles
Toulouse
SUEVI
BASQUES
VISIGOTHS
Tarragona
Toledo
Tingis
MOORS

RUGI
Milan
Ravenna
LOMBARDS
GEPIDS
OSTROGOTHS
Rome
Sirmium
Salonae
SCLAVENI
ANTAE
Serdica
Lilybaeum
Syracuse
Carthage
VANDALS
Mediterranean Sea

KUTRIGURS
UTIGURS

Black Sea
Thessalonica
Adrianople
Constantinople
Nicaea
Nicomedia
Athens
Caesarea
Cyrene
Alexandria

Caspian Sea
IBERIA
ALBANIA
Artaxata
Nisibis
Arbela
Ecbatana
Susa
PERSIAN EMPIRE
Ctesiphon
Antioch
Palmyra
Damascus
Jerusalem
Red Sea
Persian Gulf

- - - Extent of the Roman Empire in A.D. 500
——— Boundary of the Persian Empire
········ Boundaries of Barbarian Kingdoms
       Land over 1000 metres

0   500   1000   1500 km
0   500   1000 miles

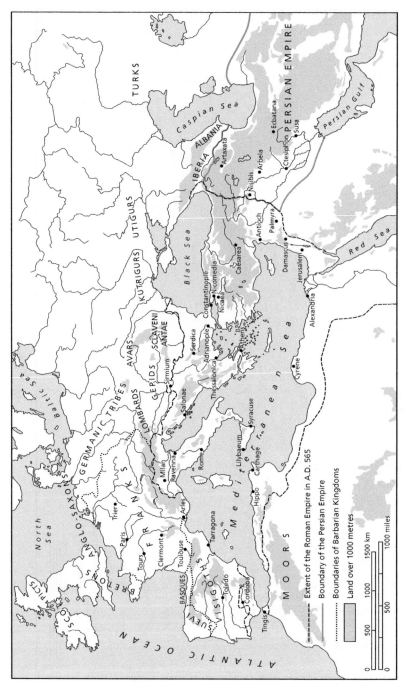

Map 3   Rome in AD 565

TURKS

UTIGURS

(KUTRIGURS)

AVARS

SCLAVENI
ANTAE

GEPIDS

LOMBARDS

GERMANIC TRIBES

ANGLO-SAXONS

BRETONS

FRANKS

SUEVI

VISIGOTHS

BASQUES

MOORS

SCOTS

PICTS

IBERIA

ALBANIA

PERSIAN EMPIRE

Caspian Sea

Black Sea

Mediterranean Sea

North Sea

Baltic Sea

ATLANTIC OCEAN

Red Sea

Persian Gulf

Artaxata
Ecbatana
Susa
Arbela
Ctesiphon
Nisibis
Antioch
Palmyra
Caesarea
Damascus
Jerusalem
Nicomedia
Constantinople
Nicaea
Alexandria
Serdica
Adrianople
Sirmium
Thessalonica
Cyrene
Salonae
Syracuse
Lilybaeum
Milan
Ravenna
Rome
Carthage
Hippo
Trier
Paris
Tours
Clermont
Toulouse
Arles
Tarragona
Toledo
Córdoba
Tingis

Extent of the Roman Empire in A.D. 565
Boundary of the Persian Empire
Boundaries of Barbarian Kingdoms
Land over 1000 metres

0   500   1000   1500 km
0   500   1000 miles

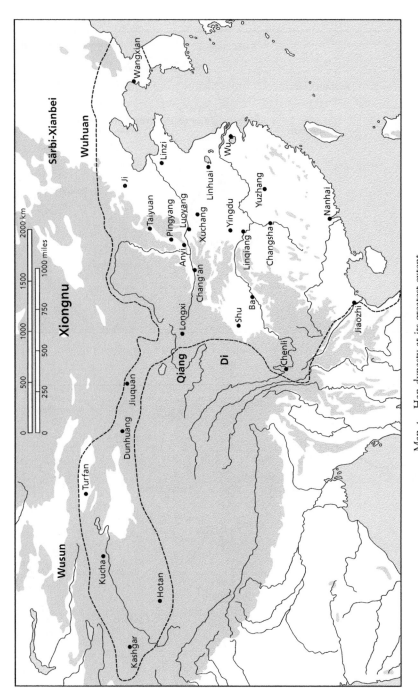

Map 4   Han dynasty at its greatest extent

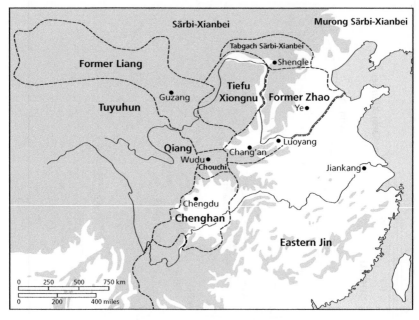

Map 5   Northern China in AD 317

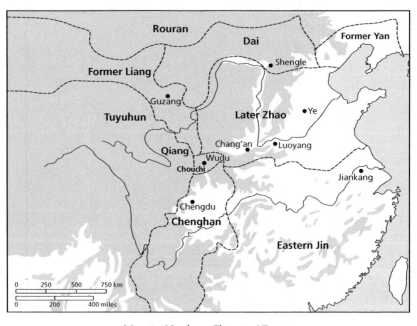

Map 6   Northern China in AD 338

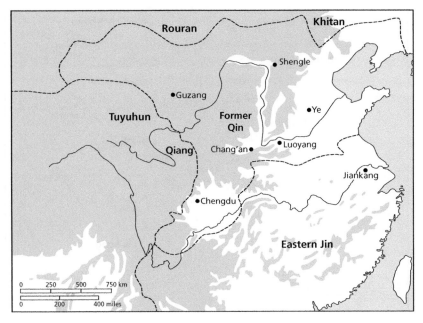

Map 7   Northern China in AD 376

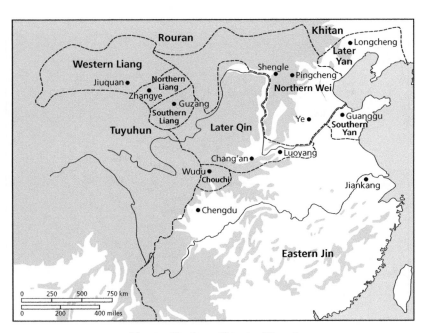

Map 8   Northern China in AD 406

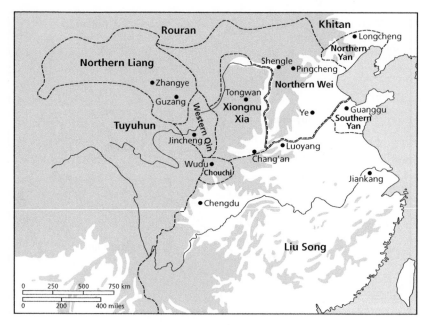

Map 9   Northern China in AD 423

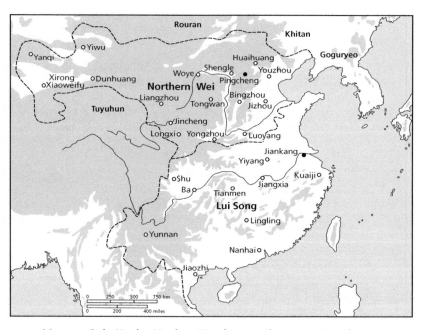

Map 10   Särbi-Xianbei Northern Wei dynasty; Chinese Liu Song dynasty

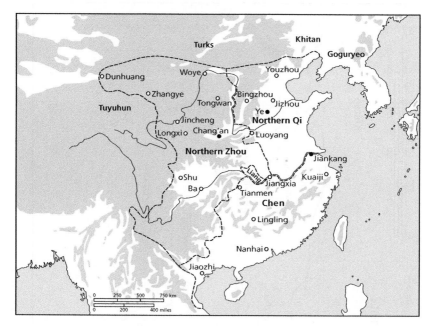

Map 11   Särbi-Xianbei Northern Zhou and Northern Qi dynasties; Chinese
Chen dynasty

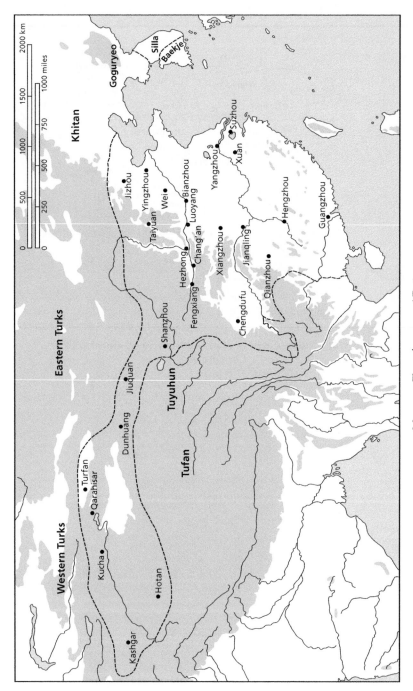

Map 12 Tang dynasty c. AD 650

Acknowledgments

There are many scholars and mentors whose teaching and generosity have made this book possible. For my early studies, I would like to thank Nick Doane, John Niles, and especially Kirsten Wolf for their guidance and instruction. For later mentorship, I am most indebted to David Levene and Nicola Di Cosmo, without whose direction this book would not have come into being. Nicola Di Cosmo took the time back in 2008 to respond to an unexpected email from an unknown student in an unrelated field and later to advise me as a member of my dissertation committee. David Levene was willing not only to take on the role of advisor to an additional student outside of his own department but also to provide invaluable and generous guidance and support throughout my graduate studies and beyond. I would also like to express my gratitude to David Konstan and Helmut Reimitz, who have both gone far out of their way to open academic doors for me and to provide most helpful direction and feedback on my research. David Konstan in particular has been extremely generous with his time and counsel, for which I am deeply indebted. For their feedback on the manuscript of this book, I would like to thank both the anonymous reviewer and Geoffrey Greatrex, whose comments have greatly improved the quality of the work. I would also like to thank Roger Bagnall, Christopher Baron, Brian Ford, Rania Huntington, Josh Mannis, Elizabeth and Tadeusz Mazurek, Hildegund Müller, William Nienhauser, Charles Pazdernik, Walter Pohl, Sören Stark, New York University's Institute for the Study of the Ancient World, and the University of Notre Dame. Lastly, my gratitude goes to my wife, daughters, father, and brother – my reduced but growing family.

A Note to the Reader

In the hope of making this book as accessible as possible to non-specialists, a number of small measures have been taken. First, abbreviations of titles of texts have been kept to a bare minimum. Second, Chinese characters will be provided on the first appearance of proper nouns in each chapter; in instances where different Chinese characters have the same Romanized written form, characters will also be provided to avoid ambiguity. Third, dates (or approximate dates) for primary texts have been supplied following the individual entry headings in the bibliography.

Introduction

Two speeches, recorded in what are among the earliest historical texts of the Greco-Roman and Chinese traditions, introduce fundamental themes of this book. The first is from the *Histories of Herodotus* (c. 484–425 BC) and appears in a conversation between Spartans and Athenians, where the Spartans are seeking assurance that the Athenians do not abandon the Greek alliance against the invading Persian Empire. The Athenians explain the reasons why an alliance with the barbarians is unthinkable. They first refer to the fact that the Persians had burned and destroyed hallowed temples to the Greek gods and that this crime must be avenged. They then proceed to explain that their shared Greek identity also precludes their abandonment of the Greek cause in favor of the Persian one:

> αὖθις δὲ τὸ Ἑλληνικόν, ἐὸν ὅμαιμόν τε καὶ ὁμόγλωσσον, καὶ θεῶν ἱδρύματά τε κοινὰ καὶ θυσίαι ἤθεά τε ὁμότροπα, τῶν προδότας γενέσθαι Ἀθηναίους οὐκ ἂν εὖ ἔχοι.[1]

> [there is the fact that we share] what it is to be "Greek": the same blood and language, common temples and sacrificial rites to the gods, and the same customs. It would not be well for the Athenians to be traitors to these things.

This passage is a cornerstone in modern discussions of Greek identity in the fifth century BC as well as of ways in which ethnicity was perceived and constructed in the classical world. In this case, the Athenians clearly mark what distinguishes not only themselves but also the greater Hellenic community from the "barbarians," a blanket term for those parts of humanity that share neither Greek cultural practices nor relations of shared kinship.

The second quotation is taken from the *Zuozhuan* 左轉, a pre-imperial Chinese text (usually dated to the fourth century BC) that is a commentary

---

[1] Hdt. 8.144.2. All translations are the author's unless otherwise noted.

I

on the events chronicled in the *Chunqiu* 春秋, the *Spring and Autumn
Annals*. The speech occurs in an episode where a chieftain of the Rong 戎
people, who had collaborated previously with the Chinese state of Jin 晉,
has been excluded from a military council of his erstwhile Chinese ally. In
response, the Rong chieftain says that

> 我諸戎飲食衣服不與華同，贄幣不通，言語不達，何惡之能為？不
> 與於會，亦無瞢焉？[2]

> We Rong people have food, drink, and clothing that is different from that
> of the Chinese; our gifts and valuables are different; our languages are
> unintelligible to one another – what basis for doing harm do we have? If
> you do not grant that we come to the council, why should we feel upset
> about that?

In this case, we see a similar delineation drawn between communities. In
the first example, what is Greek is defined in opposition to what is
barbarian, implicitly in reference to the inhabitants of the Persian Empire.
The quotation from the *Zuozhuan* is a speech from a chieftain of a people
whose ethnonym would later become synonymous with a concept of
"barbarian" in the Chinese tradition, where the speaker likewise marks
the distinctions between his own community and the Chinese, or Hua 華
as they are referred to here. In each case, the Greek and Chinese cultural
spheres, neither yet unified into a single political body and whose written
traditions would shape the discourse of political, cultural, and ethnic
identity in the later imperial traditions of the Chinese and Roman empires,
exhibit an analogous tendency to define the Self in opposition to an Other,
to mark out those features of one's own community that distinguish it
from that of another people.

These quotations are taken from two of the earliest manifestations of
wholly independent historiographical traditions. The former, Herodotus,
is generally regarded as the father of Greek historiography, and the
Zuozhuan, though still in what may be considered a developmental stage
(the "father of Chinese history" not appearing until the late second century
BC in the person of Sima Qian 司馬遷), is nevertheless a foundational
text in the Chinese historiographical tradition. Yet these two speeches
share a fundamental feature in common in that they exhibit some of the
earliest articulations of the discourse of alterity and identity that would
persist in various literary genres under succeeding empires.

---

[2] *Zuozhuan*, Xianggong 襄公.14.1007.

Centuries later, historians in the sixth and seventh centuries AD in the Greco-Roman and Chinese worlds would, in many ways, follow generic models established nearly one thousand years earlier. In particular, the bodies of ethnological discourse that historians in this later period inherited had been established in earlier centuries when the barbarians had belonged to the periphery – if not always geographically then at least culturally. However, the fall of the Western Roman and Han 漢 Chinese empires over the course of the third to fifth centuries AD witnessed large movements of populations and the entrance of increasing numbers of border peoples into the empires on their own political terms, a process that led to dramatic political dislocation and fragmentation in either case. This period was perhaps of greater significance in Europe, as the multi-centered political landscape it ushered in became a new norm that has persisted up to the present day, despite the best efforts of would-be empire builders up into the twentieth century. Yet the conceptual toolbox with which historians had to work in this later period, the representational vocabulary and ways of perceiving and describing ethnic and cultural others that they had inherited from their classical predecessors, was remarkably inconsistent with the contemporary realities of these later historians.

For no longer were the barbarians relegated to the periphery: both Rome and China witnessed groups who identified, or were identified, as non-Roman and non-Chinese not only enter imperial territory but also set up their own independent political regimes within the former borders of the empire.[3] The historian recording such unprecedented events was thus faced with the problem of renegotiating the parameters of his own political civilization. The period of ca. AD 300–600 is of additional significance because it witnessed a dramatically different outcome in the fates of Western Europe and China. By the year 600, the former remained composed of a number of successor kingdoms to the Roman Empire, whose populations would eventually be willing to subscribe to the identities of Frank, Lombard, Anglo-Saxon, or Visigoth. China, however, was reconstituted as a unified empire in the late sixth century, and, along the way, witnessed the virtual disappearance from the historical record of a number of ethnic groups (Xiongnu 匈奴, Särbi-Xianbei 鮮卑, Jie 羯, Di

---

[3] "China" and "Chinese" are of course anachronisms, but they will be employed here throughout both for the convenience of non-specialists as well as because of the lack of a single set of consistently applicable alternatives to refer to the cultural, linguistic, and political tradition that reaches from the present day back to the second millennium BC. On this point, see Brindley, "Barbarians or Not? Ethnicity and Changing Conceptions of the Ancient Yue (Viet) Peoples," 2–4.

氏 and Qiang 羌[4]) that had established some of the most powerful states in the preceding period. What happened in China was as if the Roman Empire had somehow been restored to its fourth-century extent and the identities of Frank, Goth, Anglo-Saxon, etc. had vanished. The epochs of Late Antiquity and Early Medieval China thus witnessed a renegotiation of political and cultural identities that was to have enormous consequences for the political and cultural history of both Europe and China. A parallel study of contemporary or near-contemporary histories devoted to major events of this transitional period in each civilization will shed light on the ways identities were perceived, represented, and renegotiated – processes that must have been of fundamental importance to the new status quo that was to characterize the European and Chinese experience in the succeeding centuries.

Comparative History of Greece-Rome and China

Comparative study of Greco-Roman and Chinese civilizations, though a relatively young body of scholarship, has continued to grow steadily since the 1990s.[5] Sino-Hellenic comparisons have occupied the majority of scholars who have preferred the comparative study of literary and philosophical themes, and the focus on philosophy and scientific thought in classical Greek and Warring States Chinese sources has been one of the most privileged areas of comparative study.[6] Lloyd in particular has produced several studies that examine the development of science, mathematics, and philosophical thought in ancient Greece and China.[7] Other scholars have examined topics that range from the development of Greek and Chinese poetic traditions to conceptions of geography and space.[8]

---

[4] The Qiang are something of an exception in that the term continued to be used for tribal groups in western and southwestern regions not controlled by China. The modern Qiang ethnic minority of China bears a name that was reintroduced as a specific ethnonym in the twentieth century. See Wang, Ming-ke, "From the Qiang Barbarians to the Qiang Nationality," 43–80.

[5] For an overview of this body of scholarship, see Tanner, "Ancient Greece, Early China: Sino-Hellenic Studies and Comparative Approaches to the Classical World," 89–109.

[6] For example, Raphals, *Knowing Words: Wisdom and Cunning in the Classical Tradition of China and Greece*; Hall and Ames, *Anticipating China: Thinking through the Narratives of Chinese and Western Culture*; Kuriyama, *The Expressiveness of the Body and the Divergence of Greek and Chinese Medicine*.

[7] Lloyd and Sivin, *The Way and the Word: Science and Medicine in Early China and Greece*; Lloyd, *The Ambitions of Curiosity: Understanding the World in Ancient Greece and China*; Lloyd, *Ancient Worlds, Modern Reflections: Philosophical Perspectives on Greek and Chinese Science and Culture*; Lloyd and Zhao, *Ancient Greece and China Compared*.

[8] Cai, Zong-qi, *Configurations of Comparative Poetics: Three Perspectives on Western and Chinese Literary Criticism*; Schaberg, "Travel, Geography, and the Imperial Imagination in Fifth-Century Athens and Han China," 152–91.

More in line with the interests of this project are the studies by Kim and Stuurman that have compared the treatment of foreign or "barbarian" peoples, especially the Scythians and Xiongnu in the works of, respectively, Herodotus and Sima Qian, in classical Greek and Chinese texts.[9]

Most of these studies focus on the relatively early developmental phases of Greco-Roman and Chinese civilization, a fact not surprising given that many consider the greatest efflorescence of cultural genius to have obtained in the classical ages of Greece and the Warring States period of China. Far less attention has been devoted to the seemingly parallel trajectories that led up to and beyond the establishment of the Roman and Han empires, a process through which a series of competing political entities sharing greater or lesser degrees of cultural affinity were reduced in a series of wars that left one supra-regional power standing.

Nevertheless, interest in Rome–China comparative work continues to grow. Gizewski has explored comparative approaches to periodization in Greco-Roman and Chinese antiquity and has sketched the various stages of ecumenical imperial formation in East Asia and in the Mediterranean.[10] Adshead has offered comparisons between the Tang 唐 Empire and the contemporary empires of India, the Muslim world, Byzantium, and Latin Christendom.[11] A more concentrated comparative project is Scheidel's *Rome and China* that focuses on the institutional and economic aspects of the Roman and Han Chinese empires.[12] Scheidel also launched the Stanford Ancient Chinese and Mediterranean Empires Comparative History Project (ACME), an international initiative seeking to promote collaboration between scholars in an effort to determine patterns of historical causality in imperial formation, dissolution, and reunification in China and the Mediterranean. More recently, Burbank and Cooper's volume, though not limited solely to the comparison of Rome and China, nevertheless offers a comparison of the two empires in a world-historical context, considering issues such as imperial ideology, the role of elite culture as a unifying force over diverse populations, and the role of the periphery and its inhabitants in shaping both imperial policy and worldviews.[13]

---

[9] Kim, *Ethnicity and Foreigners in Ancient Greece and China*; Stuurman, "Herodotus and Sima Qian: History and the Anthropological Turn in Ancient Greece and Han China," 1–40. Raaflaub and Talbert's edited volume examines the ethnographic and geographical traditions of a wide range of premodern societies: *Geography and Ethnography: Perceptions of the World in Pre-modern Societies*.

[10] Gizewski, "Römische und alte chinesische Geschichte im Vergleich: Zur Möglichkeit eines gemeinsamen Altertumsbegriffs," 271–302.

[11] Adshead, *T'ang China: The Rise of the East in World History*, 54–67.

[12] Scheidel, ed., *Rome and China: Comparative Perspectives on Ancient World Empires*.

[13] Burbank and Cooper, *Empires in World History: Geographies of Power, Politics of Difference*.

While there has been increasing interest in comparative study of Greco-Roman and Chinese history – often in the larger context of ancient empires – there are so far relatively few studies that offer comparative consideration of the mentalities and worldviews expressed in the Greco-Roman and Chinese historiographical traditions. An early exception is Prusek's 1970 study, which discusses features typical of Greco-Roman and Chinese historiography, considering the poetic roots of both traditions and the ways in which epic and lyric poetic forms came to influence the genre of prose historiography.[14] Since then, Lloyd, Schaberg, and Mutschler have all taken comparative approaches to historiography in these two traditions.[15] A volume edited by Mutschler and Mittag includes a variety of essays discussing the ideological representation of empire in the Roman and Chinese experience from their periods of pre-unification to dissolution in the early Middle Ages.[16]

Yet while comparative study between Rome and China is a growing field, there is not a single study to date that treats both the periods of Late Antiquity and Early Medieval China in any detail. This is unfortunate, as this period is such a critical one for those seeking to understand the nature and quality of the parallels that obtained between the two empires; it is at the point of divergence, of failed or successful imperial reunification, that some of the most significant questions may be asked about the cultural and political institutions fundamental to the integrity of the Roman and Han-Chinese states.[17] As noted above, both the late antique and early medieval Chinese worlds experienced significant influx of border peoples who established polities of their own on formerly imperial soil. The repercussions of these processes of migration and the adoption by the migrants of imperial political forms were to have enormous consequences in either sphere. The historical texts produced to describe these events are our source not only for the establishment of historical chronology but also for the attitudes, perceptions, and worldviews of the respective imperial

---

[14] Prusek, *Chinese History and Literature: Collection of Studies*, 17–34.

[15] Mutschler, "Vergleichende Beobachtungen zur griechish-römischen und altchinesischen Geschichtsschreibung," 213–53; "Zu Sinnhorizont und Funktion griechischer, römischer und altchinesischer Geschichtsschreibung," 33–54; Schaberg, "Travel, Geography, and the Imperial Imagination in Fifth-Century Athens and Han China," 152–91; Lloyd, *The Ambitions of Curiosity*, especially 1–20.

[16] Mutschler and Mittag, eds., *Conceiving the Empire: China and Rome Compared.*

[17] Scheidel, adapting the title of Pomeranz's *The Great Divergence*, has coined the phrase "the first great divergence" in reference to this period where the imperial trajectories of Rome and China diverged from one another. "From the 'Great Convergence' to the 'First Great Divergence': Roman and Qin-Han State Formation and Its Aftermath," in *Rome and China*, 11–23.

literati, those whose writings served to both prescribe and uphold the ideological framework of imperial order.

Walter Scheidel has argued that "only comparisons with other civilizations make it possible to distinguish common features from culturally specific or unique characteristics and developments, help us identify variables that were critical to particular historical outcomes, and allow us to assess the nature of any given ancient state or society within the wider context of premodern world history."[18] While this study will not share the institutional and economic focus and quantitative methodology adopted by Scheidel, its comparative approach will contribute to a better understanding of ideological currents prominent in the post-fragmentation periods of the Roman and Chinese empires, an undertaking that has not yet been attempted. By presenting a larger possible range of alternatives that could obtain under similar – though geographically isolated and distinct – circumstances, the present work will consider patterns of stasis and dynamism, of flexibility and rigidity in conceptual paradigms of ethnic and political identity. It will examine the tension inherent in efforts to emulate and restore the ideals of the past while acknowledging and coming to terms with the present, a tension that characterized the cultural and political imaginations of literary elites of these two civilizations.

It has been suggested that the comparative study of Rome and China is of a particular importance because of the fact that the classical inheritance and reception of the two empires has had great influence in shaping events in the modern period up to the present day, and that such study also heightens "our awareness of possible analogies between the present and the past, be it with regard to America or China."[19] Yet one may ask: Why not compare Rome and Sasanian Persia or Gupta India or any other ancient empire for that matter? The simple answer is that it does not, in fact, *have* to be a Rome–China comparison; other empires have offered and will continue to offer valuable points of comparison for specialists of the Greco-Roman world.[20] As has been argued by Lloyd, the comparative exercise in and of itself allows us to see the familiar from an otherwise unavailable perspective that can offer important new insights:

---

[18] Scheidel, *Rome and China*, 5.

[19] Mutschler and Mittag, "Preface," in *Conceiving the Empire*, xiv.

[20] For example, see Morris and Scheidel's *The Dynamics of Ancient Empires: State Power from Assyria to Byzantium.*

> Without a comparativist perspective, students of Greek antiquity will easily
> mistake, indeed can hardly fail to mistake, what may be distinctive, and
> what may be said to be in no way exceptional, either in the intellectual
> products of the society they study or in the circumstances and manner of
> their production.[21]

The comparison of ethnographic discourse and its relationship to Greco-
Roman and Chinese historiography undertaken in this study will enable us
to see the ways in which these two traditions perpetuated or transformed
political, cultural, and ethnic identities. More importantly, such an
approach will allow us to avoid treating different historical outcomes as
"inevitable, or as seeing them as miraculous."[22] What is particularly apt
about the comparanda selected here is the fact that China has so full a body
of documentary evidence that shares many features in common with the
literary and historical productions of the Greco-Roman world. Moreover,
for anyone familiar with the historical events of the third to seventh
centuries AD in Western Europe and in China, the comparison is
unavoidable – it has occurred to modern historians one after another,
and it is time to take some of the relevant questions beyond anecdotal
comments and footnotes that consistently point toward this direction of
research that has not yet received the sustained attention it merits. Rome
and China in this period exhibit the "extraordinary instances of 'simulta-
neity'" that call for "a world/global perspective on late antiquity" through
"thematic comparisons."[23] Is the comparison exact? That is, are the
political environments, historical processes, and literary genres and forms
of representation perfect equivalents and thereby allowing for seamless
comparison? Of course not. But with so many similarities in political
experience and circumstances on the one hand, and the convergent aspects
of genre and historiographical convention on the other, the *contrasts*
between these two traditions, specifically how they reacted to the reality
of barbarian kings and emperors ruling a lost imperial heartland, is a
necessary, and hitherto virtually untouched, direction of inquiry.

   This volume will consider the ideological climate in Roman Late
Antiquity and Early Medieval China in regards to perceptions of barbarian
identities and the degree to which such identities were compatible with
the exercise of political power. Such identities were constructed and

---

[21] Lloyd, *Methods and Problems in Greek Science*, xii.   [22] Ibid.
[23] Humphries, "Late Antiquity and World History," 25–26. The recent edited volume by Di Cosmo
    and Maas, *Empires and Exchanges in Eurasian Late Antiquity*, is an excellent example of broader,
    world-historical approaches to the period.

perpetuated in the ethnological discourse received from the early texts of either historiographical tradition; the representation of foreign peoples in Greco-Roman and Chinese classical ethnography served as a basis for the rationalization of ethnic identities that were understood to fall beyond the pale of the civilized centers but must necessarily be understood in terms of those centers. Therefore, this book will assess the adoption, manipulation, and adaptation of this discourse in a later period when, in many ways, the historians themselves had seen their conceptual world, and the representational categories employed to define it, turned upside down. Ultimately, it aims to take a step toward a new understanding of this critical period in history when continuity was restored to the Chinese imperial tradition and the Roman West remained fragmented.

Roman Late Antiquity and Early Medieval China: Brief Historical Background

The third century AD was a time of fragmentation and crisis in both the Roman and Han Chinese empires. Prior to the third century, Rome and Han China had enjoyed virtually unchallenged hegemony over their respective regions since the mid–second century BC. Although the causes and nature of the crisis that befell Rome continue to be debated, there is no disputing that a combination of plague, economic problems, and political instability led to major political disruption in this period. The result was effectively a division of the empire into thirds following the disastrous capture of the emperor Valerian by the Persians in 260: the Gallic Empire of Postumus ruling over Britain, Gaul, and Spain; the Central Empire of Gallienus holding Italy, North Africa, the Balkans, and Thrace; and the Palmyrene Empire of Odenathus and Zenobia ruling Syria, Egypt, and the other eastern provinces. This period of division lasted a relatively short time before the emperor Aurelian (r. 270–275) was able to restore unity by defeating his western and eastern rivals. His restoration would eventually be followed by the political and administrative reforms of Diocletian in the last decades of the century, which allowed the empire to persist for nearly two hundred more years in the west.

The Han Empire, which was formally dissolved in 220, also experienced a period of fragmentation that resulted in a tripartite division of the former empire into the kingdoms of Shu 蜀, Wu 吳, and Wei 魏, the last of which would ultimately destroy the other two over the course of the following decades. Before the final defeat of Wu in 280, however, the powerful Sima 司馬 family had usurped the Wei throne and declared the establishment of the Jin 晉 dynasty in 265. With the destruction of Wu, unified imperial rule was briefly restored under what has been known to historians since as the Western Jin 西晉 dynasty (265–317). The Western Jin was thus a temporary reunification of China between the fall of the Han dynasty and the nearly three-hundred-year period of division that followed the Western Jin's collapse.

The empires that were restored in the late third century, and only very briefly in the case of the Western Jin, eventually faced military pressure from foreign peoples who would ultimately overthrow imperial rule and establish their own dominance over significant portions of imperial territory. In the Roman case, this was a long process that is typically traced from the disastrous Roman defeat near Adrianople in 378 to the deposition of Romulus Augustulus in 476, after which point imperial rule in the west was never wholly reconstituted. The Jin dynasty's restoration following China's own "third-century crisis" was to be far more short-lived. The internecine warfare accompanying the "revolt of the eight princes," *ba wang zhi luan* 八王之亂, which lasted from 291 to 306, left the north of China in such a weak and unstable state that scions of the earlier non-Chinese Xiongnu Empire who had been settled in northern China within the Great Wall were able to sack both the imperial capitals Luoyang and Chang'an and usher in the period known both as the Sixteen Kingdoms, *Shiliu guo* 十六國, as well as "the Five Barbarians throw China into chaos," *Wu Hu luan hua* 五胡亂華. During this period, the majority of China north of the Yangtze River was in the hands of non-Chinese peoples who were all contending for survival and hegemony, both against one another as well as against the émigré Chinese empire in the south (referred to by historians as the Eastern Jin 東晉, which lasted from 317 to 420).

Therefore, from 476 in the West and from 316 in China (the year when the last northern capital, Chang'an, fell to the resurgent Xiongnu and the remnants of the imperial family fled to the south), the territorial heartlands of the former empires were in the hands of barbarian rulers. In the West, imperial territories were divided between the Franks and Burgundians in Gaul, the Angles and Saxons in Britain, the Visigoths in Spain, the Vandals in Africa, and the Ostrogoths in Italy. Wars of reconquest were launched by the emperor Justinian in 533, and by the middle of the sixth century Africa, the Balkans, and Italy were back in Roman hands with a foothold established on the southern coast of Spain.

One can most easily gain a sense of what was going on in China in the fourth century by keeping in mind the image of the post-Roman West and simply rotating the image such that the states of conquest are located in the north, while the imperial regime persists in the south. As with the barbarian West, northern China was ruled in this period by a variety of competing kingdoms, most of which were led by peoples of non-Chinese origin. The north was unified briefly by one of the these regimes, the Di 氐 people's Former Qin 前秦 dynasty (351–394), in the latter half of the fourth century. But following the Former Qin's fall after a failed invasion of the south in 383, its multiethnic subjects rose in revolt and reestablished a checkerboard of petty kingdoms across the northern plains. North China was again divided until the Tabgach Särbi (Chinese: Tuoba Xianbei 拓跋 鮮卑) rulers of the Northern Wei 北魏 dynasty (486-535), themselves originally from beyond the frontier, managed to eliminate their rivals. Despite aspirations to conquer the Chinese south, the Northern Wei itself collapsed and split into the Eastern and Western Wei dynasties in the 530s.[24] These two short-lived states then evolved, respectively, into the Northern Qi 北齊 (550–577) and Northern Zhou 北周 (557–581) dynasties, both of which were ruled by non-Chinese Särbi-Xianbei elites. These offspring of the Northern Wei fought one another as well as a succession of Chinese regimes in the south. In the end, it was the Northern Zhou who managed to destroy the Northern Qi in 577 and lay plans for conquest of the south. In 581, however, the Northern Zhou throne was usurped by the Chinese general Yang Jian 楊堅, who founded the Sui 隋 dynasty (581–618). The Sui succeeded in reunifying all of China in 588 before itself falling apart and being replaced by the Tang (618–907), which was to last nearly three hundred years and is considered one of the most glorious eras in Chinese history and culture, equal if not superior to the Han in its achievements.

The above sketch requires some attention to points where the two courses of events differed significantly. While by the mid-sixth century in Europe, and the late sixth century in China, symbolically significant parts or the whole of formal imperial unity had been reestablished, in the Roman case the reconquest had been accomplished by Roman forces sent from the imperial capital of Constantinople. In China, the Sui reunification had

---

[24] The name for this people often appears as "Xianbei" or "Hsien-pei," which are Romanizations of the modern Chinese pronunciation of the two characters 鮮卑. "Särbi" is a reconstructed form of the hypothesized original pronunciation of the ethnonym; see Pulleyblank, "The Chinese and Their Neighbors in Prehistoric and Early Historic Times," 452–53. The accuracy of this reconstruction has been reaffirmed more recently by Baxter and Sagart in *Old Chinese: A New Reconstruction*, 261–62. Though such reconstructions are lacking for most of the non-Chinese peoples in antiquity such as the Xiongnu, they will be preferred when available. On this point, see Mair's review of Caswell's *Written and Unwritten: A New History of the Buddhist Caves at Yungang*, 358–59.

been led by a usurping general of the otherwise "barbarian" or "barbarized" north. While the Sui is commonly seen as restoring "Chinese" rule over a unified empire,[25] the fact is that the Sui itself grew out of the Northern Zhou, a state whose royal and military elites professed a Särbi-Xianbei identity alongside or in preference to a Chinese one. Nevertheless, the Sui represented itself as a Chinese dynasty and legitimate successor to the imperial legacy of the Han Empire. This same policy was perpetuated under the Tang, whose own ruling family was of mixed or primarily non-Chinese ancestry. This newly restored Chinese empire looked back on a reunification that had not been accomplished by the self-proclaimed legitimate Chinese regimes of the south, the so-called Six Dynasties, but rather by the scions of a northern and largely barbarian political lineage. Though parts and even all of China would be conquered by foreign regimes in later centuries, the Northern and Southern dynasties period, c. 386–589, was the first age that witnessed rulers of foreign extraction establishing bureaucratic states within what had been the territories of the Han Empire.[26] The Sui and Tang – like later regimes that followed periods of partial or total foreign rule, such as the Northern Song and Ming – thus made restoration of Chinese rule an aspect of their respective political programs.

   In contrast, the Roman Empire of Justinian had not experienced centuries of rule by foreign peoples prior to its campaigns of reunification against Africa and Italy. Whereas the reconquest of Justinian may be understood as a return to an idealized status quo of sorts, where the superiority of Roman arms had again triumphed over barbarian intruders, the Chinese south never did manage to retake its lost northern territories – it was itself conquered by the "barbarized" and hybrid regime of the Sui in the north. What happened in China would thus be similar to if a hypothetical Gothic or Frankish empire of the west had conquered and incorporated not only the other western kingdoms but also the imperial territories of the eastern Mediterranean. If we then imagine that well into this process an Italo- or Gallo-Roman courtier had staged a coup and seized the throne, declaring himself a Roman ruler over Romans (and disavowing association with Gothic or Frankish ethnic identity), we have a scenario that mirrors what actually occurred in China. Would such a restored Roman Empire be truly "Roman" in our eyes? Regardless, the purpose of this thought experiment is

---

[25] Holcombe, "The Xianbei in Chinese History," 34.
[26] Liu Xueyao has divided Chinese dynastic history into four (problematic) categories: Han Chinese regimes 漢族所建王朝或政權, barbarian regimes 胡族所建王朝或政權, barbarized Chinese regimes 胡化漢族所建王朝或政權, and Sinicized barbarian regimes 漢化胡族所建王朝或政權. The category with the longest duration is that of barbarian regimes. *Wu Hu shilun*, 16–20.

to draw our attention to the extent to which *names*, the labels we give to things and the assumptions that automatically accrue to them, condition our perception of those things. One finds that within labels such as "China" – or "Byzantium," for that matter – lie always a diverse array of contradictions and alternative possibilities.[27]

Primary Questions and Approaches

The interests of this book are both historical and literary. Historical, because it examines the continuities and discontinuities within the imaginative categories used to represent foreign peoples under a defined set of historical circumstances; literary, because the materials it considers all fall within the category of historiography, whose distinction from other literary genres in the ancient world is extremely porous. Many of the models already developed for the study of comparative history are not well suited to this project, as they entail a more quantitative and/or sociological approach in their assessment of correspondences in historical phenomena. Accordingly, this study does not aim to determine historical causality or identify the "robust processes" that are sought by some comparativists.[28] Instead, it will consider two historiographical traditions whose authors shared many salient features in common.

There are several characteristics shared by Roman (whether writing in Latin or in Greek) and Chinese historians, and three in particular will be noted here that render them especially suitable for comparative study. The first is the highly rhetorical nature of historiography in both traditions. It has been argued that historians in Greco-Roman antiquity "told things not so much as they really were but as they really are."[29] This assessment is in consideration of the nature of historiography as a rhetorical exercise, a discourse of persuasion aiming to convince an audience of the truth-value of a given account of events or processes, whether truth is understood as literal fact or general probability.[30] Similarly, it has been argued that the

---

[27] On the arbitrary application of "Byzantium" to what was known throughout its existence as the Empire of the Romans, see Kaldellis, *Hellenism in Byzantium*, 42–43. As for the Holy Roman Empire established with Charlemagne's coronation as emperor in AD 800, he and his successors never ceased to be known as kings of the Franks.

[28] Goldstone, *Revolution and Rebellion in the Early Modern World*, 57–59. For analytical approaches to comparative history, see Bonell, "The Uses of Theory, Concepts and Comparison in Historical Sociology," 156–73. For a recent overview of the development of comparative methodology, see Griffiths, "The Comparative Method and the History of the Modern Humanities," 473–505.

[29] Marincola, "Speeches in Classical Historiography," 132.

[30] For exmple, see Woodman, *Rhetoric in Classical Historiography: Four Studies*, especially chapter two.

Shiji 史記 of Sima Qian, the foundational work of Chinese historiography
from the early first century BC, which at once synthesized pre-imperial
historical writings and set the template for all subsequent dynastic histories
that are recognized as *zhengshi* 正史, "official history," may ultimately be
understood as a set of anecdotes used for rhetorical persuasion that are
organized along a chronological principle.[31] Schaberg describes the accumulated historical anecdotal lore in early Chinese historical texts as having
a "fundamentally didactic form" that could be used at will for support in a
speaker's political argumentation, at times even in a manner reminiscent of
Roman *suasoriae*.[32] In formulating political narratives then, the forms of
historiography that flourished in the imperial societies of the Greco-
Roman and Chinese worlds were able, "by recording the course of events
and reflections upon it," to help "shape the collective mind and enhance
the durability of the political order."[33] The present study takes this
function of historiography as its point of departure, treating the genre as
a rhetorical representation of the world as it was perceived by the historian
(s) and assessing the worldviews that the endorsement and dissemination
of the historical text helped reinforce and perpetuate.

The construction of a particular worldview requires attention to the
second shared aspect of both Greco-Roman and Chinese historiography:
their overtly moral orientation. Roller has described the ways in which
"exemplary discourse assumes ethical and social continuity," and he has
suggested that its "transmission of moral standards and models for action"
is a constant feature of Roman historiography; indeed, that "historiography
itself is a type of monument within that discourse."[34] This interest in
moral exempla was not a prominent feature of Greco-Roman historiography alone; indeed, it has been argued that ancient Chinese historians had
an even more pronounced tendency to find prescriptive models for the
present in the exempla of the past. Dien has characterized this tendency in
terms of a notion of progress that consisted in the restoration of an earlier
age, that "precedent was the basis for change, and the sages of the past have
never been surpassed. For these reasons, the record of the past was essential
as a referent in creating policy and making decisions."[35] In either case

---

[31] Schaberg, "Chinese History and Philosophy," 403.   [32] Ibid., 396–402.
[33] Mittag and Mutschler, "Epilogue," in *Conceiving the Empire*, 427.
[34] Roller, "The Exemplary Past in Roman Historiography and Culture," 217, 219. Roller goes on to
illustrate, citing Polybius, this same phenomenon in the Greek tradition.
[35] Dien, "Historiography of the Six Dynasties Period (220–581)," 509. Rogers refers to the "traditional
didactic application of history, whereby general principles of morality and statecraft were illustrated
for the ruler's edification." *The Chronicle of Fu Chien: A Case of Exemplar History*, 40–41.

then, historiography was a literary genre that exhibited a morally prescriptive tendency in its representations of the past. This tendency, alongside the genre's intrinsically rhetorical quality, suggests that one may extend the above-quoted summation of historiography as a form of literary activity that presents things not as they were but as they are: historiography presents reality not just as it really is but *as it should be*. This reading of historical texts is in accord with that of a comparative study of Roman and Chinese historiography that argues historical texts "do not simply mirror the world: to a certain extent they also help to shape, modify, and transform it."[36]

The third shared facet of Greco-Roman and Chinese traditions of interest here is the inheritance in either case of centuries-old corpora of ethnographic literature, not so much a genre in its own right but rather a mode of descriptive digression embedded within, or appended to, a larger historical narrative. Awareness of this ethnographic inheritance is crucial in reading Greco-Roman and Chinese texts that post-date their respective classical periods.[37] For it is in the age of imperial fragmentation and states of conquest that this ethnographic material takes on a new political significance as it came to be employed in the description not of the remote but of the uncomfortably near. There are several studies aiming to assess the attitudes of Greeks, Romans, and Chinese toward the peoples that were identified as "barbarians" in the case of the former two and as Yi-Di 夷狄, Rong-Di 戎狄, Hu 胡, etc. in the case of the latter, and this area of research may be expected to grow in the coming years. None so far, however, has examined these attitudes from a comparative perspective in a period when the ethnographic and political boundaries of antiquity had broken down and new lines were being drawn.

The conclusions reached by modern classical scholars who explore these topics in earlier periods are far from uniform, ranging, on the one hand, from an emphasis on the existence of proto-racist modes of representation to, on the other hand, the argument that there was just as much if not more inclusivity and cross-cultural appropriation in the ancient Mediterranean world than there was demonization of a culturally or racially distinct Other.[38] In scholarship concerned with this question in ancient China, there is a stronger concensus that whether or not views toward the Yi-Di or "barbarians" were culturally and/or ethnically exclusive during the

[36] Mutschler and Mittag, "Preface," xv.
[37] Gillett, "The Mirror of Jordanes: Concepts of the Barbarian, Then and Now," 392–408.
[38] Isaac, *The Invention of Racism in Classical Antiquity*; Gruen, *Rethinking the Other in Antiquity*.

Spring and Autumn and Warring States periods,[39] the unification of China under the Qin 秦 and then the Han dynasties witnessed a more stark conceptual demarcation between the Chinese and their non-Chinese northern neighbors, the nomadic Xiongnu.[40] In either case, however, it remains common to conceive of the ancient relationships between Greco-Roman and Chinese centers and peripheries in terms of a barbarian dichotomy, a strict division of humankind into those who are civilized, literate, and governed by political order and those who are not. Chapters 1 and 2 examine the earlier phases of ethnographic historiography and ethnological paradigms in the traditions of Greece-Rome and China and reconsider the applicability of such a dichotomy in either case.

Modern assessments of the views toward the barbarians in Late Antiquity and Early Medieval China also vary considerably. At one end of the spectrum, one finds assertions such as that of Lechner, who has argued that "whoever was called Roman was not a barbarian; whoever was numbered among the barbarians could not be a Roman." Moreover, the barbarian was, "simply put, the negation of everything comprised by the term 'Roman.'"[41] As it has been demonstrated that many meaningful distinctions between Romans and barbarians had broken down considerably by the sixth century,[42] recent assessments are more measured. Several scholars have emphasized the stability of the Roman–barbarian dichotomy, at least in literary contexts. For example, Gillett has emphasized the continued influence of classical ethnographic discourse in Late Antiquity and the perpetuation of the concept of the barbarian as a meaningful conceptual category.[43] Heather has suggested that although specific peoples may have been perceived, or represented themselves, in different ways in this period, the basic categories of representation remained unchanged.[44] Along similar lines, Halsall has argued for the stability of

---

[39] On the potentially inclusive views of Chinese toward foreigners in this earlier period, see Creel, *The Origins of Statecraft in China Vol. One*, 211–14; Pines, "Beasts or Humans: Pre-Imperial Origins of the 'Sino-Barbarian' Dichotomy," 62.

[40] Pines, "Beasts or Humans," 90–91; Di Cosmo, *Ancient China and Its Enemies: The Rise of Nomadic Power in East Asian History*, 304; Goldin, "Steppe Nomads as a Philosophical Problem in Classical China," 234–35.

[41] "Wer sich Ῥωμαῖος nennen durfte, war nicht βάρβαρος, wer unter die βάρβαροι zählte, konnte nicht Ῥωμαῖος sein"; "der Barbar [ist] kurz gesagt die Negation alles dessen, was den Ῥωμαῖος ausmacht." Lechner, "Byzanz und die Barbaren," 292.

[42] Greatrex, "Roman Identity in the Sixth Century," 267–92. The bibliography provided here is only a small sample of the relevant scholarship on the subject, and more will be considered in later chapters.

[43] Gillett, "The Mirror of Jordanes," 392–408.

[44] Heather, "The Barbarian in Late Antiquity," 234–58.

the rhetorical dichotomy between Romans and barbarians in Late Antiquity and that it was a response of the literate elites of the empire to "emphasise this division, however much it was becoming divorced from reality."[45] This should come as no surprise if Goffart is correct in his assertion that "Western kings who ruled over Roman populations and churches ... ranked in Byzantium solely as repulsive aliens."[46] Such readings of the sources have prompted the observation that "polarity has reigned supreme" in modern scholarship on the subject of the barbarian in the later Roman world.[47]

Other scholars, however, such as Maas, point out that "the opposition of Roman and barbarian was not absolute or final"; he argues that Romans in Late Antiqutiy could draw on "diverse traditions to register the differences between themselves and their barbarian neighbors and to consider how those differences might be bridged."[48] Along similar lines, Lampinen has argued in a discussion of ethnographic motifs in this period that "whether about 'Greeks' or 'barbarians', the dynamic of cultural foreignness had clearly fragmented into a complex interplay of identities, among which religious and occupational themes played just as important a role as cultural or ethnic [ones]."[49] Pointing to other complexities, Chauvot has noted the difficulties in defining criteria of barbarism and reminds us that the Latin and Greek sources do not always employ the term in the same way.[50] Von Rummel has argued that attempts to define the concept of the "barbarian" are doomed to failure, given the range of its applications in the hands of individual authors and the complexities inherent in conceptions of "Roman" and "civilization."[51]

Scholarly consensus also remains elusive as to the ways in which foreign peoples were perceived in the early Tang era. Chinese scholars have a strong tendency to emphasize the cosmopolitanism and cultural inclusiveness of this period of Chinese history, arguing that following centuries of barbarian rule in the north of China, the traditional divisions between Chinese and barbarians had become irrelevant. This point of view has also been advanced in English-language scholarship by Ho and Wang. The

---

[45] Halsall, "Funny Foreigners: Laughing with the Barbarians in Late Antiquity," 113.
[46] Goffart, *Barbarian Tides: The Migration Age and the Later Roman Empire*, 54.
[47] Parnell, "Barbarians and Brothers-in-Arms," 809.
[48] Maas, "Barbarians: Problems and Approaches," 60.
[49] Lampinen, "Migrating Motifs of Northern Barbarism," 231.
[50] For example, Chauvot points out the term's absence in several late antique Latin authors in reference to the Persians but its almost necessary appearance in contemporary Greek texts. *Opinions romaines face aux barbares au IVe siècle apr. J.-C.*, 470–71.
[51] *Habitus barbarus: Kleidung und Repräsentation spätantiker Eliten im 4. und 5. Jahrhundert*, 3, n. 9.

former has argued that "the spirit of tolerance and cosmopolitanism exhibited by T'ang Chinese is almost the exact opposite to 'Han chauvinism', arrogance, and xenophobia, which some students of Chinese history believe to have characterized the so-called 'sinicization'."[52] Ho, therefore, rejects the existence of a Sino-barbarian dichotomy under the Tang while also suggesting that it may also have been absent under the Han. Wang accepts the presence of a demarcation between the Chinese of the Han dynasty and their northern neighbors but argues that this distinction had disappeared by the seventh century, claiming that "in a sense, the Tang empire eliminated the traditional ethnic boundary between the Han and non-Han."[53]

Modern Chinese scholarship tends to view the Tang dynasty and the preceding period of the Northern and Southern Dynasties as a period of salutary *minzu ronghe* 民族融合, "ethnic blending," a process that led to the rejuvenation of the Han Chinese people.[54] While such processes undoubtedly occurred, much of this scholarship has suffered first from the imposition of rigid Marxist teleology and, more recently, Chinese nationalism, which has a tendency to fixate on what it sees as a necessary process of Sinification of the barbarians and insists on using anachronistic, and distortive, terms such as *shaoshu minzu* 少数民族, "ethnic minorities," to label peoples originally settled beyond China's borders. The scholarship is thus in line with modern political goals of assimilating ethnic groups in peripheral regions claimed by the Chinese state. Nevertheless, this view has not remained uncontested. For example, Abramson has argued that "genealogical consciousness remained high throughout the Tang" and that "it was common ... for the elite Han [i.e., Chinese] in-group to refer to the Other as 'not of our kind', with strong implications of common descent on the part of the Han."[55] Likewise, Skaff has noted that there has been an "overemphasis on the uniqueness of Sui-Tang cosmopolitanism," and he discusses the persistence of xenophobic attitudes toward non-Chinese peoples during this period alongside more inclusive

---

[52] Ho, "In Defense of Sinicization," 134.
[53] Wang, Q. Edward, "History, Space, and Ethnicity: The Chinese Worldview," 299.
[54] A typical example: "The great migrations of various peoples, the great convergence, the great fusion, caused the Han ethnic group to absorb a great amount of new blood; [these processes] caused the Han to acquire an even greater vigor and creativity in terms of their physical constitution and culture." 各民族的大迁徙，大汇聚，大融合，使汉民族吸收了大量的新血液，使其在体质和文化方面更具活力和创造力. *Series of Chinese Ethnic History in Past Dynasties*, ed. Lu Xun et al., 2.
[55] Abramson, *Ethnic Identity in Tang China*, xi.

perspectives that advocated for the assimilation and cultural transformation of foreign groups.[56]

While also providing a comparative assessment of classical ethnographic traditions, this book reconsiders Roman and Chinese attitudes toward the barbarians in Late Antiquity and Early Medieval China through a close reading of two sources that offer some of our richest evidence for the ways in which barbarian states were perceived during the reign of Justinian and in the early Tang, periods when key territories were reincorporated into the Roman Empire and a unified empire was recreated in China. There are two reasons for limiting the scope of the study in this way. First, a comparative approach necessarily requires greater space and effort as it engages with at least two separate traditions, and it is therefore more practical to deal with a smaller set of material; a wholly comprehensive comparative study would be impossible in a single volume. Second, given the variety of not only textual but also material sources available, one could find sufficient evidence in either case to support any position; limiting the study to one major historical work in each tradition, those that are among our best and most extensive for the respective periods, at least makes it more practical to ensure a more thorough consideration of the source material.

The approach here will be to take the first texts that were produced following imperial reunification of the Roman and Chinese empires in the sixth century and consider the ways in which the ethnographic discourse of the classical era is employed in representations of foreign political actors. These texts are the *Wars* of Procopius of Caesarea (c. 500–c.565) and the *Jin shu* 晉書, or *Book of Jin*, attributed to Fang Xuanling 房玄齡 (578–648). There are several reasons to support this choice of texts. First, they were produced by historians close to the centers of power and may be assumed to present worldviews that, if not outright endorsed by the emperor as in the case of the *Jin shu*, were at least presentable to an imperial readership. Procopius was an officer close to the Roman general Belisarius, who retook North Africa from the Vandals and was in charge of the Gothic war for much of its twenty-year prosecution.[57] Procopius' *Wars*

---

[56] Skaff, *Sui-Tang China and Its Turko-Mongol Neighbors*, 10, 52–60. The same point has been argued persuasively by Yang, "Reinventing the Barbarian: Rhetorical and Philosophical Uses of the *Yi-Di* in Mid-Imperial China," xiii. Also see ibid., 71–72.

[57] For a concise overview of scholarship on the career and oeuvre of Procopius, see Greatrex, "Perceptions of Procopius in Recent Scholarship," 76–121; Treadgold, *The Early Byzantine Historians*, 176–226. Also see the recent volume edited by Lillington-Martin and Turquois, *Procopius of Caesarea: Literary and Historical Interpretations*, as well as Greatrex and Janniard's *Le monde de Procope / The World of Procopius*.

and *Buildings* were published in Constantinople and, as is clear from the suppression of his *Secret History*, he must have known that his work would come before the eyes of the emperor or at least the emperor's associates.[58] Procopius himself notes the wide circulation of his own works in his preface to book eight of the *Wars*, claiming that they "have appeared everywhere within the empire of the Romans."[59] Though his recent characterization as a "benchmark" historian of the period, "admired and imitated by his successors,"[60] may be disputed, the fact remains that Procopius provides the most extensive extant account of the age of Justinian. Moreover, there is no other historian of the period who offers so extensive a classicizing history that is also rich in ethnographic material.

Fang Xuanling was in fact not just an author but the overseer of the *Jin shu* compilation project, commissioned by the emperor Taizong 太宗 (r. 626–649) in 646 and finished in 648; the work was carried out by the Tang Bureau of Historiography, which had been established in AD 629.[61] Indeed, the emperor himself contributed a number of passages to the work and valued the *Jin shu* highly enough to use it as a gift to an ambassador from the Korean kingdom of Silla.[62] Although it may not be attributed to a single author, the corporate production of the text, as well as its imperial patronage, makes it a particularly suitable barometer for the attitudes and worldviews of the early Tang. The *Jin shu* and the *Wars*, then, may thus be taken to provide a broadly imperial perspective on the foreign states that had arisen within imperial borders during periods of division and crisis, and if not an official perspective in the case of Procopius per se, at least a perspective that was not beyond the pale of public and imperial opinion.

It must be acknowledged that the individual composition of the *Wars*, and the singular perspective of an author who was also highly critical of

---

[58] See, for example, Heather, *The Restoration of Rome: Barbarian Popes and Imperial Pretenders*, 133, 136.

[59] πανταχόθι δεδήλωνται τῆς Ῥωμαίων ἀρχῆς (*Wars* 8.1.1). Procopius' popularity is also attested by his continuator, Agathias of Myrina, who refers to him by name at several points throughout his work. The brief summary that Agathias provides of Procopius' *Wars* in his preface (22, 32), and his references to Procopius elsewhere in his work (4.26.4, 4.30.5), suggests an assumption on Agathias' part that Procopius was a well-known author.

[60] Kaldellis, *Ethnography after Antiquity: Foreign Lands and Peoples in Byzantine Literature*, 3.

[61] Though commonly attributed to Fang Xuanling, the *Jin shu* was actually the product of twenty-one scholars who worked for the official Bureau of Historiography set up in the early Tang. For the most thorough English-language discussion of the compilation and transmission of the *Jin shu* and the no longer extant texts from which it drew, see Rogers, *The Chronicle of Fu Chien*, 15–22.

[62] Rogers, *The Chronicle of Fu Chien*, 15–16; on the contributions of the emperor to the text, see ibid., 86, n. 89.

the regime, complicates any reading of the text as providing a monolithic set of contemporary cultural and political assumptions. Moreover, Procopius' elite readership was not a homogeneous group, and there was a wide range of opinion in Procopius' day regarding the nature of the Roman Empire and its place in the mid-sixth-century world. Nevertheless, the fact remains that the *Wars* was a popular and broadly disseminated work. Even if its perspective is that of individual, as opposed to corporate, authorship, it exhibits a perspective that resonated with a wide audience. The *Wars* and the *Jin shu*, then, are thus among our best sources for the attitudes, perceptions, and worldviews of the respective imperial literati – crucial components of the ideological construction of imperial landscapes, which were, to some degree, a product of the historiographical exercise itself.

Second, each of these texts employs a classicizing literary style and exhibits a culturally conservative worldview. The historians engage with inherited corpora of ethnographic discourse codified in political and demographic contexts that had long since become obsolete. Herodotus' inquiries on the peoples north of the Danube would be no better guide in the sixth century AD than would Xenophon's description of Persian military culture. Yet the works of such classical authorities continued to serve as reference points for later authors, even if only to demonstrate their erudition before a learned audience. As Kaldellis has described the classicism of Procopius, "Classicism was, after all, a way of talking about the present by using ancient paradigms whose store of accumulated meaning could be modulated to respond to new circumstances."[63] This same appeal to ancient paradigms is mirrored in the historiography of Tang China. Abramson has observed of Tang historical productions that they were "heavily indebted for their style and content to canonical Chinese works of history and thought from earlier dynasties, rendering them often anachronistic and stereotypical but revealing perhaps most clearly the mental framework that shaped Han elites' construction of non-Han ethnic identities and boundaries."[64] The *Wars* and the *Jin shu* are both works that attempt to represent a new political situation, characterized by the influx and political establishment of barbarian peoples, while working within the parameters of a conceptual toolbox inherited from centuries-old ethnographic texts. Neither interprets historical events from new religious perspectives, Buddhism and Christianity, which had developed their own

---

[63] Kaldellis, *Procopius of Caesarea: Tyranny, History, and Philosophy at the End of Antiquity*, 15.
[64] Abramson, *Ethnic Identity in Tang China*, xxii.

forms of historiography and offered new ideologies and lenses through which to view and interpret the present and the past.[65]

Indeed, one of the goals of this study is not only to compare Rome and China in the mid-first millennium AD but also to compare each tradition back on itself. Accordingly, the first two chapters consider in detail the development of the two ethnographic traditions up into the Han and Roman imperial periods. The latter three chapters then examine later classicizing historial works in light of their respective authorities. By considering this late antique/early medieval Chinese reception of classical ethnography, it is hoped that the book will be of interest to a larger audience by appealing to classical scholars and Sinologists working on pre- and high imperial periods. Accordingly, I have sought to explore how historians understood the "new" world they were faced with in the terms of the "old" world they had inherited. While Buddhism and Christianity would have had a significant impact on the socio-cultural realities on the ground in either case, the texts focused on here have been deliberately chosen because of the fact that they exhibit as little influence of these newer ideologies as possible. They thus allow the exploration of ways in which classical paradigms, employed by deliberately classicizing authors, adapted to circumstances of political and demographic change. A contention of this book is that the categories and tiers of political status created for foreign individuals and peoples in the early medieval period find precedents in either case in classical, i.e., pre-Christian and pre-Buddhist, texts of each tradition. This approach seems to me to shed much more light on our understanding of the respective imperial ideologies *in toto*, as it engages with texts exhibiting a deliberate and self-conscious continuity with their classical precedents. The aim here is to examine not simply the periods of Roman Late Antiquity and Early Medieval China, but rather the ways in which imaginative social categories, political hierarchies, and conceptions of Self and Other codified in the "classical" ages manifested themselves under drastically different circumstances.

As to the texts chosen as comparanda, the circumstances surrounding the composition of the *Wars* and the *Jin shu* were hardly identical, and there are, in fact, important differences. Procopius had been a participant in many of the actions which he describes and must have had first-hand, or near first-hand, knowledge of many of the persons represented in his

---

[65] For studies on the introduction of Christianity and Buddhism in Roman and Chinese contexts, see Poo, Drake, and Raphals' recent volume *Old Society, New Belief: Religious Transformation of China and Rome, ca. 1st–6th Centuries*.

history. Moreover, although he made use of earlier sources and was clearly influenced in terms of style and genre by the writings of earlier historians, he is credited as the sole author of his work.[66] The situation is more complex with the *Jin shu*, for it chronicles events that occurred as many as three hundred years prior to the date of the text's compilation. Moreover, the *Jin shu* incorporates historical materials compiled by earlier historians, particularly the *Shiliu guo chunqiu* 十六國春秋, or *Spring and Autumn Annals of the Sixteen Kingdoms*, by Cui Hong 崔鴻 (478–525), who lived under the Northern Wei dynasty.[67] This lost work had itself incorporated a variety of historical texts, no longer extant, produced under the regimes of the various Sixteen Kingdoms states.[68] The *Jin shu*, therefore, contains among the oldest narrative accounts of the barbarian rulers of the fourth century. The *Wei shu* 魏書, written by the Northern Qi historian Wei Shou 魏收 in the mid-sixth century, also offers accounts of some of these same foreign conquest states. However, the fact that the *Wei shu* was produced under one of the Särbi-ruled conquest dynasties of the north makes it less apt as a comparandum to the writings of Procopius.

The *Jin shu*, on the other hand, is among the first works to be produced by the office of historical writing established under the early Tang. More importantly, it is the first text produced following the imperial reunification of China to offer an account of non-Chinese regimes that had conquered parts of north China following the collapse of the Western Jin dynasty in the early fourth century. By expressing the politically mainstream voice of official history, or at least quasi-official in Procopius' case, these two texts are a window into the world-views of literate elites of the partially or fully reconstituted empires, which looked back on periods of unprecedented political upheaval and change. Procopius and the historians of the *Jin shu* had a choice of whether or not to understand and represent barbarian rule as an aberration or a politically legitimate

---

[66] On Procopius' sources, see Brodka, "Die Wanderung der Hunnen, Vandalen, West- und Ostgoten – Prokopios von Kaisereia und seine Quellen," 13–37. Perhaps more analogous to the composition of *Jin shu* is the much later collation project of Constantine VII in the tenth century, *Excerpta de Legationibus*.

[67] Historians of the period also made use of imperial proclamations, letters, memorials, official records, etc. The multiplicity of historiographical and other sources synthesized by the authors of the *Jin shu* and other historical works produced in the same period thus render the early Tang histories "the end result of a very long process of editing, rewriting, and condensation, and none can properly be characterized as a primary source." Graff, *Medieval Chinese Warfare*, 5.

[68] See Wang Zhongluo for a table of all the histories of the Sixteen Kingdoms produced between the fourth and sixth centuries, *Wei Jin Nanbeichao shi*, 832–33. Also see Rogers, *The Chronicle of Fu Chien*, 15–19. On Cui Hong's *Shiliuguo chunqiu* and its sources, see Liu Xueyao, *Wu Hu shilun*, 2–5.

phenomenon – and if illegitimate, on what terms. In a consideration of how traditional forms of historiography responded to the phenomenon of barbarian rule, these two texts offer the most extensive narrative of accounts of who the barbarians were, what they did, and how they did it. More importantly, they contain the ethical and political assessments of historians who wrote from positions of imperial strength when producing accounts of barbarian states that had come and gone. They are therefore especially useful case studies of how resilient older paradigms of ethnographic representation were in the respective historiographic corpora; a close reading of these texts that were produced when, after a fashion, the dust had settled is the best means to understand how the period of dissolution was understood and responded to in ideological terms.

Chapters 3, 4, and 5 will accordingly concentrate on these two historical works produced in the periods following barbarian invasion and imperial reconquest, which have been chosen for the sheer number of correspondences they share. This delimitation of the texts to be considered in the latter three chapters will allow for a more comprehensive analysis of these two representative works, and the study will examine ways in which they were conditioned both by their respective historiographical precedents as well as by the cultural and political circumstances that surrounded their composition.

Important to any discussion of ethnological discourse in political contexts are the concepts of ethnicity and identity, and both of these concepts have been the object of great interest in classical and late antique scholarship in recent decades.[69] Important to state at the outset is that these terms will not be used in this study as a means of understanding ways in which peoples foreign to the Chinese and Roman empires perceived or represented themselves; their use here will primarily be in the context of examining ways in which Roman and Chinese historians delineated, rationalized, and labeled these peoples. This usage will also, therefore, be understood to apply to the processes by which Roman and Chinese elites defined themselves in opposition to some sort of Other, whether conceived of in "ethnic," i.e., with reference to notions of a shared "common essence,"[70] or in cultural or ethical terms. The terms will therefore be

---

[69] For a comprehensive overview of the different ways in which these terms have been studied in late antique scholarship as well as other fields, see Pohl, "Introduction – Strategies of Identification: A Methodological Profile" 1–64; on their use in the classical world, see Hall, *Ethnic Identity in Greek Antiquity*. Also see the studies collected in Malkin's edited volume, *Ancient Perceptions of Greek Ethnicity*.

[70] Konstan, "*To Hellēnikon Ethnos:* Ethnicity and the Construction of Ancient Greek Identity," 30.

used in an analysis of the imaginative categories employed in the mapping of political landscapes and in the establishing of political hierarchies. Although the word "identity" continues to be interpreted in different ways, here it will refer to the general or specific categories into which individuals or groups were subjectively placed. It will be understood as indicating assumptions of "a fundamental and consequential *sameness* among members of a group or category . . . expected to manifest itself in solidarity, in shared dispositions or consciousness, or in collective action."[71] "Ethnicity" will refer to the perception, common in the ancient world, that social communities defined by ethnonyms – *gentes, ethnē-ἔθνη, zu* 族, *lei* 類 – all carried with them a sense of shared descent that, though the degree of its prominence could vary considerably, were often expressed through ethnogenealogies that theoretically bound individual members of a community together.[72] As has been argued by Hall, features associated with an ethnonym such as a particular physiognomy or particular cultural practices (language, religion, etc.) are only "secondary *indicia*"; the primary criteria for determining membership in an ethnic group are "a putative subscription to a myth of common descent and kinship, an association with a specific territory and a sense of shared history."[73] The use of both of these terms throughout this study takes for granted the artificiality and subjectivity of their construction, perception, and ascription.

If historiography is an exercise that shapes, modifies, and transforms political realities, analysis of the role of barbarian actors in historical texts must also include an awareness of conceptual or geographical space: the "barbarian" is a concept that necessarily implies a degree of cultural or geographical distinction. As has been argued regarding the physical frontiers established between political communities,

> boundaries do not "naturally" exist between peoples and states, between social groups and religious confessions. They tend to fade out and become permeable. Thus, the effort of maintaining boundaries and investing them with ontological significance is an essential part of the construction of communities. . . . But they are not an expression of clear, unproblematic categories and identities, but part of the effort to establish appropriate distinctions in a puzzling world.[74]

---

[71] Brubaker and Cooper, "Beyond 'Identity'," 7.
[72] On this point, see Malkin, "Introduction," in *Ancient Perceptions of Greek Ethnicity*, 9–12; Konstan, "*To Hellēnikon ethnos*," 29–31.
[73] Hall, Jonathan, *Hellenicity: Between Ethnicity and Culture*, 9.
[74] Pohl, "Frontiers and Ethnic Identities: Some Final Considerations," 265.

Ancient historiography exhibits an ideological expression of similar efforts to create distinctions. It was a crucial part of the process by which identities could be categorized, understood, and prescribed. Helpful as a means of understanding this process is the deconstructivist concept of second-order observation developed by Luhmann, who has argued that observations, i.e., descriptions of reality, "use distinctions as forms and take forms as boundaries."[75] The earliest Greco-Roman and Chinese historical authors recognized the usefulness of a distinction between the groups they identified as their own and those of an Other, or Others, that could be marked as separate, thus establishing categories defined in cultural, ethnic, or geographic terms. The debates among modern historians as to an essential conception of, or attitude toward, the barbarian in Greco-Roman or Chinese antiquity only demonstrate that the contrast between Greek-Roman and barbarian, or Chinese and Hu 胡 (or a variety of terms that may be read as having an equivalent pejorative sense to the term "barbarian"), was, despite the consistency of ethnographic stereotypes, a constantly renegotiated phenomenon. As Luhmann has pointed out, distinctions "change their use value when we use them at different times and in different contexts."[76] A historian's chosen set of historical events, as well as his inherited paradigms of style and representational vocabulary, thus leads to a second order of observation in the selection and presentation of his material. Luhmann argues that "this selective presentation is not, as most people would be inclined to think, a *distortion* of reality. It is a *construction* of reality."[77]

This study considers representations of barbarian identity as central to the process of perpetuating, creating, and rearticulating conceptual boundaries between Self and Other. Chapters 1 and 2 consider the ancient ethnographic traditions and conceptions of the barbarian codified in the canonical texts that served as models for later historians. They do so keeping in mind this question: How will these conceptions manifest themselves in an age when both Rome and China were looking back on a period of division that had witnessed external peoples enter the empire – not to raid and pillage before withdrawing again beyond the frontier or even to settle peacefully, but to establish themselves as legitimate rulers over the Roman and Chinese heartlands? Chapters 3, 4, and 5 then assess imperial views of foreign peoples, the ways in which their identities were perceived and constructed on the cusp of a "great divergence" in imperial

---

[75] Luhmann, "Deconstruction as Second-Order Observing," 769.   [76] Ibid., 764.
[77] Ibid., 776.

trajectories, a period that was for both empires one of reconquest and restoration, even if short-lived in the Roman case. Were the enormous changes in the demographics and distribution of power following imperial fragmentation enough to shock the strength of the ethnographic paradigms and constructed identities inherited from antiquity? The historical problem of how to treat barbarian states, almost a contradiction in terms, naturally resulted in an unprecedented confluence of ethnographic rhetoric on the one hand and political discourse of legitimacy on the other.

In the age of Justinian and the early decades of the Tang, *renovatio* and *restoratio* of empire were critical components of the political program. Would such an age favor a cosmopolitan and inclusive quality in its ethnographic discourse or, on the contrary, a reestablishment and re-entrenchment of a civilized–barbarian dichotomy? And in either eventuality, what consequences could this have for the legacy of the Roman and Han Chinese empires?

CHAPTER I

Ethnography in the Classical Age

As the latter part of this book will examine ethnological discourse in Late Antiquity and Early Medieval China, periods that post-date by several centuries the formulation of that discourse into a relatively stable set of norms, tropes, and conventions, this chapter will provide an introductory survey to early ethnographic practices in the Greco-Roman and Chinese traditions. Such a survey will serve as the basis for an assessment of the degree of continuity of these practices in a later age of great transformation and change, namely the sixth-century Roman Empire and the seventh-century Tang 唐 dynasty. Only by establishing the basic components of classical ethnography and ethnological thought in each tradition will it be possible to contextualize the representations of foreign peoples in the later periods in terms of their respective traditions.

The first section of this chapter gives a brief introduction to the conventions of Greco-Roman and classical Chinese ethnography, discussing the respective generic forms that characterize or constitute what modern historians refer to as "ethnography" in either case. The chapter will then turn to the ways in which both traditions employed various rationalizing and explanatory paradigms in the "writing of peoples." In considering the role of the Other in the ethnographic traditions, Chapter 2 will discuss the term "barbarian" itself, alongside its Chinese equivalents, before moving on to consider the notion of the so-called barbarian antithesis or dichotomy. While the latter chapters will examine ethnographic discourse in later historiography, the origins of ethnological thinking in each tradition derive from a variety of literary genres including philosophical, geographical, medical, and ritual texts. Therefore, a discussion of the roots of ethnological thought must necessarily consider texts from these other genres alongside early historiography. Only by demonstrating this discursive link with the classical forms of ethnographic discourse in both traditions will it be possible to analyze the strategies through which late Roman and Tang Chinese historians engaged with their literary precedents while producing accounts of later periods of invasion, crisis, and imperial fragmentation.

The Greco-Roman Ethnographic Tradition

Ethnographic discourse in the western classical world has been an object of interest for some one hundred years, and there are already many modern studies that map out its most common conventions and provide summaries of its development in antiquity.[1] However, given its centrality to the concerns of the present chapter, it is important to both provide some basic remarks by way of orientation and, more importantly, to establish a fundamental set of parameters within which inquiries into, and representations of, foreign peoples were most often conducted in antiquity.

As has frequently been noted, there was no literary genre known as "ethnography" in the Greco-Roman world, and the word itself does not appear in the English language until 1834.[2] The genre was established in its own right as one of five main branches of Greek historiography by Jacoby in the early twentieth century, although the generic distinctiveness of ethnography and the other four categories he delineates – genealogy, contemporary history, horography, chronography – has come increasingly into question in recent decades (the tenacity of his originally proposed divisions in scholarly discourse notwithstanding).[3] Given the difficulties in defining ethnography as a distinct genre of classical literature, it is not easy to determine the earliest texts that may be definitively described as being ethnographic. Yet this problem disappears if one considers ethnography to be simply one expression of a broader body of ethnographic discourse that appears in virtually all literary genres of the classical world. As far as the first-century BC geographer Strabo was concerned, the ultimate authority on the geography, genealogy, and customs of foreign peoples was Homer, as is clear from his frequent references to the authority of the poet throughout his geographical survey. Scholars have noted that at least "proto-ethnographic"

---

[1] Particularly succinct are those of Thomas, *Lands and Peoples in Augustan Poetry: The Ethnographical Tradition*, 1–7, and Rives, *Tacitus Germania*, 11–17. For a broader range of recent studies, see Almagor and Skinner, *Ancient Ethnography: New Approaches*.

[2] Dench, "Ethnography and History," 494, citing the *OED*.

[3] Ibid.; Skinner, *The Invention of Greek Ethnography: From Homer to Herodotus*, 256. For a discussion of Jacoby's division of the categories of historiography, see Fornara, *The Nature of History in Ancient Greece and Rome*, 1–32. For a summary of critiques of Jacoby's conception of historiography, see Marincola, "Genre, Convention, and Innovation in Greco-Roman Historiography," 281–301; also see his essay, "Introduction: A Past without Historians," 1–13.

passages occur at various points in both the *Iliad* and *Odyssey*. For example, *Iliad* book thirteen begins with a number of observations on the pastoral allies of the Trojans:

> ... αὐτὸς δὲ πάλιν τρέπεν ὄσσε φαεινώ
> νόσφιν ἐφ᾽ ἱπποπόλων Θρηικῶν καθορώμενος αἶαν
> Μυσῶν τ᾽ ἀγχεμάχων καὶ ἀγαυῶν Ἱππημολγῶν
> γλακτοφάγων Ἀβίων τε δικαιοτάτων ἀνθρώπων.[4]

Zeus turned back his shining eyes, gazing away upon the land of the horse-breeding Thracians, of the close-fighting Mysians, of the milk-drinking Hippe-molgi, and of the most just of men, the Abii.

In this case, the poet describes ethnographic particulars of what would later become standard points of observation, such as a people's economy, military practice, and ethical character. Elsewhere in the *Iliad*, Homer notes both the hairstyle and characteristic weapons of the Thracians, describing them as "Thracians with hair on the crown of their heads, holding long spears in their hands."[5] In the *Odyssey*, the poetic forerunner of the later geographical *periplus* or *periodos gēs*, there are more detailed descriptions of the peoples the hero meets in his travels.[6] Homer's description of the Phaeacians in particular seems to prefigure later ethnographic digressions.[7] After noting that "the Phaeacians are skilful above all men in the driving of a swift ship upon the sea, so their women are skilled at the loom,"[8] he goes on to describe the remarkable features of the local fauna as it appears in the vicinity of Alcinous' home:

> ἔνθα δὲ δένδρεα μακρὰ πεφύκασι τηλεθάοντα,
> ὄγχναι καὶ ῥοιαὶ καὶ μηλέαι ἀγλαόκαρποι
> συκέαι τε γλυκεραὶ καὶ ἐλαῖαι τηλεθόωσαι.
> τάων οὔ ποτε καρπὸς ἀπόλλυται οὐδ᾽ ἀπολείπει
> χείματος οὐδὲ θέρευς, ἐπετήσιος· ἀλλὰ μάλ᾽ αἰεὶ
> Ζεφυρίη πνείουσα τὰ μὲν φύει, ἄλλα δὲ πέσσει.[9]

---

[4] *Iliad* 13.3–6.   [5] Θρήϊκες ἀκρόκομοι, δολίχ᾽ ἔγχεα χερσὶν ἔχοντες (*Iliad* 4.533).
[6] On the *Odyssey* as a prototype for later ethnography, see Dougherty, *The Raft of Odysseus: The Ethnographic Imagination of Homer's* Odyssey, especially 7–11, 95–101. On the literary form of the *periplus* and *periodos gēs*, see Romm, *Edges of the Earth in Ancient Thought: Geography, Explanation, and Fiction*, 26–31; Rives, *Germania*, 12. For further discussion of the *Odyssey* in relation to geographical thought, see Romm, *Edges of the Earth in Ancient Thought*, 183–96.
[7] For a discussion of both this and the following passage from the *Odyssey*, see Vlassopoulos, *Greeks and Barbarians*, 173; also see Skinner, *The Invention of Greek Ethnography*, 60–62.
[8] ὅσσον Φαίηκες περὶ πάντων ἴδριες ἀνδρῶν / νῆα θοὴν ἐνὶ πόντῳ ἐλαυνέμεν, ὡς δὲ γυναῖκες / ἱστὸν τεχνῆσσαι (*Odyssey* 7.108–10).
[9] *Odyssey* 7.114–19.

Growing there were tall, bountiful trees: pear, pomegranate, and apple trees with wondrous fruit, sweet figs, and blooming olives. Their fruit never goes bad or runs out in either winter or summer, lasting throughout the year. But the west wind, always blowing, gives birth to some and ripens the rest.

The poet then describes the gathering and crushing of grapes and the stream that serves as a water source for the community, i.e., aspects of daily life, subsistence, and custom. Though such description is on a scale far smaller than that produced by later historians such as Herodotus, who sought to give an image not of a Mycenaean or Archaic Greek community but kingdoms and empires on the scale of Lydia or Persia, one nevertheless sees the interest exhibited by Homer in the economy, environment, and cultural practices of those living on the periphery of the world familiar to the Greek audiences of early epic poetry.

Also present in Homer is the element of the miraculous that appears at the edges of the known world, the *eschatiai*-ἐσχατιαί, and among their inhabitants, the *eschatoi andrōn*-ἔσχατοι ἀνδρῶν.[10] In depictions of these exotic regions, readers are confronted both with idealized portraits of human communities, such as those of the Ethiopians and Hyperboreans, as well as of their dystopic inverse as we see in the cannibalism and lawlessness of the mythical Cyclopes. The land of the Cyclopes as described in the *Odyssey* exhibits a number of features characteristic of later ethnographic description. In Odysseus' own words, the poet offers a vivid image of the society of the giants, which observes the remarkable and alien features of their customs and economy:

> Κυκλώπων δ᾽ ἐς γαῖαν ὑπερφιάλων ἀθεμίστων
> ἱκόμεθ᾽, οἵ ῥα θεοῖσι πεποιθότες ἀθανάτοισιν
> οὔτε φυτεύουσιν χερσὶν φυτὸν οὔτ᾽ ἀρόωσιν,
> ἀλλὰ τά γ᾽ ἄσπαρτα καὶ ἀνήροτα πάντα φύονται,
> πυροὶ καὶ κριθαὶ ἠδ᾽ ἄμπελοι . . .
> τοῖσιν δ᾽ οὔτ᾽ ἀγοραὶ βουληφόροι οὔτε θέμιστες,
> ἀλλ᾽ οἵ γ᾽ ὑψηλῶν ὀρέων ναίουσι κάρηνα
> ἐν σπέεσι γλαφυροῖσι, θεμιστεύει δὲ ἕκαστος
> παίδων ἠδ᾽ ἀλόχων, οὐδ᾽ ἀλλήλων ἀλέγουσι.[11]

We came to the land of the haughty and lawless Cyclopes, who, having faith in the immortal gods, neither plant nor plow with their hands; but all things grow there unsown and uncultivated: grain and barley and grapevines . . . Among the

---

[10] See Romm, *Edges of the Earth in Ancient Thought*, 45–81. On the function of *thaumata*-θαύματα, "wonders," often associated with distant lands in ethnographic accounts, see Hartog, *The Mirror of Herodotus: The Representation of the Other in the Writing of History*, 230–37.
[11] *Odyssey* 9.106–15.

Cyclopes there are neither deliberative assemblies nor laws, but they inhabit the peaks of high mountains in hollow caves; each gives the law to his own children and wives, and nor do the Cyclopes care about one another.

Although the island of the Cyclopes is clearly situated on the mythical periphery of the known world, the poet nevertheless offers a relatively detailed description of the Cyclopes' pastoral society and presents a realistic image of what Greeks might have considered to be a primitive society. As other scholars have noted, this effect is achieved through a series of negative contrasts: the Cyclopes lack the Greek practice of farming and they lack the participatory and deliberative institutions of Greek political life. Despite the fact that an imaginary people is being described, these passages nevertheless represent a "form of discourse that may legitimately be termed *ethnographic.*"[12]

While acknowledging its poetic antecedents, modern scholars trace the origins of "scientific" inquiry into the traditions and customs of non-Greeks to the late sixth and early fifth centuries BC, in particular to the lost geographical writings of Hecataeus, whose *periodos gēs* seems to have been a travel account with descriptions of individual voyages and destinations.[13] However, ethnography has its most textually intact founder, as do historiography and Greek prose itself, in the writings of Herodotus, whose first four books provide lengthy ethnographic excursuses on numerous peoples living to the north, east, and south of the Aegean Sea. Though Herodotus' immediate successor in the historiographical canon, Thucydides, did not devote nearly as much attention to the description of foreign peoples, his near contemporaries were certainly preoccupied with historical and/or ethical accounts of other peoples, e.g., Ctesias' accounts of India and Persia and Xenophon's *Cyropaedia*, a work that valorizes the Persian ruler as an ideal monarch.[14] The ethnographic excursus or digression features prominently in Polybius' history in the second century BC and was to remain a consistent component of historical narratives written in Greek and Latin from at least that time onward.

That is not to say, however, that ethnography was solely an embedded feature of historiography, and texts that are often considered paradigmatic

[12] Skinner, *The Invention of Greek Ethnography*, 49; also see Müller, *Geschichte der antiken Ethnographie und ethnologischen Theoriebildung*, 53–59.

[13] Trüdinger, *Studien zur Geschichte der griechisch-römischen Ethnographie*, 8–14; Müller, *Geschichte der antiken Ethnographie*, 94–101; also see Skinner's discussion of Lloyd on Hecataeus' influence on Herodotus, *The Invention of Greek Ethnography*, 240.

[14] On Ctesias, see Fornara, *The Nature of History in Ancient Greece and Rome*, 14. On the *Cyropaedia*, see Hirsch, *The Friendship of the Barbarians: Xenophon and the Persian Empire*, 61–97.

in their modes of representation and understanding of foreign peoples such as the Hippocratic *Airs, Waters, Places* (and even Aeschylus' *Persae*) clearly fall outside of the writing of history.[15] In the former text, the author considers the dual influences of climate and acquired characteristics in explaining differences between populations. He observes in reference to the former that

εἰσὶ γὰρ φύσιες αἱ μὲν ὄρεσιν ἐοικυῖαι δενδρώδεσί τε καὶ ἐφύδροισιν, αἱ δὲ λεπτοῖσί τε καὶ ἀνύδροισιν, αἱ δὲ λειμακωδεστέροισί τε καὶ ἑλώδεσιν, αἱ δὲ πεδίῳ τε καὶ ψιλῇ καὶ ξηρῇ γῇ. Αἱ γὰρ ὧραι αἱ μεταλλάσσουσαι τῆς μορφῆς τὴν φύσιν εἰσὶ διάφοροι· ἢν δὲ διάφοροι ἔωσι μέγα σφῶν αὐτέων, διαφοραὶ καὶ πλείονες γίνονται τοῖσιν εἴδεσιν.[16]

There are some physical natures that are similar to forested and rainy mountains, while others are like slender and waterless mountains; some physical natures are like mountains with more meadows and marshes, while others are similar to a plain and earth that is high and dry. For the seasons altering the nature of form are different. And if these should be different significantly among themselves, there will be more differences in the physical forms.

In this passage, the author of the treatise uses the general principle of climatic determinism to describe the unique physical appearance of peoples living in distant regions under particular climatic conditions. Although the description of various human forms in the following examples he provides is more theoretical than based on objective observation, he nevertheless exhibits an ethnographic gaze in attempting to describe and rationalize the physiognomy of distant peoples.

The author does not limit himself to considering the influence of climate, however, for he also allows for the transmission of acquired physical attributes from generation to generation as a result of cultural practice. The example provided to illustrate this principle is his account of the Makrokephaloi or "Longheads," who deliberately elongate the pliable skulls of their infants:

τὴν μὲν γὰρ ἀρχὴν ὁ νόμος αἰτιώτατος ἐγένετο τοῦ μήκεος τῆς κεφαλῆς, νῦν δὲ καὶ ἡ φύσις ξυμβάλλεται τῷ νόμῳ. Τοὺς γὰρ μακροτάτην ἔχοντας τὴν κεφαλὴν γενναιοτάτους ἡγέονται.[17]

---

[15] On the contribution of Aeschylus to the formation of fifth-century conceptions of Persian and eastern, non-Greek peoples, see Hall, Edith, *Inventing the Barbarian: Greek Self-Definition through Tragedy*, 76–100.

[16] *Aer.* 13.   [17] *Aer.* 14.

For in the beginning, their practice was the primary cause for the length of their heads, but now nature is added to practice. For they reckon that those having the longest head are the most noble.

In this example, one sees the ethnographer's interest not only in observable physical difference but also in particularities of local custom. This short passage is also an early illustration of the complex theoretical relationship between the competing influences of nature and nurture, *phusis*-φύσις and *nomos*-νόμος, in determining the recognizably distinct characteristics of different peoples. In a manner analogous to what one finds in the historiography of the fifth century BC, the theoretical description of foreign peoples employed in this earliest Greek medical treatise performs a rationalizing function that explains the diversity of human custom and physiognomy.

As observed by Skinner, one finds that "ethnographic description permeated everything from medical treatises to Attic drama."[18] Despite its prevalence in various media, however, ethnographic discourse remained just that: a mode of discourse that was able to transcend generic boundaries and that never crystallized into a recognizable genre in its own right.[19] There are extant titles of works from the Hellenistic era that seem to have been devoted to the exposition of a particular region or group of people and can therefore be plausibly assumed to have been ethnographic monographs, but none of these has come down to posterity.[20] Moreover, it has been suggested that even in these seeming prototypical ethnographic monographs the historical component may have overshadowed the ethnographic description in the texts, again illustrating the highly porous nature of any barrier between ethnography and its super-category historiography.[21] While the *Germania* of Tacitus is in fact an ethnographic monograph in its own right, the far more typical context for the exposition of ethnographic knowledge was that preferred by Herodotus: the digression or excursus embedded within the historical narrative. The *Germania* of Tacitus is thus highly irregular as medium for ethnographic representation;

---

[18] Skinner, *The Invention of Greek Ethnography*, 254.
[19] On the failure of ethnography to develop into a distinct textual genre, see Woolf, *Tales of the Barbarians: Ethnography and Empire in the Roman West*, esp. 54–58. I use "discourse" here in the same sense as Riggsby: "a [general] way of talking about some subject matter." *Caesar in Gaul and Rome: War in Words*, 4.
[20] Fornara, *The Nature of History in Ancient Greece and Rome*, 12; on Hellanicus of Lesbos, see Müller, *Geschichte der antiken Ethnographie und ethnologischen Theoriebildung*, 132–37; on Xanthus of Lydia, see Vlassopoulos, *Greeks and Barbarians*, 185–86.
[21] Rives, *Germania*, 13; Fornara, *The Nature of History in Ancient Greece and Rome*, 14.

far more typical is that author's treatment of the Britons in the *Agricola* or the Jews in the *Histories*.[22]

It has also been observed that ethnography was only one manifestation of a more general mode of thinking that was occupied with the "description and conceptualization of the world and its peoples" and was also embodied in material culture and even ritual performance.[23] In this sense, ethnography may be understood not merely as a genre or even a particular mode that authors might dip in and out of, but rather as a more generalized way of perceiving and categorizing identities of Self and Other. Work by Gruen and Schneider has explored the material representations of non-Greeks and non-Romans in both private and public contexts and in consideration of the discourse of alterity and otherness, which is a central feature of ethnography in general.[24] Dench has considered the ways in which ethnographic discourse was expressed in Roman triumphal processions.[25] Given this multiplicity of the types of source material that may be described as "ethnographic," the understanding of the term as it has been formulated by Skinner is particularly apt: "'Thinking about culture from the point of view of an outsider' envisages representations of peoples, customs, products, and places as all being in some way 'ethnographic'."[26] In this sense, ethnography is not limited solely to the *logoi* inserted as digressions within either a historical narrative or geographical *periplus* but also includes any instances where there is a descriptive representation of an individual or group understood to belong to a culturally or ethnically distinct category. Virgil's description of the hair, clothing, and weapons of the Gauls on the shield of Aeneas thus deserves to be considered "ethnographic" as much as does a Herodotean excursus on the sacrificial practices of Scythians. However, given the fact that the focus here will be on the textual representations of non-Roman and non-Chinese peoples, ethnographic analysis of material culture and ritual performance will fall beyond the scope of this study.

In historiography itself, it is also important to recognize that ethnographic discourse is not limited to the familiar form of the ethnographic digression. Material that refers to customs and characteristics of foreign

---

[22] *Agricola* 10–12; *Historiae* 5.2–8. On the narrative and rhetorical functions of the ethnographic digression, explicated using Sallust's *Jugurtha* as a model, see Woolf, *Tales of the Barbarians*, 55–57.

[23] Dench, *Romulus' Asylum: Roman Identities from the Age of Alexander to the Age of Hadrian*, 43–44.

[24] Gruen, *Rethinking the Other in Antiquity*, 211–20; Schneider, "Image and Empire: The Shaping of Augustan Rome," 284–95.

[25] Dench, *Romulus' Asylum*, 76–80.

[26] Skinner quoting James Clifford, *The Invention of Greek Ethnography*, 16.

peoples frequently appears also in the course of the main narrative and may
serve to exemplify the qualities ascribed to a given people elsewhere in the
same text or in that of an earlier authority. In this case, the ethnographic
description may be said to occur in real time within the narrative as
opposed to in one of the longer digressions. For example, Caesar, in
describing the beginnings of the Gallic uprising under Vercingetorix,
relates in passing that it is the custom of the Gauls to spread news in a
rapid manner by shouting reports of events throughout the countryside
and territories of the different Gallic states.[27] He also uses the phrase *suo
more* to indicate that a given behavior is characteristic of a people when he
is in the middle of describing events as they unfold.[28] In similar fashion,
Tacitus refers to the *mos gentis* of the Batavians who raise up their leaders
on a shield after their acclamation, thereby making an ethnographic
observation in medias res.[29] Likewise, Herodotus' historical narrative too
is sprinkled with ethnographic asides that are located outside any of the
longer digressions.[30] It is thus necessary to expand the notion of ethnography and ethnographic observation beyond the more or less self-conscious
historiē of the author in a digression or excursus to include any characterization or description that seems to indicate some degree of rhetorical
alterity or interest in a quality of a group that, by virtue of its needing to be
commented on and explained, is marked as somehow foreign to author
and audience.

Nevertheless, the excursus or digression in historiography remains the
most prominent platform for the exposition of ethnographic information,
a narrative mode first displayed by Herodotus that continues in virtually
unaltered form in both Greek and Latin texts up through the sixth
century AD. The ethnographic digression has several characteristic features, although these may vary between authors and even within a single
text; there is thus no hard-and-fast rule as to what types of information
will be treated. As Rives has remarked, "the only invariable subject is the
people itself, including their origin, their physical characteristics, and their

---

[27] *Bellum Gallicum* 7.3.2–3.
[28] E.g., the Gallic custom of approving a speech with the clashing of their arms (*Bellum Gallicum* 7.21.1) and the Suebic custom of holding council (*Bellum Gallicum* 4.19.2).
[29] *Historiae* 4.15.2.
[30] E.g., his observation that Lydian practice of purification is the same as that of the Greeks when Croesus receives a Phrygian with blood-stained hands (Hdt. 1.35.2); in the catalog of peoples in the army of Xerxes, he notes a wide variety of specific features of dress and armament that are particular to different peoples, though one could argue that the catalog of Persian subjects is a digression in its own right (Hdt. 7.61–96).

various religious, social, and military customs."[31] In addition to an origin myth, a historical account of a people's migrations, settlements, and interactions with other groups is often included. The particular qualities of the landscape, climate, and resources of a given area are also areas of interest to the historian.[32] As noted above, the features of a people or place that a given author sees fit to comment on may vary considerably, and even near contemporaries may give markedly different descriptions of the same people.[33]

In order to demonstrate both variation and continuity within this tradition, it will be helpful here to consider a pair of ethnographic excursuses or digressions as they appear in our earliest historian Herodotus in the fifth century BC and in his much later successor Ammianus Marcellinus in the fourth century AD. Following his account of the rise of Cyrus and the Great King's successful conquest of the Median Empire, Herodotus pauses in the narrative to introduce what he has learned about Persian society and customs.[34] He begins with a description of their religious and sacrificial practices, noting that they sacrifice to the sun, moon, and stars as well as the Greek gods Zeus and Aphrodite. He then discusses their dining habits and penchant for lavish and elaborate birthday feasts. He observes that the Persians are fond of wine, though they take care to urinate or vomit only in private. Herodotus describes greeting practices between Persians and their relative estimation of foreign peoples as correlated to greater or lesser proximity. He notes their great receptivity to foreign customs – even the practice of pederasty, which they have learned from the Greeks; otherwise they have multiple wives and concubines. He describes their high esteem of men with many sons and famously describes the three sole tenets of Persian education, "to ride, shoot, and speak the truth": ἱππεύειν καὶ τοξεύειν καὶ ἀληθίζεσθαι.[35] Herodotus praises this custom as he does aspects of their legal system, and he comments on the Persians' aversion for lying and acquiring debt. He describes their abhorrence of leprosy and observes their practice of giving personal names that accord with an individual's rank or physique, noting that all Persian names end with the Greek letter sigma. He ends the digression with a description of Persian burial practices and some of the practices of the Magi.

[31] Rives, *Germania*, 15.   [32] Ibid.

[33] For example, see Riggsby's discussion of more or less contemporary accounts of the Gauls in the first century BC, *Caesar in Gaul and Rome*, 47–71.

[34] Hdt. 1.131–40.   [35] Hdt. 1.136.2.

This general form of the ethnographic digression remained stable for over the next thousand years in the writings of historians in both Greek and Latin: at the point in the narrative where a people is introduced or at a critical juncture in the action, the historian often pulls back and offers his observations on various aspects of foreign culture and society, relying either on autopsy or inquiry. The *Res Gestae* of Ammianus, who wrote in Latin in the late fourth century AD and described himself as "a former soldier and a Greek," illustrates the continuity of this form.[36] In the midst of his account of the Emperor Julian's invasion of Mesopotamia, Ammianus offers a *periplus* of the Sasanian Empire, which he concludes with an ethnographic digression on Persian customs. Having discussed the religion of Zoroastrianism while progressing through Media in his geographical survey, he first notes their physical appearance (generally unattractive in Ammianus' eyes), before commenting as did Herodotus on their practice of taking multiple wives and concubines; however, Ammianus claims that, unlike the Greeks, the Persians do not have sexual relations with boys. Curiously, and again in contradiction of Herodotus, Ammianus claims that the Persians avoid banquets and alcohol and are extremely moderate. Yet he does observe the same modesty in regards to urination that was commented on by Herodotus. He gives a generally negative impression of Persian boastfulness and arrogance, though he notes that they are formidable warriors. Unlike Herodotus, Ammianus presents the Persians as excessively cruel and their laws harsh;[37] he does allow, however, that their judges are well chosen and appropriately appointed. He notes their constant military training and reliance on cavalry, features present in Herodotus' account of Persian education. Lastly, he comments on the gaudiness of Persian sartorial habits. Though emphases vary, and even some details are contradictory, many of the same subjects are of interest to both historians who wrote in different languages and were separated by some eight hundred years. Moreover, it is important to note that, alongside the continuity of form, there is a surprising, and almost certainly deliberate, continuity of content.[38]

---

[36] *miles quondam et Graecus* (Amm. Marc. 31.16.9); the digression occurs at 23.6.75–84. For a discussion of Ammianus' treatment of the Persians (as well as that of other historians, including Procopius), see Drijvers, "A Roman Image of the 'Barbarian' Sasanians," 67–76; Morley, "Beyond the Digression: Ammianus Marcellinus on the Persians," 10–25.

[37] That the Persians did flay criminals is, however, attested at least once elsewhere in Herodotus, Hdt. 5.25.1.

[38] See Woolf's discussion of "ethnographic ghosts" in Ammianus' ethnography of fourth-century Gaul, which Woolf argues exhibits features that belong to the reality of earlier centuries. *Tales of the Barbarians*, 105–11.

This general set of categorical and straightforwardly put observations typical of ethnographic accounts are part of a more general process of rationalization. That is, by examining the various ways in which the object of the ethnographic gaze exhibits contrasts with the frame of reference of the author, the historian produces not an "objective" representation of a foreign people but a highly subjective interpretation through the lens of his own cultural assumptions and worldview. Thereby, the ethnographic account serves to render an unintelligible phenomenon intelligible to his audience. In order to make differences comprehensible, ancient historians developed frameworks through which they were able to translate the foreign into the familiar, and this effort is visible in the terms that often precede an ethnographic account or digression: *de origine et situ*, "regarding the origin and location."[39] These two categories, origin and location, signify two of the explanatory frameworks or paradigms, identified and described by Woolf, that ancient ethnographers availed themselves of, and these are considered in detail below.[40] But before proceeding to a discussion of these rationalizing paradigms, we may first consider the formation and characteristics of the Chinese ethnographic tradition.

The Chinese Ethnographic Tradition

The representation of non-Chinese peoples in classical Chinese literature and historiography has received comparatively less attention from modern scholars, though there is growing interest in the perceptions and representations of non-Chinese and their place in the pre-imperial and imperial world order.[41] This section discusses the earliest references to, and descriptions of, peoples identified as being somehow external to the Chinese

---

[39] Thomas, *Lands and Peoples in Roman Poetry*, 126–27.

[40] See Woolf, *Tales of the Barbarians*, 32–58.

[41] I have been unable to find a work in Chinese analyzing the practice of ethnography (民族志 or 人种志) or ethnographic practice as it appears in ancient Chinese texts. More common are studies on the notion of "ancient views of the ethnicity" 古代民族观. Unfortunately, many of these studies suffer greatly from modern nationalistic ideology and repeat stock phrases (e.g., "From ancient times, China has been a country composed of many ethnic groups" 自古以来中国是一个多民族国家) that are echoes of modern policy and propaganda. Such studies tend to emphasize that xenophobia toward non-Chinese peoples as it existed in former times was part of the process of creating the modern multiethnic Chinese people (中华民族), which gradually and inevitably evolved into its current state of interethnic equality and harmony. The academic study of ethnic identities in antiquity can even be explicitly placed in the service of achieving modern political aims; the preface to a history of ethnic groups in Chinese history affirms that since ethnic issues are a crucial aspect of society, "research into ethnic questions constitutes a great mission of constructing the country and bringing stability to society": 研究民族问题就成为建设国家，稳定社会的一大使命. Wang Zhonghan, *Zhongguo minzu shi gaiyao*, 1.

cultural and political sphere in the first millennium BC and provides an introduction to the eventual development of an ethnographic component to Chinese historiography that shares many key features with the Greco-Roman tradition.

What became the standard form of historiography, which would thenceforth serve as the primary vessel for ethnographic description of foreign peoples, appeared comparatively late in China, i.e., around the year 100 BC and over one hundred years following the first unification of China under the state of Qin 秦 in 221. In the preceding Spring and Autumn and Warring States periods (c. 771–221 B.C.), ethnographic information was scattered throughout a range of literary genres, appearing in philosophical, ritual, and historical texts. It will therefore be useful to offer a brief survey of the ethnographic discourse in these pre-imperial Chinese texts before moving on to the *Shiji* 史記 of Sima Qian 司馬遷, the prototype of all later official dynastic historiography and the first text to provide a systematic and detailed inquiry into the life ways of non-Chinese peoples.

As aspects of the Greco-Roman ethnographic tradition may ultimately be traced back to Homer, foreign peoples feature in China's earliest and most influential poetic text, the *Shijing* 詩經 (*Book of Odes*). Though their appearance in this poetic collection is not accompanied by ethnographic description, the hostile relationship between them and the Shang 商 and Zhou 周 communities as presented in the *Shijing* would become a salient component of later ethnographic writing. The *Shijing* is a compendium containing poems composed over the course of several hundred years beginning around the turn of the first millennium BC, and it was to have an influence in later centuries comparable to that of Homer in the Greco-Roman world.[42] In the *Shijing*, however, the non-Chinese are not multifaceted participants in the individual poems; they are at best peripheral and murky figures who feature primarily as enemies either threatening the Chinese central domains or being defeated by the victorious kings and generals of the Shang and Zhou kingdoms. For example, the poem "Yinwu" celebrates the fact the during the reign of Shang Tang 商湯 none of the Di 氐 and Qiang 羌 peoples dared to neglect to visit the Shang court in order to offer tribute.[43] The poem "Caiwei" laments the problems

[42] On the *Shijing* and all of the Chinese primary sources cited in this chapter, see the entries in Loewe's *Early Chinese Texts: A Bibliographical Guide*. For a comparative discussion of the reception of the *Shijing* with that of Homeric epic, see Beecroft, "Homer and the Shi Jing as Imperial Texts," 153–73.

[43] 昔有成湯，自彼氐羌，莫敢不來享，莫敢不來王 (*Shijing*, Shangsong 商頌, Yinwu 殷武.1041).

caused by non-Chinese incursions, by a people here named as Xianyun 玁狁, attributing to them the loss of home, family, and peace.[44] Battles and wars over territory are recounted in the poem "Liu Yue," which praises the victories of the one of the Zhou kings over the Xianyun, who appear early in the poem as a powerful threat that necessitates an immediate military campaign in response.[45] The poem goes on to celebrate the Chinese counteroffensive, showing how they "then attacked the Xianyun and thus performed a great feat."[46] The poet then describes the magnitude and extent of the barbarian incursion:

玁狁匪茹，整居焦穫，侵鎬及方，至于涇陽.[47]

The Xianyun were not weak: they entirely occupied Jiaohuo, invaded Hao and Fang, and made it all the way to the northern bank of the Jing river.

In this poem, Zhou forces rally, however, and manage to drive the Xianyun all the way back to Dayuan in the northwest.[48] In each of these cases, the non-Chinese feature as monotone actors whose role in the poems is that of either invading aggressor or chastised rebel.

Scholars have commented on the fact that in the *Iliad* there is a marked dearth of ethnographic detail that might serve to distinguish the Trojans from the Greeks.[49] Moreover, the Trojans appear as characters exhibiting the same psychological depth and complexity as is exhibited by leaders of the besieging Greeks. And as often noted, much of the pathos in the poem is clearly engendered by the sufferings destined to befall the city of Troy and its inhabitants. The adversaries of the peoples retrospectively identified as the ancestors of the Chinese in the *Shijing* and Greeks in the *Iliad* in later centuries are thus granted little in the way of ethnographic distinction.[50] Yet it is a noteworthy contrast between these two foundational texts of either literary tradition that in the Homeric case, even individual enemies of the Greeks are represented with a great degree of sympathy and internal complexity whereas in the *Shijing*, the ancient enemies of the Shang and Zhou kingdoms are collective entities whose position in the

---

[44] 靡室靡家，玁狁之故，不遑啟居，玁狁之故 (*Shijing*, Xiaoya 小雅, Caiwei 采薇.464).

[45] 玁狁孔熾，我是用急 (*Shijing*, Xiaoya 小雅, Liuyue 六月.499).

[46] 薄伐玁狁，以奏膚公 (*Shijing*, Xiaoya 小雅, Liuyue 六月.501).   [47] Ibid.

[48] 薄伐玁狁，至于大原 (*Shijing*, Xiaoya 小雅, Liuyue 六月.503).

[49] For example, see Edith Hall, *Inventing the Barbarian*, 40–45.

[50] As noted above, the use of the terms "China" and "Chinese" (and even "Greek") in reference to early first-millennium BC contexts is of course problematic. Such terms are employed here simply to indicate what would have been fluidly defined cultural and/or linguistic communities that only in later centuries were designated by the more specific ethnonyms of "Hua" 華, "Xia" 夏, or "Greek," and they will be employed throughout because of the lack of suitable alternatives.

poems is simply one of foreign and almost elemental antagonism. We know the name of Hector, his wife Andromache, and even the name and nickname of his infant son. The barbarians of the *Shijing* are nameless.

In the above examples from the *Shijing*, the non-Chinese peoples who appear have been those associated with the northern or western regions. A last example from the *Shijing*, the poem "Caiqi," is in celebration of a Zhou victory over the foreign peoples of the south as well, claiming that

蠢爾蠻荊，大邦為讎. . . . 顯允方叔，征伐玁狁，蠻荊來威.[51]

Foolish are these Man of Jing in the south, who make themselves the enemies of [our] great country. . . . The general Fang Shu was heroic and true, he who set out and attacked the Xianyun and awed the Man of Jing into submission.

In this case, Zhou forces are shown subduing both the northern barbarians, the Xianyun, as well as the Man 蠻 of the south. In all of these examples, the various non-Chinese feature as military adversaries, relatively faceless groups distinguished only by their ethnonyms and inhabiting the various corners of the periphery surrounding the central realms of the Chinese Shang and Zhou kingdoms. Though not collated within a single "barbarian" category as would become common in later centuries, their primary function in the text is to serve as a source of danger to the Chinese community or as enemies whose defeat and subjugation provides material for the celebration of the early kings.

Given the peripheral role foreign peoples play in the *Shijing* poems, it is perhaps not surprising that one finds little ethnographic information on these various non-Chinese groups. While the paucity of ethnographic detail in regards to the Trojans in the *Iliad* seems to indicate a lack of ethno-cultural distinction between Trojans and Greeks, in the *Shijing* the peripheral role of the Xianyun and others is characterized by their arrogance, the military threat they pose, and the glory attributed to victorious Chinese kings upon repelling their incursions. It is not until the middle of the first millennium BC that there appears slightly more information in Chinese texts regarding some of the particular ways in which some of these peoples were distinct from the Zhou community, and we may now turn to the philosophical discourses that flourished between the fifth and third centuries BC.

As do their Greco-Roman counterparts, classical philosophers in China often refer to the perceived distinctions between their own society and those of their various neighbors in order to buttress rhetorical arguments. These instances, while they do not provide anything like the systematic

---

[51] *Shijing*, Xiaoya 小雅, Caiqi 采芑.510.

description of foreign customs that would appear in the *Shiji* of Sima Qian in the early first century BC, nevertheless do exhibit a degree of interest in social and ethnic particulars, an interest that intensified in later ethnographic historiography. The Confucian, or more appropriately, the Classicist tradition in particular would later exert great influence on the ethical framing of ethnographic accounts.[52] An oft-quoted passage in the the *Lunyu* 論語 (*Analects*) of Confucius refers to an episode where Guan Zhong 管仲, an official of a Chinese state, had urged his lord to come to the aid of another Chinese state being attacked by the northern Di 狄 people. Confucius praises him saying, "Were it not for Guan Zhong, we would all be wearing our hair loose and fastening our garments on the left."[53] The phrase *pifa zuoren* 被髮左衽, "wearing hair loose and fastening garments on the left," a description of two defining differences between the Chinese and the barbarians of the north, appears frequently in the historical and ethnographic works of later centuries in contexts where an author seeks to draw a rhetorical distinction between the moral orthodoxy of Classicist norms and the disorder and inversion of ritual propriety among the barbarians.[54] In the case of Confucianism, as well as the other philosophical schools of the period, such ethnographic observations and distinctions appear in a rhetorical context where scholars "served as advisers to the kings, attempting to persuade them to adopt certain policies either for governing their own people or for conquering the neighboring states."[55]

[52] Following the example of Nylan and others, the term "Classicist" will be adopted in most places instead of the more conventional, though imprecise, term "Confucian." See Nylan, "Classics without Canonization," 721–41. Still, it remains widespread for scholars to use the term "Confucian" to apply to the body of moral and political norms, rooted in a canon of authoritative texts, that formed the basis of imperial literati worldviews, especially as manifested in the practice of historiography. On this point, see, e.g., Yü, "Reflections on Chinese Historical Thinking," 294–316. For a discussion of the establishment of Ru 儒, i.e., Confucian, texts as a state canon in the late second century BC and the subsequent "*ru* intellectual hegemony," which developed over the course of the next hundred years, see Lewis, *Writing and Authority in Early China*, 337–62; Queen, *From Chronicle to Canon*, 227–40. On ways in which the term Ru itself has been contested, see Cai, Liang, *Witchcraft and the Rise of the First Confucian Empire*, 3–5.

[53] 微管仲，吾其被髮左衽矣 (*Lunyu* 14.17, Xianwen 憲問.151).

[54] The phrase appears in the *Han shu* 漢書 in reference to the barbarians in general in Ban Gu's 班固 final comments on his chapters on the Xiongnu (*Han shu* 94b.3834); a variant of the phrase is used in the *Hou Han shu* as 椎結左衽 (*Hou Han shu* 80a.2607); it appears in the *Nan Qi shu* in reference to the northern Särbi people (*Nan Qi shu* 57.983); it may even be used in reference to the Qiang peoples of the west and thus takes on a wholly generic sense of undifferentiated otherness that is not restricted to barbarians of the north, but rather indicates any who deviate from Chinese custom (*Hou Han shu* 87.2878). For an interesting challenge to such distinctions, see *Bei Qi shu* 北齊書 25.365.

[55] Lu, Xing, *Rhetoric in Ancient China: Fifth to Third Century B.C.E: A Comparison with Classical Greek Rhetoric*, 64–65.

An example of more detailed description of foreign customs appears in the primary text of the Mohist school, the *Mozi* 墨子, where ethnographic information is marshaled to argue for a measured frugality in funerary ritual. In this passage, the philosopher Mozi shows how various non-Chinese peoples, in contrast to the excessively elaborate practices of the Chinese, exhibit an array of funerary customs that include cremation and forms of cannibalism. The text suggests that foreign peoples and Chinese demonstrate two extremes of behavior and that a moderate rule must be established (by and for the Chinese) that would satisfy the requirements of piety without engaging in the wasteful ostentation being criticized by the philosopher. While on the one hand this passage might seem to offer detailed information on foreign customs, these descriptions are so obviously in the service of the rhetorical argumentation that there is little reason to assume any real interest in, or faithful reporting of, an actual foreign practice.[56] In this sense, the above example may be likened to descriptions of antithetical foreign practices as they occur in Greek ethnography in rhetorical contexts, such as the assertion in Herodotus, to be discussed below, that the Indians consumed the corpses of their dead.

In addition to philosophical works that date to pre-imperial centuries, there are also classical ritual texts in the Confucian canon that include references to non-Chinese peoples, but these too are limited in the amount of detail they provide. Nevertheless, they are important because they exhibit an emphasis on geographical schemata that would continue in later centuries to condition Chinese literary representations of foreign peoples, particularly in political contexts. Texts such as the *Shangshu* 尚書 (*Book of Documents*), the *Zhouli* 周禮 (*Rites of Zhou*), and the *Liji* 禮記 (*Book of Rites*) are not concerned with explaining or understanding non-Chinese peoples of the periphery, but focus rather on the description of a cosmological world order and the prescription of particular areas of habitation for different peoples as well as the appropriate relationships between these areas.

---

[56] The passage is also interesting for the fact that it suggests, as does a famous passage from Herodotus to be discussed below, that arbitrary custom is the determinant factor in what is or is not acceptable in a given society: 此所謂便其習而義其俗者也. However, the *Mozi* also argues for the necessity of a correct standard of funerary practice. Claiming that as there are objective standards for the uses of clothing and food because of their necessity to human life (故衣食者，人之生利也，然且猶尚有節), it asks how there cannot also be a standard for the burying of the dead: 葬埋者，人之死利也，夫何獨無節於此乎? (*Mozi* 6.187–88). Therefore, while acknowledging the primacy of *nomos*, the text nevertheless insists that there is a single standard of *phusis* that should alone dictate custom.

For example, the *Shangshu,* a text containing speeches purportedly offered to Zhou kings that urge the ruler to uphold the world order as established by the kingdom's founders and emulate the governance of these sage figures,[57] contains a passage describing the division of the known world into five different regions that proceed outward from the center. These consist of the *dianfu* 甸服, "royal region," the *houfu* 侯服, "ducal region," the *suifu* 綏服, "pacified region," the *yaofu* 要服, "border region," and the *huangfu* 荒服, "outermost region." The peoples known as the Yi 夷 are said to inhabit the *yaofu,* and those known as the Man 蠻 inhabit the *huangfu* zone.[58] A similar geographical schema in the *Zhouli* divides the inhabited world not into five but nine different regions (*zhou* 州 or *fu* 服), with royal domains comprising the central region and the foreign peoples of the Man and Yi inhabiting the sixth and seventh regions.[59] This tendency to divide the known world into different geographical zones is also accompanied by a tendency to assign numbers to the various tribes or other kinds of groups that comprise a given non-Chinese people. For example, the *Zhouli,* in describing the requisite knowledge and duties of Zhou officials, notes that it is necessary to be able to distinguish the various non-Chinese peoples: the four Yi 夷, the eight Man 蠻, the seven Min 閩, the nine Mo 貉, the five Rong 戎, and the six Di 狄.[60] These ritual texts serve primarily to lay out the system of governance of the known world, in effect providing a geopolitical map that relegates foreign peoples to a peripheral and more or less subservient status, while the Chinese Zhou community occupies the dominant position in the center. While geographical schemata are also employed in Greco-Roman texts (particularly oppositions between east and west, north and south, center and periphery),[61] they are neither as complex nor as formalized as is the case in the Chinese tradition.

In these ritual texts, one finds alongside the geographical schemata an emphasis on the political significance of, and the correlation between, a given ethnic category's political status and its physical location. These three markers are mutually reinforcing: an ethnic classification corresponds

---

[57] Lu, Xing, *Rhetoric in Ancient China,* 58–59.   [58] *Shangshu* 3, Xiashu 夏書, Yugong 禹貢.96.

[59] *Zhouli* 33, Xiaguan Sima 夏官司馬.545–47. On the formulation of the *Zhouli* and its prescription of "rules of moral conduct and harmonious relations in social, official, and family life," see Lu, Xing, *Rhetoric in Ancient China,* 59–61.

[60] 辨其邦國，都鄙，四夷，八蠻，七閩，九貉，五戎，六狄之人民 (*Zhouli* 33, Xiaguan Sima 夏官司馬.545).

[61] On these schematic divisions, see Isaac, *The Invention of Racism in Classical Antiquity,* 60–74, 82–87.

to a particular zone with its prescribed political relationship to the Chinese center. The closest Greco-Roman analogue to this practice, at least as far as its classificatory application is concerned, is in the use of ethnic super-categories such as "Scythian," which could be used to refer generically to nomadic peoples living north of the Danube.[62] As peoples in the west or north of China might be named Rong or Di, respectively, so various peoples living north of the Danube in later centuries (Goths, Huns, Avars, etc.) could also be called Scythians.

Though there is usually little ethnographic detail provided in such passages in Chinese ritual texts, one exception appears in the *Liji*. In this text there is a list of the barbarians of the four directions and some of their defining characteristics:

中國戎夷，五方之民，皆有其性也，不可推移. 東方曰夷，被髮文身，有不火食者矣. 南方曰蠻，雕題交趾，有不火食者矣. 西方曰戎,被髮衣皮，有不粒食者矣. 北方曰狄，衣羽毛穴居，有不粒食者矣. 中國，夷，蠻，戎，狄，皆有安居，和味，宜服，利用，備器,五方之民，言語不通，嗜欲不同.[63]

The Central Kingdoms and the Rong-Yi are the peoples of the five zones, who all have their own natures that cannot be changed. In the east are those called the Yi, who wear their hair loose and tattoo their bodies; some of them do not eat cooked food. In the south are those called the Man, who tattoo their foreheads and have criss-crossed feet; some of them do not eat cooked food. In the west are those called the Rong, who wear their hair loose and wear animal hides; some of them do not eat grain. In the north are those called the Di, who wear feathers and furs and live in caves; some of them do not eat grain. The Central Kingdoms, the Yi, Man, Rong, and Di all have their fixed abodes, their preferred food, suitable clothing, useful tools, and sufficient vessels. The people of the five zones all have mutually unintelligible languages and their wants and desires are different.

This last example actually gives an unusual amount of ethnographic information about the various ethnic groups inhabiting the four points of the compass, here listed as the Yi 夷, Man 蠻, Rong 戎, and Di 狄 – the so-called Si Yi 四夷 or "Four Barbarians" as they would generically be referred to in later centuries, although that particular collective term is not employed here.[64] The *Liji* shows interest in these peoples' personal *habitus*, their diet, their living conditions, and even language. It is also important to

---

[62] Amory, *People and Identity in Ostrogothic Italy*, 20–21.   [63] *Liji* 4, Wangzhi 王制.927–28.
[64] For a basic introduction to the original bearers of these ethnonyms, see Hsu, "The Spring and Autumn Period," 548–50. For a more in-depth discussion of their usage, see Bergeton's "The

note that the *Liji* clearly does not object to any of these particulars according to an objective standard, and each group's customs are implicitly considered to be appropriate to the group's given geographical location; as they inhabit different zones, so their respective mores will also differ.

Interesting to observe is that, despite the fact that it seems that each of the five ethnic categories named above deserves consideration in its own right, there is nevertheless the general categorization of all of the non-Chinese under the blanket term Rong-Yi 戎夷, which undermines the importance of particular differences between these groups such that they collectively stand in a basic opposition to the Chinese of the Central Kingdoms. There is thus a clear division between the central Chinese states of the Zhou *oikoumenê* and those on its periphery or outside of it.

This correlation between geographical environment and customs of different peoples is even more explicitly laid out in the preceding section of this same text. Here, physical conditions of the environment are understood to determine distinctive, and geographically appropriate, behaviors:

> 凡居民材，必因天地寒暖燥濕，廣谷大川異制. 民生其間者異俗，剛柔輕重，遲速異齊，五味異和，器械異制，衣服異宜. 修其教，不易其俗；齊其政，不易其宜.[65]

> Regarding their abodes and abilities, it is necessary that these should differ according to the conditions of heaven and earth, cold and heat, dryness and moisture, broad valleys and great rivers. The character of peoples differed in their customs, and they were differently regulated as they were hard or soft, light or heavy, slow or swift. The five flavors were variously blended, the implements and tools were variously made, their clothing was suitable in different ways. Their instruction was administered, but it did not change their customs. Their forms of governance were standardized, yet they did not lose their particular aptness.

This passage likewise indicates an awareness that social customs and behaviors will differ in a manner appropriate to geographical and/or climatic conditions. Yet while it assumes a causal relationship between the nature of a given environment and the appropriate response manifested in human practice, there is no discussion of climatic influence exhibited in

---

Evolving Vocabulary of Otherness in Pre-Imperial China: From 'Belligerent Others' to 'Cultural Others'."

[65] *Liji* 4, Wangzhi 王制.927. This and the above quotation from the *Liji* are both discussed by Yang in "'Their Lands Are Peripheral and Their *Qi* Is Blocked up,'" 392–93.

human physiognomy.[66] This last point represents a notable contrast to the common Greco-Roman practice of making explicit correlations between ethnic physical characteristics and environmental conditions, which will be explored below. In pre-imperial Chinese texts that deal with non-Chinese peoples, then, there is usually little interest in explaining either origins or customs of foreigners in detail.

Instead, one sees a delineation of contrasts with Chinese norms that serve to rhetorically emphasize an ascribed alterity and establish a hierarchy of political relationships and obligations. That this should be the case is not surprising given that the purpose of such ritual texts was to codify and prescribe correct modes of governance and ritual practice that were seen to perpetuate the supposed exempla established by the sage rulers of the early Zhou era. The ritual texts of the first millennium BC, as well as the philosophical rhetoric of the various competing schools, are thus directed inwards toward the Chinese social and political sphere, where foreign peoples serve as largely nonparticipatory figures in an idealized cosmology whose primary function is to acknowledge the superiority of the rulers of the center.

Turning now to the genre of historiography, pre-imperial chronicles and collections of anecdotes attest to the importance of the role that non-Chinese peoples played in relation to the expanding Chinese Zhou community. However, early historians do not yet show the interest in systematic inquiry into social and cultural differences that would later develop under the Han dynasty, as will be discussed below. That said, references to actual peoples that include brief observations on their character or nature do occur in pre-imperial historical texts such as the *Zuozhuan* 左轉 (*Commentary of Zuo*), the *Guoyu* 國語 (*Discourses of the States*), and the *Zhanguoce* 戰國策 (*Strategies of the Warring States*).[67] Nevertheless, passages that offer some description of the non-Chinese are very similar to

---

[66] An interest in geography and human exotica is on full display in the mythological-geographical treatise known as the *Shanhaijing* 山海經 or *Classic of the Mountains and Seas*. Though this text does include descriptions of foreign peoples, these fall wholly within the realm of the fantastic and are of little value in assessing Chinese attitudes towards, or forms of engagement with, their actual neighbors in antiquity. Likewise, I have omitted discussion of Greco-Roman ethnographic accounts of obviously fantastical peoples, such as the Arimaspians of Herodotus and the Kunokephaloi of Ctesias. For a discussion of both of these fantastical peoples, see Romm, *Edges of the Earth in Ancient Thought*, 67–81. For a discussion of the *Shanhaijing*, see Fracasso, "*Shan hai ching*," in *Early Chinese Texts*, 357–67; also see Di Cosmo, *Ancient China and Its Enemies*, 290–91, and Kim, *Ethnicity and Foreigners in Ancient Greece and China*, 90–91.

[67] An introduction to each of these texts is provided in Loewe, *Early Chinese Texts: A Bibliographical Guide*. The *Zuozhuan* is included under the entry "*Ch'un ch'iu, Kung yang, Ku liang*, and *Tso Chuan*," 67–76.

those discussed above: they tend to have a clearly moral orientation and usually appear in a highly rhetorical context, where ministers are advocating for or against a policy that will entail cooperation with, or aggression against, the barbarians. Still, there remains a significant amount of material in pre-imperial historiography that gives, if not detailed ethnographic description, at least some sense of ways in which the non-Chinese could be perceived to differ from the inhabitants of the Central States.

A few examples will be presented here. The *Zuozhuan* recounts an episode, dated to the year 635 BC, where the army of the state of Jin 晉 has besieged the capital city of the state of Fan 樊. A man of the city cries out that "virtue is used to placate the Central States, but force must be used to overawe the Four Barbarians [i.e., barbarians of the four directions]";[68] he then appeals to the shared kinship between the people of the city and the Zhou royal family, thus convincing the Jin army to desist – presumably to reserve its use of force for non-Chinese enemies. The notion is thus clear that Chinese and non-Chinese are expected to respond differently to the same forms of political rule; therefore, the former must be governed by a virtuous monarch, whereas only military force will subdue the latter.

Also recounted in the *Zuozhuan* is an episode where prisoners from a rebellious Chinese state are presented to the Zhou king as booty in 589 BC. However, the gift of prisoners is refused, as it is appropriate to make such an offering only when the defeated enemy is one of the Four Barbarians, who do not share the ties of kinship, *xiongdi shengjiu* 兄弟甥舅, common among the Chinese states. This instance is a striking parallel to the Greek idea, to be discussed in Chapter 2, expressed by Aristotle that barbarians are suited to slavery in a way that fellow Greeks are not. The Zhou king begins by remarking that "The Man, Yi, Rong, and Di do not heed the commands of the King. They are wholly corrupted by their lust for women and their indulgence in alcohol; their actions ruin correct order."[69] In addition to presenting ethnographic stereotypes of uncivilized barbarian behavior, this episode exhibits the rhetoric of shared kinship among the Chinese states in a manner analogous to the aggregative sense of identity based on mythical genealogies, to be discussed below, which has been observed among the Greeks. It is interesting to note, though, that while it has been argued that this aggregative sense of Greek identity was replaced by an oppositional construct, appearing first in the context of the Persian wars and pitting a

[68] 德以柔中國，刑以威四夷 (*Zuozhuan*, Xigong 僖公 25.434).
[69] 蠻夷戎狄，不式王命，淫湎毀常 (*Zuozhuan*, Chenggong 成公 2.809).

new Hellenic identity against a barbarian Other, we see in the *Zuozhuan* that an aggregative kinship community exists in tandem with a contrasting collective of barbarian peoples who tended to be the weaker parties in military conflicts.

To conclude the discussion of Chinese pre-imperial ethnographic literature, the primary interest in foreign peoples in the texts discussed above is political and rhetorical, and there is little interest in any exposition of ways of life or cultural practices that extends beyond general descriptions of their inability to conform to or understand Chinese standards of civilized behavior. The representations of non-Chinese in these texts "were neither a means to acquire knowledge about the physical realities surrounding that community nor the result of an *inquiry* into those realities."[70] References to distinctions between Chinese and non-Chinese communities are clearly in the service of a larger rhetorical argument that serves both to mark the incongruity between the Chinese and their barbarian neighbors as well as to further define proper codes of conduct by demonstrating the perversions of ritual propriety among the latter.

The monumental *Shiji* of Sima Qian (145–c. 86 BC) established what would become the standard form of Chinese historiography in later centuries. More important for the purposes of this study, Sima Qian also established the conventions of an ethnographic discourse that objectively described foreign societies and rendered them intelligible to a Chinese audience. Sima Qian is thus regarded as the "father of history" in the Chinese tradition in a manner analogous to Herodotus, and there have been a number of comparative studies in recent years that consider various aspects of these two historians' respective oeuvre and careers.[71] The first major study to describe in detail the ethnographic approach exhibited by Sima Qian is that of Di Cosmo, who argues that the significance of the Han historian's approach may be attributed to the fact that, already trained in the astronomical observation requisite for his office of *shi* 史, "historian," Sima Qian was able to apply his empirical methodology of observation to the peoples of the nomadic Xiongnu 匈奴 Empire to the north of China in an unprecedented way.[72] Sima Qian is thus the first historian in

---

[70] Di Cosmo, *Ancient China and Its Enemies*, 94.

[71] Stuurman, "Herodotus and Sima Qian," 1–40; Nienhauser, *The Grand Scribe's Records: Volume IX*, xi–xxiii; Kim, *Ethnicity and Foreigners in Ancient Greece and China*, 72–145. Martin, *Herodotus and Sima Qian: The First Great Historians of Greece and China*. It should be noted, however, that Teng had produced a comparative study on these two authors already in his 1961 article, "Herodotus and Ssu-ma Ch'ien: Two Fathers of History," 233–40.

[72] Di Cosmo, *Ancient China and Its Enemies*, 256–67.

China to exhibit what Stuurman has called "the anthropological turn."[73] Sima Qian's inquiry into the workings of Xiongnu society, the Xiongnu being the principal object of his ethnographic gaze, has been divided up by Di Cosmo under six headings: pastoral nomadism, burial customs, society and laws, military training and warfare, state sacrifices and rituals, and language.[74] As is not surprising given the authority attributed to Sima Qian by later historians, later writers of dynastic histories who described the Xiongnu and other non-Chinese peoples would likewise comment on these same features, at times repeating whole sections of the *Shiji* word for word.[75] With some variations – for example, peoples who did not inhabit the steppe would not be described as nomads, but rather be considered in light of the particulars of their own region and economy – the five headings delineated by Di Cosmo turned out to be the standard categories of ethnographic inquiry employed by later dynastic historians.

The ethnographic description of the Xiongnu by Sima Qian has already been discussed by a number of modern historians, and it would be redundant to offer a detailed account of it here.[76] Instead, we may consider a later example of this method of detailed inquiry as it was adopted by an imperial historian who followed in Sima Qian's footsteps: Fan Ye 范曄, the fifth-century AD author of the *Hou Han shu* 後漢書 (*History of the Later Han Dynasty*). In describing the customs of a people known as the Wuhuan 烏桓 who lived in the northeast, he begins by noting the earliest details of their history, relating that they were once part of a people known as the Donghu 東胡, who were destroyed and largely absorbed by the Xiongnu. But some of them managed to flee eastward, and the Wuhuan were one of these refugee groups.[77] He next describes some of the particulars of their nomadic way of life that are not dissimilar to those of the Xiongnu, including patterns of migration, life in tents, hunting, and a diet consisting of meat and dairy. Like the Xiongnu and other nomads, the Wuhuan honor the young and hold the elderly of little account.[78]

---

[73] Stuurman, "Herodotus and Sima Qian," 16, 38.

[74] Di Cosmo, *Ancient China and Its Enemies*, 271–81. The breadth of these categories suggests that Pulleyblank's assertion that the Chinese were "seldom interested in their 'barbarian' subjects or neighbors except from a narrow, military intelligence point of view" is extreme. "The Chinese and Their Neighbors in Prehistoric and Early Historic Times," 412.

[75] As has often been noted, Ban Gu's first chapter on the Xiongnu in the *Han shu* begins with an ethnographic description of the nomads and an account of their prehistory that is virtually identical to that of Sima Qian (*Han shu* 94a.3743ff.).

[76] See Di Cosmo, *Ancient China and Its Enemies*, 271–81; Stuurman, "Herodotus and Sima Qian," 24–34; Chin, *Savage Exchange: Han Imperialism, Chinese Literary Style, and the Economic Imagination*, 168–82.

[77] *Hou Han shu* 90.2979.   [78] 貴少而賤老 (Ibid.).

He notes that their *xing* 性, "nature," is *hansai* 悍塞, "fierce and simple-minded." Their society is matriarchal, though they are ruled by *daren* 大人, "chieftains," who are elected for their valor and whose station is not hereditary. The people are divided up into smaller tribal units with their own leaders who heed the commands of the chieftains, which are carved into wood with symbols, since they have no form of writing.[79] They have no consistent clan names, but rather take these affiliations according to the names of their chieftains. Fan Ye describes Wuhuan marriage custom in some detail, as he does particulars of their hairstyle and ornament; women are involved in all decision-making – only fighting is solely handled by the men.[80] The women excel in embroidery, and the men make weapons and horse fittings from metal. Their region has its own unique flora that thrives there, and they tell the seasons by observing the pregnancy and nursing of birds and beasts. The Wuhuan value a military death, and have unique burial customs and sacrifices; like the Chinese, they believe that the souls of the dead travel to a distant mountain.[81] There follows a description of their belief in gods and their sacrifices to heaven and earth, sun and moon, stars, mountains, and rivers. Their laws are few and involve obedience to the chieftain's commands; surely remarkable to a contemporary Chinese perspective, there is no penalty for the killing of one's father or elder brother.

The details provided by Fan Ye on the Wuhuan follow a similar pattern of observations first set out by Sima Qian, and the above summary from the *Hou Han shu* makes clear the extent to which ethnographic writing had departed from the terse rhetorical claims about foreign cultures found in Spring and Autumn and Warring States texts. Part of what made Sima Qian unique in relation to the ethnographic discourse he had himself inherited from pre-imperial writings is the fact that he did not take foreign peoples merely at face value; he did not simply depict them through the ethical and moral lens preferred by earlier Chinese philosophers and historians, who had sketched external communities in opposition to the prescribed cultural norms of Chinese civilization. In short, Sima Qian was the first to attempt to rationalize and understand the foreign enemies who had surrounded the Chinese cultural and political sphere from time immemorial. As will be discussed below, one of his primary strategies in so doing was to represent the Xiongnu as a manifestation in his own day

---

[79] 大人有所召呼，則刻木為信，雖無文字，而部眾不敢違犯 (Ibid.).
[80] 計謀從用婦人，唯鬪戰之事乃自決之 (Ibid.).
[81] 使護死者神靈歸赤山. . . . 如中國人死者魂神歸岱山也 (*Hou Han shu* 90.2980).

of an antagonistic relationship that had always existed between the opposed cosmological poles of the barbarians in the north and the Chinese in the south.[82]

As already noted, later dynastic histories followed the format established by Sima Qian, and accounts of the cultures and societies of non-Chinese peoples into which they inquired likewise followed the precedent of the *Shiji*, at times cutting and pasting phrases or even passages wholesale. It also became a feature of official histories to include individual fascicles in the Biographies section of the text that were devoted to the description of various foreign peoples on the near or distant periphery.[83] Such ethnographic passages also consider the tributary status between these peoples and the imperial court. For example, the *Han shu* 漢書 contains two fascicles devoted to the Xiongnu, one devoted to the non-Chinese peoples of the south and northeast, and two for the peoples of the western regions. Likewise, the third-century *Sanguo zhi* 三國志 of Chen Shou 陳壽 dedicates the last fascicle of its section on the kingdom of Wei 魏 to peoples of the north and northeast. The *Hou Han shu*, the history of the Eastern Han 東漢 dynasty produced by the fifth-century historian Fan Ye discussed above, has one fascicle devoted to the Eastern Yi 東夷, one to the Southern Man 南蠻 and Southwestern Yi 西南夷, one to the Western Qiang 西羌, one to the various peoples of the western regions, one to the Southern Xiongnu 南匈奴, and one to the Wuhuan and Särbi-Xianbei 鮮卑 of the northeast. It was thus a standard practice for historians to include ethnographic and historical information on barbarian peoples in a systematic and demarcated format. In particular, one notes the way that both the *Han shu* and the *Hou Han shu* move in a circuit, reminiscent of the Greek *periodos gēs*, to describe the foreign peoples of the four directions, and this general pattern continues in the histories produced under the Northern and Southern dynasties and up through the Tang.

Despite its similar pattern of exploring the peoples along the periphery while moving in a geographical circle, the Chinese placement of ethnographic information in the text nevertheless differs significantly from that of the Greco-Roman tradition. In Greek and Roman historical works, the ethnographic digression or excursus is a part of the larger historical

---

[82] Di Cosmo, *Ancient China and Its Enemies*, 294–304.

[83] The basic components of Chinese dynastic histories were the Basic Annals of the dynasty and then Biographies of important individuals or categories of individuals. On Sima Qian's development of this form, see Ng and Wang, *Mirroring the Past: The Writing and Use of History in Imperial China*, 63–65; on its development in later generations, see Durrant, "The Literary Features of Historical Writing," 502–03, 507–10.

narrative and is inserted at points where a foreign people is either introduced or becomes central to the related events. It was also noted above that
ethnographic observations are made by Greco-Roman historians as asides
or as an explanation for a particular action or practice. In contrast, the
majority of the ethnographic data on non-Chinese peoples in the dynastic
histories is presented in separated chapters or fascicles that are dedicated to
peoples inhabiting a given area, e.g., the "western regions," or, in the case
of foreigners of particular political or military significance, to a single non-
Chinese people, e.g., the Xiongnu or the Qiang. Other narrative sections
show little interest in dwelling on ethnographic particulars, either in
passing comments or in longer digressions inserted into the narrative, as
in the case of Greco-Roman historiography. The ethnographic treatment
of foreign peoples in the Chinese historiographical tradition thus exhibits a
degree of systemized categorization whereby the historian offers a mini-
history and contemporary description of a region or people. This organizational aspect of historical texts, the delimitation of information on
foreign peoples within discrete sections of the work (and typically relegated
to its final fascicles) instead of its being placed alongside or within the
greater narrative, is one of the greater contrasts between Greco-Roman and
Chinese ethnographic literature.

The main exception to this general rule is in the case of reported direct
speech where, when policies are being negotiated that pertain to the
imperial court's relation with non-Chinese peoples, it is common for
ministers or other interested parties to support their positions with rhetorical arguments referring to the social, economic, or cultural characteristics of the foreign group in question. For example, in the *Shiji* during a
debate on military policy against the Xiongnu, the minister Han Anguo
韓安國 offers the following description of Xiongnu military tactics before
noting that the Xiongnu have "never belonged to the human race since
ancient times":[84]

> 今匈奴負戎馬之足，懷禽獸之心，遷徙鳥舉，難得而制也。[85]
>
> These days the Xiongnu soldiers rely on the legs of their horses and possess
> the hearts of wild animals. They come and go like flocks of birds so it is
> difficult to catch and control them.

In a similar circumstance, another official warns of the difficulty of waging
war against the Xiongnu and simultaneously gives details about their
military strategy and their nomadic lifestyle, which eschews permanent

---

[84] 自上古不屬為人 (*Shiji* 108.2861).   [85] Ibid.

settlements and fortified positions where they may be easily attacked. He claims that "the Xiongnu have no dwellings in cities or fortifications and do not store any supplies. They come and go as birds and are therefore most difficult to capture and control."[86] Yet another minister of the court attempts to dissuade the emperor from campaigning against the Xiongnu, saying, "it is the nature of the Xiongnu to gather together like beasts and scatter like birds. To try and pursue them is like trying to strike a shadow."[87]

In all of these examples, despite the obviously rhetorical context, Sima Qian provides actual information on both the settlement patterns and the military strategy of the Xiongnu. Other such instances, in which characteristics of foreign peoples feature in debates over policy, exhibit the employment of ethnographic observations in service of an ethical argument, in a manner similar to that seen above in the examples from the *Zuozhuan*. In these cases, arguments are made for policies that endorse a closer or looser engagement with the barbarians based on either their capacity to be transformed by Chinese culture or their intransigence and unsuitability for incorporation within the empire.

Having sketched the general features of ethnographic discourse in the classical Greco-Roman and Chinese worlds, we may now turn to the explanatory frameworks that were employed in both traditions to rationalize and make sense of the foreign peoples and cultures that occupied the peripheries of the ancient Mediterranean and Central Plains of northern China. Despite the significant differences in the political circumstances contemporary with the development of ethnography as a literary form, it is interesting to observe that ethnologocial thinking in the Chinese tradition lends itself very well to an analysis according to three interpretive frameworks or paradigms that were used by Greco-Roman historians to explain and rationalize foreign peoples: genealogy, geography-climate, and history/historical change.[88] The following section will explore the ways in which Greco-Roman and Chinese authors employed these three different categories of information in their ethnographic representations of foreign peoples.

---

[86] 夫匈奴無城郭之居，委積之守，遷徙鳥舉，難得而制也 (*Shiji* 112.2954).

[87] 夫匈奴之性，獸聚而鳥散，從之知搏影 (*Shiji* 112.2955).

[88] The following analysis of ethnographic practices in terms of explanatory paradigms is much indebted to Woolf's discussion of ethnography in *Tales of the Barbarians*, and the categories of genealogy and geography as explanatory paradigms are attributable to him. Although Woolf does note the Greco-Roman practice of providing a summary of a foreign people's history and that this practice serves a component in their explication, he does not consider it to be a paradigm on par with, and possessing the same valence as, the genealogical and climatological paradigms. *Tales of the Barbarians*, 32–58.

Explanatory Paradigms in the Greco-Roman and Chinese Traditions

Genealogy

As a testament to the importance of genealogical origins in classical Greek thought, the first of the criteria that comprise Herodotus' conception of τὸ Ἑλληνικόν, or "Greekness," is shared blood,[89] and it is true that genealogical origins and kinship relations were one of the primary areas of interest in Greco-Roman descriptions of foreign peoples. This interest is evident both in accounts of an author's own people's ancestry as well in those devoted to that of others. While the rhetorical and ideological functions of these two different types of genealogical accounts can be markedly different, the purpose of this section is to demonstrate the prominence of ethnogenealogical thinking in Greco-Roman literature as a means of explaining not only origins in the past but also, and more importantly, relationships in the present. As succinctly remarked by Dench, "Mythological genealogies were the 'language' in which kinship, distinction, differentiation, and ethnic plurality were regularly articulated, in which the world was mapped and selves were located throughout the Mediterranean world."[90]

These ethnogenealogies, while at times seeming to be the product of "scientific" inquiry,[91] could be used just as effectively as a tool to demonstrate affinity as to create a sense of the exotic or foreign. Most often, they tended to incorporate foreign peoples into a framework that demonstrated a shared ancestry between Greeks and the peoples being explained.[92] For example, Herodotus claims that one of the origin myths of the Scythians, according to the Greeks who live along the Black Sea, is that they are the offspring of Heracles and a woman whose body was that of a snake from the waist down;[93] and in a speech attributed to a Persian ambassador, Herodotus reports the myth that the Persians are descended from the Greek hero Perseus and thus share kinship ties with the Argives.[94] Peoples

---

[89] ὅμαιμον (Hdt. 8.144.2).

[90] Dench, *Romulus' Asylum*, 12. On the creation of these ethnogenealogies, a classic study is Bickerman's "*Origines Gentium,*" 65–81; also see Kaldellis, *Hellenism in Byzantium*, 15–16; Hall, Jonathan, *Ethnic Identity in Greek Antiquity*, 40–51; Hall, Edith, *Inventing the Barbarian*, 36–37, 172; Gruen, *Rethinking the Other in Antiquity*, 223–307.

[91] Bickerman, "*Origines Gentium,*" 70–71.

[92] On this point, see especially Gruen, *Rethinking the Other in Antiquity*, 253–76.

[93] Hdt. 4.8–10.   [94] Hdt. 7.150.2.

of the west could also be given Hellenic ancestries, as in the genealogy of the Celts or Galatae who, according to Diodorus, descend from Galates, the son of Heracles and a Celtic woman.[95] And of course Romans themselves first adopted and then actively professed, an ancestry that was ultimately traceable back to the Greek world even if it preserved a degree of distinction from the Greeks themselves.[96]

While recognizing the Hellenocentricity apparent in the Greek tendency to assign Greek heroes the role of ancestor to foreign peoples, Bickerman has noted that this practice has analogues in the eastern Mediterranean. For example, the historian Xanthus of Lydia proposed a theory in the fifth century BC claiming that Greek legendary culture heroes were actually Lydians; the Egyptians may have made similar efforts at appropriating such figures for themselves and claimed credit for the founding of Babylonian civilization.[97] Greeks too could subscribe to a theory that a foreign people were actually the progenitors of the entire human race and the authors of civilization, as did Hecataeus of Abdera in the fourth century BC.[98] It is also important to note that while not tracing Greek ancestry back to a foreign people, some historians were able to claim that the Greeks had nevertheless been students of others in important spheres. Herodotus claims that knowledge of the Greek gods came from Egypt, and he elsewhere notes that the Greek image of the goddess Athena, as well as the practice of crying out during religious rites (ἡ ὀλολυγή), was learned from the Libyans.[99] Posidonius went so far as to credit geometry to the Egyptians, astronomy and arithmetic to the Sidonians, and even atomic theory to the Sidonian Mochus, believed to have lived prior to the Trojan War.[100]

Mythical founders of Greek cities or communities could also have foreign origins. The founder of the legendary house of Atreus was the Lydian or Phrygian Pelops, after whom the Peloponnese is named; the Danaans, or Danaoi-Δαναοί as they appear in the *Iliad*, were traditionally said to descend from the Egyptian Danaus; the city of Thebes had the Phoenician Cadmos for its founder.[101] It is thus important to recognize

[95] Diod. Sic. 5.24.1–3.
[96] Cornell, *The Beginnings of Rome: Italy and Rome from the Bronze Age to the Punic Wars*, 63–68; Bickerman, "*Origines Gentium*," 68. On Greek views toward Romans, see Marincola, "Romans and/as Barbarians," 347–57.
[97] Bickerman, "*Origines Gentium*," 74. [98] Ibid. [99] Hdt. 2.50–51; 4.189.
[100] Bickerman, "*Origines Gentium*," 74.
[101] For a discussion of these origin myths and a list of the sources in which they appear, see Gruen, *Rethinking the Other in Antiquity*, 227–36.

that alongside the Hellenocentric tendency to understand foreign or barbarian peoples as originally descending from Greek heroes, the opposite could also occur: Greek communities could claim as their own ancestors figures reputed to have originated in foreign lands. Gruen is therefore correct when he argues that the creation of genealogies that involved non-Greeks either as founding figures or descendants is not always indicative of an act of "rejection, denigration, or distancing," but may just as often represent a "creative mode of fashioning a collective self-consciousness."[102]

Foreign peoples were, however, not always incorporated into a larger web of Greco-Roman kinship relations, as may be seen in the case of the Germani whom Tacitus claims to be autochthonous, an origin myth that serves to underscore their intrinsic foreignness. For who, Tacitus asks, would actually choose to leave the coasts of the Mediterranean to live in the cheerless lands of Germany?[103] Moreover, in some cases multiple putative ancestries could be offered by a historian for a given people. Herodotus recounts a total of four different origin myths for the Scythians: one, attributed to the Scythians themselves, claims descent from Targitaus, the first man to inhabit Scythia; another, attributed to the Greeks living along the Black Sea, traces Scythian origins from Skythes, a son of Heracles; a third, favored by Herodotus himself, claims that the Scythians had migrated from the east, where they fought with the Massagetae and then took over the lands of Scythia, which had previously been inhabited by the Cimmerians; and lastly, Herodotus offers the testimony of the poet Aristeas, who claimed that the Scythians were pressed into the lands of the Cimmerians by the Issedones who dwelt to their northeast.[104] Given the variety of possibilities with which he presents the reader, there is little sense that Herodotus has a clear agenda of any sort, and it is thus not the case that a myth of origin was necessarily in the employ of a broader rhetorical or ideological project.

Of course, and as noted above, the construction of genealogies was hardly restricted to accounts of foreign peoples. It was a crucial means of internal self-definition undertaken by Greeks and Romans themselves and

---

[102] Ibid., 4.

[103] *Germania* 2.2. On the significance of claims to autochthony and their contribution to the exclusive xenophobia of the Athenians, see Isaac, *The Invention of Racism in Classical Antiquity*, 114–24; also see Hall, Jonathan, *Ethnic Identity in Greek Antiquity*, 53–56, Konstan, "*To Hellēnikon Ethnos*," 37–40, Bickerman, "*Origines Gentium*," 76.

[104] Hdt. 4.5–13.

has been extensively studied by modern scholars.[105] Moreover, claims of genealogical ties in the distant past could be of at least rhetorical significance in the negotiation of political relationships in the present, whether in reference to claims of shared descent from a legendary ancestor or the more recent relationship between a metropolis and its daughter city.[106] In like fashion, the understanding of foreign peoples in terms of their ancestry served as means of both explaining aspects of cultural behavior as well as of rationalizing or justifying contemporary political or social relationships.

Irrespective of the rhetorical purposes that an exposition of a foreign people's origins could serve, suffice it to say that the impulse to establish links of genealogical kinship, either within a greater Greco-Roman framework or outside of it, remained a prominent feature of ethnological discourse and played an important role in the process of understanding the relationship between a given group and other communities.

The pre-imperial Chinese texts discussed in the preceding section do not provide information as to the ancestry of non-Chinese peoples. Though many foreign ethnonyms are recognized as going back to ancient times, one finds an effort neither to recover the native stories of their progenitors nor to assign them ones from Chinese tradition. Conflicts between the Chinese and Rong 戎, Di 狄, Yi 夷, and Man 蠻 as individual peoples, or collectively under the generic labels of Rong-Di, Yi-Di, or Man-Yi, are not represented in a manner analogous to that of Herodotus, whose first four books are largely preoccupied with Lydians, Medes, Persians, Egyptians, et al., and the words and deeds of the various kings and dynasties who ruled over foreign empires. While Sima Qian traces the ancestry of the Chinese community from mythical times down to the Han dynasty, foreign peoples of pre-imperial times are not accorded anything like the same attention. There are a few exceptions to this general rule, namely the states of Wu 吳, Yue 越, and Zhongshan 中山, which were recognized as being originally foreign to the Chinese.[107] However, in

---

[105] For this "aggregative" process among the Greeks, see Hall, Jonathan, *Ethnic Identity in Greek Antiquity*, 40–51. On Greek identity, see the studies in Malkin, *Ancient Perceptions of Greek Ethnicity*. On Roman origin myths, Dench, *Romulus' Asylum*, 61–69, and Bickerman, "*Origines Gentium*," 65–68.

[106] One obvious example being the conflict between the metropolis Corinth and its colony Corcyra, the dispute that, according to Thucydides, precipitated the Peloponnesian War.

[107] On the foreign origins of these states, see Hsu, "The Spring and Autumn Period," 569–70. The states of Chu 楚 and Qin 秦 were likewise, at times, referred to as being non-Chinese, although such instances more likely reflect rhetorical arguments to undermine these two states' political ambitions rather than any significant ethnic or cultural distinction. Also see Pines, "Beasts or Humans," 87–88.

the case of these three states, all of them engaged in the political struggles of the Warring States period and adopted Chinese diplomatic and cultural norms to the extent that they were accepted, however grudgingly, into the larger Zhou community. Their claims to be branches from the same Chinese ancestral family, which the other states shared in common, may well have facilitated their inclusion, irrespective of the dubious truth-value of such claims.

Nevertheless, it is not until the history of Sima Qian that one first finds contemporary foreign peoples explained within a larger genealogical network, and this process is most clearly on display in the case of the nomadic Xiongnu, who rose to power on the northern steppes as China was itself nearing the culmination of its own process of unification.[108] Indicating genealogy's significance for the following account, he begins his chapter on the Xiongnu by saying that their ancestry may be traced back to an otherwise unknown figure called Chunwei 淳維, who Sima Qian claims was a member of the legendary Xia 夏 kingdom's royal family.[109] By naming Chunwei as the progenitor of the Xiongnu, Sima Qian thus incorporates the Xiongnu into the greater Chinese family from which the Shang and Zhou royal families were thought to ultimately descend. After establishing the primary ancestor of the Xiongnu, Sima Qian proceeds to enumerate the various other northern enemies of Chinese states (some of whom have already been mentioned, such as the Xianyun, Rong, and Di) and thereby suggests that the Xiongnu threat of the Han period was simply the latest manifestation of a very ancient enemy. As has been argued by Di Cosmo, the creation of this genealogy served, by incorporating the Xiongnu into the Chinese dynastic tradition, to rationalize their existence as an opposing hegemonic force that had always loomed to the north of China.[110] Perhaps because of the combined effect of Sima Qian's literary impact, along with the trauma engendered by the initial military superiority of the Xiongnu, this genealogy was to have a remarkable staying power in later accounts of nomadic peoples.

---

[108] Other peoples in the *Shiji* receive less detailed genealogical treatment, though several are ascribed a Chinese ancestry: the state of Chaoxian 朝鮮 is traced back to the northeastern Chinese state of Yan 燕 (*Shiji* 115.2985); that of the Southern Yue 南越 to the Chinese general Zhao Tuo 趙佗 (*Shiji* 113.2967); the Eastern Yue 東越 to the Warring States kingdom of Yue 越 (*Shiji* 114.2979); and the Southwestern Yi 西南夷 are understood to be the descendants of Chu (*Shiji* 116.2997). Various peoples of the northwest such as the Yuezhi 月氏, Wusun 烏孫, and others are granted ethnographic description, although their origins are not commented upon (*Shiji* 123.3161–62).

[109] 匈奴，其先祖夏后氏之苗裔也，曰淳維 (*Shiji* 110.2879).

[110] Di Cosmo, *Ancient China and Its Enemies*, 298–99.

The importance of the genealogical paradigm in texts produced in following centuries is also attested by the fact that many of the fascicles that offer a systematic treatment of foreign peoples begin with remarks on a people's origins. For example, in the *Hou Han shu*, Fan Ye has five fascicles dedicated to non-Chinese peoples: the Eastern Yi, the Southern Man and Southwestern Yi, the Western Qiang, the Southern Xiongnu, and the Wuhuan and Särbi-Xianbei. Though he does not here repeat the Xiongnu genealogy created by Sima Qian (and repeated by the Han-dynasty historian Ban Gu 班固) but merely begins his account of the Southern Xiongnu with events following the division of the Xiongnu Empire into northern and southern halves in the year 53 BC, Fan Ye provides genealogies for the Eastern Yi, Southern Man and Southwestern Yi, and the Qiang that go all the way back to the time of the mythical Five Emperors.[111] The Wuhuan and Särbi-Xianbei are granted less hoary pedigrees, as they are relative newcomers on the political scene, becoming a significant military threat in the north only in the second century AD. Regarding these two peoples, Fan Ye claims that they trace their ancestry back to a people known as the Donghu, who were absorbed by the expanding Xiongnu empire toward the end of the third century BC.[112] Irrespective of the antiquity of origins, there is a clear tendency when introducing accounts of foreign peoples in Chinese historiography to begin with comments on their earliest genealogical history or pseudo-history in order to place them in a broader historical context familiar to a Chinese audience.

Before moving on to discuss the impact of the Xiongnu genealogy on the imaginations of later historians, we may note two points of comparison with the above discussion of the genealogical paradigm in the Greco-Roman tradition. The first is that, like the Greeks, the Chinese clearly had a tendency to invoke their own mythological figures as putative ancestors of foreign peoples. The second is that, also like the Greeks, the Chinese were able to conceive of some of their own culture heroes as having foreign origins. For example, the Warring States philosophical text the *Mencius* 孟子 claims that the legendary emperor Shun 舜 was a man of the Eastern Yi; likewise, one of the founders of the Zhou dynasty, Zhou Wenwang 周文王, was of the Western Yi.[113] Nevertheless, this second point must be qualified, since although this pattern of ascribing foreign

---

[111] For the Eastern Yi (*Hou Han shu* 85.2807–08), the Southern Man and Southwestern Yi (*Hou Han shu* 86.2829–30), and the Qiang (*Hou Han shu* 87.2869).

[112] See the above discussion of Fan Ye's ethnography of the Wuhuan, 51–52.

[113] 舜生於諸馮，遷於負夏，卒於鳴條，東夷之人也. 文王生於岐周，卒於畢郢，西夷之人也 (*Mengzi* 8.1, Lilou B 離婁.184).

origins to legendary dynastic figures seems to have been accepted in the pre-imperial period, it falls out of official historical accounts in the foundational work of Sima Qian, who traces a seamless line from the mythical Yellow Emperor down to the Zhou royal family and does not see fit to ascribe heterogeneous origins to these same august figures. Nevertheless, the memory of these alternative narratives persisted, and even appears in rhetorical speeches in the *Jin shu* 晉書, as will be discussed in Chapter 5.

It is also the case that, for peoples who lived to the north of China, the genealogy first ascribed to the Xiongnu by Sima Qian was to be remarkably productive, in that it was applied either in explicit or implicit terms to a host of nomadic or semi-nomadic groups in later centuries.[114] It will suffice here to take the Särbi-Xianbei as an example, a people who rose to prominence on the northern steppes beginning in the second century AD. The following accounts illustrate the prominence of genealogy in representations of foreign groups as well as the influence of the invented line of descent from Chunwei, which was first ascribed to the Xiongnu by Sima Qian.

On their first appearance in dynastic historiography in the *Sanguo zhi* of Chen Shou in the third century AD, the Särbi-Xianbei are given an ancestry that ties them back to a people known as the Donghu who lived in eastern Mongolia.[115] When the Donghu are destroyed by the expanding Xiongnu Empire to their west, two of the confederation's constituent groups, the Wuhuan and the Särbi-Xianbei, take refuge by different mountains and from them receive their names.[116] This same genealogy is repeated in the next dynastic history to be produced, the *Hou Han shu* of Fan Ye, which was written in the first half of the fifth century.[117] However, the details of Särbi-Xianbei ancestry change dramatically in later histories, beginning in later part of the fifth century. The *Song shu* 宋書 of Shen Yue 沈約 abandons the former accounts that traced Särbi-Xianbei origins back to the Donghu confederation. Instead, he claims that they, or at least the Tabgach-Tuoba 拓跋 branch of the Särbi-Xianbei, who were ruling the north of China as the Northern Wei 北魏 dynasty in the fifth

---

[114] Drompp, "The Hsiung-nu Topos and the T'ang Response to the Collapse of the Uighur Steppe Empire," 1–46; Di Cosmo, "Ethnography of the Nomads and 'Barbarian' History in Han China," 319.

[115] *Sanguo zhi* 30.836. Though attributed to Chen Shou, the received text of the work includes a commentary added in the fifth century. On the Donghu, also see *Shiji* 110.2889.

[116] 鮮卑亦東胡之餘也，別保鮮卑山，因號焉 (*Sanguo zhi* 30.836).

[117] Fan Ye's account is identical in sense, if not a verbatim reproduction of the *Sanguo zhi* account: 鮮卑者，亦東胡之支也，別依鮮卑山，故因號焉 (*Hou Han shu* 90.2985).

century, are descended from the Han dynasty general Li Ling 李陵. Li Ling had settled among the Xiongnu as an exile and married a Xiongnu woman after being defeated in battle and captured in 99 BC.[118] The Särbi-Xianbei thus appear in the *Song shu* as descendants of a disgraced Chinese general who went over to China's archenemy.[119]

The manipulation of Särbi-Xianbei genealogy does not stop here. The *Nan Qi shu* 南齊書, written by Xiao Zixian 蕭子顯 in the early sixth century, dispenses with the myth of descent from Li Ling and instead claims that the Särbi-Xianbei are merely a type or branch of the Xiongnu.[120] The last and most remarkable account of Särbi-Xianbei origins appears in the *Wei shu* 魏書 of Wei Shou 魏收, who wrote in the mid-sixth century under the Särbi-Xianbei Northern Qi 北齊 dynasty. In this case, we are dealing with a dynastic history of the Northern Wei, whose legacy the Northern Qi rulers claimed as part of their bid for legitimacy. The *Wei shu* account creates an entirely new genealogy for the Särbi-Xianbei, claiming that they descend from the youngest son of the Yellow Emperor himself, the mythical progenitor of the Chinese people.[121] One sees in accounts of Särbi-Xianbei origins the following chronological progression: (1) peripheral group living in the northeast with no history going back beyond the second century BC; (2) descendants of a famous and disgraced Chinese general who defected to the Xiongnu; (3) descendants simply of the Xiongnu; (4) descendants of the illustrious mythical progenitor of the Chinese people.

Despite all of the variations in these records of Särbi-Xianbei origins, what is consistent over the course of over three centuries is the prominence of genealogical information in ethnographic accounts of them. As for the Greeks, it was important for the Chinese to know where a given people came from and from whom they descended. In a manner similar to what we have seen in the Greek tradition, these genealogies also exhibit a tendency to incorporate foreign peoples within a greater Sinitic family tree. The functions of such genealogical links, as is the case for their Greek equivalents, are variously interpreted by modern scholars. For example, it has been argued by Maenchen-Helfen that most barbarian peoples were

---

[118] Li Ling's career and life among the Xiongnu are recounted in *Han shu* 54.2451–59.
[119] 索頭虜姓託跋氏，其先漢將李陵後也 (*Song shu* 95.2321).
[120] 魏虜，匈奴種也. . . . 亦謂鮮卑 (*Nan Qi shu* 57.983).
[121] *Wei shu* 1.1. It is important to note that such genealogical contortions were not limited to those attributed to foreign peoples. The usurper Wang Mang 王莽 in the early first century AD sought to legitimate his rule by claiming descent from the Yellow Emperor and the mythical sage king Shun. See Bielenstein, "Wang Mang," 224–25.

made the "descendants of great evil-doers of the past, banished to the 'outer world'."[122] Schreiber has suggested that such fabricated lineages that claimed a common origin for Chinese and barbarians could have two purposes: the genealogies may have been produced by Chinese who "tried to pass off their foreign rulers as related to the Chinese,"[123] or they may have been actively promoted by barbarians themselves in an attempt to win over Chinese subjects to their cause.[124] Genealogies might thus assuage the fears or even the conscience of Chinese facing a barbarian threat or living under barbarian conquest. Alternatively, they could serve to shore up the political claims of non-Chinese monarchs who in later centuries seized formerly Chinese territory. Both interpretations are considered by Hinsch. Regarding the Xiongnu genealogy, he suggests that such a "mythic kinship tie" could "make the Xiongnu legitimate members of the Chinese realm, hence suitable targets for conquest and absorption."[125] Yet he notes that this strategy could cut both ways: "the same story could justify Chinese annexation of the Xiongnu, or Xiongnu annexation of China."[126] On a more fundamental level, Di Cosmo has argued that the genealogy proposed for the Xiongnu constituted a strategy of *reductio ad notum* that could "neutralise the psychological impact produced by the scary occurrence of a nomadic empire, and make its military power appear less menacing."[127] Regardless of the different functions the genealogical paradigm may have performed, it plays as prominent a role in Chinese accounts of foreign peoples as it does in the ethnographic texts of the Greeks and Romans.

Geography, Climate, and Astrology

The second major framework through which foreign peoples are often rendered intelligible in Greco-Roman and Chinese ethnographic texts is that of geography-climate. The relationship between geography and ethnography in the Greco-Roman tradition is a particularly close one and, as evident in the phrase *de origine et situ* sometimes used to title or introduce an ethnographic account, genealogical origins of a people and the

[122] Maenchen-Helfen, "Archaistic Names of the Hsiung-nu," 252.
[123] Schreiber, "History of the Former Yen Dynasty, Part I," 389.
[124] Schreiber, "History of the Former Yen Dynasty, Part II," 124.
[125] Hinsch, "Myth and the Construction of Foreign Ethnic Identity in Early and Medieval China," 91.
[126] Ibid., 103.
[127] Di Cosmo, "Ethnography of the Nomads and 'Barbarian' History in Han China," 306.

geographical environment which they inhabit are often inextricable.[128] Landscape and the particular foods, animals, and minerals that a given region produces are common areas of interest to ancient ethnographers, given that these particulars could be understood to determine the ethical characteristics of a foreign society, demonstrate the basis for distinctive behaviors, or illustrate the relationship between the barbarian periphery and the civilized center.

Herodotus explains the Scythian mobility and skill at mounted warfare in relation to the flat and treeless steppe environment in which they live; as a result, they are invincible in the face of any invading army, as Herodotus illustrates with the failed campaign of Darius.[129] Caesar describes the practice of hunting aurochs among the Germani and notes the great size, speed, and ferocity of the animals; in hunting these beasts the young men are toughened and trained, presumably for the battlefield.[130] Diodorus shows how the mining and working of tin among the Britons of the island's southwest explains both their hospitality and their relative degree of civilization, which is a result of their frequent interactions with merchants who transport the tin to the continent.[131] Tacitus describes the amber gathered on the shores of the Baltic by the Aestii, who have no notion of its value but are paid a great deal in exchange for it to satisfy the demands of Roman luxury. Tacitus thereby uses an aspect of the local geography not only to position the Aestii in relation to Rome but also to demonstrate their state of both barbaric ignorance and frugal simplicity.[132] In all of these instances, ancient ethnographers looked to the geographical particulars of a region in order to describe the sociological distinctiveness of a foreign people or to characterize that people's relationship with the historian's own polity or culture.

Equally important to ancient ethnographers were the ways in which the climate of a region directly shaped the character of a given people. This explanatory paradigm has its earliest exemplar in the Hippocratic *Airs, Waters, Places*, which explores the influence of climate on shaping not only national behavioral characteristics but also physiognomy. As summarized by Jouanna, the conclusions of this Hippocratic text show that "human beings owe their physical peculiarities mainly to the influence of climate; humanity considered in all its aspects, moral as well as physical, is shaped

---

[128] Strabo's *Geographica* is a case in point: while organized along a geographical principle, the work is full of both ethnographic, geographical, and historical information particular to each of the regions he treats.

[129] Hdt. 4.46.   [130] *Bellum Gallicum* 6.28.1.   [131] Diod. Sic. 5.22.1-4.

[132] *Germania* 45.4.

by climate."[133] This interest in the influence of climate on mankind was not limited to the genre of the medical treatise; it appears in the roughly contemporaneous historical writing of Herodotus and was taken up by later historians as well as natural and moral philosophers.[134]

Perhaps the most often-quoted example of Herodotus' use of the climatic paradigm as a means to explain the variations in characteristics of different populations appears in a speech attributed to Cyrus the Great, who, upon making himself the master of Asia, advises his fellow Persians against settling in the richer lands of conquered peoples. For he warns that, should they do so and leave the austere lands of Persia, they must "prepare themselves no longer to rule but to be ruled," for

φιλέειν γὰρ ἐκ τῶν μαλακῶν χώρων μαλακοὺς ἄνδρας γίνεσθαι· οὐ γάρ τι τῆς αὐτῆς γῆς εἶναι καρπόν τε θωμαστὸν φύειν καὶ ἄνδρας ἀγαθοὺς τὰ πολέμια.[135]

It is common for soft men to be born of soft countries; for it is not of this land here [sc. Persia] to put forth wondrous fruit but rather men who are excellent in warfare.

The implication of this statement is that the climate of a given region will be the determinative factor in shaping the disposition and even physiognomy of its inhabitants.

This passage, when considered alongside an earlier observation of Herodotus in book three, marks the unresolved tension noted above between Greek (and later Roman) conceptions of the relationship between nature and nurture, *phusis* and *nomos*. For in book three, he had recounted an episode where the Persian king Darius asks Greeks and Indians what they think of one another's burial customs, the Greeks who cremate their dead and the Indians who are said to consume theirs. As each is horrified by the practices of the other, the conclusion Herodotus draws from this episode is a sentiment he quotes from Pindar: νόμον πάντων βασιλέα, "custom is the king of all."[136] One sees in Herodotus, then, that the objective and determinative influence of climate is present alongside the subjective and arbitrary influence of particular custom.[137]

---

[133] Jouanna, *Hippocrates*, 217.
[134] For an extensive discussion of the climatic paradigm, see Isaac, *The Invention of Racism in Classical Antiquity*, 56-74, 82-109; for discussion of its development and use in *Airs, Waters, Places* and Herodotus, see Jouanna, *Hippocrates*, 211-231.
[135] Hdt. 9.122.3.   [136] Hdt. 3.38.4.
[137] On this tension between *nomos* and *phusis* in antiquity, see Konstan, "Cosmopolitan Traditions," 477. It could be argued that there is no opposition here, since Herodotus nowhere states that customary habits themselves are not simply the product of environmental conditions and that

The persistence of Hippocratic notions of climate's objective influence on distinct populations is significant in that it assumes that all humankind, Greeks and barbarians alike, are subject to the same forces and natural laws. Such a "scientific" approach to understanding human communities, in contrast to the random diversity engendered by custom, was later to receive political expression in the Augustan efforts to establish an ecumenical empire that would privilege a universalizing reason, *ratio*, over the particularities of custom, *consuetudo*.[138]

The contending influences of climatic conditions and human mores in the shaping of national character has one of its clearest articulations in Polybius' digression on Arcadian customs, where he argues that the Arcadians introduced certain cultural practices in order to counteract the forces of their harsh environment:

> ᾧ συνεξομοιοῦσθαι πεφύκαμεν πάντες ἄνθρωποι κατ' ἀνάγκην· οὐ γὰρ δι' ἄλλην, διὰ δὲ ταύτην τὴν αἰτίαν κατὰ τὰς ἐθνικὰς καὶ τὰς ὁλοσχερεῖς διαστάσεις πλεῖστον ἀλλήλων διαφέρομεν ἤθεσί τε καὶ μορφαῖς καὶ χρώμασιν, ἔτι δὲ τῶν ἐπιτηδευμάτων τοῖς πλείστοις. ... πᾶν ἐμηχανήσαντο, σπεύδοντες τὸ τῆς ψυχῆς ἀτέραμνον διὰ τῆς τῶν ἐθισμῶν κατασκευῆς ἐξημεροῦν καὶ πραΰνειν.[139]

> In this way, we are all as human beings of the nature to adapt to the necessity [of environment]. For it is on account of nothing else but this very reason that we, along the lines of ethnic and general distinctions, differ most from one another in customs, physique, even complexion, and still more in the majority of our ways of life. ... [The Arcadians] explored every contrivance, being eager to humanize and soften the hardness of their soul through the exercise of their customs.

In this case, Polybius makes clear that it is ultimately the qualities of a particular environment that determine the physical and moral differences between groups of people. Yet he recognizes that climatic factors can be

---

there is, therefore, no contradiction between nature and nurture. Yet it is elsewhere argued that these two concepts were perceived as contradictory, such as in the words of the sophist Hippias in Plato's *Protagoras*, who addresses his listeners, claiming that they are "all kin and relations and fellow citizens—by nature, not by convention [*nomos*]: for things that are similar to one another are by nature kindred, but convention, which is a tyrant over human beings, forces many things to go against nature." Konstan's translation, "Cosmopolitan Traditions," 475. Here, and as is implied by Herodotus' final comment that custom is king, custom is not conceived of as conditioned by the environmental forces that constitute nature but is rather represented as a counter force opposite to them.

[138] Wallace-Hadrill, "*Mutatio morum*: The Idea of a Cultural Revolution," 22. Also see Konstan's study of Greek and Roman cosmopolitanism (where this passage is also cited). "Cosmopolitan Traditions," 473–84.

[139] Polyb. 4.21.1–4.

mitigated and tempered by artificial human effort such as the rigorous musical training and the holding of social gatherings that were adopted by the Arcadians for this purpose. Accordingly, Polybius suggests that mankind is also able to shape itself through the conscious cultivation of particular patterns of habit and practice and thereby either temper or reverse the external forces of the elements, which cause human populations to mirror climatic conditions. The debate as to whether *nomos* or *phusis* is king remains unresolved.

Despite acknowledgment of qualifying effects that cultural practices might exert, the interest in the determinative powers of climate persisted, at least in part because of the attendant rhetorical possibilities to which such a paradigm gave room. Whereas above it was noted in the case of Herodotus that, at least in his genealogical investigations, there is little consistent sense that his ethnographic writings serve to support a political agenda, the unification of the Mediterranean world under the Romans was accompanied by a reflection of new political realities in ethnographic discourse. As the empire continued to expand beyond Italy from the third century BC to the second century AD, it is not surprising to find descriptions of distant regions of the known world attended by a particular interest in their relationship to Roman rule.

For example, Pliny the Elder describes the southern and northern extremes of the compass before explaining the political dominance of those who inhabit the center. He writes that the Ethiopians have dark skin and curly hair because of the heat and proximity of the sun; in contrast, the peoples of the far north have pale skin, straight hair, and a fierce temperament. After describing the opposite poles and the human types they produce, he goes on to describe those peoples who inhabit the middle regions of the earth, implicitly referring to the Romans and Greeks:

> medio vero terrae salubri utrimque mixtura fertiles ad omnia tractus, modicos corporum habitus magna et in colore temperie, ritus molles, sensus liquidos, ingenia fecunda totiusque naturae capacia, isdem imperia, quae numquam extimis gentibus fuerint, sicut ne illae quidem his paruerint, avolsae ac pro numine naturae urguentis illas solitariae.[140]

> Indeed, in the central part of the earth the regions are fertile in every respect by virtue of their healthy mixing [of the elements]. The condition of [the inhabitants'] bodies is moderate with a great temperance even in their complexion; their rites are mild, their perceptions lucid, their minds

---

[140] *Natural History* 2.78. On the geographical perspective of Pliny, see Honigmann, *Die sieben Klimata und die* πόλεις ἐπίσημοι, 31–33. Honigmann offers a broad introduction to cosmography and astrology in the Greco-Roman world and in the medieval Near East.

productive and able to comprehend all of nature; to these same peoples belong empires, which have never belonged to the outermost peoples. Nor thus have these latter obeyed the former, being forcefully separated and solitary on account of the power of the natural force that impels them.[141]

The political implications of this statement on the natural temperaments and dispositions of different populations are obvious: those who inhabit the central regions of the earth are, by virtue of the objective balance of the elements exhibited in their physiognomy, mental powers, and cultural institutions, destined to be the wielders of empire. Aristotle had described the suitability of the Greeks for imperial rule, but, as has been noted by Isaac, Aristotle was describing a hypothetical rather than realized political dominance of those inhabiting the center of the *oikoumenê* over those of the peripheries.[142] Moreover, Pliny further exhibits the concerns of first-century AD Romans by noting that those who are conditioned by the extreme climates at the edges of the still-expanding empire are destined to revolt from imperial control because of the immoderate impulses engendered by their environment.

In addition to the influence of geography and climate, the heavenly bodies thought to govern particular regions could also play a role in determining national characteristics. Astrological thinking was "an extreme and inflexible form of environmentalism" that precluded any mitigation of its influence through cultural practices such as those employed by the Arcadians in Polybius.[143] In book four of Manilius' astrological poem *Astronomica*, composed in the early first century AD, the poet describes at length the properties and spheres of influence of the signs of the zodiac before moving on to show the ways in which the celestial forces shape the destinies of individual men in accordance with the sign ascendant on the day of one's birth. Before listing the different regions of the earth over which each zodiac sign holds sway, Manilius describes the shape of the world, showing that different star-signs lay claim to different lands.[144] He goes on to argue that it is this astrological variety that accounts for differences amongst the nations of mankind:[145]

---

[141] The fourth-century antecedent of this passage in Pliny is in Aristotle, where he argues that Greeks ought to rule over both the intellectually dull but spirited northerners and the clever but slavish easterners, for those who inhabit the extremes of the cold and warm regions lack the balanced properties enjoyed by the Greeks in the middle (*Politica* 7.1327b.18–38).

[142] Isaac, *The Invention of Racism in Classical Antiquity*, 179.

[143] Ibid., 101. For further discussion of astrology in its ethnographic application, see Woolf, *Tales of the Barbarians*, 49–51; Rives, *Germania*, 17.

[144] *sic alias aliud terras sibi vindicat astrum* (*Astronomica* 4.710).

[145] This passage has also been discussed by Woolf, *Tales of the Barbarians*, 49–51.

Idcirco in varias leges variasque figuras
dispositum genus est hominum, proprioque colore
formantur gentes, sociataque iura per artus
materiamque parem privato foedere signant.
flava per ingentis surgit Germania partus,
Gallia vicino minus est infecta rubore,
asperior solidos Hispania contrahit artus.
Martia Romanis urbis pater induit ora
Gradivumque Venus miscens bene temperat artus,
perque coloratas subtilis Graecia gentes
gymnasium praefert vultu fortisque palaestras,
et Syriam produnt torti per tempora crines.
Aethiopes maculant orbem tenebrisque figurant
perfusas hominum gentes; minus India tostos
progenerat; tellusque natans Aegyptia Nilo
lenius irriguis infuscat corpora campis
iam propior mediumque facit moderata tenorem.[146]

Therefore, the human race is disposed to differing institutions and differing physical forms; the nations are shaped with appropriate complexion, and they attest to common laws through their limbs and the same material in accordance with particular arrangement. Blond Germania rises up through its giant offspring; Gaul is less colored by its neighbor's [i.e., Germania's] ruddiness; Spain, being harsher, produces solid limbs. The Father gives Martial appearance to the Romans of his city, and Venus, mixing with Gradivus, well measures their limbs; clever Greece brings forth through her brown-faced nations the gymnasium and the brave arts; and hair, curly from the climate, presents the mark of Syria. Ethiopians speckle the earth and adorn with shadows the poured-forth nations of mankind; India has begotten men less singed; and the Egyptian land, overflowed by the Nile, darkens their bodies more gently amid the watered fields, and since it is closer and moderate it creates a middle course.

This passage illustrates many of the same features seen above in Pliny. Just as with other climatic theorists, the properties of different geographical zones are presented as the determinative factor in both cultural and physiognomical particularities. As noted by Goold, Manilius recognizes such particular characteristics are the result of the influence of climate but believes that "these in turn depend upon the signs of the zodiac, each of which exercises paramount dominion over special areas."[147] Manilius has simply expanded the influence of climatic factors, such as proximity to the

---

[146] *Astronomica* 4.711–27.

[147] Goold, *Manilius: Astronomica*, xci. In Manilius' words, "Come now, learn the stars ruling over the various regions of the earth": *Nunc age diversis dominantia sidera terris / percipe. Astronomica* 4.585–86.

sun and variations in temperature, to include his knowledge of celestial patterns and the power they have over respective regions of the earth. In this case, the mythological marriage of the gods Mars and Venus is alluded to in the shared influence that the two stars have over their progeny, the people descended from Aeneas and Romulus.

Another astrological work that explains ethnological difference is the *Apotelesmatika*, also known as the *Tetrabiblos*, of the Alexandrian Ptolemy, who wrote in the second century AD. In this work, Ptolemy divides the world up into four quadrants, each of which is governed by its own signs of the zodiac in association with the planets. In describing the northwestern quadrant, for example, he lists the regions of Britannia, Gaul (north of the Alps), Germania, Bastarnia, Italia, Gaul (south of the Alps), Apulia, Sicily, Tyrrhennia, Celtica, and Spain, which are governed by Jupiter and Mars. By virtue of these two governing bodies and the influence of the zodiac signs Aries, Leo, and Sagittarius, he claims that it is natural, εἰκότως, for these people to be "autonomous, freedom-loving, eager for weapons, persevering, most warlike, most fit to rule, clean, and great-spirited."[148] Yet such a broad generalization is qualified by further intricacies of celestial influence, for the countries of Britannia, Gaul (north of the Alps), Germania, and Bastarnia are even more closely associated with Aries and Mars, and, as a result, their inhabitants "happen to be more wild, stubborn, and savage."[149] In contrast, the lands of Italia, Apulia, Sicily, and Gaul (south of the Alps) are associated with Leo and the sun; their inhabitants are thus "more fit to rule, beneficent, and sociable."[150] As in the case of Pliny, those inhabiting extremities of the known world are characterized by their subordinate relationship to those suited to rule from the center of the earth. These examples, along with a famous passage of Aristotle to be discussed in the next chapter, are the closest analogues to the ritual texts of ancient China that prescribe a status of political subservience to peoples inhabiting the periphery of the central Chinese kingdom.

A final example of the climatic and geographical paradigm used in interpreting the differences between nations appears in the philosophical writings of Seneca the Younger, where he describes the inability of the northern barbarians to restrain their passions. In using their behavior as a

---

[148] ἀνυποτάκτοις τε εἶναι καὶ φιλελευθέροις καὶ φιλόπλοις καὶ φιλοπόνοις καὶ πολεμικωτάτοις καὶ ἡγεμονικοῖς καὶ καθαρίοις καὶ μεγαλοψύχοις (*Apotelesmatika* 2.3.13).

[149] οἱ ἐν αὐταῖς ἀγριώτεροι καὶ αὐθαδέστεροι καὶ θηριώδεις τυγχάνουσιν (*Apotelesmatika* 2.3.15).

[150] ἡγεμονικοὶ μᾶλλον οὗτοι καὶ εὐεργετικοὶ καὶ κοινωνικοί (*Apotelesmatika* 2.3.16).

negative model for the aspiring student of philosophy, Seneca advocates the philosophical cultivation of an ability to restrain one's own impulses, as this is a prerequisite for the exercise of one's will over others:

> Deinde omnes istae feritate liberae gentes leonum luporumque ritu ut seruire non possunt, ita nec imperare; non enim humani uim ingenii, sed feri et intractabilis habent; nemo autem regere potest nisi qui et regi. Fere itaque imperia penes eos fuere populos qui mitiore caelo utuntur: in frigora septemtrionemque uergentibus "inmansueta ingenia" sunt, ut ait poeta, "suoque simillima caelo."[151]

> Then take all those peoples, free in their ferocity in the manner of lions and wolves such that as they are unable to serve, likewise, they cannot command. For they have a force not of human quality but of that which is wild and unrestrained. For no one is able to rule but he who can also *be* ruled. Generally, then, empires have belonged to those peoples who live under a milder part of the heavens. For those situated toward the frigid lands and the north have "a savage character" – as the poet says, "similar to the sky of their homeland."

As in the case of Pliny, the intractability and impulsiveness of the barbarians is attributable to factors in their physical environment. Seneca likewise imbues these northern traits with a political significance: as they are unable to even control themselves as individuals, much less as a *gens* or federation of *gentes*, they are unable to extend political sway over others. By using the climatic paradigm in this way, authors such as Pliny and Seneca manage to explain the failures of Roman imperial ventures east of the Rhine and north of the Danube while simultaneously justifying their conquest of the peoples to the west and south of those rivers. While the genealogical paradigm discussed above could be used as a means of demonstrating the appropriateness of either cooperation or antagonism in the present, the paradigm of climatic explanation could even more effectively be used in support of political projects. These could range from policies of conquest of non-Greeks or non-Romans to the opposite, i.e., the cessation of imperial expansion beyond annexed provincial boundaries.

In Seneca, however, there persists the opposing notion that artificial custom and learned behavior can temper or even transform natural predispositions, the idea that national characteristics are not impervious to change. For despite the ability of nature to foster various patterns of behavior, custom or habit is also able to condition, or even reverse, the influence of the elements – hence his warning:

[151] *De Ira* 2.15.4–5.

> Agedum illis corporibus, illis animis delicias luxum opes ignorantibus da rationem, da disciplinam: ut nil amplius dicam, necesse erit certe nobis mores Romanos repetere.[152]

> Come now, to those bodies and those minds ignorant of delights and luxury and wealth, grant them reason, grant them discipline: let me say no more, other than that it will surely be necessary for us to return to Roman customs.

Seneca's meaning here is to say that should the barbarians who still live in a state of crude and frugal simplicity acquire the reason and discipline on which the Romans believed their empire had been built, the Romans would then be forced to return to their own rustic past, free from the corrupting enervation brought on by indulgence in the riches of conquest. In fact, this passage is an excellent example of another typical feature of classical ethnography: the representation of the Other as an image of the Self at an earlier, more primitive stage.[153] But more important is the clear assumption that, just like the Roman, the barbarian could be explained by geography and climate, but he could also *change*. This point will be addressed in greater detail below in the discussion of the last of the three interpretive frameworks, i.e., that of history/historical change.

In turning now to the use of the geographical-climatic paradigm in China, one also finds a frequent co-occurrence between geographical and ethnographic information in the same text. As observed in the case of ritual and philosophical texts of the first millennium BC discussed above, such instances tend to be more explicitly prescriptive in terms of their representation of an ideal political order with a supreme ruler in the center of the Chinese community and concentric rings of increasing barbarism spreading outward from the royal zone.[154]

Given the fact that foreign peoples inhabited zones of the periphery that, typically, were regions whose environmental conditions were less suited to the practice of Chinese agriculture, the differences in flora, fauna, and the life ways that these features engendered later became common points of interest for Chinese historians. This interest is prominent in Sima Qian's account of the Xiongnu, and with good reason: the initial military superiority of the Xiongnu was attributable to their mastery of cavalry warfare, for which their nomadic economy and control of the grasslands

---

[152] *De Ira* 1.11.4.

[153] For example, see Long, *Barbarians in Greek Comedy*, 129–30; Campbell, *Strange Creatures: Anthropology in Antiquity*, 108.

[154] For a more detailed discussion of ancient Chinese cosmography, see Wang, Q. Edward, "History, Space, and Ethnicity," 287–92.

and its herds had made them ideally suited. Accordingly, after his introduction to the fasicle, beginning with the Xiongnu genealogy going back to Chunwei and then explaining that various northern enemies of the Chinese such as the Xianyun, Shanrong 山戎, and Xunyu 葷粥 were all really the Xiongnu under different names, Sima Qian turns to a description of life among the northern barbarians who "follow their flocks and move in a rotating pattern."[155] He then lists the animals in which they are rich (horses, cattle, and sheep) before listing a number of less common kinds of livestock that they keep. His oft-quoted phrase that "they migrate from place to place in pursuit of water and grass" is followed by the observation that the Xiongnu themselves "have no fixed or fortified cities or any cultivation of the soil."[156] In offering this short description, Sima Qian positions the Xiongnu geographically in the northern grasslands of the steppe and explains how their lifestyle, free from the toils of farming and of the conscript labor required for the building of fortifications, makes them ideally suited for the practice of warfare:

> 兒能騎羊，引弓射鳥鼠；少長則射狐兔：用為食. 士力能毋弓，盡為甲騎.其俗，寬則隨畜，因射獵禽獸為生業，急則人習戰攻以侵伐，其天性也.[157]

> Children are able to ride sheep, and bending their bows they shoot birds and rodents; those slightly older shoot foxes and rabbits and then eat them. Their troops are able to draw the bow and they all act as armored cavalry. It is their custom to follow their flocks at their leisure, shooting and hunting birds and beasts for a living; in times of crisis, they make wars of aggression, relying on invasion and attack: this is their inborn nature.

Sima Qian presents a sharp distinction between the demands of a nomadic lifestyle and those of the sedentary agriculture of the Chinese, emphasizing that the former makes the Xiongnu predisposed to a militaristic ethos, since even in a state of peace they are engaged in archery and hunting. Noting their lack of agriculture, he remarks on their constant mobility in implicit opposition to the farming and building of the Chinese. By demonstrating this contrast, and explaining the ways in which nomadic life creates natural warriors, Sima Qian not only makes sense of their alterity but also shows how a people who must have numbered far fewer than the inhabitants of the Han Empire could have acquired such a military advantage over China.

---

[155] 居于北蠻，隨畜牧而轉移 (*Shiji* 110.2880).
[156] 逐水草遷徙，毋城郭常處耕田之業 (Ibid.).   [157] Ibid.

However, it does not seem to be the case that Sima Qian and historians of later ages were interested in explaining foreign customs as arising directly from geographical conditions, even if they recognized that the two could be correlated with one another. More often than not, authors simply note the region in which a people lives, if that is not already clear from the name of the chapter in which they are being described.[158] A typical ethnographic account then goes on to list or describe flora, fauna, and customs of marriage, burial, and economy. Two further examples illustrate this point. Fan Ye in the *Hou Han shu* says of the Wuhuan that

> 俗善騎射，弋獵禽獸為事. 隨水草放牧，居無常處. 以穹廬為舍，
> 東開向日. 食肉飲酪，以毛毳為衣.[159]

> According to their custom, they are skilled at riding and archery, and they spend their time hunting birds and beasts. They follow grass and water and pasture their flocks. They have no fixed dwelling places. They live in tents that have an eastern opening toward the sun. They eat meat and drink milk, using furs and skins for their clothing.

The same historian, when considering the territory of the Qiang in the west and northwest, describes a similar nomadic way of life that is explained by the fact that the lands the Qiang inhabit are not especially suitable for agriculture:

> 所居無常，依隨水草. 地少五穀，以產牧為業.[160]

> They have no fixed habitations and rely on the water and grass that they migrate in order to be close to. Their land is not very productive of the five grains; they rely on the products of their flocks for a living.

In both of these cases the details regarding a geographical region and the people(s) inhabiting it are presented in matter-of-fact terms and are more descriptive than interpretative. On the whole, it is less common to see Chinese historians trying to understand general patterns of causality when writing about foreign or barbarian peoples. Whether considering the particular influences of climate or natural resources, they do not seem as

---

[158] An important exception is the early Han dynasty text the *Huainanzi* 淮南子, which explains the types of garments produced by the Xiongnu, Yu于, and Yue peoples, noting that each of them provides what is necessary and suited to the environments they inhabit. Like the long list of animals and their respective ecological niches described earlier in the passage, people who travel by boat live near water and those in the hills may breed cows and horses. Therefore, animals and humans all live according to nature: 陸處宜牛馬，舟行宜多水，匈奴出穢裘，于，越生葛絺，各生所急，以備燥濕，各因所處，以御寒暑，並得其宜，物便其所 (*Huainanzi* 1, Yuandaoxun 原道訓.37–38).

[159] *Hou Han shu* 90.2979.   [160] *Hou Han shu* 87.2869.

preoccupied as Greco-Roman authors with trying to posit generalizable patterns or forces that shape either human physiognomy or society. Nor is there an effort to postulate a set of natural or social laws that all human being should theoretically be subject to, as was observed in the ritual text, the *Liji*, discussed above. On the contrary, the emphasis is not on how the same sets of climatic forces influence human beings in different parts of the world, but rather on the correlations between certain kinds of behaviors and ethnonyms and the particular regions with which they are associated.

An important exception to this general rule, however, is in the case of astrological lore and Five Element theory. As seen in the Greco-Roman tradition, this aspect of geographical thinking could serve to explain differences between societies and their relationship to one another, and Sima Qian too attributes a correlative relationship between astronomical observations and the characteristics of human groups. An interesting difference, however, is the fact that while the Roman poet Manilius employs the interactions of the twelve signs of the zodiac to explain the variety of human diversity,[161] Sima Qian seems to prefer the construction of a dichotomous relationship between China and the northern peoples. He claims that from ancient times, the rules of the heavens have been passed down, and that in the mythical ages of the sage emperors they understood that "within are those who wear headdresses and belts, but without are the Yi and Di."[162] He goes on to describe the location of China in relation to the barbarians and explain the respective correlations with heavenly bodies:

中國於四海內則在東南，為陽 … 其西北則胡，貉，月氏諸衣旃裘引弓之民，為陰 … 太白主中國；而胡，貉數侵掠，獨占辰星，辰星出入躁疾，常主夷狄：其大經也.[163]

China in relation to the surrounding four seas occupies the regions of the southeast that are thus of the *yang* force. … To the northwest are the Hu, Mo, Yuezhi, and all of the peoples who wear furs as clothing and draw the bow – they are of the *yin* force. … Taibo [sc. Venus] governs China; however, the Hu and Mo frequently invade and pillage; they are solely aligned with Chenxing [sc. Mercury] whose comings and goings are rapid and impetuous and who thus consistently governs the Yi and Di. This is the nature of things.

---

[161] "As the stars shine, apportioned to their particular regions, they pour out upon the nations below them their own individual atmosphere": *ut certis discripta nitent regionibus astra / perfunduntque suo subiectas aere gentes* (*Astronomica* 4.742–43).

[162] 內冠帶，外夷狄 (*Shiji* 27.1342).   [163] *Shiji* 27.1347.

Sima Qian thus combines the geographical and astrological in order to reiterate a dichotomous relationship between the Chinese and the northern barbarians in a way that reinforces the genealogical paradigm he employs in his treatment of the Xiongnu. He thus preserves the pre-imperial conception of geography as a determinative factor governing not only cultural practice but also political and ethnic identity – and if geography does not determine the latter, it is at least closely correlated with it.

A similar example of ethnogeographical correlation appears in the *Hou Han shu*, although here the essential factor is not so much climate but rather the influence of one of the Five Elements, each of which is particularly strong at different points of the compass. In describing the character of the Western Qiang, who Fan Ye claims are able to endure extremes of bitter cold just like birds and beasts,[164] he says that they have "an inborn nature that is both unyielding and hard as well as bold and savage; they receive the energy that comes from the element of Metal that is prominent in the west."[165] The intricacies of Five Element correlative theory have no exact equivalent in classical Greco-Roman climatic thought, but its employment in an ethnographic context here performs a function similar to Greco-Roman speculations that attempted to explain extreme (in their eyes) forms of behavior among a distant by people by virtue of that people's location at a geographical extremity.

Interestingly, what is absent in either the geographical or astrological associations with foreign peoples, and what is so visible in Greco-Roman texts, is any interest in physiognomy. While the mythological, pseudo-geographical *Shanhaijing* does describe grotesquely or inversely formed humanoid figures, Chinese historians' interest in the role of climate and astrology does not extend beyond correlations with ethnonyms and social behaviors. One may then conclude, as other scholars have done, that there is little evidence of what might be termed racial distinctions in classical Chinese thought, at least as these may have been recognized in physical characteristics.[166]

History/Historical Change

Having considered the epistemological frameworks of genealogy and geography-climate, we may now turn to a third interpretative paradigm,

---

[164] 堪耐寒苦，同之禽獸 (*Hou Han shu* 87.2869).
[165] 性堅剛勇猛，得西方金行之氣焉 (*Hou Han shu* 87.2869). The same point is reiterated at *Hou Han shu* 87.2902: 金行氣剛，播生西羌.
[166] For example, Creel, *The Origins of Statecraft in China*, 197.

that of history/historical change. It was noted above that Greg Woolf
mentions history as a means by which ethnographers could explain foreign
peoples and their relationships with (or status within) the world of the
historian, although he does not grant it equal status alongside the genealogical and geographical paradigms. However, a framework of history/
historical change – that is, change internal and/or external to a foreign
group that is perceived as occurring over a period of time – appears
frequently in ethnographic accounts, and I would argue that it merits
the same consideration granted to the other two. Embedded historical
accounts within ethnographic digressions not only trace migrations, wars,
and other historical events, but they also serve to explain present conditions in cultural, political, and geopolitical contexts. The historical paradigm thus offers a useful means of rationalizing a current state of affairs in
reference to historical precedent while acknowledging the potential for
changes in cultural and political institutions and relationships. Its use not
only traces the history of Greek, Roman, or Chinese interaction with a
given people or that people's interactions with its other neighbors, but it
also represents that history of relations as a process that in itself serves as a
catalyst *for* historical change. Moreover, the framework of history is so
widely employed by ethnographers and historians that it deserves consideration in its own right.

In earlier Greek accounts of foreign peoples, there is at times little
interest in exploring cultural characteristics as a result of a process of
interaction with other groups. Herodotus often presents his ethnographic
inquiries without offering insights into how particular customs and features had evolved over time or came to be. One has rather the impression
that the customs of the Persians, Babylonians, Egyptians, and others have
always been as he describes them. Polybius too, when presenting general
ethnographic information on the Celts, for example, and recounting their
gradual movement into Italy and the wars they fought against Romans,
Greeks, and others, only describes the crudeness of their ways of life with
no reference to how their exposure to the culture of the Etruscans,
Romans, or Greeks might have introduced innovations or changes.[167]

Nevertheless, Herodotus was aware of the ever-present possibility of
significant ethical change, even within a relatively short period of time.
This notion is present in the warning of Cyrus discussed above, that soft
lands will weaken the Persians militarily; it is also evident in that king's

---

[167] Polyb. 2.17–18. On the use of the "ethnographic present" in historiography, see Marincola,
"Historiography," 18–19, and the references listed there.

strategy to ensure that the Lydians will not revolt against him.[168] Strabo, however, is by contrast keenly aware of the ways in which various peoples have changed over the generations, and he frequently refers to the fact that contact with Greeks or Romans had caused the customs of a given people to change dramatically. Most famous is his description of the Iberian Turdetanoi, who have been profoundly affected by Roman dominance and colonization:

> Τῇ δὲ τῆς χώρας εὐδαιμονίᾳ καὶ τὸ ἥμερον καὶ τὸ πολιτικὸν συνηκολούθ-ησε τοῖς Τουρδητανοῖς· καὶ τοῖς Κελτικοῖς δὲ διὰ τὴν γειτνίασιν ... οἱ μέντοι Τουρδητανοί, καὶ μάλιστα οἱ περὶ τὸν Βαῖτιν, τελέως εἰς τὸν Ῥωμαίων μεταβέβληνται τρόπον οὐδὲ τῆς διαλέκτου τῆς σφετέρας ἔτι μεμνημένοι· Λατῖνοί τε οἱ πλεῖστοι γεγόνασι καὶ ἐποίκους εἰλήφασι Ῥωμαίους, ὥστε μικρὸν ἀπέχουσι τοῦ πάντες εἶναι Ῥωμαῖοι· ... καὶ δὴ τῶν Ἰβήρων ὅσοι ταύτης εἰσὶ τῆς ἰδέας τογᾶτοι λέγονται (ἐν δὲ τούτοις εἰσὶ καὶ οἱ Κελτίβηρες, οἱ πάντων νομισθέντες ποτὲ θηριωδέστατοι).[169]

> To the good fortune of the country, refinement and political life have attended upon the Turdetanoi and also the Celts, on account of the latter's proximity [to them]. .... Indeed the Turdetanoi, and especially those living around Baetis, have entirely gone over to the lifestyle of the Romans, no longer remembering their own language. Most of them have become Latins and have accepted Roman colonists such that they are not far from being entirely Roman ... And however many of the Iberians who are of this type are called "toga-wearing" (and among these we find even the Celtiberians who were formerly considered to be the most savage of all).

In this passage, Strabo claims that many of those very aspects typically used to mark a foreign people as unique or distinct have here changed altogether: language, dress, political institutions, and perhaps even their status as barbarians. As enthusiastic as Strabo here appears regarding the benefits of Romanization, that is not to say he believes that foreign peoples always benefited from contact with Greeks or Romans, for he remarks that the Scythians have actually been wholly corrupted by Greek mercantile culture. The Scythians, though less happily than the Turdetanoi, have managed to survive an enormous change in their way of life and even in what were once their defining characteristics. According to Strabo, they have

---

[168] The former Lydian king Croesus advises Cyrus to forbid the people of Sardis to carry weapons, command them to wear comfortable undergarments and shoes, and teach them the arts of music. Once these measures have been taken, Croesus says to Cyrus, "You will swiftly see them, o King, having become women instead of men, and they will no longer pose a threat that they might revolt": καὶ ταχέως σφεας, ὦ βασιλεῦ, γυναῖκας ἀντ᾽ ἀνδρῶν ὄψεαι γεγονότας, ὥστε οὐδὲν δεινοί τοι ἔσονται μὴ ἀποστέωσι (Hdt. 1.155.4).

[169] *Geogr.* 3.2.15.

gone from being a nomadic people to one that relies instead on shipping and commerce for its livelihood.[170] The important point in both of these examples is that Strabo does not describe foreign peoples – even those who are characterized by a degree of cultural complexity and sophistication inferior to that of the Greeks or Romans – as static entities. Like the Greeks and Romans, they are peoples with history, and their cultural institutions are subject to the changes and forces that affect peoples of the central Mediterranean as well.

Latin authors too show a keen interest in the processes of cultural change, and this is perhaps not surprising given the great preoccupation with moral decline exhibited by some of the most prominent Roman historians. Social change among foreign peoples was generally understood in terms of either contact with, or subjugation to, Roman imperial expansion. In Caesar's long ethnographic digression in book six of the *Gallic War*, he provides a recent history of the Celtic and Germanic peoples who have played the role of either ally or enemy over the course of Caesar's campaigns. He notes that

> fuit antea tempus, cum Germanos Galli virtute superarent, ultro bella inferrent, propter hominum multitudinem agrique inopiam trans Rhenum colonias mitterent. ... Gallis autem provinciarum propinquitas et trans- marinarum rerum notitia multa ad copiam atque usus largitur; paulatim adsuefacti superari multisque victi proeliis ne se quidem ipsi cum illis virtute comparant.[171]

> There was a time before when the Gauls excelled the Germani in valor, when they would wage wars of their own volition, and when they would send out colonies across the Rhine because of their surplus population and lack of land. ... However, the nearness of our Roman provinces to the Gauls and the knowledge of overseas goods have bestowed on them many things for their material enrichment and use; by degrees they have gotten used to being defeated, and, conquered in many battles, they do not even compare themselves with the Germani as far as valor is concerned.

The Gauls, the primary barbarian adversaries of Caesar, are not a static collective entity, either in point of warfare or economic and cultural life.

---

[170] *Geogr.* 7.3.7. For a more detailed account of a process of acculturation, see Strabo's description of the civilizing influence conferred by the Massiliotes on the barbarians of Gaul who had given up warfare for farming and city life as a result of the Roman conquests (ἀντὶ τοῦ πολεμεῖν τετραμμένων ἤδη πρὸς πολιτείας καὶ γεωργίαν διὰ τὴν τῶν Ῥωμαίων ἐπικράτειαν); the Romans themselves had come to prefer Massilia over Athens as a more convenient destination for academic study, and the city had become a place where both Gauls and Romans could pursue their interests in letters and philosophy (*Geogr.* 4.1.5).

[171] *Bellum Gallicum* 6.24.1–6.

Caesar shows that they are subject to universal conditions that foster toughness and valor (omitted from the above quotation are the *inopia*, *egestas*, and *patientia* that had once made the Gauls the military equals of their eastern neighbors) and likewise may lose both their bellicosity and fitness for war through an indulgence in foreign luxuries. Here, as in many other cases, it is clear that in ethnographic contexts the Romans felt free to project onto other peoples their own perceived experience of moral decline, so famously described by Sallust, which they perceived to be a result of the great influx of wealth and licentiousness following their mastery over the Mediterranean.[172] In Caesar's eyes, and echoing the maxim of Cyrus the Great in Herodotus, Romans and barbarians are alike subject to the same environmental and habitual conditions that will make a people either tough or soft. Implicit, then, is the assumption that neither has an unchanging or somehow essential nature.[173]

While the social changes among the Gauls and Germani are represented by Caesar as occurring, as it were, offstage in *barbaricum* and prior to direct Roman intrusion into Gallic politics (though still affected by Roman influence), a more famous example of the transformation of national character appears in the *Agricola* of Tacitus, who describes the process of British acclimation to Roman governance and the subtle policies of his father-in-law Agricola:

> Namque ut homines dispersi ac rudes eoque in bella faciles quieti et otio per voluptates adsuescerent … iam vero principum filios liberalibus artibus erudire … ut qui modo linguam Romanam abnuebant, eloquentiam con-cupiscerent. inde etiam habitus nostri honor et frequens toga; paulatimque discessum ad delenimenta vitiorum, porticus et balineas et conviviorum elegantiam. idque apud imperitos humanitas vocabatur, cum pars servitutis esset.[174]

> For in order that men who were scattered about and coarse and so quick to make war should become used to peace and leisure through pleasures … he now taught the sons of the princes in the liberal arts … such that those who recently had refused the Roman language were now covetous of eloquence.

---

[172] *Bellum Catilinae* 7–12.
[173] A possible analogue to this notion of decline is the strategy of using the "five baits," *wuer* 五餌, of material luxury proposed by the Han official Jia Yi 賈誼 in the second century BC to weaken the Xiongnu. Yet this proposal was intended not so much to weaken the fighting ability of the Xiongnu as it was to undermine the Chanyu's ability to keep his loose federation of subordinates loyal to him through the distribution of wealth. See Miller, "Xiongnu 'Kings' and the Political Order of the Steppe Empire," 22–23. On the use of luxury goods to corrupt the Xiongnu, also see Chin, "Defamiliarizing the Foreigner," 335–36.
[174] *Agricola* 21.

> Then our clothing itself became a point of distinction and the toga became
> common; and by degrees they made their separate ways into the allure-
> ments of vice: colonnades, baths, and the niceties of banquets. And so
> among those ignorant men this was being called "civilization" when it was a
> part of their slavery.

Irrespective of what this passage may reveal about Roman anxieties over
the nature of their imperial expansion,[175] the point worth stressing is that
the Romans saw the characteristics of any given group as being necessarily
subject to influence from external cultural forces. While the climatic or
geographical paradigm was often used to create a sense of otherness
understood as being determined by fixed principles, one finds just as often,
if not more so in writers under the empire, a tendency to place ethnographic information in the context of dynamic historical change. In this
way, the historical paradigm could not only explain the qualities said to
characterize a foreign people but also situate them in a larger context of the
historical processes in which the historians saw their own culture or politics
as playing a crucial role.

The passages quoted above thus undermine assumptions that Greeks
and Romans always perceived foreign peoples as existing in an ahistorical
equilibrium impervious to change. It also requires a reconsideration of
such statements that "ethnography did not lead to greater appreciation of
the complexity of change because the studies . . . portrayed their subjects as
always having had such customs and practices, rather than as developed
over time and in relation to or in reaction against external or internal
stimuli."[176] On the contrary, there is ample evidence that a diachronic
perspective illustrating processes of historical change was central to explanations of present conditions among a foreign people. Greco-Roman
authors operated under the assumption that the same social trends and
patterns observable in their own experience should be equivalent to those
found elsewhere. While they do often use the "ethnographic present"
when describing what they perceive to be the defining characteristics of a
group, they are nevertheless cognizant of changes that occurred over time
and as a result of interactions between different peoples. It may be argued
that this feature of ethnography was particularly significant following the

---

[175] On the capacity of the Romans to not only question the legitimacy of, but even regard with a
degree of moral anxiety, their wars of expansion and conquest, see Adler, *Valorizing the Barbarians:
Enemy Speeches in Roman Historiography*, 171–74.

[176] Marincola, "Historiography," 19. Also see Webster, "Ethnographic Barbarity: Colonial Discourse
and Celtic 'Warrior Societies'," 111–23; Geary, *The Myth of Nations: The Medieval Origins of
Europe*, 49.

establishment of Roman hegemony in the Mediterranean, since imperial expansion, and the concomitant absorption of new peoples into the Roman sphere of influence, necessitated an awareness of the fact that foreigners and barbarians could eventually become Romans – as of course was to eventually happen en masse by imperial decree in AD 212.

This gradual process of incorporation has one of its clearest expressions in the words attributed by Tacitus to the emperor Claudius, who, in this instance, is shown debating with members of the senate who opposed the incorporation of Gallic provincials into the senatorial body. The emperor argues,

> at conditor nostri Romulus tantum sapientia valuit, ut plerosque populos eodem die hostes, dein cives habuerit. ... ac tamen, si cuncta bella recenseas, nullum breviore spatio quam adversus Gallos confectum: continua inde ac fida pax. iam moribus artibus adfinitatibus nostris mixti aurum et opes suas inferant potius quam separati habeant.[177]

> But our founder Romulus so excelled in wisdom that on the same day he might end up considering a great many peoples as fellow citizens who had been enemies. ... and regardless, if you should consider all those wars [of Roman expansion], none was completed in a shorter space than that fought against the Gauls; and since then there has been continual and faithful peace. So now let them bring in their gold and wealth having mixed with us in customs, arts, and marriage rather than hold these things separately.

Claudius reminds the senate that even his own Sabine ancestors had once been enemies of the *populus Romanus* and that the citizen body of his own day is full of individuals who must ultimately trace their ancestry to once-foreign peoples who had made war upon the Romans. The open reality of the expansion of Roman power and the constant growth of its citizen body, facilitated as it was by the granting of individual or collective rights of citizenship and the manumission of slaves, must have made it far more difficult to conceive of ethno-cultural differences as a fixed set of lines along which political allegiances could be drawn. As has been demonstrated by Farney, non-Roman origins were not only acknowledged but even served as points of pride for Roman aristocrats in the late Republic, and this same phenomenon has also been observed half a millennium later in fifth-century Gaul, where pre-Roman Celtic tribal names came back

---

[177] *Annales* 11.24.4–6. The historian's account of the senate speech has been corroborated by the discovery of the *Tabula Lugdunensis*, part of a bronze inscription that matches much of the speech attributed to Claudius by Tacitus. See Griffin, "The Lyons Tablet and Tacitean Hindsight," 404–18.

into use.[178] The preservation of such pre-Roman ethnic or tribal markers does not necessarily indicate any actual perpetuation of distinct communities; but it does show that the Roman people was conceived of as an amalgam of originally diverse groups and that this diversity was not only acknowledged but could even serve as a point of pride and distinction for individuals or regional communities. Not surprisingly, this awareness of the Roman state's fundamental heterogeneity is clearly visible in the way authors living under its hegemony employed the framework of history/historical change in their ethnographic writings.

In turning now to the framework of history/historical change as employed by Chinese historians, an obvious point to notice is that descriptions of foreigners typically appear in an ethnographic present as is apparent, though far from ubiquitous, with Greco-Roman authors. Though one might suggest that this tendency is due to the absence of a tense system in Classical Chinese, the language is fully able to make clear that certain conditions may have obtained in the past but had undergone change by the time of the historian's own day. Yet a sense of a static ethnographic present is strongly underscored by frequent allusions to certain characteristics as being representative of a described people's essence or nature. This idea is expressed in the terms *xing* 性, "nature," *benxing* 本性, "fundamental nature," or *tianxing* 天性, "inborn nature," terms that imply constancy and immutability over time.[179] One sees this sense of the term explained in a passage from the philosophical text the *Lüshi chunqiu* 呂氏春秋, which actually argues the much rarer position that certain kinds of behaviors associated with foreign peoples are in fact the result of habit and not expressions of an essential nature:

---

[178] See Farney, *Ethnic Identity and Aristocratic Competition in Republican Rome*, 1–38. On the above speech of Claudius in particular, see ibid., 229–33. On the use of Celtic tribal names in fifth-century Gaul, see Geary, *The Myth of Nations*, 104–08. Yet even in the late third century, the orator Eumenius identified as a citizen of the Aedui, a people conquered by Rome centuries earlier but whose tribal name was still in use. See Woolf, *Becoming Roman: The Origins of Provincial Civilization in Gaul*, 1–4.

[179] In contrast to the use of the term *xing*, ethnographic descriptions also make use of the term *su* 俗, "custom, habit," which is understood to mean a practice that is susceptible to change. The relationship between the two terms is analogous to that between *phusis* and *nomos* discussed above. Lin's gloss of *tianxing* 天性, "inborn nature," in Sima Qian's description of the Xiongnu as actually having the meaning of *xisu* 習俗, "custom," ignores the obvious sense of the former term and its rhetorical force. Lin Gan, *Xiongnu shi*, 17. The *Lüshi chunqiu* makes this distinction perfectly clear when it states that "*xing* 性 is that which is received from Heaven; it is not something that can be chosen and thus put into practice.": 性也者，所受於天也，非擇取而為之也 (*Lüshi chunqiu* 12, Chenglian 誠廉.267).

姦偽賊亂貪戾之道興，久興而不息，民之讎之若性，戎，夷，胡，
貉，巴，越之民是以，雖有厚賞嚴罰弗能禁.[180]

When the Way of wicked deception, theft, disorder, and covetousness is in
resurgence and when it has been preeminent for a long period with no
respite, the people's reflection of these characteristics *seems as though it were
their nature* [my emphasis]. Such is the case for peoples of the Rong, Yi,
Hu, Mo, Ba, and Yue [sc. barbarians]: although one uses rich rewards and
strict punishments, they cannot be restrained.

This passage may be read in two different ways. The first is to suggest that
when Chinese behave poorly, it is *as though it were* their nature (but it
isn't), whereas the fact that barbarians behave this way indicates that *this is
in fact* their nature. A second reading, and the interpretation I find more
likely, is that the passage implies that just as wicked behavior among the
Chinese is more a matter of habitual practice over time, and therefore not
their essential nature, the same may be true for the non-Chinese.[181] Yet
the passage is ambiguous, for it does not make explicit how the analogy
between the behavior of a Chinese population and other barbarian peoples
works. The important point, however, is that the idea of *xing* 性, "nature,"
stands for an essential quality in opposition to the relativity and mallea-
bility of social habit.[182]

References to a people's *xing* have already appeared in a number of the
examples discussed above. For example, Fan Ye notes in the *Hou Han shu*
that the Wuhuan people's *xing* is one that is *hansai* 悍塞, "fierce and
simple-minded."[183] The same historian describes the Eastern Yi as a
people with an inborn nature (*tianxing* 天性) that is gentle and agreeable,
in this case modifying the term *xing* with the character *tian* 天, "heaven,"
emphasizing the inexorability of this quality. Sima Qian also uses this
expression, *tianxing*, in describing the Xiongnu, claiming that "it is their
custom to follow their flocks at their leisure, shooting and hunting birds

[180] *Lüshi chunqiu* 14, Yishang 義賞.327. For an introduction to this text, see Carson and Loewe, "Lü
shih ch'un ch'iu," 324–30.
[181] This interpretation is supported by that of Chen Qiyou, *Lüshi chunqiu jiaoyi*, 782–83. However,
I disagree that this passage refers to foreign peoples in a way that is analogous to the examples he
cites from the *Zuozhuan*. Also see Pines, "Beasts or Humans," 68.
[182] For an extensive discussion of the usage of this term in the second-century BC text the *Huainanzi*,
see Vankeerberghen, *The* Huainanzi *and Liu An's Claim to Moral Authority*, 101–05.
Vankeerberghen argues that, in the *Huainanzi*, *xing* 性 identifies "the characteristics that
distinguish things of one kind from things of another kind. For instance, that humans have
preferences that run contrary to those of birds and beasts or those of apes and monkeys is explained
by a difference in *xing*." Ibid., 102.
[183] See above, 52.

and beasts for a living; in times of crisis, they make wars of aggression, relying on invasion and attack: this is their inborn nature."[184] In describing Xiongnu tactics on the battlefield, Sima Qian has a Chinese official describe the *xing* of the nomads as being "to gather together like beasts and scatter like birds," and he notes that "to try and pursue them is like trying to strike a shadow."[185] In this case the comparison with animals underscores the notion that *xing* denotes an essential quality that is analogous to animal instinct.[186]

The most explicit statement that the *xing* of the barbarians is inborn and essential appears in the above-quoted passage from the *Liji*: "The Central Kingdoms and the Rong-Yi are the peoples of the five regions who all have their own natures (sc. *xing* 性) that cannot be changed."[187] While the actual dating of this text is controversial,[188] parts of it may well date to the pre-imperial period, a likelihood that might suggest a reconsideration of Goldin's claim that pre-imperial Chinese texts never argued that an inborn nature could determine the distinctions between Chinese and others.[189] While the Greek *phusis*-φύσις and Latin *natura* can be used in such a sense, these terms occur, to the best of my knowledge, only in highly rhetorical contexts and not in texts or passages that seek to impart a sense of objective or "scientific" description.[190] Of all the examples cited so far, only the passage from Seneca refers to something "inborn" when noting the "savage character" (*inmansueta ingenia*) of northern barbarians. The frequent use of the term *xing* as a collective signifier implies that a people's nature is a fixed quality and one that is not susceptible to alteration; and indeed, one sometimes sees, as in the example from the *Liji*, the use of the term followed by an assertion that *xing* cannot be changed.

Nevertheless, there is ample evidence for the belief in changeability of non-Chinese peoples in pre-imperial philosophical literature. Perhaps most famous is the dictum found in the *Mencius*: "I have heard of using ways of

---

[184] See above, 74.   [185] See above, 55.

[186] The same notion may be expressed in other terms. For example, in the *Guoyu* the barbarians are said to have "a moral quality that is the same as that of jackals and wolves": 狄，豺狼之德也 (*Guoyu* 2, Zhouyu B 周語.49).

[187] See above, 46.   [188] See Riegel's "*Li chi*," 293–97.

[189] Goldin argues that Sima Qian's reference to the Xiongnu's *tianxing* "could scarcely be a more radical repudiation of the traditional belief that foreigners differ in their habits rather than in their inborn nature." Goldin, "Steppe Nomads as a Philosophical Problem in Classical China," 229. As Goldin notes elsewhere, "at least some of the Li-chi goes back to c. 300 B.C.E." "The Thirteen Classics," 92. It is possible that Sima Qian was not so great an innovator in this respect.

[190] For example, a speech Livy attributes to a Roman consul describes the Carthaginian enemy (*Poenus hostis*) as a people "harsh and wild in nature and customs whose very leader has made even more savage": *hunc natura et moribus inmitem ferumque insuper dux ipse efferavit* (23.5.12).

the Xia [sc. Chinese] to transform the Yi [sc. barbarians]; I have never heard of the former being transformed by the Yi."[191] This statement is in line with a common notion in Chinese political thought, that the sage ruler will use his superior virtue or *de* 德 to draw people in from afar and transform them. The correctly ordered kingdom, in harmony with the cosmos, thus acts as a transformative and civilizing beacon, a boon for the moral improvement of others.[192] It is important to stress, however, that this is only one line of thought in classical Chinese ethnological thinking. Just as, if not more, prominent are assertions that the Chinese–foreign divide transcends ethics and is either genealogically or geographically determined. The notion that foreign or barbarian peoples have an essential nature that, at least in theory, could make such change impossible has already been encountered. This notion stands in marked contrast to what we have seen from Greco-Roman ethnography, which frequently expresses interest in the changes that have occurred, and are presently occurring, in the author's own day.

If we turn to the historical narratives appearing in accounts of foreign peoples in Chinese historiography, there is a consistent tendency, analogous to the Hellenocentric and Romanocentric examples cited above, to position them in terms of their historical relationship to China. Often, an opening statement of genealogical origin that begins an ethnographic section is followed by a centuries-long record of contacts with China. These historical accounts thus describe a political and cultural relationship that has persisted for as far back in time as may be imagined.

In this respect the *Hou Han shu* of Fan Ye is particularly rich. As noted above, Fan Ye provides genealogies for the Eastern Yi, Southern Man, Southwestern Yi, and the Qiang, which extend all the way back to the time of the mythical Five Emperors.[193] In the case of the Eastern Yi, the relationship is described in relatively positive terms, it being noted that the Eastern Yi are a people whose inborn nature is gentle and agreeable and that Confucius wished to spend time among them.[194] Although they revolted from the control of the legendary Xia dynasty when its ruler

---

[191] 吾聞用夏變夷者，未聞變於夷者也 (*Mengzi* 5.4, Tengwen Gong A 滕文公.125).

[192] Also see Poo, *Enemies of Civilization: Attitudes toward Foreigners in Ancient Mesopotamia, Egypt, and China*, 123ff. Yet some of the evidence that Poo cites for the assimilation of barbarians as described in texts is problematic. For example, consider the passage he cites from the *Lüshi chunqiu* – "The skillful ruler is one to whom the Man and Yi, on the contrary, with their remarkable tongues and strange customs will all submit": 善為君者，蠻夷反舌殊俗異習皆服之，德厚也 (*Lüshi chunqiu* 2, Gongming 功名.54). What is being described here is the political subservience of the barbarians to the Chinese, not their transformation.

[193] See above, 61.   [194] 故天性柔順. . . . 故孔子欲居九夷也 (*Hou Han shu* 85.2807).

Taikang 太康 lost his virtue, they returned to their allegiance and allowed themselves to be civilized by the reign of the ruler Shaokang 少康.[195] The Yi revolted again and invaded in the final years of the Xia dynasty before being subdued by the Shang king Tang 湯; from the reign of Zhongding 仲丁, however, there began a period of the three hundred years when they would revolt and submit in turn.[196] The account then moves through the centuries of rule under the Zhou kings, when the Yi peoples either fought against or proved loyal to the Chinese. The unification of China under the Qin dynasty saw the dispersal and incorporation of Yi peoples under direct Chinese rule.[197] There were further conflicts and raids when China was in turbulence under various Han emperors, but following the restoration of the Eastern Han dynasty, relations with the Four Barbarians were stable.[198] The historical introduction ends with a description of Eastern Yi peoples as being fond of dancing and drinking, and it notes that some of them wear proper caps and embroidered garments and perform ritual sacrifices.[199] This observance of correct etiquette and civilized behavior prompts the historian to remark, "hence the expression that if ritual propriety is lost in China, it may be sought among the Four Barbarians."[200]

This long historical introduction serves to demonstrate a close relationship between the Chinese regimes leading up to the historian's period of focus, which is, in this case, the latter half of the Han dynasty. Over the course of the many centuries of this relationship, the fact that it oscillates between hostility and peace does not obscure the fact that Eastern Yi have allowed themselves to be improved by Chinese civilization and have somehow always been in its orbit. Important to point out, however, is that despite changes in the relationship over the centuries, the status of the Eastern Yi remains consistently that of semi-civilized border peoples in a more or less close relationship to the Chinese.

The historical background provided in accounts of other non-Chinese peoples may also illustrate a very different kind of relationship. Fan Ye's chapter on the Western Qiang, despite its references to periods of

---

[195] 夏后氏太康失德，夷人始畔. 自少康已後，世服王化 (*Hou Han shu* 85.2807-08).
[196] 桀為暴虐，諸夷內侵，殷湯革命，伐而定之. 至于仲丁，藍夷作寇. 自是或服或畔，三百餘年 (*Hou Han shu* 85.2808).
[197] 秦并六國，其淮、泗夷皆散為民戶 (*Hou Han shu* 85.2809).
[198] 自中興之後，四夷來賓 (*Hou Han shu* 85.2810).
[199] 東夷率皆土著，憙飲酒歌舞，或冠弁衣錦，器用俎豆 (*Hou Han shu* 85.2810).
[200] 所謂中國失禮，求之四夷者也 (*Hou Han shu* 85.2810). The third-century historian Chen Shou implies that the proper etiquette and ritual preserved among the Eastern Yi may be traced back to Chinese who had previously lived in the area (*Sanguo zhi* 30.840–41).

submission and cooperation, is dominated by military conflicts between the Chinese and the Qiang (or Rong, with whom they are equated for most of the events of the second and first millennia BC). This relationship is best summed up with a line from the colophon to the chapter where Fan Ye says that "the trouble from the Qiang and Rong has existed since the age of the Three Sage Kings!"[201] The identification of the Qiang with the Rong, and the even earlier Sanmiao 三苗, one of the so-called *si xiong zu* 四凶族, "Four Wicked Peoples," in mythological times, thus contextualizes the military conflicts between the Qiang and Chinese during the Han dynasty within a much deeper historical and mythological pattern.[202] One may say that the historical framework, therefore, does explain the Qiang, although it does so by representing them not as subject to various cultural or political forces, but rather in a static opposition to China since time immemorial.

Moreover, the Qiang, like other foreign peoples, can be remarkably resistant to change. Even when settled among the Chinese, they are shown to preserve their own language and remain beyond a cultural divide. Fan Ye, in a speech attributed to the Chinese official Ban Biao 班彪 in AD 33, claims that the settlement of large numbers of Qiang in the western region of Liangzhou has had little success, partly because of the Qiang inability or unwillingness to assimilate:

今涼州部皆有降羌，羌胡被髮左衽，而與漢人雜處，習俗既異，言語不通.[203]

Today the Liangzhou districts all have surrendered Qiang living there. The Qiang wear their hair loose and fasten their garments on the left; although they live mixed with the Chinese, their customs and habits are completely different and their spoken language is unintelligible.

The official goes on to blame the problem of Qiang revolts on the abuse they suffer from greedy and exploitive Chinese administrators and makes the unusual critique of Han imperialism by saying that such abuse is the reason for all barbarian invasions.[204] But the official nevertheless highlights the persistence of Qiang cultural practices that distinguish them from their Chinese neigbors, among whom they have presumably been living for some time. This instance provides an interesting contrast with the passages considered above from Strabo and Tacitus where, for better

---

[201] 羌戎之患，自三代尚矣 (*Hou Han shu* 87.2899). The Three Sage Kings are the mythical rulers Yao 堯, Shun 舜, and Yu 禹.
[202] 西羌之本，出自三苗 (*Hou Han shu* 87.2869).   [203] *Hou Han shu* 87.2878.
[204] 夫蠻夷寇亂，皆為此也 (Ibid.).

or for worse, the barbarians are represented as adopting Greek or Roman habits and tastes.[205]

Fan Ye's history of the Qiang, which goes back to the early legendary figures in the Chinese tradition, is perhaps modeled on the one composed by Sima Qian for the Xiongnu. As already discussed above, Sima Qian claims that the Xiongnu descend from a member of the legendary Xia dynasty royal family; he then traces the conflicts with various northern peoples such as the Xianyun, Shanrong, and Xunyu, who waged wars with China in ancient times. Sima Qian then describes various non-Chinese northerners, often using the generic term Rong-Yi, and traces the history of these conflicts down to the Qin dynasty. Before providing a list of Xiongnu titles and describing their legal, funerary, and other customs, Sima Qian rounds off this long account by saying,

自淳維以至頭曼千有餘歲，時大時小，別散分離，尚矣，其世傳不可得而次云．然至冒頓而匈奴最彊大，盡服從北夷，而南與中國為敵國．[206]

From the time of Chunwei down to the age of Touman[207] it has been over one thousand years; the power of the Xiongnu was at times large and at times small as they were scattered and divided for such a long time. Their dynastic succession cannot thus be obtained and recounted in order. But in the time of Modu, the Xiongnu were at the apex of their power, forcing all of the northern barbarians to obey them and representing an enemy nation to China in the south.

In the prehistory Sima Qian provides for the Xiongnu, the various wars that he recounts contextualize Xiongnu history in reference to centuries of warfare waged by Chinese kings or emperors against foreign tribal groups. In tracing the conflicts between China and the north, what is remarkable is that Sima Qian gives the Xiongnu so long a history – not, as one might think, to demonstrate the great historical change that had occurred over the course of time but rather to show the remarkable stability of the antagonistic relationship between the Xiongnu in the

---

[205] The inclusion of the phrase *pifa zuoren* 被髮左衽, "they wear their hair loose and fasten their garments on the left," should not be taken as an objective observation but rather as an allusion to generic barbarian practice that reinforces an image of the Qiang as a foreign antitype to the Chinese. On this phrase, see above, 43.

[206] *Shiji* 110.2890.

[207] Touman was the Xiongnu Chanyu 單于, the Xiongnu title for their hereditary supreme leader, whose son Modu greatly increased the power and territory of the Xiongnu empire at the end of the third century BC and led his people to many victories against the Chinese Han dynasty.

north and the Chinese in the south. The picture is one of stasis, not dynamism, over the centuries.

This use of the historical paradigm constitutes one of the most significant contrasts between the ethnographic histories produced by Greco-Roman and Chinese historians. In both traditions, we have seen that it is common for the history of foreign or barbarian peoples to be included alongside ethnographic accounts, since it was recognized that a people's history impinged upon the community in the present as well as the societies of the respective historians. In this way, the paradigm of history/historical change could be applied in either case as a means to rationalize and explain the relationship between a foreign group or region and the world of the historian. The traditions differ, however, in that it was not uncommon for historical accounts ascribed to non-Chinese peoples to exhibit a remarkable antiquity when compared with the comments of Greco-Roman authors such as Strabo, Caesar, and Tacitus who, despite mentioning a legendary genealogical founder, do not discuss events predating a few generations earlier than the historian's own age – at least when discussing peoples to the north and northwest.[208]

Yet such ethnohistorical accounts have important implications for a basic understanding of common humanity in both traditions. The framework of history/historical change in fact only seems to fully apply to the Greco-Roman tradition, where ethnographic historians were interested in tracing the ways in which the customs and institutions of a people changed as a result of broader interactions with other communities. It is taken as a given that *gentes* and *ethnē-ἔθνη* change under the influence of such interactions, just as the Greeks and Romans, perhaps the latter in particular, were aware was the case for themselves. In the Chinese tradition, we see the use of a historical paradigm put to opposite ends. That is, ethnographic history is used not to demonstrate fluctuation and change in the observable features that comprised a people's identity, but rather to assert those features' consistency over time and, occasionally, even immutability. While there is a clear awareness that characteristics of foreign peoples could in fact be subject to outside natural or cultural influence, there persists a convention in Chinese ethnography of representing ethnic characteristics as static. This convention is in line with what one scholar has dubbed a "cardinal concern idealized by Chinese historiography": "to discover and articulate within the recording of the flux of events that principle of

---

[208] Accounts of the Carthaginians, Jews, Persians, and Egyptians, however, go back to eras contemporaneous with or preceding the founding of Rome.

permanence in eternal, patterned recurrence."[209] Therefore, the paradigm of history/historical change is used in the Chinese ethnographic tradition not so much to explain the processes of change that had culminated in a present state of affairs, but rather to demonstrate a continuity between a present state and an earlier age.

Conclusions

In the above survey of Greco-Roman and Chinese ethnographic practices, there are several points that stand out from the general comparison. The first is simply the fact that both traditions lend themselves remarkably well to an analysis that considers the division of ethnographic discourse into three rationalizing frameworks that, collectively, manage to encompass much of the information Greco-Roman and Chinese historians thought worthy of mention in accounts of their foreign neighbors. More illuminating, however, are the ways in which these frameworks are weighted differently in either case.

A keen interest in the foreign is exhibited by the earliest Greek prose text, the *Histories* of Herodotus, which devotes extensive attention to the origins and history of non-Greek peoples. Moreover, the most fundamental literary texts in the Greco-Roman tradition, the epics of Homer, position the non-Greek Trojans and their diverse array of allies as central, sympathetic figures in the narrative. The contrast with early Chinese poetry and prose writing is quite stark: the earliest poetic traditions codified in the *Shijing* and early historical prose works such as the *Zuozhuan*, *Guoyu*, and others all mention contacts with foreign peoples but do so usually in a manner that neither expresses sympathy with them nor offers ethnographic observation that might reflect an interest on the part of the author or his audience as to how these peoples might differ from the Chinese in ways beyond a general moral inferiority.

While each tradition adopts the practice of incorporating foreign peoples within a greater genealogical network of the historian's own culture, there is a much stronger sense of interest on the part of Greco-Roman authors in the genealogical history of foreign peoples. Greeks and Romans might even espouse particular genealogical lineages for themselves that did not suppose Hellenic or Roman progenitors. In the case of early Chinese texts, little to no interest is expressed in the origins of Yi, Di, or other foreign peoples in pre-imperial Chinese literature; it is only with the *Shiji*

---

[209] Yu, "History, Fiction, and the Reading of Chinese Narrative," 15.

of Sima Qian in the early first century BC that we find a genealogy that explains the origins of the Xiongnu and their relations with the Chinese. Yet while genealogy was clearly a critical component to political thinking in pre-imperial China, it was not a framework that either granted attention to the origins of foreign peoples or considered how they may have participated in establishing noteworthy lineages within the Chinese Zhou community, unless of course such foreign ancestry could discredit the claims of political rivals.

Moreover, the Xiongnu genealogy, linking the Xiongnu to the Chinese but doing so in a way that presents their relationship as consistently antagonistic since mythical times, renders the northern nomads as a dichotomous force opposite to China in the south. This approach stands in marked contrast to the almost haphazard variety of origin myths presented by Herodotus in reference to, for example, the Scythians. While Herodotus does conceive of an opposition between Greeks and barbarians – the term in Herodotus' case referring primarly to Persians and other inhabitants of Asia – the opposition lacks the genealogical consistency and rhetorical strength evident in representations not only of the Xiongnu but also of later northern peoples.

While both traditions devote considerable attention to the framework of geography-climate, the Greco-Roman texts considered above do so with an emphasis on attempting to understand the influence of natural forces that will be determinative in shaping not only physiognomic but also ethical characteristics of different peoples. Although early Chinese texts do refer to the influence of astrology and forces exerted by the Five Elements in the molding of a given people's ethical norms, there is little interest in explaining or even commenting on foreign peoples' physiognomy as a feature that needs to be explained.

A more significant contrast in the employment of the geography-climate paradigm is the political implications that the paradigm offers in each case. Thinkers from Aristotle to Pliny the Elder commented on the fact that those situated in the center of the Mediterranean, where the balance of natural forces was at a state of greatest equilibrium, are best suited to rule over other peoples. Yet the influence of these philosophers and natural scientists cannot compare with the *gravitas* exerted by pre-imperial Chinese ritual texts on later political practice and conceptions of an orthodox world order. While Greco-Roman authors explored the influence of geography-climate as a means of explaining their political and cultural achievements, early Chinese texts explicitly *prescribe* the subservience of foreign peoples to a Chinese center – not as a hypothetical series of relationships, but rather as an ideal achieved in the mythical golden age and one that any legitimate ruler must strive to restore and perpetuate. The fact that works such as the *Shangshu* and the *Zhouli* were incorporated into the canon of Confucian Classics under the Han dynasty, a body of texts central to the education of ministers and bureaucrats of succeeding dynasties, the prescriptive geographical schemata these works contained acquired a political and even cosmological authority. Accordingly, these notions of political space correlated with ethnic categories became a central component in the formulation of imperial foreign policy. That these schemata employed particular ethnonyms to mark the subservient inhabitants of concentric zones was of critical significance in later centuries as these same ethnonyms (Yi, Di, etc.) continued to be applied to new peoples inhabiting the margins of the Chinese realm. Whereas the framework of geography-climate in the Greco-Roman case featured as part of a body of medical and philosophical discourse, in China it was a component of canonical, sacro-political texts that prescribed an orthodox political and moral order, where ethnonyms were assigned to specific spatial, ethical, and political statuses.

The last framework, that of history/historical change, explains political and cultural relationships in a manner that overlaps at times with that of genealogy, i.e., relationships in the present could be understood in terms of historical precedent and records of earlier contacts between peoples. The two traditions' employment of the framework differs, however, in Chinese historians' tendency to provide accounts of a people's history in a manner that explains the present primarily by projecting it into the past, by demonstrating continuity with earlier ages and a lack of fundamental change. The Greco-Roman texts considered above demonstrate an opposite tendency: foreign peoples are typically seen as subject to the same vicissitudes of fortune, as well as the same kinds of cultural and political change, experienced by the Greeks and Romans themselves. As in the case of the geography-climate paradigm, while the Greco-Roman description of foreign peoples was approached, on the whole, more as an objective description of natural phenomena, the Chinese tradition exhibits a markedly prescriptive tendency that perpetuates the categories set down in the most authoritative political and ritual texts thought to preserve an ideal world order established in antiquity. Greek and Roman authors, lacking an equivalent tradition of a golden age in which their own communities were a dominant political and moral force, recognized their own achievements as a relatively recent phenomenon. They were thus more concerned with understanding processes of historical change than they were in determining which modern phenomena corresponded to established categories in an inherited cosmological system.

While these contrasts between the two traditions may simply be a reflection of the fact that both Greece and Rome were relatively late-arriving participants in a broader Near Eastern/Mediterranean cultural nexus, it nevertheless indicates an awareness of cultural and social engagement with other societies with which the Greeks and Romans saw themselves as sharing a larger *oikoumenê*. As later chapters will argue, the above-sketched features of the Chinese and Greco-Roman ethnographic traditions persisted in later centuries and contributed significantly to the perception and representation of new foreign peoples who would challenge, and ultimately overthrow, the Chinese and Roman political orders.

CHAPTER 2

The Barbarian and Barbarian Antitheses

The Term "Barbarian" and Its Chinese Equivalents

While the previous chapter examined the different conceptual frameworks within which foreign peoples could be represented, rationalized, and understood in Chinese and Greco-Roman antiquity, a study of ancient ethnography must also consider the concept of the "barbarian" itself. In particular, the notion of a "barbarian antithesis," a dichotomous division of mankind in Greco-Roman thought that places Greeks and then Romans on one side of an ethno-cultural barrier and everyone else – the uncivilized, ungoverned, immoderate, bestial portion of humanity – on the other is a commonplace in modern scholarship. In some ways, the notion of a binary division of humanity into civilized and barbarian categories may be understood as an interpretative or rationalizing framework in its own right, on a par with those considered in Chapter 1. It differs, however, in that it is not only a far more simplistic response to the realities of human diversity but also to the extent that it has been identified by many scholars as a fundamental principle in Greek and Roman worldviews and attitudes. The same notion has been exported to the study of ancient China, as several scholars have identified a comparable bipartite schema that developed in ancient Chinese philosophical and political thinking. Therefore, a discussion of the civilized–barbarian dichotomy in the Greco-Roman and Chinese classical periods is essential before moving on to consider texts of a later period, when the geographical and cultural distance between these two categories, the civilized Self and the barbarian Other, had narrowed considerably.

In approaching this subject from a comparative perspective, the first problem one is confronted with is that of the word "barbarian" itself. One must ask whether the Greek or Latin term βάρβαρος-*barbaros-barbarus* is suitable as a translation for an equivalent term in Classical Chinese. So far in this study, the term has been applied relatively loosely in reference to foreign peoples surrounding ancient China, and the use of "barbarian" in reference to non-Chinese peoples in antiquity requires some justification.

First, it is important to note that the word *barbaros* is fundamentally a word that, originally at least, described the act of speech and seems only later to have been generalized to include other behavioral domains.[1] The term first occurs in the *Iliad* of Homer, where the Carians, allies of the Trojans, are described as βαρβαροφώνων-*barbarophōnōn*.[2] Despite the appearance of the notion of a barbarian *genos* in fifth century tragedy, i.e., ascribing to the category "barbarian" an inherent sense of shared kinship among all non-Greeks, the term itself nevertheless lacks any of the genealogical information that Greeks and, to a much lesser degree, Romans were interested in.[3] There was no eponymous figure named Barbaros in mythical times from whom the barbarians in later ages were thought to descend.[4] It is simply too broad a term to have an ethnic significance in itself, that is, to include a perception of shared genealogical descent for a given group of people.

There are several terms in Classical Chinese that are often translated as "barbarian" in English or other European languages, and many of these have been encountered already. The most common are Rong 戎, Di 狄, Man 蠻, and Yi 夷, and these terms seem to have referred initially to distinct peoples surrounding the early Chinese cultural sphere and corresponding to populations inhabiting the west, north, south, and east, respectively.[5] They thus came to be known as the Si Yi 四夷, "Four Barbarians." However, by the Spring and Autumn period (c. 771–476 BC), these terms were already appearing in binomial form, i.e., they could

---

[1] See Nippel, "The Construction of the 'Other'," 281, and the references provided there, n. 24. Also see Munson, *Black Doves Speak: Herodotus and the Languages of the Barbarians*, 1–4.

[2] *Iliad* 2.867. For an intriguing discussion of the term and its development, see Kim, "The Invention of the 'Barbarian' in Late Sixth-Century B.C. Ionia," 25–48.

[3] Hall, Edith, *Inventing the Barbarian*, 161. A reference to a barbarian *genos* also occurs in Isocrates in the fourth century, where he notes that human beings are superior to animals just as the *genos* of the Greeks is to that of the barbarians (*Antidosis* 293–94) – yet even here there is a reference to language, which distinguishes the Greeks, who have been better educated than others both in reason and in language: καὶ πρὸς τὴν φρόνησιν καὶ πρὸς τοὺς λόγους ἄμεινον πεπαιδεῦσθαι τῶν ἄλλων.

[4] Hall, Edith, *Inventing the Barbarian*, 13.

[5] Creel, *The Origins of Statecraft in China*, 197–98. Goldin claims that "these ethnonyms were all derogatory and never denoted any specific ethnic group." "Steppe Nomads as a Philosophical Problem in Classical China," 221. While Goldin is of course right that terms like Yi or Rong are frequently used singly or in pairs in a nonspecific, derogatory manner equivalent to the use of the term "barbarian," it is also clear from the sources that these terms could be used individually to indicate non-Chinese peoples of a given area or those perceived to have descended from them. The fact that they could, at least in Chinese imagination, is clear enough from the examples cited above from the *Shijing* (above, 41–42) and from the *Lüshi chunqiu* where the Rong and Yi are listed beside clearly historical peoples such as the Hu, Mo, Ba, and Yue (above, 85).

be combined in pairs such as Rong-Di 戎狄 or Man-Yi 蠻夷, and in these cases they usually convey an unspecified sense of "non-Chinese" rather than any reference to particular pairs of peoples. In this way, generic terms composed of what were originally two distinct ethnonyms were later combined to form a more or less pejorative expression to describe various types of non-Chinese (i.e., non-Hua 華 or non-Xia 夏 peoples).[6] Although the geographical associations with individual ethnonyms were often preserved,[7] one notes that already in the pre-imperial text the *Mencius* 孟子 there is a reference to the Western Yi 西夷, the Yi otherwise typically associated with the east.[8] Sima Qian 司馬遷, writing in the first century BC, could refer to the northern barbarians as Northern Yi 北夷.[9] It is clear in such instances that, even individually, these terms could be used to denote a generic sense of non-Chinese or foreign. The use of "barbarian" as a translation for the frequent and indiscriminate use of these obsolete ethnonyms, though not perfect, is quite apt. I would argue that the most crucial difference is that "barbarian" is etymologically a behavioral distinction referring to the act of speech, whereas the Chinese terms have their roots in distinctly geographical and/or ethnic origins.

These various Chinese terms that I would translate as "barbarian" – Rong 戎, Di 狄, Man 蠻, Yi 夷, Hu 胡, or their binomial forms of Rong-Di 戎狄, Yi-Di 夷狄, etc. – do in fact seem to have referred once to coherent communities of some sort, at least as they were perceived by the Chinese.[10] In later centuries when the original use of these terms as ethnonyms had become obsolete, they continued to be used interchangeably or in binomial constructions that nevertheless carry a sense reminiscent of particular and distinct groups. That this legacy was preserved is illustrated by the fact these terms themselves became organizational

---

[6] See Di Cosmo, *Ancient China and Its Enemies*, 102; Creel, *The Origins of Statecraft in China*, 197–98.

[7] The example from the *Liji* quoted in Chapter 1 lists characteristics of the Rong, Di, Man, and Yi – each associated with a point of the compass – while also referring to them collectively as Rong-Yi. See above, 46.

[8] See above 61, for a reference to the Western Yi and the association of the Yi with east, respectively. Also see Poo, *Enemies of Civilization*, 46.

[9] *Shiji* 129.3263.

[10] Creel, *The Origins of Statecraft in China*, 197. The term Hu 胡 was originally associated with northern nomads and appears later than the other four terms. Nevertheless, it eventually came to be used in the same sense as the others when referring to non-Chinese, and Hu 胡 remains a shorthand in modern scholarship as a general term for all foreign peoples contrasted to Han 漢 Chinese, each term used to constitute a single ethnic collective, *zuqun* 族群. On its usage, see Liu Xueyao, *Wu Hu shilun*, 14. For a discussion of the semantic development of the term, see Di Cosmo, "The Northern Frontier in Pre-Imperial China," 951–52; Dien, *Six Dynasties Civilization*, 425; Chen Yong, *Hanzhao shilun gao*, 20–21.

categories in formal historiography, such that under the headings of Rong, Di, Man, and Yi, historians could list and describe the foreign peoples of their own day who inhabited the west, north, south, and east, respectively. As will be considered in detail in later chapters, rhetorical contexts also exhibit a strong tendency to refer to a contemporary foreign people not by its own name but under one of these traditional ethnonyms in order to more forcefully argue for a policy based on historical precedent. Indeed, it is not unusual for speeches put in the mouths even of non-Chinese in historical texts to identify themselves as Yi, Rong, etc. when noting the political implications that such a form of identification could have, and several examples of this phenomenon will be discussed in later chapters. Likewise, the framing of a contemporary history of a foreign people could be presented in terms that recalled other ancient peoples known to have been non-Chinese but who either inhabited the same regions or had a similar relationship with China.

For example, in the third-century AD history, the *Sanguo zhi* 三國志, the author Chen Shou 陳壽 begins his chapter on the Wuhuan 烏桓, Särbi-Xianbei 鮮卑, and other peoples of the northeast (Dong Yi 東夷) with two quotations from canonical texts discussed in Chapter 1, the *Shijing* 詩經 and the *Shangshu* 尚書, which frame the coming account in the context of the predatory and antagonistic threat posed by the northern barbarians to the Chinese:

書載「蠻夷猾夏」，詩稱「玁狁孔熾」，久矣其為中國患也。[11]

> It says in the *Shangshu* that "the Man and Yi have caused chaos for the Xia [sc. Chinese]"; in the *Shijing* that "the Xianyun are most powerful." Thus for a great length of time they have been a trouble to the Central States.

The author has omitted the following phrase from his quotation from the *Shangshu*: 寇賊姦宄 "pillaging thieves and wicked miscreants";[12] likewise, he has omitted the next line of verse following his quotation from the *Shijing*: 我是用急 "because of this one must respond swiftly," i.e., it is necessary to be on high alert in the face of such a military threat.[13] A literate audience, however, would have been able to supply the missing content in allusions to such canonical texts, and thus clearly understand that the Wuhuan and Särbi-Xianbei are to be recognized as modern manifestations of China's northern enemies since time immemorial. By beginning the chapter in this way, the historian Chen Shou suggests that

---

[11] *Sanguo zhi* 30.831.   [12] *Shangshu* 1, Yushu 虞書, Shundian 舜典.84.
[13] *Shijing*, Xiaoya 小雅, Liuyue 六月.499.

the particular origins or traditions of the Wuhuan, Särbi-Xianbei, and peoples with whom they are associated ought to be understood as new manifestation of an age-old phenomenon. This strategy is of course analogous to the one employed by Sima Qian in his chapter on the Xiongnu 匈奴 and would continue to be used by historians up through the seventh century, as will be discussed in the following chapters.

It has been argued that this practice is equivalent to the Greek and Roman tendency to apply ethnonyms of ancient peoples to new groups who appeared on the frontier. The Goths could thus be described as "Scythians" until the Huns appeared farther to the northeast and took over the title.[14] Similarly, the Franks could be referred to in late antiquity as "Germani," since they lived in areas that were inhabited by peoples who were categorized under that label in earlier centuries. Huns could be called either "Scythians" or "Massagetae," the latter ethnonym serving to link them with a people known to Herodotus and located further to the northeast beyond Scythia. The function performed by this recycling of ancient ethnonyms is not always consistent; at times it may be used for literary or rhetorical effect, effectively providing a comparison between a contemporary and ancient people, while at other times, and particularly in ethnographic digressions, it may serve to explain a contemporary group by claiming that they are, in fact, descended from a people known to have inhabited the same regions in earlier centuries.

While Roman authors in later centuries did indeed avail themselves of the device of associating barbarian incursions of their own day with enemies of an earlier age, e.g., the pairing by Claudian of the Gothic invasions of the early fifth century with the Cimbrian wars, or *Cimbrica tempestas*,[15] of the late second century BC, the antagonism is not conceived of as taking place between Romans on the one hand and an eternal northern or otherwise foreign threat on the other. For the Romans did not have a set of obsolete ethnonyms that could be used more or less interchangeably with one another and thus produce a collective sense of a single "barbarian" entity. The use of the term "Cimbri" had its specific associations with time and place; terms like "Rong," "Yi," "Di," and "Man" could be used indiscriminately over the centuries to indicate non-Chinese. More importantly, names such as "Cimbri," "Germani," and "Scythians" do not have the moral or philosophical associations that the

[14] Amory, *People and Identity in Ostrogothic Italy*, 20–21; Gillett, "The Mirror of Jordanes," 398; Kaldellis, *Ethnography after Antiquity*, 113–17.
[15] Claudian, *Bellum Geticum* 641.

obsolete barbarian ethnonyms in China carried with them. In China, these ethnonyms also featured in the geopolitical schemata of ritual and philosophical texts, discussed in Chapter 1, that were central to early Chinese conceptions of cosmology and political landscapes.

Indeed, the very words themselves, i.e., the Chinese characters used to represent the names of foreign peoples, contain derogatory associations that frequently suggest either a bestial, warlike, or servile quality – a practice that, no doubt at least partially due to the peculiarities of alphabetic and logographic writing systems, is absent from Greco-Roman practice. For example, the ethnonym Di 狄 has the semantic signifier, or radical, 犭 "dog" attached to it; the same is the case for both of the characters of the ethnonym Xianyun 獫狁 and the first of those for the Xunyu 獯粥. The Mo 貊 people's name has another radical affixed to it, 豸, which suggests a meaning of "insect." The character for the Man 蠻 is marked by the radical 虫 meaning "worm" or "reptile."[16] The character for the Rong 戎 is itself a word that means "weapon" or "martial." Contemporary ethnonyms could also contain pejorative elements: the Xiongnu ethnonym is composed of the characters *xiong* 匈, which could stand as a variant for the anatomical term *xiong* 胸 "chest," but here more likely means "noise," and *nu* 奴 "slave." For the Rong, Di, Man, and Yi – often referred to collectively as the Si Yi 四夷, "Four Barbarians" or "Barbarians of the Four Directions" – Loewe has remarked that these ethnonyms carry "an implication of living creatures that should not properly be classified as human beings."[17]

As discussed in Chapter 1, the generic terms for non-Chinese featured in early philosophical and historical texts where they could be used to oppositionally define proper or improper ethical norms. Greco-Roman authors were of course aware of wars against Celtic, Germanic, and trans-Danubian peoples in the distant past, but these conflicts did not come to be either remembered or represented in terms of an eternal, almost cosmological struggle of Rome against the Germani or Greece against the Persians.[18] While the memory of former wars against foreign

---

[16] Remarkably, at least one modern scholar manages to suggest that although this obviously dehumanizing strategy is an indicator of "a considerable degree of cultural pride," this "need not imply a general xenophobic attitude." Poo, *Enemies of Civilization*, 46.

[17] Loewe, "The Heritage Left to the Empires," 992–93.

[18] On the memory and use of former conflicts with foreign peoples in Republican Roman literature, see Bellen, Metus Gallicus-Metus Punicus: *Zum Furchtmotiv in der römischen Republik*, 3–46. And yet even Rome's nemesis Carthage received praise for its political system from Greek and Roman philosophers. See Scullard, "Carthage and Rome," 486.

peoples, or even particular foreign adversaries like Hannibal, could be evoked in poetic or rhetorical contexts in order to imbue a contemporary theme with a sense of both immediacy and historical continuity, this practice lacks the essentializing quality of the Chinese geopolitical schemata, which place a dominant Chinese moral power in the center, surrounded by forces of barbarism and disorder. While Romans may have highlighted the lack of cultural sophistication and political organization of northern peoples, their greatest enemies were imperial powers such as the Carthaginians, Parthians, and Persians. Irrespective of whom the Romans fought, battles were won or lost and many barbarian peoples were conquered and eventually became provincials. However, if writers chose to avail themselves of the concept of an ancient antagonism between two poles of humanity, the hostile side was the "barbarians" – a term that, despite its pejorative associations, lacks both the stasis and specificity of even an obsolete ethnonym such as Mede or Scythian or Teuton.

In this way, barbarism, or specifically the labels *barbaros-barbarus*, whether in the singular or plural, indicate an abstract category that a given individual or community might or might not be associated with. The intrinsic vagueness and even relativism of this concept is most clearly expressed in a fragment of Antiphon, for which Isaac has tentatively suggested a possible date of 420 BC:

> ... ρων ἐπ[ισατάμε]θά τε κ[αὶ σέβομεν·] τοὺς δὲ [τῶν τη]λοῦ οἰκ[ούν]των οὔτε ἐπι[στ]άμεθα οὔτε σέβομεν. ἐν τ[ο]ύτῳ οὖν πρὸς ἀλλήλους βεβαρβαρώμεθα· ἐπεὶ φύσει γε πάντα πάντες ὁμοίως πεφύκ[α]μεν καὶ βάρβαροι καὶ Ἕλλην[ες] εἶναι.[19]

> ... (the laws of those near by) we know and observe, the laws of those who live far off we neither know nor observe. Now in this we have become barbarians in one another's eyes; for by birth, at least, we are all naturally adapted in every respect to be either Greeks or barbarians.

Absent from this understanding of what it means to be a barbarian, itself a purely relative concept, is any notion of specific genealogical descent that is inevitably associated with an ethnonym. The latent sense that is preserved in such Chinese terms as Yi, Di, etc. or any of their combined forms must have made it problematic, to say the least, to suggest that Chinese

---

[19] Quoted in Pendrick, *Antiphon the Sophist: The Fragments*, 180. Pendrick's translation. For further discussion of this passage, and a summary of the various interpretations it has engendered, see ibid., 358–59.

themselves could be "Yi" or "Rong" in the eyes of peoples usually so labeled; just so, one never sees a Greek or Roman suggest that, in the eyes of Scythians or Caledonians, the Greeks or Romans themselves may appear to be Scythians or Caledonians and vice versa – they could only say that they might appear as "barbarians" to one another.[20]

The fact that "barbarian" could be used as a relative term is because it was ultimately conceived of as a performative category in a way that ethnonyms were not.[21] The term still had linguistic associations in the later fifth century and beyond, as is clear in Herodotus' rationalization of the legend regarding the speaking dove at Dodona, which Herodotus concludes must have originally been an account of a woman speaking a barbarian language.[22] Into the second century AD and even into the fifth, one finds references to "barbarism" specifically in the context of flawed speech.[23] This linguistic component is important, since there is a tendency in scholarship dealing with conceptions of the barbarian in either the Greco-Roman or Chinese traditions to assume that in China the division between the civilized Chinese and their uncivilized neighbors was one of culture and behavior (not genealogical descent) while in classical Greece the construction of Greek identity was based on a belief in shared blood. While this may at least partly be the case in delineating notions of what it meant to be Greek, what constituted a barbarian was far less defined given that the term referred to peoples as different from one another as Egyptians, Persians, and Celts, each of which had an extensive body of distinct ethnographic associations that developed over the course of several centuries. Even in relation to the archetypical barbarians of the east, "the ancient discourse was anything but uniform."[24]

However, in China, the category of the Other could be indicated by a variety of terms that were all at one time ethnic designations but later lost all of their ethnonymic signification short of general, though not consistent, geographical associations. As the subsequent discussion will

---

[20] As Herodotus indeed shows with his comment that "the Egyptians call all those who speak a language different from their own 'barbarians'": βαρβάρους δὲ πάντας οἱ Αἰγύπτιοι καλέουσι τοὺς μὴ σφίσι ὁμογλώσσους (Hdt. 2.158.5).

[21] As Almagor has demonstrated, the first-century BC geographer Strabo approaches the question of Carian barbarian identity in Homer in reference to their manner of speaking. Almagor, "Who Is a Barbarian? The Barbarians in the Ethnological and Cultural Taxonomies of Strabo," 44–47.

[22] Hdt. 2.57.

[23] Lucian 41.23; Aulus Gellius 5.20.3–5, 5.21.4–5; Sidonius Apollinaris *Epistles* 5.5.3.

[24] "Der antike Diskurs alles andere als stromlinienförmig war." Gehrke (citing Gerold Walser), "Gegenbild und Selbstbild," 88.

demonstrate, the notion of genealogical descent shared among various non-Chinese peoples continued to be a common rhetorical feature in Chinese historiography. The fact that the Greek term βάρβαρος initially described the performative act of speech whereas the Chinese generic terms for foreigners were based on obsolete ethnic markers suggests that the aforementioned comparison between Greek and Chinese attitudes toward the Other needs to be reconsidered: while a belief in shared blood was a criterion for determining Hellenicity, the term "barbarian" itself, at least under the Roman Empire, had no such implications. In China, however, the cluster of labels that represented foreign peoples *all* carried with them notions of genealogical descent simply because these terms are derived not from an aspect of cultural behavior, such as language or degree of civilizational refinement, but rather from ethnonyms, labels used to describe more or less coherently imagined kinship communities.

Therefore, I would suggest that there is a fixity inherent in the categories of Yi, Di, Rong, and Man, and their various combinations, that is absent in the term "barbarian." As the former were understood as ethnonyms, they carried with them a sense of ethnic identity when they were assigned to either a specific group or a larger category of non-Chinese. "Barbarian," on the other hand, did not share anything like the same degree of ethnogenealogical baggage; "barbarian" was a loose category into which and out of which it was understood that individuals or peoples could move. As Dauge has argued, "barbarism" was not a separate class of humanity, but rather an inferior state of human evolution. Yet this distinction was dynamic and mutable: "access to *humanitas* is always possible as is the fall, or relapse, into barbarism."[25]

Although this assessment refers to an understanding of the term only in the Roman period, there is evidence in the examples cited above that alongside the more xenophobic attitudes expressed in the Greek world in the fifth and fourth centuries BC, there was also a counter-discourse arguing that the category of barbarian was a highly subjective one, providing little in the way of meaningful or absolute distinctions.

Despite the fact that one often sees discussion and even interrogation of what it means to be Yi or Di in Chinese classical texts, no one, as far as I am aware, ever challenged the objective reality of Yi or Di-ness per se.

---

[25] "l'accès à l'*humanitas* est toujours possible, de même que la chute, ou rechute, dans la barbarie." Dauge, *Le Barbare: Recherches sur la conception romaine de la barbarie et de la civilization*, 19–20. Yet the absolute conceptual duality between notions of "Roman" and "barbarian" as a fundamental component of Roman thought is perhaps overstated; ibid., 34–37.

The stability and validity of the Si Yi, "Four Barbarian," category itself remained in place. While it is indeed true that in pre-imperial China there is ample evidence to indicate that the Chinese could consider the barbarians to be changeable and thus to have the potential to enter the civilized league of Chinese central states, the peoples categorized under the generic barbarian labels in later centuries are often represented as the actual descendants of their namesakes, as will be discussed at length in later chapters. Such an association confers on, or prescribes for, the ethnonym and its bearer a particular set of expectations of collective behavior. Accordingly, the same characteristics attributed to the bearers of the earlier ethnonyms may thus be conferred on their latter-day descendants as their *benxing* 本性 or "basic nature," attested by its purportedly unchanged quality over the centuries. While it was clear that the barbarians could adopt Chinese language and cultural practice (i.e., to Sinify, *Hanhua* 漢化) and vice versa, the basic ethnic categories remained the same.

The purpose of calling attention to this distinction is to demonstrate that the terms that came to be used in ways that seem virtually equivalent – *barbaros-barbarus*, Yi, Di, etc. – nevertheless maintained nuances of meaning that, though often latent, might serve to condition the available parameters of description, and thus the perception, of the realities of social difference. Whether or not ethnonyms such as Yi and Di when generalized to refer to non-Chinese peoples collectively always had ethnic connotations is not the point; what matters is that they *could* have such connotations to an extent that "barbarian" could not. Moreover, given the fact that such ethnonyms were correlated with geopolitical schemata (as exhibited in the ritual texts discussed in Chapter 1), there was an added significance to these categories, absent in Greco-Roman representations of political landscapes, which prescribed political statuses and relationships along "ethnic" lines.[26]

Although it is an imperfect solution to translate terms such as Rong, Di, Man, or Yi with "barbarian," it is not an inappropriate one.[27] Given their nonspecific nature and the generally negative connotations associated with the Chinese terms Yi, Di, etc. either in single or compound form, the use of "barbarian" as a translation is actually quite suitable in most cases where its function is to serve as a collective label for a people or peoples

---

[26] On the actual impact such theoretical geopolitical schemata could have on real political choices, see Yü, "Han Foreign Relations," 379–83.

[27] Also see Yang, "'What Do Barbarians Know of Gratitude'," 28, n. 1.

recognized by the audiences of Chinese authors as ethically, if not ethnically, inferior to themselves.

Views of Barbarians in the Greco-Roman Tradition

As for the conclusions reached by modern classical scholars who explore the question of Greco-Roman attitudes toward the barbarians, these are far from uniform. They range from, on the one hand, an emphasis on the existence of proto-racist modes of representation to, on the other hand, the argument that there was far more inclusivity and cross-cultural appropriation in the ancient Mediterranean world than there was demonization of a culturally or racially distinct Other.[28] The bibliography on this subject alone would justify a monograph-length treatment even with a focus limited to either Greek or Roman literature; as this section intends to address the phenomenon as it appears in ancient China as well as in the Greco-Roman tradition, only a brief introduction will be provided here.

It remains common in modern scholarship to conceive of ancient worldviews in terms of a barbarian dichotomy, a conceptual division of humankind into those who are civilized, literate, and governed by political order and those who are not.[29] It has been influentially argued by Hartog that in any representation of two peoples in Herodotus, one of them is inevitably represented as somehow "Greek" while the other represents the barbarian. For example, the Persian cavalry are useless against Greek hoplites at Plataea but Persians, otherwise characterized by their use of cavalry, become quasi-infantry against the nomadic Scythians; however, the Scythians are also assimilated to the Greeks as, in the face of Persian invasion, the Scythians become lovers of freedom and defenders of independence.[30] A binary view opposing Greeks and barbarians remains constant. The dichotomy has a further articulation by O'Gorman, who applies Hartog's theoretical approach to the *Germania* of Tacitus:

---

[28] Two excellent studies that demonstrate this diversity of opinion are the above-cited works by Isaac, *The Invention of Racism in Classical Antiquity*, and Gruen's *Rethinking the Other in Antiquity*. The former stresses what he terms "proto-racist" aspects of Greco-Roman thought, and the latter emphasizes strategies of ethno-cultural inclusion and appropriation in the ancient Mediterranean.

[29] Müller, *Geschichte der antiken Ethnographie und ethnologischen Theoriebildung, Teil I*, 152–53; Gillett, "The Mirror of Jordanes," 397–99. On Greek binary thought, see Cartledge, *The Greeks: A Portrait of Self and Others*, 11–16. For a discussion of modern scholarly assessments of the barbarian dichotomy, see Vlassopoulos, *Greeks and Barbarians*, 1–4.

[30] *The Mirror of Herodotus*, 35–57.

> The discourse of barbarian representation in the ancient world is very much a discourse of duality, polarity, of being either one or the other. . . . Three-way splitting does not, in practice, occur. In other words, if two types of barbarianism are represented, one will be assimilated to the Roman.[31]

Such a strict dichotomy is far more simplistic than a careful reading of many texts indicates, as is acknowledged by many scholars who note the absence of any static definition of the term "barbarian" or means of determining non-barbarian status.[32] Yet it nevertheless remained a rhetorical possibility for ancient authors depicting the relationship between those who lived within the borders of the author's community and those who lived without, whether from the point of view of Greece threatened by the Persian Empire or in the context of Roman imperial expansion.

The notion of a barbarian dichotomy is generally thought to have appeared in the fifth century in Greece immediately following the Persian Wars in the first decades of the century. As described by Diller, "the barbarian designation acquired the sense of a political antithesis to the Greek world that it had not had before."[33] It was the Greek opposition to an external and potentially overwhelming foreign enemy that precipitated the development of a new sense of Hellenic identity that was no longer aggregative, as has been argued by Hall, but that now defined itself in terms of what it was not, i.e., the barbarian that was personified initially by the Persian Empire.[34] It was the prospect of invasion by, and subjugation to, the Achaemenid Great Kings Darius and Xerxes that precipitated the formation of this new sense of Greek identity. An important corollary to this new sense of Hellenicity was the development of the barbarian antithesis: "the idea of the barbarian as the generic opponent to Greek civilization was a result of this heightening in Hellenic self-consciousness caused by the rise of Persia."[35] The resulting image of the barbarian in the fifth century was characterized not only by an inability to speak Greek and "an absence of the moral responsibility required to exercise political

---

[31] O'Gorman, "No Place like Rome: Identity and Difference in the *Germania* of Tacitus," 147. In fact, three-way splitting does occur in Greco-Roman authors (see Almagor, "Who Is a Barbarian?," 46–47, for a discussion of one such instance), and it was common from the first century BC to conceive of a continuum along which there were several positions between barbarism and *humanitas* or *civilitas*.

[32] Kennedy et al., *Race and Ethnicity in the Classical World: An Anthology of Primary Sources in Translation*, xv; Skinner, *The Invention of Greek Ethnography*, 249–50.

[33] "In dieser Zeit gewinnt die Barbaren-Bezeichnung den Sinn einer politischen Antithese zum Hellenentum, den sie vorher nicht hatte." Diller, "Die Hellenen-Barbaren-Antithese im Zeitalter der Perserkriege," 39.

[34] Hall, Jonathan, *Ethnic Identity in Greek Antiquity*, 47–51.

[35] Hall, Edith, *Inventing the Barbarian*, 9.

freedom" but also by the trope that "barbarians are marked by a lack of control regarding sex, food, and cruelty."[36] Based on these criteria of distinction, humanity could be conceived of as being divided between Greeks on the one hand and everyone else on the other.

The notion of such a division of humanity between Greeks and barbarians, however, was problematized from the start by Herodotus himself, who noted that the concept of the barbarian was relative to one's point of view. As far as the Egyptians were concerned, all peoples other than themselves were the barbarians.[37] The concept of the barbarian was thus a relative matter contingent upon particular subjectivity. Even though Herodotus begins his history with the expressed plan of recording the deeds of the Greeks and barbarians, he also recognizes that the Self–Other binary implicit in this dichotomy is one in which the superior position is always that of the beholder. It has also been argued by Nippel that "the connection between self-definition and observation of the foreigner is shown in the fact that the Barbarians were understood as the incarnation of a cultural stage through which the Greeks themselves had at one time passed."[38] This view was even more pronounced under the Roman Empire, as has been discussed in Chapter 1, though in that case not so much through a process of self-definition as through self-observation and critique of contemporary society.

Following Herodotus, the idea of a dichotomy between Greeks and barbarians was perpetuated in the fourth century,[39] as illustrated by the following excerpt from Plato:

> φημὶ γὰρ τὸ μὲν Ἑλληνικὸν γένος αὐτὸ αὑτῷ οἰκεῖον εἶναι καὶ συγγενές, τῷ δὲ βαρβαρικῷ ὀθνεῖόν τε καὶ ἀλλότριον. ... Ἕλληνας μὲν ἄρα βαρβάροις καὶ βαρβάρους Ἕλλησι μαχομένους πολεμεῖν τε φήσομεν καὶ πολεμίους φύσει εἶναι, καὶ πόλεμον τὴν ἔχθραν ταύτην κλητέον.[40]

> "For I say that the Greek race is related and congenital to itself, but that it is foreign and unfamiliar to the barbarian one." ... "We shall say that it is in accord with nature that the Greeks fight against the barbarians as enemies and that they are at war with them and likewise barbarians with Greeks; and this hostility ought to be called war."

---

[36] Wiedemann, "barbarian," in *The Oxford Classical Dictionary*, 223. For a summary and discussion of the most stereotypical qualities associated with barbarians in general, see Dauge, *Le Barbare*, 424–40.

[37] See above, 103, n. 20.

[38] Nippel, "The Construction of the 'Other'," 288. Also see Bonfante, "Classical and Barbarian," 7–8.

[39] For an excellent discussion of Greek identity in the fourth century, see Saïd, "The Discourse of Identity in Greek Rhetoric from Isocrates to Aristides," 275–86.

[40] *Respublica* 5.470c.1–7.

In this case, there is a clear articulation of a pan-Hellenic identity, conceived of in terms of genealogical descent, which may be opposed to a putative barbarian *genos*. This opposition has important political implications, as Plato argues that Greeks should naturally be on good terms with one another and that their own internecine conflicts ought to be regarded not as warfare but rather as *stasis*-στάσις, "faction." It is important to note, however, that the Greek–barbarian dichotomy was not the only lens through which to see the world, and another of Plato's works critiques this very notion. While noting that it is common for Athenians to divide humanity into these two parts, one of the dialogue's speakers actually describes the logical absurdity of such a dichotomy:

τὸ μὲν Ἑλληνικὸν ὡς ἓν ἀπὸ πάντων ἀφαιροῦντες χωρίς, σύμπασι δὲ τοῖς ἄλλοις γένεσιν, ἀπείροις οὖσι καὶ ἀμείκτοις καὶ ἀσυμφώνοις πρὸς ἄλληλα, βάρβαρον μιᾷ κλήσει προσειπόντες αὐτό, διὰ ταύτην τὴν μίαν κλῆσιν καὶ γένος ἓν αὐτὸ εἶναι προσδοκῶσιν.[41]

separating the Hellenic race [sc. *genos*-γένος] from all others while applying the term "barbarian" as a single name to all other races together – these being countless, mutually distinct, and linguistically unintelligible to one another – they suppose this to be a single race in its own right because of the name they have given it.

Plato thus both illustrates the perpetuation of a barbarian dichotomy in Greek thought while also showing that at least some individuals recognized the impossibility of reducing the vast range of ethnographic diversity described by Herodotus, for example, to a single, generic category.[42]

Yet despite voices that may have argued for a more rational conception of Greek relations with their neighbors, the fourth century witnessed, in some cases, a sharpening of anti-barbarian rhetoric alongside the expression of a more clearly articulated pan-Hellenic ideology, as exemplified by such authors as Aristotle and Isocrates. Aristotle notoriously argued that some portions of humanity were natural slaves,[43] and that it is proper for Greeks to rule over them:

διὸ φασιν οἱ ποιηταὶ "βαρβάρων δ᾽ Ἕλληνας ἄρχειν εἰκός," ὡς ταὐτὸ φύσει βάρβαρον καὶ δοῦλον ὄν.[44]

Therefore, the poets say that it is proper for Greeks to rule barbarians, since that which is barbaric and that which is slavish are by nature the same thing.

---

[41] *Politicus* 262d.2–6.   [42] Also see Long, *Barbarians in Greek Comedy*, 129.
[43] *Politica* 7.1333b.38–1334a.1.   [44] *Politica* 1.1252b.7–9.

In this instance, Aristotle combines his doctrine of natural slavery with the suggestion that it is barbarians, in contrast to Greeks, who are the people most suitable for slavery.[45] This idea is echoed by Isocrates, who notes as a matter of common knowledge that Greeks "consider it proper to make use of barbarians as servants."[46] The same orator, in a manner analogous to what appears in a number of the Chinese texts discussed above, also describes the antagonism between Greeks and Persians as one rooted in nature, asking rhetorically, "is it not fitting [to make war] against those who are enemies by nature and hateful to the Greeks as part of their own inheritance?"[47]

Interestingly, though, while the writings of Isocrates may be considered a high point of anti-barbarian sentiment, the orator nevertheless takes an unwitting step toward undermining the thesis of a naturally determined distinction between Greeks and others. For in this same text, his praise of Athens reevaluates the criteria of Hellenicity, enumerated by Herodotus as "shared blood, the same language, shared temples and sacrifices for the gods, and the same customs":[48]

τὸ τῶν Ἑλλήνων ὄνομα πεποίηκε μηκέτι τοῦ γένους, ἀλλὰ τῆς διανοίας δοκεῖν τεκμήριον εἶναι καὶ μᾶλλον Ἕλληνας καλεῖσθαι τοὺς τῆς παιδεύσεως τῆς ἡμετέρας ἢ τοὺς τῆς κοινῆς φύσεως μετέχοντας.[49]

[Athens] has made the name of the Greeks no longer seem to be a designation of birth, but rather of a state of mind, and that those ones who have partaken in our form of education ought to be called "Greeks" more than those who are of a shared nature.

Even if this statement is interpreted as restricting rather than extending inclusion within the Greek community – i.e., if, far from including non-Greeks within a larger Hellenic community, it excludes both barbarians *and* other Greeks who had not devoted themselves to the school of Hellas[50] – it

---

[45] Cf. this theory to the episode cited above, 49, from the *Zuozhuan* where the Zhou king is quoted as saying that as all the Chinese are of one family, it is not proper to offer them as captive slaves to the ruler.

[46] τοῖς βαρβάροις οἰκέταις ἀξιοῦν χρῆσθαι (*Panegyricus* 181).

[47] Οὐκ [προσήκει στρατεύειν] ἐπὶ τοὺς καὶ φύσει πολεμίους καὶ πατρικοὺς ἐχθροὺς (*Panegyricus* 184). It is worth pointing out, however, that what is described as being determined "by nature" is the relationship between Greeks and barbarians, not any particular quality characteristic of a barbarian people.

[48] τὸ Ἑλληνικόν, ἐὸν ὅμαιμόν τε καὶ ὁμόγλωσσον, καὶ θεῶν ἱδρύματά τε κοινὰ καὶ θυσίαι ἤθεά τε ὁμότροπα᾽ (Hdt. 8.144.2).

[49] *Panegyricus* 50.

[50] On this point, see Walbank, "The Problem of Greek Nationality," 239–40; Saïd, "The Discourse of Identity in Greek Rhetoric from Isocrates to Aristides," 282.

nevertheless represents a step away from the centrality of blood lineage as a determinative factor of Hellenicity.[51] For it is worth noting that shared blood, τὸ ὅμαιμον, was the first of the three features that Herodotus puts in the mouth of an Athenian who defines what it means to be "Greek," τὸ Ἑλληνικόν. This shift from absolute ethnic distinctions to more, potentially, inclusive cultural ones has been observed by Dauge, who has argued that the Greeks of the fourth century considered not only the possibility of barbarian participation in Greek culture but also the corresponding value of foreign civilizations.[52]

The Hellenistic Age produced one of the most powerful visual monuments to the notion of the barbarian antithesis in the gigantomachy depicted on the Pergamon altar under the reign of Eumenes II.[53] Nevertheless, the concept of the barbarian continued to be challenged in the third century BC, if we accept as genuine the ideas of Eratosthenes of Cyrene that have been transmitted by Strabo. According to Strabo, Eratosthenes advocated a division of humankind into two categories, but the opposing categories of Greek and barbarian were rejected as the basis of any meaningful distinction:

> Ἐπὶ τέλει δὲ τοῦ ὑπομνήματος οὐκ ἐπαινέσας τοὺς δίχα διαιροῦντας ἅπαν τὸ τῶν ἀνθρώπων πλῆθος εἴς τε Ἕλληνας καὶ βαρβάρους καὶ τοὺς Ἀλεξάνδρῳ παραινοῦντας τοῖς μὲν Ἕλλησιν ὡς φίλοις χρῆσθαι, τοῖς δὲ βαρβάροις ὡς πολεμίοις, βέλτιον εἶναί φησιν ἀρετῇ καὶ κακίᾳ διαιρεῖν ταῦτα. πολλοὺς γὰρ καὶ τῶν Ἑλλήνων εἶναι κακοὺς καὶ τῶν βαρβάρων ἀστείους, καθάπερ Ἰνδοὺς καὶ Ἀριανούς, ἔτι δὲ Ῥωμαίους καὶ Καρχηδονίους, οὕτω θαυμαστῶς πολιτευομένους.[54]

> At the end of his account, and neither praising those who divide the entire mass of humanity in two – into Greeks and barbarians – nor those who were advising Alexander to treat the Greeks as his friends and the barbarians as his enemies, [Eratosthenes] says that it is better to make these distinctions

---

[51] It has often been observed that Isocrates may here have been influenced by the problem of Macedonian identity, which was an issue of some controversy. Isocrates' rhetoric illustrates the complexities inherent in uses of a Greek–barbarian dichotomy; it has been argued that "uses of the Hellenic-barbarian opposition ... served to effect assimilation with or differentiation from non-Greek external powers." Champion, *Cultural Politics in Polybius' Histories*, 34.

[52] "On conçut la possibilité de communiquer, dans certaines conditions, cette culture aux meilleurs parmi les barbares, et l'on se mit, corrélativement, à reconnaître la valeur de civilisations étrangères à la grecque." Dauge, *Le Barbare*, 11.

[53] Gillett has commented on the significance of the monument as a Hellenistic representation of the barbarian antithesis. "Barbarians, *barbaroi*," in *The Encyclopedia of Ancient History Vol. V*, 1044. For a detailed discussion of ethnography in the Hellensitic period, see Dihle, "Zur hellenistischen Ethnographie," 207–39.

[54] *Geogr.* 1.4.9.

according to virtue and vice. For many of the Greeks are evil and many of the barbarians are civilized, such as the Indians and Aryans and still more so the Romans and Carthaginians, who are so remarkably well organized politically.

This passage returns to the relativism of Herodotus, who recognized that the division of Greek and barbarian, though he makes use of it himself, is ultimately subjective and has no absolute ethnic or ethical value. More logical to Eratosthenes is a division between those who are virtuous and civilized and those who are wicked and brutish. Such a formulation challenges any assumption of Greek ethical supremacy while allowing that some Greeks themselves may well be inferior to certain foreign peoples.

The Romans, while initially regarded as barbarians by the Greeks, were in time to adopt this same binary division of mankind as one among a variety of strategies for representing foreign peoples.[55] Although some scholars have suggested that Roman thinking internalized the notion of two exclusive communities, the civilized community characterized by its *humanitas* and the barbarian community characterized by its savagery and immoderation,[56] others have argued that the Roman view was far more nuanced than this and allowed for a wide range of possibilities between these two extremes. Browning has proposed that, following the Roman entrance into the larger Hellenistic community, there was a threefold division of Greeks, Romans, and barbarians.[57] However, such a formulation is still in many ways simply a conflation of the first two categories (albeit with the former inevitably enjoying a degree of sophistication and refinement beyond that of its junior partner in civilization) that are joined in opposition to the barbarian.

Nevertheless, the complete absence of a *tertium quid* as proposed by Hartog and O'Gorman is not borne out by the sources. For example, Riggsby has demonstrated that Caesar's commentaries exhibit a great deal of plasticity in the concept of the barbarian, representing the Germani as far more barbaric than the Gauls and the latter as more and more civilized over the course of the narrative.[58] Caesar's manipulation of the concept shows both the mutability of any fixed conception of the barbarian as well as the ways in which this flexibility could be employed in the service of conquest. More evident in the commentaries of Caesar is the

---

[55] On Greek views of the Romans and the ambivalence that accompanied the Roman entrance in the Hellenistic world, see Champion, *Cultural Politics in Polybius' Histories*, 30–63.

[56] For example, see Veyne, "*Humanitas*: Romans and Non-Romans," 342–69, esp. 359.

[57] Browning, "Greeks and Others: From Antiquity to the Renaissance," 262–63.

[58] Riggsby, *Caesar in Gaul and Rome*, 101–05.

above-mentioned continuum described by Dauge, which allows for a variety of intermediate positions in between the poles of highest refinement and rudest barbarism.

Notions of a barbarian antithesis were further undermined by the historical circumstances of Rome's rise to hegemony. Barbarians in the eyes of Greeks like Eratosthenes, the Romans saw little to gain from upholding a worldview in which they themselves necessarily occupied an inferior position. For example, Cicero directly challenges the Greek binary division, while also claiming Roman membership within the Hellenistic civilized world. In book one of *De Republica*, the question is asked whether or not the subjects of Rome's founder Romulus were themselves barbarians.[59] Cicero's answer is that

> Si ut Graeci dicunt, omnes aut Graios esse aut barbaros, vereor ne barbarorum rex fuerit; sin id nomen moribus dandum est, non linguis, non Graecos minus barbaros quam Romanos puto.[60]

> If, as the Greeks say, all people are either Greeks or barbarians, I am afraid that he may have been a king of barbarians. But if that name should be given to *customs* [my italics] and not to languages, I should not think the Greeks to be barbarians any less than I do the Romans.

Cicero suggests that the Greeks saw barbarism's defining characteristic in linguistic terms and not those concerned with genealogical descent or affinity. Nevertheless, he makes clear in this passage that a Roman conception of identity is not only distinct from the criteria voiced in fifth-century Greece but even more susceptible to processes of change and assimilation. While language itself is a performative, cultural act, it nevertheless does have an element of perceived heredity that supports its place beside genealogy and religious custom as an aspect of identity inherited from one's ancestors. After all, people learn to speak from their parents, and the acquisition of a second language later in life is not only difficult but also (in most cases) imperfect. Much easier is the donning of a toga and the frequenting of baths. In an analysis of this passage, Woolf has convincingly argued both that "Romans conceived of a continuum along which it was relatively easy to progress" and that "in common usage, the disengaging of civilization from ethnicity was a commonplace among Roman writers" – indeed, as Woolf points out, this had to be the case, since not all civilized men were Romans.[61] Moreover, Cicero does not

---

[59] *num barbarorum Romulus rex fuit?* (*De Republica* 1.58).   [60] *De Republica* 1.58.
[61] Woolf, *Becoming Roman*, 59.

refute the suggestion that the early Romans were barbarians by claiming that they were something else; he simply allows that if one accepts language as the decisive criterion, then that must indeed have been the case. However, in terms of ethics and behavior, the things Cicero deems to be of actual importance, the Romans and Greeks should be reckoned as equals. In a further departure from fifth-century BC thought, not only is barbarism a concept devoid of genealogical content, but even Greek exceptionalism has fallen by the wayside. Neither half of the Greek–barbarian dichotomy maintains any valence in Cicero's view.

In light of the emperor Claudius' speech on including Gauls in the Roman senate, it was noted in Chapter 1 that the Romans were particularly aware, or at least particularly comfortable acknowledging, the heterogeneous origins of their empire. Nevertheless, it is instructive to consider the way even Greek-speaking provincials could acknowledge the idea of an empire that had abandoned the concept of a barbarian antithesis. After describing the Roman Empire's fusion of the continents of Asia and Europe and the disappearance of any meaningful geographical boundaries, Aelius Aristides claimed in the latter half of the second century AD that

> πρόκειται δ' ἐν μέσῳ πᾶσι πάντα· ξένος δ' οὐδεὶς ὅστις ἀρχῆς ἢ πίστεως ἄξιος ... καὶ τὸ Ῥωμαῖον εἶναι ἐποιήσατε οὐ πόλεως, ἀλλὰ γένους ὄνομα κοινοῦ τινος, καὶ τούτου οὐχ ἑνὸς τῶν πάντων, ἀλλ' ἀντιρρόπου πᾶσι τοῖς λοιποῖς. οὐ γὰρ εἰς Ἕλληνας καὶ βαρβάρους διαιρεῖτε νῦν τὰ γένη ... ἀλλ' εἰς Ῥωμαίους τε καὶ οὐ Ῥωμαίους ἀντιδιείλετε, ἐπὶ τοσοῦτον ἐξηγάγετε τὸ τῆς πόλεως ὄνομα.[62]

> All things are now in the middle for everyone: no one is a stranger, whoever is worthy to govern or to be trusted ... And you have made "Roman" not the name of a city but of a common race – not of this one race out of all the others, but rather a race that is complementary to all others. For you do not now divide the nations into Greeks and barbarians ... but you have rather divided them up into Romans and non-Romans – to such an extent have you extended the name of the city.

The panegyric suggests that what was hubris in the Persian transgressions of continental barriers in their efforts to subjugate the Massagetae, Ethiopians, Scythians, and finally Greeks stands here to the greater glory of Rome. But more importantly, Aristides acknowledges the artificiality of the Roman imperial project. He was doubtless aware of the city's own mythological origins, both the myth of Aeneas who wedded his people to

---

[62] *Oration* 14.213–14. For an analysis of the speech, as well as a translation and commentary, see Oliver, *The Ruling Power.*

the Latins and created "a race mixed with Ausonian blood,"[63] as well as the legend of Romulus' asylum, which attracted Rome's future inhabitants out of an "obscure and humble crowd" that was drawn from various neighboring peoples, "a throng without any care for a man's free or slave status."[64] While acknowledging the artificial creation of a "common race" by Rome, Aristides is not interested in emphasizing the unity of a new people out of heterogeneous origins so much as he wishes to claim that the Roman people is a new kind of community that has transcended earlier divisions. The only meaningful distinction according to Aristides is a political one: those who are subject to, and whose freedom and prosperity are guaranteed by, the political and legal institutions of the empire and those who are not. Yet Roman citizenship did not stand in opposition to other forms of identity. Aristides goes on to note that many inhabitants of individual cities of the empire are no less Roman citizens than they are members of their own respectives ethnic groups.[65] Roman identity is thus not in opposition to either the "barbarian" or alternative ethnicities; it is a super-category that binds even those who have not yet seen the city of Rome to the Roman community.

While the notion of a barbarian antithesis continued to be exploited in rhetorical contexts well beyond the second century AD and even beyond the sixth, there is nevertheless a clear sense that what originally began as a xenophobic and defensive Greek response to the threat of imperial conquest was greatly attenuated in the Hellenistic Mediterranean world under the Roman Empire. Though the conceptual schema of a world divided between the civilized and the barbarians remained among the tools of the orator or historian, the concept of the barbarian antithesis was balanced by the heterogeneity of Roman mythical and historical ancestry and the diversity of imperial cosmopolitanism.

Views of Barbarian Others in Ancient China

In scholarship concerned with the barbarian antithesis in ancient China, it is agreed that there was a range of views toward the barbarians or foreign peoples during the Spring and Autumn and Warring States periods.[66] This

---

[63] *genus Ausonio mixtum . . . sanguine* (*Aeneid* 12.838).

[64] *obscuram atque humilem . . . multitudinem. . . . turba omnis, sine discrimine liber an seruus esset* (Livy 1.8.5–6).

[65] πολλοὶ μὲν ἐν ἑκάστῃ πόλει πολῖται ὑμέτεροι οὐχ ἧττον ἢ τῶν ὁμοφύλων (*Orat.* 14.214).

[66] On the potentially inclusive views of Chinese toward foreigners in this earlier period, see Creel, *The Origins of Statecraft in China*, 211–14; Pines, "Beasts or Humans," 62.

should come as no surprise, as this was the era of the so-called Hundred Schools of philosophical thought, which were all engaged in vigorous debate with one another until the establishment of Classicist, "Confucian" orthodoxy under the Han 漢 became the dominant political and philosophical ethos. Yet despite this plurality of voices in the pre-imperial period, there remained a tendency to conceive of the relationship between the Chinese and their foreign neighbors in dichotomous terms. Such a view is present already in Confucius, who states that "Should the Yi-Di have a ruler, they would still be inferior to the Chinese without one."[67] Confucius' praise for the Chinese minister who convinced his lord to come to the aid of another Chinese state under barbarian attack – thus assuring the generations down to Confucius' day would wear their hair and clothing correctly – has been considered in Chapter 1 and underscores the importance of a distinction between Chinese and barbarian norms in this most influential of early Chinese thinkers. That same episode as recounted in the *Zuozhuan* 左轉, to be discussed below, was used to emphasize the belief in shared kinship between the various Zhou 周 states that excluded foreign communities.

Although Pines has argued that texts exhibiting an ethnic or cultural exclusivity in the pre-imperial period are rare, they are nevertheless not difficult to find. Moreover, the rarity observed by Pines is due not to a countervailing prevalence of passages that exhibit a relativistic, sympathetic, or inclusive view, but rather to the fact that the non-Chinese are seldom a topic of interest at all, outside of the political and military repercussions of their wars and alliances with Chinese states. As Pines acknowledges, pre-imperial Chinese authors developed a notion akin to the barbarian antithesis, what Pines has dubbed the Sino-barbarian dichotomy.

An example of anti-barbarian rhetoric typical of the pre-imperial period appears in the historiographical text the *Guoyu* 國語. In this instance an envoy from the Chinese state of Jin 晉 comes to the court of the Zhou king, the nominal ruler over the other Chinese states; while the envoy is told that the state of Jin is the kindred of the Zhou ruling house,[68] the Rong-Di barbarians are not so, and the Zhou king has the following remarks for them:

---

[67] 夷狄之有君，不如諸夏之亡也 (*Lunyu* 3.5, Bayi 八佾.24).

[68] 女，今我王室之一二兄弟 (*Guoyu* 2, Zhouyu B 周語.58). Cf. the episode discussed in Chapter 1, where the Zhou king is quoted as acknowledging the ties of kinship between the Chinese states that do not include the barbarians.

夫戎，狄，冒沒輕儳，貪而不讓. 其血氣不治，若禽獸焉.[69]

As for the Rong and the Di, they are recklessly grasping and make no
distinction between the different status of the young and the aged; they are
greedy and do not ever yield with propriety; their blood and breath are
chaotic; they are like birds and beasts.

Not only are the barbarians relegated to subhuman status in this passage,
but they are also clearly represented as the cultural antithesis of the
Chinese: cardinal Confucian values of filial piety and refined modesty
have their inverse manifestation in the barbarian world. In an oppositional form of self-identification, analogous to that of the Greeks in
opposition to Persia, ethnographic description of the barbarians is
employed to define what constitutes Chinese ethical behavior by describing its antithesis.

Interestingly, and similar to the formulation appearing in Plato above,
this passage also represents the relationship between different Chinese
kingdoms as one of a shared kinship that excludes barbarian peoples.
The *locus classicus* for this notion appears in the *Zuozhuan*, where the
Chinese minister Guan Zhong 管仲, later praised by Confucius, admon-
ishes his lord, who hesitates to come to the aid of a Chinese state under
barbarian attack:

戎狄豺狼，不可厭也；諸夏親暱，不可棄也.[70]

The Rong-Di are jackals and wolves and they cannot be restrained; all of the
Chinese states are close relatives who cannot be abandoned.

As in the case of Greece composed of its competing *poleis*, which, by the
fourth century, had increasingly come to conceive of a pan-Hellenic
consanguinity, the various states under the nominal lordship of the Zhou
royal family could also be thought of in terms of a network of kinship
relations that served not only to define the Zhou community but also to
exclude an antithetical foreign threat.

There is ample evidence that for much of the first millennium BC the
Chinese perceived a stark, theoretical divide between themselves and the
Barbarians of the Four Directions, the Si Yi 四夷. This is the view taken
by Dikötter, who critiques, perhaps in too strong terms, the suggestion by
some modern scholars that such a divide was largely rhetorical, what
Dikötter describes as the "delusive myth of a Chinese antiquity that
abandoned racial standards in favor of a concept of cultural universalism

---

[69] *Guoyu* 2, Zhouyu B 周語.58.   [70] *Zuozhuan*, Mingong 閔公.1.256.

in which all barbarians could ultimately participate."[71] Indeed, the example quoted above from Confucius where he claims that even if the barbarians should acquire sage kings they would still be inferior to the Chinese with no ruler suggests that it is not simply a matter of cultural norms that separates Chinese and non-Chinese: even if they should follow the Chinese example, they would still be inferior.

Yet it has been demonstrated that although such a division is a prominent feature of the political rhetoric of the period, such a dichotomous worldview is certainly not reflected in the pragmatic political choices of the various Chinese states in the Spring and Autumn and Warring States periods. Di Cosmo has shown that political opportunism and the constraints of realpolitik far outweighed abstract notions of pan-Chinese solidarity vis-à-vis the barbarians.[72] Ethno-cultural ideology did not prevent rulers of Chinese states from marrying barbarian wives who would produce legitimate heirs.[73] It has also been noted that two of the last major political powers to enter the competition among the warring states were the barbarian states of Wu 吳 and Yue 越, which claimed ultimate descent from the Zhou and Xia 夏 royal families, respectively.[74] Even if there was skepticism regarding the veracity of such claims, these two states nevertheless entered into the greater Chinese political sphere and were dominant political players for a time. Although we do not have evidence of whatever genealogical claims its rulers may have made for themselves, the state of Zhongshan 中山 in the northeast was widely considered to have been of Di 狄 origin;[75] yet based on the archeological evidence from Zhongshan, there is little that would lead one to any conclusion that this state was somehow culturally distinct from its peers.[76]

The case of Zhongshan seems to be a real-life corroboration of one of the philosophical arguments in the *Mencius* 孟子, namely that it was

---

[71] Dikötter, *The Discourse of Race in Modern China*, 3. While Pines offers multiple examples from pre-imperial texts that suggest a view contrary to the one espoused by Dikötter, that does not make the passages clearly expressing ethnic xenophobia any less significant – especially when they appear in the sayings of as authoritative a thinker as Confucius or in works later incorporated into the Confucian canon.

[72] Di Cosmo, *Ancient China and Its Enemies*, 124–26.

[73] Hsu, "The Spring and Autumn Period," 569–70.   [74] Ibid., 563.

[75] The *Lüshi chunqiu*, for example, refers to the people of Zhongshan as *Di ren* 狄人, "Di people" (*Lüshi chunqiu* 8, Jianxuan 簡選.185).

[76] "Without the historical knowledge of the Di origins of the Zhongshan kings, it is unlikely that anyone would ever have thought of interpreting their funerary remains as reflecting 'alien', non-Zhou cultural traditions." Falkenhausen, *Chinese Society in the Age of Confucius (1000–250 BC): The Archaeological Evidence*, 288. Also see Di Cosmo, *Ancient China and Its Enemies*, 126.

possible for barbarians to be transformed, and presumably civilized, by their exposure to Chinese culture:

吾聞用夏變夷者，未聞變於夷者也.[77]

> I have heard of using ways of the Xia [sc. Chinese] to transform the Yi [sc. barbarians]; I have never heard of the former being transformed by the Yi.

This passage, from which the idiom *yong Xia bian Yi* 用夏變夷 "use [the civilization of] China to transform the barbarians" is thought to derive, makes it clear that there is a sense in pre-imperial texts that while the supremacy of Chinese civilization may not be in question, there is at least the possibility that barbarians, classified as Rong, Yi, Di, Man or some combination of any two of these ethnonyms, might shed their barbarism.

A similar notion appears in the passage discussed in Chapter 1 from the *Lüshi chunqiu* 呂氏春秋 that suggests that all behaviors are the result of practices that build up over time;[78] though they can be difficult to change, it is not impossible. That a notion of the changeability of the barbarian should find expression in this period is not surprising given that such a view was far more in accord with the reality of the times. The Warring States period saw continued expansion of the Chinese states at the expense of their neighbors and the incorporation of different peoples into their subject populations. Indeed, the formation of the people who would comprise the majority of the subjects of the Qin 秦 and Han dynasties must have incorporated large numbers of other peoples historically known to have inhabited areas both surrounding and in between different Chinese states but who had largely disappeared by the late third century BC.[79] Nevertheless, an interest in describing this process is not clearly articulated in the classical period to the extent that we see it acknowledged in the narratives of Roman expansion and conquest. In contrast to later detailed accounts of Roman wars, treaties, and alliances with Latins, Volscians, Samnites, and others, the Si Yi in the historical record were more quietly absorbed into the expanding Chinese cluster of states.

It has been argued, however, that the establishment of a unified empire under the Qin and then the Han dynasties witnessed a more exclusive conceptual demarcation of the Chinese sphere that had its physical man-ifestation in the northern border fortifications dividing the agricultural territories of China from the nomadic world of the Xiongnu and other

---

[77] See above, 86–87.   [78] See above, 84–85.
[79] Eberhard, *China's Minorities: Yesterday and Today*, 25–26; Pines, "Beasts or Humans," 85.

peoples of the steppe.[80] As the unification of China under the Qin and then the Han was accompanied by an unprecedented militarization and consolidation of power on the steppe, the military threat posed from the north seems to have proved ideologically threatening enough to necessitate the construction of a monolithic barbarian enemy that loomed larger in the Chinese imagination than had the scattered non-Chinese peoples on the periphery of the Zhou sphere. Ironically, what led to such a formulation in the Greek context was the threat of the massive and ecumenical empire of Persia against a disunited and peripheral people; in the case of China, the expanding empire itself was checked by a nomadic people it considered to be culturally and politically inferior. From this point on, it became more common, despite the sympathetic and relativistic approach hinted at by Sima Qian, to see xenophobia and hostility toward the foreign expressed in Chinese historiography.[81] Even in Sima Qian, this view appears in his depiction of the Xiongnu as a constant "northern threat [that] had faced China since the mythical beginning of its existence."[82] The fact that such a consistently menacing portrait of the Xiongnu is somewhat belied by periods of peace and diplomatic success under the *heqin* 和親 treaty only underscores the ideological potence of the nomadic threat to the north.[83]

Sima Qian's historiographical successor, Ban Gu 班固 (AD 32–92), was to continue the theme of an inexorable antagonism between China and the Xiongnu. However, Ban Gu did not temper his representation of the nomads with the sort of embedded speeches employed by Sima Qian that served to question, or at least problematize, the assertions of Han Chinese cultural superiority.[84] While Sima Qian lived in an age that witnessed an

---

[80] Pines, "Beasts or Humans," 90–91; Di Cosmo, *Ancient China and Its Enemies*, 302.

[81] On this point, see Pines, "Beasts or Humans," 91; Wang, Q. Edward, "History, Space, and Ethnicity," 297–98. For Sima Qian's sympathetic treatment of the Xiongnu and implicit critique of the Han Empire, see Di Cosmo, *Ancient China and Its Enemies*, 275–76; Chin, "Defamiliarizing the Foreigner," 324–36.

[82] Di Cosmo, *Ancient China and Its Enemies*, 304.

[83] For example, the first of three visits of the Xiongnu Chanyu Huhanye 呼韓邪 to the Chinese imperial capital in 51 BC heralded decades of peace between China and the southern branch of the Xiongnu. See Barfield, *The Perilous Frontier: Nomadic Empires and China*, 64–66. For a discussion of the *heqin* policy during the Han dynasty, see Di Cosmo, *Ancient China and Its Enemies*, 193–205; Barfield, *The Perilous Frontier*, 45–48, 64–67.

[84] In a discussion Sima Qian recounts between a former Chinese living among the Xiongnu and envoys from China, many of the Xiongnu customs are argued to be, contrary to expectation, actually superior to those of the Chinese – at least in the context of nomadic life on the steppe (*SJ* 110.2899–2900). In this instance, Sima Qian exhibits a relativist approach analogous to that of Herodotus. This episode has been discussed in detail by Di Cosmo, *Ancient China and Its Enemies*, 269–76; Stuurman, "Herodotus and Sima Qian," 30–34; Chin, *Savage Exchange*, 174–82. Perhaps Sima Qian's relativism contributed to the limited circulation of the text; on its circulation, see Nienhauser, "Sima Qian and the *Shiji*," 475–78; Durrant, "The Han Histories," 486.

expansion of Chinese power at the expense of the Xiongnu, Ban Gu was more aware of the limits of Chinese expansion as well as the long-term unfeasibility of efforts to control nomadic peoples and states in the western regions. Moreover, much of his work was carried out with imperial patronage such that the "*Han shu* [漢書] became an official government project."[85] His ethnographic worldview is thus more conservative, advocating a distinction between the Chinese and non-Chinese worlds. In his concluding remarks to the second of his two fascicles on the Xiongnu, Ban Gu begins by harking back to the distant past and asserts that the Xiongnu are a modern manifestation of an ancient threat:

> 書戒「蠻夷猾夏」，詩稱「戎狄是膺」，春秋「有道守在四夷」，久矣夷狄之為患也.[86]

> The *Shujing* refers to the "Man-Yi who have caused chaos for the Xia"; the *Shijing* says, "this is to fight off the Rong-Di"; the *Chunqiu* that "the ruler who knows the Way maintains defense against the Four Yi." How long it has been that the Yi-Di have posed such danger!

Marshalling the support of these three authoritative classics from the preimperial age, Ban Gu employs a strategy similar to that of Sima Qian. The Xiongnu are assimilated to the earliest enemies of Chinese civilization who challenged or were chastised by the kings of the Zhou dynasty. After describing the policies of the Han dynasty, Ban Gu returns to the precedents of antiquity and the ways they impinge upon his present day:

> 故先王度土，中立封畿，分九州，列五服，物土貢，制外內，或脩刑政，或詔文德，遠近之勢異也. 是以春秋內諸夏而外夷狄. 夷狄之人貪而好利，被髮左衽，人面獸心，其與中國殊章服，異習俗，飲食不同，言語不通[…].[87]

> Therefore, the ancient kings measured the land, establishing the royal domains in the Center, dividing the Nine Regions, arranging the Five Zones, determining products for tribute, establishing the domestic and the foreign. Over some they created punishments and governance, over others they proclaimed their civility and virtue, for the conditions of distance and proximity varied. Thus are the words of the *Chunqiu*: "The Chinese are regarded as internal but the Yi-Di are held without." The people of the Yi-Di are covetous and eager of gain; wearing their hair loose and fastening their garments on the left, they have the faces of humans but the hearts of beasts. Their habits of dress are different from those of China; their customs are different; they eat and drink different things; their languages are unintelligible.

---

[85] Durrant, "The Han Histories," 491.   [86] *Han shu* 94b.3830.   [87] *Han shu* 94b.3833–34.

Ban Gu clearly wishes to argue for a policy of non-engagement with the Xiongnu and draws on the precedent of ancient sage kingship to buttress his argument. In this passage, there are a number of features that have already appeared in quotations discussed in earlier sections, in particular the confluence of geographical conceptions of space, political relationships, and ethnic identities or ethnonyms. However, what Ban Gu emphasizes most is an essential and absolute alterity that divides the Xiongnu from the Chinese and extends from the most mundane facets of life to the most profound: while the Xiongnu have the appearance of human beings, their hearts are those of wild animals. Because of this fundamental division between Chinese and barbarians, "the ancient sage kings treated them like birds and beasts."[88] After delineating his policy of defensive disengagement, he sums up with the assertion that "in sum, this is the constant Way of the sage kings in treating the Man-Yi."[89] It is also important to note that in making his final remarks, he abandons the Xiongnu ethnonym in favor of the anachronistic and generalized barbarian binomes Yi-Di and Man-Yi, which are clearly used interchangeably. One understands that he is not talking simply about the Xiongnu, but rather extending this concept of alterity beyond the confines of a single, specific ethnonym to a broader category of a barbarian Other. Writing in the mid-first century AD, Ban Gu poses an interesting contrast to Roman imperialism's own dilution of the barbarian antithesis.

Nevertheless, it is important to point out that also under the Han, there continued to be a body of discourse that did not assert the objective superiority of Chinese culture in comparison with those of its neighbors. For example, the Daoist text the *Huainanzi* 淮南子, compiled in the second century BC, exhibits a clearly relativistic approach to cultural difference, claiming that

故秦，楚，燕，魏之謳也，異轉而皆樂，九夷八狄之哭也，殊聲而皆悲，一也.[90]

The songs of the state of Qin, Chu, Yan, and Wei may have their different tunes but they are still all music. The nine Yi and the eight Di have their cries of sadness, which are different in sound but are all sorrowful. All are one and the same.

The *Huainanzi* is uninterested in drawing significant distinctions between human groups, suggesting that the differences people perceive are not only

---

[88] 是故聖王禽獸畜之 (*Han shu* 94b.3834).   [89] 蓋聖王制御蠻夷之常道也 (Ibid.).
[90] *Huainanzi* 19, Xiuwuxun 脩務訓.1327.

relative but also superficial. Moreover, this passage suggests in the parallel structure of its two examples that just as the differences between the Chinese and Yi-Di groups are inconsequential among themselves, so too do the Chinese and barbarian worlds comprise a fundamental unity. Irrespective of whether one's provenance was among the Chinese states or from among one of the various Yi or Di peoples, the human experience is understood to be essentially the same.

Although the above quotation from the *Huainanzi* may be informed by the integration of Man, Yi, Rong, and Di peoples as they were incorporated into the pre-imperial Chinese states and subsequently disappeared, one may also hypothesize that a spirit of relativism may also have arisen from the constant interactions of Chinese and non-Chinese along the frontiers, whether in border markets or in connection with the military garrisons established for the empire's expansion and defense.[91] There is not space here to explore these exchanges on the frontiers, but it is certain that in some cases hybrid populations formed in border regions between Chinese and Qiang 羌, and probably with Xiongnu and others as well. In the latter part of the Han dynasty these hybrid populations, those mixed with the Qiang in particular, had a dubious allegiance to China and eventually broke out in revolt.[92] Regardless of the xenophobic rhetoric of political figures such as Ban Gu, the reality for civilian populations on the ground must have been very different from his envisaged ideal of a Chinese empire isolated from the barbarians.[93]

In considering aspects of the Roman and Chinese imperial experience, the expression of the barbarian antithesis offers one of the most interesting points of comparison. As has been shown above, the Roman Empire seems to have been characterized by an increasing cosmopolitanism and reduction of meaningful ethnic distinctions, as more and more foreign nations and individuals were either manumitted from slavery or otherwise obtained citizenship through military service or imperial grant. That is not to deny the fact that the Roman process of imperial expansion was

---

[91] See de Crespigny, *Northern Frontier: The Policies and Strategy of the Later Han Empire*, 1–53, for the administration of the western and northern frontier. On the establishment of military colonies in the western regions, see Yü, "Han Foreign Relations," 418–21.

[92] Ibid., 433–34.

[93] China's expansion into the western regions also resulted in extensive contacts with urbanized societies that established diplomatic relations with the Han court. Such relations often involved the marriage of a Chinese princess to a local ruler, a strategy that was intended to place half-Chinese rulers on the thrones of western states who would be sympathetic to China and offer necessary logistical support its trade and military ambitions in the west. See Hulsewé, *China in Central Asia*, 60–61. On the Chinese expansion into the west more generally, see ibid., 39–66.

accompanied by horrific massacres and what would today be characterized as appalling episodes of ethnic and cultural genocide.[94] Even the philanthropic and philosophical Marcus Aurelius is reported to have desired the wholesale extermination of the Sarmatian Iazyges in the later second century.[95] But the Roman imperial experience has also been shown to have been characterized by a fluidity in the conceptual categories of civilized and barbarian, where the binary construct breaks down to allow for not just a *tertium quid* but rather a continuum of possible stations ranging from the hard primitives of outer Germania to the toga-clad and refined citizens of the post-barbarian provincial cities. In China, however, the final forging of imperial unity by the state of Qin and the establishment of large-scale conflict in the north against the Xiongnu seems to have heralded the end of an era that had allowed for a much more porous border, both physically and philosophically, between the Chinese *oikoumenê* and the barbarian world.

Yet lest this characterization become too absolute, it is important to note that even Ban Gu, author of the *Han shu* and one of the most xenophobic (in the eyes of modern scholars) of ancient Chinese historians, could represent a barbarian not only adapting his nature to the ways of the Chinese but also rendering great service to the emperor and setting an example for his descendants to follow in turn. Ban Gu includes a biography of the surrendered Xiongnu prince Jin Midi 金日磾, who became a trusted minister of the emperor Han Wudi 漢武帝, the emperor who reversed the policy of appeasement with the Xiongnu toward the end of the second century BC and adopted an aggressive military strategy instead. In his account of Jin Midi's career, and those of his several descendants, Ban Gu refers to the surrendered Xiongnu's loyalty, piety, sincerity, and diligence;[96] at one point Jin Midi even executes one of his own sons who dares to flirt with the emperor's concubines – an act of severity for which Jin Midi is at first criticized but then even more revered by the emperor.[97] Likewise, the descendants of Jin Midi's brother Jin Lun 金倫 distinguish themselves for their service to the empire and are noted in their own day both for their filial piety as well as their thorough mastery of Confucian

---

[94] For example, several such episodes that occurred during Caesar's subjugation of Gaul have been discussed by Collins, "Caesar as Political Propagandist," 933–35.

[95] ὁ γὰρ αὐτοκράτωρ ἤθελε μὲν αὐτοὺς καὶ παντάπασιν ἐκκόψαι (Cassius Dio 72.16.1).

[96] 繇是著忠孝節 (*Han shu* 68.2961); 其篤慎如此，上尤奇異之 (*Han shu* 68.2962). Despite the fact that members of the imperial family disapprove of the emperor showing such favor to a "Hu" 胡 barbarian, Han Wudi persists in holding Jin Midi in the highest esteem: 貴戚多竊怨，曰：「陛下妄得一胡兒，反貴重之！」上聞，愈厚焉 (*Han shu* 68.2960).

[97] Ibid.

canonical texts.[98] The biography of Jin Midi and his family is a testament to the fact that men of barbarian origins could indeed rise to great heights in imperial service and excel in the study of Classicist learning. Despite the existence of the chasm Ban Gu elsewhere seeks to establish between the Chinese and barbarian worlds, he nevertheless recognized that a Xiongnu exile could become one of the emperor's most prized ministers.

Conclusions

In closing this chapter, and before moving on to the periods of Late Antiquity and Early Medieval China, we may consider two character portraits of barbarian figures that appear in major histories produced during the respective high imperial periods of the Roman Empire and the Han dynasty: the *Annals* of Tacitus and the *Han shu* of Ban Gu. The succeeding three chapters of this study will deal extensively with representations of barbarian peoples and their leaders, and it will be interesting to keep these two portraits in mind while proceeding further to explore conceptions of identity and alterity in a later age.

The first major military disaster under the Roman Principate was the loss of three full legions in Germania in AD 9, the trauma from which was perhaps not to be equaled until the defeat of Roman forces in Mesopotamia and the capture of the emperor Valerian himself by the Persians in 260. The architect of this disaster in Germania was Arminius, a man of the tribe of the Cherusci, who betrayed the Roman commander Varus into leading Roman forces into an ambush. The historian Tacitus, however, gives Arminius a striking eulogy, conspicuously placed at the close of book two of the *Annals*:

> ceterum Arminius, abscedentibus Romanis et pulso Maroboduo regnum adfectans, libertatem popularium adversam habuit, petitusque armis cum varia fortuna certaret, dolo propinquorum cecidit: liberator hau[d] dubie Germaniae et qui non primordia populi Romani, sicut alii reges ducesque, sed florentissimum imperium lacessierit, proeliis ambiguus, bello non victus. septem et triginta annos vitae, duodecim potentiae explevit, caniturque adhuc barbaras apud gentes, Graecorum annalibus ignotus, qui sua tantum mirantur, Romanis haud perinde celebris, dum vetera extollimus recentium incuriosi.[99]

---

[98] For example, Jin Chang 金敞 is "famous through the ages for his loyalty and piety": 敞以世名忠孝; Jin She 金涉 is "thoroughly versed in the classics, of a virtuous and courteous character, and praised by all of the Confucian scholars": 涉明經儉節，諸儒稱之 (*Han shu* 68.2963–64).

[99] *Annales* 2.88.2–3.

Hence Arminius, after Roman withdrawal and the defeat of [his enemy] Maroboduus, maintained the defiant freedom of his people while striving for his kingdom. Attacked in combat, he fell to the treachery of his relatives while he was fighting with mixed success. Without doubt, he was the liberator of Germania and a man who had challenged not the early years of the Roman people – as had other kings and leaders – but the empire at its mightiest, a man who won and lost battles, but was never conquered in war. He completed thirty-seven years of his life, twelve of them in power; and his name is still sung among barbarian nations, unknown to the annals of the Greeks, who only marvel at their own affairs, and not much more famous among the Romans, since we, careless of present matters, celebrate those of the past.

There are several features of this eulogy worth noting. First, this is not a portrait of a noble barbarian leader who is granted one last heroic and defiant speech by the historian before his dramatically satisfying death and his people's subjugation to Rome. Such valorizing speeches were a consistent feature of Roman historiography and have perhaps their most famous example in the speech of Calgacus in Tacitus' *Agricola* where the Caledonian famously declares that Roman practice is to "create a desert and to call it peace."[100] In the case of Arminius, we are not dealing with either an individual or even a people who has been conquered. Arminius had inflicted a massive defeat on the Romans – the three legions he destroyed, the seventeenth, eighteenth, and nineteenth, were never reestablished – and lived to get away with it. Despite the campaigns across the Rhine of Drusus, Tiberius, and Germanicus under the early Principate, no coin was ever issued with the legend *Germania capta* that attested to anything like conquest in fact. It is therefore striking that, in the words of Tacitus, Arminius is not a rebel but a liberator. Although Arminius suffered setbacks and ultimately fell to treachery, Tacitus recognizes him as a hero and seems even to chide the myopia of both Greek and Roman historians who are unable to recognize that barbarian *res gestae* deserve commemoration and reflection.[101] Arminius' own brother Flavus had abandoned his people and was a loyal soldier in the Roman army, and the historian even includes a heated debate between the two brothers, who meet to parley between the opposing Roman and Cheruscan armies.[102]

---

[100] *ubi solitudinem faciunt, pacem appellant* (*Agricola* 30.5).

[101] Though of course this criticism of the Greeks is unfair – at least in respect to figures such as Herodotus, Xenophon, and Polybius. As Fornara has noted, Roman historiography, in contrast to the universality common in Greek practice, did tend to place Rome in the center, although this practice was not absolute. *The Nature of History*, 53.

[102] *Annales* 2.9–10.

Yet it is not Flavus whom Tacitus wishes to eulogize. In this case, Tacitus exhibits Roman historiography's tendency to fixate on exemplary deeds in a remarkable way: even a barbarian and enemy of the empire could be deemed worthy of praise – not for his *civilitas*, loyalty to the emperor, or embrace of Hellenistic civilization, but rather for his defiance and rejection of these very things.

The character portrait from China is of the Xiongnu chieftain Jin Midi, who has been discussed above as an example of the positive treatment a barbarian figure could receive from a historian traditionally considered one of the most hostile toward the barbarians in general and the Xiongnu in particular. Following his biography of Jin Midi, Ban Gu includes the following remarks in his colophon to the chapter:

金日磾夷狄亡國，羈虜漢庭，而以篤敬寤主，忠信自著，勤功上將，傳國後嗣，世名忠孝，七世內侍，何其盛也!¹⁰³

Jin Midi the barbarian's nation was destroyed and, taken prisoner, he was brought to the Han court. Because of his sincerity and reverence he was recognized by his superiors; with loyalty and good faith he acquired his fame. For his great effort and achievements he was promoted to a general's rank. He passed on the lands granted to him to his descendants, who were all conspicuous for their loyalty and filial piety, and seven generations of them were ministers of the inner court. What remarkable glory this is!

Ban Gu clearly acknowledges what he perceives to be the virtues of this surrendered Xiongnu, and Jin Midi is held up as an exemplum of the ideal Confucian minister, exhibiting the virtues of sincerity, loyalty, and filial piety, virtues whose opposites otherwise characterize his former people. Although Jin Midi himself declines an appointment to a particularly distinguished office on account of his foreign origin saying, "I am a foreigner; moreover, [for me to accept this] would cause the Xiongnu to look on China with contempt,"¹⁰⁴ this portrait nevertheless demonstrates that even in the eyes of a historian otherwise hostile to the barbarians, it was not only possible for a Xiongnu to learn the civilized ways of the Chinese but also to perfect them and pass them on to his descendants. Yet it also indicates that even if a barbarian had merited both office and distinction in service of the state, a fact that demonstrates the potential inclusivity of the Han Empire, his foreign origins nevertheless delimit his participation in the governance of it. Indeed, his very acknowledgment of the fact that his Xiongnu ethnicity bars him from accepting the offered

¹⁰³ *Han shu* 68.2967.   ¹⁰⁴ 臣外國人，且使匈奴輕漢 (*Han shu* 68.2962).

position is, paradoxically, further testament to his mastery of Classicist imperial ethics: having so thoroughly absorbed the tenets of the imperial moral-political system, he is able to recognize that that very system pre-scribes limits to his status in imperial society in appropriate accordance with his foreign origins.

The contrast between these two eulogies of barbarian figures is stark. The one offers praise for an enemy of the imperial order who at every turn fought off the military and even cultural inroads made by the supposedly superior civilization of the Romans. The other praises a barbarian who had left his people and pledged his services to the revanchist and expansionist emperor Han Wudi. In either case of imperial historiography, there is a clear acknowledgment that it is possible for a barbarian to join the side of the empire and abandon his earlier ethno-cultural loyalties. Arminius' fierce resistance to Rome has its counterpoint in his brother Flavus' collaboration. In either case, barbarian identities do not necessarily have to be perceived as fixed qualities – at least not in the case of individuals. How is it that Tacitus could see fit to give such a eulogy to Arminius while Ban Gu, traditionally hostile and xenophobic toward the Xiongnu in particular, could only praise one of them who had abandoned his own people and adopted the cause of the Han?

Perhaps the answer lies in the pre-imperial inheritance of both tradi-tions. The Romans had adopted the Greek tradition whose founders in poetry and prose, Homer and Herodotus, had presented a worldview where the foreign, and even the inimical, could be perceived and repre-sented with admiration and empathy. While the fifth and fourth centuries BC developed an at times virulent form of pan-Hellenic hostility toward the barbarian, this worldview never managed to dominate the discourse of the period entirely. Moreover, a crucial factor in shaping Greek worldviews was the simple fact that the Greeks recognized that their near eastern neighbors, from whom the Greeks learned so much, were the scions of civilizations much more ancient and sophisticated than their own. Yet for Ban Gu, looking back to the *Shijing* and ritual texts of the Confucian canon, there was not a legacy of interest in the foreign that extended beyond an awareness of its threat, or the necessity of its subservience, to the dominant Chinese power or Sinitic cultural sphere. The result was an "ethnographic tradition that either commemorates political domination or facilitates conquest by creating as its epistemological object an inferior Other awaiting civilization."[105] One might dispute this "postcolonial"

---

[105] Chin, "Defamiliarizing the Foreigner," 313.

reading of Ban Gu as an author who envisioned the eventual military victory over the barbarians and argue, on the contrary, that his view was conditioned by failed policies to assimilate surrendered tribal groups within the imperial frontiers. The result, however, is the same: an appeal to an ancient ethnogeographical and exclusionary cosmology inherited from pre-imperial times. Surrounded by peoples whom the Chinese considered to be less developed and sophisticated than themselves, the primacy of the Chinese political order was a largely uncontested fact in the eyes of pre-imperial authors. Their worldviews would exert a great influence on the historians who would record the dynastic records of imperial China in the succeeding centuries.

CHAPTER 3

Ethnography in a Post-Classical Age
The Ethnographic Tradition in the Wars *and the*
Jin shu 晉書

Whereas the previous chapter discussed the barbarian antithesis in the pre-imperial and imperial literature of the Greco-Roman and Chinese traditions, this chapter will turn to the later periods of Late Antiquity and Early Medieval China. It will first consider the expression of this concept in the *Wars* of Procopius and the *Jin shu* 晉書 of the Tang 唐 Bureau of Historiography, before examining the perpetuation of the three ethnographic frameworks discussed in Chapter 1. After considering the aspects of classical ethnography treated in Chapters 1 and 2, i.e., the notion of the barbarian antithesis and the epistemological frameworks used by both Greco-Roman and Chinese authors to rationalize and represent foreign peoples, the chapter will then turn to the two texts' representations of the main non-Roman and non-Chinese peoples who will be the primary focus of the remaining chapters. Central to the concerns of this study, these were the peoples who had moved into the empires and claimed to be legitimate rulers over formerly imperial territories, counting both their own original followers as well as the Roman and Chinese populations of their domains among their subjects. Procopius and the authors of the *Jin shu* were not treating the unknown quantities situated beyond the frontiers, peoples who had been in a relationship of either subjugation to the empire or one of independent hostility or alliance. Accordingly, the historians were presented with a new and unprecedented phenomenon: How does one represent a barbarian people that has not only entered the empire but also assumed the reins of state along with royal or imperial prerogatives? This chapter provides a critical link between the classical past of each tradition and the new realities of the early to mid-first millennium AD. By establishing continuity with the respective classical traditions, the chapter allows us to consider the later legacy of ancient worldviews while also offering a window onto the way those worldviews were adapted to represent new realities.

Though this topic has not been extensively explored in either case, several scholars have commented on the quality of ethnographic discourse in both the *Wars* and the *Jin shu* as well as on the implications that such discourse has for the mentalities and worldviews of the authors and their respective milieu. Writing on the *Wars*, Benedicty has emphasized the influence of the classical tradition in Procopius and argues that it pervades every facet of the work, not least its ethnographic discourse.[1] He accordingly infers that Procopius exhibits the ethnographic biases and commonplaces established in classical authors. Müller has stressed Procopius' familiarity with classical authors and compares his ethnographic representations to those of Poseidonius, Caesar, and Tacitus, noting that Procopius' achievement is not to be found in any innovation in ethnological theory, but rather in his successful imitation of the classics.[2] Börm has pointed to the "classicizing, conservative tendency" in Procopius in which "essential elements of the barbarian concept" were perpetuated. He notes the continued use of ancient ethnonyms and the supposed transference of characteristics of ancient groups to new peoples.[3] Revanoglou argues that Procopius provides a fuller definition of barbarism than did many of his classical models, extending it to include not only speech but also dress and the spiritual plane; while allowing for the detached and matter of fact treatment of the Persians, she concludes that Procopius' ethnological thought serves to underscore the cultural superiority of the Byzantines, who are surrounded by an anonymous barbarian world.[4] All of these scholars thus emphasize a conceptual conservatism in Procopius' ethnological discourse.

Other scholars offer a more complex view. Veh has pointed to various stereotypical barbarian failings in Procopius, and he notes that Procopius at times shares xenophobic attitudes found in other authors. But he also sees in Procopius "the desire to arrive at a state of equality with the barbarian world" that is exemplified by the historian's admiration and even idealization of barbarians such as Theoderic; even the Persians are at least treated with a degree of toleration.[5] Cesa has argued that Procopius

---

[1] "Nicht nur die Sprache und der Aufbau des Prokopschen Werkes zeigt dieses Gepräge, sodern auch die charakteristischen stereotypen Wendungen und Formeln wie auch einige Erzählungen historischer Episoden und nicht zulezt die ethnographischen Gemeinplätze (τόποι), die zur Charakterisierung der Barbarenvölker dienen, bezeugen die antike Einwirkung." Benedicty, "Die Milieu-Theorie bei Prokop von Kaisareia," 1.

[2] Müller, *Geschichte der antiken Ethnographie und ethnologischen Theoriebildung, Teil II*, 474–75, 479.

[3] "Aufgrund einer klassizistischen, konservativen Tendez wurden wesentliche Elemente der Barbarentopik über große Zeiträume hinweg immer wieder perpetuiert; neben den Namen älterer Ethnien wurden so auch ihre vermeintlichen Eigenschaften auf „neue"Völker übertragen." Börm, *Prokop und die Perser*, 89.

[4] Revanoglou, Γεωγραφικά και εθνογραφικά στοιχεία στο έργο του Προκοπίου Καισαρείας, 246–48.

[5] "der Wunsch nämlich, zu einem gewissen Ausgleich mit dem Barbarentum zu kommen." "Zur Geschichtsschreibung und Weltauffassung des Prokop von Caesarea," 23–24.

exhibits a hostile tone toward barbarians who attack the empire from without or who have embarrassed (*hanno messo in difficoltà*) Roman armies. However, she notes that there is a critical distinction between the negative representation of peoples such as Franks, Moors, Slavs, and Heruli on the one hand and the Ostrogoths and Vandals on the other; indeed, these latter two groups may be depicted with equanimity and sympathy.[6] Cesa thus concludes, in contradiction to the view of Benedicty, that Procopius' ethnographic discourse is not dominated by traditional topoi and biases in general; hostility toward some barbarians and sympathy toward others is not determined by commonplaces of classical ethnography, but rather by conditions particular to the mid-sixth century.[7] Cameron, however, while acknowledging that some barbarian leaders are sympathetically portrayed in the *Wars* and that the Persian Empire was recognized as being "essentially civilized in the diplomatic sense,"[8] nevertheless reads Procopius as preserving a strong demarcation between Roman civilization and the barbarian world,[9] and this is reflected partly in his own ethnographic descriptions, which are heavily influenced by classical topoi.[10]

More recently, Cataudella has characterized Procopius' ethnographic approach as one divided between the barbarians who are "faithless, cruel, lawless, etc." and those of the west who are "moderate, tolerant, wise in government, etc."[11] She concludes that Procopius' contrasting views are attributed to his willingness to legitimize the barbarian rulers of the west while those of the east are the true enemies of the empire.[12] Kaldellis has likewise offered a nuanced discussion of the functions of ethnography in the writings of Procopius and explores the ways in which the ethnographic mode was used for rhetorical purposes: "ethnography could serve to reinforce (or create) the distinction between Roman and barbarians, but it could also question that distinction or even critique Roman preconceptions about it."[13] While noting that late antique ethnography was "premised on the difference between Romans and barbarians,"[14] he concludes that it served less as a mode of expressing elitist and chauvinistic opinions

---

[6] "i Vandali e i Goti (ma soprattutto questi ultimi e i loro sovrani) sono caratterizzati con molta equanimità e non senza una certa simpatia." Cesa, "Etnografia e geografia nella visione storica di Procopio di Caesarea," 214.

[7] A recenty study by Sarantis also argues that even among barbarian groups beyond the frontiers one sees a variety of different barbarian types portrayed in Procopius' work. "Procopius and the Different Types of Northern Barbarian," 355–78.

[8] Cameron, *Procopius and the Sixth Century*, 239–40.   [9] Ibid.   [10] Ibid., 218.

[11] Cataudella, "Historiography in the East," 411–12.   [12] Ibid., 412.

[13] Kaldellis, *Ethnography after Antiquity*, 11.   [14] Ibid., 10.

than as a means of self-reflection and self-criticism.[15] Greatrex acknowledges the difficulty in characterizing Procopius' views one way or another, remarking that Procopius' "attitude to barbarians is remarkably variable, ranging from the admiring … to the bitterly hostile."[16]

There is thus a range of views as to whether or not and how Procopius' classicizing aesthetic determined the tone of his ethnographic representations: while some have suggested that, for the most part, Procopius exhibits a conservative, anti-barbarian point of view, others have stressed not just his tendency to hold up the barbarians as a mirror to Roman moral and political failings but also his willingness to sympathetically portray, and even recognize as legitimate, the barbarian conquerors of the empire's former western provinces. As the following discussion will demonstrate, there is evidence in the *Wars* to support both of these views. It will be argued here, however, that in the case of those peoples who established independent regimes within former imperial borders, Procopius largely abandons traditional anti-barbarian biases.

Turning to the *Jin shu*, there is a certain unanimity of opinion among Chinese-language scholars. Researchers have long noted the prominence of Chinese–barbarian interactions in the period covered by the *Jin shu* as well as the text's value as a source for exploring mentalities and attitudes toward these interactions. Li claims that the historians who produced the *Jin shu* employed the emperor Tang Taizong's 唐太宗 principle of *Hua Yi yijia* 华夷一家, "Chinese and barbarians are one family," and suggests that in the content of the Chronicles section of the work, there is a "considerable spirit of treating both barbarians and Chinese fairly."[17] This same popular phrase, "treating [both barbarians and Chinese] fairly," *yishi tongren* 一视同仁, appears in a nearly verbatim assessment of Cao, who adds that this view is the common consensus.[18] Zhu has argued that the work was produced under a guiding principle: "the progressive ethnic theory that Chinese and barbarians are one family";[19] not surprisingly, he sees an

---

[15] Ibid., 21, 25. Kaldellis also notes that Procopius "treated Romans and barbarians impartially, condemning the former as often as he praised the latter." *Procopius of Caesarea*, 221.

[16] Greatrex, "Perceptions of Procopius in Recent Scholarship," 95. Also see his recent study, "Procopius' Attitude towards Barbarians," 327–54.

[17] 也颇体现对胡汉一视同仁的精神. Li, "*Jin shu* yanjiu xia," 88. The Chronicles are the final section of the *Jin shu* where the accounts of barbarian conquest states of north China are appended. The structure of the *Jin shu*, and the Chronicles in particular, will be discussed in greater detail below.

[18] 从载记的内容看，大家一致认为它体现了对胡汉一视同仁的精神. Cao, "*Jin shu* yanjiu shulüe," 56.

[19] 唐修晋书在华夷一家进步民族理论指导下. Zhu, "*Jin shu* de pingjia yu yanjiu," 46.

even-handed approach exhibited in the text's treatment of ethnic relations. Ma argues that the Chronicles reflect an age of unification between north and south and, in somewhat abstruse terms, a "historical psychology of ethnic blending" (民族融合后的历史心理); he concludes that these factors make the Chronicles "positive" and "healthy" for the formation of an "ethnic nation."[20]

This trend is moderated, however, by Qu, who, contrary to the more mainstream interpretation, stresses not only the ubiquity in the *Jin shu* of the notion that only the Chinese Eastern Jin 東晉 regime in the south was politically legitimate but also the consistent division between Chinese and barbarians, *Hua Yi zhi bie* 华夷之别.[21] He notes that this "distinction between Chinese and barbarians often reaches an extreme," and suggests that such an approach was therefore unable to satisfy the requirements of the emperor Tang Taizong – a curious assertion given that Taizong not only contributed to the work but also seems to have held it in high esteem.[22] Nevertheless, Qu elsewhere argues that the *Jin shu* "is preoccupied with questions of political legitimacy and abandons an exaggeration of the differences between Chinese and barbarians."[23] He argues that the *Jin shu*, among other histories produced in the early Tang, "reflects the Sui-Tang post-unification era's mentality of 'all under heaven are one family'."[24]

It will become clear in the following pages that many of these studies, as is often the case with scholarship concerning broader questions of ethnicity and interethnic relations in ancient China, suffer significantly from modern ideological constraints. Indeed, it could hardly be otherwise when even basic terms of the discussion are both anachronistic and distortive: foreign peoples beyond the Chinese frontiers are consistently referred to in modern Chinese scholarship as "ethnic minorities," *shaoshu minzu* 少数民族.[25] The indiscriminate use of such a term suggests that by virtue of appearing in Chinese historical texts and having hostile or peaceable interactions with

---

[20] 对于民族国家的熔铸来说，它是积极的，健康的. Ma Tiehao, "*Jin shu* zaiji de zhengtongguan ji qi chengyin," 27.

[21] 但史论之中以东晋为正统的观念，以及华夷之别的观念，处处显示出来. Qu, "Lun Wei Jin Sui Tang jian de shaoshu minzu shixue shang," 78.

[22] 华夷的区别往往走向极端 ... 未能完全反映出唐太宗修晋书诏的本意. Ibid., 77. As noted in the Introduction, not only did the emperor Tang Taizong contribute essays of his own composition to the *Jin shu*, but he also presented it as a gift to foreign envoys and his own son. One may assume that he approved of its contents. See Ng and Wang, *Mirroring the Past*, 120.

[23] 着眼于僭伪，不再渲染华夷. Qu, "Lun Wei Jin Sui Tang jian de shaoshu minzu shixue shang," 74.

[24] 反应了隋唐统一后 "天下一家" 的思想. Ibid.

[25] This practice has also been observed and criticized by Kim, *Ethnicity and Foreigners in Ancient Greece and China*, 30–31.

a Chinese empire, these peoples, and the lands they inhabited, may be incorporated into the modern conception of a Chinese nation state that is projected back in time.[26] The "precedents" of ancient history may thus be made to serve modern political ends in a manner not dissimilar to ideologies typical of European ethno-nationalistic historians of the nineteenth and early twentieth centuries.

There are very few works in western-language scholarship that treat the *Jin shu* in any detail, and the studies of Rogers and Honey are the most in-depth.[27] Honey has argued that the Chronicles section of the *Jin shu* is characterized by its employment of ethnographic topoi on the nomads and that it perpetuates the classical stereotypes and conventions that delineate the proper place for barbarians outside of the empire and in a subservient status to the Chinese.[28] Yet Honey also notes that the attitudes toward barbarians expressed in the *Jin shu* are careful to make clear that it is the behavior of the nomads, not their ethnic background, that is worthy of censure.[29] He thus accepts the interpretation of Creel and others that any notion of "Chinese-ness" in ancient China was defined according to cultural rather than ethnic criteria.[30]

Other scholars have made broader assessments of early Tang historiography of which the *Jin shu* is a part. Ng and Wang have characterized the era's historiography by its lack of interest in the legitimacy or illegitimacy of earlier regimes, and they argue that it exhibits a "cosmopolitan strain" in its treatment of Chinese interactions with non-Chinese.[31] Wang elsewhere

---

[26] An explicit example of this sort of reasoning appears in the work of Mi, who, while arguing that a site in Manchuria is the original homeland of the Särbi founders of the Northern Wei dynasty, claims, "This place is the original homeland of the Northern Wei emperors; of course it belongs to China" (这里就是北魏皇帝的故乡，当然属于中国). "Gaxian dong beiwei shike zhuwen kaoshi," 363. Similarly, Lin Gan has described the *heqin* treaty terms imposed by the Xiongnu on the Han dynasty in the following way: "Within the national boundaries of a single country – China – the Han and Xiongnu ethnic groups respectively divided and defended their own territories in their original areas of habitation, and mutually refrained from transgressions" (在一个国家-中国-的国境内，汉匈两族彼此在原来生活的地区分疆自守，互不侵犯). *Xiongnu shi*, 46. In its historical context, this is as absurd as arguing that the Romans and trans-Rhenine or Danubian Germanic peoples were two ethnic groups of a single "country."

[27] Rogers, *The Chronicle of Fu-Chien: A Case of Exemplary History*; Honey, *The Rise of the Medieval Hsiung-nu*; Honey, "History and Historiography on the Sixteen States: Some T'ang Topoi on the Nomads." Also see Honey's dissertation, "Sinification and Legitimation: Liu Yüan, Shi Le, and the Founding of Han and Chao."

[28] Honey, "History and Historiography on the Sixteen States," 168.

[29] Honey, "Sinification and Legitimation," 227–28.　　　[30] See above, 15–16, n. 39.

[31] Ng and Wang, *Mirroring the Past*, 118. In a surprising error, though one illustrative of the period's neglect in modern scholarship, the authors incorrectly state that the Chronicles section of the *Jin shu* comprises accounts of sixteen Särbi states in the north of China. Ibid., 120. Of the Sixteen

argues that historiography of the period exhibits no concerns about the northern frontier or the peoples living beyond it, since he claims, "the Tang Empire eliminated the traditional ethnic boundary between the Han and non-Han."[32] Regarding attitudes toward ethnic identities during the Tang in general, modern scholarship has tended to emphasize the "cosmopolitanism" of the Tang dynasty. It is easy to find idyllic descriptions of life under the Tang that emphasize "the open-mindedness and large-heartedness" of Tang society and the way the "Chinese watched with amusement the adoption of certain steppe ways and customs by the playful aristocrats and commoners."[33] Key words in Chinese-language scholarship that typify modern assessments of Tang culture are *baorong* 包容, "tolerance," *xina* 吸纳, "appropriation/adoption," and *hexie* 和谐, "harmony," all of which are used to indicate the breakdown in perceived barriers of ethnic or cultural distinction.[34]

While the significant influx and influence of Central Asian cultures under the Tang is undisputed, the majority of descriptions of Tang worldviews ignore the persistence of xenophobic ethnographic rhetoric that is rooted in Han 漢-dynasty historiography. The work of Abramson, however, has served as an important challenge to the dominant view, arguing in reference to Tang dynasty historiography that

> the historical and statecraft works were heavily indebted for their style and content to canonical Chinese works of history and thought from earlier dynasties, rendering them often anachronistic and stereotypical but revealing perhaps most clearly the mental framework that shaped Han elites' construction of non-Han ethnic identities and boundaries in a variety of official and nonofficial contexts.[35]

Contrary to the conclusions of many other scholars, Abramson argues that ethnic identities were in fact a matter of great anxiety in the Tang and that this anxiety is reflected in the textual sources of the period. In a similar

---

Kingdoms, only *five* were founded by the Särbi. Though some of these ethnic classifications are problematic, of the remaining eleven kingdoms *three* were founded by Xiongnu leaders, *one* by a Jie, *three* by Di, *one* by a Qiang, and *three* by Chinese. Such oversights are not unusual. Even a recent volume on early medieval China credits the sacking of Luoyang in 311 and the capture of Chang'an in 317 to the Xiongnu ruler Liu Yuan – he died in 310.

[32] Wang, Q. Edward, "History, Space, and Ethnicity," 299.

[33] Ho, "In Defense of Sinicization," 136–37.

[34] For example, see Ye: "[Chinese culture when in an ascendant period such as under the Tang] was not characterized by resistance and conflict but rather by respect, appropriation, tolerance, seeking of the similar while preserving the different, and harmonious coexistence": 它对于外来文明，不是拒绝，冲突，而是尊重，吸纳，包容，求同存异，和谐相处。"Zhonghua wenming de kaifang xing he baorong xing," 5.

[35] Abramson, *Ethnic Identity in Tang China*, xxii.

challenge to the prevalent image of the Tang dynasty as an era when distinctions between Chinese and non-Chinese were of little significance, Yang has suggested that early Tang discourse was in fact characterized by "barbarophobic" sentiment.[36] It will be argued here that, despite the frequent assessments of the Tang (and in particular of the reign of the emperor Taizong) as a period characterized by its cosmopolitanism and tolerance, the image of the barbarian as it is reflected in the *Jin shu*, one of the major historical productions of the Tang Bureau of Historiography, exhibits an at times intensely xenophobic tenor.

It remains the case, however, that the predominant assessment of ethnographic discourse in early Tang historiography, and in the *Jin shu* in particular, is that it reflects the cosmopolitanism and ethnic blending of the period, the applauded process through which the once ethnically distinct conquerors of parts of the empire – the Wu Hu 五胡, or Five Barbarians: Xiongnu 匈奴, Jie 羯, Di 氐, Qiang 羌, and Särbi-Xianbei 鮮卑 – disappeared as relevant cultural or political entities. The following chapters will argue that alongside the cosmopolitanism so often attributed to the Tang, there existed a perpetuation of the xenophobia and anti-barbarian hostility that has often been noted by scholars of the Han era.

Perpetuation of the Barbarian Antithesis

Prior to beginning an analysis of the texts, a brief historical review of the basic contexts will be provided here (readers may also refer back to the Introduction). At the start of the reign of emperor Justinian I (r. 527–565), the territories of the western part of the Roman Empire were in the hands of a number of different regimes whose ruling elites were of foreign origin. Beginning in the late fourth century AD, foreign groups began to penetrate Roman frontiers in numbers that imperial forces were unable to manage effectively. In contrast to the experience of earlier centuries, many of these barbarian groups managed to maintain or acquire a degree of coherence as distinct political entities within the empire, either under the auspices of a *foedus* or treaty with the Roman state or in outright conflict with it. Increasing pressure on imperial finances eventually led to the complete inability of the western emperors to assert imperial authority and collapse of Roman rule in the west. By the beginning of the reign of

---

[36] Yang, "Reinventing the Barbarian: Rhetorical and Philosophical Uses of the *Yi-Di* in Mid-Imperial China," 2.

Justinian, the rich provinces of North Africa were in the hands of the Vandals, Spain was held by the Visigoths, Gaul was under the sway of the Franks, and Italy and much of the western Balkans were ruled by the Ostrogoths. It is in this context that emperor Justinian launched his wars of reconquest in 533, first targeting the Vandal kingdom of North Africa before beginning what was to become a twenty-year war of attrition fought in the Italian peninsula. Over the course of some three decades, imperial forces were engaged in simultaneously fighting barbarian kingdoms in the western Mediterranean, a host of tribally organized peoples in the northern Balkans, and the Sasanian Empire of Persia to the east, an old enemy of Rome with whom relations had deteriorated after a prolonged period of peace. It was against this backdrop that Procopius' account of the *Wars* of Justinian is set.

The authors of the *Jin shu* were charged in 646 by the emperor Taizong (r. 626–649) to produce a record of the Western and Eastern Jin 晉 dynasties (265–316 and 317–420, respectively). This period includes the massive disturbances of the early fourth century when foreign peoples settled within the empire revolted against Chinese rule and other groups entered the neglected frontiers. The result of these events was that the Western Jin regime crumbled in the north of China and abandoned the imperial capitals, fleeing to south of the Yangtze River where the city of Jiankang was established as the seat of the Eastern Jin dynasty. Throughout most of the fourth century, the northern part of China was carved up among a series of competing states, mostly of foreign origin. Although one of these peoples eventually unified the north in the fifth century under the Northern Wei 北魏 dynasty (386–534), China was not reunified until the Sui 隋 dynasty (581–619) conquered all of its rivals in north and south. The Sui was soon replaced by the Tang, and its second emperor Taizong was keen to produce an account of the several regimes that had preceded the founding of his own dynasty. The *Jin shu* is one of these commissioned works, and it includes the most detailed extant accounts of the barbarian conquest states that claimed legitimate rule over northern China throughout the fourth century, the first time that such an event had occurred in Chinese history. In each case, the subject under consideration here is the unprecedented phenomenon of foreign peoples ruling imperial heartlands: Italy and the rest of the western Mediterranean in one case, and the north China plain in the other.

Irrespective of how one characterizes the overall ethnographic tenor of either work, there are frequent examples in the *Wars* and *Jin shu* that evidence a dichotomous division between the Romans or Chinese on the one side and the barbarians on the other. Even the opening sentence of the *Wars*, in homage to Herodotus, introduces Procopius' subject as an account of conflicts between the Roman emperor Justinian and the barbarians of the east and west. As the fifth century BC was the age in which it seems that the mutually exclusive categories of Hellenicity and barbarism were first clearly articulated,[37] Procopius prepares his audience to see the coming narrative in the familiar context of Romans (no longer Greeks) fighting against the aggressive Persian Empire in the east. Even more to the glory of the emperor, however, *this* history will also relate the wars fought against the barbarians of the west as well, thereby elevating Procopius' theme with a universality surpassing that of his predecessor(s):

> Προκόπιος Καισαρεὺς τοὺς πολέμους ξυνέγραψεν, οὓς Ἰουστινιανὸς ὁ Ῥωμαίων βασιλεὺς πρὸς βαρβάρους διήνεγκε τούς τε ἑῴους καὶ ἑσπερίους, ὥς πη αὐτῶν ἑκάστῳ ξυνηνέχθη γενέσθαι, ὡς μὴ ἔργα ὑπερμεγέθη ὁ μέγας αἰὼν λόγου ἔρημα χειρωσάμενος τῇ τε λήθῃ αὐτὰ καταπρόηται καὶ παντάπασιν ἐξίτηλα θῆται, ὧνπερ τὴν μνήμην αὐτὸς ᾤετο μέγα τι ἔσεσθαι καὶ ξυνοῖσον ἐς τὰ μάλιστα τοῖς τε νῦν οὖσι καὶ τοῖς ἐς τὸ ἔπειτα γενησομένοις, εἴ ποτε καὶ αὖθις ὁ χρόνος ἐς ὁμοίαν τινὰ τοὺς ἀνθρώπους ἀνάγκην διάθοιτο.[38]

> Procopius of Caesarea has recorded these wars that Justinian, emperor of the Romans, waged against the barbarians of the east and west; he made a record of how it turned out in each case lest the expanse of time overwhelm such laborious deeds, bereft of mention, and lest it consign them to forgetfulness and render them faded to all. He considered that the memory of these matters would be a great thing and of much help – both to those now living as well as to those of future generations if at some point a future age should present a similar crisis before men.

Also alluding to Thucydides, Procopius presents his history as a work of utility for future generations that will benefit from consideration of the historical processes, and vicissitudes of fortune, that he will recount.[39] Most important to note, however, is that the entire work is framed with these opening lines as an exposition of the *res gestae* of Romans and barbarians, an oppositional construct in historiography that may ultimately

---

[37] Hall, Edith, *Inventing the Barbarian*, 1–3; Kim, *Ethnicity and Foreigners in Ancient Greece and China*, 29. See Chapter 2, 107–08.

[38] *Wars* 1.1.1.

[39] Evans, "The Attitudes of the Secular Historians of the Age of Justinian towards the Classical Past," 356. For a recent discussion of Procopius' *mimesis* of Herodotus and Thucydides here, see Basso and Greatrex, "How to Interpret Procopius' Preface to the Wars," 59–72.

be traced back through Herodotus to Homer and that had remained in use well into the Roman imperial period.[40]

This opposition between Romans and barbarians appears at multiple points throughout the work. For example, in an exhortation of the general Belisarius to his troops, Procopius notes that the Libyans whom Roman armies have come to liberate are former Romans who have been oppressed by the barbarian Vandals.[41] When the city of Rome is abandoned by the Gothic king Vitigis and is occupied by the Roman army, the city is said to again be under Roman sway, implicitly in opposition to the period of non-Roman rule, after a period of sixty years.[42] Elsewhere, Procopius makes no distinction between the ethnic identities of the conquerors of the western provinces, stating at different points that "the barbarians had divided up the empire of the Romans"[43] and that "the barbarians had become the clear lords of the entire west."[44] Illustrating the impossibility of the odds faced by the Roman inhabitants of Rome itself, Procopius claims that the Romans preserved their city even under barbarian rule,[45] going so far as to keep intact the ship of Aeneas himself, which Procopius claims to have seen.[46] There are thus many instances throughout the work where the dichotomy between Romans and barbarians is clearly articulated.

Other aspects of the Roman–barbarian dichotomy – particularly the pejorative, collective characterizations of peoples labeled as barbarian – occur frequently throughout the eight books of the *Wars*. For example, in describing Diocletian's ultimately unsuccessful policy of paying the Nobatae and Blemmyes not to cause trouble in Egypt, he concludes with the statement that "no contrivance will keep all barbarians in good faith towards the Romans without the fear of the soldiers there to keep them at bay."[47] Faithlessness is a charge often imputed to foreign peoples in Greco-Roman literature, and this stereotype is elsewhere well attested in the *Wars*. The perfidy toward the Romans of the allied and migrating Visigoths is also noted, Procopius observing that "good faith towards the Romans does

---

[40] Like Herodotus, Arrian avails himself of the convenient division of the world between Greeks and barbarians (*Anabasis* 1.12.4).
[41] *Wars* 3.20.19.   [42] *Wars* 5.14.14.
[43] Οὕτω μὲν οἱ βάρβαροι διεδάσαντο τὴν Ῥωμαίων ἀρχήν (*Wars* 7.34.1).
[44] κύριοι τῆς ἑσπερίας οἱ βάρβαροι διαρρήδην ἐγένοντο πάσης (*Wars* 7.33.1).
[45] οἵ γε καὶ πολύν τινα βεβαρβαρωμένοι αἰῶνα τάς τε πόλεως διεσώσαντο οἰκοδομίας καὶ τῶν ἐγκαλλωπισμάτων τὰ πλεῖστα (*Wars* 8.22.6).
[46] *Wars* 8.22.7–8.
[47] βαρβάρους ἅπαντας οὐδεμία μηχανὴ διασώσασθαι τὴν ἐς Ῥωμαίους πίστιν ὅτι μὴ δέει τῶν ἀμυνομένων στρατιωτῶν (*Wars* 1.19.33).

not know how to live amongst barbarians."[48] This charge is applied at various points to most of the enemies of the Romans: to the Lombards, Moors, Franks, and others.

In his approval of the Herulian Pharas' conduct and perhaps with a touch of humor, Procopius takes the opportunity to iterate the familiar stereotypes of barbarian perfidy and intemperance: "For a Herulian man not to be given over to faithlessness and drunkenness but to lay claim to virtue – that is a difficult thing and worthy of much praise."[49] Lest it seem that this negative treatment is Herulian-specific, the same Pharas himself ascribes his lack of refinement to his general barbarian identity saying, "I myself am a barbarian and unfamiliar with letters and speeches, and I am otherwise unskillful."[50] Though it is clear from Pharas' example that it was possible for a barbarian, even a Herulian such as Pharas, to transcend the general stereotypes associated with his general or particular non-Roman identity, the expectation on the part of Procopius that barbarians are typified by "barbarian" behaviors is clear.[51] Taragna has argued that the speeches Procopius crafts for barbarian characters depict the speakers as ignorant and arrogant by virtue of their tone and content.[52]

Indeed, there are multiple examples where the term "barbarian" is associated with, or indicative of, a variety of more or less negative stereotypes. Though in most cases, barbarian vices are not so often commented upon as they are in relation to the Heruli, for whom Procopius appears to have had a particular distaste,[53] they are nevertheless visible in a wide range of peoples. The Lombard envoys refer to their own "barbaric simplicity," ἀφελείᾳ βαρβαρικῇ, and "scarcity of words," λόγων σπανιζούσῃ.[54] Barbarian "simplicity" is also said to describe the Abasgi's belief that trees are gods.[55] Indeed, the Huns, or rather the Turkic Utigurs whom Procopius

---

[48] οὐ γὰρ οἶδε βαρβάροις ἐνδιαιτᾶσθαι ἡ ἐς Ῥωμαίους πίστις (*Wars* 3.2.7).

[49] ἄνδρα δὲ Ἔρουλον μὴ ἐς ἀπιστίαν τε καὶ μέθην ἀνεῖσθαι, ἀλλ᾽ ἀρετῆς μεταποιεῖσθαι, χαλεπόν τε καὶ ἐπαίνου πολλοῦ ἄξιον (*Wars* 4.4.30). It would seem that the reputation of the Heruli for drunkenness was so pervasive that it extended to those associated with them: a Roman commander of Heruli troops, unless he was a Heruli with a Roman name, was a notorious drunk (*Wars* 7.27.5).

[50] Εἰμὶ μὲν καὶ αὐτὸς βάρβαρος καὶ γραμμάτων τε καὶ λόγων οὔτε ἐθὰς οὔτε ἄλλως ἔμπειρος γέγονα (*Wars* 4.6.15).

[51] Of course, Pharas' opening to his speech to Gelimer should be read as a *captatio benevolentiae*, where he disavows his oratorical ability prior to launching in on a rhetorical speech. Nevertheless, appearance here of the trope of barbarian ignorance indicates the valence of the trope in the expectations of Procopius and his audience. For further discussion of Pharas and his barbarian identity, see Parnell, "Barbarians and Brothers-in-Arms," esp. 814–20.

[52] Taragna, Logoi historias: *Discorsi e lettere nella prima storiografia retorica bizantina*, 87.

[53] Greatrex, "Roman Identity in the Sixth Century," 269.

[54] *Wars* 7.34.23. The same comments in n. 51 apply here as well.

[55] θεοὺς γὰρ τὰ δένδρα βαρβάρῳ τινὶ ἀφελείᾳ ὑπώπτευον εἶναι (*Wars* 8.3.14).

anachronistically calls Huns, are completely illiterate and without any form of education; in a message sent to Justinian, their king Sandil refers to himself as an "uncouth barbarian"[56] and, since he is illiterate, delivers his message orally through his envoys in a "more barbaric manner."[57]

The drunkenness of the Heruli has been noted above, and intemperance is a trait shared by other barbarian peoples as well. For example, a group of Massagetae is involved in a drunken brawl that prompts Procopius to make the comment that "of all men the Massagetae are truly the most unrestrained drinkers."[58] This stereotype is repeated in the case of the Massagetan Chorsamantis who, along with his countryman Bochas, plays the role of a hero among the Roman forces during the Gothic siege of Rome. When Chorsamantis is wounded in a display of almost suicidal valor, Procopius relates that "since he was a barbarian he did not bear this peacefully," and Chorsamantis then vows vengeance against the Goths for the injury; upon recovery, he rides out against the Goths "having gotten himself drunk at breakfast as he was accustomed to do."[59]

Depictions of the barbarian rank and file in Roman armies are not always characterized by such tropes, however, and figures who are identified as barbarians can also be represented in a decidedly positive light; the heroism of the Massagetan Chorsamantis and his compatriot Bochas is one such example.[60] While the Goths are about to take the Roman-held fortress of Ancon, the Massagetan Gouboulgoudou and the Thracian Ulimuth manage, while suffering great wounds, to drive the Goths off the battlements.[61] When the two Roman garrisons of Asise and Spolitium are besieged by the Goths, the former fortress is defended by Sisifridus,

[56] ἀγροικιζόμενον βάρβαρον (*Wars* 8.19.11).

[57] βαρβαρικώτερον (*Wars* 8.19.8). Procopius notes that "the Huns are completely ignorant and unpracticed when it comes to letters up to this time, and they have neither a schoolmaster nor do their children enrich themselves with any labor over their letters": γραμμάτων παντάπασιν Οὖννοι ἀνήκοοί τε καὶ ἀμελέτητοι ἐς τόδε εἰσὶ καὶ οὔτε γραμματιστήν τινα ἔχουσιν οὔτε τῷ περὶ τὰ γράμματα πόνῳ συναύξεται αὐτοῖς τὰ παιδία (*Wars* 8.19.8).

[58] πάντων γὰρ ἀνθρώπων μάλιστά εἰσιν ἀκρατοπόται οἱ Μασσαγέται (*Wars* 3.12.8). The particular association of heavy drinking with peoples of the far northeast appears on multiple occasions in Herodotus: Hdt. 1.106.2, 1.207–212, 6.84.3.

[59] ἅτε ἀνὴρ βάρβαρος οὐκ ἤνεγκε πρᾴως. ... ἔν τε ἀρίστῳ οἰνωμένος, ὥσπερ εἰώθει (*Wars* 6.1.27-28).

[60] On barbarians in Roman armies in the sixth century, see Parnell, "Barbarians and Brothers-in-Arms," 809–25, and, more recently, "Procopius on Romans, non-Romans, and Battle Casualties," 249–62.

[61] Ulimuth is identified as being "from Thrace," ἐκ Θρᾴκης (*Wars* 6.13.14). While it is beyond the scope of this study to determine the ethnic identities of participants on either side of Justinian's wars, it is clear that "Thracian" may suggest Gothic origin rather than Roman provincial. The Roman officers Godidisklus and Bessas are referred to as a Goths, Γότθοι ἄνδρες (*Wars* 1.8.3), but Bessas is elsewhere simply identified as being from the lands of Thrace, ἐκ τῶν ἐπὶ Θρᾴκης χωρίων

"a Goth by birth," Γότθος μὲν γένος, but most loyal to the Romans and the emperor's affairs; the fortress is only taken after Sisifridus dies fighting his former Gothic countrymen.[62] In contrast, the Roman commander Herodian surrenders Spoletium to the enemy and saves his own life. Even Roman administration may be unfavorably compared with barbarian occupation, for Procopius notes that the citizens of the city of Rome itself long for the days of barbarian rule when they find themselves oppressed by the presence of a Roman army that cannot even guarantee their own safety.[63] These examples, and the last one in particular, indicate that tropes of barbarism, as was common in classical ethnography, could be introduced by Procopius to serve as a critical mirror of either Roman policy or military virtue.

A similar tendency to praise individual barbarians also appears in Agathias. After a successful battle against the Alamanni in Italy when Agathias claims that all the soldiers in the Roman army had exhibited courage, the only men he honors by name are a Goth and a Herulian.[64] More remarkable is that even an enemy Persian commander, a certain Mermeroes, is described by Agathias as having been "masterly in counsel, the greatest in warfare, and exceptionally courageous in spirit."[65] Agathias takes this same Mermeroes to illustrate the fact that "it is thus to be granted that generalship is not a matter of strength of the body, but rather of wisdom."[66] Even to an author otherwise hostile toward Persia, a Persian general embodies all of the virtues to be desired in his Roman counterparts, and there is no indication that his origin among, and allegiance to, a barbarian people should qualify such praise.

To summarize, it is clear that Procopius is working within the general parameters of classical ethnological worldviews, whose typical features are widely present throughout the *Wars*. Whether it is the persistence of a binary division between Romans and barbarians or any number of stereotypes assigned to foreign peoples in classical texts, Procopius is obviously comfortable in his application of traditional tropes to the enemies of the empire.

While the *Wars* is a work dedicated in its opening lines to the conflicts between the Romans and the barbarians of the east and west, the *Jin shu* is

---

(*Wars* 5.5.3). On the difficulty of assessing ethnic affiliation of individuals from Thrace, see Greatrex, "Roman Identity in the Sixth Century," 268–69.

[62] *Wars* 7.12.12–17.   [63] *Wars* 7.9.1–6.   [64] Agathias 2.9.13.

[65] δεινὸς μὲν ἐς εὐβουλίαν, ἄριστος δὲ τὰ πολέμια καὶ σφόδρα τὴν ψυχὴν ἀνδρειότατος (Agathias 2.22.5).

[66] οὕτως ἄρα τὸ στρατηγεῖν οὐ σώματος ῥώμῃ, μᾶλλον μὲν οὖν φρονήσει δοτέον. Ibid.

not defined so narrowly. It is rather a general history of the Western and Eastern Jin dynasties that is organized according to the basic format of earlier dynastic histories, covering all aspects of the regimes considered to be of interest and importance. The *Jin shu* is divided up into four major sections: the Basic Annals, the Monographs, the Biographies, and the Chronicles. This arrangement follows the general format of the dynastic history, wherein ethnographic material is featured in the Biographies section, which typically contains an individual fascicle or fascicles devoted to accounts of prominent barbarian peoples and where information on the non-Chinese is otherwise organized according to the four points of the compass.[67] Speeches in the Basic Annals and Biographies also contain ethnographic content, and topically organized Monographs dedicated to subjects such as astrology or geography likewise make reference to barbarian peoples. The *Jin shu* is unique, however, in comparison to other dynastic histories in that it includes a new section: the Chronicles, which narrate the affairs of the various barbarian states, the so-called Sixteen Kingdoms, which ruled parts of northern China from the early fourth century to the mid-fifth century. Given this study's concentration on ethnographic discourse, it is fascicle 97 from the Biographies section, which is devoted to the Si Yi 四夷, "The Four Barbarians," and the Chronicles, the accounts of barbarian states, that will be the focus here.[68]

As Procopius' prologue has been shown to follow the schema of Herodotus, which introduces a conflict between Romans and barbarians, the two sections of the *Jin shu* dedicated to the discussion of foreign peoples are, likewise, firmly rooted in the Sino-barbarian discourse of earlier centuries. In some ways, fascicle 97 and the Chronicles in their entirety function as works in their own right, as each is preceded by a

---

[67] See above, 53–54. The length of an individual fascicle varies considerably. To give non-Sinologists a rough sense of how long fascicles are, fascicle 97 of the *Jin shu* is twenty-two pages long in the Zhonghua shuju edition; the first three fascicles of the Chronicles section of the *Jin shu* contain thirteen, twenty-six, and twenty-three pages, respectively. The *Jin shu* itself runs to 3,216 pages and contains 130 fascicles in total. There is great variety in terms of how much space is granted to individual kingdoms within the last thirty fascicles of the Chronicles, due to discrepancies in the length of a kingdom's existence and the number of rulers: some of the barbarian states are given three fascicles, whereas others receive only one or even just part of a fascicle. In comparison, the eight books of Procopius' *Wars* range from book three at 110 pages to book eight at 192 pages in the Teubner edition used here.

[68] It is important not to confuse the Si Yi 四夷, the four barbarian groups associated in ancient times with the four points of the compass – the Rong 戎, Man 蠻, Di 狄, and Yi 夷 – with the Wu Hu 五胡, the Five Hu or Five Barbarians. The latter are the five dominant ethnic groups who conquered parts of northern China beginning in the fourth century AD: the Xiongnu 匈奴, Jie 羯, Di 氐, Qiang 羌, and Särbi 鮮卑.

rhetorical preface and each has a clearly delineated theme: fascicle 97 describes the various foreign peoples who had some contact with China during the Jin era, whereas the thirty fascicles of the Chronicles cover the history of the barbarian conquest states. In a manner somewhat analogous to Procopius' preface to the *Wars*, the preface to fascicle 97 calls to mind historical conflicts of earlier ages:

夫恢恢乾德，萬類之所資始；蕩蕩坤儀，九區之所均載．考羲軒於往統，肇承天而理物；訊炎昊於前辟，爰制地而疏疆．襲冠帶以辨諸華，限要荒以殊遐裔，區分中外，其來尚矣．九夷八狄，被青野而互玄方；七戎六蠻，緜西宇而橫南極．繁種落，異君長，遇有道則時遵聲教，鍾無妄則爭肆虔劉，趨扇風塵，蓋其常性也．詳求遐議，歷選深謨，莫不待以羈縻，防其猾夏．．．．既而惠皇失德，中宗遷播，凶徒分據，天邑傾淪，朝化所覃，江外而已，賝貢之禮，於茲殆絕，殊風異俗，所未能詳．故採其可知者，為之傳云．北狄竊號中壤，備於載記；在其諸部種類，今略書之．[69]

Regarding vast celestial power, it is the originating force of the Ten Thousand Kinds; regarding the boundless expanse of earth, it is that which supports all the Nine Regions. Examining Fuxi and the Yellow Emperor and their ancient governance, [one sees that] they began to follow the way of Heaven and order the material world. Inquiring into the way in which the Fire Emperor and Fuxi formerly administered, [one sees that] they thus established territory and opened up the peripheries. They wore hats and belts in order to signify all of the Xia [sc. China]; they delimited the marches in order to differentiate the distant regions and to separate the central and the external. Since then a great expanse of time has passed. The Nine Yi and the Eight Di peoples cover the verdant wilderness and extend throughout the far north. The Seven Rong and the Six Man reach out through the western lands and crisscross the farthest south. Their tribal groups proliferate, and they have their different chieftains. When they interact with China when it follows the Way, they then give heed to the civilized teachings. When catastrophe gathers, they fight to expand while killing and pillaging, rushing about and stirring up wind and dust. On the whole, this is their general nature. If one examines in great detail the ancient discussions and deliberately selects profound strategies, there was none who did not control them with the "loose rein" system in order to prevent their treacherous chaos against Xia [sc. China]. ... At the time when Emperor Hui [r. 290–307] lost his power and the imperial clan was forced into migration and exile and the evildoers divided and occupied, the imperial capitals were overwhelmed and drowned; the reach and influence of the imperial court were relegated to south of the Yangtze River. The ritual acceptance of precious tribute missions was well nigh broken off. Regarding

---

[69] *Jin shu* 97.2531–32.

strange customs and alien mores, this is the reason it has not been possible to be precise. Therefore, in taking what things can in fact be known about them, these will now be put into record. The account of the Northern Di, who illegitimately usurped the imperial title of the central territory, is to be told in the Chronicles. As for all their various tribes and kinds, a summary will be written here now.

While Procopius introduces his work with a literary allusion to Herodotus, whose own introduction recalls the Homeric conflict between Achaeans and Trojans, the *Jin shu* preface to the fascicle on the Four Barbarians goes back to the mythological origins of the Chinese people, showing how culture heroes such as the Yellow Emperor, Fuxi 伏羲, and the Fire Emperor brought order and civilization to the world. An aspect of this ordering process was the determination of what is internal, i.e., China or the Sinitic cultural sphere, and what is external, i.e., barbarian. In these introductory lines and in the passage that follows, the reader is prepared to understand a fundamental division between the Chinese and barbarian worlds where the latter are restrained by the superior virtue of China when it is correctly governed but who revert back to violent disorder when China fails to adhere to the Way of virtuous governance. The barbarians thus have a collective *xing* 性, "nature," which rulers of China have always been required to restrain politically and militarily by means of the "loose rein" system (*jimi* 羈縻 or *jimi fuzhou* 羈縻府州), a policy implemented in the early Tang but whose origins go back to the Han dynasty. The purpose of the "loose rein" system was to organize and control foreign peoples who had surrendered to the Chinese by organizing them into units that would be under the supervision and control of Chinese generals along the frontiers.[70]

These two introductory passages, when looked at simultaneously, offer a telling contrast. While Procopius has been taken by some scholars to uphold the traditional biases of a Greek– or Roman–barbarian dichotomy,

---

[70] Pan, *Son of Heaven and Heavenly Qaghan*, 197. It is important to point out that the compound *jimi* 羈縻 itself suggests the restraint of animals, not human beings. *Ji* 羈 is a word for "bridle" or may be used as a verb meaning "restrain/fasten" and contains the graph 馬 for "horse"; *mi* 縻 has a similar range of meanings with the distinction that it is associated with cattle rather than horses. As the name for a policy to manage non-Chinese peoples, *jimi* is clearly a term with explicitly dehumanizing connotations. It is in line with Ban Gu's assertion in the *Han shu* that "the ancient sage kings treated them [sc. the barbarians] like birds and beasts": 是故聖王禽獸畜之 (*Han shu* 94b.3834). Also see Hulsewé, *China in Central Asia*, 128, note 314. It also stands in marked contrast to the language of *amicitia* and *foedus* employed by the Roman state with its tribal neighbors; however euphemistic and veiling they may be of the brutal realities of Roman power, there is at least a vestigial notion of agreements concluded between diplomatic equals.

a comparison with the preface to fascicle 97 of the *Jin shu* shows that his presentation of the theme of his work is suggestive of a parity between the Romans and the barbarians, military and political adversaries in contention with one another. The struggle between the emperor of the Romans and the barbarians of the east and west presents the Roman community contending with antagonists whose deeds, alongside those of the Romans, are worthy of recounting, lest they be forgotten by posterity. In contrast, the *Jin shu* characterizes the conflict between the Chinese and barbarians, while equally adversarial, as one that is explicitly defined in xenophobic moralizing terms: the barbarians are those who have rebelled, whose nature is to be violent and chaotic, whose proper status is one of subservience to be expressed in the offering of tribute to China. Not fully human, their proper status is to be controlled by the reins of a morally virtuous and powerful Chinese emperor. While these features of the *Jin shu* are commonplaces in Chinese historiography, they stand out all the more clearly when compared with the preface to the *Wars*. In Procopius' formulation, the barbarians have not rebelled; they have no morally inferior nature; and their status as military or political adversaries is not conceived of as an inversion of the cosmological or even political order. Irrespective of the ideological baggage with which the term "barbarian" may be accompanied, the barbarians in the preface to the *Wars* are represented as one half of an antagonistic relationship, whose deeds, along with those of the Romans, are to be commemorated for the benefit of future generations.

The context within which the Si Yi, the Four Barbarians, are to be discussed in the *Jin shu* is one that takes for granted that those peoples should be, in theory, in a state of precariously controlled subservience to China. However, in reality it is clear that many of these peoples were far beyond the frontiers, and knowledge of their cultural practices was vague at best, only scattered details being known by report. The preface suggests that the ideal state of relations, however unrealistic, between China and the barbarians is that of the *jimi* system, under which foreign peoples acknowledge the supremacy of China irrespective of their distance from it and express their subservience through tribute missions.[71] The preface concludes with a reference to the fact that during the first decades of the fourth century AD, the barbarians had actually taken control of north China and expelled the Jin royal family to the south, the crisis that divides the Western Jin and Eastern Jin periods. As this overthrow of Chinese power

---

[71] On this aspect of the traditional Chinese worldview, see Rossabi, "Introduction," 2–4; Pan, *Son of Heaven and Heavenly Qaghan*, 24–28.

was an unprecedented break in the traditional world order, the details regarding these barbarian states are reserved for special treatment in the Chronicles, the last section of the *Jin shu*.

The Sino–barbarian antithesis is thus clearly expressed in the preface to fascicle 97, and one sees throughout the *Jin shu* a common opposition between Chinese and any of the five major ethnic groups who ruled over parts of northern China in the period. It is typical when referring to Chinese and non-Chinese at the same time to speak of Hua-Yi 華夷, an expression that denotes Chinese as Hua 華 and barbarians as Yi 夷; an equivalent formulation is Hua-Di 華狄. Otherwise the Chinese may be referred to as Xia 夏 or *Jinren* 晉人, "people of Jin." A notable difference between the general ethnographic discourse in the *Wars* and the *Jin shu* is the relative lack of barbarian tropes in the actual narrative sections. While it has been shown above that Procopius not infrequently comments on either the barbarian origin of a particular figure or notes that his behavior is characteristic of a particular ethnic group, the *Jin shu* tends to treat barbarian actors more at face value; the ethnographic description is typically relegated either to speeches in various parts of the work or to those sections traditionally dedicated to ethnographic exposition.

As discussed in Chapter 1, ethnographic material in Chinese historiography is much more systematically presented than it is in the Greco-Roman tradition; instead of being scattered throughout the work in the form of lengthy digressions or short authorial comments, it is largely contained in geographically or topically arranged sections that are dedicated to the treatment of either a single people or several peoples of a particular region. This is an important contrast in the way the two traditions represent foreign peoples and their relation to the events that are considered to be of primary interest. In the Chinese dynastic history format, the first section of the text is always that of the Basic Annals, which focus on the events at court. Information on foreign peoples is relegated to discrete, appropriately named fascicles that are placed near or at the end of the work. The very arrangement of a dynastic history, therefore, is almost a reflection of the geopolitical zone schemata, discussed in Chapter 1, that envision a central Chinese domain surround by concentric areas of increasing barbarism and degrees of submission to the center. The reader, therefore, recognizes that the fascicles devoted to the barbarians are of, literally, peripheral importance.

Such an arrangement could not be more different from the approach exhibited by Herodotus and Procopius, historians separated by nearly one thousand years, whose prologues to their histories profess that they will commemorate the deeds of Greeks and barbarians (or Romans and barbarians) lest these events be forgotten. Like the Trojans and Achaeans in the *Iliad*, Greeks/Romans and barbarians are placed side by side in a relationship that, if antagonistic, recognizes them both as contestants on par with one another.[72] These two forms of arrangement necessarily prepare the reader to encounter the barbarians with differing expectations: in the Greco-Roman case, with the assumption that the barbarians are participants and actors whose *res gestae* are worthy of the same note as are those of the Greeks or Romans;[73] in the Chinese case, with the knowledge that barbarian peoples are those whose geographical and textual marginalization corresponds to their lower level of civilization and necessary submissiveness to the Chinese emperor.

While the *Jin shu*'s fascicle devoted to the Si Yi by its very form demonstrates continuity with the ethnographic writing of earlier centuries, one of the most commonly cited passages from the *Jin shu* regarding attitudes toward barbarians actually appears in the biography of the Jin official Jiang Tong 江統. While the rhetorical arguments quoted therein are typically taken by Chinese scholars to reflect attitudes of the late third century AD, they nevertheless exhibit a marked similarity to the worldview expressed in the prefaces to the both the Si Yi fascicle and the Chronicles composed centuries later under the early Tang when the *Jin shu* was compiled. Following a revolt of the Di 氏 people in the west against the Jin regime in the late 290s, Jiang Tong delivered his famous memorial to the emperor advocating for the mass removal of Di and Qiang people who, having surrendered to China and been relocated within imperial territory, had come to make up a total of half the population in the Guanzhong region.[74] He begins in a manner reminiscent of that employed by Ban Gu 班固 in the *Han shu* 漢書,[75] by describing the dichotomous geographical

---

[72] Prusek has argued that "Whereas in Greece literature begins with the *epos*, in China it begins with lyrical songs. In Greece historiography imitates the epic mode of expression; in China the categorization and systemization of facts by free linking of rough material reminds one of lyric methods." *Chinese History and Literature: Collection of Studies*, 31. While the poetic precedents of historiography are certainly crucial to an understanding of both traditions, it is also important to note the influence of politically and geographically schematized worldviews of Chinese ritual texts in the structure of dynastic historiography.

[73] For example, in Sallust's *Bellum Jugurthinum* the two commanders, the Roman Caecilius Metellus and the Numidian Jugurtha, appear as "two commanders fighting one against one the other, men of the highest quality and equals": *inter se duo imperatores, summi viri, certabant, ipsi pares* (*Bellum Iugurthinum*. 52.1).

[74] 且關中之人百餘萬口，率其少多，戎狄居半 (*Jin shu* 56.1533). For a discussion of this passage, see Chen Yinke, *Wei Jin Nanbeichao shi jiangyan lu*, 74–81

[75] See above, 121.

relationship between the Chinese and barbarians as it is recorded in the
most authoritative of ancient texts:

夫夷蠻戎狄，謂之四夷，九服之制，地在要荒. 春秋之義，內諸夏
而外夷狄. 以其言語不通，贄幣不同，法俗詭異，種類乖殊.[76]

The Yi, Man, Rong, and Di are called the Si Yi; according to the system of
the Nine Zones, their land is in the outermost wastes. This is the essence of
the *Chunqiu*: the Xia [sc. Chinese] are all within and the Yi-Di are without.
Accordingly, their languages are unintelligible, their gifts and currency are
different, their laws and habits are treacherous and foreign, and their various
ethnicities are strangely disparate.

Jiang Tong offers a worldview that is firmly in accord with classical
Chinese ethnographic views: the barbarians as a collective, irrespective
of their internal diversity, belong outside the Chinese community. While
he notes that the Rong and Di are the worst offenders, the Si Yi as a
whole share a common essence: "their inborn nature is greedy and
covetous, violent and cruel."[77] While the preface to fascicle 97 quoted
above described the barbarians' nature or *xing* 性 as one that yields to a
well-governed China but invades and pillages when China is ruled
inappropriately, Jiang Tong offers a more consistently negative view of
the pan-barbarian ethos. As is common in ancient Chinese rhetoric, he
sets forth his case with an appeal to ancient precedent going back to the
Great Yu 大禹, the founder of the mythical Xia 夏 kingdom, and
followed by references to the Shang 商, Zhou 周, Qin 秦, and Han
regimes up to his own day. He praises, as did Confucius, the minister
Guan Zhong 管仲 who saved China from adopting the coiffure and
costume of the barbarians; Jiang Tong even finds praise for the first
emperor of Qin who expanded the borders of the empire such that "at
that time China saw no trouble from the Si Yi."[78]

Throughout Jiang Tong's proposal there are references to a fundamental
incompatibility between the Chinese and the barbarians; he asks rhetorically whether it is not the case that previous success in defending the
frontier was due to keeping the barbarians out of the empire and separate
from the Chinese.[79] He insists that "those who are not of our kindred
must have a heart that is incompatible; the Rong-Di have a mentality that
is other than that of the Hua [sc. Chinese]."[80] The *Jin shu* notes that

---

[76] *Jin shu* 56.1529.   [77] 其性氣貪婪，凶悍不仁，四夷之中，戎狄為甚 (*Jin shu* 56.1530).
[78] 當時中國無復四夷也 (Ibid).
[79] 豈不以華夷異處，戎夏區別，要塞易守之故，得成其功也哉 (*Jin shu* 56.1532).
[80] 非我族類，其心必異，戎狄志態，不與華同 (*Jin shu* 56.1531–32).

although the emperor did not adopt Jiang Tong's recommendation of barbarian deportation, "within ten years' time the Yi-Di had thrown China into chaos and the people of the age admired the depth of Jiang Tong's perception."[81] While there are certainly indicators of anti-barbarian sentiment in the *Wars*, one does not find the same kind of categorical dismissal of, and hostility toward, the collective non-Roman world. While Jiang Tong's speech is primarily concerned with only two contemporary peoples, the Di 氐 and Qiang, he nevertheless subsumes their particular ethnic identities within the archaic binome Yi-Di 夷狄, a generic term referring to all non-Chinese and carrying with it the most pejorative aspects associated with the Greco-Roman term "barbarian."

Yet despite the overt xenophobia that appears in some places, there is at least one instance in the *Jin shu* where a barbarian people is held up for explicit praise, and that is in the case of the Tuyuhun 吐谷渾, whose history is recorded in fascicle 97. The Tuyuhun were a Särbi-Xianbei people who took their name from their founder, the eldest and illegitimate son of the chieftain Shegui 涉歸. Shegui granted Tuyuhun control over many of his subject families while conferring the formal position of leadership on his legitimate heir Murong Wei 慕容廆. The *Jin shu* recounts an incident when horses of the two brothers' respective herds are fighting one another, and Murong Wei becomes angry and blames his brother for it. In anger and frustration, Tuyuhun vows to lead his followers away. Despite Murong Wei's regret and efforts to persuade his brother to return, Tuyuhun guides his people out of the northeast and into the northwestern regions where he establishes a kingdom. As recorded elsewhere, Murong Wei never recovered from his grief and regret and composed a song *Agan zhi ge* 阿干之歌, "Song of Elder Brother," which he often sang.[82]

The two brothers' careers in the *Jin shu* form a stark contrast: while Murong Wei goes on to found the powerful Former Yan 前燕 dynasty in the northeast of China, one of the Sixteen Kingdoms treated in the Chronicles section of the *Jin shu*, Tuyuhun, while living in de facto independence, never disavows his allegiance to the legitimate Chinese Jin dynasty.[83] Tuyuhun and his descendants thus represent a barbarian

---

[81] 帝不能用. 未及十年，而夷狄亂華，時服其深識 (*Jin shu* 56.1534).

[82] 廆追思之，作阿干之歌，歲暮窮思，常歌之 (*Jin shu* 97.2537). The *Jin shu* explains that in the Särbi language, *agan* 阿干 means "elder brother": 鮮卑謂兄為阿干 (Ibid.).

[83] For accounts of these two states, see Schreiber, "History of the Former Yen Dynasty," parts I and II, and Carroll, *Account of the Tu-Yü-Hun in the History of the Chin Dynasty*. Carroll has translated this section of fascicle 97 and provides a brief introduction to the history of the people.

alternative to the usurpers and conquerors who claimed to rule their conquered territories *suo iure*. Indeed, throughout the history of the Tuyuhun provided in fascicle 97, Tuyuhun and his descendants, with one or two exceptions, are portrayed in the most virtuous terms. His son Tuyan 吐延 is described as being *xiongzi kuijie* 雄姿魁傑, "heroically poised and of heroic stature," though his nature, *xing* 性, is *kuren* 酷忍, "cruel"; his grandson Yeyan 葉延 is *zhixiao* 至孝, "extremely filial," and the *Jin shu* recounts edifying anecdotes regarding his grief for his father and attentiveness to his sick mother. His son Bixi 辟奚 is described as having a nature that is *renhou cihui* 仁厚慈惠, "graciously benevolent and compassionately kind"; Bixi's son Shilian 視連 is described as *lianshen you zhixing* 廉慎有志性, "diligently virtuous and having deep feeling," in his youth, and he abstains from governmental affairs, alcohol, and hunting for seven years in grief for the death of his father. Shipi 視羆 has a nature that is *yingguo* 英果, "heroic and decisive," and is able to produce *xionglüe* 雄略, "remarkable strategies." According to the *Jin shu*, one of these Tuyuhun leaders was even able to quote from the classical text the *Yijing* 易經.[84] In these instances, we do not find a barbarian antithesis but barbarians who behave with Chinese virtues and, accordingly, recognize the authority of the rightful Chinese Jin emperor.

It is of course true that non-Romans too may receive high praise from Procopius. For example, he says regarding the Armenian Artabanes that "in Byzantium the common people marveled at his deeds and otherwise loved him; for he was tall and handsome, free-spirited in his manner, and sparing of his speech."[85] However, such positive representations of individuals identified as non-Roman do not generally compare with the highly moralizing praise lavished on Tuyuhun and his descendants – a critical exception will be Procopius' assessments of some barbarian rulers, to be discussed in the following chapter.[86] For the most part, positive comments Procopius offers for non-Romans such as Artabanes are typically made offhand and not imbued with great significance.

The *lun* colophon to fascicle 97 of the *Jin shu* exhibits extremes of moral condemnation and praise in its treatment of the two brothers, Murong Wei and Tuyuhun: while the former is represented as a lawless, defiant

[84] These attributes of Tuyuhun's descendants appear at *Jin shu* 97.2538–40.

[85] τὸν Ἀρταβάνην ἐν Βυζαντίῳ ὁ μὲν δῆμος τῶν πεπραγμένων ἐθαύμαζε καὶ ἄλλως ἠγάπα. ἦν γὰρ εὐμήκης τε τὸ σῶμα καὶ καλός, τό τε ἦθος ἐλευθέριος καὶ ὀλίγα ἄττα φθεγγόμενος (*Wars* 7.31.8–9).

[86] An important exception to this general rule is the treatment of Theoderic to be discussed in Chapter 4.

usurper – for he had disavowed allegiance to the Jin court and set up his own independent state, the Former Yan – the latter is noble and loyal to the Chinese. After praising Tuyuhun and his successors, the colophon offers an explicit moral lesson in its juxtaposition of the noble and ignoble barbarian brothers:

且渾廆連枝，生自邊極，各謀孫而翼子，咸革裔而希華. 廆胤姦凶，假鳳圖而竊號；渾嗣忠謹，距龍涸而歸誠. 懷姦者數世而亡，資忠者累葉彌劭，積善餘慶，斯言信矣.[87]

> Murong Wei and Tuyuhun were branches from the same tree and were born at the farthest edges of the frontier. Each took counsel for and aided his descendants; both reformed the border regions and looked to the Chinese. Wei led the wicked and evil; he appropriated royal ambitions and usurped the imperial title. The rightful heir Tuyuhun was loyal and sincere; he arrived at Longhe and offered his sincere allegiance. Those who were bent on wickedness lasted for several reigns before being destroyed; those who put their faith in loyalty brought their excellence to fruition through the generations. To accumulate virtue and pass it on to one's descendants – this is proof of that.

This pairing of the brothers Tuyuhun and Murong Wei is a perpetuation of two contrasting barbarian types that appear in Chinese historiography, going back at least to the first century AD. While the negative portrayal of Murong Wei satisfies expectations of barbarian wickedness, the praise lavished on Tuyuhun and his progeny recalls Ban Gu's eulogizing of the surrendered Xiongnu minister Jin Midi 金日磾.[88] It is thus too simplistic to assert that views of the barbarians were universally negative in classical and early medieval Chinese texts; while there were firmly entrenched, and frequently reiterated, notions of barbarian character and collective "nature," there was nevertheless room for noble barbarians as well – those who emulated Chinese Confucian virtues and, crucially, recognized the political and moral authority of a Chinese emperor.

Yet despite the barbarian capacity to adopt a righteous path, there persists in the *Jin shu* a worldview that takes for granted a physical and ethical barrier between the Chinese and the barbarians. That the geographical division between these two sections of humanity is both ancient and necessary has already been noted not only in the Han-dynasty history of Ban Gu but also in the *Jin shu*'s preface to fascicle 97. The colophon to fascicle 97 begins with the same idea:

---

[87] *Jin shu* 97.2551. [88] See above, 124–25, 127–28.

夫宵形稟氣，是稱萬物之靈；繫土隨方，迺有羣分之異. 蹈仁義者
為中寓，肆凶獷者為外夷，譬諸草木，區以別矣.[89]

The primordial matter receives energy,[90] and this may be called the spirit of
the Ten Thousand Things. Correlated with the soil and according to
region, one then finds the division of groups into races. Those who tread
the path of benevolence and righteousness comprise the central region;
those who flaunt their violence and ferocity are the outer Yi. Take the
example of plants and trees: they can be distinguished by their
different types.

One notes the emphasis on a geographical schema, familiar from classical
Chinese texts discussed in Chapter 1, that is characterized by its moral and
ethnological distinctions. While the Chinese are not named in the above
passage, it is clear that it is they who are the benevolent and righteous
inhabitants of the center whose corollary is the variety of peripheral
peoples, violent and fierce, who are collectively referred to here as *wai* Yi
外夷, outer Yi. The breakdown of this dichotomy, when foreign peoples
were settled along and within the imperial borders in increasing numbers
during the third century, is lamented in the final lines of the fascicle, which
is concluded with a short *zan* 贊 poem:[91]

逖矣前王，區別羣方.... 武后升圖，智昧遷胡. 遽淪家國，多謝明謨.[92]

How distant are the ancient kings who delineated the nations and regions. ...
Under Emperor Wu,[93] ambitions were lofty; when wisdom failed, the Hu
barbarians were settled within the empire. Then home and country were overwhelmed; there was a great decline in wise policies.

One observes here, and in other examples quoted above, an emphasis on a
clearly delineated political world order, where distinctions between Chinese
and barbarians are of great importance and upheld by the policies of wise
rulers who will keep different peoples in their appropriate places. The
absence of such a consistently expressed schema in the Greco-Roman
tradition has already been discussed in Chapter 1, and this contrast between
the classical Greco-Roman and Chinese traditions remains visible in the
Wars and the *Jin shu*. While Procopius recounts the follies and blunders of

---

[89] *Jin shu* 97.2550.
[90] The term *qi* 氣, translated here with "energy," is difficult to translate accurately. For a discussion of
its cosmological significance, see Lewis, *Sanctioned Violence in Early China*, 214–26.
[91] *Zan* were, by the time of the *Jin shu*, "rhymed eulogistic poems appended to the *lun*" colophons
that concluded either a fascicle or a narrative that spanned multiple fascicles. Honey, "History and
Historiography on the Sixteen States," 165.
[92] *Jin shu* 97.2551.
[93] Emperor Jin Wudi 晉武帝 (r. 266–290) was the founder of the Western Jin dynasty.

western Roman emperors and generals under whose tenure the western provinces were lost to the barbarians, his account does not explicitly decry the dissolution of an ethical world order that is premised upon a demarcation between Roman civilization and the disorder of the barbarians. The *Jin shu*, on the other hand, repeatedly returns to the notion of an ideologically correct, ethno-political landscape in which barbarians are held in control, in a state analogous to that of animals, on either the borders of the empire or farther afield. While the *Wars* certainly exhibits disdain toward barbarians and is at times categorically dismissive of them, Procopius' xenophobia lacks a systematic, moralizing, and frequently reinforced conception of a barbarian antithesis to the Roman world – much less of the dangers inherent when the physical divisions between the barbarians and Romans are not observed and diligently maintained.

Ethnographic Continuity

As the general notion of a barbarian antithesis persists in the *Wars* and *Jin shu*, if to varying degrees, so too does the formal exposition of ethnographic information on foreign peoples. Just as we have seen in earlier Greco-Roman historiography, Procopius mixes ethnographic material into his narrative of the wars in the form of digressions that are periodically inserted into the text as well as in shorter descriptive references amid his account of events. Typical of this latter practice is an account of a battle in which the Heruli fight for the Romans against the Persians; Procopius observes amid the action that it is Herulian custom to fight without a helmet or proper armor.[94] In similar fashion, and prior to an engagement between Roman and Vandal forces in North Africa, he notes that among Hunnic armies it is a custom for a certain person to have the honor of taking first blood in battle, and that "it was not lawful for a Massagetan [sc. a Hun] to rush forward and take one of the enemy before someone of his household had struck the first blow against them."[95]

More common in Procopius, however, are the ethnographic digressions that appear in the classical form established by Herodotus and his successors. Since a thorough discussion of all of these digressions would only offer a series of different accounts of the various peoples Procopius describes, a single example will suffice to demonstrate that Procopius

---

[94] *Wars* 2.25.27.
[95] οὐ γὰρ ἦν θεμιτὸν ἀνδρὶ Μασσαγέτῃ προτύψαντι ἐν μάχῃ τῶν τινα πολεμίων λαβεῖν, πρίν γε δή τινα ἐκ ταύτης τῆς οἰκίας ἐς τοὺς πολεμίους τῶν χειρῶν ἄρξαι (*Wars* 3.18.14).

approaches the ethnographic digression in a fashion wholly congruent with his classical models.[96] In book seven of the *Wars*, Procopius recounts the recruitment of a large force of Heruli who have been persuaded to accompany Roman forces to Italy. While passing through Thrace, they encounter a host of invading Sclaveni and Antae; the episode prompts Procopius to offer a short history of these latter two peoples' depredations in Thrace and of their activities north of the Danube. He begins by relating various particulars about their political organization (they have democratic rule rather than monarchy),[97] and he observes that they have always shared the same customs and believe in a single deity but are ignorant of fate. He goes on to describe sacrificial practices and their reverence for rivers, nymphs, and other spirits. The poverty of their dwellings and crudeness of their clothing is matched by the scarcity of their military equipment. Alluding to the original associations of the word "barbarian" with the act of speech, Procopius notes that an entirely barbarous language is common to them both.[98] More detail than is typical for Procopius is provided as to their appearance: Sclaveni and Antae look the same, being tall, especially sturdy, having complexion and hair that is neither fair nor dark but reddish colored. He compares the severity of their lifestyle with that of the Massagetae and notes that despite the fact that they are constantly covered up with dirt, "they are in fact not in the least worthless or wicked but maintain the Hunnic ethic in their artlessness."[99] The digression ends with the observation that the Sclaveni and Antae were both called Sporoi-Σπόροι, in ancient times and are descended from one and the same people, thereby explaining their linguistic, physiognomic, and cultural affinity in Procopius' own day in genealogical terms. Procopius seems to make a pun with the ethnonym, as he infers that it derives from the fact that they are scattered "sporadically," σποράδην, over a wide stretch of territory north of the Danube.[100]

If one were to change the names of the people being described, the above ethnographic digression could just as well appear in Herodotus or

---

[96] More or less detailed ethnographic digressions are devoted to the Hephthalites (1.3.1–7), the Tzani (1.15.21–25), the Heruli (6.14.1–42), the Scrithiphinoi (6.15.16–23), and the people of Brittia (8.20.42–58).

[97] οὐκ ἄρχονται πρὸς ἀνδρὸς ἑνός, ἀλλ᾽ ἐν δημοκρατίᾳ ἐκ παλαιοῦ βιοτεύουσι (*Wars* 7.14.22).

[98] φωνὴ ἀτεχνῶς βάρβαρος (*Wars* 7.14.26).

[99] πονηροὶ μέντοι ἢ κακοῦργοι ὡς ἥκιστα τυγχάνουσιν ὄντες, ἀλλὰ κἂν τῷ ἀφελεῖ διασώζουσι τὸ Οὐννικὸν ἦθος (*Wars* 7.14.28).

[100] *Wars* 7.14.29–30. For a discussion of early sources on the Sclaveni (i.e., the Slavs), see Curta, *The Making of the Slavs*, 36–73. For an analysis of this particular ethnographic digression, see Sarantis, "Procopius and the Different Types of Northern Barbarian," 358–60.

Ammianus. All the typical features of classical ethnography are present along with the familiar mixture of objectivity, disgust, curiosity, and bemused, or even sincere, admiration. More or less the same range of categories of inquiry – political institutions, religious practices, military matters, cultural particularities, etc. – are present in the other digressions contained in the *Wars* and are among the most commonly noted features of Procopius' classicizing style.

The *Jin shu* too perpetuates the highly systematic mode of ethnographic accounts that was common in earlier dynastic historiography by virtue of its containing a fascicle devoted to the Si Yi, the Four Barbarians, in the Biographies section of the work. While other histories such as the *Hou Han shu* 後漢書 may have divided this material up into different fascicles, the *Jin shu* combines them into one, treating the Eastern Yi 東夷, Western Rong 西戎, Southern Man 南蠻, and Northern Di 北狄 in turn. It is clear, however, that these four subsections are themselves archaic ethno-geographical labels, as neither Yi, Rong, Man, or Di is actually treated as a real people. These labels are rather categories that organize contemporary peoples who live in more or less distinct geographical regions. Yet these obsolete terms retain their former semantic content as ethnonyms belonging to peoples once perceived as enemies of the Chinese in the early first millennium BC, as is clear from their frequent use as rhetorical alternatives to contemporary names such as Xiongnu, Qiang, etc.

Like Procopius, the *Jin shu* exhibits a classicizing approach in its description of foreign peoples. Although the preface to fascicle 97 discussed above makes it clear to the reader that there is an underlying hostility toward the barbarians, the *Jin shu* at times also exhibits a relatively objective, and at times even explicitly laudatory, ethnographic gaze. Typical of its approach is its treatment of the Woren 倭人 people, who inhabited what are today the islands of Japan. After locating their country, the *Jin shu* remarks that it has many mountains and forest and lacks good land for fields, hence a reliance on seafood.[101] After noting the number of their kingdoms and size of their population, it is said that all of the men, irrespective of age, tattoo their faces and bodies.[102] This custom is explained by the fact that the Woren themselves claim to be descended from Taibo 太伯, a figure of the Zhou kingdom royal family, who may have lived during the late second millennium BC and who also tattooed his body. Shaokang 少康, a ruler of the legendary Xia kingdom, according

---

[101] 地多山林，無良田，食海物 (*Jin shu* 97.2535). [102] 男子無大小，悉黥面文身 (Ibid.).

to the *Jin shu* also marked himself in this way in order to avoid the danger of a river dragon. As the Woren like diving for fish, the *Jin shu* claims that they tattoo their bodies in order to protect themselves from beasts in the water.[103] The *Jin shu* proceeds to describe their sartorial habits, noting that they wear their hair loose and go barefoot.[104] After describing their crops and noting that they do not have cows or horses, their weapons are listed, and it is observed that they live in buildings where parents and children sleep in separate rooms. Their marriage and burial customs are described, as are their methods of divination and manner of reckoning time. Many of them live to be eighty, ninety, or one hundred years old. After noting the harshness of their legal system, the *Jin shu* comments that while they used to have men for their rulers, they began to take women for their kings during the latter part of the Han dynasty, a somewhat unusual observation of historical change in a foreign cultural practice. The section ends by noting the dates of their tribute missions to China. Throughout, there is no indication of a change in the ethnographic conventions standardized by Sima Qian 司馬遷 and Ban Gu.

Ethnographic Paradigms

Both the *Wars* and *Jin shu* exhibit a clear continuity with their respective classical precedents, and it is not surprising that the three explanatory frameworks considered in Chapter 1 are likewise evident in these two texts. The first of these frameworks, that of genealogy, has already been noted in the ethnographic digression on the Sclaveni and Antae, and it also appears in the *Jin shu* where the ancestry of the Woren is traced back to the family that founded the Zhou dynasty. Various other peoples in the *Wars* are given genealogies that indicate their earliest origins and/or their relationship to other peoples.[105]

The most extensive of these genealogies is the one Procopius provides for the Moors, who posed major military problems for Roman forces following the destruction of the Vandal kingdom in 534.[106] Following an episode where a detachment of Roman forces is trapped and killed,

---

[103] [少康] 斷髮文身以避蛟龍之害，今倭人好沈沒取魚，亦文身以厭水禽 (*Jin shu* 97.2535–36).
[104] 皆被髮徒跣 (*Jin shu* 97.2536).
[105] Müller underestimates Procopius' interest in genealogy in the *Wars*, claiming that he for the most part only exhibits interest in barbarian events directly impinging on his own day. *Geschichte der antiken Ethnographie und ethnologischen Theoriebildung, Teil II*, 474.
[106] Amitay offers an analysis of Procopius' account of Moorish ancient history in its historical and literary context in "Procopius of Caesarea and the Girgashite Diaspora," 257–76.

Procopius begins his account of how the Moors arrived in and settled Libya. Their story begins with the exodus of the Jews from Egypt and their arrival in Palestine. Because of the Jews' military supremacy, some of the Phoenician peoples fled to Egypt and, finding no place to settle there, moved on to Libya. He recounts how there were autochthonous peoples living there already whose king Antaeus wrestled with Heracles. Dido, the leader of the Phoenicians, and her followers were permitted to settle among them, founding the city of Carthage, and the settlers eventually subdued the Moors and forced them to live inland. This was the state of affairs until the Romans conquered Carthage and made both peoples subject to themselves, resettling the Moors in the outer reaches of Libya. Procopius then moves quickly forward to his own day, stating that the Moors had won many victories against the Vandals and conquered the land of Mauritania.[107] The genealogy thus includes both mythological and historical elements that serve to situate the Moors in the broader history of the Mediterranean world.

Other peoples too, excepting for now the barbarian conquerors who will be the focus of the latter part of this chapter, appear with their own genealogical histories. For example, the Utigurs living along the eastern shores of Lake Maeotis are said to be descendants of the ancient Cimmerians, a people whose deeds are recounted by Herodotus.[108] In the following chapter, Procopius repeats this origin myth but now associates the name of the Huns with the Cimmerians as well.[109] He claims that there was once a king over this Hunno-Cimmerian people who had two sons, named Utigur and Kutrigur, to whom he bequeathed his power; these were of course the eponymous ancestors of Utigurs and Kutrigurs of Procopius' own day. Farther to the west were a people known as the Tetraxitae, whom Procopius says are a Gothic people but located far away from other Gothic nations.[110] While Procopius had noted that the Huns, Utigurs, and Kutrigurs may all be recognized as descendants of the Cimmerians, he says that the Tetraxitae "were called Scythians in earlier times since all of the nations who were controlling the lands in that region were in common called 'Scythian', some also being called

---

[107] *Wars* 4.10.13–29.

[108] Κιμμέριοι μὲν τὸ παλαιὸν ὠνομάζοντο, τανῦν δὲ Οὐτίγουροι καλοῦνται (*Wars* 8.4.8).

[109] Πάλαι μὲν Οὔννων, τῶν τότε Κιμμερίων καλουμένων, πολύς τις ὅμιλος τὰ χωρία ταῦτα ἐνέμοντο (*Wars* 8.5.1). Procopius tends to use the ethnonyms Huns, Massagetae, and Scythian interchangeably.

[110] Γότθοι οἱ Τετραξῖται καλούμενοι (*Wars* 8.4.9); πολλῷ δὲ αὐτῶν ἄποθεν Γότθοι τε καὶ Οὐισίγοτθοι καὶ Βανδίλοι καὶ τὰ ἄλλα Γοτθικὰ γένη ξύμπαντα ἵδρυντο (*Wars* 8.5.5).

Sauromatae-Σαυρομάται, or Melanchlainoi, Μελάγχλαινοι, or something else."[111]

All of these examples demonstrate that Procopius is still employing the rationalizing paradigm of genealogy, which locates foreign peoples within the Greco-Roman historical and ethnographic tradition and thereby confers a greater intelligibility upon them, irrespective of its dubious accuracy. While he continues the practice of ascribing genealogical origins to foreign peoples seen in classical texts, it is important to note that Procopius neither sees these origins as indicative of a certain moral quality nor represents them as a manifestation of an ancient threat. As will be argued at the end of this chapter and elsewhere, the relative lack of moral significance attributed to ethnic origins in Procopius exemplifies one of the greatest distinctions between Greco-Roman and Chinese historiography.

Also employing the framework of genealogy, the *Jin shu*'s preface to fascicle 97 on the Si Yi quoted above makes clear that the various barbarian peoples to be described therein are to be understood as descendants of those four archetypical non-Chinese peoples: the Yi, Di, Rong, and Man. Accordingly, the contemporary peoples inhabiting the four peripheral points of the compass are understood to fall into these four general ethnic categories. In a manner parallel to that of the preface to fascicle 97, the fascicle's colophon reiterates that barbarian peoples of ancient times are the ancestors of the various contemporary ethnic groups just described:

夷狄之徒，名教所絕，闚邊候隙，自古為患，稽諸前史，憑陵匪一. 軒皇北逐，唐帝南征，殷后東戡，周王西狩，皆所以禦其侵亂也.[112]

The people of the Yi-Di have refused the teachings of ritual hierarchies; they keep their eyes on the frontiers and wait for a breach, a source of trouble since ancient times. Examine all of the former histories – [the barbarians'] reliance on banditry has been constant. The Yellow Emperor drove them to the north; Emperor Yao campaigned in the south; King Zhou of the Shang defeated them in the east; the King of Zhou hunted them in the west. These were all efforts to prevent the barbarians' invasion and disruption.

The reader had learned from the preface, or had rather been reminded, that the world is divided between those who inhabit the civilized center and the barbarians without, who are characterized by a brutish existence.

---

[111] οἳ δὴ καὶ Σκύθαι ἐν τοῖς ἄνω χρόνοις ἐπεκαλοῦντο, ἐπεὶ πάντα τὰ ἔθνη, ἅπερ τὰ ἐκείνῃ χωρία εἶχον, Σκυθικὰ μὲν ἐπὶ κοινῆς ὀνομάζεται, ἔνιοι δὲ αὐτῶν Σαυρομάται ἢ Μελάγχλαινοι, ἢ ἄλλο τι ἐπεκαλοῦντο (*Wars* 8.5.6).

[112] *Jin shu* 97.2550.

This same lesson is reiterated in the concluding passage of the fascicle. By using the ethnonyms Yi and Di, the *Jin shu* connects the barbarians of the Jin-dynasty era with the enemies of both mythical and historical dynastic figures. This use of ancient ethnonyms differs from that adopted by Procopius in that it places an explicit and recurring emphasis on a conflict between barbarians and Chinese that is articulated in highly moralizing terms. When assigning a Cimmerian, Massagetan, or even Hunnic ancestry to the Utigurs and Kutrigurs, Procopius does so with an eye to their geographical origins in the lands to the north and east of the Black Sea and likely to their nomadic way of life on the steppe. Yet he does not represent these peoples as posing an ancient political, much less cosmological, threat to Roman or pre-Roman civilization.

As has already been observed in relation to the Woren said to descend from the Chinese figure Taibo, individual peoples receive their own genealogies as well. According to the *Jin shu*, the Chenhan 辰韓 "themselves say that they are descended from [Chinese] refugees who fled from the labor conscriptions of the Qin dynasty in the late third century B.C."[113] As testament to this claim, the *Jin shu* adds that "their language is similar to that of the people living in the area that constituted the heartland of the Qin state, and for this reason some people call them Qinhan 秦韓."[114] In this case, the genealogical paradigm is situated in historical times and, as with the example of the Woren, claims a certain affinity between the Chinese and this foreign people. It is interesting to note the discrepancy between the general notions of pan-barbarian (Yi, Yi-Di, Rong-Di, etc.) genealogy expressed in the preface and colophon and the particular genealogies attributed to individual peoples: while the barbarians in general are an inferior and hostile force to be kept under control and at arm's length, several peoples described under that very rubric are nevertheless granted genealogical connections with the Chinese.

As discussed above, the *Jin shu*'s fascicle 97 on the Si Yi notes in its preface that it will not treat the barbarian peoples who conquered parts of north China in the fourth and fifth centuries but will rather reserve this subject matter for the Chronicles section of the work. It is curious, therefore, that the Xiongnu are also included as descendants of the Northern Di 北狄 in fascicle 97. In contrast to the subsections for the Eastern Yi, Western Rong, and Southern Man, which discuss multiple peoples under each heading, the section of the fascicle dedicated to the

[113] *Jin shu* 97.2534
[114] 自言秦之亡人避役入韓 …言語有類秦人，由是或謂之為秦韓 (Ibid.).

Northern Di in fact only treats the Xiongnu. It notes that in the time of
the legendary Xia kingdom the Xiongnu were known as the Xunyu 薰鬻;
under the Shang, they were called the Guifang 鬼方; under the Zhou,
the Xianyun 獫狁; and under the Han, they were called Xiongnu.[115]
However, the *Jin shu* notes that as their particular characteristics and
customs have been treated in other histories, it will only provide a
summary of Xiongnu relations with the Chinese since the latter part of
the Western Han dynasty (c. 50 BC).[116] Perhaps their inclusion in the Si
Yi fascicle is attributable to the status of the Xiongnu as the archetype of
the northern barbarian in the Chinese imagination. As the last people to
be treated in fascicle 97, the contemporary history provided for the
Xiongnu provides a logical transition to the Chronicles section of the
Jin shu – the first of the barbarian states to be recounted in the Chronicles was founded by a Xiongnu chieftain. While ancestries are not
provided for all of the foreign peoples treated in the fascicle, the paradigm of genealogy as it is introduced in the preface and reiterated in the
final colophon nevertheless indicates its importance in the framing of the
ethnographic accounts in between.

Regarding the framework of geography-climate, there is only limited
interest in either text in explaining either physiognomical or ethical difference in geographical terms. There are several instances in the *Wars* where
Procopius describes the physical appearance of foreign peoples in an either
positive or negative light;[117] likewise, the *Jin shu* makes occasional remarks
on physiognomy and comments on peoples' robustness, ugliness, or
physical similarity to the Chinese.[118] Yet neither text goes beyond simply
commenting on these features, and they do not seek to explain any of them
as a result of climatic forces. While Procopius does describe various

---

[115] 夏曰薰鬻，殷曰鬼方，周曰獫狁，漢曰匈奴 (*Jin shu* 97.2548).

[116] 其強弱盛衰，風俗好尚，區域所在，皆列於前史 (Ibid.).

[117] For example, the Hephthalites are "the only Hunnic people who are fair complexioned and not
ugly in appearance": μόνοι δὲ Οὔννων οὗτοι λευκοί τε τὰ σώματα καὶ οὐκ ἄμορφοι τὰς ὄψεις εἰσίν
(*Wars* 1.3.4); Goths, Gepids, and Vandals are "all fair complexioned, blonde haired, tall, and good
looking in appearance": λευκοί τε γὰρ ἅπαντες τὰ σώματά εἰσι καὶ τὰς κόμας ξανθοί, εὐμήκεις τε
καὶ ἀγαθοὶ τὰς ὄψεις (3.2.4); to the west of Mauritania "are men not dark-colored like the Moors
but very fair complexioned and blonde haired": ἄνθρωποί εἰσιν οὐχ ὥσπερ οἱ Μαυρούσιοι
μελανόχροοι, ἀλλὰ λευκοί τε λίαν τὰ σώματα καὶ τὰς κόμας ξανθοί (4.13.29). The appearance
of the Sclaveni and Antae has been discussed above.

[118] For example, "the people [of Fuyu 夫餘] are strong and spirited": 其人強勇 (*Jin shu* 97.2532);
the people of Dayuan 大宛 "all have deep-set eyes and much facial hair": 其人皆深目多鬚
(97.2543); the people of Daqin 大秦 [sc. the Roman Empire] "are tall with an appearance similar
to the Chinese": 其人長大，貌類中國人 (97.2544); the people of Funan 扶南 are "all ugly and
dark with curly hair": 人皆醜黑拳髮 (97.2547).

geographical settings as part of his excursuses, he never explicitly draws a correlation between the nature of a given climate and the ethical qualities of the people who inhabit it.[119] Even in describing the land of Thule in the extreme north, Procopius notes that despite the remarkable primitivism of the Scrithiphinoi and the savagery of their practice of human sacrifice that he goes on to describe, "all the other peoples of Thule differ in no great respect so to speak from the rest of mankind."[120] Discussing the absence of the climatic paradigm as an explanatory factor in the *Wars*, Kaldellis has pointed out that the description of the poverty of Moors' lifestyle is juxtaposed with the luxury of the Vandals – the two opposite ways of life are thus seen to co-occur in the same geographical area, indicating that climate itself is not determinative.[121] There is not an explicit correlation between geography and physiognomy, nor is there any interest in explaining physical difference in terms of climatic variation.

The situation is somewhat more complex in the case of the *Jin shu* when it comes to the association of ethical disposition, geographical location, and climate. As discussed at some length in Chapter 1, particular regions and their corresponding ethnic categories were correlated not only with a number of specific ethnonyms but with also a relatively stable set of cultural, but mostly political, conditions. The relationship between the Chinese who inhabit the center and the various barbarian peoples who occupy the periphery in a subservient status is a recurring theme in the *Jin shu* – as is the basic assumption that these peoples have it as their inborn nature to revolt and plunder China when given the opportunity. In this sense, the geographical paradigm is very much in evidence in the *Jin shu*. The preface to fascicle 97 discussed above notes that mythical Chinese culture heroes had "delimited the marches in order to differentiate the distant regions and to separate the central and the external." This notion is even more explicit in the colophon of the fascicle, already quoted in part:

蹈仁義者為中寓，肆凶獷者為外夷，譬諸草木，區以別矣. 夷狄之徒，名教所絕，闚邊候隙，自古為患.[122]

---

[119] Cameron argues that Procopius' biases toward barbarians were heavily influenced by climatic theory, citing as the most illustrative example the ethnographic digression on the Sclaveni and Antae discussed above. Yet in this passage, Procopius does not make a single reference to the climate in which these people live, and his only remark on geography is that they inhabit most of the northern bank of the Danube. *Procopius and the Sixth Century*, 218.

[120] οἱ μέντοι ἄλλοι Θουλῖται ὡς εἰπεῖν ἅπαντες οὐδέν τι μέγα διαλλάσσουσι τῶν ἄλλων ἀνθρώπων (*Wars* 6.15.23). Cf. Procopius' representation of the Scrithiphinoi (*Wars* 6.15.16–22) with the Fenni of Tacitus, *Germania* 46.

[121] Kaldellis, *Ethnography after Antiquity*, 3.   [122] *Jin shu* 97.2550.

> Those who tread the path of benevolence and righteousness comprise the central region; those who flaunt their violence and ferocity are the outer Yi. Take the example of plants and trees: they can be distinguished by their different types. The people of the Yi-Di have refused the teachings of ritual hierarchies; they keep their eyes on the frontiers and wait for a breach, a source of trouble since ancient times.

The Chinese sphere, which is correlated with civilization, and the barbarian world characterized by violence and lawlessness are clearly conceived of in geographical terms. Indeed, the analogy is drawn between a region's influence on various ethical predispositions and the types of flora that are produced in different climatic zones. As in earlier Chinese texts, climate and geography are factors that determine not only the brutish nature of the barbarians but also their necessarily antagonistic relationship with the Chinese.

Along similar lines, the climatic aspect also appears in some of the Monographs in the *Jin shu* that prescribe certain types of behaviors or qualities for geographically correlated ethnonyms, referring by implication to the contemporary peoples who inhabit those regions. In particular, there are references to the ways in which different peoples are governed by astrological or astronomical bodies. For example, the Särbi-Xianbei, Wuhuan 烏丸, and Woqie 沃且 are governed by the four stars of the southeastern sky that are known collectively as Gouguo.[123] The *Jin shu* notes that when these four stars are under the influence of Yinghuo [sc. Mars], "the outer Yi revolt."[124] Four stars of the southern sky are known as Changyuan, and they are said to govern the frontier regions and the Hu barbarians, Hu-Yi 胡夷.[125] The *Jin shu* explains that "when Yinghuo enters among them, the Hu invade China; when Taibo [sc. Venus] enters among them, the nine ranks of ministers hatch plots."[126] Likewise, it is observed that when "Chenxing [sc. Mercury] moves to and fro rapidly, it generally controls the Yi-Di. It is also said that it is the star of the Man-Yi."[127] While it is clear from the above reference to the behavior of Chinese ministers at court that the motions of the heavens exerted an influence on Chinese and barbarians alike, it does seem to be the case that

---

[123] 東南四星曰狗國，主鮮卑，烏丸，沃且 (*Jin shu* 11.296). In similar fashion, the Dingling and Xiongnu, referred to collectively as Northern Yi, are governed by thirteen stars known collectively as Tianleicheng 天壘城: 主北夷丁零，匈奴 (11.305).

[124] 熒惑守之，外夷為變 (*Jin shu* 11.296).

[125] 南四星曰長垣，主界域及胡夷 (*Jin shu* 11.299).

[126] 熒惑入之，胡入中國；太白入之，九卿謀 (Ibid.).

[127] 辰星出入躁疾，常主夷狄。又曰，蠻夷之星也 (*Jin shu* 12.320).

the various barbarian groups are represented as essentially physical phenomena whose actions are governed according to the same laws as other
elemental forces. Particular *aspects* of Chinese society are influenced by the
stars; barbarian peoples are influenced by them *in toto*. The last-quoted
passage goes on to indicate that while Chenxing also governs the proper
functioning of the penal system, it is also correlated with earthquakes and
floods.[128] Incursions of barbarian peoples are thus analogous to other
natural disasters.[129]

Lastly, it should be noted that the *Jin shu* exhibits a particular interest in
the products typical of the geographical areas inhabited by foreign peoples,
since these products often comprised the articles of tribute that would be
brought to the imperial court. As stated in the preface to fascicle 97,
tribute relations were an essential component of Chinese foreign relations
in ancient times, and all relationships with foreign peoples assumed the
latter's tributary status – in theory if not in practice.[130] For example, it is
noted that the land of the Fuyu 夫餘 produces fine horses, mink and sable
pelts, and large pearls;[131] the Xiaoshenshi 肅慎氏 send stone arrowheads
to the Eastern Jin court;[132] the people of Dayuan 大宛 send fabled
"blood-sweating horses";[133] the people of Funan 扶南 even sent a trained
elephant, which the Eastern Jin emperor Jin Mudi 晉穆帝 (r. 344–361),
fearing that such an exotic beast might prove dangerous, had sent back.[134]
While Procopius does note aspects of climate and landscape that are an
inevitable part of his geographical and ethnographical digressions, these
details are not explicitly correlated with an ethnic group's customs, inherent qualities, or relationship with the Roman state.

The last of the three interpretative frameworks discussed in Chapter 1 is
that of history/historical change. In this case, both the *Wars* and the *Jin shu*
perpetuate the patterns of their classical precedents that were discussed
in Chapter 1: the *Wars* offers frequent examples of peoples changing

---

[128] 亦主刑法之得失. 色黃而小，地大動. 光明與月相逮，其國大水 (Ibid.).

[129] There is an analogy here with Procopius, even if the correlation is not so explicit: a comet appears
prior to a devastating "Hunnic" invasion across the Danube (*Wars* 2.4.1–6). Yet while he clearly
indicates that the comet is an omen, he does not suggest that tribal incursions are a result of
heavenly movements.

[130] For a brief introduction to the tribute system in ancient China, see Rossabi, "Introduction," 2–4.
Its importance in Chinese geographical-political thinking has its earliest detailed expression in the
Shangshu. See *Shangshu* 3, Xiashu 夏書, Yugong 禹貢.93–96.

[131] *Jin shu* 97.2532.   [132] *Jin shu* 97.2535.   [133] 汗血馬 (*Jin shu* 97.2544).

[134] 遣使貢馴象. 帝以殊方異獸，恐為人患，詔還之 (*Jin shu* 97.2547). References to the time
and frequency of tribute missions are the final notes for each of the peoples described in the *Jin shu*,
although the individual items are not always referred to. In the case of Daqin [sc. the Roman
Empire], it is said that a tribute mission was received at some point in the 280s.

significant elements of their cultural practices over a period of time, whereas the *Jin shu* tends to represent foreign peoples, while chronicling their migrations and interactions with China, in a comparatively static light.

Though Procopius does not always discuss the ways in which barbarian peoples have changed as a result of their contact either with Romans or other barbarians, this feature is nevertheless not infrequent in his ethnographic excursuses. For example, on introducing the Tzani who live at the eastern end of the Black Sea, Procopius describes how their way of life has undergone a radical change. Although they had been deceitful antagonists of Rome and Armenia in earlier times, Procopius explains that the Roman general Sittas managed to effect an enormous change upon them such that the Tzani,

> τήν τε γὰρ δίαιταν ἐπὶ τὸ ἡμερώτερον μεταβαλόντες ἐς καταλόγους αὐτοὺς Ῥωμαϊκοὺς ἐσεγράψαντο καὶ τὸ λοιπὸν ξὺν τῷ ἄλλῳ Ῥωμαίων στρατῷ ἐπὶ τοὺς πολεμίους ἔξίασι. τήν τε δόξαν ἐπὶ τὸ εὐσεβέστερον μετέθεντο, ἅπαντες Χριστιανοὶ γεγενημένοι.[135]

> transforming their lifestyle to one of a more civilized kind, were having themselves entered into the Roman conscription lists, and they have been setting out alongside the army of the Romans against [the Romans'] enemies ever since. They also transformed their beliefs in a more pious direction, having all become Christians.

The Tzani thus go from being adversaries of the Roman Empire and its allies to willing supporters. This change of political orientation is accompanied by a change of faith and an unspecified move toward a more refined way of life – a chauvinistic expression for moving more closely into the Roman political orbit.[136]

Even the people whose collective behavior is most commonly frowned upon by Procopius have the capacity to make significant ethical changes. The Heruli, at least one of whom was considered by Procopius to be remarkable for his sobriety and keeping of good faith,[137] turn out to be capable of improvement if conditions are favorable. When the emperor

---

[135] *Wars* 1.15.25.

[136] For a detailed discussion of Procopius' ethnography on the Tzani, see Maas, "'Delivered from Their Ancient Customs': Christianity and the Question of Cultural Change in Byzantine Ethnography," 160–69. One should not overemphasize the significance of conversion to Christianity in such contexts as providing a radically new framework for incorporation into the Roman community; the description of cultural changes among the Tzani is more reminiscent of Strabo's characterization of Romanization in the Iberian peninsula than it is redolent of Christian ideology. See above, 79.

[137] See the example of Pharas above, 141.

Justinian gives them land and property, he manages to win their allegiance and convince them to convert to Christianity.[138] Procopius describes the affect of the Heruli's alliance with Rome and their adoption of the Roman religion:

διόπερ τὴν δίαιταν ἐπὶ τὸ ἡμερώτερον μεταβαλόντες τοῖς Χριστιανῶν νόμοις ἐπὶ πλεῖστον προσχωρεῖν ἔγνωσαν, καὶ Ῥωμαίοις κατὰ τὸ ξυμμαχικὸν τὰ πολλὰ ἐπὶ τοὺς πολεμίους ξυντάσσονται.[139]

Therefore, transforming their lifestyle to one of a more civilized kind, they learned to come over to Christian laws to a great extent, and, for the most part, they take the field for battle alongside the Romans in alliance against [the Romans'] enemies.

It is true that the Heruli's capacity for change is undermined by Procopius' following assertions that, despite their conversion and alliance with Rome, they continue to be faithless, greedy, shameless, and sexually perverse. Indeed, he concludes the passage with a statement that the Heruli "are the most worthless of all mankind and, being wicked, they are wickedly forlorn."[140] Nevertheless, Procopius has demonstrated that even the Heruli are able to attempt some faltering steps out of barbarism: they fight for, as opposed to against, the Romans and give at least some heed to the laws of the Roman Christians.

A more successful case of barbarian transformation appears in the case of the Abasgi who live along the northeastern shore of the Black Sea. After noting the simplicity of their barbarian religion,[141] Procopius describes their practice of making eunuchs of the most beautiful of their young men, such that the Abasgi had become "wretched because of the deadly beauty of their children."[142] Yet both their pagan beliefs and this salient cultural practice are subject to change, for in the time of Justinian, Procopius notes that

ἅπαντα Ἀβασγοῖς ἐπὶ τὸ ἡμερώτερον τετύχηκε μεταμπίσχεσθαι. τά τε γὰρ Χριστιανῶν δόγματα εἵλοντο [. . .].[143]

it fell to the Abasgi in all respects to become restrained in a more civilized manner. For they took up the teachings of Christianity [. . .].

---

[138] χώρα τε ἀγαθῇ καὶ ἄλλοις χρήμασιν αὐτοὺς δωρησάμενος, ἑταιρίζεσθαί τε παντελῶς ἴσχυσε καὶ Χριστιανοὺς γενέσθαι ἅπαντας ἔπεισε (*Wars* 6.14.33).
[139] *Wars* 6.14.34.
[140] καί εἰσι πονηρότατοι ἀνθρώπων ἁπάντων καὶ κακοὶ κακῶς ἀπολούμενοι (*Wars* 6.14.36).
[141] Noted above, 141.   [142] παίδων θανάσιμον δεδυστυχηκότες εὐπρέπειαν (*Wars* 8.3.17).
[143] *Wars* 8.3.18–19.

The Abasgi, like the Tzani and even the Heruli, are shown to move toward a way of life that is "more civilized," ἡμερώτερον, by adopting Roman religion and abandoning practices that serve to distinguish them from other peoples. While exhibiting a self-assured sense of superiority in making such remarks, Procopius clearly recognizes that the cultural practices of a given people are dynamic and subject to influence and change.

Lest it appear that such instances are all examples of enthusiastic cheerleading for the civilizing influence of the Roman state, it should be noted that Procopius can also be cynical, in Tacitean fashion, of this very process.[144] For in the case of the Abasgi he notes, following his discussion of their conversion and abandonment of the practice of castration, that they did away with their own form of government under a native dual kingship and "were straightway seeming to live in freedom."[145] Procopius indicates here that a cultural shift toward Roman norms heralds the loss both of the Abasgi's ethical distinctiveness as well as their political independence. Irrespective of whether or not Procopius applauds or critiques the cultural and political influence of Rome on the barbarians, the important point is his acknowledgment, if not assumption, that peoples and their cultural traits are subject to change. The cultural and political identity of the Roman state does not seem dependent on a static and unchanging *barbaricum* against which it could be defined.

The *Jin shu*'s ethnography of the peoples comprising the Si Yi in fascicle 97 also chronicles historical interactions between China and various barbarian peoples, which often reach implausibly far back in time.[146] These interactions and the ethical qualities of individual ethnic groups remain, for the most part, characterized by continuity and stasis; there is usually little or no reference to ways in which their societies may have changed over time.[147] As discussed in Chapter 1, classical Chinese ethnography often makes use of references to a given people's *xing* 性,

---

[144] On the contradictions between empire and freedom in ancient historiography in general and Procopius in particular, see Pazdernik, "A Dangerous Liberty and a Servitude Free from Care," 73–126, 302–12.

[145] τούς τε βασιλεῖς ἄμφω Ἀβασγοὶ καθελόντες αὐτίκα ἐν ἐλευθερίᾳ βιοτεύειν ἐδόκουν (*Wars* 8.3.21).

[146] For example, the account of the Xiaoshenshi claims that they had sent tribute to China during the time of King Wu of Zhou, sometime in the mid-eleventh century BC (*Jin shu* 97.2535).

[147] In the case of the Tuyuhun, who migrated from the northeast to the northwest of China, the *Jin shu* indicates that even when a nomadic people had moved to an area with fixed habitations and agriculture, they continued to prefer their earlier lifestyle: "although they live an a land with walled cities, they do not dwell in them, but rather migrate in pursuit of water and grass; they use tents for their houses and rely on meat and dairy instead of grain": 然有城郭而不居，隨逐水草，廬帳為屋，以肉酪為糧 (*Jin shu* 97.2537).

"nature," and this tendency is prominent in the *Jin shu* as well. The preface to fascicle 97 has already been quoted, saying that it is the *changxing* 常性, "general nature," of the barbarians to obey China when it is ruled virtuously but to rebel and pillage when it is not. Elsewhere in fascicle, the Mahan 馬韓 are said to have a nature that is *yonghan* 勇悍, "courageous and fierce";[148] the nature of the Xiaoshenshi is *xionghan* 凶悍, "violent and fierce";[149] that of the Linyi 林邑 is also *xionghan* 凶悍;[150] that of the Funan is *zhizhi* 質直, "upright and straightforward."[151] Irrespective of whether these attributes are positive or negative, they are nevertheless seen to categorize a people in an essential and static way. Although the term *xing* 性 is also used to describe the specific character of individuals, both Chinese and barbarian, its employment in the collective description of entire peoples is analogous to its use to describe a species of the animal kingdom. As the eponymous ancestor of the Tuyuhun people remarks, "given that horses are domesticated beasts, for them to fight is their *general nature*," *changxing* 常性.[152]

Though the term *xing* is not used in the *Jin shu* in reference to the Xiongnu, the historical narrative tracing their interactions with the Chinese since the first century BC assumes that the Xiongnu as a whole remain a hostile force that has not been mollified by their proximity to the Chinese. For while the *Jin shu* makes clear that the Xiongnu had been in close contact with the Chinese for several centuries and that many of them were settled both along and inside the frontier and even among the Chinese population, there is no indication that they became any less dangerous a threat.[153] In fact, the *Jin shu* argues that the contrary is the case because of their closer proximity, a reality that would be borne out by the establishment of the Xiongnu Former Zhao 前趙 state in the early fourth century, whose commanders finished off the civil war–ravaged Western Jin dynasty and sacked the two ancient capital cities of Luoyang and Chang'an.

---

[148] *Jin shu* 97.2533.   [149] *Jin shu* 97.2535.   [150] *Jin shu* 97.2545.   [151] *Jin shu* 97.2547.

[152] 馬為畜耳，鬥其常性 (*Jin shu* 97.2537). While Roman authors do at times compare barbarians to animals to indicate ethical deficiencies, such practice is far from ubiquitous. To take as an example the fourth-century historian Ammianus, Wiedemann has observed that Ammianus just as often applies animal metaphors to Romans (emperors, the mob, senators, Christians, etc.) as he does to barbarians, and that "bestiality is not a special mark of non-Roman barbarians." "Between Men and Beasts," 201.

[153] The *Jin shu* states that by the end of the Han dynasty, the Xiongnu settled in the north were "largely the same as the registered [Chinese] population": 與編戶大同. Even so, "their population gradually grew until their numbers covered the north central part of the frontier and they eventually became difficult to control": 戶口漸滋，彌漫北朔，轉難禁制 (*Jin shu* 97.2548).

The closest Procopius comes to an equivalent of the Chinese term *xing*
性 is his use of the word *phusis*-φύσις, "nature," and he occasionally
employs this term to signify a quality or qualities associated with collective
groups. For example, when Procopius describes the Moors as being a people
most suspicious of others, he suggests that a person who is himself untrust-
worthy *by nature*, φύσει, will also be untrusting of others.[154] Though
Procopius does not explicitly refer to a collective nature of the Moors, it
is implied that the characteristic of being both faithless and suspicious
applies to them as a whole, just as it does to an individual Moor whose
nature it is to be so. Likewise, in a speech put in the mouths of Gothic
commanders who are exhorting their troops, the Romans are referred to as
"Greeks" who are cowardly by nature.[155] A speech of Frankish envoys to
the Goths argues that the Roman nation or race, τὸ Ῥωμαίων γένος, has
been faithless toward all barbarians, since it is inimical to them by its very
nature.[156] While Procopius is unlikely to have shared these estimations of
his own people's character, such ways of generalizing ethnically or politically defined communities do occasionally appear in the *Wars*.

But while these examples show that ethnic groups could at least on
some occasions be imagined to possess a fundamental nature or φύσις,
far more common in the *Wars* are references to a shared nature of
mankind.[157] In an address to his troops, the Roman general Belisarius
observes that "no human beings are by nature disposed towards others
either affectionately or the opposite," but rather it is their actions, πράξ-
εις, and congruence or divergence of their mindset, τῆς γνώμης, that
determine whether or not there will be peace or hostility.[158] The notion
of a common human nature appears when Procopius recounts the Goths'
criticism of a tactical error made by their king Totila. He notes that such
criticisms are the result not of barbarian fickleness (for they had not found
fault with Totila's strategy when the events seemed to be transpiring in
their favor), but rather of "what it is by nature for men" to do.[159]

---

[154] *Wars* 4.26.3.   [155] Γραικοί τε εἰσι καὶ ἄνανδροι φύσει (*Wars* 8.23.25).
[156] ὅλως δὲ ἄπιστον πᾶσι βαρβάροις τὸ Ῥωμαίων καθέστηκε γένος, ἐπεὶ καὶ φύσει πολέμιόν ἐστιν
(*Wars* 6.28.14).
[157] On human nature in Procopius, see Brodka, *Die Geschichtsphilosophie in der spätantiken
Historiographie*, 109–14.
[158] φύσει μὲν γὰρ οὐδένες τῶν πάντων ἀνθρώπων οἰκείως ἂν ἢ ἐναντίως ἀλλήλοις ἔχοιεν (*Wars*
4.15.22).
[159] οὕτω τοῖς ἀνθρώποις ἐμπέφυκε (*Wars* 7.24.28). Veh has also commented on the notion of shared
humanity in Procopius, although he attributes it not to classical cosmopolitanism but rather to the
Christianization of the empire. "Zur Geschichtsschreibung und Weltauffassung des Prokop von
Caesarea," 24.

Procopius concludes his discussion of the episode by asserting that such inconsistency of judgment will always be exhibited by human beings, "since it is by nature the wont of such things to happen."[160] This instance would seem to be a prime opportunity for Procopius to suggest that barbarians or Goths are either fickle or stupid by nature, but instead he merely observes that the Goths are characterized by the same nature as other men are. Totila himself argues the same point when he notes in a speech to the Goths that "by nature men do not seem to be different from one another in any great respect."[161]

The notion of a shared human nature common to Romans and non-Romans alike appears in other contexts featuring barbarian actors as well. In a letter sent by the Persian general Mermeroes to Gabazes, king of the Lazi, Mermeroes describes the attributes of power and wisdom that govern the relations amongst human beings, saying that

> ταῦτα οὐ παρὰ μὲν τῶν ἐθνῶν τισι σφίσι φέρεται οὕτως, παρὰ δὲ τοῖς ἄλλοις οὐ ταύτῃ πῃ ἔχει, ἀλλὰ ἀνθρώποις ὡς εἰπεῖν ἅπασι πανταχόθι γῆς τῆς οἰκουμένης ὥσπερ ἄλλο τι ἐμπέπηγε φύσει.[162]

> These things are not borne out thus for some nations alone while they are not so for others in the same way; but they are thus, so to speak, for all men in every part of the inhabited world, just as is anything else that is fixed by nature.

"Nature" can occasionally appear as a concept that explains an essential quality of either the Roman people or a barbarian nation; far more often, "nature" is a principle that does not serve to divide mankind into separate categories, but rather subsumes all peoples into a single entity.[163] While both historical works chronicle events transpiring in a context of intense political and military conflict, this practice differs markedly from the use of *xing* 性 in the *Jin shu*, where "nature" is understood not as a universal but as a particular phenomenon. Such usage necessarily assumes fundamental and essential differences between peoples that may be called on to reflect political antagonisms.

---

[160] ἐπεὶ καὶ φύσει γίγνεσθαι εἴωθε (*Wars* 7.24.30).

[161] φύσει μὲν γὰρ ἄνθρωποι οὐδέν τι μέγα διαφέρειν ἀλλήλων δοκοῦσιν (*Wars* 7.25.10). Pazdernik has discussed this speech and its intertextual relationship to a speech of Pericles in Thucydides in "Belisarius' Second Occupation of Rome and Pericles' Last Speech," 207–18.

[162] *Wars* 8.16.24.

[163] This point has also been observed by Veh: "Auch Pr. teilt die Vorstellung, wonach alles, was Menschenantlitz trägt, letzlich einer großen Familie angehört." "Zur Geschichtsschreibung und Weltauffassung des Prokop von Caesarea," 24.

Ethnography and the New Barbarians

The discussion thus far has demonstrated that not only is the notion of a barbarian antithesis perpetuated in the *Wars* and the *Jin shu* but also that the ethnographic modes and rationalizing frameworks developed in earlier antiquity were still viable for much later historians. This connection is critical to the broader aims of this study, as it intends to assess the ways in which traditional worldviews associated with the classical and high-imperial eras of ancient China and Greece-Rome adjusted to the upheavals of the mid-first millennium AD. As the authors of the *Jin shu* and the *Wars* both exhibit a great deal of continuity with classical texts in their employment of ethnography and their ethnological views, these two historical works allow us to explore how authors writing within the Chinese and Greco-Roman historiographical traditions responded to the ideological challenge of barbarian peoples and chieftains claiming to rule over parts of the fragmented empires.

Having established these continuities between the *Wars* and the *Jin shu* and their ethnographic precedents, we may now turn to the question of how this relatively stable set of ideas and approaches is applied to the barbarians of conquest states. For the material considered thus far represents the application of classical modes of thinking to a familiar subject, i.e., to the barbarians living in tribal communities either on the borders of the empire or serving as federate military units alongside imperial troops. But barbarian kings and emperors were a wholly novel phenomenon. Will we find the same degree of continuity in the representation the peoples who managed both to maintain a significant political coherence after moving into the empire and to carve out their own states of conquest?

In both texts, one notes a marked change in the subjection of the barbarian conquerors to the formal ethnographic gaze of the historian; for in neither case is there the same tendency to explain the rise of barbarian states by relying on the same rationalizing paradigms already discussed in Chapter 1. Instead, these peoples seem, to varying degrees, to have graduated into a new category that occupies something of a middle ground: they are distinguished from the barbarians of the past whose foreignness and alterity necessitated detailed description of origins, life ways, and geographical setting – yet they are still perceived as belonging to the barbarian world. The formal excursus in the Greco-Roman tradition, and the standard introductory passages that precede ethnographic description of foreign peoples in the Chinese tradition, are generally not applied to the Goths, Vandals, Särbi-Xianbei, Qiang, etc., although there are one or two exceptions to this general rule. But while detailed ethnographic accounts have been set aside, the paradigm of genealogy appears consistently in representations of the barbarian conquerors of the *Wars* and the *Jin shu*. As this section of the chapter will demonstrate, however, it is applied in significantly different ways.

Some may object to the lack of attention granted to the Persians in the discussion thus far. There are two reasons for this omission. First, the Persians as an independent political entity were hardly a new phenomenon in the sixth century, and the aim of this part of the study is to assess the ways in which newly established barbarian political entities were represented in an ethnographic context. The second reason, and related to the first, is the fact that Procopius simply offers little in the way of ethnographic observation on the Persians – far less than did Ammianus, for example, writing in the late fourth century. Procopius does not deem it necessary to comment on or explain Persian origins, life ways, or processes of social change. The Persians as a politically distinct entity were recognized as a people with a long history that was known to Procopius' audience and could be taken for granted, provided that the author was not interested in employing ethnographic discourse in the service of a broader rhetorical argument.[164] They therefore feature little in this discussion of the application of classical ethnological paradigms to politically *new* phenomena. Persia in the sixth century could fit comfortably into ancient conceptions of an antagonism between east and west; Procopius and his contemporaries were not faced with a new relationship when looking toward the east in the way that they were when confronted with Gothic control of the Italian peninsula. For Procopius, Sasanian Persia could easily be represented as a point of continuity with the past, not change, and this point is most clearly demonstrated by Procopius' lack of interest in subjecting the Persians to the ethnographic gaze. Indeed, he seems to consider the Persian Empire to be a fully legitimate state according to Roman criteria, noting that they live in a state, *politeia*-πολιτεία, organized according its own laws; in discussing the Persian succession, he notes that *themis*-θέμις, or customary justice, was a decisive factor.[165]

---

[164] On this point, see also Kaldellis who notes that the Vandals and Goths are also not given "full-fledged ethnographies"; *Ethnography after Antiquity*, 3.

[165] *Wars* 1.5.1. The reference to the Persian regime occurs in a remarkable account of the Hephthalite Huns, about whom Procopius says they have a "lawful state," πολιτείαν ἔννομον, and "engage rightly and justly with those near to them, no less than do the Romans and Persians": τοῖς πέλας ἀεὶ ὀρθῶς καὶ δικαίως ξυμβάλλουσι, Ῥωμαίων τε καὶ Περσῶν οὐδέν τι ἧσσον (*Wars* 1.3.5). As Kaldellis points out, Procopius implies a fundamental equivalence between the Roman and Persian

The same may not be said, however, for Procopius' successor Agathias. Agathias offers an extensive, and generally hostile, account of Persian culture and history, as well as a harsh critique of the Khosrow I Anoshirvan, even if he begrudgingly acknowledges the Great King's martial prowess.[166] Yet even Agathias was willing to praise Persia at Rome's expense, even if only when availing himself of the device of the reported speech. In a discussion held by the Lazi, who inhabited the eastern edge of the Black Sea and were perpetually an object of contention between Rome and Persia, one of their orators argues for a Persian alliance. Agathias writes that Aeëtes, "an excellent speaker more than is usually the case among the barbarians," pointed out many of the vices not only of Roman policy but also in the character of the Romans themselves.[167] Aeëtes accuses them of "impudence"; their emperor is "extremely wicked"; the Romans have committed "most unholy acts" against the Lazi; they have acted as though "full of savagery, madness, and hatred."[168] The Romans employ "deceitful gentleness" as they "commit injustice."[169] They are also guilty of cowardice and a "voluntary injustice has been added to those wicked by nature."[170] The speaker arguing for an alliance with Persia contrasts all of this with the loyalty and goodwill shown by the Persians to their allies. Unlike the Romans, the Persians "do their best to show kindness to those they have had as friends to begin with"[171]; likewise, the Persians are "honest," χρηστοί, and "magnanimous," μεγαλόφρονες.[172] Despite his above-noted hostility toward the Persians, the presence of such arguments in Agathias is yet another example of a consistent tendency in the Greco-Roman historiographical tradition to place the

---

states. Ibid., 18. This equivalency has also been noted by Revanoglou, Γεωγραφικά και εθνογραφικά, 247. For Procopius' treatment of the Persians, see Drijvers, "A Roman Image of the 'Barbarian' Sasanians," 72-73. Also see Maas, "The Equality of Empires," 175-85, which discusses Procopius' accounts of diplomatic relations between Rome and Persia. The most extensive study of relations with Persia in the age of Justinian is Börm's *Prokop und die Perser*. Although the deterioration of Rome–Persia relations after 540 shattered hopes of peaceful coexistence, Börm notes that Procopius' positive assessments of the Persians (alongside negative ones as well) were part of a broader trend in the eastern empire in the early decades of the sixth century. *Prokop und die Perser*, 326.

[166] The digression on Persian customs and the character of Khosrow appear in Agathias at 2.23-32 and conclude the second book of his history. Yet just prior to the digression, Agathias includes an encomium for the Persian commander Mermeroes, who is praised for his courage, tactical skill, endurance, and wisdom (Agathias 2.22.6). Greatrex offers a short comparison of Procopius' and Agathias' respective assessments of Persia accompanied by useful references. "Procopius' Attitude towards Barbarians," 333-34.

[167] ἦν γὰρ καὶ λέγειν δεινὸς πλέον ἢ κατὰ βαρβάρους (Agathias 3.8.8).   [168] Agathias 3.9.5–7.

[169] Agathias 3.9.12.

[170] τοῖς ἐκ φύσεως μοχθηροῖς τὸ αὐθαίρετον ἀδίκημα προστεθὲν (Agathias 3.10.1).

[171] φίλους τε γὰρ οὓς ἂν ἐξ ἀρχῆς κτήσαιντο, βεβαιότατα στέργειν πειρῶνται (Agathias 3.9.8)

[172] Agathias 3.10.11

sharpest critiques of imperial policies, often argued in high rhetorical style, in the mouths of barbarian speakers. Even in the work of an author perfectly at ease with anti-barbarian rhetoric, there thus remains a place for the imagined sentiments of the barbarians that expose imperial hypocrisy. Yet while Agathias is generally hostile to Persia, Procopius seems largely indifferent.

But to return to the employment of ethnographic description of barbarian peoples in the *Wars*, the barbarian rulers of the west are likewise largely exempted from interest or scrutiny. In fact, of the barbarian peoples who had established their own kingdoms following the dissolution of the western Roman Empire, only three figure in any prominence in the *Wars*: the Vandals, Goths, and Franks. This is because by the 530s, the Burgundian kingdom of southeastern Gaul had been absorbed by the expanding Franks in the north; by this time, the Franks had also taken control over former Visigothic territories in the southwest following the Frankish victory at the battle of Vouillé in 507. While the Visigoths would continue to rule the Iberian Peninsula until the Muslim invasions of the early eighth century, they are nevertheless remote actors in Procopius' narrative and receive little attention.

The fact that the prominence of roles played by different barbarian peoples in the text varies considerably is also not surprising given the theme of the *Wars* as a historical work: the campaigns waged by the Romans and the emperor Justinian against the barbarians of the east and west. Accordingly, of the four still-extant major barbarian realms in the west at the time of Justinian's wars of reconquest, only the Vandals, Franks, and Goths play a significant part in Procopius' narrative. The scope narrows even further, however, for the Franks occupy a much smaller role, given that it is only against the kingdoms of the Vandals and Goths that Justinian sent his armies. Accordingly, the Franks are also considered in a slightly different ethnographic light from that applied to the other two peoples, as will be shown below.

While books one and two of the *Wars* recount campaigns in the east against the Persian Empire, books three and four are concerned with Justinian's invasion of North Africa and the reconquest of Roman territories there.[173] As book three introduces the North African theater of the *Wars*, Procopius takes the opportunity to trace the origins of the enemies

---

[173] It should be noted, however, that the majority of book four is taken up with fighting against the Moors and Roman usurpers who contested Roman control of the region following the swift destruction of the Vandal kingdom by Belisarius in 534. Unlike the Vandals, however, the Moors did not establish a unified kingdom based in the regional capital Carthage.

of the empire, saying that "it will first be discussed whence the army of the Vandals fell upon the country of the Romans."[174] Procopius is explicit about the importance of explaining the existence of the Vandal kingdom by beginning with their origins, i.e., availing himself of the paradigm of genealogy. Before doing so, however, he first proceeds through a geographical excursus that describes the extent of the Roman Empire in ancient times before marking the limits of the eastern and western halves, which had been administered separately by the sons of Theodosius since that emperor's death in 395.

Procopius claims that Vandals, Goths, Visigoths, and even Gepids all fall into the same ethnic category and have common origins, perhaps simply because they all first became known to Romans while inhabiting lands north of the Danube. This collectivizing of western barbarians suits his statement in the opening lines of book three that "during the reign of Honorius over the Western Empire, the barbarians took control over his country."[175] Procopius then provides a genealogy and historical background for the peoples who are about to occupy the center stage of his narrative:

> Γοτθικὰ ἔθνη πολλὰ μὲν καὶ ἄλλα πρότερόν τε ἦν καὶ τανῦν ἔστι, τὰ δὲ δὴ πάντων μέγιστά τε καὶ ἀξιολογώτατα Γότθοι τέ εἰσι καὶ Βανδίλοι καὶ Οὐισίγοτθοι καὶ Γήπαιδες. πάλαι μέντοι Σαυρομάται καὶ Μελάγχλαινοι ὠνομάζοντο· εἰσὶ δὲ οἳ καὶ Γετικὰ ἔθνη ταῦτ' ἐκάλουν. οὗτοι ἅπαντες ὀνόμασι μὲν ἀλλήλων διαφέρουσιν, ὥσπερ εἴρηται, ἄλλῳ δὲ τῶν πάντων οὐδενὶ διαλλάσσουσι. λευκοί τε γὰρ ἅπαντες τὰ σώματά εἰσι καὶ τὰς κόμας ξανθοί, εὐμήκεις τε καὶ ἀγαθοὶ τὰς ὄψεις, καὶ νόμοις μὲν τοῖς αὐτοῖς χρῶνται, ὁμοίως δὲ τὰ ἐς τὸν θεὸν αὐτοῖς ἤσκηται. τῆς γὰρ Ἀρείου δόξης εἰσὶν ἅπαντες, φωνή τε αὐτοῖς ἐστι μία, Γοτθικὴ λεγομένη· καί μοι δοκοῦν ἐξ ἑνὸς μὲν εἶναι ἅπαντες τὸ παλαιὸν ἔθνους, ὀνόμασι δὲ ὕστερον τῶν ἑκάστοις ἡγησαμένων διακεκρίσθαι. οὗτος ὁ λεὼς ὑπὲρ ποταμὸν Ἴστρον ἐκ παλαιοῦ ᾤκουν.[176]

> There were many Gothic peoples in former times as there are now, the greatest and noteworthy being the Goths, Vandals, Visigoths, and Gepids. Indeed, in the past they were named Sauromatai and Melanchlainoi. And there are also those who call these same nations "Getan." For these peoples all differ from one another in their names, just as has been said, but in all other respects distinguish themselves in no way. For they are all fair of complexion and blonde of hair; they are tall and good looking in

---

[174] λελέξεται δὲ πρῶτον ὅθεν ὁ Βανδίλων στρατὸς τῇ Ῥωμαίων ἐπέσκηψε χώρᾳ (*Wars* 3.1.1).

[175] Ὁνωρίου δὲ τὴν πρὸς ἡλίου δυσμαῖς ἔχοντος βασιλείαν βάρβαροι τὴν ἐκείνου κατέλαβον χώραν (*Wars* 3.2.1).

[176] *Wars* 3.2.1–6.

appearance. They use the same customs, and likewise the same matters are observed by them in respect of the divine; for they are all of the Arian belief. There is a single language among them that is called Gothic. And they seem to me to be of old from a single nation, but later to have split off according to the individual names of their leaders. This people lived beyond the Danube River since ancient times.

Like other peoples introduced in the Wars, the "Gothic" groups who had conquered much of the western empire are given ancestors known in the time of Herodotus. Interestingly, however, Procopius does not refer to the Gothic peoples' ancestors as Scythians, but rather as Sauromatae and Melanchlainoi – peoples either living near the Scythians or related to them but not Scythians proper. This may be because the ethnonyms "Scythian" and "Massagetan" had come to be associated with the Huns and even more recently appearing peoples such as the Utigurs and Kutrigurs, as has been noted above. The avoidance of the Scythian ethnonym nevertheless seems to represent a conscious choice on the part of Procopius, since classical authors from the third to fourth centuries had themselves referred to the Goths as "Scythians."[177] By avoiding an association of Gothic peoples with the Scythian ethnonym – and preferring instead to assign them the Sauromatae and Melanchlainoi for their ancestors – Procopius marks a distinction between the Gothic peoples and other tribal groups to come from the same regions.

Also noteworthy is the fact that peoples who are of central importance to the *Wars* as enemies of the Roman Empire, the Goths and Vandals, are given ancestors of only marginal importance in ancient times. While the Scythians were a people whose primitive society could represent an opposite pole to the far more complex civilization of Egypt and an extreme of spirited barbarism in contrast to the balance of Greek rationality, the Sauromatae and Melanchlainoi are peoples of much less importance in classical texts.[178] By naming them the ancestors of the Gothic nations,

---

[177] Dexippus, who wrote in the 270s AD, referred to the Goths as "Scythians," Σκύθαι, as did Synesius of Cyrene some one hundred years later. For Dexippus' use of the term, see Christensen, *Cassiodorus, Jordanes, and the History of the Goths: Studies in a Migration Myth*, 233; for Synesius, see Cameron and Long, *Barbarians and Politics at the Court of Arcadius*, 109 ff.

[178] Amory ignores the significance of this choice of ethnonyms in his characterization of Procopius' "ethnographic ideology," which he detects in this passage. In order to support his interptretaion, Amory also skips over several sentences of text to append the phrase "they became the most savage of all men," γίνονται ὠμότατοι ἀνθρώπων ἁπάντων, to this ethnographic passage (*Wars* 3.2.11). In fact, the reference to a people becoming savage does not refer to the "Gothic" peoples collectively, but rather to the Visigoths alone after they had split from the rest, entered Italy, and found it undefended. Moreover, the use of the verb "became," γίνονται, indicates not a general quality, but rather a change as a result of particular circumstances. Procopius nowhere

Procopius gives these peoples of his own day an ancient pedigree that is relatively devoid of cultural or political significance but simply correlates with the known place of origin of Goths, Vandals, and others. As will be discussed below, this relative obscurity of the Gothic ethnogenealogy is markedly different from the symbolically loaded origin myths attributed to the barbarians in the *Jin shu*.

While noting that the Gothic peoples are also known as "Getan races," Γετικὰ ἔθνη, Procopius also associates them with the Getae, a people discussed at some length by classical authors such as Herodotus and Strabo. The Getae too are distinct from the Scythians, and while the Scythians are known for their hostility toward Greek and other foreign customs, the Getae are associated with the Greek philosopher Pythagoras through their mystical figure Salmoxis.[179] More than the Scythians, they are praiseworthy in the eyes of Herodotus, who describes them as "the bravest and most just of the Thracians."[180] While not as obscure as the Sauromatae and Melanchlainoi, the Getae are nevertheless not a people characterized by a particular hostility or savagery in the classical imagination.[181] Because of their habitations around the Danube in earlier centuries and the obvious orthographic similarity between the names Getae-Γέται and Goths-Γότθοι, the Getae serve as an additional ancient people from whom Procopius may trace Gothic origins.

Procopius also notes the physical distinctiveness of these peoples as he does with some other non-Romans in the *Wars*, commenting on their complexion, height, and hair color. He likewise notes their shared Arian faith, common language, and observance of the same laws. These details are of the sort typical of other ethnographic passages in Procopius and his predecessors. Absent from this formal ethnographic introduction, however, is any negative judgment passed on these peoples who would eventually take control of the western Roman Empire. As discussed below, this matter-of-fact presentation of "Gothic" peoples

---

suggests, as Amory claims, that "Gothic" physiognomy, "fierceness in war" (not even mentioned by Procopius), and Arian faith are "characteristics derived from their original habitation of one place, the Danube." *People and Identity in Ostrogothic Italy*, 141–42.

[179] I have discussed the distinction between Scythians and Getae in classical ethnography at length in a chapter in the forthcoming volume, *Historiographies of Identity, Vol. 2: Post-Roman Multiplicity and New Identities*.

[180] οἱ δὲ Γέται . . . Θρηίκων ἐόντες ἀνδρηιότατοι καὶ δικαιότατοι (Hdt. 4.93.1).

[181] Procopius is of course not the first historian to associate the Goths with the Getae, an association likely based on both the linguistic similarity of their names and their habitations along the Danube. On the Goth–Getae correlation, see Christensen, *Cassiodorus, Jordanes, and the History of the Goths*, 51, 232–34.

stands in marked contrast to the treatment received by the barbarian rulers in parts of the *Jin shu*.

After introducing the "Gothic" nations whose individual groups presumably trace their origins back to a shared line of descent, Procopius describes how the Visigoths broke off from the rest in the late fourth century and, since "good faith towards the Romans does not live among barbarians,"[182] became enemies of both the western and eastern divisions of the Empire under the leadership of Alaric. Visigothic atrocities are recounted as they move through Italy sacking cities and killing all they meet indiscriminately. At the end of this historical digression, Procopius notes that the Goths who ruled over Italy in his own day were at this time dwelling in Pannonia prior to settling in Thrace under imperial sanction. Procopius says that their deeds, however, will be related in the section of his history dedicated to them.

Having thus treated the origins of all "Gothic" peoples and narrating the Visigothic sack of Rome in 410, Procopius finally begins his historical narrative of the war against the Vandals. However, he offers little information on their specific prehistory, saying simply,

Βανδίλοι δὲ ἀμφὶ τὴν Μαιῶτιν ᾠκημένοι λίμνην, ἐπειδὴ λιμῷ ἐπιέζοντο, ἐς Γερμανούς τε, οἳ νῦν Φράγγοι καλοῦνται, καὶ ποταμὸν Ῥῆνον ἐχώρουν, Ἀλανοὺς ἑταιρισάμενοι, Γοτθικὸν ἔθνος.[183]

The Vandals living around Lake Maeotis, because they were oppressed by famine, set out to the Germanoi – who are now called Franks – and the Rhine River, joining company with the Alans, a Gothic people.

The entire migration of the Vandals from their homes east of the Don river is narrated in a mere two sentences, which state that the Vandals moved into the lands of the Franks, known as the Germanoi in earlier times, and associated themselves with the Alans, also considered by Procopius to be a "Gothic" people. The narrative quickly traces the Vandal migration into Spain where they are settled per an agreement between their leader Godigisclus and the emperor Honorius. At this point, Procopius shifts his attention to the quarrels between different

[182] οὐ γὰρ οὐδὲ βαρβάροις ἐνδιαιτᾶσθαι ἡ ἐς Ῥωμαίους πίστις [οὐδὲ has been substituted for οἶδε following Dewing's note] (*Wars* 3.2.7). This comment is the only place I have found in the *Wars* where Procopius attributes a stereotypically barbarian and negative trait, identified by him as such, to any of the "Gothic" peoples who entered the western provinces of the empire in large numbers. It is perhaps significant that it occurs in a description of events taking place over one hundred years prior to the contemporary events chronicled in the *Wars* and in reference to the Visigoths alone, a people who eventually settled in Spain and who, therefore, appear only sporadically in the text.

[183] *Wars* 3.3.1.

western Roman commanders that ultimately resulted in the invitation of
the Vandals into North Africa, where they seize power for themselves. In
providing this historical backdrop, Procopius has little to say regarding
events in Vandal early history. After he has provided the common origin
story for all the Gothic peoples discussed above, the story of the Vandals
simply begins with their emigration from Lake Maeotis and rapidly
follows their movements through Gaul and Spain until they establish
their kingdom in North Africa.

The prehistory of the Goths in book five is even more sparing in its
detail. The Goths who held Italy in the fifth and sixth centuries had
already been included under the larger category of "Gothic" peoples,
which also includes Visigoths, Vandals, Gepids, and even Alans. When
Procopius begins book five, and thus shifts his focus from the North
African to the Italian theater of the *Wars*, he has nothing to add about
their particular genealogy. In introducing the Gothic war ("I will now
come to the Gothic war, first relating however many things happened
both to the Goths and the Italians prior to the war"),[184] he instead
provides a history of the kingdom that only goes back to the 470s, which
saw the deposition of Romulus Augustulus in 476 and the establishment
of the barbarian Odoacer as king in Italy. He notes that the Roman
alliance with the Sciri and Alans, both identified by Procopius as
"Gothic" peoples, led to the barbarians' eventual usurpation of both land
and power in Italy.

It is at this point that Procopius turns to a history of the Goths proper,
whom he says were at that time settled in Thrace in accordance with a
former agreement with the empire. Although they had been engaged in
hostilities with the imperial armies of the east, the emperor Zeno urges the
Gothic ruler Theoderic to win a kingdom for himself in the west by
driving out Odoacer instead of making war against the eastern empire.
No other information is supplied regarding either the genealogy of the
Gothic royal family of Theoderic or their particular branch of the larger
"Gothic" family of peoples.

In sum, although a shared genealogy is provided for the Vandals and
Goths, there are scant indications that they exhibit a cultural distinctiveness that merits particular ethnographic description. Later in the *Wars*,
there are some scattered instances where Procopius does provide details
on Vandal or Gothic custom; for example, he observes that the Vandals

---

[184] ἐγὼ δὲ ἐπὶ πόλεμον τὸν Γοτθικὸν εἶμι, ἐπειπὼν πρότερον ὅσα Γότθοις τε καὶ Ἰταλιώταις πρὸ
τοῦδε τοῦ πολέμου γενέσθαι ξυνέβη (*Wars* 5.1.1).

prefer to fight only on horseback, using only swords and spears and foregoing the use of missile weapons.[185] In like fashion, he notes that while Roman troops, and their Hunnic contingents, are mounted archers, the Gothic cavalry use swords and spears while Gothic bowmen are deployed among the infantry.[186] However, these observations only occur in passing and are not imbued with any ethical or characterizing significance.

There is, however, one notable exception to this general rule, and that is the passage that describes the luxury of the Vandals in contrast to the poverty and hardiness of the Moors. When the Vandals and their king Gelimer are besieged on Mt. Papua by the Romans, Procopius observes that "of all the peoples we know of, that of the Vandals is the most decadent while that of the Moors is the most wretchedly poor."[187] He goes on to explain that the Vandals, following their conquest of North Africa, wasted themselves in excessive luxury, "spending every day in the baths and at a table overflowing with all things, whatever most sweet and good the earth and sea bring forth."[188] The Moors, on the contrary, "live in stifling tents during winter, the summer season, and every other time ... they have neither bread nor wine nor anything else that is good ... [and] they eat [their food] in a fashion no different from that of the other animals."[189] In this juxtaposition of two peoples destined to be defeated by Roman armies, Procopius follows the tropes of classical ethnography to represent their opposite, though ultimately shared, flaws of excess: the one people a slave to its luxuries and the other, while perhaps displaying a primitive frugality, nonetheless inferior to the Romans because of its extreme poverty and savagery.[190]

While in this passage it seems that the Vandals are subjected to the traditional ethnographic gaze, it has been observed that the practices that characterize the Vandals are stereotypically Constantinopolitan, i.e.,

---

[185] *Wars* 3.8.27.   [186] *Wars* 5.27.27–28.

[187] ἐθνῶν γὰρ ἁπάντων ὧν ἡμεῖς ἴσμεν ἁβρότατον μὲν τὸ τῶν Βανδίλων, ταλαιπωρότατον δὲ τὸ Μαυρουσίων τετύχηκεν εἶναι (*Wars* 4.6.5).

[188] βαλανείοις τε οἱ ξύμπαντες ἐπεχρῶντο ἐς ἡμέραν ἑκάστην καὶ τραπέζῃ ἅπασιν εὐθηνούσῃ, ὅσα δὴ γῆ τε καὶ θάλασσα ἥδιστά τε καὶ ἄριστα φέρει (*Wars* 4.6.6).

[189] Μαυρούσιοι δὲ οἰκοῦσι μὲν ἐν πνιγηραῖς καλύβαις, χειμῶνί τε καὶ θέρους ὥρᾳ καὶ ἄλλῳ τῷ ξύμπαντι χρόνῳ ... ἔχουσι δὲ οὔτε ἄρτον οὔτε οἶνον οὔτε ἄλλο οὐδὲν ἀγαθὸν ... οὐδὲν ἀλλοιότερον ἢ τὰ ἄλλα ζῷα ἐσθίουσι (*Wars* 4.6.10–13).

[190] The opposition between Vandals and Moors appears elsewhere, such as when the Moor Cabaon instructs his people to observe the abuses that the Vandals had committed against their Roman subjects and then do the opposite. The Moors thus become noble savages in opposition to the Vandals, who in their vices appear as decadent Romans (*Wars* 3.8.15–22).

Roman, indicators of excess.[191] The Vandals' devotion to luxury and refinement is also to be understood as a quality that postdates their entrance into the wealthy Roman world. It is curious then that in the only passage that really seems to consider either Goths or Vandals in an ethnographic light following the brief comments in the first introduction of "Gothic" tribal groups, one sees a people characterized by the wholesale adoption of behaviors not associated with tribes beyond the frontiers, but rather with the inhabitants of the rich cities of the empire. Procopius had noted that the Vandals had suffered from hunger in their original homeland, and one may assume that they lived a life of relative poverty prior to crossing the Rhine and entering Roman provinces. It is therefore interesting to observe that they are not distinguished by any traits typical of barbarian life north of the Black Sea; on the contrary, the Vandals have changed to become "Roman" to a fault.

The last of the three barbarian peoples to feature as a coherent political entity in the *Wars* is the Franks. It is important to repeat, however, that the Franks are not adversaries in Justinian's wars of reconquest; they are unreliable and opportunistic allies who, though their actions are of diplomatic and military interest to the historian, are nevertheless not granted the attention accorded to the Vandals and Goths, whose political destruction was the primary aim of the emperor's western campaigns. It is this difference in their role in the narrative, as peripheral rather than primary barbarian enemies, that seems to earn the Franks an ethnographic portrait differing from that accorded to the Goths and Vandals.

In a sense, the Franks are treated as barbarians in the traditional manner. At the point where they begin to play a significant part in the events of the Gothic war in book five, Procopius furnishes them with a genealogy, noting that "these Franks were of old named Germanoi."[192] After describing the limits of Europe and the territory of Gaul, Procopius then offers an early history of the Franks, whose ancestors the Germanoi, "a barbarian people not worthy of much account in earlier times,"[193] lived among the many lakes near the Rhine estuary. Procopius then describes how by the time of the Visigothic acquisition of Spain and Gaul west of the Rhone, a

---

[191] Kaldellis, *Ethnography after Antiquity*, 21. Conant offers three possible interpretations: Vandal decadence may be inspired by contemporary North African culture, Mediterranean urbanized lifestyles in general, or the historiographical trope of degeneration and decadence brought on by luxury. *Staying Roman*, 56–58. Also see Wood, "Being Roman in Procopius' Vandal *Wars*," 431–33.

[192] οἱ δὲ Φράγγοι οὗτοι Γερμανοὶ μὲν τὸ παλαιὸν ὠνομάζοντο (*Wars* 5.11.29).

[193] βάρβαρον ἔθνος, οὐ πολλοῦ λόγου τὸ κατ᾽ ἀρχὰς ἄξιον (*Wars* 5.12.8).

people known as the Arborychoi, formerly conquered by the Romans and employed as soldiers by the empire, were attacked by the Franks. As the Franks were unable to conquer the Arborychoi, they offered to intermarry with them, a process facilitated by the fact that both peoples were Christians. As a result, "coming together into a single people they markedly rose to a position power."[194] Interestingly, Procopius seems to dwell on the hybridity of the Franks: after noting their union with the Romanized Arborychoi, he goes on to explain how former Roman soldiers who had guarded the frontiers joined the Franks, now understood as a union between Germanoi and Arborychoi, while still maintaining their Roman military standards, military organization, and even manner of dress.[195]

Compared to the scarcity of genealogical background and prehistory Procopius provides for the Vandals and Goths, his treatment of the Franks stands out for its detail. But that is not the only way in which the Franks receive a greater amount of traditional ethnographic attention. In book six of the *Wars*, when Gothic and Roman armies are fighting one another in the north of Italy, the Franks disregard the pacts they had previously made with both peoples and invade Italy under the leadership of their king Theudibert.[196] Upon reaching the river Po, they begin sacrificing the women and children of the Goths whom they find there by throwing them into the river. Procopius explains their shocking behavior:

οἱ γὰρ βάρβαροι οὗτοι, Χριστιανοὶ γεγονότες, τὰ πολλὰ τῆς παλαιᾶς δόξης φυλάσσουσι, θυσίαις τε χρώμενοι ἀνθρώπων καὶ ἄλλα οὐχ ὅσια ἱερεύοντες, ταύτῃ τε τὰς μαντείας ποιούμενοι.[197]

For these barbarians, though having become Christians, maintain their religion of old in most respects: using sacrifices of human beings and performing other unholy rituals, making their prophecies in this way.

The Franks thus exhibit an incongruent mixture of semi-Roman origins and some of the most savage of barbarian practices. The only other peoples to whom Procopius attributes the practice of human sacrifice are the Heruli and various barbarians of the distant northern land of Thule.[198] One might expect that it would be the declared enemies of the emperor

---

[194] οὕτω τε ἐς ἕνα λεὼν ξυνελθόντες δυνάμεως ἐπὶ μέγα ἐχώρησαν (*Wars* 5.12.15).
[195] *Wars* 5.12.16–19.
[196] At this point Procopius appositely observes that the Franks "are the most wavering of all mankind when it comes to keeping faith": ἔστι γὰρ τὸ ἔθνος τοῦτο τὰ ἐς πίστιν σφαλερώτατον ἀνθρώπων ἁπάντων (*Wars* 6.25.2).
[197] *Wars* 6.25.10.
[198] For the Heruli, see *Wars* 6.14.1–2; for the peoples of Thule, see 6.15.24–25.

Justinian, the Vandals and Goths, who should exhibit such uncouth behaviors that would impugn their pretensions to rule over Roman territories. Yet these latter two peoples are instead largely, if not completely, exempt from the stereotypical representations that otherwise tend to characterize barbarian peoples, both in classical ethnography as well as in the *Wars* itself. In this case, Procopius differs considerably from Agathias, who picks up where Procopius' narrative breaks off in 552 and offers an extensive and surprisingly positive ethnography of the Franks. Agathias not only draws on ethnographic climatic theory in his depiction of the Franks as a northern people but also attributes to them a reputation for orthodox Christian piety, justice, and political order, claiming that they are scarcely different from the Romans themselves with exception of their strange language and clothing style.[199]

While Procopius does offer some ethnographic observations on "Gothic" peoples when he introduces them at the beginning of book three (physique, complexion, etc.), these characteristics are of a neutral sort and offer no indications of anti-barbarian prejudice or hostility on the part of the author. The closest Procopius comes to such sentiments appears in his account of the reign of the young Gothic king Athalaric, when he notes that some of Athalaric's Gothic subjects desire the young king to be raised "to virtue according to barbarian custom," i.e., in such a way that would allow them to abuse Roman citizens.[200] Yet even this instance is offset by the example of the Gothic queen Amalasuintha and the elder Gothic counselors whom she appoints to give the youth a proper Roman education.

Also rare in the *Wars* is any clear sense of inter-barbarian solidarity in opposition to the Romans. Despite the best efforts of a Frankish envoy to foster inter-barbarian sympathy and his claim that "the race of the Romans is faithless to all barbarians alike since it is inimical by nature," Procopius nowhere else suggests that there are any meaningful ethnological ties between barbarian groups.[201] For elsewhere, Justinian convinces the Franks to enthusiastically support him against their shared Gothic enemy

---

[199] Agathias' lengthy ethnography of the Franks appears at 1.2.1–8. As noted by Greatrex, this contrast between Procopius' and Agathias' respective ethnographies of the Franks is likely the result of changing political conditions over the course of the sixth century. "Procopius' Attitude towards the Barbarians," 334.

[200] ἀρετὴν κατά γε τὸν βάρβαρον νόμον (*Wars* 5.2.17). Procopius explains that "in their desire of injustice against their subjects, they wanted to be ruled by him in a more barbarous way": τῆς γὰρ ἐς τοὺς ὑπηκόους ἀδικίας ἐπιθυμίᾳ βαρβαρικώτερον πρὸς αὐτοῦ ἄρχεσθαι ἤθελον (*Wars* 5.2.8). On this episode, see Goltz's recent study, "Anspruch und Wirklichkeit," 291–95.

[201] *Wars* 6.28.14. This passage was noted above, 170.

with an appeal to their common Catholic faith;[202] and Vitigis does not hesitate to name the "Franks ancient enemies of the Goths."[203] It seems that such appeals to a putative barbarian solidarity would have been far too incongruous with sixth-century realities for Procopius to use them even as a literary trope, given the fact that different peoples were fighting on all sides of the conflict, irrespective of their ethnic backgrounds.[204] Procopius is clear that Goths, Vandals, and Franks are barbarians and, therefore, may be represented in opposition to the Romans. But the dichotomous arrangement that appears in Procopius' introduction to the work, a self-consciously Herodotean pitting of Romans against a pan-barbarian Other, was too fraught with the complexities of actual political allegiances to be applied with any consistency throughout the work.

To summarize, the primary barbarian enemies of the *Wars* – the Vandals, Goths, and even Persians – are largely exempt from the ethnographic gaze.[205] On introducing the various "Gothic" peoples that include the Goths and Vandals, Procopius makes several remarks on their physiognomy and social practices (their shared laws and profession of the Arian Christian faith), but these details do not lend a moral coloring to the overall representation; Procopius does not suggest an ethical approval or disapproval of any "Gothic" characteristics. Also noteworthy is that of the three ethnographic paradigms observed in classical and even late antique texts, only that of genealogy is applied to the barbarian rulers of the west to any significant degree. While Vandals and Goths are attributed a shared ethnogenealogy connecting them to peoples known in earlier centuries to inhabit regions around and north of the Danube, Procopius exhibits little interest in describing whatever cultural traits, if any, may be inferred from such an association. Moreover, while he does represent the Franks as likely to commit atrocities in accord with their barbarian customs, the Goths and Vandals are free from any such practices that may be correlated with non-Roman origins. While one might suggest that this ethnographic exemption

---

[202] *Wars* 5.5.8–9. As noted above, Procopius does not have a high opinion of Frankish "orthodoxy."

[203] οἷς ἐκ παλαιοῦ πολεμίοις οὖσι (*Wars* 5.13.19).

[204] There is at least one instance, in a speech attributed to Vitigis, where Procopius suggests at least an intra-Gothic solidarity: Vitigis claims that death or loss of life is of little consequence as long as a fellow Goth should take his place, i.e., one of his fellow countrymen. *Wars* 5.29.5–8.

[205] While the absence of ethnographic observations may to a degree be related to familiarity, i.e., the fact that these groups were known quantities to author and audience at this point, centuries of contact did not preclude a lengthy ethnographic digression. As noted above, Agathias includes a long, and quite hostile, assessment of the Persians in his history. A historian's employment of the ethnographic mode, therefore, has just as much to do with rhetorical strategy as it does with providing accounts of the exotic.

may be analogous to the *Jin shu*'s omission of ethnographic digressions on barbarian conquest regimes to be discussed below, a critical difference is that the barbarian conquerors in China are rhetorically assimilated to barbarians of the ancient, pre-imperial past in symbolically potent terms.

Also lacking in the *Wars* is a sense that the barbarians somehow formed a conceptually coherent, collective entity in opposition to the Romans, despite the fact that the work is introduced as an account of Justinian's wars against the barbarians of the east and west. Procopius does not provide a narrative that is contextualized as an ancient antagonism between Roman civilization and the forces of chaos that, while perhaps individually distinct from one another, may ultimately be reduced to a monochrome category that threatens, while it defines, the Roman world order. Although the blanket term "barbarian" is indeed used to indicate a distinction between Romans and all others, the term "barbarian" itself had, by the sixth century, ultimately come to signify those who were not politically identified with the Roman emperor and state.[206] Other than this crucial distinction, its use in the *Wars* indicates little in the way of an essential or irreconcilable opposition between the civilization of the empire and the savagery of the barbarians. This is most clearly exhibited in the treatment of the Vandals and Goths who, beyond being labeled as barbarians, scarcely exhibit anything like a "barbarian" nature.

Having considered the ethnographic representation of the new barbarians in the *Wars*, we may now turn to the *Jin shu*. However, it will first be necessary to reiterate some fundamental ways in which the *Jin shu* differs from the *Wars* in terms of the organization of its contents. As discussed above, the *Jin shu* follows the general form of the Chinese dynastic history as established by the historians Sima Qian and Ban Gu in the first centuries BC and AD. Accordingly, it is composed of Basic Annals, Monographs, and Biographies. Yet one of the reasons the *Jin shu* is particularly suitable for the exploration of worldviews and mentalities of early Tang China as they are expressed in the ethnographic discourse of the period is because the *Jin shu* adds a new component: the Chronicles, *zaiji* 載記. The Chronicles treat the establishment of barbarian conquest states within the former empire, a new phenomenon in Chinese imperial history. Whereas the *Wars* is a work focused on the classical topic of Greco-Roman

---

[206] Greatrex, "Roman Identity in the Sixth Century," 274. For an argument not only against this definition but also the assumption that adherence to Orthodox Christianity was equivalent to Roman identity in Byzantium, see Kaldellis, *Hellenism in Byzantium*, 75. On sixth-century Roman identity, also see Moore, "Constructing 'Roman' in the Sixth Century," 115–40.

historiography, i.e., the war narrative and its *res gestae*, the Chronicles of the *Jin shu* comprise only one section of a larger work, and they are deliberately placed last in accordance with the traditional practice of putting narratives dedicated to barbarian peoples amid the final fascicles of a dynastic history.

The term *"zaiji"* was not wholly new; it was actually borrowed from the *Dongguan hanji* 東觀漢記, a historical work compiled by the Han dynasty historian Ban Gu and others. In the *Dongguan Hanji*, there is only a single *zaiji* fascicle (fascicle 23) that contains accounts of the various illegitimate regimes established following the collapse of Wang Mang's 王莽 short-lived Xin 新 dynasty in AD 23.[207] Nevertheless, in the *Jin shu* the category of *zaiji*, i.e., Chronicles, takes on a new significance, since they contain the accounts of the barbarian states that ruled over parts of north China from the early fourth century to the mid-fifth century in the period known as that of the Sixteen Kingdoms.[208] An often overlooked fact, which it is important to point out, is that of these sixteen states, two were ruled by indisputably Chinese royal houses and are therefore considered to have been "Chinese" states: the Former Liang 前涼 and the Western Liang 西涼. A third dynasty to rule part of the northeast, the Northern Yan 北燕, is either identified as being a Chinese or barbarian state; at any rate, there is no doubt that the Northern Yan royal family represented itself as a scion of the Särbi-Xianbei Later Yan 後燕; even if its ruling house was not of Särbi-Xianbei origin, its political tradition was.

It is therefore significant that of the sixteen states for which histories are provided in the *Jin shu*, only *fourteen* are actually recounted in the Chronicles; the remaining two regimes, those considered by Tang historians to have been ruled by indisputably Chinese sovereigns, are instead treated in the Biographies section of the work. The explanation for this difference in organization is simple: the Chronicles serve as a new category for the recording of barbarian political history, and the two Chinese regimes that ruled independent kingdoms in northern China in this period are therefore exempted from inclusion therein.

---

[207] Rogers, *The Chronicle of Fu Chien*, 16–17, and ibid., nn. 100 and 101.

[208] The term "Sixteen Kingdoms" is itself quite arbitrary, as the total of short-lived states that were established in northern China in this period exceeds this number – Corradini has identified a total of forty-one states to appear in this period. "The Barbarian States in North China," 166–71. The period derives its name from the work of the lost work of Cui Hong 崔鴻 (478–525), the *Shiliu guo chunqiu* 十六國春秋, *Spring and Autumn Annals of the Sixteen Kingdoms*, in which he recognized only sixteen of these competing states as meeting his criteria for inclusion in his work: sufficient length of reign and the production of a national history. See Han, "Bei Wei shiqi 'Shiliu guo shi' zhuanshu de shixue chengjiu," 77.

The Northern Yan poses an interesting test of this theory. Its founder, Feng Ba 馮跋, is said to have been of Chinese ancestry.[209] Yet there remain reasons to argue that the Northern Yan, despite the Chinese ancestry of its founder, is included in the Chronicles on ethnic grounds. First of all, the Northern Yan emphasized its continuity with the previous Särbi-Xianbei regimes of the Murong 慕容 clan; the *Jin shu* states that on Feng Ba's taking the throne, "he nevertheless did not change the former name [of the state], and thus his realm was called Yan."[210] Moreover, in overseeing the funeral for the last emperor of the Later Yan, Gao Yun 高雲 (also known as Murong Yun 慕容雲, whom Feng Ba had himself formerly placed on the Later Yan throne), Feng Ba intimately associates himself with Gao Yun: "my relationship with Gao Yun is that of a minister to a lord in terms of duty, and it surpasses that of younger brother to elder brother in terms of affection."[211] Feng Ba also had an ancestral temple built for Gao Yun and arranged for offerings to be made there each season of the year.[212] Moreover, while the chronicle of the Northern Yan is placed in the same fascicle as that of the Särbi-Xianbei Western Qin 西秦 state, it nevertheless has its own *lun* colophon which, like so many of the others, begins by situating its assessment of the regime in the context of barbarian invasions (this particular passage will be discussed below).

The case of the Northern Yan thus demonstrates *e contrario* that even if the lineage of the state's ruling house was not a barbarian one, the fact that its own political ancestors *were* barbarians automatically conferred the status of barbarian usurpation and illegitimacy on it.[213] By contrast, the only two Chinese states that dared to lay claim to rule parts of the north have their histories told in the Biographies part of the *Jin shu* rather than among barbarian usurpers. The Chronicles, which make up the last thirty fascicles of *Jin shu*, are thus a separate category especially for the barbarian states, which are all deemed illegitimate. That these barbarian regimes were seen in such a light is made abundantly clear in the preface to the Chronicles as well as in many of the individual colophons that will be discussed below.

Scholars who ignore this relatively obvious ethnic categorization have proposed other theories as to why the Chinese states of Former Liang and

[209] *Jin shu* 125.3127.   [210] 而不徙舊號，即國曰燕 (*Jin shu* 125.3128).
[211] 吾與高雲義則君臣，恩踰兄弟 (*Jin shu* 125.3129).   [212] Ibid.
[213] It is worth pointing out the contrast here with the "Chinese" Sui dynasty, which replaced the Särbi Northern Zhou in the late sixth century. In that case, a new dynasty was proclaimed; in the case of the Northern Yan, its founder Feng Ba had claimed to *restore*, not replace, the Murong Särbi state of Yan.

Western Liang should be exempted from inclusion in the Chronicles. It has been noted in the case of the Former Liang that one of its rulers declared himself emperor in 354 and established a new regnal era.[214] He himself was murdered the next year, and his successor gave up the imperial title and also dispensed with the recently proclaimed regnal era and reverted to the regnal era of the Western Jin that was now in its forty-third year (建興四十三年), thereby pledging his allegiance to the Western Jin dynasty, which had fallen some forty years earlier.[215] Therefore, although the Former Liang lasted from 314 to 376 in a state of de facto independence, it was only in outright rebellion for one of those years. The prevailing explanation as to why the Former Liang was not included by the Tang historians in the Chronicles is because this lapse of loyalty toward the Western Jin was so fleeting.[216] Nevertheless, at least one modern scholar does in fact note that there was really not much difference between the Former Liang and the other barbarian kingdoms in political terms.[217] Yet the fact that its Chinese identity might be the reason the Former Liang is exempted from the Chronicles, the category of illegitimate usurpers, is not considered.

The case of the other state not to be included in the Chronicles but rather placed in the Biographies section of the *Jin shu*, the Western Liang, has a simpler explanation: the Western Liang's royal family had the surname Li 李, the same as that of the Tang royal house. The early Tang emperors, themselves of at least semi-barbarian ancestry, traced their lineage back to this very family.[218] Moreover, as Ma notes, the Western Liang family was, after all, Chinese.[219] Therefore, despite the fact that the

---

[214] The establishment of a new regnal era according to which the calendar was reckoned was solely the prerogative of the ruling dynasty. New regnal eras "were frequently inaugurated to mark a new beginning for political reasons, often on the occasion of an auspicious astronomical sign or splendid event such as a military victory, and always as an affirmation of the sovereignty of the ruler." Wilkinson, *Chinese History: A Manual*, 182.

[215] The episode is recounted at *Jin shu* 86.2245–48. The case of the Former Liang's allegiance to the Western Jin is discussed in Ma Tiehao, "*Jin shu* zaiji de zhengtongguan ji qi chengyin," 25–27, and Rogers, *The Chronicle of Fu Chien*, 9–13.

[216] As noted by Ma, this logic is problematic, since the Former Liang, by perpetuating the regnal era of the Western Jin, failed to recognize the legitimacy of the Eastern Jin, which had succeeded it. For a discussion of the Former and Western Liang's inclusion in the Biographies as opposed to the Chronicles section of the *Jin shu*, see Ma Tiehao, "*Jin shu* zaiji de zhengtongguan ji qi chengyin," 25–27.

[217] Ibid., 26.

[218] Doubt has been cast upon this genealogical claim in both the seventh and twentieth centuries, and modern scholars recognize it as a fabrication of the early Tang. On this point, see Chen, Sanping, *Multicultural China in the Early Middle Ages*, 4–14; Ma Tiehao, "*Jin shu* zaiji de zhengtongguan ji qi chengyin," 26–27.

[219] 且为汉人. Ibid., 25.

Western Liang made no show of allegiance to the Eastern Jin, and its first ruler both took the imperial title and established his own regnal era on assuming power, the Western Liang is, nevertheless, not included among the barbarian states treated in the Chronicles. If one acknowledges the prominence of ethnicity in the discourse of political legitimacy in the early Tang, the reasons for the exoneration of the Former Liang and Western Liang become far more clear.[220]

Yet if the missing taint of ethnic barbarian origins were not enough to explain the exemption of the Former and Western Liang states from inclusion in the Chronicles, the preface to the Chronicles and the *lun* colophons appended to accounts of the various conquest dynasties make perfectly clear that these last thirty fascicles of the *Jin shu* are to be understood as a record of the disaster that began with the claim of a Xiongnu chieftain to the title of Son of Heaven. The preface to the Chronicles begins in a manner similar to that of *Jin shu* fascicle 97 on the Si Yi, the Four Barbarians:

古者帝王乃生奇類，淳維，伯禹之苗裔，豈異類哉？反首衣皮，餐羶飲湩，而震驚中域，其來自遠. 天未悔禍，種落彌繁. 其風俗險詖，性靈馳突. 前史載之，亦以詳備.[221]

The ancient emperors gave birth to a strange race: the offspring of Chunwei and of the Great Yu; is this not a different race of beings? They wear their hair loose and wear skins; they eat sheep meat and drink milk. Moreover, they shock and terrify the central regions; their place of origin is far away. Heaven has not regreted the disaster; their tribes grow and proliferate. Their customs are treacherous and wicked; their nature is agile and they gallop swiftly. Earlier histories give an account of these things and have recorded them in detail.

The preface introduces the accounts of barbarian states with Chunwei 淳維, the mythical ancestor of the nomadic Xiongnu discussed in Chapter 1. It was the Xiongnu who posed the gravest military threat to the Han dynasty and around whom the sense of a barbarian archetype antithetical to Chinese civilization crystallized as early as the early first

---

[220] It has also been observed by Honey that there is a markedly more positive tone in the treatment of the Former Liang. "History and Historiography on the Sixteen States," 168. Ma Tiehao observes this difference as well, yet he curiously reads it as an emphasis on the "distinction between legitimate and illegitimate," 正偽之別, rather than between Chinese and barbarian. "*Jin shu* zaiji de zhengtongguan ji qi chengyin," 26.

[221] *Jin shu* 101.2643. For an alternative translation of the entire preface with extensive commentary, see Honey, "History and Historiography on the Sixteen States," 175–83.

century BC.[222] As in the examples below, there are references here both to ethnographic details of barbarian life as well as tropes associated with the northern barbarian: perfidy, particulars of the nomad economy, and superior employment of cavalry in warfare.[223] Right from the start, the barbarian threat is represented in terms of foreign practices and an ethnogenealogy that ultimately connects the barbarians to the Chinese of the mythical past but does so via the greatest enemy to face the first unified Chinese empire. These opening lines of the preface to the Chronicles, beginning with this ethnogenealogy and then listing ethnographic particulars of nomadic life, stands in contrast to the simpler preface of the *Wars* as a whole. Paraphrasing Herodotus, Procopius tells the reader that the following narrative will be a war between Justinian and the barbarians of the east and west. The *Jin shu* is much more specific: not only do we know from whom the barbarians are descended; we also know what they eat, how they dress, and that they are essentially the same ones who have been threatening China since time immemorial.

Such a coherent image of the barbarian world is absent in the *Wars*. It is true that the Goths and Vandals are ascribed a shared ancestry by Procopius, and they are both peoples who have taken control of western Roman regions. Yet the Franks too are a major barbarian power, but they are left wholly outside of the larger "Gothic" family – not to mention the Persians who, referred to as barbarians throughout, have no association with the peoples of the far north and west. The *Jin shu* thus presages its forthcoming accounts of barbarian conquest states by reducing them in their entirety to a much more clearly defined, monolithic, and opposite pole to Chinese civilization. The ethnogenealogy embracing all barbarian peoples as descendants of Chunwei and the ancient ancestors of the Xiongnu has more in common with the biblical schema of a cursed line descending from Cain than it does with the diverse and polycentric barbarian world found in Procopius.

The preface to the Chronicles goes on to recount events from the earliest age in Chinese mythology: the time of the Yellow Emperor himself,

---

[222] See Di Cosmo for a discussion of the Xiongnu genealogy going back to Chunwei, *Ancient China and Its Enemies*, 297–304; for the notion of the Xiongnu as an antithesis to Chinese civilization, see ibid., 304–06. Honey offers an opposite analysis of the function of this genealogy, claiming that it served to soften "the abrasiveness of the contemptuous tone of these accounts, and directed this abuse to the nomad's behavior, not their race." "History and Historiography on the Sixteen States," 171.

[223] Honey has provided a study on four such *topoi* that he sees employed in the *Jin shu* Chronicles: the *topos* of common ancestry, of moral efficacy, of nomad greed, and of nomad disloyalty. "History and Historiography on the Sixteen States," 169–74.

with whose era the foundational work in Chinese historiography, Sima Qian's *Shiji* 史記, begins. The *Jin shu* states that there has been constant conflict between the Chinese and this other branch of human kind:

> 軒帝患其干紀，所以徂征; 武王竄以荒服，同乎禽獸。 而於露寒
> 之野，候月覘風，覘隙揚埃，乘間騁暴，邊城不得緩帶，百姓靡有
> 室家. 孔子曰: 「微管仲，吾其被髮左衽矣.」此言能教訓卒伍 [...].²²⁴

The Yellow Emperor was troubled by their lawlessness and began to fight them; King Wu scattered them to the outermost wastes where they lived as birds and beasts. Then in the exposed cold of the wilderness they watched the moon and gazed upon the wind, waiting for a chance to kick up dust, to seize a breach where they could exert their violence. The border fortresses could not relax their belts, and the common people lost their homes. Confucius said, "Were it not for Guan Zhong, we would all be wearing our hair loose and fastening our clothes on the left." This statement serves as a principle of instruction for our troops [. . .].

There are several aspects of this passage that are familiar at this point. First, the Yellow Emperor, mythical progenitor of the Chinese people and their first sovereign, is shown here in conflict with the barbarians who live like animals beyond the pale of civilization. The Zhou dynasty monarch King Wu, who is thought to have ruled in the eleventh century BC, is shown expelling them from the Chinese heartlands. As Procopius alludes to Herodotus and Thucydides in his preface, so the *Jin shu* includes a direct quotation from Confucius that further serves to represent the wars of barbarian invasion and conquest in fourth to fifth-century AD China as a later manifestation of the ancient pan-Chinese struggle against barbarian encroachments onto the Central Plains. The quotation is in reference to a seventh-century BC Chinese statesman, Guan Zhong, who urged his lord to come to the aid of another Chinese state being invaded by barbarians from the north, an early expression of inter-Chinese solidarity against foreign peoples. Had the Chinese not ignored their internecine rivalries in the face of the external threat, Confucius warns, the rules of propriety essential to Chinese civilization would have been confounded.²²⁵ While Procopius presents his narrative in terms of a conflict between these two sides of humanity, perhaps implicitly from time immemorial but more likely only since the fifth-century BC Persian wars, the preface to the Chronicles is much more explicit. For the *Jin shu* describes an even more

---

²²⁴ *Jin shu* 101.2643.
²²⁵ On Guan Zhong featuring as a Chinese hero in the face of barbarism, also see above, 43, 117, 150.

ancient opposition, beginning in mythical times, between the Chinese and the northern nomads who were expelled by the progenitors of the Chinese people to the wastes of the north and who have pillaged and plundered China ever since.

Moreover, the reiteration in the preface to the Chronicles of many of the rhetorical figures present in the preface to fascicle 97 on the Si Yi of the barbarian periphery indicates that the conquest states are to be understood in the same context. For example, in both cases the *Jin shu* refers to the collective *xing* 性, "nature," of the peoples described that sets them apart from the Chinese. Honey has argued that the "historiographical outlook" of the *Jin shu* involved treating "the nomadic barbarians rather carefully; conduct, not race, was the focus of criticism."[226] Yet this interpretation, while it may pertain to the narrative sections of the individual states, is clearly not valid for those sections of the *Jin shu* that may be attributed with confidence to the historians of the early Tang, i.e., the preface to the Chronicles and the various *lun* colophons to the accounts of individual regimes. The usage of a collective *xing* for the non-Chinese is clearly not to be understood as a reference to conduct or culture; as the *Lüshi chunqiu* 呂氏春秋 makes quite clear, "*xing* 性 is that which is received from Heaven; it is not something that can be chosen and thus put into practice."[227] What is being described with the use of *xing* is an immutable and essential difference that is naturally inherited. It is thus far closer to conceptions of "race" than it is to culture. Characterized by their essential otherness, the barbarian regimes are thus automatically recognized as an aberration from the correct world order established by Chinese rulers in the mythical past; accordingly, the period to be recounted in the Chronicles is referred to as a *huo* 禍, "disaster." The discrete category of the Chronicles, therefore, indicates that the very organization of material in the *Jin shu* marks out a deliberate distinction between the Chinese and the illegitimate barbarian usurpers.

How then are the barbarian peoples individually represented in the text? After all, the so-called Wu Hu, "Five Barbarians," were a diverse group who hailed from different regions: the Xiongnu and Jie were nomads from the north, the Di and Qiang were semi-nomadic peoples from the west and northwest, and the Särbi-Xianbei were a nomadic people from the

---

[226] Honey, *The Rise of the Medieval Hsiung-nu*, 14.
[227] 性也者，所受於天也，非擇取而為之也 (*Lüshi chunqiu* 12, Chenglian 誠廉.267).

northeast.[228] Interestingly, and in a manner similar to Procopius' treatment of the barbarian conquerors in the *Wars*, the Wu Hu in the *Jin shu* are, for the most part, not subjected to the traditional forms of ethnographic description that appear throughout fascicle 97. As already noted, the one exception to this rule is the passage in fascicle 97 dedicated to the Xiongnu, which recounts events of their history from the mid-first century BC. But when one actually comes to the history of Xiongnu rulers of the Former Zhao dynasty in the Chronicles, the barbarian people who first conquered much of north China in the early fourth century, the narrative of the Xiongnu is generally free of ethnographic coloring. There are of course frequent references to things like the use of cavalry and Xiongnu titulature and tribal organization, but these are presented matter-of-factly and without the explanatory context that otherwise characterizes classical Chinese ethnography.

The same holds true for the other ethnic groups whose affairs are recounted in the Chronicles; they are generally represented in terms no different from those of other Chinese political narratives. If one did not know, thanks to the preface to the Chronicles, that the fourteen states treated therein were of barbarian origin, it would be easy to lose sight of this fact given that, although they do appear from time to time, direct references to non-Chinese ethnic identities are relatively rare. It is impossible to know whether this is because the thirty fascicles that make up the Chronicles are a composite work, largely copied and pasted from earlier histories produced during the actual reigns of the barbarian states themselves or after their fall, or rather because of the editorial choices of Fang Xuanling 房玄齡 and the other early Tang historians who were assigned to the project.[229]

However, the same cannot be said regarding the *lun* 論 colophons that are appended to the end of many of the fascicles in the Chronicles. The

---

[228] Again, it is important not to confuse the Si Yi 四夷, the Four Barbarians of antiquity (the Rong, Di, Yi, and Man) whose ethnonyms had become generalized to refer either to the foreign peoples at the four points of the compass or barbarians in general, with the five barbarian peoples who managed to carve out several states in northern China for themselves beginning in the fourth century AD, the so-called Wu Hu 五胡, or "Five Barbarians." This latter group have given rise to one of the more colorful phrases conventionally used to the describe the fourth century: *Wu Hu luan Hua* 五胡亂華, "The Five Barbarians throw China into chaos." Moreover, it is important to note that even though the Romanized forms are identical, the Di 氐 of the Wu Hu, a western people often associated with the Qiang, are not the same as the Di 狄, the northern barbarian group of the Si Yi.

[229] See Wang Zhongluo for a table of all the histories of the Sixteen Kingdoms produced between the fourth and sixth centuries. *Wei Jin Nanbeichao shi*, 832–33. Also see Honey *The Rise of the Medieval Hsiung-nu: The Biography of Liu Yüan*, 10–13.

inclusion of such statements at the end of narrative segments was a consistent practice of Chinese historiography that may be traced back to Sima Qian.[230] These colophons, introduced in the *Jin shu* by the phrase *shichen yue* 史臣曰, "The historian says," provide a moralizing assessment of the regime, its rulers, and its most prominent statesmen. It is in these *lun* assessments that the official ethical verdict of the historian(s) is most clearly expressed, and it is here that one finds a direct window onto early Tang attitudes and worldviews as far as non-Chinese peoples are concerned.[231]

Perhaps unfortunately for modern historians, authors in the Greco-Roman tradition did not offer such succinct and accessible summaries of their moral views; instead, authorial comments must be gathered throughout the narrative and ethical standpoints must be further extrapolated from quoted speeches and an author's general representa-tion of a people or figure's character and deeds. Even so, representation of conflicts between individuals and groups is often characterized by a complexity and balance of opposing perspectives that eludes simple moralizing in black and white terms. Scholars continue to debate where the sympathies of Herodotus, Thucydides, Sallust, and Tacitus actually lay. Given the semi-official nature of Chinese dynastic history writing prior to the Tang, and then the wholly official nature of it after the establishment of the Bureau of Historiography in 629, it may be argued that one cannot always take the *lun* as faithfully and completely repre-senting the historian's point of view. What the *lun* do represent, however, is a moral view that elites and figures in power deemed appropriate and necessary; in short, they are a barometer of the *zeitgeist* and ethical preoccupations of any given era, and it is on these that the following discussion will concentrate.

It is interesting to note that in the *lun* colophons, the *Jin shu* historians not only provide an assessment of the various barbarian regimes but also interpret these regimes' historical significance using the only ethnographic framework employed by Procopius in his representation of barbarian conquerors, i.e., that of genealogy. However, as the following discussion will show, this paradigm is not only more prominent in the *Jin shu* than it is in the *Wars*; it also interprets many of the barbarian kingdoms that arose

---

[230] Honey: "The *lun* was a short evaluation or appraisal, normally appended to the *lieh chuan* [fascicle] biographies and annalistic chronicles, which recorded the direct judgment of the historian on the subject of his account." "History and Historiography on the Sixteen States," 164.

[231] On the significance of authorial comments appended to individual fascicles in Chinese historiography, also see Chin, "Defamiliarizing the Foreigner," 314.

following the collapse of the Western Jin in terms of a unified genealogical schema linking most of the usurpers with the barbarian antithesis defined centuries earlier in pre-imperial and Han-dynasty texts. The same concept of a barbarian antitype to Chinese civilization visible in the preface to the Chronicles appears with striking consistency throughout the colophons for different regimes. Moreover, there is no ambiguity as to the moral verdict placed on the rise of independent barbarian regimes within the frontiers.

The first state to establish itself in the early fourth century was the Former Zhao dynasty founded by the Xiongnu, who rose to power in the chaos caused by a civil war between members of the Western Jin royal family.[232] The *lun* colophon dedicated to the Former Zhao dynasty begins by re-contextualizing the Xiongnu dynasty in the tradition of the predatory northern barbarian:

> 彼戎狄者，人面獸心，見利則棄君親，臨財則忘仁義者也.　投之遐遠，猶懼外侵，而處以封畿，窺我中釁.[233]

> Who are those who are the Rong-Di? Those who have the faces of humans and hearts of beasts; seeing profit causes them to abandon loyalty to lord and kindred; the nearness of wealth causes them to forget benevolence and justice. To expel them to the farthest reaches is to fear their invasions from the outside, but to settle them with lands inside the empire causes them to seek for a breach in our central kingdom.

In framing the *lun* with the ancient and generic category of Rong-Di, within which the Xiongnu and all other barbarians are necessarily included, the historians return to the mythological conflict presented in the preface. Also present here are the tropes of representing the barbarians as subhuman and as a constantly faithless and hostile entity. Located on or beyond the borders of the empire, the barbarians are oriented toward the political center against which it is their nature to rebel. The consistency of this political cosmology in the *Jin shu*, as will be seen in succeeding examples, is rooted in the pre-imperial ethnological thought discussed in earlier chapters and has already been observed in the *Jin shu*'s fascicle 97 on the Si Yi.

---

[232] For an overview of the settlement and distribution of the Xiongnu in this period, see de Crespigny, *Northern Frontier*. Also referred to as the Han Zhao 漢趙, a history of this dynasty is provided in Wang Zhongluo, *Wei Jin Nanbeichao shi*, 218–23. Also see Liu Xueyao, *Wu Hu shilun*, 108–19; Corradini, "The Barbarian States in North China," 183–87.

[233] *Jin shu* 103.2702. The *lun* colophons to fascicles 103 and 107 have also been translated by Honey with a commentary, "History and Historiography on the Sixteen States," 183–97.

The same strategy of combining an ancient genealogy with the traits of barbarian wickedness, represented as an eternal and elemental threat to the Chinese world order, is repeated in the *lun* for the Later Zhao 後趙 dynasty, which was established by a ruler belonging to the Jie ethnic group, a people often loosely associated with the Xiongnu.[234] Irrespective of the particular flaws or achievements of the dynasty, one is struck by the rhetorical similarity between the *Jin shu*'s assessment of this regime and that of its predecessor:

夫拯溺救焚，帝王之師也；窮凶騁暴，戎狄之舉也. 蠢茲雜種，自古為虞，限以塞垣，猶懼侵軼，況乃入居中壤，窺我王政，乘弛紊之機，覘危亡之隙，而莫不嘯羣鳴鏑，汨亂天常者乎！[235]

Regarding the rescue of the drowning and the saving from fire – these are the guiding principles of emperors and kings; to exercise wickedness and carry out wanton violence – these are the deeds of the Rong-Di. How stupid are these motley hordes; troublemakers since ancient times and checked by the border fortifications, yet we still fear the flood of their incursions. How much more so now that they have entered into the central territory and settled here; they cast a covetous eye on our state and take the opportunity provided by our relaxed vigilance and disorder; they look upon the cracks in our defenses for themselves to spread devastation. Moreover, none of them fails to howl among his herds and whistle with his arrows. This throws even the celestial order into chaos!

Again, many of the themes here are familiar: ancient antagonism between the civilized Chinese and the barbarians of the north, the use of generic and obsolete ethnonyms, and the danger posed by the barbarians who have been resettled within the frontiers. There is again the graphic representation of militaristic nomads in the wilderness, and in this case their presence in Chinese territories is presented not just as a political but even a cosmological catastrophe. The respective *lun* assessments of the above two regimes exhibit the same tendency to equate the Xiongnu and Jie peoples with the moral depravity that defined the barbarians in opposition to the Chinese in classical philosophical and ritual texts.

What about barbarians from other quarters? The Murong branch of the Särbi-Xianbei who originated in Manchuria to China's northeast were one of the most politically successful groups to enter China in large numbers in

---

[234] For a discussion of this relationship, see Liu Xueyao, *Wu Hu shilun*, 34–37; for a history of the dynasty, 125–34. Also see Wang Zhongluo, *Wei Jin Nanbeichao shi*, 223–34; Corradini, "The Barbarian States in North China," 187–90.

[235] *Jin shu* 107.2797–98.

this period, founding three different dynasties: the Former Yan, the Later Yan, and the Southern Yan 南燕.[236] Other branches of the Särbi-Xianbei formed the Western Qin and the Southern Liang 南涼 dynasties. Most important of all is the Tabgach-Tuoba 拓跋 branch of the Särbi-Xianbei who founded the state of Dai 代, destroyed in the mid-fourth century but reestablished in 386. It was the Tabgach Särbi-Xianbei state of Dai, renamed the Northern Wei 北魏 following its resurgence in the late fourth century, that would reunite all of northern China and bring the period of the Sixteen Kingdoms to an end in the 440s. The Northern Wei thus ushered in the period of the Northern and Southern dynasties, when the north of China was ruled by the Särbi-Xianbei and the south by a succession of weak Chinese regimes.[237] However, of all of these different branches of the Särbi-Xianbei, the Murong clan was the first to establish itself as the Former Yan state in the northeast in the period of chaos in the early years of the fourth century.

Interestingly, fascicle 108, the first of the Chronicles to discuss the Murong, begins by stating that their ancestors are traced back to Youxiongshi 有熊氏, an ambiguous term that would seem to link the Murong Särbi-Xianbei to the mythical age of the Chinese Central Plains. It then goes on to say that "for generations they had lived amongst the northern barbarians," before eventually becoming known as the Donghu 東胡.[238] Although the Donghu seem originally to have been a distinct people, they were conquered and largely absorbed by the Xiongnu in the third century BC; only what became the Wuhuan and Särbi-Xianbei branches of the Donghu managed to escape. This perhaps explains the fact that in the *lun* colophon concluding the account of the Former Yan dynasty, the Murong are characterized in a fashion analogous to the treatment received by the Xiongnu and Jie dynasties of the Former and Later Zhao discussed above:

---

[236] The most extensive account in English of the Murong Särbi are Schreiber's "History of the Former Yen Dynasty," parts I and II. Also see Corradini, "The Barbarian States in North China"; Liu Xueyao, *Wu Hu shilun*, 134–55; Wang Zhongluo, *Wei Jin Nanbeichao shi*, 238–44, 269–87. More recently, see Holcombe, "The Xianbei in Chinese History," 1–38.

[237] On the founding of the Dai state and the early history of the Tabgach, see Holmgren, *Annals of Tai: Early T'o-pa History According to the First Chapter of the* Wei-shu. For a cultural, not historical, overview of the Northern and Southern dynasties, see Lewis, *China between Empires*. A comprehensive guide to the political history of the period in English remains to be written.

[238] 其先有熊氏之苗裔，世居北夷…號曰東胡 (*Jin shu* 108.2803). The Donghu have been discussed above as the ancestors of the Särbi peoples. See above, 62. On their conquest by the Xiongnu, see *Shiji* 110.2889.

觀夫北陰衍氣，醜虜彙生，隔閡諸華，聲教莫之漸，雄據殊壤，貪悍成其俗，先叛後服，蓋常性也。[239]

> Consider how the northern region spreads its energy, and the wicked enemies gather and proliferate; divided and alienated from all the Chinese, no civilized teachings reach them; they hold their distant lands with force. Greed and ferocity have become their custom; first they rebel and then submit in turn – this is their general nature.

The *lun* begins with the familiar description of the predatory enemies in the far north. Noticeably absent are the archaic barbarian terms Rong-Di or Yi-Di to denote their general barbarian identity. However, not much should be made of this, for it remains perfectly clear that the Murong find themselves on the far side of the same cultural and ethnic divide. This distinction is made clear with references to *jiao* 教, "teaching," and *su* 俗, "custom," which refer to the refinements of Chinese civilization that have never reached them. These details are remarkable given that several members of the Murong family had clearly managed to not only learn about the teachings of civilization but also put those very teachings into the service of constructing a powerful state, as will be discussed in the next chapter. An ethnic component is also present in the familiar use of the word *xing* 性, "nature," here referring to the familiar barbarian trope of perfidy, which implies not simply a learned behavior but one that is genealogically inherited. As was the case with the assessments of the Former and Later Zhao dynasties, the *Jin shu* presents the Murong Särbi-Xianbei as a people whose proper place is far away from China and whose natural state is one of savagery, violence, and faithlessness. Moreover, they are characterized by an elemental, and unchanging nature that is correlated with geopolitical and moral inferiority.

The case of the Northern Yan dynasty was discussed above as one that might challenge the argument that a barbarian classification determined a regime's inclusion in the Chronicles. For this state's founder, Feng Ba, was himself believed to be of Chinese ancestry, which, according to the theory put forth above, ought to exempt him and the state he founded from inclusion amongst the other barbarians in the Chronicles. Yet the *lun* colophon for the Northern Yan state makes it clear that the Northern Yan, if only by virtue of its own claim to succeed the Särbi-Xianbei Later Yan, was ranked among the non-Chinese regimes:

---

[239] *Jin shu* 111.2862. For an alternative translation of this passage, see Schreiber, "History of the Former Yen Dynasty, Part II," 128.

自五胡縱慝，九域淪胥，帝里神州，遂混之於荒裔；鴻名寶位，咸
假之於雜種. 嘗謂戎狄凶嚚，未窺道德，欺天擅命，抑乃其常. 而馮
跋出自中州，有殊醜類，因鮮卑之昏虐，亦盜名於海隅.²⁴⁰

Since the time when the Five Barbarians gave free rein to their wickedness,
the Nine Regions have all been overthrown; the imperial capital and sacred
domains were then confounded with the descendants of the outer wastes.
The great name and precious seat have all been taken up by these motley
hordes. One attempts to describe the malice and evil of the Rong-Di: they
have never glimpsed the Way or Virtue; they insult Heaven and usurp
authority – truly this is their way of being. Although Feng Ba came from
the central domains [sc. China], he was of an especially wicked race; in
succession from the chaotic violence of the Särbi-Xianbei, he too stole his
title among the coastal regions.

In this passage, the Northern Yan monarch Feng Ba is introduced following the conventional descriptions of the disaster that had befallen China
when non-Chinese peoples had taken control of the north in the early
fourth century. The *lun* goes on to note that Feng Ba was indeed of
Chinese ancestry, yet this is qualified by stating that he "was of a particularly wicked race," *you shu chou lei* 有殊醜類. This term *lei* 類, having a
sense of "race" or "type," is modified by *chou* 醜, "wicked" or "ugly,"
forming a compound that is periodically used in descriptions of barbarian
peoples.²⁴¹ It is almost as though the *lun* deliberately employs terms
associated with ethnic distinction in order to more effectively associate
Feng Ba with other non-Chinese peoples; and indeed the next sentence
shows his close association with the Särbi-Xianbei states who had ruled
over the northeastern coastal regions before him. The result is that the
Chinese Feng Ba is barbarized in order to be associated more closely with
the political line of succession within which he had positioned himself.
While his career is testament to the possibility of crossing the divide
between Chinese and non-Chinese identities and seems to indicate a
degree of porousness along the lines of any such dichotomy, it is interesting that in the case above, the distinction is nevertheless conceived of in
ethnic rather than behavioral terms.

Curiously, even the *lun* that concludes the chronicle of a people living to
the southwest of China, the Di (or Ba-Di 巴氐) people who founded the

---

²⁴⁰ *Jin shu* 125.3134–35.
²⁴¹ For other examples of this compound in the *Jin shu*, see 74.1949 (in reference to the Di 氐
people), 81.2113 (here even more clearly associated with the non-Chinese in the phrase "Yi-Rong
chou lei" 夷戎醜類), 103.2703 (in reference to the Xiongnu), 107.2798 (in reference to the Jie
leader Shi Le 石勒), 108.2810 (in reference to the Jie people).

Chenghan 成漢 state, begins by relegating them too into the barbarian category of Rong-Di, archaic ethnonyms often used for nomads of the north and northwest.[242] The use of Rong-Di here may have seemed appropriate since the Ba-Di people's state was at least located in the (south)west.[243] However, more likely is that, as has been suggested, the term Rong-Di was simply a term denoting "barbarians," irrespective of their provenance or way of life. Given the range of peoples it is applied to, the term can just as well be used to describe the proto-Mongol/Turk nomads of the northern steppes, the Särbi-Xianbei of northeastern Manchuria, and the proto-Tibetan sheep herders and farmers of the west and southwest. Irrespective of where the barbarians come from, however, the problems are the same:

是知戎狄亂華，釁深自古，況乎巴濮雜種，厥類實繁，資剽竊以全生，習獷悍而成俗.[244]

This is what it means to understand that the Rong-Di throw China into chaos; the strife has been deep since ancient times. Moreover, there are the Ba-Pu[245] motley hordes of the southwest, whose race is truly numerous; they store up plunder and booty for a livelihood, while studying rudeness and ferocity has become their custom.

What is interesting about the case of the Chenghan state is the way in which the peoples of the southwest are incorporated in an ancient conflict that does not merely see China at war with the nomads of the steppe, but also against the non-Chinese of other directions as well – even regions that in ancient times had been well outside the Chinese cultural sphere. The vices of the Ba-Di people appear markedly akin to those of peoples originating at the opposite point on the compass, i.e., the Murong Särbi-Xianbei of Manchuria. The fact that barbarian moral inferiority may be generalized to any non-Chinese people of the periphery that has claimed former imperial territory for its own indicates a lack of interest in the particulars of any of these people – the fundamental concern is their

---

[242] The most extensive work in Chinese on the Di and Qiang is Ma Changshou's *Di yu Qiang*. Rogers also offers a history of the Di in *The Chronicle of Fu Chien*, 4–6. For an account of the Chenghan dynasty, see Liu Xueyao, *Wu Hu shilun*, 193–96; Corradini, "The Barbarian States in North China," 180–83.

[243] Note that in the binome Ba-Di 巴氐, the second component Di 氐 is distinct from the ethnonym Di 狄 of Rong-Di, Yi-Di, etc., which was used generically to signify "barbarian."

[244] *Jin shu* 121.3049.

[245] The compound Ba-Pu refers, in its first part Ba 巴, to a kingdom based in the southwest of China in the first millennium BC; the character 巴 may also mean "large snake." The second component, Pu 濮, also denotes a people in the southwest of China in ancient times. See Hu, "Puren," 186–90.

common affinity with an antagonistic, non-Chinese entity that looms over China from all sides.[246]

There are, however, exceptions to this generally hostile and xenophobic tone, and a number of the conquest regimes in the Chronicles are not condemned in terms of their barbarian identity in their respective *lun* assessments. For example, the Di 氐 ethnic group's Former Qin 前秦 and Later Liang 後涼 dynasties (fascicles 115 and 122), the Qiang Later Qin 後秦 dynasty (fascicle 119), and the Särbi-Xianbei Western Qin and Southern Yan dynasties (fascicles 125 and 128) are not discussed in terms of their non-Chinese ancestry in the colophons, even though there are other indications of their barbarian identity at certain points in their preceding narratives. In other cases, such references to ethnicity are present, although they are somewhat less conspicuous. For example, the dynastic founder of the Xiongnu state of Northern Liang 北涼 is simply said to have come from the *yizou* 夷陬, "barbarian regions."[247] The *zan* following the colophon to fascicle 124, which is devoted to the Särbi-Xianbei Later Yan dynasty, simply states that "the Rong-Di invade and harass; mountains and rivers seethe and boil."[248] In the case of the Southern Liang state, its Särbi-Xianbei people are shown to exhibit the barbarian tendencies that appear both in the preface to the Chronicles and in assessments of other dynasties:

候滿月而窺兵，乘折膠而縱鏑，禮容弗被，聲教斯阻.[249]

They gazed upon the full moon and spied with their warriors; taking advantage of the cold weather they let fly their arrows. Ritual propriety has not come to them, and the civilized teachings make no headway among them.

While the generic barbarian names of Rong, Di, or Yi are not mentioned in this case, it is clear that the Särbi-Xianbei of Southern Liang are to be understood in the same terms as their barbarian Särbi-Xianbei fellows. The practice of reiterating the pan-barbarian genealogy introduced in the Chronicles' preface is therefore not ubiquitous in the *lun* colophons, even if it is common. But even in instances where the associations with the ancient enemies of China are not expressed genealogically, the *Jin shu* authors have other ways to make clear that the people in question has its place among the other barbarians of the periphery. As this last example

---

[246] Nevertheless, the frequent applicability of the traditional ethnonymns Rong, Di, and Yi to various foreign peoples is not shared by the term Man 蠻, which maintains a relatively strong association with non-Chinese peoples of the south.
[247] *Jin shu* 129.3199.   [248] 戎狄憑陵，山川沸騰 (*Jin shu* 124.3110).   [249] *Jin shu* 126.3158.

demonstrates, even when barbarian ethnonyms are omitted, one finds the same consistent correlation between geographical/cosmological schemata and ethical characteristics that allows Chinese historians to represent the rise of barbarian kingdoms as an inversion of the prescribed political and moral order inherited from antiquity.

Conclusions

This chapter has demonstrated the ways in which the *Wars* and *Jin shu* both exhibit a significant degree of continuity with the earlier ethnographic texts in their respective traditions. Whether it is the notion of a barbarian antithesis, the manner and forms of presenting ethnographic information, or the epistemological paradigms used to rationalize and make the barbarians intelligible to Roman and Chinese audiences, both texts may clearly be positioned in a direct line of literary descent from their models, even if some innovations or changes obtain. As noted above, the classicism of Procopius is taken for granted by modern scholars, and the authors of the *Jin shu* exhibit an analogous literary conservatism. The binary construct that marks a division between barbarians and Romans is clearly articulated in the opening lines of the *Wars*, and the term "barbarian" continues to be used for non-Roman enemies and allies throughout the work. Yet over the course of the above discussion, the *Jin shu*'s organized consistency in reinforcing the Sino-barbarian dichotomy stands out more starkly. Part of this contrast is attributable simply to the standard form of the dynastic history, which includes a chapter on barbarian peoples, complete with its own preface and allusions to earlier literary precedents. But with the novel form of the Chronicles, the *Jin shu* also creates a new literary category consisting of accounts of illegitimate barbarian regimes, where the central focus is necessarily on political figures whose shared characteristic is their non-Chinese identity.

In contrast to this organized and schematized delineation of the Chinese and barbarian spheres, the *Wars* offers a comparatively haphazard and almost offhand representation of the barbarian dichotomy, following as it does the pattern of the classical war narrative with ethnographic digressions and shorter passages inserted at various points therein. More significant is that while the *Wars* does in fact perpetuate the notion of the barbarian dichotomy, the "new" peoples of the era – primarily the Vandals and Goths who are the most significant barbarian players – are in a number of ways exempted from conventional ethnographic treatment. Procopius notes that these new barbarians may be associated with other ethnonyms known to historians in earlier centuries, obscure peoples such as the Sauromatae, Melanchlainoi, and Getae. Yet these associations carry nothing like the weight that the *Jin shu* ascribes to the Rong, Yi, Man, and Di, whose names serve not just as ethnonyms but as moral, political, and geographical categories serving to define the Chinese and the Chinese Empire by their opposition to it.[250]

The use of "Germanoi" as an alternative ethnonym for the Franks appears with some frequency, especially in describing events of the centuries and decades prior to the beginning of the wars of reconquest, and one could argue that such usage was intended to conjure up images of the Germani who had resisted Roman expansion under the early principate and ultimately proved unconquerable. Yet even if this were Procopius' intention, the ethnonym itself does not have the resonance even of contemporary barbarian ethnonyms in China such as that of the Xiongnu, whose components *xiong* 匈 and *nu* 奴 mean respectively "noisy, violent" and "slave," or that of the Jie, the character for whom, 羯, contains the "sheep" radical 羊 with clear animal associations. By contrast, Germanoi-Γερμάνοι is orthographically almost identical to the Latin adjective *germanus* meaning "genuine, fraternal," not to mention the name of the emperor Justinian's own cousin Germanus-Γερμάνος, who is a great hero in Procopius' narrative. Indeed, Procopius explicitly downplays any significance the Franks may have had in the past, describing them as "a barbarian people not worthy of much account in earlier times."[251] While several modern scholars have read Procopius as reaffirming traditional anti-barbarian biases, this chapter has shown that his representation of non-Romans is hardly so simplistically constructed.

In the *Jin shu*, by contrast, the reader is again and again reminded that the barbarians of the fourth and fifth centuries AD are simply a contemporary expression of an ancient, almost existential antagonism that is clearly defined and has deep ethical and political resonances. Compared with those of the *Jin shu*, the ethnogenealogies attributed to the barbarians in the *Wars*, while clearly illustrating familiarity with classical texts and drawing connections between the barbarians of Procopius' own day and those of an earlier age, seem random and almost perfunctory, lacking the morally and politically loaded significance that one finds attributed to the barbarian lineages recorded in the *Jin shu*. I would argue that this difference between the two texts points to a deeper anxiety in worldviews of

---

[250] These associations are discussed at length in Chapter 1.
[251] βάρβαρον ἔθνος, οὐ πολλοῦ λόγου τὸ κατ' ἀρχὰς ἄξιον (*Wars* 5.12.8).

early Tang elites regarding the instability both of the new regime as well as the need to assert a political orthodoxy that was necessarily defined, based on the absolute authority of classical philosophical and political texts, as "Chinese" in opposition to the surrounding world of the "barbarians." The comparison with Procopius indicates a deep preoccupation with ethnic identities and the political connotations associated with given ethnonyms in the *Jin shu* that is simply absent in the *Wars*.

Procopius on the other hand, in turning to the classical ethnographic models of antiquity perpetuates instead the relativism and objectivity that characterized the work of the first historian Herodotus. This is in itself remarkable in an age that had witnessed the loss of half of the Roman Empire to barbarian peoples, but it may perhaps be more easily understood in light of the above noted classicism of Procopius: while self-consciously seeking to emulate the style, lexicon, and authorial voice of the ancients, he describes his own "present by using ancient paradigms whose store of accumulated meaning could be modulated to respond to new circumstances."[252] In this sense, the classical authorities to which Procopius looked for instruction and inspiration, texts whose composition was not carried out under the dominance of a single imperial power but rather in the multi-polar world of the pre-Roman Mediterranean, lent his account of his own times a capacity to view events from a relatively objective standpoint and unencumbered by a single dominant ideology.

Combined with the inheritance of Greek and Roman historiography is also the history of incorporating foreigners into the Roman citizen body, attested even in accounts of the founding of the city and continuing up through the centuries of the principate. There is no doubt that pre-imperial and imperial China also witnessed similar processes of conquest, incorporation, and assimilation, but the Chinese tradition does not seem to have either tolerated or exhibited interest in the perpetuation of alternative ethnic identities once peoples had become imperial subjects to the extent that the Roman tradition did. This phenomenon has been discussed at length by Farney, who has shown that various non-Roman Italian identities, marked by ethnonyms once borne by enemies of Rome, were much in use in the first century BC, long after these peoples had ceased to exist as coherent political entities.[253] Alternative, sub-Roman identities even enjoyed a resurgence in fifth-century Gaul, over four centuries after the Celtic peoples there had been conquered and

[252] Kaldellis, *Procopius of Caesarea*, 15.
[253] Farney, *Ethnic Identity and Aristocratic Competition in Republican Rome*, 1–38.

"Romanized."[254] Julius Caesar had referred to the Gauls as "barbarians"; but Claudius arguing for the inclusion of Aedui tribal elites from *Gallia comata* into the Roman Senate in AD 48 did not – yet everyone knew that the peoples were one and the same. As evidenced in the speech of Claudius on the incorporation of Gauls into the Senate discussed in Chapter 1, the reality of this diversity was an aspect of Roman mainstream political discourse in a way that one does not see in China, where once foreign peoples were incorporated into the empire, alternative ethnic identities that their ancestors may have espoused ceased to maintain their valences. After the Romans conquered and absorbed their neighbors, the latter's ethnonyms were perpetuated as sub-Roman markers of identity, and native *patriae* persisted as constituents of the greater legal-consitutional *patria* of Rome. Aelius Aristides in his fourteenth oration of the late second century AD notes that citizens of the empire continue to guard their "fatherlands," πατρίδας, on behalf of the empire.[255] While the original peoples of the Rong, Di, Man, and Yi must largely have been incorporated by expanding Chinese states in the first millennium BC, these names did not become alternative identities within the Chinese political tradition but, instead, remained the signifiers of inimical and hostile peoples.

Moreover, while the Classicist texts canonized under Han China dictated a formalized Chinese ethical and political superiority over the barbarians, the relativism and dogged heterodoxy of Greco-Roman historiography allowed for a more complex response to the rise and fall of kingdoms and empires. As Herodotus had observed, "the deeds of both Greeks and barbarians were great and worthy of admiration,"[256] and "there are many cities that were great in the past, but of these many have become small; those that were great in my time were formerly of little account."[257] Greco-Roman historians envisioned themselves as part of a pluralistic world in which there was not one but rather multiple great empires of both past and present. In contrast, the tradition from the Han onwards imagined a world dominated by the single and central Chinese community; such a worldview that defined its sense of natural order, both moral and cosmological, by the political supremacy of the Chinese in opposition to the external barbarians was perhaps bound to represent barbarian kingdoms in a harsh light.

---

[254] Geary, *The Myth of Nations*, 104–08.   [255] *Oration* 14.214–15.

[256] ἔργα μεγάλα τε καὶ θωμαστά, τὰ μὲν Ἕλλησι, τὰ δὲ βαρβάροισι (Hdt. 1.0).

[257] τὰ γὰρ τὸ πάλαι μεγάλα ἦν, τὰ πολλὰ αὐτῶν σμικρὰ γέγονε, τὰ δὲ ἐπ' ἐμεῦ ἦν μεγάλα, πρότερον ἦν σμικρά (Hdt. 1.5.4).

In terms of their ethnographic discourse, the use of ancient barbarian ethnonyms to explain contemporary peoples (or in the case of the *Jin shu*, contemporary to the period whose history is being recounted) is thus a critical difference between the two texts. While Procopius often notes that a people were called such and such in ancient times, the *Jin shu* uses obsolete ethnonyms such as Rong, Yi, Di, etc. as though they were still current, as indeed their ethnic and political symbolism clearly still was. The purpose of using these terms, then, was not simply to explain who the Xiongnu, Jie, Särbi-Xianbei, and others *were* in the past – it was to show who they really *are* in the present. A similar practice does of course obtain in the *Wars* with respect to peoples whom Procopius identifies as both Huns and Massagetae, but we do not see it in relation to the peoples who occupy the most significant roles, i.e., those who adopt the trappings of statehood in more or less Roman fashion and who are the main enemies of the empire. The *Jin shu* thereby constructs a remarkably stable sense of continuity in its representation of Chinese and non-Chinese peoples in a way that contrasts sharply with the near constant change and dynamism observable in the *Wars*. This is particularly remarkable given that the northern half of China had been under barbarian rule for close to three centuries prior to the founding of the Tang, and the preceding centuries had undoubtedly witnessed significant blurring of ethnic or cultural distinctions on the ground. The ethnic conservatism exhibited in the *Jin shu* is a testament, therefore, to the enormous power of canonical texts to shape not only the representation but perhaps also the perception of the world; despite the centuries of Chinese-barbarian interaction and mutual influence, the ethno-political rhetoric of the *Jin shu* remains unchanged. While the Xiongnu, Jie, and Särbi-Xianbei are reduced to the familiar ethnic and politically symbolic categories of the first millennium BC, the Vandals and Goths appear as relatively new phenomena whose present and future are not pre-determined by specific barbarian categories to which they have been assigned.

In either case, the political events described in the *Wars* and *Jin shu* represent a massive upheaval in the established imperial world order, which had witnessed the barbarians of the border regions and beyond lay claim to the political prerogatives of the imperial heartlands. It is important to keep in mind the contrast of historical contexts surrounding the composition of the two texts. Procopius described contemporary events and wrote from the imperial capital of Constantinople, which had never fallen to the barbarians, even if it had witnessed the rise of barbarian kingdoms of the west. The *Jin shu* was compiled some two hundred years after the last of the Sixteen Kingdoms had been destroyed by the Särbi-Xianbei Northern Wei dynasty, and the historians of the early Tang who worked on the project were in the service of a regime that had itself risen from the culturally and ethnically mixed north of China. It is, therefore, almost counterintuitive that the historical treatment of foreign regimes in either case turn out to be as they are: the authors of the *Jin shu* exhibit an insistence on an anachronistic delineation of the boundaries between the civilized and the barbarian as defined in ancient times, an insistence on understanding a new age with the concepts and signifiers of the past. The premier historian of the Roman sixth century, in contrast, is shown by virtue of the above comparison to treat his present age, and the barbarian peoples who had in many ways come to define it, on its own terms.

CHAPTER 4

New Emperors and Ethnographic Clothes
The Representation of Barbarian Rulers

The previous chapter demonstrated the continuity of classicizing ethno-graphic discourse in the *Wars* and the *Jin shu* 晉書, paying particular attention to the presence and function of the "barbarian" antithesis in the two works, the dichotomous division of humanity into a civilized center and a barbarian periphery. This chapter will further explore the intersec-tion of traditional concepts of barbarian alterity and the political discourse of sixth-century Constantinople and seventh-century Chang'an, as histo-rians in either capital included accounts of individual barbarian political figures in their works. It will seek to determine the degree to which ethnic labels, and the connotations associated with them (whether vague as in the case of "barbarian" – in Chinese Rong 戎, Yi 夷, Di 狄, Hu 胡, or combinations of these – or specific as in the case of Goth, Vandal, Xiongnu 匈奴, Särbi-Xianbei 鮮卑, etc.), condition the representation of barbarian political figures who had risen above the status of generals, allies, or federates to become leaders of their own independent states.

The chapter will address this question by analyzing the authorial assessments and characterizations of political figures of barbarian origin and, by extension, of their regimes.[1] Such characterizations of personae are morally significant in the historiography of both traditions. Vasaly has pointed to the role of individual characterization in Roman historiography as a central component of its didactic functions, arguing that historians "portrayed events as dependent on the actions of individuals and these actions, in turn, as 'indexes of goodness or badness of character'."[2] In reference to ancient Chinese historiography, Watson has similarly noted the prevalence of stereotypical kinds of action or "conventional patterns of

---

[1] Some of the material discussed in this chapter will appear in the author's contribution to forthcoming volume, *Historiography and Identity IV: Writing History across Medieval Eurasia*, Brepols Publishers.

[2] Vasaly, "Characterization and Complexity: Caesar, Sallust, and Livy," 245. Vasaly is quoting from Gill, "The Character-Personality Distinction."

behavior," observing that "certain types of personalities in history would appear almost automatically to attract to themselves certain types of anecdotes, anecdotes that in the past had been applied to examples of the same personality type."[3] In either case, individual personalities or character types were a central component of the didactic quality of Greco-Roman and Chinese historiography, which presented exempla of the past as a means of establishing an ethical and moral coherence for both the past and present.[4]

The question here will once again be: How do classical conceptions of the barbarian manifest themselves in a new era when both Rome and China were looking back on an age of division that had witnessed external peoples enter the empire? These barbarians did not simply raid and pillage before withdrawing again beyond the frontier, or even settle peacefully as they had in previous centuries; rather, they established themselves as rulers over the Roman and Chinese heartlands. Under such circumstances, how were politically prominent individuals characterized when the figures in question were of barbarian origin?

As to how ethnic identity, in particular barbarian identity, was perceived and represented in this period, consensus remains elusive. General views of the barbarians in the period have already been discussed in Chapter 3. It has been argued in the case of the Roman Empire of late antiquity that "the stereotyped views of Roman and barbarian of late imperial ideology ... emerged unscathed from the political revolution of the fifth century," with reference here to the penetration of large groups of barbarians into the empire en masse who maintained a significant enough degree of political cohesion to become political entities distinct from the imperial court.[5] The same study argues that "the destruction of the western Roman empire did not see the collapse of traditional notions of 'Roman' and 'barbarian'. Individuals and groups were recategorised, or recategorised themselves, for a variety of purposes. ... The actual categories, however, remained the same."[6] If this is the case, we should expect, especially in a deliberately classicizing work such as the *Wars* of Procopius, to find

---

[3] Watson, "Some Remarks on Early Chinese Historical Works," 39.
[4] On didacticism in Greco-Roman historiography, see Fornara, *The Nature of History in Ancient Greece and Rome*, 104–20; Roller, "The Exemplary Past in Roman Historiography and Culture," 214–15. In Chinese historiography, see Olberding, *Dubious Facts: The Evidence of Early Chinese Historiography*, 13–14; Durrant, "The Literary Features of Historical Writing," 507–08; Rogers, *The Chronicle of Fu Chien*, 40–41; Dien, "Historiography of the Six Dynasties Period (220–581)," 509; Yu, "History, Fiction, and the Reading of Chinese Narrative," 10–11.
[5] Heather, "The Barbarian in Late Antiquity," 254.   [6] Ibid., 254–55.

barbarian rulers represented with conventional tropes and the familiar ethnographic signposts.

Other scholars, such as Maas, have observed a renegotiation of categories of identity in this period, arguing that "the opposition of Roman and barbarian was not absolute or final," and that citizens of the empire could take advantage of a variety of "diverse traditions to register the differences between themselves and their barbarian neighbors and to consider how those differences might be bridged."[7] Lampinen has similarly downplayed the significance of a Roman–barbarian ideological division in Late Antiquity, arguing that "whether about 'Greeks' or 'barbarians', the dynamic of cultural foreignness had clearly fragmented into a complex interplay of identities, among which religious and occupational themes played just as important a role as cultural or ethnic [ones]."[8]

As for the ethnographic landscape of the early Tang 唐, there is a similar diversity of views. Likely because of the widespread perception that the Tang was among the most cosmopolitan eras in Chinese history, it has been argued that "the Tang empire eliminated the traditional ethnic boundary between the Han and non-Han."[9] If this view is correct, a distinction may thus be drawn between the historiography of the early Tang and that of the Han 漢 dynasty; while Han historians "showed a strong concern for the threat coming from the north, this concern was absent from Tang historiography because the threat itself had gone."[10] According to this view, we should expect to find the non-Chinese rulers of the conquest states of the fourth and fifth centuries appearing without ethnographic coloring or characterized by the ethnic stereotypes that were consistently employed in earlier periods of Chinese classical literature.

Although such views of the period are not infrequent in Chinese-language scholarship and even appear in some western scholarship, there are other assessments of the period that see a much greater sense of ideological division between Chinese and barbarian in the early Tang. For example, Abramson has observed that it was common practice "for the elite Han in-group to refer to the Other as 'not of our kind', with strong implications of common descent on the part of the Han."[11] He has argued that there was a strong antipathy toward foreign peoples, even those living within the empire, and

---

[7] Maas, "Barbarians: Problems and Approaches," 60.
[8] Lampinen, "Migrating Motifs of Northern Barbarism," 231.
[9] Wang, Q. Edward, "History, Space, and Ethnicity," 299.   [10] Ibid., 300.
[11] Abramson, *Ethnic Identity in Tang China*, xi.

that "from the viewpoint of the imperial bureaucracy, their presence was ultimately an aberration that acculturation and assimilation would eventually eradicate."[12] Skaff has pointed to the complexity of early Tang attitudes toward ethnicity and demonstrates that multiple, and even contradictory, views were present in the ethnological discourse of the period and at times even attributed to the same individual.[13]

There is, then, a lack of concensus in scholarly assessments of ethnographic discourse in both Late Antiquity and Early Medieval China. Some scholars argue for the stability of the barbarian antithesis in the later Roman Empire and under the Tang, while others claim that the ethnological divide between center and periphery broke down and had become, or at least was on its way to becoming, meaningless. The previous chapter demonstrated that traditional ethnological biases are on full display in both the *Wars* and the *Jin shu*, although the latter text exhibits a marked tendency to assimilate foreign peoples of a later age to ancient barbarian categories. Through a close reading of depictions of barbarian monarchs in the texts and a consideration of the degree to which ethnic origins condition the representative strategies of the historians, this chapter will argue that, when it comes to the assessment of foreign political actors, the already noted contrasts between *Wars* and the *Jin shu* become even more stark. Procopius largely exempts the barbarian antagonists of Justinian from traditional forms of ethnographic representation, and this impulse is even more pronounced in his depiction of barbarian kings. In contrast, the *Jin shu* consistently characterizes rulers of non-Chinese ethnicity in a negative light defined by their foreign identities and their association with barbarian peoples of the distant and even mythological past.

Barbarian Figures in the *Wars*

As discussed in Chapter 3, the treatment of foreign peoples in the *Wars* abounds with pejorative representations of non-Romans that have clear precedents in the ethnographic tradition. In his descriptions of peoples either still beyond the imperial periphery or whose presence inside the empire was restricted to the capacity of serving as auxiliaries in Roman armies, Procopius freely employs the ethnographic tropes used by his predecessors.[14] Yet despite the presence of familiar, and pejorative,

---

[12] Ibid., 117.   [13] Skaff, *Sui-Tang China and Its Turko-Mongol Neighbors*, 52–60.
[14] See, for example, his treatment of the Hephthalites (*Wars* 1.3.2–7), the Tzani (1.15.21–5), the Heruli (6.14.1–7), and the Sclaveni and Antae (7.14.22–30).

anti-barbarian rhetoric throughout, the depiction of barbarian political actors, i.e., barbarian kings, exhibits a dearth of ethnographic signification. Traditional ethnological discourse does not, therefore, survive the transfer to the higher levels of the political sphere, to the representation of political actors of barbarian origin. It should be reiterated, however, that throughout the *Wars* there is no ambiguity regarding the fact that Goths and Vandals belong to the barbarian category; collectively they are referred to as barbarians whether on or off the battlefield. It is therefore surprising that their leaders are rarely, if at all, referred to as such, even when they may be clearly unviable political alternatives to Roman rule in Procopius' view.

As already observed, some scholars have argued that the conceptual categories of Roman and barbarian did not break down in Late Antiquity, even though barbarian peoples had entered the empire and taken up the reins of state in several of its former provinces.[15] Regarding Procopius in particular, it has been suggested that

> Like most members of the late Roman literary elite, Procopius was convinced of his own cultural superiority over the peoples whose lands surrounded the empire. In his thought, a sharp line divided the Roman world and the poverty, violence, and faithlessness of the barbarians.[16]

The following discussion will argue that such an assessment of Procopius' views does not hold up to scrutiny. In what one might assume to be the most appropriate place for the expression of anti-barbarian sentiment – in the representation of the barbarian kings who were not only members of politically coherent groups that had renounced obedience to the emperor but had presumed to claim legal rights of sovereignty over their newly won domains – ethnographic rhetoric, the means by which cultural hierarchies of superiority and inferiority were traditionally constructed, is virtually absent.[17] This absence problematizes the often-invoked stability of the "barbarian" as a conceptual category. For if the Vandals and Goths are barbarians, what does one make of Procopius' decision to have his barbarian kings, even the bad ones, consistently appear without their ethnographic clothes? It will be argued here that the barbarian rulers of Vandal

---

[15] E.g., Heather, "The Barbarian in Late Antiquity," 254–55.

[16] Conant, *Staying Roman: Conquest and Identity in Africa and the Mediterranean*, 256.

[17] An important exception here is the treatment of the Franks (particularly at *Wars* 6.25.1–10), who were the masters of much of Gaul by the mid-sixth century. However, as discussed in Chapter 3, they are only peripheral actors in the *Wars* and not the declared enemies of the empire in the campaigns narrated by Procopius.

Africa and Ostrogothic Italy are represented by Procopius in ethnically neutral terms and, as a corollary to this, that in a widely and popularly circulated narrative of Justinian's wars of conquest, the non-Roman ethnicity of his chief enemies was not politicized.

The Vandals

Procopius begins book three by providing a detailed account of events in the west covering much of the fifth century, including the migration, conquest, and depredations of the Vandals. He traces their migration from its origins around the Maeotic Lake to their final seizure of the city of Carthage in 439, at which point their leader Gaiseric is believed to have adopted the title *rex*.[18] Gaiseric was the most notorious of the Vandal kings,[19] who led his people from Spain into Africa and established their kingdom in the city of Carthage. Throughout this history of the Vandal kingdom, there are several points at which Procopius offers observations on Gaiseric's character. In several instances he seems to be an archetype of the rapacious barbarian, sacking the city of Rome itself in 455. In the following years, Gaiseric spends his time "making attacks against Sicily and Italy . . . and pillaging everything such that the land became empty of both men and money."[20] However, Gaiseric is not presented as a figure wholly subject to his impulses of greed and violence. Procopius shows that the Vandal king is also capable of restraint and prudence, noting that after a victory, "[Gaiseric] was not exalted by the things he had been lucky in, but rather became moderate because of the things he feared."[21] The barbarian tendency to be elevated to recklessness by success and driven to despair by failure is a traditional feature in Roman ethnography that serves to highlight the *constantia* of the Roman character by contrast.[22] In this case, the attribution of moderation to Gaiseric serves to temper the barbarian stereotypes of cruelty and greed that he elsewhere displays.

---

[18]　On the employment of this royal title by the Vandals, see Conant, *Staying Roman*, 42, 44. Also see Chrysos, "The Title Βασιλεύς in Early Byzantine International Relations," 53, n. 150; 55, n. 168.

[19]　I will use the conventional spellings of Vandal and Gothic names as they appear in the *OCD* or *The Cambridge Ancient History* in place of their Greek spellings, i.e., "Gaiseric" for "Gizerikos."

[20]　ἔς τε Σικελίαν καὶ Ἰταλίαν ἐσβολὰς ἐποιεῖτο . . . ληισάμενός τε ἅπαντα, ἐπεὶ ἀνθρώπων τε ἡ χώρα καὶ χρημάτων ἔρημος ἐγεγόνει (*Wars* 3.5.22).

[21]　οὐχ οἷς εὐημέρησεν ἐπηρμένος, ἀλλ᾽ οἷς ἔδεισε μέτριος γεγονώς (*Wars* 3.4.13).

[22]　See Lampinen on the stereotypical *levitas* and *infirmitas* of northern barbarians, "Migrating Motifs of Northern Barbarism," 210–11. Yet Gaiseric exhibits less of the northern barbarian than of Horace's *sapiens*, whose "well-prepared breast in adversity hopes – in success it fears – for the contrary event": *sperat infestis metuit secundis/ alteram sortem bene praeparatum/ pectus* (*Odes* 2.10).

However, in all of the references to Gaiseric's cunning and cruelty, as well as occasional prudence and foresight, none of these qualities is ever explicitly correlated with his Vandal, and hence barbarian, ethnicity. In terms of a general assessment of Gaiseric's character, Procopius only offers the brief remark on introducing him in the narrative with the words: "Gaiseric was most excellently practiced in the arts of war and of all men was the most to be reckoned with."[23] While Gaiseric posed a grave threat to the empire, and his conquest of North Africa was surely an economic and political catastrophe, so much so that four expeditions were wholly or in part sent from Constantinople prior to the invasion of Belisarius under Justinian, Procopius chooses not to portray this most notorious Vandal king in language that calls attention to either his barbarian or Vandal origins.[24]

Following the death of Gaiseric in 477, Procopius moves quickly through the reigns of Gaiseric's successors down to the accession of Hilderic in 523. He has relatively little to say about the three Vandal kings in between. Of Gaiseric's son Huneric, Procopius merely notes that "Huneric became the most savage and most unjust of all men towards the Christians in Libya."[25] Procopius' main interest here is the persecution of Catholics under the Arian king, and he goes on to list the atrocities committed against them. A similarly brief assessment is offered for Huneric's successor, Gunthamund, who perpetuated the policies of his predecessor amid his struggles against Moorish neighbors. Yet Procopius offers little moral assessment of his reign either, observing merely that he died "having compelled the Christians with greater sufferings."[26] In the above three examples, Procopius is dealing with barbarian kings who had taken control of one of the most lucrative provinces of the western empire, yet he takes no note of the barbarian identity of the Vandal kings. Rather, he is only interested in the political, economic, and military problems they caused for the empire and in their treatment of their orthodox Christian subjects.

Slightly more information appears in assessments of the reigns of the Vandal kings who follow. After the death of Gunthamund from sickness, Thrasamund succeeded to the throne and is described as

---

[23] Γιζέριχος δὲ τά τε πολέμια ὡς ἄριστα ἐξήσκητο καὶ δεινότατος ἦν ἀνθρώπων ἁπάντων (*Wars* 3.3.24).

[24] For a discussion of Constantinople's interest in restoring stability to the west and North Africa to imperial control prior to the reign of Justinian, see Heather, *The Fall of the Roman Empire*, 385, 388–89.

[25] γέγονε δὲ Ὀνώριχος ἐς τοὺς ἐν Λιβύῃ Χριστιανοὺς ὠμότατός τε καὶ ἀδικώτατος ἀνθρώπων ἁπάντων (*Wars* 3.8.3).

[26] μείζοσι δὲ τοὺς Χριστιανοὺς ὑπαγαγὼν πάθεσιν (*Wars* 3.8.7).

εἴδους τε καὶ ξυνέσεως ἐς τὰ μάλιστα καὶ μεγαλοψυχίας εὖ ἥκων. τοὺς μέντοι Χριστιανοὺς ἐβιάζετο μεταβαλέσθαι τὴν πάτριον δόξαν, οὐκ αἰκιζόμενος τὰ σώματα ὥσπερ οἱ πρότεροι, ἀλλὰ τιμαῖς τε καὶ ἀρχαῖς μετιὼν καὶ χρήμασι μεγάλοις δωρούμενος. ... ἐγένετο δὲ φίλος καὶ Ἀναστασίῳ βασιλεῖ ἐς τὰ μάλιστα.[27]

particularly well endowed with good looks, intelligence, and magnanimity. However, he compelled the Christians to change the faith of their fathers, not by harming their bodies as had his predecessors, but pursuing them with honors and positions of authority and giving great gifts of money ... and he became a great friend of the emperor Anastasius.

Though Thrasamund perpetuated the Vandal policy of persecuting orthodox Christians, Procopius nevertheless confesses that Thrasamund had his positive qualities, not least of which were his friendly relations with the emperor. It is not clear in the narrative if this friendship between Thrasamund and Anastasius was merely of a diplomatic nature, such as that attested between Huneric and Zeno in a fragment of Malchus (φίλος τε τῷ βασιλεῖ), or whether it is actually meant to indiciate a personal connection.[28] Nevertheless, the amicable relations, formal or otherwise, between Thrasamund and the emperor are represented in terms that exhibit no interest in the Vandal's non-Roman identity.

As he nears the beginning of the Vandal war in 533, Procopius slows down the pace of the narrative and provides more detail on the character of the Vandal king Hilderic, whose deposition by his cousin Gelimer would serve as a pretext for Justinian to launch his attack on North Africa – the fifth effort to reclaim the province since the Vandals had crossed the strait of Gibraltar in 429:

Ἰλδέριχος δὲ Ὁνωρίχου τοῦ Γιζερίχου παῖς τὴν βασιλείαν παρέλαβεν, ὃς τὰ μὲν ἐς τοὺς ὑπηκόους εὐπρόσοδός τε ἦν καὶ ὅλως πρᾷος, καὶ οὔτε Χριστιανοῖς οὔτε τῳ ἄλλῳ χαλεπὸς ἐγεγόνει, τὰ δὲ ἐς τὸν πόλεμον μαλθακός τε λίαν καὶ οὐδὲ ἄχρι ἐς τὰ ὦτα τὸ πρᾶγμά οἱ τοῦτο ἐθέλων ἰέναι. ... Ἰλδέριχος δὲ φίλος ἐς τὰ μάλιστα Ἰουστινιανῷ καὶ ξένος ἐγένετο ... χρήμασί τε μεγάλοις ἀλλήλους ἐδωροῦντο.[29]

Hilderic, the son of Huneric who was the son of Gaiseric, took over the empire; he was both approachable to his subjects and very mild, nor was he harsh towards the Christians or any other person; he was altogether weak in respect of warfare, not wishing the matter to come so far as to his ears. ... Hilderic was a great friend of Justinian and became his guest-friend ... they made great gifts of money to one another.

---

[27] *Wars* 3.8.8–14.　　[28] "A friend to the emperor." Quoted in Conant, *Staying Roman*, 33.
[29] *Wars* 3.9.1–5.

In great contrast to the cunning and rapaciousness of the founder of the Vandal kingdom, Hilderic is a wholly pacific figure, and it would seem that the friendship between him and Justinian indicated by Procopius is intended to be understood as a sincere connection. The Vandal king is not only free of any charge of barbarism but appears a cooperative partner of the emperor, perhaps even hinting at a collegial relationship such as that between the eastern and western emperors of the Theodosian dynasty. It is easy to see how this representation serves the narrative of the *Wars*, however, as it is the deposition of Hilderic by his cousin Gelimer that provides the pretext for Justinian to launch his attack on the Vandal kingdom. But this would suggest that in Procopius' eyes, the justification for the campaign is rooted not in the barbarian illegitimacy of the Vandal kingdom, but rather in a legal and moral imperative precipitated by Gelimer's usurpation. Indeed, a letter of Justinian quoted in the text urges Gelimer to await his proper turn in the succession and to take the title of power solely according to the proper time and law of Gaiseric.[30] Not only does Procopius here acknowledge the legality of the polity established by Gaiseric; he also goes on to have Justinian claim that, far from being a campaign against the successor to the *basileia* of Gaiseric, the coming invasion will avenge the Vandal progenitor himself.[31] For Gaiseric had declared that his oldest direct descendant should hold the Vandal throne. The explicit justification for the reconquest of North Africa, therefore, is the illegality of Gelimer's usurpation, a formulation that necessarily recognizes the otherwise legitimate status of Vandal rule. The deposed Vandal king Hilderic appears in the *Wars* more as an imperial colleague on equal diplomatic footing than a barbarian ruling a conquest state.[32]

The last ruler of the Vandal kingdom was Gelimer, who, impatient of the proper order of the succession laid down by his grandfather Gaiseric, deposed, imprisoned, and eventually murdered his cousin Hilderic. On introducing him in the narrative, Procopius sketches a brief, negative portrait of Gelimer:

---

[30] προσδέχου τε ἀπὸ τοῦ χρόνου καὶ τοῦ Γιζερίχου· νόμου μόνον λαβεῖν τὸ τοῦ πράγματος ὄνομα (*Wars* 3.9.12).

[31] τῷ γὰρ ἐκδεξαμένῳ τὴν ἐκείνου βασιλείαν ἐρχόμεθα οὐ πολεμήσοντες, ἀλλὰ τὰ δυνατὰ τιμωρήσοντες (*Wars* 3.9.19).

[32] As Procopius was surely aware, Hilderic was himself the son of the imperial princess Eudocia and thus a descendant of Theodosius I. Yet Procopius makes no mention of his blood connection to a Roman dynasty as either a basis for his friendly relations with Justinian or for the legitimacy of the Vandal kingdom.

ὃς τὰ μὲν πολέμια ἐδόκει τῶν καθ' αὑτὸν ἄριστος εἶναι, ἄλλως δὲ δεινός τε ἦν καὶ κακοήθης καὶ πράγμασί τε νεωτέροις καὶ χρήμασιν ἐπιτίθεσθαι ἀλλοτρίοις ἐξεπιστάμενος.[33]

This man seemed to be the most excellent in warfare of those in his own day; otherwise he was a man to be reckoned with and wicked, knowing full well how to make use of untoward deeds and other people's money.

While calling attention to Gelimer's moral failings and at the same time noting his skill in the arts of war, Procopius highlights the contrast with the peaceful and amicable Hilderic. The contrast heightens expectations of the campaign to be launched against the Vandal usurper, whose seizure of the throne reintroduces both the violence exemplified by Gaiseric and the threat posed to Constantinople. However, as with previous Vandal kings, the criticism offered by Procopius is in strictly moral terms that make no mention of Gelimer's barbarian origin. As far as Procopius is concerned, the fact that Gelimer and his predecessors are all Vandals, and therefore barbarians, has neither explanatory nor delegitimizing force. The critique of Gelimer is in ethical and legal terms, not ethnological ones.

It is interesting to note that Gelimer is the only Vandal king who is actually labeled as a "tyrant" by Procopius, a distinction that implies the legitimacy of his royal predecessors extending back to Gaiseric. Indeed, in a letter addressed to Gelimer by Justinian, Procopius quotes the emperor urging the Vandal not to exchange the name of tyrant, *tyrannos*-τύραννος, for that of emperor, *basileus*-βασιλεύς, by seizing power unlawfully.[34] In fact, the term *tyrannos*-τύραννος appears in several places throughout the *Wars*, but Procopius never suggests an ethnic association with the label. The Romans Vitalianus, John, Boniface, both Maximus the elder and younger, Stotzas, Maximinus, and Gontharis are all named tyrants either by Procopius or by characters speaking in the narrative.[35] By contrast, only three barbarians are referred to as tyrants in the *Wars*.[36] The first is the Goth Godas, initially in the service of the Vandals, who rebels and seizes control of Sardinia, setting up a tyranny (τυραννίδι) there. Odoacer, who had

---

[33] *Wars* 3.9.7.

[34] μήτε τοῦ βασιλέως ὀνόματος ἀνταλλάξῃ τὴν τοῦ τυράννου προσηγορίαν (*Wars* 3.9.11).

[35] Vitalianus: *Wars* 1.8.3; John: 3.3.7; Boniface: 3.3.17; Maximus the elder: 3.4.16; Maximus the younger: 3.4.36; Stotzas: 4.15.26–7; Maximinus: 4.18.2; Gontharis: 4.25.1.

[36] The case of Gontharis is a perfect example of the problems with assuming a Germanic name must indicate a non-Roman identity. Procopius nowhere suggests that the tyrant Gontharis is anything but a Roman in the service of Roman armies, despite the fact that he bears the same name as the Vandal Gaiseric's own brother. On the problems of trying to determine who is a Roman and who is a barbarian in this period, see Greatrex, "Roman Identity in the Sixth Century," 267–92; Chrysos, "Romans and Foreigners," 119–36.

deposed Romulus Augustulus in 476 and thus brought an end to the western empire, is described by Procopius as setting up a tyranny (τυραν-νίδα).[37] Lastly, Theoderic himself is said to be a tyrant, although, as will be shown below, the term in Theoderic's case is only introduced to be subverted. The Roman generals Belisarius and Narses both refer to Gothic rule as a tyrrany, and the former claims that Theoderic was just as much a tyrant as Odoacer.[38] However, in no case is this label determined by ethnicity such that a barbarian ruler is a tyrant by default. Tyranny is, as in earlier centuries, limited to a designation for unlawful usurpation of political power, irrespective of ethnic identity. Indeed, even Roman rule itself is labeled a tyranny by the Lazi in an embassy to the Persian king Khosrow.[39]

It is also important to consider the implications of the titles *basileus*-βασιλεύς and *rex*-ῥήξ as they are used throughout the *Wars*. As will be discussed below, Procopius notes that the title *rex*-ῥήξ is the preferred title of barbarian rulers in the west.[40] However, this word appears only on two occasions in all eight books of the *Wars*,[41] and the two instances where it does appear are remarkably distinct from one another in context. The first is when Procopius recounts the reign of Theoderic when providing his history of the Ostrogothic kingdom. In that case he describes how Theoderic

> καὶ βασιλέως μὲν τοῦ Ῥωμαίων οὔτε τοῦ σχήματος οὔτε τοῦ ὀνόματος
> ἐπιβατεῦσαι ἠξίωσεν, ἀλλὰ καὶ ῥὴξ διεβίου καλούμενος (οὕτω γὰρ σφῶν
> τοὺς ἡγεμόνας καλεῖν οἱ βάρβαροι νενομίκασι) [...].[42]

> did not think it proper to claim either the title or regalia of the emperor of the Romans but rather lived his life being called *rex*, as it is customary for the barbarians to call their rulers.

The second use of the word *rex*-ῥήξ occurs in a somewhat random circumstance in reference to a king of the Heruli living north of the Danube; and even then the Heruli king is referred to as *basileus* in the following

---

[37] Godas: *Wars* 3.10.27; Odoacer: *Wars* 5.1.8.
[38] Only in one instance do we see tyranny qualified by the word "barbarian": in a speech of Belisarius that refers to the rule of "barbarian tyrants," βαρβάρων τυράννων (*Wars* 5.8.27). The general Narses makes no such distinction (8.30.2). Belisarius' comparison of Theoderic to Odoacer appears at 6.6.23.
[39] *Wars* 2.15.19.
[40] See Arnold for the actual titulature employed by Theoderic, *Theoderic and the Roman Imperial Restoration*, 75–76, and also Chrysos, "The Title Βασιλεύς in Early Byzantine International Relations," 52–57. On titulature in general in the barbarian kingdoms, see Gillett, "Was Ethnicity Politicized in the Earliest Medieval Kingdoms?" 85–121.
[41] Also noted by Chrysos, "The Title Βασιλεύς in Early Byzantine International Relations," 56–57.
[42] *Wars* 5.1.26.

sentence.[43] It is difficult to see why Procopius uses *rex*-ῥήξ in this latter context at all. It is significant, though, that *basileus* is the default term used by Procopius for any barbarian figure who exercises a degree of sovereignty over his own people, particularly given the fact that neither Goths nor Vandals, or even Franks, ever actually assumed the imperial titles of *augustus* or *imperator*.[44] Chrysos, citing Helm and Vetter, has observed that, with the exception of Malalas and Olympiodorus, who preferred the terms ῥῆγες or φύλαρχοι, most Greek literary sources of the period did in fact use the term *basileus* in referring to Germanic kings.[45] Procopius' usage of *basileus* for the new rulers of the west is therefore not unique.

Over the course of the sixth century, *basileus* had already begun to replace the title of *autokratōr*-αὐτοκράτωρ, the Greek version of Latin *imperator*, becoming prominent during Justinian's reign, although not officially denoting the imperial office until the seventh century.[46] In virtually all other instances than the two appearances of *rex*-ῥήξ, Procopius refers to barbarian "kings," be they Goths, Vandals, Persians – even Heruli north of the frontier – as "emperors," using the same term to denote their political position as he does that of Justinian, i.e., *basileus*-βασιλεύς.[47] Moreover, he refers to the barbarian kingdoms themselves as "republics," *politeia*-πολιτεία, and the institutions of rulership as either *archē*-ἀρχή or *basileia*-βασίλεια – again, the same terms as those used for the Roman Empire. Chrysos explains this usage, in the case of two letters sent from Justinian to Gelimer and quoted by Procopius, by virtue of "the fact that these two letters were written originally in Latin, and the 'purist' Procopius contented himself with translating *rex* and *regnum* of the original into βασιλεύς and βασίλεια."[48] The important point, as has been argued by

---

[43] *Wars* 6.14.38. Procopius, therefore, cannot be said to avoid using *basileus* in reference to the Heruli king as Chrysos claims ("The Title Βασιλεύς in Early Byzantine International Relations," 57). Perhaps Procopius uses the term ῥήξ here to underscore that this is a barbarian practice? Regardless, the fact that this is the only other occurrence of the title is peculiar.

[44] Chrysos, "The Title Βασιλεύς in Early Byzantine International Relations," 53, 56.   [45] Ibid., 54.

[46] McCormick, "Emperor and Court," 142. Kaldellis has pointed out that *basileus* had been an informal imperial title already for centuries prior to its purported official adoption by Heraclius in the seventh century. *Hellenism in Byzantium*, 66.

[47] For a discussion of analogous usage in Priscus of Panium, see Blockley, *The Fragmentary Classicizing Historians of the Later Roman Empire*, 53. Blockley concludes that there is no significance in Priscus' choice of different Greek terms employed for barbarian royal titulature. Yet the fact that the use of even an informal Roman imperial title for barbarian rulers carried with it no taboo is in itself a significant fact.

[48] Chrysos, "The Title Βασιλεύς in Early Byzantine International Relations," 55. This explanation is virtually the same as that of Ennslin, which is quoted by Chrysos: "Procopius as a 'purist' avoided using non-Greek words as much as possible" (Prokop als Purist vermeidet es möglichst nichtgriechische Wörter zu gebrauchen). Ibid., 54, n. 164.

Veh, is that the language used in the letters quoted by Procopius is a reflection of the historian's chosen mode of expression and not that of the chancellery.[49] In the case of Theoderic, Procopius thus deviates from his preferred practice of referring to barbarian kings as "emperors" in the one case where he wishes to emphasize the fact that Theoderic actually embodies and exemplifies the imperial ideal: "[T]he moral and political image of the true ruler, which Procopius attributes to Theoderic, is not that of a 'king', but that of a Roman emperor."[50]

That Procopius uses *basileus* to refer to barbarian rulers is often obscured by the fact that *basileus* is usually translated as "emperor" when referring to Justinian or other emperors of the Romans but "king" when referring to a ruler of the barbarian kingdoms. It is important to keep in mind that Procopius himself does not make this distinction. The barbarian kingdoms are thus recognized in Procopius as occupying a status of legitimate sovereignty, on par with the empire of Persia, rather than of illegitimate conquest. Procopius' extension of the title of supreme imperial power to barbarian kings implicitly recognizes the legitimacy of the rulers in question, or at least exhibits a lack of any interest in using titulature to refute their claims to power. It also stands in significant contrast to the terms *jian* 僭 and *wei* 偽, which denote usurpation and illegitimacy and are consistently used in reference to the barbarian states of north China in the *Jin shu*.[51] While these terms do not contain any ethnographic undertones and are used for Chinese as well as non-Chinese actors, the fact that any assumption of royal or imperial power by barbarian figures is generally accompanied by such terms leaves no ambiguity regarding the invalidity of such claims.

To return to the destruction of the Vandal kingdom, it is interesting to observe that even though Gelimer is an unlawful usurper, he is not a wholly unsympathetic figure. In the closing scene of book three and following the Vandals' first disastrous encounter with the invading Roman armies and withdrawal from their capital city of Carthage, Gelimer is reunited with his brother Tzazon and the elite Vandal troops previously

---

[49] "Indessen tragen auch sie in ihrer Schlichte nicht das rhetorische Gewand der byzantinischen Kanzlei, sondern der Ausdrucksweise Prokops [...]." Veh, "Zur Geschichtsschreibung und Weltauffassung des Prokop von Caesarea," 16. Also noted by Chrysos.

[50] Chrysos, "The Title Βασιλεύς in Early Byzantine International Relations," 57.

[51] Just to offer a pair of examples from one of the fascicles in the Chronicles: when the Xiongnu Liu Cong of the Former Zhao takes the throne, the *Jin shu* notes the year in which he "usurped the imperial throne," 僭即皇帝位 (*Jin shu* 102.2658); on his death, the *Jin shu* notes that he was "illegitimately given the posthumous title 'Emperor Zhaowu'," 偽諡曰昭武皇帝 (102.2677).

sent to put down the rebellion of Godas in Sardinia. Having received word of the Roman invasion, Tzazon had hastened back to North Africa and joined his troops with what remains of his brother Gelimer's Vandal army. When the forces of Gelimer and Tzazon meet, there is an arresting scene of which Procopius says, "even if it should fall to one of their enemies to observe it, even he would pity the Vandals and indeed [the caprice of] human fortune."[52] He goes on to describe how Gelimer and Tzazon embrace one another, and each man of their respective entourages embraces one from the other group in silent lamentation; they stand entwined "as though grown together," ὥσπερ ἀλλήλοις ἐμπεφυκότες, neither asking the other about the events in either Sardinia or Africa.[53] The pathos is increased with the final lines of book three:

οὐ μὴν οὐδὲ γυναικῶν ἢ παίδων ἰδίων λόγον ἐποιοῦντό τινα, ἐξεπιστάμε-
νοι ὡς, ἤν τις αὐτοῖς ἐνταῦθα οὐκ εἴη, δῆλον ὅτι ἢ ἐτελεύτα ἢ ὑπὸ τῶν
πολεμίων ταῖς χερσὶ γέγονε. ταῦτα μὲν δὴ ταύτῃ πῃ ἔσχεν.[54]

Nor indeed did they say a word about their own women and children, understanding fully that if one of their own was not there, there was no doubt but that the loved one had either died or was in the hands of the enemy. Matters were in such a state.

This scene is one of the most emotionally evocative to be found in the *Wars*, and it is curious that in a text that covers over twenty-five years of warfare, it is the misfortune of the barbarian Vandals that receives such delicate treatment. Of course the descriptions of the plague in Constantinople and the famine in Italy depict horrific suffering, but it is always generalized to the populations at large and relatively anonymous.[55] But Procopius often uses the reverses suffered by figures on either side of the battle lines, irrespective of Roman or barbarian identity, to serve as an opportunity to comment on the instability of chance and fragility of human endeavor. Another such example is the philosophical reflection of Gelimer while being led in a triumphal procession in Constantinople; the Vandal king quotes from the Book of Ecclesiastes, uttering the words "vanity of vanities, all is vanity."[56] Gelimer appears not as a conquered savage fit for the arena, but rather as a Christian who has studied scripture and has the wisdom to recognize the same fickleness of fortune,

---

[52] εἰ καὶ αὐτῶν πολεμίων ἀνδρὶ θεατῇ γενέσθαι τετύχηκε, τάχα ἂν καὶ αὐτὸς Βανδίλους τε τότε καὶ τύχην τὴν ἀνθρωπείαν ᾠκτίσατο (*Wars* 3.25.23).
[53] *Wars* 3.25.25.   [54] *Wars* 3.25.26.
[55] For the plague in Constantinople, see *Wars* 2.22–23; for the famine in Italy, 6.20.15–33.
[56] ματαιότης ματαιοτήτων, τὰ πάντα ματαιότης (*Wars* 4.9.11).

tyche-τύχη, so often commented on by Procopius. The selection of barbarian actors for such scenes undermines a distinction between them and the Romans, since it demonstrates that all are subject to the same temptations and punishments of hubris and the folly of putting faith in man's ability to control his fate. It thus illustrates what Cesa has described as Procopius' choice to present the barbarian kings "characterized with great equanimity and not without a certain sympathy."[57]

The Goths

Following the swift destruction of the Vandal kingdom in 534, the imperial armies were next sent against the Ostrogothic kingdom of Italy. On the arrival of the Roman general Belisarius, Italy was being ruled by the Goth Vitigis, who had been acclaimed king by his people and had overthrown the house of Theoderic. In Italy, imperial forces initially met with considerable successes. But following the surrender of Vitigis in Ravenna in 540, Roman mismanagement of reconquered territory allowed the rapid rise of the Gothic king Totila, who managed to win back significant amounts of the peninsula, largely undoing the achievements of Belisarius. If Procopius' assessments of Vandal rulers seemed free of ethnographic "othering," this tendency is even more pronounced in his account of the campaigns to retake the city of Rome and the Italian peninsula.

It is a great irony, when considered in light of xenophobia and exclusivity often purported to characterize representations of non-Greeks and non-Romans in classical literature, that the most idyllic depiction of a political figure in the *Wars* is that of the Gothic king Theoderic.[58] Following an account of Theoderic's invasion of Italy at the behest of emperor Zeno, defeat of the barbarian king Odoacer, and subsequent decades of Theoderic's rule, Procopius offers a summary of the deceased king's tenure. First, as noted above, he claims that Theoderic neither saw fit to take the imperial title of *basileus* nor assume the trappings of imperial office but rather contented himself with the title *rex* preferred by barbarian custom. This being the case, however, Procopius goes on to give a glowing account of Theoderic's reign:

---

[57] "caratterizzati con molta equanimità e non senza una certa simpatia." Cesa, "Etnografia e geografia nella visione storica di Procopio di Caesarea," 214.

[58] This point has been observed by several scholars, e.g., Kaldellis, *Procopius of Caesarea*, 160; Goltz, "Anspruch und Wirklichkeit," 287–91.

τῶν μέντοι κατηκόων τῶν αὐτοῦ προὔστη ξύμπαντα περιβαλλόμενος ὅσα
τῷ φύσει βασιλεῖ ἥρμοσται. δικαιοσύνης τε γὰρ ὑπερφυῶς ἐπεμελήσατο
καὶ τοὺς νόμους ἐν τῷ βεβαίῳ διεσώσατο, ἔκ τε βαρβάρων τῶν περιοίκων
τὴν χώραν ἀσφαλῶς διεφύλαξε, ξυνέσεώς τε καὶ ἀνδρίας ἐς ἄκρον ἐληλύθει
ὡς μάλιστα. καὶ ἀδίκημα σχεδόν τι οὐδὲν οὔτε αὐτὸς ἐς τοὺς ἀρχομένους
εἰργάζετο οὔτε τῳ ἄλλῳ τὰ τοιαῦτα ἐγκεχειρηκότι ἐπέτρεπε, πλήν γε δὴ
ὅτι τῶν χωρίων τὴν μοῖραν ἐν σφίσιν αὐτοῖς Γότθοι ἐνείμαντο, ἥνπερ
Ὀδόακρος τοῖς στασιώταις τοῖς αὐτοῦ ἔδωκεν. ἦν τε ὁ Θευδέριχος λόγῳ
μὲν τύραννος, ἔργῳ δὲ βασιλεὺς ἀληθὴς τῶν ἐν ταύτῃ τῇ τιμῇ τὸ ἐξ ἀρχῆς
ηὐδοκιμηκότων οὐδενὸς ἧσσον, ἔρως τε αὐτοῦ ἔν τε Γότθοις καὶ Ἰταλιώταις
πολὺς ἤκμασε, καὶ ταῦτα ἀπὸ τοῦ ἀνθρωπείου τρόπου. ... ἔτη δὲ
ἐπιβιοὺς ἑπτὰ καὶ τριάκοντα ἐτελεύτησε, φοβερὸς μὲν τοῖς πολεμίοις γεγο-
νὼς ἅπασι, πόθον δὲ αὐτοῦ πολύν τινα ἐς τοὺς ὑπηκόους ἀπολιπών.[59]

Indeed, he governed his subjects having embraced all those things that
characterize a man who is an emperor by nature. He showed an extraordinary attention to justice and preserved the laws most securely; and he
guarded the land safely against the barbarian peoples on the borders and
arrived at the pinnacle of intelligence and courage. And he himself did
hardly any wrong to those he ruled, nor did he permit anyone else trying to
do so – except for the fact that the Goths apportioned among themselves
the allocation of the lands which Odoacer had given to his supporters.
Theodoric was a tyrant in name, but he was a true emperor in deed, no less
than any of those who have been esteemed in that office from the very
beginning; and a great love of him flourished among both the Goths and
Italians – these things being very much out of the ordinary in mens'
affairs. ... He died having been in power for thirty-seven years and having
become a terror to all of his enemies, leaving behind him a great yearning
for his presence among his subjects.

In this case, Theodoric's barbarian identity is in fact noted in a political
context with reference to his choice of title, as "the barbarians are accustomed to do."[60] But what is striking is that it occurs in a wholly neutral
sense, and neither undermines nor impugns Theodoric's political status.
He upheld justice and the rule of law, two essential qualities in Roman
political ideology that were particularly prominent in the propaganda of
Justinian's reign.[61] As ruler over the Romans, he defended them from the
barbarians on the borders, i.e., the Gepids and the Franks, and there is a
suggestion that he also defended them from some of his own people:
Procopius offers the apology that the land appropriations that occurred
under his tenure were merely a perpetuation of those that had already been

---

[59] *Wars* 5.1.26–31.   [60] οἱ βάρβαροι νενομίκασι (*Wars* 5.1.26).
[61] Pazdernik, "Justinianic Ideology and the Power of the Past," 185–212.

instituted under Odoacer, whom Theoderic had removed from power at the behest of the emperor Zeno. Despite his barbarian identity, Theoderic himself "by nature" possessed the qualities of a Roman sovereign and was worthy to be ranked alongside the likes of Augustus and Trajan. Pazdernik has pointed out that the eulogy for Theoderic shares significant intertextual features with Thucydides' obituary for Pericles; he also suggests that a later eulogy for Belisarius in book seven is intended to pair both of these men, Theoderic and Belisarius, as "superlative figure[s], whose personal qualities are for the most part admirable and whose accomplishments are unmatched."[62] For the king of an unambiguously barbarian people to receive such praise indicates that any dichotomy between barbarians and Romans was far from firm.

This valorization of Gothic royalty does not end with Theoderic's death. His daughter Amalasuintha, who ruled as a steward for her young son Athalaric after Theoderic's death in 526, receives an obituary that does not fall far short of that accorded to her father:

Ἀμαλασοῦνθα δὲ ἅτε τοῦ παιδὸς ἐπίτροπος οὖσα, τὴν ἀρχὴν διωκεῖτο, ξυνέσεως μὲν καὶ δικαιοσύνης ἐπὶ πλεῖστον ἐλθοῦσα, τῆς δὲ φύσεως ἐς ἄγαν τὸ ἀρρενωπὸν ἐνδεικνυμένη. ὅσον τε χρόνον τῆς πολιτείας προὔστη, οὐδένα τῶν πάντων Ῥωμαίων ἐς τὸ σῶμα ἐκόλασεν ἢ χρήμασιν ἐζημίωσεν. οὐ μὴν οὐδὲ Γότθοις ξυνεχώρησεν ἐς τὴν ἐς ἐκείνους ἀδικίαν ὀργῶσιν [...].[63]

Amalasuintha, being the guardian of her son, governed the empire – on the one hand arriving at the culmination of intelligence and justice, and on the other revealing the very masculine quality of her nature. As long as she governed the state, she neither harmed the body of any of the Romans nor punished anyone by taking his property. Indeed, she did not comply with the Goths who were eager to commit injustice against them.

The beneficent rule of Theoderic is thus perpetuated under his daughter Amalasuintha, who embodies all of the desirable qualities in a monarch. She does seem to possess one trait at which there might be room for

---

[62] Pazdernik, "Reinventing Theoderic in Procopius' *Gothic War*," 138–40, 148. Another possible correlation between Belisarius and Theoderic is the fact that each of them, in the eyes of Procopius, is guilty of only a single crime. In the case of Belisarius, it is the murder of the Roman general Constantius, and "this was the only unholy act performed by Belisarius, which was in no way worthy of his character": τοῦτο Βελισαρίῳ εἴργασται μόνον οὐχ ὅσιον ἔργον καὶ ἤθους τοῦ αὐτοῦ οὐδαμῶς ἄξιον (*Wars* 6.8.18). For Theoderic, it is the well-known murder of the senatorial philosopher Boethius, and Theoderic himself died after "having committed this first and last injustice against his subjects": ἀδίκημα τοῦτο πρῶτόν τε καὶ τελευταῖον ἐς τοὺς ὑπηκόους τοὺς αὐτοῦ δράσας (5.1.39).

[63] *Wars* 5.2.3–5.

reservation: it is not her Gothic ancestry, but rather her female gender, which Procopius assures is in fact compensated for by her "masculine nature."[64] Although masculinity exhibited in a woman who engages in political life could be considered a matter of censure, Procopius gives no indication of his disapproval. Moreover, he describes Amalasuintha in the *Anecdota* in similarly positive terms, as "most attractive," εὐπρεπὴς ἄγαν, and possessing "greatness," μεγαλοπρεπές, and "exceptional masculinity," διαφερόντως ἀρρενοπόν.[65] As seen in the eulogy for Theoderic, the reign of Amalasuintha also bears witness to a certain tension between the impulses of the Goths and the restraint imposed upon them by their rulers who are determined to protect the interests of their Roman subjects. However, neither Amalasuintha nor her father is implicated in this tendency of the Goths to seek their own enrichment at the expense of the Romans.

The tension between Gothic rulers and the Gothic nobility in Italy culminates in a conflict where members of the latter object to Amalasuintha's desire to give her son Athalaric, now king of the Goths following the death of Theoderic, a Roman education. For the Goths object to Athalaric's being forced to learn his letters and to heed the counsels of senior Gothic men, preferring instead that he be prompted toward "virtue according to barbarian custom,"[66] i.e., in such a way that would allow the Gothic elites to abuse Roman citizens.[67] They cite the example of Theoderic himself, who had supposedly frowned upon the enervating effects of Roman education.[68] And when Athalaric comes of age, he ends up indulging in drinking and sex, thanks to the exhortations of his Gothic companions, and turns out to be "exceptionally wicked and less willing to heed his mother on account of his stupidity."[69]

---

[64] Amalasuintha's masculine qualities are also explicitly attested at *Wars* 5.2.21. This may perhaps be a reference to the trope of the masculine barbarian woman, the classic example of which is, of course, the Amazons, but which elsewhere appears in representations of the British queen Boudica in Tacitus and Cassius Dio. See Adler, *Valorizing the Barbarian*, 117–61.

[65] *Anecdota* 16.1.   [66] τὴν ἀρετὴν κατά γε τὸν βάρβαρον νόμον (*Wars* 5.2.17).

[67] "In their desire for injustice against their subjects, they wanted to be ruled by him in a more barbarous manner": τῆς γὰρ ἐς τοὺς ὑπηκόους ἀδικίας ἐπιθυμίᾳ βαρβαρικώτερον πρὸς αὐτοῦ ἄρχεσθαι ἤθελον (*Wars* 5.2.8).

[68] On the implausibility of assertions that Theoderic himself was uneducated or illiterate, see Hen, *Roman Barbarians: The Royal Court and Culture in the Early Medieval West*, 37–39. Hen also suggests that it is likely that Theoderic was a patron of the arts during his reign, and he certainly saw to a thorough education for his daughter Amalasuintha. Procopius leaves it to the reader to decide as to the authenticity of the claims of the Goths who desire royal sanction for their revels.

[69] ἐπειδὴ τάχιστα ἐς ἥβην ἦλθεν, ἔς τε μέθην καὶ γυναικῶν μίξεις παρακαλοῦντες, κακοήθη τε διαφερόντως εἶναι καὶ τῇ μητρὶ ὑπὸ ἀβελτερίας ἀπειθέστερον κατεστήσαντο (*Wars* 5.2.19).

This reference to "barbarian custom" is the closest Procopius comes to explaining the shortcomings of a Gothic or Vandal ruler in reference to his or her barbarian origins. The wishes of the Gothic nobility to reject the civilizing effects of Roman education and instead pursue their vices of excess does indeed seem to be an expression of familiar barbarian stereotypes. But even here it is significant that the stereotype appears in a juxtaposition of the civilized behavior of Amalasuintha and that of the Gothic elites who desire a more permissive sovereign – not between a Goth and a Roman. It is also important to note that the noble Goths' objection to the boy's Roman education also includes their demand that Amalasuintha dismiss the three elderly Goths whom she had appointed to be the boy's tutors. If she "wished to have the boy grounded in the same way of life as that of rulers of the Romans,"[70] it is curious that she "chose three old men of the Goths whom she knew, more than all others, to be wise and reasonable and ordered them to live with Athalaric."[71] Yet this detail only serves to underscore that what befits a Roman and what befits a Goth are not antithetical.

Moreover, the behaviors that Procopius presents as comprising the barbarian way of life in this case (typified by excesses of wine, women, and violence) are not an innate feature of young Athalaric's character. Indeed, this particular example explicitly indicates that the person the young man will become is determined by his education, for which there are two alternatives: the Roman path of letters and *civilitas* – a virtue that Procopius suggests may be acquired under the tutelage of senior Gothic mentors – or the barbarism of the Gothic nobility. Implicit, then, is the possibility that, should his mother have had her way, Athalaric would have grown up to emulate the virtues of both his mother and grandfather. A student of Herodotus (and perhaps Pindar), Procopius makes clear that *nomos*, not blood, is king.[72] The comparative element of this study has shown that in Chinese historiography one sees frequent reference to an immutable nature that defines not only whole groups but also individuals. While some of the Goths are shown to behave in stereotypically barbarian ways, the contest over Athalaric's education makes it clear that the youth's eventual character was hardly a foregone conclusion.

---

[70] Ἀμαλασοῦνθα τὸν παῖδα ἐβούλετο τοῖς Ῥωμαίων ἄρχουσι τὰ ἐς τὴν δίαιταν ὁμότροπον καταστήσασθαι (*Wars* 5.2.6).

[71] τρεῖς τε ἀπολεξαμένη τῶν ἐν Γότθοις γερόντων, οὕσπερ ἠπίστατο μᾶλλον ἁπάντων ξυνετούς τε καὶ ἐπιεικεῖς εἶναι, ξυνδιαιτᾶσθαι Ἀταλαρίχῳ ἐκέλευε (*Wars* 5.2.7).

[72] καὶ ὀρθῶς μοι δοκέει Πίνδαρος ποιῆσαι νόμον πάντων βασιλέα φήσας εἶναι (Hdt. 3.38.4). Also see above, 66.

Halsall reads this episode relating to Athalaric's education, as well as the account of the literary preoccupations of Theodahad to be discussed below, as an ironic satire of barbarian failure at playing Roman.[73] Yet Halsall overstates the "heavy, deliberate irony," "punchlines," and "outright joke [s]" he envisions in the text. He assumes that instances in which a barbarian behaves in a stereotypically "Roman" way are evidence of a deliberate inversion that is intended to be humorous. While drawing on examples from other Greek and Roman authors, Halsall argues that representing a known barbarian with behaviors typical of Greeks and Romans "was ludicrous, it was ridiculous, and it could be funny."[74] This may well be the case in some instances, yet it is a gross overstatement to assume that such inversions are always intended to be humorous or are even inversions in the first place. If Halsall is right, then the humor in classical historiography has been massively underappreciated: we have not realized that Herodotus' recorded debate among the Persian Darius and his fellow conspirators over the ideal political constitution is supposed to be comical,[75] that Xenophon was being ironic when in his eulogy of Cyrus he claimed that Persian youth "learn both to rule and be ruled,"[76] that the rhetorical speech of Calgacus in Tacitus, which is one of the harshest known critiques of Roman imperialism, is supposed to be amusing.[77] Even the description of the barbarian usurper Magnentius as "quick in his eagerness for reading" has not been appreciated for the joke that it must be.[78] After all what could be more ridiculous than barbarians, who are unfree and uncouth, holding forth on topics of political organization or proclaiming, in high oratorical style, their determination to live free from the slavery of a foreign empire?

It is also problematic to assume that any time a barbarian behaves in a way that we assume to be stereotypically "Roman" this represents an inversion, yet when a Roman exhibits some flaw in character such as greed, stupidity, perfidy, etc., it is simply a facet of that individual's character. Such an approach takes for granted an absolute stability of a barbarian antithesis in the minds of Greeks and Romans that is not borne out by the evidence in our sources. To take an example from the *Wars*: Halsall claims that Procopius makes "much play on the traditional

---

[73] Halsall, "Funny Foreigners," 106–08.   [74] Ibid., 96–97.   [75] Hdt. 3.80–83.

[76] παῖδες ὄντες μανθάνουσιν ἄρχειν τε καὶ ἄρχεσθαι (*Anabasis* 1.9.4). This very formulation is offered by Seneca as one of the crucial distinctions between barbarians and Romans, i.e., "no one is able to rule but he who is able to be ruled": *nemo autem regere potest nisi qui et regi* (*De Ira* 2.15.4).

[77] *Agricola* 30–32.

[78] *Ortus parentibus barbaris, qui Galliam inhabitabant; legendi studio promptus* [...] (*Epitome de Caesaribus* 42.7)

barbarian inability to carry on siege warfare," citing an episode in book five when the Goths build a siege engine that, when brought forward, is unable to get close enough to the wall of Rome to do any damage, and the oxen drawing it are all shot down by Belisarius' bowmen.[79] Granted, Procopius attributes this failure to barbarian simplicity, and one may infer that ineptitude in siege warfare is thus a barbarian attribute.[80] Yet in book eight, when the Romans are in despair at their inability to make headway in their siege of the fortress of Petra, they are saved by a device designed by the barbarian Sabiri, a Hunnic people. Procopius notes that such an idea had never occurred to Romans or Persians, peoples with centuries of experience in siege warfare, which now occurred to these barbarians.[81] In the following chapter, Procopius notes that the Roman efforts to take the fortress, though eventually successful, are plagued by their own negligence, ὀλιγωρία, in contrast to the diligence, ἐπιμέλεια, of the Persians. By Hallsall's logic, these instances must also be examples of comical irony. One is prompted to ask: In what case could one not make the same argument? To always assume that an inversion, comical or otherwise, is necessarily intended when non-Roman figures do not act or speak strictly in accord with barbarian stereotypes is based on modern assumptions of the conceptual rigidity of ancient authors, not on the myriad examples where distinctions have been shown to break down between the civilized and the barbarian. Such arguments are reductive and only serve to flatten the complexity of views expressed by ancient authors.[82]

Moreover, Halsall seems to suggest that "the ludicrously incongruous concept of barbarian education" exemplified by Amalasuintha and Theodahad was an invention of Procopius. Yet this is of course not the case. Cassiodorus, the Roman senator employed by the Gothic regime in Italy, writes in a letter to the senate in 534 that Amalasuintha is "expert in the clarity of Attic diction; she shines with the adornment of Roman eloquence; she exults in the fecundity of her native speech; she excels all others on their own terms as she is equally remarkable in all respects."[83] Theodahad's erudition too, "ludicrously incongruous" to Halsall, finds corroboration in Cassiodorus' letter to the senate on behalf of Amalasuintha that introduces the new king to Roman elites. According to Cassiodorus,

---

[79] Halsall, "Funny Foreigners," 110.   [80] τὴν τῶν βαρβάρων εὐήθειαν (*Wars* 5.22.9).

[81] ἀλλ' αὐτῶν οὐδενὶ τὸ ἐνθύμημα τοῦτο γεγένηται, ὅπερ τούτοις δὴ τοῖς βαρβάροις τανῦν γέγονεν (*Wars* 8.11.28).

[82] On this point, also see Greatrex, "Procopius' Attitude towards the Barbarians," 331.

[83] *Atticae facundiae claritate diserta est: Romani eloquii pompa resplendet: nativi sermonis ubertate gloriatur: excellit cunctos in propriis, cum sit aequaliter ubique mirabilis* (*Variae* 11.1.6).

Theodahad is "resolute in adversity, measured in prosperity, and, what is the most difficult kind of mastery [to obtain], he has been a governor of himself. He adds to these qualities the much sought after erudition of letters which lends ornament to a very praiseworthy nature."[84] One assumes that Cassiodorus was not trying to be funny.

Moreover, there is certainly precedent for well-educated barbarians who were not somehow corrupted by their erudition. For example, there is the case of the emperor Julian's teacher, whom he identifies as "a barbarian, by the gods and goddesses, and a Scythian by birth" – the man to whose instruction the emperor credits his own love of philosophy and virtue.[85] In instances where an author such as Procopius notes the erudition elsewhere accorded to barbarian figures in other sources, there is little basis for a humorously inverted representation of Roman *civilitas*. Lest this response to Halsall's reading of the text seem excessive, it is engaged with at such length here because there remains a tendency, particularly in late antique scholarship, to embrace the notion of a barbarian dichotomy in Greco-Roman thought as an absolute principle that may be taken for granted. Yet as has been argued in Chapter 1, such a notion was frequently problematized in earlier centuries, and even the earliest texts of the Greco-Roman tradition exhibit views challenging the validity of such a distinction.

To return to Procopius' representations of Gothic kings or nobles in the *Wars*, it is of course not the case that they are all represented as exemplars of ethical behavior. The Gothic king Theodahad, who ruled briefly and indecisively, is clearly not a figure worthy of emulation:

> Ἦν δέ τις ἐν Γότθοις Θευδάτος ὄνομα, τῆς Θευδερίχου ἀδελφῆς Ἀμα-
> λαφρίδης υἱός, πόρρω που ἤδη ἡλικίας ἥκων, λόγων μὲν Λατίνων μετα-
> λαχὼν καὶ δογμάτων Πλατωνικῶν, πολέμων δὲ ἀμελετήτως παντάπασιν
> ἔχων, μακράν τε ἀπολελειμμένος τοῦ δραστηρίου, ἐς μέντοι φιλοχρηματίαν
> δαιμονίως ἐσπουδακώς.[86]

> There was a man by the name of Theodahad among the Goths, the son of Theoderic's sister Amalafrida, who was now well into his adulthood and with a share of Latin literature and Platonic philosophy; he was completely untrained in warfare being wholly bereft of vigor, but was incredibly attentive to his love of money.

---

[84] *patiens in adversis, moderatus in prosperis, et, quod difficillimum potestatis genus est, olim rector sui. Accessit his bonis desiderabilis eruditio litterarum, quae naturam laudabilem eximie reddit ornatam* (*Variae* 10.3.3–4).

[85] βάρβαρος νὴ θεοὺς καὶ θεάς, Σκύθης μὲν τὸ γένος (*Misopogon* 352b).

[86] *Wars* 5.3.1. A more nuanced reading of the representation of Theodahad and other Gothic rulers appears in Kaldellis, *Procopius of Caesarea*, 107–15.

Procopius goes on to describe Theodahad's insatiable appetite for real estate in Tuscany, which leads him to dispossess his neighbors. As will be discussed in the next chapter, Theodahad's devotion to literature is one of his defining characteristics and, curiously, the very thing that disqualifies him from the kingship. But despite the fact that Theodahad reigns for only a short time before being deposed by the more vigorous Vitigis, Procopius never sees fit to correlate Theodahad's flaws of character or insuitability for the throne with his Gothic or barbarian origins. As noted, it has been argued that Theodahad's appreciation of Roman literary culture is a trope of the corrupting effect that the fruits of civilization may have on the barbarian who is unable to exercise moderation, analogous to the Vandals' unrestrained enjoyment of baths and fine dining that dissipates their vigor.[87] The logic in such tropes is that what ennobles and refines the Roman leads the barbarian into unwitting corruption and even slavery, as in the case of the Britons under the imperialist policies of Agricola.[88] However, even if one allows that Procopius is indeed employing this trope, he does not do so explicitly and limits its use to Theodahad.

Theodahad was supplanted by the more warlike Vitigis, who ruled the Goths from 536 to 540. For whatever reason, Procopius never offers a summary statement of Vitigis' character for better or for worse, only noting his middling birth and that he had distinguished himself in Theo-deric's war against the Gepids in the Balkans.[89] His reign is characterized by a number of tactical mistakes and ultimate defeat by Belisarius, who manages to hold the city of Rome against Vitigis for over a year and then trap Vitigis in turn in Ravenna. Throughout the four years of Vitigis' reign, Procopius offers little insight into the Gothic king's character. On the one hand, he is able to make measured tactical decisions, as is shown when he advocates the initial abandonment of Rome in order to first deal with the Frankish threat in the north, displaying in his speech a Fabian willingness to adopt a strategy of tactical, though inglorious, delay instead of aggression.[90] However, at other points Vitigis appears wholly unable to accurately assess military conditions, and his failed use of siegeworks has already been noted. Further difficulties in pressing the siege against Rome drive Vitigis into anger and despair, under the influence of which he orders Roman senatorial hostages to be executed.[91] Vitigis is also out-generalled in a series of engagements where he fails to realize that his lack of mounted

---

[87] See Kaldellis for a discussion of the rhetorical representation of Vandal luxury, *Ethnography after Antiquity*, 19–21; also see above, 181–82.

[88] *Agricola* 21.2.   [89] *Wars* 5.11.5.   [90] *Wars* 5.11.12–15.   [91] *Wars* 5.26.1.

archers will lead to huge losses in a series of battles where his Gothic troops are pitted against the Romans and their Hunnic allies.[92]

So far, it is clear that not all of the Goths are worthy of the praise accorded to Theoderic and Amalasuintha, and it has already been noted that both Goths and Vandals are indeed collectively referred to as "barbarians" throughout the eight books of the *Wars*. As seen in the case of the Gothic followers of the young Athalaric, a barbarian origin or identity can also be explicitly correlated with stereotypically barbarian behaviors. However, in only three cases does Procopius use the classifier "barbarian" in association with any of the Gothic kings. The first of these has been discussed above in the case of Theoderic where Procopius refers to his abstention from taking the imperial title and preference for styling himself as *rex*, as Procopius says the barbarians are accustomed to do. In this case, the use of the term "barbarian" is ethically neutral and only serves to qualify a cultural practice that, while indicating distinction from Romans, does not involve negative moral judgment.

The second instance involves the Gothic king Totila, who was raised up as king following Vitigis' surrender to Belisarius in 540 and who becomes the real hero of the final book of the *Wars*.[93] After the Gothic capture of the city of Naples, Procopius says that Totila "showed a humaneness to the prisoners that was not to be expected from either an enemy or a barbarian."[94] Implicit here is the expectation that, as a ruler of a barbarian people and being a barbarian himself, Totila ought to behave in a manner that accords with the audience's preconceived notions associated with this label. Tellingly, however, this direct correlation between Totila's barbarian origin and any stereotypically uncivilized behavior is only introduced in a context that thwarts this very expectation. For Totila takes great care that the citizens, being in a state of starvation from the siege, do not gorge themselves, but are rather steadily given more food until they are restored to a state of health.

The third such example, and similar to the previous one, also involves Totila and occurs in a letter he sends to the Roman senate in which he puts forward a case for the legitimacy of Gothic rule and upbraids the inhabitants of the city for betraying the cause of both Goths *and* Italians to the "Greeks," the term used by enemies of Justinian to refer to his otherwise

---

[92] *Wars* 5.27.15–29.
[93] Kaldellis, *Procopius of Caesarea*, 198; also see Moorhead on the positive representation of Totila in Procopius and even in the *Liber pontificalis*. "Totila the Revolutionary," 382.
[94] φιλανθρωπίαν ἐς τοὺς ἡλωκότας ἐπεδείξατο οὔτε πολεμίῳ οὔτε βαρβάρῳ ἀνδρὶ πρέπουσαν (*Wars* 7.8.1).

"Roman" troops.[95] In this instance, Totila urges his hearers not to make light of his remarks and assume that his reproaches are brought against them either because of the ambition of his youth or because, being a leader of barbarians, he makes boastful speeches.[96] In both of these examples, the pejorative baggage associated with the barbarian label is clear: barbarians are not expected to exhibit clemency and restraint, particularly after the taking of a city;[97] nor are their leaders supposed to speak with moderation and restraint.[98]

What is interesting is that these assumptions that accompany the barbarian category, to which Gothic kings indisputably belong, are only introduced to be subverted. Though Totila is identified, and indeed identifies himself, as a barbarian, he is not only freed of censure on this count but is, if anything, the more worthy of praise for it. Just as with Theoderic's adherence to a barbarian custom, the barbarian label is again only introduced to be subverted in a context where traditional expectations turn out to be false.[99] Moreover, these episodes are not isolated examples of Totila acting in "Roman" fashion; throughout books seven and eight, Totila consistently appears as a wise and just ruler.

As was the case with Vitigis, Procopius does not offer significant character assessments of the last two Gothic kings Totila and Teias. The lengthiest description is devoted to Totila, and that no more than a sentence:

Τουτίλας ἦν τις, Ἰλδιβάδου ἀνεψιός, ἐπὶ πλεῖστον ξυνέσεως ἥκων καὶ τὸ δραστήριον ὡς μάλιστα ἔχων καὶ λόγου ἐν Γότθοις πολλοῦ ἄξιος.[100]

---

[95] The term was already in use to describe eastern Romans in the fifth century by Sidonius Apollinaris, referring to the emperor Anthemius appointed in Constantinople as *Graeco imperatore* (*Epist.* 1.7.5), although not with the diminutive sense, "Greekling," attributed to the term by Heather. "The Western Empire, 425–76," 28–29. Nor did the term always reflect a western hostility toward Romans from the east; Priscus meets a man among the Huns who claims to be a "Greek": ἔλεγεν Γραικὸς μὲν εἶναι τὸ γένος (*Excerp. de legat.* 8.97).

[96] ὑμῶν δὲ οἰέσθω μηδεὶς μήτε ὑπὸ νέου φιλοτιμίας τὰ ὀνείδη ταῦτα ἐς αὐτοὺς φέρεσθαι μήτε με ἅτε βαρβάρων ἄρχοντα κομπωδεστέρους ποιεῖσθαι τοὺς λόγους (*Wars* 7.9.15).

[97] Cf. the concerns of Belisarius as to his being able to restrain the barbarians in his army before entering the newly won city of Naples (*Wars* 5.9.27).

[98] As the Herulian Pharas says explicitly. See above, 141.

[99] Again, I disagree with Halsall's assessment that "Procopius uses inversion to ridicule the barbarians, and especially makes fun of those barbarians who try to emulate Romans." "Funny Foreigners," 113. The rhetorical technique of inversion occurs so frequently throughout the *Wars* that the whole work should become a satire if every instance be read as comic. Kaldellis has argued that "Procopius' view of Theoderic as a statesman is very positive and has never been doubted by modern scholars" – the concensus, at least, is to take Procopius at his word. *Procopius of Caesarea*, 107.

[100] *Wars* 7.2.7.

> There was a man named Totila, a cousin of Ildibad; he was a possessed of
> the fullness of intelligence and had a great deal of vigor, being considered
> worthy of great reputation among the Goths.

However, these last two Gothic kings, Totila and Teias, rejuvenated the
fortunes of the Goths following the lackluster reigns of Theodahad and
Vitigis. In a short period of time, Totila managed to win back many of the
territories re-conquered by the Romans by 540, and the war in Italy turned
into one of attrition. Within this period, Totila displays occasional acts of
cruelty, but Procopius takes care to present his reign as being typified by a
consistent attention to justice and care for the well-being of his Gothic and
Italian subjects.

For example, at several points Totila shows clemency to those who have
fallen into his power, and the justice of his leadership draws Italians and
Roman troops to fight on his side.[101] In situations where civilians are at his
mercy, he gives express orders that forbid the killing of Romans, and, if he
does take their property, he at least leaves their persons unharmed.[102]
Totila is also shown taking thought for the vulnerability of women; when
he sees to the protection of the wives of senators and treats them kindly,
"his name was great among all the Romans for his understanding and
benevolence."[103] When judging the case of a Goth who had raped a young
woman, Totila has the man executed and gives the offender's money to the
girl, despite the initial protests of the man's Gothic companions, who are
eventually persuaded of the correctness of their leader's actions. Totila uses
the event to make a point of demonstrating his conviction that only rule
according to justice will secure the divine favor necessary to win the war.[104]
Totila even lets himself be dissuaded from razing the city of Rome to the
ground by the arguments of Belisarius, who appeals to the beauty of the
city, the civilizing genius of the ancients, and the crime the destruction of
the memory of antiquity would constitute.[105] Though no savior of Rome,
neither is Totila a barbarian who would destroy it.

That is not to say that Totila is perfect in Procopius' eyes, and one
occasionally senses that Totila has a faint barbarian shadow hanging over
him. At one point he cuts off the hands of a priest who had tried to
smuggle grain from Sicily to relieve beleagured Romans.[106] Elsewhere, he

---

[101] For example, *Wars* 7.5.19; 7.8.6–9.   [102] *Wars* 7.20.25; 7.30.24.

[103] μέγα τε ἀπ' αὐτοῦ ὄνομα ἐπί τε ξυνέσει καὶ φιλανθρωπίᾳ ἐς Ῥωμαίους ἅπαντας ἔσχε (*Wars* 7.6.4);
also see 7.20.29–31, where Totila again protects vulnerable women and augments his reputation
for *sōphrosynē*-σωφροσύνη, "temperance," the most stereotypically un-barbarian of traits.

[104] *Wars* 7.8.12–25.   [105] *Wars* 7.22.6–17.   [106] *Wars* 7.15.15.

is overcome by passion and fury, and, giving in to his anger, allows himself to be deprived of an easy victory.[107] Procopius even says in one instance that Totila collects his forces in a place where Hannibal himself had encamped, perhaps suggesting a barbarian affinity with republican Rome's greatest enemy.[108] Yet despite these instances, the general picture Procopius offers of Totila is of a just ruler of Italy, free of pride and presumption, who tries to persuade Justinian to accept the collegial arrangment enjoyed by Anastasius and Theoderic, "who ruled as emperors not long before."[109] Such an arrangement would yield the senior role to Justinian and allow him to call Totila his son. Totila is willing to go further than this, offering to declare himself subject and ally of Justinian, paying tribute and taxes while also ceding control of Sicily and Dalmatia.[110] And when Totila dies after his dramatic leadership at the battle of Busta Gallorum, Procopius says with seeming regret that his end was not worthy of the deeds he had performed.[111] Despite occasional and sublte reminders by Procopius that Totila is, after all, a barbarian, the historian is more interested in representing him as a model ruler who is neither characterized nor delimited by his non-Roman origins.[112]

The last of the Gothic kings, Teias, also lacks a character portrait at either his entrance into the narrative or at his death, and his reign takes up only a short part of the eighth and final book. However, in a battle that constitutes the last major engagement of the war and marks the destruction of the Gothic kingdom, Procopius glorifies Teias' final encounter with Narses:

> Ἐνταῦθά μοι μάχη τε πολλοῦ λόγου ἀξία καὶ ἀνδρὸς ἀρετὴ οὐδὲ τῶν τινος λεγομένων ἡρώων, οἶμαι, καταδεεστέρα γεγράψεται, ἧς δὴ ὁ Τεῖας δήλωσιν ἐν τῷ παρόντι πεποίηται.[113]

> Here I will write of a battle fully deserving report and of a man's virtue that, I think, is no lesser than that of any of the sung heroes, a demonstration of which Teias made in this circumstance.

Procopius goes on to describe a bitter fight in which the Gothic king places himself in the front of his troops and kills an impossible number of

---

[107] *Wars* 7.26.19–20.   [108] *Wars* 7.22.24.

[109] οἳ βεβασιλεύκασι μὲν οὐ πολλῷ πρότερον (*Wars* 7.21.23). On the imperial collegiality of Theoderic and Anastasius, see Arnold, *Theoderic and the Roman Imperial Restoration*, 78–82.

[110] *Wars* 8.24.4.   [111] *Wars* 8.32.28.

[112] Totila has been characterized by Brodka as one of the "main heroes" of books seven and eight of the *Wars*, and he appears as a "representative of ethics in the political realm" in a critique of Justinian: Auf diese Weise wird Totila zum Vertreter der Ethik in der Politik und zu einem Mittel, Justinians Politik zu kritisieren. *Die Geschichtsphilosophie in der spätantiken Historiographie*, 124.

[113] *Wars* 8.35.20.

enemies before finally being mortally struck in the chest by a javelin thrown from an unknown hand. The battle occurs in the last chapter of book eight and is the dying gasp of Gothic rule in Italy. The following day, the Romans and Goths come to terms on which the majority of the Gothic forces agree to leave Italy and "to live according to their own laws among other barbarians,"[114] although some thousand Goths under the leadership of Indulf head north to Pavia to continue the resistance. Though far less developed than other Gothic kings, the character of Teias in his brief reign is nevertheless valorized and given a tragic quality; his downfall, far from being celebrated as a final vindication of the Roman cause and a victory of Justinian over the barbarians of the west, is followed by a brief and uncelebratory summary of the immediate events on the ground in Italy, which takes up only a few paragraphs of text.[115]

Given Procopius' limited employment of ethnographic rhetoric in his representation of barbarian kings, several of the former assessments of Procopius need to be reconsidered. For example, it has been argued in a discussion of dominant themes in Procopius that he is much concerned with "preserving the established order, and for Procopius the established order includes a strong demarcation between civilized people and barbarians."[116] Likewise, Procopius has been read as "convinced of his own cultural superiority" and conscious that "a sharp line divided the Roman world and the poverty, violence, and faithlessness of the barbarians."[117] Although this assessment may be true in Procopius' treatment of the Huns, Sclaveni, Kutrigurs, and even Franks as discussed in Chapter 2, it does not hold up when applied to the representation of the Gothic and Vandal kings who are the most prominent barbarian actors in the *Wars*.

Although it is abundantly clear that Romans and barbarians fight in both imperial and Gothic armies and that ethnic affiliation did not determine political allegiance,[118] the lack of ethnic hostility – even

---

[114] ἀλλὰ ξὺν τῶν ἄλλων βαρβάρων τισὶν αὐτόνομοι βιοτεύσοντες (*Wars* 8.35.33).

[115] Of course, many scholars have pointed out Procopius' disillusionment and even hostility towards the regime of Justinian. For example, see Cameron, *Procopius and the Sixth Century*, 137–43; Moorhead, "Totila the Revolutionary," 382; and Kaldellis, *Procopius of Caesarea*, 118–64.

[116] Cameron, *Procopius and the Sixth Century*, 239. Cameron recognizes the different treatment accorded to certain barbarian rulers, although this very fact complicates her assertion that Procopius "operates with a strong sense of borderlines, which makes his judgments easy." Ibid., 240.

[117] See above, 213.

[118] This point has been discussed in detail by Greatrex. "Roman Identity in the Sixth Century," 267–92. Also see Mathisen's excellent study "*Peregrini, Barbari*, and *Cives Romani*: Concepts of Citizenship and the Legal Identity of Barbarians in the Later Roman Empire," 1011–40.

when Romano–Gothic distinction is made clear both nominally and even in reference to language – can be striking. In book six, Procopius describes an episode where a Gothic and a Roman soldier find themselves trapped together in a pit on the battlefield, but instead of killing one another, the two end up pledging their friendship, each vowing to ensure the other's safety should they be rescued by soldiers of either army. The men shout for help, each in his own language, and when Goths respond first to the clamor, the Gothic soldier in the pit insists that the Roman be hauled up first. The two recognize that this is the only way they can ensure that the Goth's comrades will not abandon the Roman in the pit if they should rescue the Goth first. Once the men are lifted to safety, the two part company in friendship, each to his own army.[119] This brief friendship is particularly interesting in that it occurs in warfare, the ultimate expression of an irreconcilable conflict, where Gothic claims to legitimate rule over Italy are pitted against Justinian's mission of imperial *renovatio* and reconquest. But more importantly, it is remarkable that in a widely circulated and popular text, in an age governed by an explicit ideological program that aimed at reclamation of the west from the barbarians and the restoration of the empire, the historian was so willing to avoid representing the hostility of the rival claimants to power in ethnological terms.

Barbarian Figures in the *Jin shu*

In turning now to the *Jin shu*, we will consider the same questions central to the above discussion of the *Wars*: How are the rulers of barbarian kingdoms represented by historians looking back from a restored empire? Does the use of ethnographic discourse in the text's depiction of barbarian political figures indicate a breaking down of the barbarian antithesis or, on the contrary, a reestablishment and reentrenchment of a civilized–barbarian dichotomy?

It is common for scholars to read the *Jin shu*, in particular the Chronicles, which comprise the last section of the work and which will be the focus here, as a text that exemplifies the Tang emperor Taizong's 唐太宗 policy of *hua yi yi jia* 华夷一家, "Chinese and barbarians are one family," and to claim that the *Jin shu* Chronicles "exhibit an equally benevolent spirit towards both Chinese and barbarians."[120] Zhu Dawei has described

---

[119] *Wars* 6.1.11–19.
[120] 在载记的内容上，也颇体现对胡汉一视同仁的精神. Li, "*Jin shu* yanjiu xia," 87–88.

what he sees as the "progressive ethnic theory of *hua yi yi jia* 华夷一家"
serving as a guiding principle in the *Jin shu*, and he believes that the work
"demonstrates a relatively even-handed treatment towards ethnic relations."[121] While it is one of the main contentions of this book that western
scholarship has often overstated the presence of a conceptual dichotomy
between Romans and barbarians, I will argue here that the opposite is true
for Chinese-language scholarship on the *Jin shu* and early medieval China
in general.

Early Tang literati discourse on barbarian rulers who founded states in
north China during the fourth and fifth centuries, as it appears in the *Jin
shu*, asserts that the barbarians pose a threat not only to the Chinese
political order but even to the order of the cosmos. This clarity of an
ideological distinction between the civilization of China and the barbarism
of the periphery stands in great contrast to the *Wars* of Procopius, which,
while including the ethnographic conventions of the past that often
represent barbarians in a decidedly negative light, nevertheless allows the
rulers of barbarian kingdoms to largely transcend the limitations of the
barbarian category. The remainder of this chapter will demonstrate that
the Chronicles of the *Jin shu* exhibit a consistent tendency to define the
rulers of conquest states in terms of their barbarian identities and the
ethnographic characteristics traditionally employed in the creation of a
barbarian Other.

Like Procopius, the compilers of the *Jin shu* had access to an extensive
body of ethnographic literature from earlier ages, and as the introductory
preface to the Chronicles indicates, this material goes at least as far back as
the age of Confucius in the fifth century BC.[122] Yet in contrast to the
examples cited from Procopius above, the authorial comments on barbarian political actors offered in the *Jin shu* are not merely influenced by
classical conceptions of the barbarian Other – they are often dominated by
them. As we will see, the assessments of barbarian rulers presented in the
Jin shu display a consistently hostile and xenophobic tenor that is reinforced by frequent reference to the barbarian origins of the individuals in
question. Because of the fact that the number of barbarian rulers featured
in the *Jin shu* is far larger than in the *Wars* (there are not two barbarian
kingdoms that have come and gone in China, but rather fourteen), there

[121] 唐修晋书在华夷一家进步民族理论指导下，对民族关系的处理上较为公允. Zhu, "*Jin shu*
de pingjia yu yanjiu," 46. However, see Qu, "Lun Wei Jin Sui Tang jian de shaoshu minzu shixue
shang," 67–78, for an important exception to this general trend.

[122] See above, 190–93, for a discussion of the preface to the Chronicles.

will not be place to give them all equal treatment; and only parts of a few of the *lun* 論 colophons will be analyzed that exhibit the ethnological context within which the barbarian regimes and their rulers are represented.

Still, it is important to note that in the course of the narrative accounts of the conquest states, there is no dearth of laudatory passages on the political achievements of barbarian rulers, and these examples of praise and political success serve to temper the overall impression of Chinese hostility toward the notion of barbarian kingship or emperorship. In fact, a number of the conquest rulers or their officials admirably fulfill the standards of Confucian political orthodoxy in their management of their states. For example, the *Jin shu* describes how the Ba-Di 巴氏 ruler of the Chenghan 成漢 state, Li Xiong 李雄, "had a nature that was magnanimous and great; he simplified penal statutes and confirmed the laws ... therefore he brought stability to both barbarians and Chinese and was regarded with awe in the western lands."[123] Moreover, Li Xiong "established schools and set up a bureau of historiography; when he had leisure from his administrative duties, his hand was never without a book."[124] Not only is Li Xiong's personal character praiseworthy; his ability to manage the state in the best interests of his people is also exemplary, and he himself embodies the ideal of a scholar who devotes his energy to his studies when he is not preoccupied with the affairs of state.

A similarly idyllic portrait is painted of the Qiang 羌 ruler Yao Hong 姚泓 of the Later Qin 後秦 state, described as "filial and friendly, magnanimous and peaceful."[125] Even though he lacks experience of affairs and has a weak physical constitution, Yao Hong is distinguished by his respect for his teacher of the Confucian classics. When this teacher falls ill, Yao Hong goes to his bedside and attends him there personally. The *Jin shu* says that "from that time onwards, whenever princes and lords came across teachers they would pay their respects."[126] Yao Hong is not only virtuous in his own conduct, but his example inspires others to imitate his standards of piety and reverence for scholars and teachers.

These kinds of character sketches of non-Chinese dynastic figures in the *Jin shu* are not infrequent. Even figures such as Shi Le 石勒, the founder of the Later Zhao 後趙 dynasty, which was notorious for the cruelty of its rulers, takes a great interest in ancient history and has Classicist scholars read to him even when in military camp; he becomes so well versed in classical

---

[123] 雄性寬厚，簡刑約法. ... 由是夷夏安之，威震西土 (*Jin shu* 121.3040).
[124] 雄乃興學校，置史官，聽覽之暇，手不釋卷 (Ibid.).   [125] 孝友寬和 (*Jin shu* 119.3007).
[126] 泓受經於博士淳于岐. 岐病，泓親詣省疾，拜于牀下. 自是公侯見師傅皆拜焉 (Ibid.).

texts that scholars at court are impressed at his erudition.[127] Not content to edify himself with his intellectual curiousity, Shi Le's governance also seeks to cultivate and reward the virtuous and diligent among his subjects. The *Jin shu* recounts an inspection tour of his realm, during which whenever Shi Le "met the elderly, filial, agriculturally industrious, or scholarly, he gave them appropriate awards of grain and silken fabric."[128] In this case, even an illiterate barbarian who had lived much of his early life as a slave is able to exemplify scholarly virtues and benevolent governance.

However, it is essential to keep in mind that much of the material in the *Jin shu* Chronicles was stitched together from a large number of earlier works, some of which had been produced under the patronage of alien dynasties themselves. Therefore, these sympathetic portrayals present a major interpretive problem: it is impossible to know if they are the work of early Tang historians or, what is perhaps more likely, sections and exercepts taken from multiple earlier sources that reflect the attitudes and biases of earlier centuries.[129] Nevertheless, whatever material made it into the final text of the *Jin shu* was deemed acceptable by the Bureau of Historiography and, one must assume, by the emperor Taizong himself. It is these passages of praise for barbarian rulers that have led to the modern readings of the *Jin shu* as a testament to the ethnic harmony and inclusivity otherwise attributed Tang era.

Yet the most explicit source of information on contemporary Tang attitudes toward non-Chinese peoples is necessarily to be found in the historians' comments that form the concluding moral assessments of the barbarian dynasties. As noted in the previous chapter, these *lun* colophons are the only sections of the Chronicles that we may attribute with certainty to historians of the Tang Bureau of Historiography. While sections of individual fascicles may praise and even valorize barbarian rulers, it is the *lun* colophons that deliver the final assessments on those regimes and their rulers as they were viewed in the early Tang.

The following discussion will demonstrate that the *lun* colophons exhibit an aspect of ethnological thinking that has no equivalent in the

---

[127] 勒雅好文學, 雖在軍旅, 常令儒生讀史書而聽之, 每以其意論古帝王善惡, 朝賢儒士聽者莫不歸美焉 (*Jin shu* 105.2741).

[128] 引見高年, 孝悌, 力田, 文學之士, 班賜穀帛有差 (*Jin shu* 105.2745).

[129] Wang Zhongluo offers a table of all the histories of the Sixteen Kingdoms that appeared between the fourth and sixth centuries, *Wei Jin Nanbeichao shi*, 832–33. The most thorough available narrative in English for the period of the Sixteen Kingdoms is provided by Corradini, "The Barbarian States in North China," 163–232. For a discussion of this and other aspects of the *Jin shu*'s composition and arrangement, see above, 20, 23.

Wars, i.e., a consistently repeated hostility toward barbarian rulers that is often expressed in ethnological terms. Again, it must be noted that not all of the barbarian rulers are so strongly associated with their non-Chinese ethnicities in the *Jin shu*, and the ethnographic rhetoric tends to be more prominent in the accounts of the first conquest state of a given ethnic group. For example, the *lun* for the Särbi-Xianbei Former Yan 前燕 dynasty is charged with pejorative references to barbarian ethnicity, whereas in the respective *lun* colophons for that regime's later offshoots, the Later Yan 後燕 and Southern Yan 南燕, there is far less emphasis on their ethnic origins. Nevertheless, while the *Jin shu* and the *Wars* share many features in common, and indeed that is the reason for their selection as comparanda, it is at the points of divergence where the comparison becomes most instructive. The remainder of this chapter will consider the *lun* colophons for four of the fourteen alien regimes represented in the Chronicles. While it is possible that the *Jin shu* historians may have tried to attenuate their final assessments in the *lun* by means of more sympathetic characterization over the course of the preceeding individual narratives, the official pronouncement reiterated frequently throughout reveals a deeply entrenched antagonism between the Chinese and non-Chinese that is conceived of in ethnological terms.

The Xiongnu 匈奴 *Former Zhao* 前趙 *Dynasty*

While its first emperor Liu Yuan 劉淵 receives praise at certain points for his adoption of Chinese cultural practices and his attempts to establish just and stable rule, he is nevertheless described as "the head of the disaster" at the end of the preface to the Chronicles.[130] The disaster referred to is the 136 years of barbarian rule in northern China, which the above-discussed preface to the Chronicles presents as an expression of the ancient antagonism between China and the barbarians. By placing the various conquest states in the context of this antagonism, the *Jin shu* emphasizes that although some of them may have exhibited positive qualities, their place in the ethno-geographical schema inherited from antiquity demands a condemnation for their presumption in claiming to rule part of China. The simple fact of a barbarian kingdom within China thus logically constitutes an inversion of an ancient principle fundamental to Chinese political thought.

---

[130] 元海為之禍首云 (*Jin shu* 101.2644).

Nevertheless, throughout the chronicle of Liu Yuan's reign, the *Jin shu* recounts several instances where he appears as a virtuous figure by Chinese standards. For example, when still a seven-year-old child, his filial grief for his deceased mother moves his relatives to sigh with admiration.[131] As a youth he is an avid scholar and learns many historical, poetic, and philosophical texts by heart.[132] Such details are typical in Chinese historiography for sketching the early years of a man who is destined for great things in adulthood. Moreover, Liu Yuan is initially stubborn in his allegiance to the legitimate Western Jin 西晉 dynasty, despite the exhortations of his fellow Xiongnu, whose tribes had been settled along the northern frontier of China for centuries. Liu Yuan only decides to revolt when his Chinese commander ignores his advice and suffers a major military defeat. Yet despite his otherwise laudable traits as a statesman, Liu Yuan's depiction in the *lun* colophon to the Former Zhao dynasty casts him as a scion of the ancient enemies of the Chinese imperial order:

況元海人傑，必致青雲之上；許以殊才，不居庸劣之下. 是以策馬鴻騫，乘機豹變，五部高嘯，一旦推雄，皇枝相害，未有與之爭衡者矣.... 單于無北顧之懷，獫狁有南郊之祭，大哉天地，茲為不仁矣！[133]

As for Liu Yuan, he was heroic and must be ranked above the celestial; granting that he had rare talents, he cannot be placed below the mediocre or inferior. In spurring his horses he soared aloft; he seized the opportunity and rebelled like a leopard; the five [Xiongnu] tribes acclaimed him aloud. Once he had been raised up as a warlord, the imperial factions warred against one another, and there was none to compete with him. ... When the Chanyu has no thought for the north, when the Xianyun hold their sacrifices in the southern outskirts of the capital – however great are Heaven and Earth, this is not benevolence!

While the military abilities of Liu Yuan are praised, these very qualities underscore the lamentation over his career, which had led him to seize imperial territory as the leader of a Xiongnu rebellion. The *lun* describes his elevation by his fellow tribesmen who urge him first to take the title of Chanyu 單于, the ancient Xiongnu title accorded to the ruler of their steppe confederation, though of mostly symbolic significance by the late

---

[131] 七歲遭母憂，擗踴號叫，哀感旁鄰，宗族部落咸歎賞 (*Jin shu* 101.2645).
[132] 幼好學，師事上黨崔游，習毛詩，京氏易，馬氏尚書，尤好春秋左氏傳，孫吳兵法，略皆誦之，史，漢，諸子，無不綜覽 (Ibid.).
[133] *Jin shu* 103.2702.

third century.[134] Not satisfied with this, Liu Yuan goes on to take the title of emperor, and it is this that the Tang historians decry. For it would have been clear to the Tang historians and their audience that the Xiongnu Chanyu belongs in the north among the barbarians; for him to abandon the steppe in favor of the plains of China, holding his sacrifices in the southern suburbs of the city in Chinese imperial fashion – that was a disaster in both political and cosmological terms. For the Son of Heaven was an office through which the emperor ensured harmony between the celestial and terrestrial realms by means of the appropriate ritual sacrifices.[135] The *lun* also refers to Liu Yuan, or the Xiongnu collectively, as Xianyun 獫狁, another ethnonym for a barbarian people of the early to mid-first millennium BC.[136] By doing so, it emphasizes that not only the Xiongnu as a whole but also their leaders are to be associated with the ancient enemies of Chinese civilization.

The image of the barbarians offering the proper ritual sacrifices is an example of a theme that appears repeatedly in the Chronicles: the notion that a barbarian acting in Chinese fashion *when in a position of independent political power within the empire* is an aberration to be deplored, not a sign of assimilation to be lauded. The anxiety exhibited in the *Jin shu* regarding the appropriation of Chinese models of governance is striking, given that there is certainly precedent for the representation of the assimilated barbarian in positive terms in earlier Chinese historiography. As discussed in Chapter 2, the otherwise relatively xenophobic first-century AD historian Ban Gu 班固 extols the character of the surrendered Xiongnu chieftain Jin Midi 金日磾, who was himself a close confidant of the emperor Han Wudi 漢武帝, and Jin Midi's descendants went on to hold imperial offices for generations.[137] Yet clearly a line is crossed when a barbarian is no longer in the service of a Chinese monarch but rather upon the throne himself. The above assessment of Liu Yuan also makes clear that the proper place for the Chanyu is not in the south but in the northern lands beyond the frontier, reiterating the familiar principle that different peoples have

[134] On later usage of the title Chanyu and its decline in significance, see Luo, *Zhonggu beizu minghao yanjiu*, 43–48. Also see Klein, "The Contributions of the Fourth Century Xianbei States to the Reunification of the Chinese Empire," 82.

[135] The function of the monarch in ancient Chinese political thinking will be discussed at greater length in Chapter 5.

[136] Sima Qian, *Shiji* 110.2879. Liu Xueyao discusses this ethnonym's association with the Xiongnu and enemy peoples of previous eras in the second and first millennia BC in *Xiongnu shilun*, 3–5. Also see Pulleyblank, "The Chinese and their Neighbors in Prehistoric and Early Historic Times," 449.

[137] *Han shu* 68.2959–67. See above, 124–25, 127–28.

their proper place and customs, but that these are boundaries not to be transgressed.

A further example of the inherent tension between the prospect of barbarian assimilation to Chinese political culture and their independent exercise of power appears in the *lun*, when it assesses the Former Zhao rulers' attempts at proper administration:

若乃習以華風，溫乎雅度；兼其舊俗，則罕規模. ... 終為夷狄之邦，未辯君臣之位. 至於不遠儒風，虛襟正直，則昔賢所謂并仁義而盜之者焉.[138]

> If they had studied the ways of the Chinese and taken heed of the proper rites of governance while still keeping their old customs, that would have been a remarkable model. . . . In the end it was still an Yi-Di state that could not distinguish between the ranks of lord and minister. As for the fact that they were not far from the Confucian teachings, that they were selfless and upright, their condition was still what the ancient wise men called "those who appropriate benevolence and virtue and yet defraud them."

This passage reaffirms the distinction between the barbarians and the Chinese, remarking that even if the Xiongnu had adopted Chinese ways, they were still barbarians, Yi-Di 夷狄, unable to distinguish the hierarchical proprieties of Confucian orthodoxy; they are thus inevitably unfit to rule according to the correct tenets of Chinese governance. The contrast between this view and Procopius' equation of Theoderic with the greatest emperors of the earlier Roman Empire is here at its most pronounced. Yet the Xiongnu of the Former Zhao came close, and it is striking that, although they attained a state of uprightness and moral cultivation, it is these very achievements that serve as part of their condemnation. Explicit in the case of Liu Yuan and the Former Zhao state is the notion that the barrier between the Chinese and the barbarians is insurmountable and that attempts to cross this divide result in the perversion of virtue itself. While the adoption of *civilitas* by barbarian rulers such as Theoderic and Amalasuintha is a matter of praise for Procopius, the efforts of the Former Zhao to adopt Chinese ways are worthy of censure in the eyes of the *Jin shu* historians.[139]

[138] *Jin shu* 103.2702.
[139] The closest possible analogy of this phenomenon in Procopius is the erudition of the Gothic king Theodahad, which may be interpreted as somehow corrupting in and of itself, i.e., what is virtuous in a Roman serves to corrupt a barbarian nature. Even if such a reading is correct, Procopius leaves it wholly up to the reader to infer and suggests no incongruity between Theodahad's Gothic/barbarian ethnicity and his literary pursuits.

The Jie 羯 *Later Zhao* 後趙 *Dynasty*

Shi Le, the founder of the Later Zhao state, belonged to the Jie ethnic group, a people often associated with the Xiongnu, although the actual relationship between the two peoples is unclear. Shi Le was originally an escaped slave who rose to prominence as an official under the Former Zhao state before breaking away to establish his own dynasty in 319. In some ways Shi Le is not an unsympathetic figure, as has been pointed out above: though illiterate, he greatly esteemed Chinese historical classics and enjoyed discussion of the merits of ancient rulers, and he took steps in his governance of the state to encourage virtue and industry in his subjects. He at least ruled without the egregious abuses demonstrated by his adopted son Shi Hu 石虎, which will be discussed below.

Yet despite the virtues of the dynasty's founder, the assessments of the Later Zhao rulers do no turn out to be much better than did those of the Former Zhao. Shi Le himself is a man not unworthy of praise at various points in the narrative, yet his ethnic background and genealogical descent remain a central concern in the *lun*:

石勒出自羌渠，見奇醜類. ... 雖曰凶殘，亦一時傑也. 而託授非所，貽厥無謀，身隕嗣滅，業歸攜養，斯乃知人之闇焉.[140]

Shi Le was a descendant from Qiangqu [a Chanyu of the Xiongnu]; he revealed his remarkably hideous race. ... Although he is called wicked and cruel, he was also the most heroic man of his day. However, he conferred and appointed inappropriately; he took no thought for the succession; he himself perished, his descendants were destroyed, and his achievements went to his adopted son – this is an inability to assess men's character.

Though noted for his heroism, Shi Le is stigmatized by his genealogy and ethnic background. After first noting his descent from a barbarian lineage, the *Jin shu* then shows how he revealed the qualities inherent in his foreign identity, described as his "remarkably hideous race" or "kindred."[141] Unquoted above, there follows a series of references to the destruction and harm he caused in the north of China that proves Heaven must have indeed hated the Western Jin dynasty to set upon it such an evil monster.[142] According to the *lun*, he had attempted throughout his reign to rule according to the correct system of government, but he failed in his

---

[140] *Jin shu* 107.2798.   [141] The use of this expression, *choulei* 醜類, has been discussed above, 200.
[142] 豈天厭晉德而假茲妖孽者歟! (*Jin shu* 107.2798).

attempt to follow the Confucian principles that require a sovereign to be able to recognize and reward talent appropriately. As in the case of Liu Yuan, there is an association between his inability to rule according to the tenets of Chinese political philosophy and his barbarian origin, a notion expressed by the reference to his genealogy and its determinative force. The prevalence of this explanatory device challenges assessments by scholars that "the fundamental criterion of 'Chinese-ness', anciently and throughout history, has been cultural."[143] Based on the examples discussed thus far, there is a very strong indication that, in some contexts, not only was "Chinese-ness" inaccessible to the barbarians, but the very attempt at trying to attain it could be worthy of condemnation.

Shi Le's successor Shi Hu, a figure noted for his decadence and violence, receives a much harsher portrait. This comes as no surprise, as the narrative account of his reign mentions several instances of cruelty, decadence, and sadistic violence. For example, when taking cities in his younger years, Shi Hu would not discriminate between guilty and innocent, "burying and beheading men and women alike such that hardly anyone would be left over."[144] Perhaps his most outrageous habit was to have sex with and then murder attractive Buddhist nuns; afterwards he would cook their flesh, mixed with cow and sheep meat, and distribute it to his courtiers to see if they could tell what they were eating.[145] His character in the *lun* is accordingly presented in colorful terms:

季龍心昧德義，幼而輕險，假豹姿於羊質，騁梟心於狼性，始懷怨懟，終行篡奪。...戎狄殘獷，斯為甚乎![146]

Shi Hu's heart was blind to virtue and justice; as a youth he cared nothing for danger. He disguised the likeness of a leopard in the disposition of a sheep. He let an owl's heart fly with the nature of a wolf. Initially, he cherished resentment and malevolence, but he finally turned to usurpation and rapine. The Rong-Di are cruel and uncivilized – this is the extreme example!

Especially prominent in the assessment of Shi Hu is the use of animal imagery, a feature common in Chinese representations of the barbarians and typified in the phrase *ren mian shou xin* 人面獸心, "human face animal heart," which has a long textual tradition and has appeared in

---

[143] Creel, *The Origins of Statecraft in China*, 197.
[144] 至於降城陷壘，不復斷別善惡，坑斬士女，尟有遺類 (*Jin shu* 106.2761).
[145] 又內諸比丘尼有姿色者，與其交褻而殺之，合牛羊肉煑而食之，亦賜左右，欲以識其味也 (*Jin shu* 106.2766).
[146] *Jin shu* 107.2798.

previous chapters.[147] What is important to point out here is that, as with other barbarian individuals and groups, Shi Hu is defined by the generic barbarian labels Rong and Di, archaic ethnonyms that recall classical ritual texts and their schematized representation of peripheral and morally inferior barbarians tributary to the Chinese emperor. Associating these terms with Shi Hu's wickedness provides further corroboration of the thesis that the Rong-Di, and all later barbarians who fall into that category, are by nature vicious and barbaric. Classical ethnographic rhetoric thus serves a dual purpose of rationalizing the phenomenon of barbarian conquest – a lamentable consequence of moral decline under an otherwise legitimate Chinese dynasty that failed to subjugate Rong-Di barbarians – while also undermining the political legitimacy of a barbarian ruler. While we have seen that Vandal and Gothic kings may be represented in a harsh light, such critiques are never formulated in ethnological terms; in such instances, negative qualities are never ascribed either to a particular group or even the broader barbarian categoy.

The *Särbi-Xianbei* 鮮卑 *Former Yan* 前燕 *Dynasty*

The three figures discussed above – Liu Yuan, Shi Le, and Shi Hu – belonged to the Xiongnu and Jie ethnic groups, both of which were originally nomadic peoples who lived to the north of China and along its northern borders. As the Xiongnu of the fourth century shared their name with the steppe empire that had posed so severe a threat to the Han dynasty, it is easy to see why these two groups might be likely to be stigmatized because of their perceived relationship to enemies of China's imperial past. But lest one think that the employment of othering ethnographic discourse was limited to the treatment of northern pastoralists, it is important to consider the ways in which other ethnic groups hailing from other regions are represented in analogous terms.

Throughout the narrative account of the various members of the Former Yan ruling house, there are several points where different rulers exhibit qualities of just or efficient rule that would seem to merit praise. For example, the founder of the dynasty, Murong Wei 慕容廆, displays great respect for ritual propriety[148] and governs his territory in so principled a fashion that many Chinese flock to him and there is a "flourishing of propriety and civility" in his kingdom.[149] His son Murong Huang 慕容皝

---

[147] The phrase appears in passages discussed above at 121 and 196.   [148] *Jin shu* 108.2804.
[149] 禮讓興矣 (*Jin shu* 108.2806).

is noted for his knowledge of the classics and astronomy,[150] and his illegitimate son Murong Han 慕容翰 enjoys great popularity among officials and soldiers alike, exhibiting a love of Confuciansim.[151] Murong Huang's son Murong Ke 慕容恪 also follows the tenets of both virtuous governance as well as Confucian ethics, and thus manages to put the affairs of state into good order.[152]

Yet despite such positive qualities, which are clear in the preceding narrative sections of the *Jin shu*, the rulers of the Murong clan appear in a predominantly negative light in the *lun* colophon, which delivers the early Tang historians' final assessment of them.[153] Regarding the dynastic founder of the Former Yan state, Murong Wei, the *lun* says,

慕容廆英姿偉量，是曰邊豪，釁迹姦圖，實惟亂首. 何者? ... 況乎放命挺禍，距戰發其狼心；剽邑屠城，略地騁其螯賊.[154]

Murong Wei had a heroic nature and enormous capacity; he is what is called a hero of the marches. Searching for a breach and plotting wickedness, he is truly the sole beginner of the chaos. How did this happen? ... Moreover, he revolted and spread the catastrophe. In fighting off enemies he let loose his wolf's heart. Plundering towns and massacring cities, he seized territory and gave free rein to his locust bandits.

As in the case of Shi Le, praise is allowed for Murong Wei's martial prowess, but he too is cast as a stalker along the borders of the empire, looking for a chance to cause trouble. Even if no reference is made to ancient barbarian ethnonyms such as Rong, Di, etc., the trope of the predatory barbarian in the border regions, a consistent feature in the Chinese texts considered throughout this study, is unmistakable. This is particularly striking in Murong Wei's case, because he had actually cooperated with the Eastern Jin 東晉 dynasty in the south and initially expressed reluctance to assert his independence from Chinese rule, accepting titles bestowed by the Eastern Jin emperor.[155] Yet as has been noted above, the *lun* colophons often express a harshness of judgment that seems at times at odds with the depictions of barbarian figures in the preceding narrative sections of a given fascicle. Also prominent in the assessment of Murong Wei is familiar animal imagery that likens his character to that of

---

[150] 尚經學，善天文 (*Jin shu* 109.2815).
[151] 愛儒學，自士大夫至于卒伍，莫不樂而從之 (*Jin shu* 109.2827).
[152] 虛襟待物，諮詢善道. ... 盡心色養，手不釋卷. 其百僚有過，未嘗顯之，自是庶僚化德，稀有犯者 (*Jin shu* 111.2859).
[153] This contrast in tone between the narrative and *lun* sections on the Former Yan state has also been noted by Schreiber, "History of the Former Yen Dynasty, Part II," 128.
[154] *Jin shu* 111.2862.   [155] *Jin shu* 108.2804–07.

an animal and compares his armies to swarms of locuts. These particular qualities are not necessarily indicative of a non-Chinese identity, yet in the context of a barbarian ruler they may be easily assimilated into the broader constellation of subhuman associations typical of ethnographic rhetoric. Such associations are emphasized in the *zan* 贊 poem appended to the *lun*, which uses the phrases "stupid like insects are these motley hordes," 蠢茲 雜種, "taking advantage of the crisis to rise up like hedgehogs," 乘危蝟起, and "they spread their wings [like birds of prey]," 鴟張.[156]

Murong Wei's son Murong Jun 慕容儁 possesses qualities indicating that, in the eyes of the historians, he was in fact not so far beyond the civilizational pale as the opening lines of the colophon suggest. For the *lun* had begun by stating that the people of the northern regions are "divided and alienated from all the Chinese, no civilized teachings reach them."[157] But as in the case of several other barbarian figures, even Murong Jun's positive attributes do not exempt him from a critique of his character that refers back to his barbarian origins:

宣英文武兼優，加之以機斷.... 宰割黎元，縱其鯨吞之勢.... 非夫 天厭素靈而啟異類，不然者，其鋒何以若斯![158]

> Murong Jun possessed the excellence of both letters and warfare, and added to these his decisiveness ... But he carved up the common people and let loose the power of his whale-like engulfing appetite. .... Is it not true that Heaven must have hated the Eastern Jin and thus given rise to this alien race? If not, how could its ferocity be like this!

Despite his cultivation of Chinese literature and natural abilities on the battlefield, Murong Jun is ultimately characterized in terms of his ethnic background, an alien kindred that is opposed to the Chinese Eastern Jin dynasty in the south. While his father had the heart of a wolf, Murong Jun has the appetite of a whale. Also visible here is the tendency to describe behavior perceived as hostile to the Chinese as being directly correlated to barbarian identity. This distinction is underlined by frequent references to genealogy and terms such as *lei* 類 (which I have translated as "race") that indicate a strong sense of not only cultural but also ethnic demarcation. Again, it must be noted that this tendency is not always explicit, and there are several *lun* colophons where there is no overt indication of barbarian ethnicity; however, in those cases there are usually elsewhere in the preceeding chronicle clear indications that the ruling family is non-Chinese

---

[156] *Jin shu* 111.2863.   [157] 隔閡諸華，聲教莫之漸 (*Jin shu* 111.2862). See above, 198–99.
[158] *Jin shu* 111.2863.

and that this fact necessitates different expectations on the part of the reader.[159] Regardless, the important point for the comparison with the *Wars* is that the rhetorical strategy of discrediting barbarian claims to legitimacy and critiquing their regimes in explicitly ethnological terms, while nearly absent in Procopius, appears consistently in the *Jin shu*.

The Ba-Di 巴氐 *Chenghan* 成漢 *Dynasty*

It is interesting to consider the case of the Chenghan dynasty, as it was founded not by a foreign people of the north or northeast but by one from the southwest known variously as the Ba, Di, or Ba-Di.[160] While there were precedents for destructive foreign invasion coming from the northern regions, both ancient and more recent, the south and southwest had witnessed far more expansion on the part of the Qin 秦 and Han Empires and much weaker resistance on the part of the indigenous peoples.[161] It is therefore indicative of the general anti-barbarian sentiment in the *Jin shu* that even the Ba-Di are assimilated into the larger category of the predatory barbarian:

> 是知戎狄亂華，釁深自古，況乎巴濮雜種，厥類實繁，資剽竊以全生，習獷悍而成俗．李特世傳凶狡，早擅梟雄，太息劍門，志吞井絡．[162]

> This is what it means to understand that the Rong-Di throw China into chaos; the strife has been deep since ancient times. Moreover, there are the Ba-Pu[163] motley hordes of the southwest, whose race is truly numerous; they store up plunder and booty for a livelihood, while studying rudeness and ferocity has become their custom. Li Te is known by tradition as a man evil and wily, excelling early on in ferocity and ambition; he sighed [covetously] over Jianmen pass and his ambition swallowed all of Shu.

The first lines of this passage have already been discussed in Chapter 3, but they are worth reiterating here as they contextualize the following assessment of the Chenghan state's progenitor Li Te 李特 by making him into a barbarian exemplar who treacherously covets lands that are not his own. Interestingly, and in a manner seen in the *Jin shu*'s

---

[159] Examples relating to the Di 氐 Former Qin 前秦 state and the Qiang 羌 Later Qin 後秦 state will be discussed in the following chapter.

[160] Note the distinction between the Di 氐 of Ba-Di 巴氐 and the ancient northern barbarian ethnonym Di 狄 used compounds such as Rong-Di 戎狄, Yi-Di 夷狄, etc.

[161] Brindley, "Barbarians or Not? Ethnicity and Changing Conceptions of the Ancient Yue (Viet) Peoples," 10–15; Holcombe, *The Genesis of East Asia*, 147–55.

[162] *Jin shu* 121.3049.   [163] On the two-word compound Ba-Pu, see above, 201, n. 245.

treatment of other conquest regimes, a number of Li Te's successors are given much more positive assessments in contrast, both in the preceeding narrative section of the fascicle and in the *lun* colophon. For example, Li Ban 李班, the nephew of Li Xiong already mentioned above, was "modest and widely learned, showing reverence and respect for Confucian men of talent."[164] His qualities are superseded by Li Shou 李壽, one of Li Xiong's cousins who went on to take power for himself. The *Jin shu* says that Li Shou was "perceptive and eager to study, magnanimous and enlightened; as a child he revered ritual propriety and set himself apart from the other sons of the Li clan."[165] Yet even these positive descriptions of barbarian individuals struggle against the generalizations about their inherent flaws, which ultimately serve to characterize both the people and the state. For the fascicle's concluding *zan* poem, devoted to the Chenghan state ruled by many virtuous barbarian figures, seems to obliquely refer to the Five Barbarians, Wu Hu 五胡, who for generations had "captured, murdered, and usurped the state, bringing chaos to the proper [imperial] succession."[166] The final word on the Chenghan state thus recalls the cosmopolitical maps described in pre-imperial texts, which conceive of a legitimate moral and political Chinese center opposed to a pan-barbarian outer world.

The Xiongnu Xia 夏 Dynasty

It has been demonstrated that barbarian tropes and terminology in the *Jin shu* encompass a wide range of non-Chinese peoples, and that different ethnonyms in various combinations may still carry a generic pejorative sense equivalent to the term "barbarian," which is applied to foreign peoples indiscriminately. Yet it remains true that the steppe nomads do seem to be singled out for especially negative treatment. This fact is no doubt partly attributable to their easy association with the Xiongnu Empire of the Qin and Han periods. But contributing to the negative predisposition of the Chinese against the northerners is the fact that it was rebels in the north in the early fourth century who first threatened and then took control of the ancient capital cities of Chang'an and Luoyang, cities whose political and symbolic significance was not less than that of the

---

[164] 班謙虛博納, 敬愛儒賢 (*Jin shu* 121.3041).
[165] 敏而好學, 雅量豁然, 少尚禮容, 異於李氏諸子 (*Jin shu* 121.3043).
[166] 世歷五朝, 年將四紀. 篡殺移國, 昏狂繼軌 (*Jin shu* 121.3049). Even if the identification of the *wu chao* 五朝, "five dynasties," with the Wu Hu Five Barbarians is incorrect, the following sentence certainly refers to the period of barbarian conquests.

city of Rome to the Romans. Hence the reference to the Xiongnu Liu Yuan as the "head of the disaster."[167]

Among the most reviled of the barbarian rulers to be presented in the *Jin shu* is Helian Bobo 赫連勃勃, another Xiongnu chieftain who founded the Xia state in 407. The *lun* concluding the fascicle chronicling the Xia says,

> 赫連勃勃獯醜種類，入居邊宇，屬中壤分崩，緣間肆慝，控弦鳴鏑，據有朔方．遂乃法玄象以開宮，擬神京而建社，竊先王之徽號，備中國之禮容，驅駕英賢，闚覦天下．[168]

> Helian Bobo was of a wicked Xun race; he entered the frontier regions and came upon the central territory, which was cracked and divided. Within the breaches of the frontier he indulged in wicked deeds; drawing his bow-strings amid the whistling of arrows, he seized control of the northern frontier. In time he followed the patterns of celestial signs in the building of palaces; he contrived the establishment of a capital and founding of a state. He usurped the magnificent title of the former kings and appropriated the system of rites and propriety of the Central Kingdom. He compelled and made use of those who were heroic and excellent and cast a covetous eye over the empire.

Lest there be any doubt of his genealogical background, Helian Bobo is identified as being of the Xun 獯 "race," an abbreviation for the ancient ethnonym of a hostile northern people, the Xunyu 獯粥. The predatory, arrow-shooting barbarian on the frontier again appears in vivid ethnographic colors that associate him with enemies of the past and exemplify the moral failings of his kindred. Like many of the barbarian rulers of the other fourteen states treated in the Chronicles, Helian Bobo is shown to adopt a number of the cultural trappings of Chinese royalty: he gives up his mobile tents for a proper capital and even has his palaces built according to the dictates of astrological science.[169] But as observed in some of the other examples above, the eventual efforts of the Xiongnu monarch to rule in Chinese fashion and display his adoption of Chinese cultural practices are presented as acts of usurpation and presumption, as an inversion of the proper world order. No doubt this is partly because, in contrast to the restraint Procopius tells us was exercised by Theoderic in deference to the emperors of the east, Helian Bobo takes the title of Son of Heaven for himself alone and presumes to perform the ritual acts of a sovereign while

[167] See above, 241, n. 130.   [168] *Jin shu* 130.3213.
[169] The fascicle's *zan* includes the phrase 爰創宮宇，易彼氈廬: "He changed [his lifestyle] and built palaces, adopting them in exchange for blankets and tents" (*Jin shu* 130.3214).

attempting, in Confucian style, to recognize and employ the virtuous and worthy in the service of his ambition. Yet even in the context of decades of armed Gothic resistance to Roman armies from the east, the rulers of Gothic Italy never appear reduced to simple ethnological categories and ethnographic tropes – nor are they subject to any xenophobic hostility of the historian. Yet as seen in many of the *lun* colophons to the *Jin shu* Chronicles, it is clear that the greatest crime a barbarian could commit was to adopt the ways of the Chinese while attempting to rule legitimately over both barbarians and Chinese subjects.

Conclusions

This chapter has sketched the prevalent use of barbarian ethnogenealogy and identity in the *Jin shu* as an explanatory and delegitimizing force in its representation of several of the barbarian rulers of the states featured in the Chronicles, a rhetorical strategy virtually absent in the *Wars* of Procopius. Although Procopius makes free use of the term "barbarian" when referring to his non-Roman protagonists, he never uses barbarian identity, either general or specific, as a causal factor in the narrative or as means of rationalizing or understanding their behavior. He never suggests in the case of Goth, Vandal, or even Frankish monarchs that X being a barbarian, it is only reasonable that Y may be inferred.[170] Contrary to the assumptions of a number of modern scholars, Procopius therefore exhibits little or no interest in making use of the category of the "barbarian" to rationalize or characterize barbarian kings, and the absence of this tendency in Procopius is only thrown into stark relief by the examples discussed above from the *Jin shu*. For in the latter case, we see how the historians make frequent use of ethnological thinking and biases in order to reinforce the distinctions between barbarians and subjects of the empire, a strategy that represents barbarian statehood as a catastrophic aberration from the patterns and hierarchies established in antiquity.

It is important to reiterate, however, that Procopius was a historian who was highly critical of the regime of Justinian, as has often been pointed out.[171] That he should represent the enemies of the emperor in a more

---

[170] At least one such instance occurs in Agathias, where a Roman speaker claims that a murdered king of the Lazi, Gubazes, was "led by his passions by virtue of his being born a barbarian and having the affliction of the common faithlessness of his race": ὁ Γουβάζης ὑπῆκτο τοῖς πάθεσι τῷ βάρβαρος τε πεφυκέναι καὶ τὴν κοινὴν τοῦ γένους νοσεῖν ἀπιστίαν (4.8.6).

[171] For example, see Cameron, *Procopius and the Sixth Century*, 137–43; Moorhead, "Totila the Revolutionary," 382; and Kaldellis, *Procopius of Caesarea*, 118–64.

sympathetic light is, therefore, not surprising, and it has been observed that even his praise of the barbarian Theoderic may be interpreted as an "indirect indictment of Justinian."[172] That the notion of the "barbarian" could be unambiguously pejorative in a political context is attested by Procopius' use of this very word in reference to Justinian himself in the *Anecdota*.[173] Nevertheless, the use of the term in the *Wars* is not employed as a delegitimizing, or otherwise significant, aspect of Gothic or Vandal rule. If Procopius had intended his work to offer a series of virtuous barbarian kings in mirror opposition to the flaws of Justinian, such an objective should, nevertheless, reveal a consistent preoccupation with barbarian imagery and tropes in his representation of foreign rulers – the very thing that this chapter has shown is not in evidence in his treatment of Vandal or Gothic kings. His history does not offer a valorization of barbarian rule; it simply fails to express interest in barbarian kings' ethnic or barbarian otherness whatsoever.

Yet as has repeatedly been observed, there are plenty of examples from the *Jin shu*, in the respective narratives of the fourteen barbarian regimes and in the *lun* colophons themselves, that do not represent barbarian rulers or states in ethnological or ethnographic terms; perhaps most notably in the assessment of Fu Jian 符堅, the ruler of the Di 氐 ethnic group's Former Qin 前秦 state, which was among the most militarily and politically successful of them all, if only briefly.[174] But even in the case of Fu Jian, who "transformed the barbarians to follow the ways of the Chinese" and "promoted the Confucian teachings of the ancient sages," there is still an occasional trace of ethnographic imagery, such as when he is described relying on his non-Chinese troops under the pejorative and collective expression for foreign enemies, *quanyang* 犬羊,

---

[172] Kaldellis, *Procopius of Caesarea*, 160. Also see Pazdernik, "Reinventing Theoderic in Procopius' Gothic War," 140; Goltz, *Barbar-König-Tyrann*, 252–55. Yet Procopius' own personal aims in the work, as they have variously been interpreted, do not detract from the fact that his work is part of a larger discourse where ethnic origins and political legitimacy were rarely correlated. As Gruen has argued regarding the interpretation of Augustan-age attitudes toward empire, as expressed by the poets of the late first century BC, the "ideas and attitudes repeatedly voiced by the poets evoke the prevailing atmosphere of public discussion." Gruen, "The Expansion of the Empire under Augustus," 190.

[173] *Anecdota* 14.2. In this case, it is important to note that the word appears, in a critique of Justinian's ability to pronounce Greek (as well as his disposition and dress), as a form of the verb *barbarizein*-βαρβαρίζειν. Its use in this context thus preserves the original sense of the word as something one does rather than what one is.

[174] On the Former Qin in general and for a translation of the narrative account of its most important emperor (though the *lun* colophon for the dynasty is not translated), see Rogers, *The Chronicle of Fu Chien*.

"dogs and sheep."[175] And even this otherwise successful state, which grew to such strength that it defeated all of its enemies in the north and even attempted to destroy the Chinese Eastern Jin dynasty in the south, is ultimately reduced to a pitiful laughingstock and an absurdity.[176]

As stressed above, the purpose of this study is not to draw attention to all of the facets that the *Wars* and *Jin shu* have in common, but rather, in focusing on the two texts' deployment of ethnographic and ethnological discourse in political narratives, to consider the crucial points at which they diverge. The fact that this prominent feature in the *Jin shu*, i.e., the attention granted to barbarian ethnicity or identity in assessing the character and reigns of barbarian rulers, is virtually absent in the *Wars* of Procopius should give us pause when considering a recent scholar's statement regarding ethnic boundaries in Late Antiquity: "[S]ince identity is generally created and hardened in conflict, the disappearance of the Roman state [in the west] removed the force which had sustained the old separate identities and drawn a firm line between Romans and outsiders."[177] How firm could this line have been if, from the point of view of the triumphant Roman Empire of Justinian, such a purported ideological dichotomy turns out to be as porous as the frontier zones themselves? Procopius did not write with the perspective of a western Roman provincial, one of those who may have come to terms with the new rulers and would certainly have had incentives to do so; much less was he under the patronage of a barbarian king. Yet his Constantinopolitan worldview exhibits neither a hardening of identities throughout a twenty-year war of attrition nor a significant political distinction between Romans and barbarians.

This chapter has also shown how fraught are assertions of ethnic harmony and equanimity in the early Tang, and even in the *Jin shu* itself. On the contrary, the officials of the Tang Bureau of Historiography, despite the fact that they worked under a ruling dynasty with strong ties to the steppe and Inner-Asian traditions, seem to have been at pains to redraw a clear line of distinction between a Chinese center and a

---

[175] 變夷從夏: "He tranformed the barbarians to follow the Chinese"; 闡先聖之儒風: "he promoted the Confucian teachings of the ancient sages"; 負其犬羊之力: "he relied on the strength of his dogs and sheep" (*Jin shu* 115.2956). That this phrase, "his dogs and sheep" *qi quanyang* 其犬羊, is pejorative in an ethnographic sense has also been assumed by Yang. "Reinventing the Barbarian," 80, n. 10.

[176] "He became a laughingstock for the whole world. How pitiful! How absurd!": 取笑天下，豈不哀哉! 豈不謬哉! (Ibid.). That the regime was also considered illegitimate on ethnic grounds will be discussed in the next chapter.

[177] Heather, "State, Lordship and Community in the West," 454.

barbarian periphery – this after any such distinction in reality had broken down for centuries in the north of China. Why should this be? In each case we are dealing with texts produced in a political climate where there was a dominant ideology of restoration of an imperial past, a program that professed to reclaim and rejuvenate the empire in self-conscious reflection of ancient precedent. But only in China's case did this involve establishing a stark demarcation between a barbarian Other and an imperial Self, a demarcation that delegitimized the political and civilizational ambitions of barbarians on ethnological grounds. As has been argued in the previous chapter's conclusion, part of the explanation lies in the classical ritual and historical texts that provided the lexical and conceptual framework for the representation of foreign peoples, the authoritative precedents for how to rationalize and make sense of a diverse and complex world. The fact that our main classicizing Roman source on the reconquest of Italy and North Africa from the Goths and Vandals does not apply such a demarcation in its accounts of barbarian dynasts and their followers, or does so to an extremely limited extent, raises the question of whether the dichotomy's presence in earlier classical thought has been exaggerated to begin with.

CHAPTER 5

The Confluence of Ethnographic Discourse and Political Legitimacy
Rhetorical Arguments on the Legitimacy of Barbarian Kingdoms

The preceding two chapters discussed the presence of ethnographic discourse in representation of the barbarian peoples and individuals who had come to rule portions of the former Roman and Chinese empires. Thus far, a central focus has been the ways in which Procopius and the historians of the *Jin shu* 晉書 offer critical evaluations of individual barbarian actors and the presence or absence of ethnographic rhetoric in those assessments. An underlying theme that has run throughout the discussion is the question of political legitimacy and its relationship to assumptions inherent in the respective bodies of ethnological discourse. While the preceding chapters have focused more on general forms of ethnic or individual representation, this chapter will address the question of political legitimacy directly: How was political legitimacy conceived of in Rome and China in this period and to what degree did perceptions of ethnic identity function as criteria in its construction and articulation?

In order to answer this question, this chapter will consider the extent to which ethnographic discourse appears in the form of reported speeches that appear in political contexts. While the preceding chapters considered historians' collective representation of foreign peoles of varied political status and the assessments of individual figures in the historians' own voice, the present chapter will analyze the rhetorical speeches attributed, for the most part, to barbarian speakers. Such passages offer deeper insight into the mentalities and worldviews that characterized either period, and the multiplicity of perspectives therein grants modern scholars access not only to what may have been official points of view but also to politically critical interpretations of imperial policy. Perhaps even more importantly, the speeches attributed to barbarian actors represent an imaginative leap on the part of the historian and his audience into the minds and motivations of foreign individuals; they show how Roman and Chinese historians imagined the barbarians might perceive themselves in relation to the Roman and Chinese imperial traditions. As the narratives of the *Wars* and the *Jin shu* Chronicles are characterized by political conflict, it is not surprising that a recurring theme in either text is that of the legitimation of political claims. Analysis of the speeches dealing with this question in light of their ethnological content will shed light on the degree to which ethnic identity was politicized in either case. This issue is critical to the larger context of this study, which examines the way Roman and Chinese historical traditions rationalized and represented a period of unprecedented political and demographic change, when the barbarian Others against whom modern scholars often assume the imperial communities of ancient Rome and China were defined had taken possession of the imperial heartlands.

Political Legitimacy

Political legitimacy has been referred to loosely at several points in previous chapters, but given its centrality to the subsequent discussion, it will be helpful to discuss the concept at greater length here. "Legitimacy" has been broadly defined by Suchman as "a generalized perception or assumption that the actions of an entity are desirable, proper, or appropriate within some socially constructed system of norms, values, beliefs, and definitions."[1] Important for the purposes of a study concerned with the representation of barbarian peoples entering the political sphere is Suchman's recognition of the subjectivity of the concept: the presence of legitimacy is determined by perceptions and assumptions that are sufficiently generalized within a population. Notions of legitimacy, like the tropes and commonplaces that typify ethnographic representations, may be remarkably stable over centuries, but they are nevertheless subject to the variations and changes that characterize any body of discourse. While he does not include it in his definition of legitimacy, Suchman goes on to emphasize that it is "socially constructed" and that it "reflects a congruence between the behaviors of the legitimated entity and the shared (or assumedly shared) beliefs of some social group."[2] Like ethnic identity, legitimacy is therefore a social construct that must necessarily accord with the particular norms and worldview of the group or society by which it is conferred.[3]

---

[1] Suchman, "Managing Legitimacy: Strategic and Institutional Approaches," 574. For a discussion of older theoretical conceptions of the term beginning with Max Weber, see the references in Wechsler, *Offerings of Jade and Silk: Ritual and Symbol in the Legitimation of the T'ang Dynasty*, 10–12. Also see Ando, *Imperial Ideology and Provincial Loyalty in the Roman Empire*, 19–29.

[2] Ibid.

[3] The concept of ethnicity and its application to the study of the historical periods in question has been discussed above, 24–25.

In her discussion of the concept in a specifically political context, Tamvaki has described the necessity of a congruence between legitimacy and the body of norms and expectations characteristic of a given society. She argues that "political authority is legitimate to the extent that it is exercised according to established rules (legality) and is subsequently confirmed by the consent of subordinates."[4] According to Tamvaki, legitimacy may ultimately be reduced to "a function of a system's capacity to persuade members of its own appropriateness so that it will be granted wider legitimation."[5] While legality is an integral aspect of legitimacy, as indicated by its very etymology, Tamvaki makes clear that legality is ultimately subsumed under a larger body of social assumptions that in the aggregate determine what is appropriate and therefore acceptable to the society at large. This broader description of the determinative factor of legitimacy – the necessary congruence between the qualities of a governing body and the socio-cultural norms and expectations of its subjects – is the understanding of the term "legitimacy" that will be adopted here. Both of the imperial traditions discussed in this study had their own set of criteria, their own "constructed system of norms, values, beliefs, and definitions," according to which political power was awarded to groups and individuals, and a brief summary of them now follows.

The Roman imperial system established under the Principate of Augustus was essentially a monarchy that was still conceived and spoken of in the terms of a representative republic. While elections continued to be held and offices were filled, absolute authority now rested in the hands of the emperor rather than in the multiple hands of a competitive aristocracy. In order to reconcile this disconnect between what was a *res publica* in name but a *monarchia* in practice, forms of ritual behavior were adopted by the emperors that served to persuade the citizenry and senatorial aristocracy that he was merely the first among equals.[6] In addition to "judicial and administrative responsibilities, and religious and ceremonial roles" fulfilled by the *princeps*, McEvoy has described the traditional virtues of "courage, justice, wisdom, and temperance" that served to legitimate an emperor's reign; military competence and success

---

[4] Tamvaki, "European Polity: Layers of Legitimacy," 236.   [5] Ibid.

[6] For an in-depth discussion of the political theater that served to reconcile these contradictions, see Wallace-Hadrill, "*Civilis Princeps*: Between Citizen and King," 32–48; Eck, *The Age of Augustus*, 41–84. For an in-depth discussion of political symbolism and performance in the late Republic, see Flaig, *Ritualisierte Politik: Zeichen, Gesten und Herrschaft im Alten Rom*. Wienand's edited volume on the imperial office in the fourth century offers a comprehensive collection of essays. *Contested Monarchy: Integrating the Roman Empire in the Fourth Century AD*.

were of course also important.[7] Yet the tensions at the heart of the new form of government under the Principate never disappeared, the result being that the empire was left with "a constitutionally undefined and indefinable regime."[8]

This essential ambiguity was particularly marked in relation to the question of succession. Kaldellis has explained the absence of any clearly articulated right of imperial succession by virtue of the fact that the state remained a *res publica*, even under a monarchical regime: "what was not owned privately could not be bequeathed."[9] While the office of emperor was theoretically elective and subject to the discretion of the senate and army, as was to remain the case until the fifteenth century,[10] it has been observed that a dynastic component was clearly visible already in the first century AD, as Julio-Claudian emperors publicly associated themselves with Augustus.[11] This dynastic aspect of the imperial office was perpetuated under the Flavians and seems to have "reached maturity" during the reign of Hadrian who "stressed the genealogical connection between Trajan and Aeneas and between Trajan and Augustus."[12] Despite this appeal to a Roman genealogical tradition, there is little evidence that a potential candidate's ethnic background was a critical factor in the degree of legitimacy he could command. As is well known, Rome's alternative to the myth of Trojan origins, i.e., the motley community attracted by the city's founder Romulus, emphasizes the heterogeneity of the founding population. Even the second of its kings, Numa Pompilius, was a non-Roman Sabine, and two of the last three kings prior to the founding of the Republic were of Etruscan origin. Quoting Coleridge, who asserted that "Rome under Trajan was an empire without a nation," Purcell argues that "the imperial character could subsist without the foundations of ethnic pride."[13] Dynastic continuity, nevertheless, remained an important aspect of imperial legitimation as evidenced by Septimius Severus' self-proclaimed adoption as the son of Marcus Aurelius and the brother of Commodus,

---

[7] McEvoy, "Rome and the Transformation of the Imperial Office in the Late Fourth–Mid Fifth Centuries," 159–60. An alternative list is supplied by Norena: *aequitas, pietas, virtus, liberalitas,* and *providentia. Imperial Ideals in the Roman West,* 99; see ibid., 37–100, for an in-depth discussion of the various virtues that were considered to characterize the ideal emperor.

[8] Lo Cascio, "The Emperor and his Administration: The Age of the Severans," 138. For a concise summary of the emperor's constitutional position, see Stein, *Geschichte des spätrömischen Reiches von 284 bis 476 n. Chr.,* 46–49.

[9] Kaldellis, *The Byzantine Republic,* 44. Also see Börm, "Born to Be Emperor," 239–64.

[10] Bury, *History of the Later Roman Empire from the Death of Theodosius I to the Death of Justinian,* Vol. 1, 5.

[11] Ando, *Imperial Ideology and Provincial Loyalty in the Roman Empire,* 33.   [12] Ibid., 37–39.

[13] Purcell, "Rome and Italy," 443.

thus perpetuating the Antonine dynasty, which had itself traced its legitimacy back to the Julio-Claudians.[14]

The third century was a period of immense upheaval in the Roman Empire, which witnessed barbarian invasion, economic crisis, and territorial fragmentation, exacerbated by the rapid succession of emperors that began in the 230s and did not end until the accession of Diocletian. The late fourth-century *Historia Augusta* would label many of these emperors "tyrants," and the rapid turnover of rulers makes the third century the most politically unstable era of Roman history. Moreover, as dynastic continuity became increasingly difficult to establish with so many contenders for power, the combination of military acclamation and claims to divine prerogative became more prominent.[15] Nevertheless, the role of the senate in conferring legitimacy upon an emperor retained at least some significance; this is evidenced by the care exhibited by Philip the Arab to seek senatorial approval, in contrast to Maximinus Thrax, who had contented himself with the acclamation of the army alone and lost the loyalty of the capital city and its elite as a consequence.[16] But the third century made manifest the potential instability inherent in the constitutionally undefined republic: because his position was itself basically illegitimate in constitutional terms, the emperor could theoretically be overthrown without harm done to anyone else but him.[17]

Perhaps in response to the disastrous implications of this aspect of the Principate, one of the lasting changes that the later decades of the third century produced was a shift in the legitimizing discourse of the imperial office, although it is important to note that this development built upon earlier precedents. As has been discussed by Kaldellis, the regimes of Diocletian, the tetrarchs, and Constantine perpetuated innovations of their recent predecessor Aurelian and exhibited a particular emphasis on the divinity of the emperor.[18] Of course, notions that the *princeps* enjoyed the favor of the gods and that he could even be revered as a deity himself go back to the reign of Augustus, though the latter practice ended with the fall

[14] Kulikowski, *The Triumph of Empire*, 85.

[15] This earlier tradition of associating a ruling dynasty with divine favor reached its culmination in the reign of Aurelian, who for the first time represented the emperor as a sole ruler on earth mirrored by a single divinity in heaven. Alföldi, *Studien zur Geschichte der Weltkrise des 3. Jahrhunderts nach Christus*, 375–76.

[16] Potter, *The Roman Empire at Bay*, 240. On the decreasing significance of senatorial ratification of elected emperors, see Seston, *Dioclétien et la tétrarchie*, 194–99.

[17] "[W]eil er grundsätzlich illegitim war, konnte der Kaiser gestürzt werden, ohne daß man jemand anderem übel tat als ihm selbst." Pfeilschifter, *Der Kaiser und Konstantinopel*, 2.

[18] Kaldellis, *The Byzantine Republic*, 175–78; Jones, *The Later Roman Empire*, 284–602, 40–41.

of Julio-Claudians. While the adoption of Christianity rendered any explicit deification of the emperor impossible, "the consecration of the ruler's person was maintained in the epithets *sacred* and *divine*; and the Emperors came to regard themselves rather as viceregents of God than as rulers set up by their people."[19] Yet several scholars have noted that this conjoining of the divine and terrestrial spheres in the imperial office is hardly illustrative of an innovation by the early tetrarchic regime, which identified its two principal figures, Diocletian and Maximian, with the Roman divinities of Jupiter and Hercules through the titles Iovius and Herculius.[20] Seen in terms of this precedent, the conversion of Constantine to Christianity and his official patronage of the religion are a merely a reflection of the imperial religiosity that had become more prominent since the 270s and that itself had roots in the early reigns of the Principate.

While the Tetrarchy was characterized by a system where authority was delegated to four monarchs ruling simultaneously, if in junior and senior capacities, it is recognized that the dynastic element of the political system nevertheless persisted through marriage alliances between the tetrarchs.[21] It is at least clear that Constantius I wished his son to occupy the office of Caesar when Constantius himself was promoted to that of Augustus, as is the fact that the exclusion of Maxentius, the son of the retiring Augustus Maximian, from the office of Caesar precipitated Maxentius' revolt. In any case, the dynastic principle was firmly reestablished under Constantine, and the significance of imperial blood is evident in the massacre conducted by Constantius II against nearly all of his living relatives who might be eligible for the throne by virtue of descent from Constantius I.[22]

Yet despite the persistence of a conception of legitimacy encompassing both dynastic and divine aspects, the republican legacy remained stubbornly in place. As Jones has put it, "the imperial office never became legally hereditary, and its divine right did not depend on birth: in theory always, and on occasion in practice, the empire was elective."[23] This

---

[19] Bury, *History of the Later Roman Empire from the Death of Theodosius I to the Death of Justinian*, *Vol. 1*, 12. For examples of the awe this could inspire in the emperor's subjects, see Kelly, *Ruling the Later Roman Empire*, 192–93.

[20] See, for example, Kolb, *Diocletian und die Erste Tetrarchie*, 88–114; Seston, *Dioclétien et la tétrarchie*, 211–30.

[21] For a discussion of imperial succession and legitimacy under the Tetrarchy, see Rees, *Diocletian and the Tetrarchy*, 76–85.

[22] For discussion of the persistence of the dynastic principle following the end of the Constantinian dynasty, see Errington, *Roman Imperial Policy*, 13–42.

[23] Jones, *The Later Roman Empire*, 322.

elective component to imperial legitimacy was borne out in several points of succession crisis, such as in the death of the emperor Julian during his failed invasion of Persia. With the army leaderless and in hostile country, its leaders elevated Jovian, who soon died and was replaced by the officer Valentinian I following a similar conclave. The fifth century also witnessed the appointment of emperors from wholly outside the royal family, such as Leo and Zeno. For Leo, there was not even a woman of the imperial family whom he might marry, as his predecessor Marcian had done when he joined the Theodosian family through marriage to Pulcheria, the daughter of the emperor Arcadius. Leo's successor Zeno was not only unrelated to Leo and the Theodosian dynasty; he was also an Isaurian chieftain who changed his name from Tarasicodissa to the more Hellenic-sounding Zeno.[24] As several scholars have observed, Theodosius II was the last emperor until the seventh century to inherit the throne from his father.[25] In the sixth century, the uncle of Justinian himself rose through the ranks of the army from his humble origins as a shepherd in the Balkans to become emperor. While Justinian's candidacy for the purple was doubtless facilitated by his blood relationship to Justin, this particular case nevertheless exemplifies the elective component to Roman imperial legitimacy, according to which "either the Senate or the army could proclaim an Emperor, and the act of proclamation constituted a legitimate title."[26]

The reign of Justinian also illustrates another legitimating component in Roman political discourse: the role of the emperor as lawgiver. In his discussion of the sixth-century official John the Lydian's *On Offices*, Pazdernik has pointed out the importance of the legal nature of imperial rule, suggesting that, in contrast to tyranny,

> lawful emperorship is characterized by the elective character of the office, by an unstinting determination on the part of the emperor to disturb neither the laws nor the form of the state, and by an approach to government that involves the leading men of the state in the formulation of policy.[27]

Justinian's efforts in the legal sphere have been much discussed, since they resulted in an unprecedented codification and organization of Roman laws and legal precedents reaching back centuries. As has been argued by

---

[24] On the status of the Isaurians in Late Antiquity, see Elton, "The Nature of the Sixth-Century Isaurians," 293–307.

[25] McCormick, "Emperor and Court," 145.

[26] Bury, *History of the Later Roman Empire from the Death of Theodosius I to the Death of Justinian,* Vol. 1, 5.

[27] Pazdernik, "Justinianic Ideology and the Power of the Past," 195.

Pazdernik, Justinian's project of legal codification was "set on par with the restoration of imperial authority over the west," and these two endeavors "constituted equal parts of a double legacy that Justinian became determined to rehabilitate."[28] In Justinian's case, legislative control was actively employed by the emperor as a "vehicle of political legitimization";[29] it served the propagandistic needs of an emperor who sought to embody the inherited ideal of a legislating monarch.

This active interest in legislation, however, was combined with an intensification of the religious nature of the imperial office, which had been developing for centuries. While on the one hand the legislation of Justinian could be seen by John the Lydian as an expression of continuity with the Roman republican legacy, Justinian himself "insisted … that God had entrusted the government of the empire to him alone and that his laws should attempt to restore on earth the order that God had established in heaven."[30] Therefore, while the legislative and legal component of the imperial office seems to have reached an apogee under the reign of Justinian, this activity was accompanied by an increasingly prominent assertion of the divine prerogatives that accrued to the emperor's own person.

Though the Roman Empire had never witnessed the rise of a barbarian state prior to the kingdoms founded in the fifth century – that is, a dynasty similar to any of those that appeared in north China in the fourth century – there were emperors from various parts of the empire who spoke different languages and who had ethnic identities that seem to have coexisted comfortably with their Roman ones. Indeed, credit for Rome's greatness is explicitly attributed by Aurelius Victor in the late fourth century to the emperors who were born outside the city and even Italy:

> Hactenus Romae seu per Italiam orti imperium rexere, hinc advenae quoque. … Ac mihi quidem audienti multa legentique plane compertum urbem Romam externorum virtute atque insitivis artibus praecipue crevisse.[31]

> Up until this time [the reign of Domitian, d. AD 96], if men originating from throughout Italy wielded the imperial power, henceforth men from elsewhere also ruled. … And to me, hearing and reading many accounts, it seems a plain fact that the city of Rome grew especially thanks to the virtue and imported skills of foreigners.

---

[28] Ibid., 199.
[29] Ibid., 204. On the essential role of law in imperial conceptions of legitimate authority, see ibid., 189–90.
[30] Maas, "Roman Questions, Byzantine Answers: Contours of the Age of Justinian," 6.
[31] *Liber de Caesaribus* 11.12–13.

The trend of non-Italian emperorship was perpetuated by the first of the Severan emperors, Septimius Severus, who was from North Africa and is believed to have spoken the Punic language;[32] he himself was of mixed Punic and Italian ancestry, and his first wife bore names indicating Punic origin.[33] Severus' second wife was a native of Syria, and his sons, the emperors Geta and Caracalla, were thus of mixed Italian, North African, and Syrian descent. While Elagabalus claimed descent from Severus' son Caracalla, he himself was from Roman Syria and was ascribed the name of a Syrian sun god following his death.[34] The period of turmoil in the third century following the death of Alexander Severus in 235 is described by Aurelius Victor as one in which "both good and bad men were variously invested with imperial power, men both noble and low-born as well as many barbarians."[35] Reference to the fact that barbarians had won control over the empire is quite understated, and Victor does not dwell on the point or grant it especial significance. The anonymous, late fourth-century *Epitome de Caesaribus* is similarly understated when it notes the barbarian origins of two soldiers who are elevated to the throne by the army, Magnentius and Silvanus. It comments that the former was an avid reader, sharply spoken, and cowardly while the latter had a "most gentle character" and, "although born of a barbarian father, was nevertheless sufficiently civilized and hardy from his Roman education."[36] Ammianus expresses nothing but sympathy for the Frank Silvanus, whose unwilling usurpation ended in his being assassinated by agents of Constantius II.[37] Even if one discounts the significance of these examples, the Roman Empire had witnessed military figures of peripheral, and perhaps even barbarian, origin proclaimed emperor in the third

---

[32] Birley, *Septimius Severus: The African Emperor*, 35, 63.

[33] Ibid. For Septimius' ancestry, see ibid., ix–x, 212–21; for that of his first wife, see 225, n. 56.

[34] If this posthumous use of a foreign title was intended to have discredited the memory of the emperor (in a manner similar to the use of the nickname "Caligula" for the emperor Gaius), it was, nevertheless, recognized as being a foreign name and reflecting a foreign cult practice that marked his exogenous origins. Whatever eastern stereotypes may be evident in posterity's representation of Elagabalus, his reign was not deemed illegitimate because of his provincial or foreign origins.

[35] *immissique in imperium promiscue boni malique, nobiles atque ignobiles, ac barbariae multi* (*Liber de Caesaribus* 24.9). Victor makes no comment on the barbarian origins attributed to Maximinus Thrax by the *Historia Augusta* and Herodian, lending support to Potter's assertion that such "wild slanders" of barbarian ancestry were fabrications of Maximinus' detractors. Potter, *The Roman Empire at Bay*, 168. Barbarian origins are also dismissed by Kulikowski, *The Triumph of the Roman Empire*, 112.

[36] *Fuit ingenio blandissimus. Quamquam barbaro patre genitus, tamen institutione Romana satis cultus et patiens* (*Epitome de Caesaribus* 42.10–11).

[37] Amm. Marc. 15.5.32–34.

and fourth centuries, and at least some of our sources close to the period do not appear scandalized over the fact.[38]

Yet despite the sometimes diverse origins of Roman emperors, there seems to be a belief, at least among modern historians, that a barbarian could never have legitimately held the throne. The fourth and fifth centuries were a period that saw the increased participation of barbarians in imperial politics in both the west and east. The Frank Arbogast wielded considerable power during the reign of Valentinian II, and his career terminated when his preferred candidate for the throne, Eugenius, was defeated by Theodosius at the battle of the Frigidus in 394. The Alan Aspar seems to have had an opportunity to succeed the eastern emperor Marcian in 457, but he is quoted as having claimed that he did not wish to set a precedent[39] – Anastos has pointed out that exactly what kind of precedent is not made clear, although it has been assumed that this statement refers to the precedent of a barbarian succeeding to the throne.[40] Still, having a clearly foreign name did not prevent Aspar's great-grandson Areobindus from being proclaimed emperor during a riot in 512.[41]

Similar arguments have been put forward regarding the half-Vandal general Stilicho, who was the de facto ruler of the western empire during the minority of the emperor Honorius in the last years of the fourth, and early years of the fifth, century. Although he had married the adopted niece of Theodosius, it has been assumed that Stilicho's barbarian ethnicity would have disqualified him from the imperial power: "as the son of a Vandal, he could never aspire to the purple himself."[42] One of the most prominent political figures of the fifth-century west was the barbarian Ricimer of mixed Suevic and Gothic ancestry;[43] Jones has asserted

---

[38] This does not mean that there was not intense hostility and xenophobia expressed toward the barbarian enemies of the empire in the third and fourth centuries in other media and genres such as on coins or in panegyric. See Ladner, "On Roman Attitudes toward Barbarians in Late Antiquity," 12–21.

[39] On this episode, see Anastos, "*Vox Populi Voluntas Dei* and the Election of the Byzantine Emperor," 193–94. Anastos cites the testimony of Zonaras to demonstrate that it was Aspar's Arian faith rather than ethnic background that barred him from becoming emperor. Moreover, any assumption that the "precedent" should have referred to Aspar's Alan ethnicity is also problematic, since he wished his own son Patricius to be named Leo's successor. Lee, Doug, "The Eastern Empire: Theodosius to Anastasius," 47. On the remarkable career of Aspar and his relatives, see McEvoy "Becoming Roman?: The Not-So-Curious Case of Aspar and the Ardaburii," 483–511. Also see Pfeilschifter on Aspar's role in East Roman politics in *Der Kaiser und Konstantinopel*, 512–36; on the succession in 457, see ibid., 517.

[40] Bachrach, *A History of the Alans in the* West, 44.

[41] *Areobindam sibi imperatorem fieri clamitant* (Marcellinus Comes 512.4).

[42] Cameron, "Theodosius the Great and the Regency of Stilico," 274.

[43] Gillett, "The Birth of Ricimer," 380–81.

that "Ricimer as a barbarian and an Arian would have been unacceptable as emperor," and the same point has been argued by Woods, who claims that Ricimer "realised that his barbarian origin rendered him an unacceptable candidate for the throne."[44] While it may have been the case that the barbarian *magistri militum* were in fact excluded from the imperial office on ethnic grounds, the evidence for this argument is only loosely inferred from the sources and never explicitly attested.[45] What is clear, however, is that from the second century AD, the empire became accustomed to emperors and leading political figures who were not only of non-Italian origin but even, in the case of the kingmakers and generals of the fourth and fifth centuries, seem to have openly professed barbarian identities.

In sum, political legitimacy under the Roman Empire incorporated a number of different factors, though these were of varied weight at different times: a superficial rhetoric of continuity with the republican past, the legality conferred by an "elective" process and acclamation by the senate and people, support of the armies and success in battle, dynastic continuity, and divine favor. Absent from these criteria is any reference to genealogies connecting would-be rulers to mythical Roman ancestors, and there are many instances where emperors of provincial origin were openly recognized as belonging to sub-Roman ethnic categories.

In turning to the case of political legitimacy in ancient China, the following summary will be similarly brief. While the English term "emperor" derives from Latin *imperator*, an originally military designation denoting the significance of military leadership in the Roman conception of its highest office, the supreme position of political power in ancient China, typically translated as "emperor," was *huangdi* 皇帝, or *tianzi* 天子, "Son of Heaven."[46] The source of the emperor's authority in China "derived from a belief, embodied in the Mandate of Heaven [*tianming* 天命] concept, that his surpassing wisdom and exemplary virtue had prompted Heaven to confer upon him (and his descendants) a divine

---

[44] Jones, *The Later Roman Empire*, 240; Woods, "A Misunderstood Monogram: Ricimer or Severus?" 19. Heather is more careful in his interpretation, noting only that "Ricimer himself never sought the throne." "The Western Empire," 21.

[45] As put by Mathisen in his excellent study, "we have plenty of evidence for barbarians behaving as if they were Roman citizens. They held office, owned and transferred property, made wills, went to Roman courts, and generally made use of *ius civile*, all without formally receiving citizenship." "*Peregrini, Barbari*, and *Cives Romani*," 1036.

[46] The terms *caesar, augustus, autokratōr*-αὐτοκράτωρ, and *basileus*-βασιλεύς are all typically translated as "emperor" in modern scholarship.

mandate to rule the land."[47] Two features of this description of the imperial office in ancient China are familiar from the discussion of Roman conceptions of imperial legitimacy: the divine significance of the imperial office and the dynastic or hereditary nature of political power. Aihe Wang has traced the origins of both of these features to the practice of ancestor worship first introduced by the Shang 商 kings in the second millennium BC, describing how political authority and sacral practice were "fused into a continuity of being in the king's body, an unbroken chain in the royal ancestral line."[48]

Following the establishment of the Zhou 周 dynasty at the end of second millennium, the notion of supreme rulership witnessed innovations such as the introduction of the concept of the ruler's *de* 德 – "potency accumulated over time by the ruler"[49] or simply "virtue" – as well as the conceptualization of *tian* 天, "Heaven." At the same time, the centrality of ancestor worship retained its prominence and contributed to the formulation of the notion that the supreme ruler was the "Son of Heaven," who was graced by its mandate.[50] Once formulated and established, the Mandate of Heaven as a legitimating principle for the temporal power exercised by the emperors was to remain in place until the beginning of the twentieth century.[51] The Warring States period of the fifth to third centuries BC witnessed further changes in the conception of political power that eventually arrived at "the unquestioned supremacy of a single, cosmically potent autocrat who ruled as the image of heaven on earth, and the reconstitution of the public order around this figure."[52] Such a conception is markedly different from Roman experimentation with collegial rule under the adopted brothers Marcus Aurelius and Lucius Verus in the second century, the Tetrarchy in the third and fourth centuries, and then the division of the empire between the members of the Constantinian, Valentinian, and Theodosian dynasties thereafter. While such arrangements stressed the necessary unity of the empire even amid bitter and violent internal struggle, imperial titulature, even at the highest level, allowed for multiple bearers. In contrast, the Chinese imperial tradition from the start was characterized by the notion that "there was

---

[47] Wechsler, *Mirror to the Son of Heaven: Wei Cheng at the Court of T'ang T'ai-tsung*, 2–3. For more in-depth discussions of the nature and evolution of imperial authority in ancient China, see Loewe, "The Concept of Sovereignty," 726–46; Wechsler, *Offerings of Jade and Silk*, 10–20; Creel, *The Origins of Statecraft in China*, 81–100.

[48] Wang, Aihe, *Cosmology and Political Culture in Early China*, 56.

[49] Wang's translation. Ibid., 60.   [50] Ibid., 58–60.

[51] Creel, *The Origins of Statecraft in China*, 93.   [52] Lewis, *Sanctioned Violence in Early China*, 246.

no alternative to the singularly legitimate 'universal' monarch," "the sole mediator with and representative of the highest diety, Heaven."[53]

That is not to say that Chinese notions of emperorship were not beset by political tensions and complexities. As has been pointed out by Wechsler, the Mandate of Heaven was contingent upon the virtuous exercise of power and could be transferred from an unworthy individual or dynasty to a more appropriate candidate.[54] Moreover, the mythical tradition that told how the rulers Yao 堯 and Shun 舜 both conferred their power onto the worthiest potential successor, passing over their own sons, was to have an important exemplary power that was often invoked in periods of political crisis and usurpation.[55] Therefore, neither the dynastic principle nor the Mandate of Heaven was exempt from challenge. The precedent of ritualized abdication and the accompanying bestowal of the divine mandate on a new candidate could be utilized to claim the legitimate transfer of power from one regime to another at times of political upheaval. While the exception rather than the rule in patterns of succession in ancient China, the "meritocratic" precedent nevertheless remained, in a manner not dissimilar to the republican legacy in Roman imperial politics, a means by which political and dynastic discontinuity could be justified and legitimated.

The concept of emperorship in ancient China was further elaborated and codified under the Han 漢 dynasty, as was the case with many other political and philosophical ideas that would remain influential throughout the imperial period. In particular, the further articulation of cosmological correlative theory provided new ways of understanding both the legitimation of the imperial office and the cosmological significance of the role of the sovereign. During the Warring States period, the growing study of *wuxing* 五行 (Five Element or Five Phases) theory had "transformed the nature of rulership from a hereditary king, legitimized by an ancestral cult, to a territorial ruler of a bureaucratic state, legitimized by his imitation of and conformity to the cosmos."[56] The interpretation of omens as a reflection of the relationship between imperial virtue and ritual performance on

---

[53] Pines, *The Everlasting Empire*, 27, 44. Pines points to a significant contrast between the insistence on a single orthodox faith in medieval Europe in a context where multiple secular powers were more or less on par with one another. In China, there were multiple religious faiths but all were subject to the sole and sacral authority of the emperor. See ibid., 58.

[54] Wechsler, *Offerings of Jade and Silk*, 12.

[55] Wechsler, *Offerings of Jade and Silk*, 13. For two examples of the continued relevance of these mythical instances of imperial abdication, see Knechtges, "The Rhetoric of Imperial Addiction and Accession in a Third-Century Chinese Court," 3–35; and Leban, "The Accession of Sima Yan, AD 265," 1–50.

[56] Aihe Wang, *Cosmology and Political Culture in Early China*, 91.

the one hand and the functioning of the cosmos on the other became a specialty of scholarly officials who used their expertise to "to constrain the emperor's person, to construct emperorship as the core institution of empire building," and "to monopolize divine and moral authority."[57] In a manner similar to the function performed by the legal constraints upon imperial activities in the Roman Empire, the status and powers of the Han emperors were "constantly contested and reproduced through the discursive actions of interpreting omens and theorizing the cosmos."[58]

In an interesting contrast to the case of the Roman Empire and the period in which the *Wars* of Procopius were written, China in the early seventh century had already witnessed centuries of barbarian rule of the northern heartlands of China under the Northern Wei 北魏, Northern Qi 北齊, and Northern Zhou 北周 dynasties, all of which had ruling houses that professed a non-Chinese, Särbi-Xianbei 鮮卑 identity, spoke a different language, and even wore clothes different from those of their Chinese subjects.[59] Compared to the position of the Tang 唐 dynasty in the early seventh century, the emperor Justinian in the sixth century was faced with a situation where Roman political supremacy, even if it had fallen away in the western provinces, remained unshaken. While Roman authority had never been overwhelmed, the early fourth century in China witnessed the flight of the imperial family and elites to the south, which was still undergoing a process of Chinese colonial expansion.[60] The succession of weak regimes that they established south of the Yangtze would ultimately end with the destruction of the Chen 陳 dynasty by the northern Sui 隨 dynasty armies in 589. As has been discussed in greater detail in the Introduction, an important point to remember is that it was one of the barbarian dynasties in the north that had given rise to the Sui, which was in turn rapidly succeeded by the Tang. To reiterate: the "Chinese" Empire was restored not by any of the southern Chinese dynasties, but rather by the barbarian, or at least semi-barbarian, north. Unlike the Roman Empire of Procopius' own day where the historian could write from the perspective of the eastern imperial capital, which had launched successful (even though they proved to be short-lived) wars of reconquest, the *Jin shu* historians wrote following a 300-year period that had been ushered in with the sack

---

[57] Ibid., 179.
[58] Ibid., 206. For a discussion of correlative cosmology under the Han, see Queen, *From Chronicle to Canon*, 206–26.
[59] Still, the cultural boundaries in this period came to blur to the point of becoming indistinguishable. See Dien, *Six Dynasties Civilization*, especially 424–29; Lewis, *China between Empires*, 167–69.
[60] Holcombe, *In the Shadow of the Han*, 25–27; Lewis, *China between Empires*, 56, 166–67.

of both imperial capitals and the flight of the imperial family and elites to the south, and during which the north had been ruled for centuries by non-Chinese. Procopius could continue to write with a degree of confidence in the continuity and stability of the Roman political system and ideology in a way that was impossible for the historians of the Tang.

It should therefore be a question of great interest how the Tang articulated its own claim to political legitimacy. Not surprisingly, the thinking on this issue was complicated. The modern scholar Deng Lequn has described three different criteria according to which a particular dynasty could be considered legitimate. However, he begins by noting that the necessity of Han Chinese ethnicity was taken for granted in the centuries of the Qin-Han dynasties and afterwards:

> among Han-Chinese the political view naturally developed that Han-Chinese regimes of the Central Plains [professing] a hereditary succession from older dynasties should be considered legitimate [*zhengtong* 正统] whereas states of barbarian ethnic groups [*huzu* 胡族] should be considered illegitimate [*jianwei* 僭伪, or "usurping"].[61]

Deng suggests, therefore, that the fundamental criterion for political legitimacy was that a regime should profess a Chinese identity distinguishable from a variety of barbarian alternatives, which were disqualified on ethnic grounds. He argues that this ethno-political distinction may be traced back to the pre-imperial texts that assert the political superiority of Chinese over barbarians and decry the possibility of barbarian rule, claiming that by later centuries these ideas had been embraced by both Chinese and non-Chinese alike.

Nevertheless, the period of the Sixteen Kingdoms *did* witness rule by several non-Chinese peoples, and Deng goes on to discuss three alternative ways in which legitimacy could be claimed: legitimacy of virtuous government, *youde zhengquan* 有德政权; legitimacy of rule over the Central Plains, *zhongyuan zhengquan* 中原政权; and legitimacy of unified rule, *da yitong zhengquan* 大一统政权. Deng describes how these arguments for legitimacy were put forward by various non-Chinese states that attempted to circumvent the prescribed exclusion of the barbarians, which was integral to imperial political discourse as has been discussed in the preceding chapters. Accordingly, they resorted to claims of virtuous governance or geographical control that could trump those of their rivals.

---

[61] 视中原汉族世袭旧王朝为正统，胡族部落政权为僭伪的政治观念，也就在汉人中自然生发而成. Deng, "Shiliuguo huzu zhengquan de zhengtong yishi yu zhengtong zhi zheng," 84.

Yet Deng notes that the traditional view that political legitimacy must rest solely in Chinese hands proved resistant to such efforts.[62] The foreign ethnic group that ultimately won out in the wars of north China was the Särbi-Xianbei, who he claims were able to establish a legitimate state in the north only through a thorough process of Sinification – never mind that the existence of such a "politically, economically, and culturally thorough Sinification" of the Särbi-Xianbei is precluded by historical evidence.[63] A successor of this state, the Northern Zhou, would eventually produce the Sui dynasty, which was swiftly followed by the Tang. By the time of the early Tang, however, the various barbarian regimes of the fourth and fifth centuries whose reigns are recounted in the *Jin shu* Chronicles were clearly deemed illegitimate, and as was shown in the previous chapter, their non-Chinese identities were a prominent feature in the determination of that illegitimacy.

What then was the early Tang to do with its own political pedigree, which was traced back through the Sui and then to the Särbi-Xianbei Northern Zhou and Northern Wei dynasties? Given the prominence of Chinese, or Hua-Xia 華夏, ethnic identity not only in the discourse of political legitimacy in classical times but also in the *Jin shu* of the early Tang, this became a particularly significant question. The conflict between barbarian ethnic identities and notions of political legitimacy that appears in the Chinese sources considered thus far makes it unsurprising that the first century of Tang rule exhibited a wide-ranging debate on the dynasty's own line of legitimate succession.[64] Liu Pujiang sketches three possible alternatives that traced Tang legitimacy from (a) the Särbi-Xianbei and

---

[62] 传统的汉民族正统观具有顽强的生命力. Deng, "Shiliuguo huzu zhengquan de zhengtong yishi yu zhengtong zhi zheng," 87.

[63] 政治，经济，文化习俗的彻底汉化. Ibid. It is common for modern Chinese-language scholarship to praise the far-sightedness of the Northern Wei emperor Tuoba Hong 拓跋宏 (r. 471–499), also known as emperor Xiaowen 孝文, who instituted reforms that banned Särbi language and clothing from use in the imperial court and required the translation of Särbi clan names into Chinese equivalents. Sanguine appraisals of the civilized barbarian who realized that it was best for his people to renounce their own culturally distinctive practices and identity tend to ignore the fact that these reforms led to an alienation of tribal elites that ultimately tore the dynasty apart. Moreover, Särbi traditions were still much in favor in the two successor dynasties of the Northern Wei: the Northern Zhou and Northern Qi. The Northern Zhou witnessed the translation of surnames *back* into their earlier Särbi forms and even the bestowal of Särbi clan names on Chinese subjects. For a detailed discussion of this period, see Lee, John, "Conquest, Division, Unification: A Social and Political History of Sixth-Century Northern China." On the Sinification question in particular and the ways in which there has been an unhelpful "obsession" with it as an inevitable historical process among scholars, see Holmgren, "The Northern Wei as a Conquest Dynasty," 1–50.

[64] The various hypotheses proposed are discussed in Liu Pujiang's excellent study, "Nanbeichao de lishi yichan yu Sui Tang shidai de zhengtong lun," 127–51.

Särbi-Chinese Northern Dynasties 北朝: the Northern Wei, Northern Zhou, and Sui; (b) the Chinese Southern Dynasties 南朝: the Eastern Jin 東晉, Liu Song 劉宋, Southern Qi 南齊, Southern Liang 南梁, and Chen 陳; and (c) from the Han alone. According to this last alternative, all of the regimes between AD 220 and 618 were considered illegitimate! Each of these alternatives had its own cosmological explanation according to the logic of Five Element theory, which dictates the ascendancy and decline of the five elements (wood, earth, fire, water, metal) in succession.

The non-Chinese identity of the Northern Wei and Northern Zhou rulers proved problematic in later decades of the seventh century and thereafter, since some voices at court argued that legitimacy ought to be accorded only to the southern states founded by Chinese émigrés. Supporters of this position argued on the basis of "ethnic Chinese blood and the orthodoxy of Confucian culture."[65] The charge of barbarian identity was also brought against the Northern Wei by the scholars Liu Zhiji 劉知幾 (661–721) and Huang Fushi 皇甫湜 (777–835). The former argued that "Northern Wei origins stem from mongrels who committed a theft and claimed to call themselves true lords";[66] the latter claimed that "the race of the Tabgach [Chinese *Tuoba* 拓跋, the ruling clan of the Northern Wei] are actually Xiongnu."[67] Yet while the legitimacy of the Northern Dynasties was increasingly disputed in later decades of the Tang and again in later centuries, it was the dominant alternative for much of the dynasty and under its first emperors in particular.[68]

To summarize, we can see that there are several shared features between the sets of politically legitimating factors in Rome and China: both had a monarchical, at least in practice, form of government; a conception of an imperial office granted by divine forces and fulfilled in accord with them; and a notion that both the divine and temporal powers wielded by the emperor were contingent, in theory, upon his own virtuous conduct, which should be reflected in the peace and prosperity of his subjects. There are of course crucial differences such as the absolute acceptance of monarchical rule in China as opposed to the Roman form of monarchy, which was unable to give up the rhetoric and symbology of republican government.[69]

---

[65] 華夏種族的血統和儒家文化的道統. Ibid., 138.

[66] 魏本出於雜種，竊亦自號真君. Quoted in ibid., 141. The use of the term *zhenjun* 真君 is perhaps a reference to the regnal era *taiping zhenjun* 太平真君, "True Ruler of Great Peace," taken by the Northern Wei emperor Tuoba Tao 拓跋燾 in the 440s.

[67] 拓跋氏種實匈奴. Quoted in ibid.　　[68] Ibid., 128–33.

[69] For an interesting comparative study on this contrast in the early imperial historiography, see Mutschler, "The Problem of 'Imperial Historiography' in Rome," 119–41.

Nevertheless, there remain far more points of similarity than difference between the two political systems.

But of the various criteria of political legitimacy discussed above that were prevalent in the Roman Empire of the sixth century and the Tang Empire of the seventh, one notes that ethnic identity was only an explicit feature of the political discourse in China. The reason for this is obvious: the previous centuries in China had witnessed not only the establishment of barbarian states but also their great success, which the Tang emperors appropriated for themselves. Contrary to the assertions of several modern scholars who argue that ethnic distinction was no longer of any political significance by the Tang period, ethnic concerns have already been shown above to be clearly visible in both the classical Chinese tradition and in the historiography of the early Tang. It is therefore to be expected that barbarian or non-Chinese identity would become one of the issues discussed in contexts of political legitimacy. In contrast, the empire of Justinian's day had seen the rise of barbarian states, but it had also seen the destruction of two of the most powerful ones and the restoration of Roman rule over symbolically important territories. The empire of Justinian's day, unlike the Tang, was not itself forced to reach a verdict on the legitimacy of a barbarian state or states that its own regime had itself grown out of. Recognizing that the respective positions of either empire in relation to the phenomenon of barbarian conquest states were markedly different, we may now turn to the final question of this study: To what degree is barbarian identity a factor in the discourse of political legitimacy as it appears in the *Wars* and the *Jin shu*?

Speeches in Greco-Roman and Chinese Historiography

In addressing this question, the texts will be considered according to one of the most notable shared features of Greco-Roman and Chinese historiography: the inclusion of direct speeches attributed to actors in the historical narrative. In the Greco-Roman historiographical tradition, this practice goes back to Herodotus and is given explicit methodological discussion soon thereafter by Thucydides in book one of his *Histories*.[70] Inclusion of rhetorical speeches in historiography was taken up by Romans writing in

---

[70] Thuc. 1.22.1. For a discussion of the practice of recorded speech in Greco-Roman historiography, see the contributions in Pausch (ed.), *Stimmen der Geschichte: Funktionen von Reden in der antiken Historiographie*. Also see Fornara, *The Nature of History in Ancient Greece and Rome*, 142–68; Woodman, *Rhetoric in Classical Historiography: Four Studies*, 11–15; Marincola, "Speeches in Classical Historiography," 118–32.

Latin and has left posterity with some of the most interesting perspectives on Roman imperialism and expansion as well as relations with non-Roman or barbarian peoples. As has often been noted, the practice of recording direct speech allowed historians to express points of view that challenged or even vilified Roman military conquest using the same kind of moral logic that the Romans used to defend their *bella iusta*.[71] That quoted speeches could be used to problematize, and even criticize, Roman policy has been argued by Adler who has produced a monograph devoted to the analysis of barbarian speeches in the historical works of Sallust, Polybius, Tacitus, and others. Others have pointed to other rhetorical functions of barbarian speeches in historiography, for example in the service of Caesar's justification for the subjugation of Gaul.[72]

Explicit comment on the use of direct speech in historical writing, equivalent to the methodological statement of Thucydides referred to above, does not appear as far as I am aware until the *zaiyan* 載言, "Recording Words," chapter of the *Shitong* 史通 by Liu Zhiji in the seventh century AD and postdating the composition of the *Jin shu*. Nevertheless, modern scholars have discussed the practice of incorporating speeches in early Chinese historiography.[73] It has been argued that Chinese historiography in later centuries built upon the basic form of the historical anecdote, consisting of speeches and deeds, present in pre-imperial texts; collections of anecdotes, organized in a "chronological sequence," constituted the fundament of Sima Qian's *Shiji*, which would serve as a model for later historians.[74] Similarly to the conclusions reached by Adler, Di Cosmo has discussed the way in which speeches from *barbaricum* recorded in the *Shiji*, if not reported as being from the mouth of a non-Chinese per se but rather from a Chinese who had taken up life

---

[71] The most classic example of such a speech is that of the Caledonian Calgacus in Tacitus' *Agricola* who famously declares, "where they make a wasteland, they call it peace": *ubi solitudinem faciunt, pacem appellant* (*Agricola* 30.5). For a full discussion of the function of these speeches and their importance for assessing Roman ambivalence toward their own imperialism, see Adler, *Valorizing the Barbarian*. For a contrary view, see Veyne, "*Humanitas*: Romans and Non-Romans," 361–62.

[72] Riggsby, *Caesar in Gaul and Rome*, 107–32. Also see Dué, "Tragic History and Barbarian Speech in Sallust's *Jugurtha*," 311–25.

[73] Dien, "The Disputation at Pengcheng: Accounts from the *Wei shu* and the *Song shu*," 36–38; Schaberg, *A Patterned Past: Form and Thought in Early Chinese Historiography*, 21–56. Although Dien is inclined to grant greater credence to the verbatim use of actual documents in the presentation of letters and speeches in dynastic histories, he still allows for the centrality of their rhetorical function in the text and a significant degree of editing to suit the concerns and biases of individual historians. For the didactic and moralizing function of rhetorical speeches in the *Zuozhuan*, also see Egan, "Narratives in *Tso Chuan*," 325–31.

[74] Schaberg, "Chinese History and Philosophy," 396, 403.

among them, could serve as a safe medium through which to offer covert, and easily disavowed, criticism of imperial policy.[75]

The reason for focusing on recorded speeches in the *Wars* and the *Jin shu* is that both historiographical traditions share the practice of composing speeches not only for Greco-Roman or Chinese political figures but also for barbarian figures themselves, and these two works are replete with speeches occurring in a wide variety of contexts.[76] As Marincola has argued, "speeches indicated the reasons and rationale of the historical characters, why they did what they did and with what aims, goals, and expectations."[77] Speeches thus serve as a window onto the internal life of characters in a narrative from the point of view of the historian. This quality makes them particularly suitable for an analysis of attitudes toward non-Romans, as speeches reveal the ways in which the historian and his audience imagined that barbarians perceived themselves in relation to the empire and its citizens. Schaberg has recognized recorded speeches in Chinese texts as an equally if not even more significant component of Chinese historiography, observing in reference to early historical writings that "reflections on the workings of the world, formulations of the laws of history, thoughts on morality, and elaborations of theory belong ... to the speech."[78] In his analysis, recorded speech is the central action of the "historical anecdotes" that, in the aggregate, comprise classical Chinese historiography.[79] As in the Greco-Roman tradition, the recorded speech played an important role in the exemplary and didactic discourse engaged in by the historian. An analysis of its function when placed in the mouths not only of Greco-Roman and Chinese figures but also of foreign or barbarian individuals may be expected to offer insights onto the worldviews and imaginative categories shared by historians and their audiences alike.

What follows will be a close reading of speeches attributed to Romans, Chinese, and the barbarians as they occur in the *Wars* and the *Jin shu*. The selection of speeches will be limited to those passages that engage with the question of political legitimacy claimed by the conquest states of the respective periods, where this legitimacy is either being asserted or denied. More explicitly than in previous chapters, the fundamental question will

---

[75] Di Cosmo, *Ancient China and Its Enemies*, 272.

[76] Taragna's Logoi historias: *Discorsi e lettere nella prima storiografia retorica bizantina* provides the most extensive overview of speeches not only in Procopius but also in the histories of Agathias and Theophylact. Pazdernik's study of an intertextual link between speeches in Procopius and Thucydides has been cited above.

[77] Marincola, "Speeches in Classical Historiography," 119.   [78] Schaberg, *A Patterned Past*, 22.

[79] Schaberg, "Chinese History and Philosophy," 396, 403.

be the extent to which the ethnic identities assigned to individuals and groups are imbued with a political significance, i.e., the extent to which ethnicity is politicized in either text. Within the historiographical device of direct speech, with all of its rhetorical and discursive dimensions, to what extent do the descriptive categories of ethnic identity and the culturally specific parameters of political legitimacy intersect?

Speeches in the *Jin shu*

While previous chapters have begun with the *Wars* and then moved on to the *Jin shu*, the remaining part of this chapter will reverse the order. The purpose of this change is to draw greater attention to one of the most salient aspects of the comparision: while the *Wars* exhibits minimal use of ethnological thinking in contexts where political legitimacy is debated by Romans and barbarians, the *Jin shu* reveals a consistent preoccupation with ethnic origins and their connotations under similar circumstances. Rather than begin with a discussion of the *Wars* that explains in negative terms what is *not* to be found in the text, it will be more helpful to trace this phenomenon as it appears in the *Jin shu* first and only then turn to examine the variety of other justifications for, or condemnations of, the political claims of barbarian kings that appear in the *Wars*.

It is important to state at the outset that the amount of relevant material in the *Jin shu* is much greater than that which appears in the *Wars*. While the Roman Empire of Procopius' day was confronted with four barbarian conquest states, and only three of these receive significant attention in his narrative, the *Jin shu* covers fourteen such kingdoms in its Chronicles. The passages considered here are therefore only a limited selection of speeches attributed to barbarian rulers. What will become clear, however, is that these passages in the *Jin shu* reveal not only the presence of ethnological modes of thinking through frequent references to ethnogenealogies particular to (or shared among) the barbarian regimes but also an intense interest in them. While there are multiple instances in the Chronicles where political legitimacy is contested according to the range of factors according to which it was constituted in ancient China, the *Jin shu*, in contrast to the *Wars*, exhibits a large number of cases where ethnicity and genealogical links to non-Chinese peoples of an earlier age are made crucial components of the debate.

The first of the conquest regimes, and the one to take control of the ancient imperial capitals of Luoyang and Chang'an in the beginning of the fourth century, was the Xiongnu 匈奴 Former Zhao 前趙 state. In the late third and early fourth centuries, the Western Jin 西晉 dynasty was embroiled in a convulsion of violence, the "revolt of the eight princes," *ba wang zhi luan* 八王之亂, in which members of the royal family contended among themselves for control of the throne. It was in the course of these events that Xiongnu tribes, some of whom had been settled for centuries inside the northern frontier, decided to revolt from Chinese control. This decision was advocated by Liu Xuan 劉宣, the uncle of the founder of the first barbarian state to establish itself in the north, the Former Zhao. In a speech to his nephew Liu Yuan 劉淵, Liu Xuan makes an argument for Xiongnu independence:

> 晉為無道，奴隸御我. … 單于之恥也. 今司馬氏父子兄弟自相魚肉，此天厭晉德， 授之於我. 單于積德在躬，為晉人所服，方當興我邦族，復呼韓邪之業，鮮卑，烏丸可以為援，奈何距之而拯仇敵！今天假手於我，不可違也. 違天不祥，逆眾不濟；天與不取，反受其咎.[80]

> The Jin have lost the Way and control us as though we were slaves. . . . This is the shame of the Chanyu. Now the [imperial] Sima clan are murdering one another indiscriminately; this shows that Heaven has grown weary of Jin's Virtue and has conferred it upon us. The Chanyu has accumulated Virtue in his person, and you are the one obeyed by the Jin people. It is now that you ought to rejuvenate our people and restore the dominion of Huhanye; the Särbi-Xianbei and Wuhuan will be our support. How can you refuse them and help a hated enemy? Now Heaven exerts its will through us and cannot be defied. To defy Heaven is inauspicious, to resist the multitude is inexpedient.

In this passage, Liu Xuan begins by referring to the political crisis of the late third and early fourth centuries, and argues that the Western Jin has strayed from the way of proper governance. He laments the fact that even Liu Yuan, the bearer of the once imperial Xiongnu title Chanyu 單于 but now of much less prestige and significance, is subject to the commands of the Jin emperor's officials. He argues that Liu Yuan should restore the Xiongnu Empire of the Chanyu Huhanye 呼韓邪, who surrendered along with his tribesmen to the Chinese some 350 years before. He argues that the other nomadic peoples of the north and east, the Särbi-Xianbei and Wuhuan 烏桓, will assist the Xiongnu in their endeavor, and he asks how Liu Yuan can continue to fight in the service of the Western Jin, which was, at the moment, fighting against its own internal rebels and those rebels' barbarian allies, the Särbi-Xianbei and the Wuhuan.

---

[80] *Jin shu* 101.2648–49.

This speech is replete with typical features of Chinese political rhetoric, arguing that the Jin dynasty has strayed from the Way, *dao* 道, and that this has led Heaven, *tian* 天, to revoke its mandate from the Jin house. In contrast, Liu Xuan claims that his nephew Liu Yuan has accumulated the requisite Virtue, *de* 德, which legitimizes a ruler, and that this is reflected in the obedience shown to him by the Chinese subjects of Jin. Arguing further for his nephew's right to disavow his allegiance to the Chinese, Liu Xuan asserts that not only does the divine power of Heaven wish for Liu Yuan to seize power for himself, but that it is perilous not to heed the call of its mandate. Liu Xuan thus argues that the time has come for the Xiongnu to return to their ancient position of imperial strength.[81] He also advocates for alliance with other barbarian groups, rather than conflict with them, as part of his plan to restore dignity and independence to the Xiongnu.

Liu Yuan proved amenable to these exhortations and in 304 declared independence from the Western Jin, moving his people to the city of Zuoguo. Prior to this action, the *Jin shu* records a speech in which Liu Yuan rationalizes the legitimacy of his position. Yet he goes much further in this speech. Having already claimed the legacy of the Xiongnu Empire on the grounds of a genealogical link to Huhanye Chanyu, he now asserts his right to the legacy of the Chinese Han Empire in genealogical terms as well:

> 夫帝王豈有常哉，大禹出於西戎，文王生於東夷，顧惟德所授耳....
> 雖然，晉人未必同我. 漢有天下世長，恩德結於人心 ... 吾又漢氏
> 之甥，約為兄弟，兄亡弟紹，不亦可乎？且可稱漢，追尊後主，以懷
> 人望.[82]

> Indeed, do emperors and kings have a consistent principle? The Great Yu came from the Western Rong; King Wen was born among the Eastern Yi. It is only Virtue that is a criterion for reception of authority. ... Nevertheless, the people of Jin are not necessarily similar to us. The Han held the empire for many generations and bound itself to the people's hearts with benevolent Virtue ... but I am a nephew of the Han and in a pact of brotherhood; when the elder brother dies, the younger succeeds – is that not proper? Moreover we can proclaim the title of Han, showing posthumous honor to the last rulers and embracing the people's hopes.

---

[81] On a previous occasion, Liu Xuan expresses similar sentiments, arguing that the present "is the time to restore the nation and take back our dominion": 興邦復業，此其時矣 (*Jin shu* 101.2647).
[82] *Jin shu* 101.2649.

Liu Yuan asks rhetorically whether there is any set principle in the determination of legitimate kings or emperors.[83] He claims that the mythical emperor and culture hero the Great Yu 大禹 came from the Rong barbarians of the west, and that one of the founding figures of the Zhou dynasty, King Wen of Zhou 周文王, was from the Eastern Yi 東夷 barbarians.[84] Reference to these ancient figures is only understandable if it was otherwise assumed that, being a Xiongnu Chanyu, Liu Yuan should be ineligible for the imperial title. If the Great Yu and King Wen had risen to such preeminence despite their origins, why should he not be able to do the same? He therefore invokes these legendary and ancient figures in order to counter the assumption that his ethnic background should refute his claims, arguing that Virtue alone determines political legitimacy. Irrespective of the strength of his position, the fact that it needs to be presented in terms that are preoccupied with ethnicity and ethno-genealogies is clear.

Genealogy and ethnicity continue to be central concerns in Liu Yuan's speech when he notes the distinction between his own people and the Chinese of the Western Jin Empire. Yet despite this ethnic distinction, he argues his case by actually claiming genealogical continuity with the Han dynasty itself. In naming himself a nephew or descendant of the Han dynasty, he refers to the treaty relations between the Xiongnu and the Chinese of the early Han dynasty, which were conducted in the language of familial connections, the so-called *heqin* 和親 policy.[85] One aspect of the *heqin* policy was that the imperial ruler of the Xiongnu Empire, the Chanyu, would marry a princess of the Han royal house, thereby symbolically cementing the treaty. Yet following the later internal disputes among the Xiongnu and victories of the Chinese, who had abandoned the *heqin* arrangement in favor of a more aggressive policy under the emperor Han Wudi 漢武帝 (r. 141-87 BC), the Xiongnu grew progressively weaker over the generations. Many Xiongnu groups were settled along and within the Chinese frontier, and remaining tribes were either absorbed under the

---

[83] Virtually the same question is also posed by the Särbi-Xianbei chieftain Tufa Wugu 禿髮烏孤: 帝王之起，豈有常哉 (*Jin shu* 126.3142).

[84] The pre-imperial Confucian philosopher Mencius had made similar claims regarding the mythical ruler Shun and Zhou Wenwang. See above, 61.

[85] For a discussion of the *heqin* policy during the Han dynasty, see Di Cosmo, *Ancient China and Its Enemies*, 193–205. Also see Barfield, *The Perilous Frontier*, 45–48, 64–67. One may note that this policy was not limited to diplomatic relations with the Xiongnu; other states also received brides from the imperial family whose offspring, it was hoped, would produce heirs sympathetic to the Chinese and their interests. Such a connection in the case of a vassal state also provided a pretext for imperial intervention in peripheral regions. See Hulsewé, *China in Central Asia*, 60–61.

ascendant Särbi-Xianbei tribes on the steppe or migrated to the west. Liu Yuan here argues that, as a scion of the Han dynasty, he is able to restore not only the Xiongnu Empire but also the Han Empire simultaneously.[86]

So the ethnic dimension of the question of his legitimacy functions on two levels: on the one hand, he looks to ancient precedent to anticipate arguments against his claim, pointing to the irrelevance of ethnic origins; on the other, he points to his lineage, which he ultimately traces back to the intermarriage of his Xiongnu ancestors with the Chinese of the Han Empire. The case is thus somewhat self-contradictory, for while Liu Yuan seeks to discount the importance of ethnic background, he nevertheless stresses his professed genealogical connection to the Chinese Han dynasty. While arguing from both sides of the issue, his claim to power revolves around the question of his ethnic and genealogical origins.

The Former Zhao dynasty established by Liu Yuan was succeeded by the Later Zhao 後趙 dynasty, which was founded by a man of the Jie 羯 ethnic group named Shi Le 石勒, as has been discussed in Chapter 3. In Shi Le's case, there is not a speech similar to that of Liu Yuan where Shi Le puts forth arguments for the legitimacy of his own state. However, the *Jin shu* does record an exchange between him and the Chinese general Liu Kun 劉琨, who was still in the service of the Jin Empire, which had been overthrown in the north but reestablished south of the Yangtze River as the Eastern Jin dynasty. While campaigning in the north, Liu Kun seeks to recruit Shi Le, at that time still a general in the Former Zhao Xiongnu army, to come over to the Chinese side. He includes the following claim as part of his proposal:

自古以來，誠無戎人而為帝王者，至於名臣建功業者，則有之矣。[87]

> Since ancient times, there has truly never been a person of the Rong barbarians who has acted as an emperor or king. But as to famous ministers who established great careers with their accomplishments – well there are those.

As part of his effort to recruit Shi Le, Liu Kun attempts to discredit the legitimacy of the Xiongnu Former Zhao against whom he himself is fighting. Employing one of the archaic ethnonyms of the Si Yi Four Barbarians, the Rong 戎, to refer to the Xiongnu and others, he claims that the barbarians have never acted as legitimate rulers. That said, he allows the fact that there is historical precedent for non-Chinese to serve as

---

[86] Accordingly, he proclaimed his new dynasty the Han 漢; the name was changed to Zhao 趙 under one of his successors, Liu Yao 劉曜, over a decade later. See Corradini, "The Barbarian States in North China," 183–87.

[87] *Jin shu* 104.2715.

ministers to Chinese kings and emperors with great distinction.[88] The intent of the argument is to persuade Shi Le to feel bound to turn against the Xiongnu whom he serves, since Xiongnu origins render their regime illegitimate; in so doing, however, Shi Le may himself be assured that it is possible for him to have an illustrious career in the service of the rightful Chinese dynasty, in this case the Eastern Jin. Either way, the fact that an individual or ruling house is of barbarian origin, in this case identified with a generic barbarian ethnonym, Rong, determines its political status and the proper extent of its aspirations.

Shi Le is unimpressed by this argument. He offers a succinct reply to the offer that both excuses his refusal to join with Liu Kun and includes a jab at the ethnocentricity of Confucian political thinking:

事功殊途，非腐儒所聞. 君當逞節本朝，吾自夷，難為效.[89]

> There are different paths that lead to success; this is something that corrupt Confucianists have never heard about. You yourself ought to show off your moral refinement to the ruling dynasty; I come from the Yi and can't be of much use.

This is an interesting case where a barbarian, self-identified with an alternative archaic barbarian ethnonym Yi 夷, adopts Chinese ethnocentric thinking for his own purposes, i.e., to excuse his unwillingness to accept Liu Kun's offer. After all, as Shi Le argues, being a barbarian puts him outside of such matters. Nevertheless, he exhibits his courtesy after the exchange by sending gifts of pearls and horses to Liu Kun and treats his envoys with great hospitality. The conversation between the two men not only underscores the centrality of ethnological thinking in contests of political legitimacy but also emphasizes the familiar principle that barbarians are welcome to participate in imperial politics – as long as it is in a position of subservience to a Chinese emperor.

At other points in the *Jin shu*, ethnic identity becomes the focus of heated exchanges, where pejorative slurs accompany assertions that a barbarian identity not only disqualifies a people from legitimate rule but also carries with it other stigmas inherited from ancient times. The Later Zhao state was overthrown by Ran Min 冉閔, the ethnically Chinese adopted son of the Later Zhao emperor Shi Hu 石虎.[90] After Ran Min

---

[88] This point has been discussed above, 124–25, 127–28.   [89] *Jin shu* 104.2715.

[90] For the short-lived regime established by Ran Min, most notable for its ethnic massacre of over 200,000 Jie people who were recognizable by their high noses and facial hair, see Corradini, "The Barbarian States in North China," 190. The massacre is described at *Jin shu* 107.2791–92. The case of the Jie is interesting, as they are the only people in the Chronicles whose physiognomy is clearly

himself has been defeated by the Former Yan 前燕 army and captured, he is confronted by the Särbi-Xianbei Murong Jun 慕容儁. Murong Jun upbraids him for trying to take the imperial title for himself, saying, "You lowly and talentless slave, how could you take the initiative to absurdly declare yourself the Son of Heaven?"[91] Ran Min replies:

天下大亂，爾曹夷狄，人面獸心，尚欲篡逆. 我一時英雄，何為不可作帝王邪！[92]

The world is in a state of great chaos, and all you Yi-Di, with faces of humans and hearts of beasts – you still desire to usurp and rebel. I was a great warrior for a short while; why should I not be able to be an emperor or king!

Ran Min points to the disorder of the wars raging in north China and attributes them to the lawless ambition of the "barbarians" in general. As a compliment to his use of the generic term Yi-Di 夷狄, Ran Min employs the now familiar barbarian characterization of classical literature, that the barbarians have the faces of humans and the hearts of animals. The context is telling: the conversation occurs following a contest between the Chinese Ran Min, who had sought to restore Chinese rule to the north, and a Särbi-Xianbei prince whose own state, the Former Yan, was in its ascendancy. At a moment when the right to legitimate rule had just been contested by arms, the conversation between the two is a rhetorical perpetuation of the same struggle. Interesting to note is the reappearance of the tension between two prominent strains in ancient Chinese political thinking: the criterion of Virtue on the one hand and that of Chinese ethnic identity on the other. Murong Jun, a barbarian, critiques Ran Min's imperial pretensions with an attack on the latter's personal abilities; Ran Min's response is to delegitimate Murong Jun with a reference to his barbarian Särbi-Xianbei ethnicity.

One of the most poignant expressions of this tension appears in a speech attributed to Murong Wei 慕容廆, the founder of the Särbi-Xianbei Former Yan state. In this case, we have a near inversion of the conversation discussed above between Liu Kun and Shi Le; now it is the barbarian ruler Murong Wei trying to enlist a Chinese as a general in the service of his

---

distinguished from that of other peoples. In one case a doctor makes a joke about deep-set eyes, typical of the Jie, to a Later Zhao official. When this is reported to the crown prince Shi Xuan 石宣, who is said to have "more than anyone else a *hu* 胡 [sc. "barbarian"] appearance and deep-set eyes," (宣諸子中最胡狀，目深), Shi Xuan is furious and has the doctor and his children all executed (106.2776).

[91] 汝奴僕下才，何自妄稱天子? (*Jin shu* 107.2796).   [92] *Jin shu* 107.2796–97.

own state, a captive named Gao Zhan 高瞻. Gao Zhan feigns illness and refuses to accept the offer. However, Murong Wei greatly values Gao Zhan's qualities and persists in trying to win him over. In pointing to the political disorder and violence of the period, Murong Wei appeals to the argument that his own barbarian background should not dissuade virtuous officials from serving as ministers in his court:

今天子播越，四海分崩. .... 奈何以華夷之異，有懷介然. 且大禹出于西羌，文王生于東夷，但問志略何如耳，豈以殊俗不可降心乎!⁹³

At the present time the Son of Heaven has fled and the [land between the] four seas has fallen into ruin ... what purpose does it serve to have a feeling of anxiety regarding the difference between Chinese and barbarians? Moreover, the Great Yu came from the Western Qiang, and King Wen was born among the Eastern Yi; but if one asks about their aspirations and talent, how could you not be perfectly at ease about their foreign customs?

Murong Wei concedes that his barbarian ethnicity is a cause for hesitation on the part of Chinese who have scruples about pledging their allegiance to a barbarian dynasty, yet he argues that the chaos of the period should render such scruples irrelevant. He thereby acknowledges that his foreign origins represent an obstacle to his acceptance as a legitimate alternative to the Eastern Jin dynasty in the south. Murong Wei appeals then to the same argument employed by Liu Yuan above: great figures from the Chinese past have been said to have come from the peoples of the periphery, the Qiang 羌 in the west and the Yi in the east. He concludes that these distinctions of ethnicity and descent, and even different cultural practices, cannot be weighed alongside the crucial distinction of aspirations and talent. Yet despite his best efforts, Murong Wei fails to persuade, and Gao Zhan demurs, citing his feigned ill health to the great dismay of his would-be employer.⁹⁴

The *Jin shu* also contains professions of illegitimacy on the part of barbarians themselves, and this has already been hinted at in the above exchange between Liu Kun and Shi Le, although in that instance Shi Le was only referring to his capacity to serve as a general for the Chinese Eastern Jin dynasty. But there are other examples where the issue of imperial power itself is at issue. One of these appears in the case of Murong Jun, the Särbi-Xianbei prince mentioned above, who would soon become emperor of the Särbi-Xianbei Former Yan dynasty. Prior to his accession,

⁹³ *Jin shu* 108.2813.   ⁹⁴ 瞻仍辭疾篤，廆深不平之 (Ibid.).

Murong Jun declares his own ineligibility for the imperial office, and his speech is a showcase of ethnographic tropes that will be familiar from earlier chapters:

吾本幽漠射獵之鄉，被髮左衽之俗，曆數之籙寧有分邪! 卿等苟相褒舉，以覬非望，實匪寡德所宜聞也.[95]

I am originally from the northern deserts, the land where men shoot with bows and hunt. My custom is to wear my hair loose and fasten my robe on the left. How could I have a share in the prerogatives of imperial succession! If you ministers all wish to elevate me in order to covet presumptuous hopes, this is truly not what my humble self should be listening to.

Even if Murong Jun's modesty is a mere formality – and the ritual of refusal was a requisite for a "sincere" accession to the throne in the Chinese tradition – the criteria according to which he illustrates his ineligibility are telling. First, there is the geographical reference to the northern regions, a place alien to the agricultural and sedentary society of China. This point is interesting, as the Särbi-Xianbei were a people not from the northern deserts but from the mixed steppe and forest zone of Manchuria to the east of the Kinghan mountains. This description of his lifestyle would be more appropriate to the Xiongnu of the Han era than to the Särbi-Xianbei of the fourth century. He also uses the classic trope of the northern barbarian, which has appeared in earlier chapters: that of wearing one's hair loose and fastening garments on the left. This expression is a form of ethnographic distinction between the Chinese and the northern barbarians that goes back to Confucius.[96] Being a barbarian, therefore, Murong Jun claims that he could not adequately perform the duties of the emperor, which are to regulate the human world in harmony with the cosmos. There is thus a juxtaposition between the traditional role of a legitimate emperor and the barbarian tropes that disqualify Murong Jun for the office. One could argue that Murong Jun only addresses cultural factors rather than ethnic or genealogical ones; yet the stereotypes he employs are so loaded by ethnographic tradition that they are inseparable from an image of the non-Chinese nomad whose foreign identity is correlated with a set of moral and political expectations. While Murong Jun does, in the end, yield to the exhortations of his people to become emperor, this speech nevertheless shows the prominence of ethnological thinking in the question of political legitimacy.

---

[95] *Jin shu* 110.2834.
[96] This trope has been discussed in the preceding chapters. See above, 43, 192.

The above instance is not the only case where a barbarian himself disavows the possibility of a barbarian claim to the throne. While Murong Jun engages in the political theater that required a new sovereign to protest his own unworthiness, there are other instances in the *Jin shu* where the argument of barbarian illegitimacy is intended to be sincere. When Fu Jian 苻堅, the emperor of the Di 氐 Former Qin 前秦 dynasty, has conquered all of the other kingdoms in the north in the 370s, he contemplates a major invasion of the Eastern Jin dynasty in the south. His brother Fu Rong 苻融, however, opposes the plans. In addition to the logistical arguments that he puts forward against the campaign, Fu Rong expresses concern over the Di origins of his own state:

且國家，戎族也，正朔會不歸人. 江東雖不絕如綖，然天之所相，終不可滅.[97]

Moreover, our kingdom is of the Rong barbarian ethnicity; the dynastic prerogative will not come to us. Although the kingdom east of the Yangtze is fragile and weak, nevertheless it has the favor of Heaven and cannot be destroyed in the end.

Fu Rong reminds his brother the emperor that their state, though belonging to the Di ethnic group, is ultimately to be associated with the ancient Rong barbarians of the west. This simple fact precludes the possibility that Heaven would ever confer its mandate on the barbarian Former Qin in favor of the Chinese émigré Eastern Jin dynasty in the south. As in the above speech of Murong Jun, the traditional features of dynastic legitimacy are still in play, namely the crucial favor of Heaven and the mandate that it confers. Present too is reference to the omens according to which the will of Heaven may be ascertained. Although the Eastern Jin regime is in a state of clear military inferiority, Fu Rong argues that it still bears the heavenly mandate, and his own people's barbarian ethnicity – it does not matter *which* ethnicity they actually have, as simply being described under the ancient ethnonym Rong is enough – precludes the possibility of their obtaining it for themselves.

The identification of the Di Former Qin state with the Rong is particularly interesting given that, in a another context, its emperor Fu Jian makes a speech regarding the fact that his general Lü Guang 呂光 is to set out for the western regions to pacify the "Rong." It is remarkable that this same ethnonym is used here to refer to those in need of civilization:

[97] *Jin shu* 114.2935.

西戎荒俗，非禮義之邦. 羈縻之道，服而赦之，示以中國之威，導以
王化之法 [...].⁹⁸

The Western Rong have uncultivated customs; they are not a nation of
proper ritual and justice. The Way of the "loose rein" system, by pacifying
and then releasing them – this makes a demonstration of the majesty of the
Central Kingdom and directs them according to the principles of a royal
system.

If one did not know that Fu Jian is himself a man of the non-Chinese Di
people, there is no clue here to suggest that he is not a Chinese emperor,
hostile to foreign peoples who need to be restrained by a superior civilization. The very incongruity in representing Fu Jian in this fashion actually
demonstrates the consistency of ethnological political thought and perhaps
the absurdity inherent in his aspirations to universal empire.⁹⁹ Remarkably, the *Jin shu* represents him as a would-be civilizing conqueror of the
very Rong to whom his brother claims that their own Di ethnic group
ultimately belongs.

In the end, Fu Jian ignored his brother Fu Rong's advice, and he
mobilized an enormous army to invade the south in an attempt to destroy
the Eastern Jin dynasty and unify China. The expedition, launched in 383,
was a spectacular catastrophe, and the Former Qin Empire rapidly disin-
tegrated thereafter. As a result, the various peoples whom the dynasty had
conquered were quick to return to their original homelands and reestablish
their own states. One of the most powerful of these was the Later Qin
後秦, which was founded by the Qiang ethnic group.¹⁰⁰ Yet Yao Yizhong
姚弋仲, the father of the Later Qin's first emperor, goes even further than
did Fu Rong in his disavowal of imperial claims. While Fu Rong had
advised against risking everything on an invasion of the south, claiming
that Heaven still favored the Eastern Jin and would never confer its
mandate on a Rong people, Yao Yizhong urges his sons that, after he has
passed away, they should give up their independence and pledge their
obedience to the Chinese in the south:

---

⁹⁸ *Jin shu* 114.2914.
⁹⁹ The tone taken by Fu Jian here is similar to the sentiments expressed by Theoderic the Ostrogoth as
we have them in the official correspondence composed on his behalf by Cassiodorus. In a letter
addressed to the Roman population of Gaul in 508, Theoderic urges them to adhere to their Roman
customs and resist those of the barbarians (*Variae* 3.17.1). His grandson Athalaric draws similar
distinctions between the primitive ignorance of the barbarians and the Roman cultivation of letters
and rhetoric (*Variae* 9.21.4). Yet the purpose of this study is not to assess the "realities" of actual
policy under the barbarian states of conquest; it is rather to assess the deployment and function of
ethnographic discourse in the deliberate representations of the past constructed by historiography.
¹⁰⁰ On the Later Qin, see Corradini, "The Barbarian States in North China," 221–24.

今石氏已滅，中原無主，自古以來未有戎狄作天子者. 我死，汝便
歸晉，當竭盡臣節，無為不義之事.[101]

Now the [Later Zhao imperial] Shi clan has been destroyed and the Central
Plains are without a ruler. From ancient times, there has never been a man
of the Rong-Di who could be the Son of Heaven. When I die, you must
return your allegiance to Jin and exhaust all your efforts in the duties of a
loyal official; do no act that is unjust.

Yao Yizhong died in 352 following the destruction of the Jie Later Zhao
dynasty, whose rulers used the clan name Shi 石. In this exhortation to his
sons, he brings forth the argument, familiar at this point, that only ethnic
Chinese may be legitimate rulers over the Central Plains of north China.
Now that the Later Zhao dynasty has been destroyed, of which Yao
Yizhong had been a loyal supporter, he urges his sons to help restore the
political situation to its proper state, which by necessity entails the reestablishment of a Chinese empire that may rule over barbarians and
Chinese alike. Although allowing for the possibility of active and loyal
service to the Eastern Jin, Yao Yizhong acknowledges the impossibility of a
legitimate barbarian emperor.

As seen in the above examples, ethnogenealogical concerns were a
decisive factor in the discourse of political legitimacy as it is presented in
the *Jin shu*. In order to get around this problem, several of the barbarian
rulers represented in the Chronicles argue that mythological or ancient
sage monarchs of the past were in fact of barbarian origin and that virtue
and merit should be the criteria in selecting an emperor, although these
arguments were not always successful. There was one way, however, in
which the centrality of ethnogenealogical thought could be put in the
service of a foreign state's claims to legitimacy rather than simply serving to
undermine them. This strategy has already appeared above in the case of
Liu Yuan, the founder of the Xiongnu Former Zhao dynasty, when he
claims that although he is a Xiongnu, his ancestors also include members
of the Han dynasty's imperial household, thus making him a legitimate
heir to the Han imperial legacy. If a barbarian wished to become emperor,
he simply needed to prove that he was also of Chinese ancestry.[102]

The Xiongnu Xia 夏 dynasty, which was founded in the late fourth
century, also looked to a Chinese genealogical line for legitimation,

---

[101] *Jin shu* 116.2961.

[102] This practice was present even in the Warring States period of pre-imperial times, as has been
discussed in the case of the states of Wu 吳 and Yue 越, which both either formulated or were
ascribed ethnogenealogies linking them to Chinese mythical ancestors. See above, 59–60. For the
Xiongnu genealogy, see above, 60–64, 190–91.

although the *Jin shu* does not show its founder asserting descent from the royal family of the Han dynasty.[103] The Xia state's founder Helian Bobo 赫連勃勃 opts for a more grandiose claim:

> 朕大禹之後，世居幽朔．祖宗重暉，常與漢魏為敵國．中世不競，受制于人．逮朕不肖，不能紹隆先構，國破家亡，流離漂虜．今將應運而興，復大禹之業 [...].[104]

> Our imperial person is descended from the Great Yu; through the generations we have dwelt in the farthest north. Our ancestral lineage performed glorious achievements, and we were often in a hostile relationship with the empires of the Han and Cao-Wei. In the generations since then, we were weak and controlled by others. In my own day, I was not worthy and was unable to inherit and perpetuate the ancestral establishment; our nation was destroyed and our family exiled; wandering abroad we drifted as slaves. But now taking advantage of opportunity we rise up and restore the dominion of the Great Yu.

In this case, the speech of Helian Bobo takes advantage of the ethnogenealogy attributed to the Xiongu by Sima Qian 司馬遷 in the first century BC, which was perpetuated by later historians.[105] Sima Qian had given the Xiongnu an ancestry that linked them to descendants of the legendary Xia 夏 kingdom's royal family. In choosing the same name, Xia, for his own state, Helian Bobo seeks to claim for himself the legacy not only of the Han but also of the first regime in the Chinese dynastic tradition. Accordingly, he names the Great Yu, the mythical Chinese culture hero who was the founder of the Xia state, as his imperial ancestor. This claim perhaps dovetails with the speeches discussed above that use the example of the Great Yu, who originated among the barbarians, to argue for the possible legitimacy of non-Chinese rule. Helian Bobo outdoes these claims by naming that same figure as his ancestor: whether or not one accepts the precedent set by the Great Yu, Helian Bobo argues that he is descended from him anyway, thereby indicating the primacy of ethnogenealogical lines in political discourse.

The examples from the *Jin shu* discussed so far show that ethnic identity, and particularly its constituent parts genealogy and notions of shared kinship, was frequently a factor in either affirming or discrediting dynastic claims. Yet it is far from always the case that legitimacy is conceived in solely these terms. For example, the above quotation occurs

---

[103] On the Xia, see above, 252–53.   [104] *Jin shu* 130.3205.
[105] See above, 60. If the Xiongnu are descended from the ancient Xia, it follows that they should also claim descent from the kingdom's mythical founder the Great Yu.

when Helian Bobo is in conversation with the Chinese official Wang Maide 王買德, who had formerly served the Qiang ethnic group's Later Qin dynasty but was now in the service of Helian Bobo's Xia state. In the above speech, Helian Bobo had just presented the above account of his family and dynastic pretensions; in response, Wang Maide offers a flattering response as to why Helian Bobo is a legitimate alternative to the Chinese Eastern Jin in the south:

自皇晉失統，神器南移，羣雄岳峙，人懷問鼎，況陛下奕葉載德，重光朔野，神武超于漢皇，聖略邁于魏祖，而不于天啟之機建成大業乎！[106]

Since the time when the Jin Empire lost its legitimacy and its tokens of government migrated to the south, crowds of heroic contenders have surged up like mountains, and the hearts of people have sought to know who is the legitimate ruler. Furthermore, your majesty has accumulated Virtue through successive generations, inheriting the former glories in the northern wastelands. Your awesome prowess transends that of the Han Empire, and your sage strategems surpass those of Cao-Wei – and yet you do not take advantage of the heavenly omens and achieve your great undertaking!

Even in a context where the ethnogenealogical argument has been prominent, this speech from Wang Maide demonstrates the persistence of other traditional forms of dynastic legitimation at the same time: the acquisition of Virtue the blessings of military success, and the omens of Heaven that express divine favor and the bestowal of its mandate. He makes no mention of the role ethnicity or genealogy might play in validating Helian Bobo's claims to power. There are many other such examples in the Chronicles where figures, both Chinese and non-Chinese, argue for the legitimate rule of foreign regimes. Yet while there are various criteria according to which political legitimacy is articulated in the *Jin shu*, the text reveals a consistent interest in one aspect of the question that is almost wholly absent from the *Wars*: the ethnic background of the claimants.

Speeches in the *Wars*

As the wars recounted by Procopius were initiated by the emperor Justinian, it is fitting to begin with a letter the emperor sends to the Vandal usurper Gelimer, who had violated the sequence of the succession as established by his grandfather Gaiseric, that the throne should always go

---

[106] *Jin shu* 130.3205.

to the eldest of his direct living descendants.[107] Impatient to take power himself, Gelimer had staged a coup and had his cousin Hilderic deposed and imprisoned. At this point, Procopius includes a letter that he claims was sent by Justinian to North Africa, in which the emperor attempts to persuade the usurper Gelimer to restore Hilderic to the throne and await his own turn in the succession:

Οὐχ ὅσια ποιεῖς οὐδὲ τῶν Γιζερίχου διαθηκῶν ἄξια ... ἐξὸν αὐτὴν ὀλίγῳ ὕστερον χρόνῳ κατὰ νόμον λαβεῖν. μήτε οὖν ἐργάσῃ περαιτέρω κακὸν μήτε τοῦ βασιλέως ὀνόματος ἀνταλλάξῃ τὴν τοῦ τυράννου προσηγορίαν ... ἀλλὰ τοῦτον μὲν, ἄνδρα ὅσον οὔπω τεθνηξόμενον, ἔα φέρεσθαι τῷ λόγῳ τὴν τῆς βασιλείας εἰκόνα, σὺ δὲ ἅπαντα πρᾶττε ὅσα βασιλέα πράττειν εἰκός· προσδέχου τε ἀπὸ τοῦ χρόνου καὶ τοῦ Γιζερίχου· νόμου μόνου λαβεῖν τὸ τοῦ πράγματος ὄνομα.[108]

You are doing things unholy and unworthy of the testament of Gaiseric ... it being possible to take power in a short time according to the law. Therefore do no further evil nor exchange the name of emperor for that of tyrant ... but allow this man not yet dead to bear the semblance of empire; but do you all the things there are that it is proper for an emperor to do. Be patient enough to take up the name of the office only at the proper time and according to the law of Gaiseric.

Perhaps surprisingly, the basis throughout Justinian's letter for his threat of involvement in the Vandal succession dispute never calls into question the legitimacy of the kingdom itself. On the contrary, Justinian exhorts Gelimer to respect the legacy of the dynastic founder and to wait for the proper time at which he may legally assume the throne according to Gaiseric's will and testament, διαθηκῶν. In what may be an allusion to Procopius' description of Theoderic as a tyrant in name while being a true emperor by nature, Justinian urges Gelimer to follow an analogous

---

[107] *Wars* 3.7.29. The question of whether or not the letters quoted in Procopius represent actual documents translated from Latin into Greek by Procopius has been taken up by Chrysos, "The Title Βασιλεύς in Early Byzantine International Relations," 54–55. Yet even if some of the letters quoted in Procopius may be more or less faithful versions of the documents themselves, there are other secret letters whose contents he records that it seems highly implausible he may have had access to. I am inclined to treat the letters in the *Wars* as rhetorical creations of Procopius himself. For irrespective of whether or not Procopius had actual official correspondence in front of him, he nevertheless chose which material to include and went through the editorial process of translating the letters from Latin into Greek. Either way, he is ultimately following the principle laid down by Thucydides of what he finds to be most probable and appropriate to the circumstances of the narrative. For an approach to a similar instance where a document is reproduced in a Roman historical work, see Adler who discusses Sallust's *Epistula Mithridatis, Valorizing the Barbarian,* 17–18.

[108] *Wars* 3.9.10–12.

principle by taking power in practice while respecting the outer semblance of his cousin Hilderic's authority. The central issue is the current illegality of Gelimer's action, and the phrasing of the emperor's words in this way necessarily implies the otherwise valid legal status of the Vandal position in North Africa. This impression is underscored by the use of the terms *basileus*-βασιλεύς and *basileia*-βασιλεία that have been translated as "emperor" and "empire" here, respectively, which establish a parity between the Roman Empire and the Vandal Kingdom rather than undermine its legitimacy.[109]

A second letter follows in which Justinian makes clear that "the treaties between us and Gaiseric will not be a hindrance"[110] to the coming invasion that will be launched to "avenge" Hilderic, the one "who has received the empire from Gaiseric."[111] Though obvious pretexts, the fact remains that Procopius represents the justification for Justianian's campaign as an obligation to restore the proper functioning of the barbarian state rather than destroy it. The basic assumption in these letters from the emperor Justinian is something that does not appear in the *Jin shu*: the possibility of legitimate barbarian rule. For although Justinian urges Gelimer to accept the testament of Gaiseric and to temporarily yield precedence to his cousin Hilderic, he never calls into question the legal foundations of the kingdom's right to exist. Even when war is declared and the invasion is launched, the professed ideological justification of the campaign is not to punish the Vandals and to drive them from Roman lands, but rather to *avenge* their deposed barbarian king. This is particularly remarkable given the deposed king Hilderic's own ancestry: his mother was the imperial princess Eudocia, descended from Theodosius I himself. While the Vandal regime seems to have emphasized Hilderic's imperial Roman ancestry for its own legitimating propaganda, Procopius expresses no interest in the fact.[112]

Gelimer's reply contends that he is well within his rights to have seized power, since, according to him, Hilderic had been preparing a revolution, νεώτερα πράσσοντα, against the house of Gaiseric. Gelimer also argues in legalistic terms and accuses Justinian of interfering with other peoples' affairs. Moreover, Gelimer warns Justinian not to break the treaties former Roman emperors had made with the Vandals. If he should invade,

---

[109] On the significance of these terms, see above, 219–21.
[110] αἵ τε σπονδαὶ ἡμῖν αἱ πρὸς Γιζέριχον ἐκποδὼν στήσονται (*Wars* 3.9.19).
[111] τῷ γὰρ ἐκδεξαμένῳ τὴν ἐκείνου βασιλείαν ἐρχόμεθα . . . τιμωρήσοντες (Ibid.).
[112] On the significance of Huneric's marriage to Eudocia, and their son Hilderic's Theodosian descent, to the Vandal political program, see Conant, *Staying Roman*, 43–44.

however, Gelimer assures him of Vandal resistance, adding, "we will do so invoking the oaths Zeno swore, the one from whom you hold your throne in succession."[113] In both the effort on the part of Justinian to persuade Gelimer of the illegitimacy of the Vandal king's seizure of power, as well as in Gelimer's defense thereof, the arguments are strictly presented in legalistic and diplomatic terms. These refer to agreements, formal or informal, between the Vandals and the emperor Zeno on the one hand and the testament of the Vandal kingdom's founder on the other. One notes that in Gelimer's reply he suggests a parity between his political status and that of Justinian, each of the two holding his respective throne by legal right of succession. In neither case does the barbarian or Vandal ethnicity of the North African kingdom even enter into the discussion.

Personal correspondence between Justinian and a barbarian potentate appears soon after in book three when the emperor writes to the Goth Godas, a rebellious lieutenant of Gelimer. Godas had revolted and taken control over the island of Sardinia, which had been part of the Vandal realm. Concerned about the vulnerability of his position, Godas writes to Justinian to request troops that may help him resist the military force the Vandals will send against him to reclaim the island. He gives his reasons for abandoning the Vandal king Gelimer and pledging his allegiance to the Roman emperor instead:

> Οὔτε ἀγνωμοσύνη εἴκων οὔτε τι ἄχαρι πρὸς δεσπότου παθὼν τοῦ ἐμοῦ εἰς ἀπόστασιν εἶδον, ἀλλὰ τἀνδρὸς ἰδὼν τὴν ὠμότητα ἰσχυρὰν οἵαν εἴς τε τὸ ξυγγενὲς καὶ ὑπήκοον μετέχειν τῆς ἀπανθρωπίας οὐκ ἂν δόξαιμι ἑκών γε εἶναι. ἄμεινον γὰρ βασιλεῖ δικαίῳ ὑπηρετεῖν ἢ τυράννῳ τὰ οὐκ ἔννομα ἐπαγγέλλοντι.[114]

> Neither yielding to arrogance nor suffering anything disagreeable from my lord did I look to revolt; but seeing what great savagery the man had towards relative and subject, it did not seem right for me voluntarily to take part in his inhuman behavior. For it is better to serve a just emperor than a tyrant who commands things unlawful.

Here we see a direct effort to disparage the reign of Gelimer that impugns the Vandal's character and his treatment of those over whom he wields power. However, as in the case of the above examples, the argument is represented in legal, if also moralistic, terms. Godas stresses the legitimacy of Justinian to whom Godas wishes to ally himself on account of the

---

[113] μαρτυρόμενοι τοὺς ὅρκους τοὺς Ζήνωνι ὀμωμοσμένους, οὗ τὴν βασιλείαν παραλαβὼν ἔχεις (*Wars* 3.9.23).
[114] *Wars* 3.10.29–30.

emperor's "justice," signified by the adjective δικαίῳ. In contrast, Gelimer is not a *basileus* but rather a *tyrannos* whose reign is characterized by its "illegality," τὰ οὐκ ἔννομα – not of the state itself, but rather of the way in which it is governed.[115] While the legitimacy of the Vandal king Gelimer is indeed contested, that of the Vandals' authority over their territories is not. Moreover, there is no mention of the barbarian origins of the Vandal regime or even of its new and illegitimate usurper, an indication that while Procopius elsewhere clearly refers to the Vandals as barbarians, the fact that they are so has no bearing on legitimacy of their polity.

In turning to the Gothic war, there is significantly more material to consider, since the Gothic War takes up over three books in the *Wars* in comparison to the little more than one book dedicated to the Vandal campaign. Following the death of Theoderic in 526, the throne passed to his grandson Athalaric as has been discussed in the previous chapter. When the youth died from poor health induced by an excessive lifestyle, his mother Amalasuintha assumed the reins of the state. During her tenure as sole ruler of the Goths, Procopius records exchanges between her and both Justinian and the Justinian's general Belisarius regarding control of the coastal fortress of Lilybaeum on Sicily. In response to Belisarius' demand that control of the fortress be returned to the Romans, Amalasuintha replies that

> ἡμεῖς γὰρ οὐδὲν τῶν βασιλέως Ἰουστινιανοῦ λαβόντες ἔχομεν ... Σικελίαν δὲ ξύμπασαν προσποιούμεθα ἡμετέραν οὖσαν, ἧς δὴ ἄκρα μία τὸ ἐν Λιλυβαίῳ φρούριόν ἐστιν. εἰ δὲ Θευδέριχος τὴν ἀδελφὴν τῷ Βανδίλων βασιλεῖ ξυνοικοῦσαν τῶν τινι Σικελίας ἐμπορίων ἐκέλευσε χρῆσθαι, οὐδὲν τοῦτο πρᾶγμα. οὐ γὰρ ἂν τοῦτο δικαιώματος ὑμῖν ὁτουοῦν ἀξίωσιν φέροι. ... ἡμεῖς μὲν οὖν Ἰουστινιανῷ βασιλεῖ περὶ τούτων διαιτᾶν ἐπιτρέψομεν, ὅπη ἂν αὐτῷ δοκῇ νόμιμά τε εἶναι καὶ δίκαια.[116]

> We possess nothing having taken it from the property of Emperor Justinian ... We claim all Sicily as being our own, a single promontory of which is the garrison at Lilybaeum. And if Theoderic let his sister who was marrying the emperor of the Vandals make use of one of the markets of Sicily, that is of no consequence.[117] For this could not offer any sort of claim of justification for you. ... Therefore we will entrust the judgment of these things to the Emperor Justinian, whichever alternative seems to him to be in accord with the law and justice.

[115] On the significance of these terms, see above, 218–21.   [116] *Wars* 4.5.20–24.

[117] Amalasuintha refers here to the fact that Lilybaeum had been included in the dowry of Theoderic's sister Amalafrida, who was married to the Vandal king Thrasamund in 500 (*Wars* 3.8.12–13). Upon the destruction of the Vandal regime, Belisarius counted Lilybaeum among the spoils, but the Goths in possession of it refused him entry and drove his forces off (4.5.11).

The argument put forward by Amalasuintha for the retention of Lily-baeum following the Vandal war rests on the justification that the Goths had provided decisive assistance to the Romans and thus helped secure the Roman victory. The Goths should therefore be entitled to enjoy at least this small portion of the spoils that had previously belonged to the Goths anyway. Yet even so, she allows that the matter be referred to the arbitra-tion of the emperor in Constantinople; the legitimate rule of the territory is thus to be determined by the things which, in the view of the emperor, are "lawful," νόμιμα, and "just," δίκαια.

Belisarius duly reports her reply to the emperor and then lets the issue drop. Discussion of the garrison comes up again in book five, however, when the emperor sends a secret message to Amalasuintha, who, following the onset of her son Athalaric's sickness, is contemplat-ing the handing over of Gothic rule of Italy to Justinian in exchange for her own safety. Justinian sends to her a secret letter, in which he merely states that Lilybaeum is simply "ours," ἡμέτερον ὄν.[118] It is interesting to note that Justinian's claim in this case, as stated in the letter, is prompted by his displeasure at the Goths' defense of Lilybaeum, the refuge given to ten Huns who had deserted from the Roman army in Africa, and the fact that the Goths had attacked a Roman town in the Balkans in the course of fighting against the Gepids.[119] As shown above in Justinian's charges against Gelimer, Roman claims over territory held by the Goths are devoid of any anti-barbarian rhetoric whatsoever that might assert Gothic illegitimacy on ethnological grounds. Unlike the various barbarian peoples to found states in the north of China in the *Jin shu*, neither Goths nor Vandals find their position undermined by their barbarian identities.

Amalasuintha writes in response that it was the fact that the Goths had offered the use of Lilybaeum to Belisarius during the Vandal war, in addition to supplying horses and provisions, that led to the Roman victory in Africa:

> ὥστε σοι τὸ τῆς νίκης κεφάλαιον ἐξ ἡμῶν ἐστιν. ὁ γὰρ τοῖς ἀπόροις τὴν
> λύσιν διδοὺς καὶ τὴν ἐντεῦθεν ἀπόβασιν φέρεσθαι δίκαιος. . . . νῦν δὲ καὶ τὸ
> Σικελίας Λιλύβαιον, ἄνωθεν Γότθοις προσῆκον, ἀξιοῖς ἀφαιρεῖσθαι ἡμᾶς,
> πέτραν, ὦ βασιλεῦ, μίαν ὅσον οὐδὲ ἀργυρίου ἀξίαν, ἣν ἀνθυπουργεῖν σε
> Ἀταλαρίχῳ εἰκός γε ἦν, ἐν τοῖς ἀναγκαιοτάτοις ξυναραμένῳ, εἴπερ ἄνωθεν
> τῆς σῆς βασιλείας οὖσα ἐτύγχανε.[120]

---

[118] *Wars* 5.3.17.   [119] These episodes are both recounted at *Wars* 5.3.15.   [120] *Wars* 5.3.25–27.

> Thus the crown of the victory [over the Vandals] stems from us. For whoever offers the solution in dire straits has full rights to bear the profit therefrom. . . . But now you see fit to take Lilybaeum of Sicily from us, it belonging to the Goths from old; a single rock not worth a silver coin, O Emperor, which it would be reasonable for you to grant to Athalaric as a return kindness, as he helped you in times of great need – if indeed it had in fact belonged to your empire from of old.

While this passage is quoted from a letter that Procopius claims Amalasuintha wrote to Justinian, the historian adds, however, that she agreed in secret to put all of Italy in his power. Nevertheless, she still puts forth an argument for the Gothic right to retain Lilybaeum that is based on precedent, i.e., the fact that the Goths had ruled Lilybaeum for decades. In addition, she presents the Goths' claim of compensation for services rendered in support of the Roman reconquest of North Africa. While Justinian had simply stated that Lilybaeum is "ours," none of his claims makes any mention of the fact that the Goths' control of it is illegitimate for any other reason. There is no sense that the Romans should have a more rightful claim to the territory on the basis of its once having been "Roman" or that the Goths or other barbarians by default have no business governing territories Justinian clearly feels should be in the power of the Roman state.

Before she could put her secret plan of abdication into action, however, her son Athalaric died in 534, and Amalasuintha decided to associate her cousin Theodahad with her reign and make him emperor,[121] hoping in this way to redeem this member of the royal family from the ill will he had engendered among both Goths and Italians.[122] Unknown to Amalasuintha, Theodahad had already contacted Justinian in secret with his own plans of turning over lands in Tuscany to the emperor in exchange for money, a seat in the senate in Constantinople, and a comfortable living.[123] Following his elevation to the throne, however, Theodahad abandoned these plans and also contrived to have Amalasuintha murdered. Theodahad then made an offer to Justinian that would allow the Gothic king to maintain his rule in Italy while taking second place in all official and public matters to Justinian, a proposition swiftly rejected by the emperor.[124] However, Theodahad had anticipated Justinian's refusal of an imperial colleague in the west and had prepared a second set of terms

---

[121] ἐς τὴν βασιλείαν παρακαλεῖν (*Wars* 5.4.8).

[122] For the reputation of Theodahad and his treatment of his neighbors, see above, 230–31, and *Wars* 5.4.1.

[123] *Wars* 5.3.4.   [124] See *Wars* 5.6.2–5 for the terms of Theodahad's offer.

that should be offered as a last effort to ward off a Roman invasion from the east. In this letter, he offers all of Italy to the emperor, making the following remarks on his own *unsuitability* for the throne:

> Οὐ γέγονα μὲν βασιλικῆς αὐλῆς ἐπηλύτης, τετύχηκε γάρ μοι τετέχθαι τε ἐν βασιλέως θείου καὶ τεθράφθαι τοῦ γένους ἀξίως, πολέμων δὲ καὶ τῶν ἐν τούτοις θορύβων εἰμὶ οὐ παντελῶς ἔμπειρος. περὶ λόγων γὰρ ἀκοὴν ἄνωθεν ἐρωτικῶς ἐσχηκότι μοι καὶ διατριβὴν ἐς τοῦτο ἀεὶ πεποιημένῳ ξυμβαίνει τῆς ἐν ταῖς μάχαις ταραχῆς ἑκαστάτω ἐς τόδε εἶναι. ὥστε ἥκιστά με εἰκὸς τὰς ἐκ τῆς βασιλείας ζηλοῦντα τιμὰς τὸν μετὰ κινδύνων διώκειν βίον, ἐξὸν ἀμφοῖν ἐκποδὼν ἵστασθαι.[125]

I have been no outsider to the imperial court, for it befell me to be born and raised in that of my uncle the emperor [sc. Theoderic] and in a fashion worthy of my lineage; but I am wholly inexperienced in wars and their tumults. It has befallen me to always devote my attention and spend my effort in the study of logical arguments since I was young up until now, and likewise to be as far as possible from the chaos of battles. So therefore it is least fitting for me to envy the honors of imperial power, to pursue a life among dangers – it being possible for me to stand out of the way of both.

As a prelude for Theodahad's proposal to confer on Justinian "the rule over both Goths and Italians," these remarks are intended to demonstrate why Theodahad is ineligible as a ruler.[126] In order to argue why this is so, he points to his own lack of military experience and his preference for leisurely study instead of dangerous combat. Indeed, concern for his own personal happiness is a factor of his unsuitability for political power, as he asserts, "I would thus be happier as a farmer in peace and quiet than I might live among royal cares and going from one set of dangers to another."[127] Accordingly, he deems that it is only "fitting that [he] should hand over both Italy and the matters of the empire."[128] Given the extent to which some modern scholars have argued that the Roman–barbarian dichotomy was firmly in place not only in Late Antqituity but even in the writings of Procopius, it is notable that any ethnic component to this profession of illegitimacy on the part of Theodahad is wholly absent. One might expect that a Gothic ethnic distinction from either Italians or Romans might somehow factor into his argument, such that he might represent the offered transfer of power as that of a restoration of rule over

---

[125] *Wars* 5.6.15–17.   [126] τὸ Γότθων τε καὶ Ἰταλιωτῶν ... κράτος (*Wars* 5.6.19).

[127] ὡς ἔγωγε ἥδιον ἂν ξὺν τῇ ἀπραγμοσύνῃ γεωργὸς εἴην ἢ ἐν μερίμναις βασιλικαῖς βιῴην, κινδύνους ἐκ κινδύνων παραπεμπούσαις (*Wars* 5.6.20).

[128] Ἰταλίαν τε καὶ τὰ τῆς βασιλείας πράγματα παραδοῦναι προσήκει (*Wars* 5.6.21).

Italy to its rightful owners from either foreign usurpers or stewards. Yet this is not the case.

This self-profession of illegitimacy on the part of a barbarian ruler is an anomaly in the *Wars*, and the majority of instances in which the issue is discussed occur in contexts where cases for or against the legitimacy of barbarian rule are pitted against one another. Such instances provide our most explicit evidence for assessment of the terms in which political legitimacy over imperial territories was understood. For example, in the year 537 when Vitigis is besieging the Roman general Belisarius in Rome, he sends envoys from the Goths to negotiate with Belisarius in front of members of the Roman senate.[129] In this case, the Gothic envoys address themselves to Belisarius personally, blaming him in the presence of Roman senators for the hardships endured by the besieged populace of the city and urging him neither to prolong the suffering of the Romans, "whom Theoderic nourished in a way of life not only soft but also free, nor stand in the way of the lord of both Goths and Italians."[130] They then point to the senators themselves while still addressing Belisarius, asking,

> ἡδέως δ' ἂν καὶ Ῥωμαίους ἔτι ἐροίμεθα τούσδε, τί ποτε ἄρα Γότθοις ἐπικαλεῖν ἔχοντες ἡμᾶς τε αὖ καὶ σφᾶς αὐτοὺς προὔδοσαν, οἵ γε τῆς μὲν ἡμετέρας ἐπιεικείας ἄχρι τοῦδε ἀπήλαυσαν, νῦν δὲ καὶ τῆς παρ' ὑμῶν ἐπικουρίας εἰσὶν ἔμπειροι.[131]

We would happily ask these Romans: what have they ever had to accuse the Goths of such that they betray both us and themselves – these who until now have enjoyed our fairness but now have experienced "help" from you.

The case of the Goths is based on two things: the beneficent rule of Theoderic and the fairness, ἐπιείκεια, of the Goths in general. It is rather the faithlessness of the Romans toward the Goths, and the role played by

---

[129] The Goth Vacis had shortly before this been sent to reproach the Roman populace for betraying the rule of the Goths by welcoming the invading army from the eastern empire. This accusation is presented in indirect speech where he labels the eastern Romans as "Greeks," charging that no "Greeks had ever come to Italy other than actors, mimes, and pirates": ἐξ ὧν τὰ πρότερα οὐδένα ἐς Ἰταλίαν ἥκοντα εἶδον, ὅτι μὴ τραγῳδούς τε καὶ μίμους καὶ ναύτας λωποδύτας (*Wars* 5.18.40). On the lack of significant distinction between direct speech, *oratio recta*, and indirect speech, *oratio obliqua*, see Laird, *Powers of Expression, Expressions of Power: Speech Presentation and Latin Literature*, 79–115. For a discussion of this and other episodes where the Goths make a case for their own legitimate rule, see Pazdernik, "A Dangerous Liberty and a Servitude Free from Care," 270–83.

[130] οὓς δὴ Θευδέριχος ἐν βίῳ τρυφερῷ τε καὶ ἄλλως ἐλευθέρῳ ἐξέθρεψε, μήτε τῷ Γότθων τε καὶ Ἰταλιωτῶν δεσπότῃ ἐμποδὼν ἵστασο (*Wars* 5.20.11).

[131] *Wars* 5.20.14.

Belisarius in the prolonging of the besieged city's sufferings, that are deserving of reproach.

The most extensive argument presented by the Goths for the legitimacy of their rule over Italy occurs in a similar diplomatic context when, later during the siege that was to last a total of one year and nine days,[132] Vitigis sends another embassy. This embassy consists of three men, two of whom are Goths and a third who is "a Roman man of reputation among the Goths."[133] There ensues a debate of some length between these envoys and Belisarius over the legitimacy of the Gothic position and the possible terms according to which peace may be achieved. The Goths begin by addressing not merely Belisarius but the Romans in general, saying, "You have acted unjustly towards us, Roman men, taking up arms against friends and allies unnecessarily."[134] In this case "Romans" in the vocative seems to indicate not the inhabitants of the city but the imperial army under the command of Belisarius. The first part of the speech presents the Gothic version of events that led to their arrival in Italy and the establishment of their rule there:

> Γότθοι γὰρ οὐ βίᾳ Ῥωμαίους ἀφελόμενοι γῆν τὴν Ἰταλίας ἐκτήσαντο, ἀλλ᾽ Ὀδόακρός ποτε τὸν αὐτοκράτορα καθελὼν ἐς τυραννίδα τὴν τῇδε πολιτείαν μεταβαλὼν εἶχε. Ζήνων δὲ τότε τῆς ἑῴας κρατῶν καὶ τιμωρεῖν μὲν τῷ ξυμβεβασιλευκότι βουλόμενος καὶ τοῦ τυράννου τήνδε τὴν χώραν ἐλευθεροῦν, Ὀδοάκρου δὲ καταλῦσαι τὴν δύναμιν οὐχ οἷός τε ὤν, Θευδέριχον ἀναπείθει τὸν ἡμῶν ἄρχοντα, καίπερ αὐτόν τε καὶ Βυζάντιον πολιορκεῖν μέλλοντα, καταλῦσαι μὲν τὴν πρὸς αὐτὸν ἔχθραν τιμῆς ἀναμνησθέντα πρὸς αὐτοῦ ἧς τετύχηκεν ἤδη, πατρίκιός τε καὶ Ῥωμαίων γεγονὼς ὕπατος, Ὀδόακρον δὲ ἀδικίας τῆς ἐς Αὐγούστουλον τίσασθαι, καὶ τῆς χώρας αὐτόν τε καὶ Γότθους τὸ λοιπὸν κρατεῖν ὀρθῶς καὶ δικαίως.[135]

For the Goths did not acquire the land of Italy depriving the Romans of it by violence, but formerly Odoacer held it after having deposed the emperor and turning the Republic into a tyranny. But Zeno, then ruling the east and wishing to avenge his imperial colleague as well as liberate this land from the tyrant, was himself not able to end the power of Odoacer; he convinced our leader Theodoric, although Theodoric was about to lay siege to Byzantium and Zeno himself, to put down his hatred towards Zeno and, mindful of the honor awarded to him by Zeno already in making him a patrician and Roman consul, to avenge the injustice done against Augustulus by Odoacer; [and Zeno convinced] both him and the Goths to rule over the country in the future both rightly and justly.

---

[132] *Wars* 6.10.13.   [133] Ῥωμαῖον ἄνδρα ἐν Γότθοις δόκιμον (*Wars* 6.6.3).

[134] Ἠδικήκατε ἡμᾶς, ἄνδρες Ῥωμαῖοι, ἐπὶ φίλους τε καὶ ξυμμάχους ὄντας ὅπλα οὐ δέον ἀράμενοι (*Wars* 6.6.14).

[135] *Wars* 6.6.15-16.

It is made clear that the Gothic entrance into Italy in the first place was at the behest of the emperor Zeno and not at their own initiative; they came as avengers of the crimes of Odoacer, who had set himself up as an illegal tyrant and tried to do away with the Republic, πολιτεία.[136] The Goths' action in deposing the barbarian tyrant was therefore in the interests of *restoring*, not destroying, Roman rule. The Goths were thus liberators in this action, not conquerors. Crucially, the Goths argue that it was given to the Goths "to rule over the country in the future both rightly [ὀρθῶς] and justly [δικαίως]." This last sentence of the passage asserts that not only were the Goths persuaded by the emperor himself to take up rule in the west on terms both right and just, but that their tenure has indeed lived up to these standards. To prove that this is the case, the Gothic envoys proceed to demonstrate how their reign over Italy has not only been to the benefit of their subjects but has also maintained appropriate deference to the superior authority and prerogatives of the emperors in the east:

οὕτω τοίνυν παραλαβόντες τὴν τῆς Ἰταλίας ἀρχὴν τούς τε νόμους καὶ τὴν πολιτείαν διεσωσάμεθα τῶν πώποτε βεβασιλευκότων οὐδενὸς ἧσσον, καὶ Θευδερίχου μὲν ἢ ἄλλου ὁτουοῦν διαδεξαμένου τὸ Γότθων κράτος νόμος τὸ παράπαν οὐδεὶς οὐκ ἐν γράμμασιν, οὐκ ἄγραφός ἐστι. τὰ δὲ τῆς εἰς θεὸν εὐσεβείας τε καὶ πίστεως οὕτω Ῥωμαίοις ἐς τὸ ἀκριβὲς ἐφυλάξαμεν, ὥστε Ἰταλιωτῶν μὲν τὴν δόξαν οὐδεὶς οὐχ ἑκὼν οὐκ ἀκούσιος ἐς τήνδε τὴν ἡμέραν μετέβαλε, Γότθων δὲ μεταβεβλημένων ἐπιστροφή τις οὐδαμῶς γέγονε. καὶ μὴν καὶ τὰ Ῥωμαίων ἱερὰ τιμῆς παρ' ἡμῶν τῆς ἀνωτάτω τετύχηκεν. οὐ γὰρ οὐδεὶς εἴς τι τούτων καταφυγὼν πώποτε πρὸς οὐδενὸς ἀνθρώπων βεβίασται, ἀλλὰ καὶ πάσας τὰς τῆς πολιτείας ἀρχὰς αὐτοὶ μὲν διαγεγόνασιν ἔχοντες, Γότθος δὲ αὐτῶν μετέσχεν οὐδείς. ἢ παρελθών τις ἡμᾶς ἐλεγχέτω, ἢν μὴ μετὰ τοῦ ἀληθοῦς ἡμῖν εἰρῆσθαι οἴηται. προσθείη δ' ἄν τις ὡς καὶ τὸ τῶν ὑπάτων ἀξίωμα Γότθοι ξυνεχώρουν Ῥωμαίοις πρὸς τοῦ τῶν ἑῴων βασιλέως ἐς ἕκαστον ἔτος κομίζεσθαι. ὑμεῖς δέ, τούτων τοιούτων ὄντων, Ἰταλίας μὲν οὐ προσεποιεῖσθε, κακουμένης ὑπὸ τῶν Ὀδοάκρου βαρβάρων, καίπερ οὐ δι' ὀλίγου, ἀλλ' ἐς δέκα ἐνιαυτοὺς τὰ δεινὰ εἰργασμένου, νῦν δὲ τοὺς δικαίως αὐτὴν κεκτημένους, οὐδὲν ὑμῖν προσῆκον, βιάζεσθε.[137]

---

[136] Cassiodorus gives us Theoderic's own statement to this effect: "We are happy to live under Roman law, [the law of those] whom we wish to avenge by means of arms; nor are we concerned any less with moral matters than with wars. For what good would it have been to have driven out a horde of barbarians if we should not then live according to the laws?": *Delectamur iure Romano vivere quos armis cupimus vindicare, nec minor nobis est cura rerum moralium quam potest esse bellorum. quid enim proficit barbaros removisse confusos, nisi vivatur ex legibus?* (*Variae* 3.43.1).

[137] *Wars* 6.6.17–21. The most thorough overview of Theoderic's reign as represented in a wide variety of sources is provided by Goltz, *Barbar-König-Tyrann*; for discussion of Procopius' account in particular, see ibid., 210–67.

Thus taking over the rule of Italy we have safeguarded both the laws and the Republic no less than any of those ruling as emperors before us; and there has not been a single piece of legislation, either written or unwritten, from Theoderic or any other who has succeeded to the Gothic rule. We have diligently protected the worship and faith toward God for the Romans such that none of the Italians, whether willing or unwilling, has converted to our tenets of belief, but there was no concern at all [on our part] if any of the Goths converted [to orthodox Christianity]. And indeed the holy places of the Romans have enjoyed respect from us to the utmost degree. For no one fleeing into any of them has ever been compelled by anyone; otherwise [the Romans] themselves have carried on holding all the appointments of the Republic, and not one Goth has participated. Or let someone come forth and disprove us if he does not think these things said in accordance with the truth. One could even add that the Goths have agreed that each year the honor of those made consuls among the Romans should come from the emperor of the east. But you all, things being thus, did not lay claim to Italy when it was being abused by the barbarians of Odoacer – and not just for a little while but with him keeping on terribly for ten years – and now you abuse the ones who have acquired the land justly, a matter not at all seemly for you.

In describing the Gothic rule over Italy, the Goths explicitly represent their rulers according to the same legitimating factors that apply to Roman emperors: the safeguarding of the laws and the Republic, τούς τε νόμους καὶ τὴν πολιτείαν διεσωσάμεθα. Yet even in their military supremacy, having defended the state when the emperor in the east was unable to do so, the Goths yielded the prerogative of legislation to their senior partners in Constantinople. Not only that; in one of the relatively few instances where Procopius notes the doctrinal differences that divided the Christian communities of the age, the Goths argue that they have not interfered in any way in the orthodox faith of their Roman subjects.[138] The envoys go on to point out that Gothic deference to the emperors of the east has extended even to the appointing of secular offices, from which they claim the Goths have abstained entirely. The argument ends with a reminder of the fact that it was the Goths, not the imperial armies, who ended the barbarian tyranny of Odoacer, an outrage that the emperor in the east had tolerated for over a decade. As it had begun, the

---

[138] The religious views of Procopius continue to elude scholarly consensus. For two markedly different interpretations, see Cameron, *Procopius and the Sixth Century*, 113–33, and Kaldellis, *Procopius of Caesarea*, 165–221. For a recent response to Kaldellis's arguments, see Cameron, "Writing about Procopius Then and Now," 16–17. Also see Murray, "Procopius and Boethius: Christian Philosophy in the *Persian Wars*," 104–08; Conterno, "Procopius and non-Chalcedonian Christians: A Loud Silence?," 95–99.

speech ends with an emphasis on the fact that the Goths have ruled justly, δικαίως, again underscoring the legal and moral framework of their political case.

Throughout this detailed apology, we find nothing analogous to the frequent references in the *Jin shu* to the barbarian ethnicity of political claimants. Liu Yuan, Murong Wei, and Helian Bobo all based part of their claims to legitimate rule on either their own descent from mythical or Chinese figures or on the precedent set by ancient monarchs who were themselves said to have been of barbarian ancestry. Whether they argue for legitimacy by asserting that they themselves may lay claim to the same genealogical line professed by the Chinese or by that position's inverse, i.e., arguing that their own barbarian origins should not undermine their political status as it did not for mythic sage rulers of the past, a crux of the argument in either case is ethnic identity. The same is true for those instances where barbarian poltical legitimacy is undermined on ethnological grounds, whether in the case of Shi Le, who excuses himself from serving a Chinese state, or in the case of Fu Rong and Yao Yizhong, who argue that their barbarian status is an insurmountable impediment to any imperial ambitions entertained by their own people. Having considered these debates regarding the political legitimacy of barbarian kingdoms in China, the fact that such ethnological rhetoric is not even in evidence in the *Wars* stands out all the more clearly.

In response to the above claims of the Gothic envoys, Belisarius answers with a speech, only a third the length of that of the Goths, in which he dismisses their claims categorically:

> ἡ δὲ ῥῆσις μακρά τε καὶ οὐ πόρρω ἀλαζονείας ὑμῖν γέγονε. Θευδέριχον γὰρ βασιλεὺς Ζήνων Ὀδοάκρῳ πολεμήσοντα ἔπεμψεν, οὐκ ἐφ᾽ ᾧ Ἰταλίας αὐτὸς τὴν ἀρχὴν ἔχοι· τί γὰρ ἂν καὶ τύραννον τυράννου διαλλάσσειν βασιλεῖ ἔμελεν; ἀλλ᾽ ἐφ᾽ ᾧ ἐλευθέρα τε καὶ βασιλεῖ κατήκοος ἔσται. ὁ δὲ τὰ περὶ τὸν τύραννον εὖ διαθέμενος ἀγνωμοσύνῃ ἐς τἆλλα οὐκ ἐν μετρίοις ἐχρήσατο. ἀποδιδόναι γὰρ τῷ κυρίῳ τὴν γῆν οὐδαμῆ ἔγνω. ... ἐγὼ μὲν οὖν χώραν τὴν βασιλέως ἑτέρῳ τῳ οὔποτε οὐκ ἂν παραδοίην.[139]

Your speech was both lengthy and not far from false pretension. Emperor Zeno did not send Theodoric to fight Odoacer on condition that he himself should hold sway over Italy. What would it have behooved the emperor to trade one tyrant for another? [He sent Theodoric] rather on condition that Italy would be free and subject to the emperor. But acquitting himself well regarding the tyrant, he [sc. Theodoric] showed unfairness on other points

---

[139] *Wars* 6.6.22–25.

well beyond measure. In no way did he understand that he should hand over the land to its master. . . . Therefore, I would never confer the land of the emperor to any other.

Without responding to the Gothic arguments, Belisarius simply states that the Goths were never intended by Zeno to do anything other than act as a federate contingent of the imperial army. In establishing themselves as rulers of Italy, their position is no more valid in Belisarius' eyes than was that of Odoacer, whom the Goths under Theoderic had overthrown some fifty years earlier. In this back and forth between the Gothic and Roman negotiators, therefore, there is nothing to suggest that the Gothic claims are either supported or undermined by their ethnicity. As presented by Procopius, the conflict is strictly a legal dispute in which the political legitimacy of the Goths is butressed by alleged agreements with the emperor, the military supremacy that enabled them to remove the tyrant Odoacer, their safeguarding of the laws and religious institutions of the state, and, most importantly, their preservation of the *politeia*.

The above is the most extensive argument for or against the legitimacy of the Gothic kingdom in the west, although Procopius continues to insert speeches in the later books of the *Wars* that address the issue. Totila, the ruler of the Goths for the majority of the war following the surrender of Vitigis in 540, brought about a revival of Gothic fortunes, and his success is often represented in the *Wars* as a result of his sense of justice and piety.[140] Taragna has argued that the large number of speeches and letters attributed to Totila by Procopius underscores the Gothic king's prominence in the narrative; she argues that Totila is also clearly paired with Belisarius as a heroic and righteous figure through the placement, length, and content of his speeches.[141]

Totila is not accorded many speeches where he defends the legitimacy of Gothic rule, although there is at least one case where, in chastising the Roman senate in a letter, he asks if they "happen to be ignorant of the beneficence of Theodoric and Amalasuintha or did these become obscured by time and poor memory?"[142] In fact, in the majority of cases, Totila is more concerned with the injustice and illegitimacy of the Roman claims. For example, prior to an engagement with a Roman force he exhorts his

---

[140] On Procopius' depiction of Totila, especially Totila as the embodiment of justice, *die Verkörperung der Gerechtigkeit*, see Brodka, *Die Geschichtsphilosophie in der spätantiken Historiographie*, 124–26.

[141] *Logoi historias: Discorsi e lettere nella prima storiografia retorica bizantina*, 131–32.

[142] πότερα ὑμᾶς ἀγνοεῖν τὰς Θευδερίχου τε καὶ Ἀμαλασούνθης εὐεργεσίας τετύχηκεν, ἢ χρόνῳ τε αὐτὰς καὶ λήθῃ ἐν ὑμῖν ἐξιτήλους εἶναι; (*Wars* 7.9.10).

troops with the promise that "we may with good hope go against the arms of our enemies, being emboldened by the injustice of these men,"[143] a reference to the abuses suffered by the population of Italy at the hands of the Roman armies. Elsewhere, he refers to the Goths as "liberating," ἀπαλλάξαντες, the people of Italy from their "most hated overlords," ἐχθίστων δεσποτῶν, i.e., the Romans of the east.[144]

Totila also allows for critique of the Gothic regime prior to his assumption of the kingship because of its negligence of justice under king Theodahad. In an episode already discussed in Chapter 4, he at one point insists on the execution of one of his own Gothic bodyguards who had raped a Calabrian girl, even though the man's comrades protest the severity of the punishment. Totila explains the necessity of justice and observance of the law:

> ἐπεὶ δὲ ὑπὸ Θευδάτῳ ταττόμενοι, ἀνδρὶ τὸ δίκαιον περὶ ἐλάσσονος τῆς ἐς τὸ πλουτεῖν ἐπιθυμίας πεποιημένῳ, ἵλεων ἡμῖν αὐτοῖς τὸν θεὸν παρανομίᾳ τῇ ἐς τὴν δίαιταν ὡς ἥκιστα κατεστήσαμεν, ὅπη ποτὲ κεχώρηκεν ἡμῖν ἡ τύχη ἐπίστασθε δή που, ὑφ᾽ οἵων τε καὶ ὁπόσων ἡσσημένοις ἀνδρῶν. . . . οὐ γὰρ ἔστιν, οὐκ ἔστι, τὸν ἀδικοῦντα καὶ βιαζόμενον ἐν τοῖς ἀγῶσιν εὐδοκιμεῖν, ἀλλὰ πρὸς τὸν βίον ἑκάστου ἡ τοῦ πολέμου πρυτανεύεται τύχη.[145]

> When marshaled under Theodahad, a man who valued justice less than his eagerness for being rich, we made God most ungracious toward ourselves with the lawlessness of our way of life; wherefore at some point fortune withdrew from us as I suppose you know, being defeated by men of such a sort and in such numbers. . . . For it is impossible, impossible, for one who does wrong and commits violent acts to win good fame in a struggle, but the fortune of war is guided by the life of each individual.

While acknowledging the earlier failures of Gothic governance, Totila demonstrates by his own example the importance of adhering to just action: he has his bodyguard executed and all of the man's property given to the young woman he had raped. Totila demonstrates that strict adherence to justice that ignores ethnic loyalty is necessary for the propitiation of divine favor, which legitimates political rule by virtue of the military success that it confers. By the end of his speech, Totila has succeeded in persuading the Goths that the ebb and flow of their fortunes have been contingent upon their observance of law and justice and not simply attention to military

---

[143] ἄξιον δὲ ἡμᾶς μετὰ τῆς ἀγαθῆς ἐλπίδος τοῖς πολεμίοις ἐς χεῖρας ἰέναι, τῇ τῶν ἀνδρῶν ἀδικίᾳ θαρροῦντας (*Wars* 7.4.15).
[144] *Wars* 7.7.11.   [145] *Wars* 7.8.21–24.

matters. He acknowledges shortcomings of the regime thus far, yet these are never associated with their barbarian or Gothic identity.

The prerequisite of just and lawful rule for the enjoyment of divine favor is something of a theme of Totila's reign. Elsewhere, Totila again refers to the period when the Goths "formerly were reckoning justice lower than all other things."[146] Yet he goes on to argue that divine support is contingent only on this single virtue:

> οὐ γὰρ ἀνθρώπων γένει οὐδὲ φύσει ἐθνῶν ξυμμαχεῖν εἴωθεν, ἀλλ᾽ οἷς ἂν μᾶλλον ὁ τοῦ δικαίου λόγος τιμῷτο. πόνος τε οὐδεὶς αὐτῷ τἀγαθὰ ἐφ᾽ ἑτέρους μετενεγκεῖν.[147]

> For [God] is not accustomed to fight as an ally alongside any race of men or any kind of nation, but rather whichever ones among whom the word of justice is honored. It is no trouble for him to share his grace with one side or the other.

In this passage it does in fact seem as though, at last, Procopius addresses the issue of ethnicity as a factor of political legitimacy, if only insofar as he anticipates the unsustainable argument that divine favor might adhere to one ethnic group, one *genos-*γένος or *ethnos-*ἔθνος, more than to another. Yet Totila's point is to argue that there is no such meaningful distinction in the eyes of the divine, and he names no specific groups or communities. There is thus no mention of a Roman–barbarian divide, the type of division taken for granted as a central factor in political contests in the *Jin shu*, where the distinction between Chinese and barbarians is repeatedly, and explicitly, addressed. Moreover, in the *Jin shu* there are clear assertions that the Son of Heaven simply cannot be a barbarian; such assertions are exactly opposite to Totila's conviction that divine favor is contingent upon neither ethnic identity nor genealogy. In the *Jin shu*, the importance of ethnic terms and categories as objective realities is not in doubt; the only issue is to determine what the implications are if one is Yi, Di, Rong, Xiongnu, etc. By contrast, in the political speeches in the *Wars* in which legitimacy is contested, the issue does not even appear.

A last example from the *Wars* where the political legitimacy of the Gothic kingdom is challenged appears prior to Procopius' account of the climactic battle, where the Roman general Narses won a decisive victory over the Goths in 552. While stubborn resistance continued following this Gothic defeat, Gothic fortunes were in irrevocable decline from this point

---

[146] Γότθοι μὲν πρότερον τῶν ἄλλων ἁπάντων περὶ ἐλάσσονος πεποιημένοι τὸ δίκαιον (*Wars* 7.21.6).
[147] *Wars* 7.21.9.

onward. In his pre-battle harangue of his troops, Narses is dismissive and contemptuous of Gothic political claims. He urges his troops to

> ἐπαγόμενοι πολλῷ τῷ καταφρονήματι ἐπὶ τούτων δὴ τῶν λῃστῶν τὴν ἐπικράτησιν ἔσεσθε, οἵ γε δοῦλοι βασιλέως τοῦ μεγάλου τὸ ἐξ ἀρχῆς ὄντες καὶ δραπέται γεγενημένοι τύραννόν τε αὐτοῖς ἀγελαῖόν τινα ἐκ τοῦ συρφετοῦ προστησάμενοι ἐπικλοπώτερον συνταράξαι τὴν Ῥωμαίων ἀρχὴν ἐπὶ καιροῦ τινος ἴσχυσαν.[148]

> rush forth to the victory, being driven on with great disdain of these bandits. They, being slaves of the great emperor from the beginning, having become runaways and setting up a common man of the mob as tyrant over themselves, have had the strength to thievishly confound the Roman Empire for a time.

These words are typical insults that serve to debase the Goths in the eyes of Narses' own troops for the sake of morale.[149] Yet while these charges of banditry, cowardice, and ochlocracy are all intended to make the Goths look like easy prey for the Roman army, none of the ways in which Narses characterizes them takes notice of the Goths' non-Roman identity. However, Narses goes on to provide a more cogent argument for the illegitimacy of the Gothic position in terms that have appeared throughout the *Wars* when political legitimacy has been at stake. He assures his troops that

> ὑμεῖς μὲν πολιτείας εὐνόμου προκινδυνεύοντες καθίστασθε εἰς ξυμβολὴν τήνδε, οἱ δὲ νεωτερίζουσιν ἐπὶ τοῖς νόμοις ζυγομαχοῦντες, οὐ παραπέμψειν τι τῶν ὑπαρχόντων ἐς διαδόχους προσδοκῶντές τινας, ἀλλ' εὖ εἰδότες ὡς συναπολεῖται αὐτοῖς ἅπαντα καὶ μετ' ἐφημέρου βιοτεύουσι τῆς ἐλπίδος. ὥστε καταφρονεῖσθαι τὰ μάλιστά εἰσιν ἄξιοι. τῶν γὰρ οὐ νόμῳ καὶ ἀγαθῇ πολιτείᾳ ξυνισταμένων ἀπολέλειπται μὲν ἀρετὴ πᾶσα, διακέκριται δέ, ὡς τὸ εἰκός, ἡ νίκη, οὐκ εἰωθυῖα ταῖς ἀρεταῖς ἀντιτάσσεσθαι.[150]

> While you who face danger on behalf of the lawful Republic have taken your stand in this campaign, they are revolutionaries fighting together

---

[148] *Wars* 8.30.2.

[149] There is perhaps an allusion here to the invasion of Greece by the Persian king Xerxes as it appears in Herodotus. Though I have translated βασιλέως τοῦ μεγάλου as "of the great emperor," the title is the same as that of the Great King Xerxes. The implicit critique of Justinian's reconquest and the representation of empire as an enslaving, rather than liberating, process and institution is a common motif throughout the *Wars* and lies solidly within the Greco-Roman historiographical tradition's larger preoccupation with the tension between ideals of liberty and realities of monarchy. This tension was an integral part of Roman imperial political discourse and lacks an equivalent in the Chinese tradition. However, a thorough discussion of this theme in the *Wars* would fall beyond the scope of this study. For the representation of the emperor Justinian as an oriental despot, see Kaldellis, *Procopius of Caesarea*, 119–42.

[150] *Wars* 8.30.5–6.

against the laws and not expecting to pass on anything that they have to any successors, but knowing well that everything that is theirs will be destroyed at once and along with the transient hope they live on. Thus are they most worthy to be despised. For all virtue has abandoned them as they stand bound together not by law or a proper republic; and victory has been decided, as to be expected, since she is not accustomed to stand in battle opposite the virtues.

This passage is one of the most explicit critiques of just what it is that disqualifies the Goths as legitimate rulers of Italy. Narses, who is commanding a heterogeneous force of Roman troops and barbarian federate contingents, represents the Romans as the sole defenders of the lawful Republic, πολιτείας εὐνόμου.[151] In opposition, the Goths are despised as a band that fights against the very laws, ἐπὶ τοῖς νόμοις, which constitute Roman order. The Gothic state is thus defined by its very lack of those things that the Romans possess: law, νόμῳ, and a proper republic, ἀγαθῇ πολιτείᾳ. As in previous examples, the legitimacy or illegitimacy of the barbarian political regime is conceived of and represented in terms taken from legal and political discourse. There is no indication of a disqualifying element of barbarian identity that is drawn from ethnological rhetoric. Even on the cusp of a climactic final battle where Procopius might have been expected to heighten his audience's expectations with rhetorical flourish, he makes no use of ethnographic tropes or imagery that could represent the conflict as a struggle between barbarians and Romans. He does allow Narses to delineate the opposing sides of this struggle – but it is a distinction that only has meaning when defined in political and legal terms, not ethnological ones.

In sum, none of the arguments for and, more significantly, against barbarian rule in the *Wars* appeals to an ethnological argument where the non-Roman background of the figures involved is either a matter of interest or of relevance. Again, that this should be the case is surprising given the fact that Goths, Vandals, and others are all indiscriminately and consistently referred to as barbarians throughout the work. Even the

---

[151] Indeed, when Totila perceives his own troops' fear of the Roman army, τὴν Ῥωμαίων στρατιάν, in his own harangue he points to the heterogeneity of the Roman army, arguing that "the crowd of enemies deserves only disdain, collected from a vast number of ethnicities. For an alliance gathered from many places offers neither secure trust nor strength, but it is naturally fractious and is divided among its races and its intentions": τοῦ δὲ τῶν πολεμίων ὁμίλου ὑπερφρονεῖν ἄξιον, ἐξ ἐθνῶν ξυνειλεγμένων ὅτι μάλιστα πλείστων. ξυμμαχία γὰρ πολλαχόθεν ἐρανισθεῖσα οὔτε τὴν πίστιν οὔτε τὴν δύναμιν ἀσφαλῆ φέρεται, ἀλλὰ σχιζομένη τοῖς γένεσι μερίζεται καὶ ταῖς γνώμαις εἰκότως (*Wars* 8.30.17). Yet as discussed in a by Greatrex, ethnic heterogeneity was a consistent feature of either side of the conflict. See "Procopius' Attitude towards Barbarians," 327–54.

Franks, a people who in at least one case Procopius represents as savage and murderous, are exempt from ethnic delegitimation of their political claims. In responding to the Roman envoy Leontius, their king Theudibald argues,

> ὁ πατὴρ ὁ ἐμὸς Θευδίβερτος οὔτε βιάσασθαι πώποτε τῶν ὁμόρων τινὰ ἐν σπουδῇ ἔσχεν οὔτε κτήμασιν ἀλλοτρίοις ἐπιπηδᾶν. τεκμήριον δέ· οὐ γάρ εἰμι πλούσιος. οὐ τοίνυν οὐδὲ τὰ χωρία ταῦτα Ῥωμαίους ἀφελόμενος, ἀλλὰ Τουτίλα ἔχοντος ἤδη αὐτὰ καὶ διαρρήδην ἐνδιδόντος καταλαβὼν ἔσχεν, ἐφ᾽ ᾧ χρῆν μάλιστα βασιλέα Ἰουστινιανὸν συνήδεσθαι Φράγγοις.[152]

> My father Theudibert neither had a desire to use force against any of his neighbors nor to assault the property of others. And the proof is that I am not wealthy. Indeed, he did not hold these lands having deprived the Romans of them but rather taking them from Totila, who was already in possession of them and explicitly conferring them – in respect of which Emperor Justinian ought to have rejoiced for the Franks.

While Procopius is clear about the rapacious opportunism of the Franks throughout the *Wars*, the argument presented by Theudibald for his rightful acquisition of the territories he holds, that he received them through a formal agreement from Totila who already held sovereignty over them, is fundamentally a legal one. Even in the case of the most barbarous of the barbarian kingdoms, Procopius is willing to suspend whatever anti-barbarian prejudices he may have entertained and allow their rulers to appear as a political claimants in ethnically neutral terms.

Conclusions

This chapter has considered the question of political legitimacy in the *Wars* and the *Jin shu* as it appears in the rhetorical speeches recorded in either text. It began with the question of how political legitimacy was conceived of in the Roman and Chinese empires and the degree to which perceptions of ethnic identity served to influence these conceptions. As has been shown, many of the traditional aspects of political legitimation remain visible in either text. Both the *Jin shu* and the *Wars* exhibit interest in a similar mix of divine, ethical, and, in the Roman case, legal factors. Moreover, both the Roman and Chinese empires had a tradition of barbarians serving with distinction in imperial service, and this tradition is visible in the frequent examples where political loyalties are not determined by ethnic background. The alliances between states and the

---

[152] *Wars* 8.24.26–27.

indiscriminate participation of soldiers in armies led by either "native" or barbarian regimes indicates that the exigencies of political survival and advantage trumped theoretical notions of ethnic status in either case. What is crucially different, however, is the way the two texts treat the possibility of legitimate barbarian rule.

It was indicated early in this chapter that the Roman Empire of Justinian and the Tang Empire of Taizong 唐太宗 were situated in markedly different positions in relation this question. Justinian's armies had conquered the Vandal and Gothic kingdoms of North Africa and Italy, and Roman imperial power, though severely humbled in the fifth century with the deposition of the last emperor in the west, had never been superseded in the east. The Tang dynasty, in contrast, had been born out of a succession of non-Chinese Särbi-Xianbei, or at least Särbi-Chinese, regimes, which it recognized as politically legitimate. One might expect that given this contrast in their respective standpoints, the historian of the Roman Empire, secure and confident, might triumphantly declare the superiority of Roman institutions and perhaps a primacy of an ethnic conception of *Romanitas*, if only through rhetorical attacks against a barbarian Other. Indeed, this is the reading of the *Wars* that some scholars have preferred, as has been discussed in previous chapters. Yet this is not what one finds if one looks at the passages of the text that deal directly with the question of barbarian political legitimacy. Again and again, Procopius presents rhetorical arguments both for and against the barbarian position that ignore the question of ethnic background and are free from the wealth of ethnological tropes otherwise so common in Greco-Roman literature.

Given its own rise from the semi-barbarized north of China, we might expect, on the other hand, that historians of the early Tang might represent the period of foreign conquest states of earlier centuries in a forgiving light, at least as regards the non-Chinese ethnic origins of those states. Moreover, one might assume, based on the assertions of many modern scholars, that the concept of a Sino-barbarian dichotomy would have no prominent place in political discourse because such distinctions had, by the early seventh century, become vague at best. Yet here too, the text belies such assumptions. The above discussion has shown that, time after time, the stigma of barbarian identity discredits the claims of non-Chinese rulers to political legitimacy. Although there are many instances where claims of legitimacy are articulated in terms consonant with those common in earlier imperial China, one finds alongside these instances a consistent awareness of the ethnic origins of barbarian political figures and the consequent charge of illegitimacy and usurpation that attends them. The arguments for and against are thus often phrased in the very kinds of ethnological terms that characterize earlier Chinese historiography's representations of foreign peoples.

In short, while the political debates represented in the *Wars* are conducted with little interest in the ethnic backgrounds of the participants, the historians of the *Jin shu* exhibit a consistent preoccupation with, and delegitimation of, the non-Chinese origins of the regimes it chronicles. While many western scholars have been inclined to suggest that Procopius, as a self-consciously classicizing historian, maintains the conceptual boundaries between Romans and barbarians and, as a citizen of Constantinople, should have viewed barbarian kings "solely as repulsive aliens,"[153] the above discussion of the *Wars* alongside the *Jin shu* demonstrates the degree to which ethnic biases and barbarian prejudice did not condition his representation of barbarian rulers. The conclusion of this study will address the implications of this marked contrast and assess not only its significance for the fate of the Roman and Chinese empires in the middle ages, but also how it may condition our understanding of the worldviews and mentalities that characterized the broader Chinese and Greco-Roman historiographical traditions.

[153] Goffart, *Barbarian Tides*, 54.

Conclusion

Questions with which this study began are intimately tied to the ways in which the two imperial traditions were understood in antiquity and how they have been perceived in the modern period. Why was a Roman Empire never firmly restored in the western Mediterranean following the deposition of the last western emperor in 476? And, more importantly, why did the several states that succeeded it in the west choose not to identify as Romans, as rightful descendants and perpetuators of the Roman name who could trace their ancestry back to such august figures as Aeneas and Romulus? This question becomes all the more necessary when one considers that, under similar circumstances, a Chinese empire thousands of miles away did reestablish itself in the late sixth century under the Sui 隨 and Tang 唐 dynasties. After nearly three hundred years of division, the empire was restored and the barbarians who had entered China eventually abandoned their respective barbarian identities for a "Chinese" one. Comparative historians are therefore presented with a similar set of circumstances that led to radically different outcomes. Western scholars, following in the footsteps of Edward Gibbon, have long been vexed by this question of how and why the Roman Empire, at least its western half, ultimately dissolved. Why did a great ecumenical empire that was, and still is, recognized as the source of so many fundamental ideas and institutions valued by modern western nations ultimately fail?

Chinese scholars, however, have not been faced with such a problem, for under the restoration of "Chinese" rule under the Sui, the inevitability and inexorability of a unified Chinese empire was established beyond doubt. Though China would again be invaded, divided, and even conquered, the largely uncontested assumption has remained, at least up to the twentieth century, that the natural state of the geographical space identified today as "China" should be of a unified political and cultural entity. Modern Chinese scholars have also addressed the question with the confidence imparted by Marxist teleological thinking: it is a law of history that peoples possessing a less advanced culture will imitate and be assimilated into a superior one.[1] While such a view of historical processes has little to recommend it, it is important to point out that its basic premises are not markedly different from those that have preoccupied western scholars for centuries; it is only in the European case, where the political civilization considered to be superior actually failed to be reconstituted and perpetuated, that one finds a problem of understanding events.

Faced with such a contrast in historical outcomes, the necessity of a comparative study is particularly clear. For in the Roman case, scholars have emphasized, at times excessively, the complete reliance of the Germanic peoples of the Roman west on Roman cultural and political institutions, arguing that these foreign peoples imitated Roman forms and practices and looked to the Roman legacy and tradition for their own political legitimation in virtually all respects. Yet the Roman west remained fractured into single entities that, crucially, forewent an identification with the legal construct of the Roman *res publica* in favor of identities that were defined in genealogical terms – people who had once been "Romans" eventually became "Franks," "Goths," "Lombards," etc. There was thus a reversal, or rejection, of the dual identity articulated in Cicero's notion of two *patriae*, a framework within which local or ethnic categories persisted as constituent components of a legally defined Roman community. Eventually, the new kingdoms of Europe would be defined by the ethnonyms of their respective ruling elites.

The case is very different in China. While the invaders and conquerors did adopt many features of Chinese culture, political and otherwise, they nevertheless exhibited a comparatively staunch adherence to barbarian identities in many cases – a fact often passed over by modern Chinese historians. While it is common for scholars to praise the Särbi-Xianbei 鮮卑 Northern Wei 北魏 emperor Tuoba Hong 拓跋宏 for his wisdom and providence in promulgating edicts that banned his own people's language, dress, and naming practices in favor of their Chinese equivalents, it is much less often noted that these measures resulted in political instability and tensions between tribal elites and a Sinified aristocracy that would ultimately tear the dynasty apart. The praises lavished upon Tuoba Hong

---

[1] For a typical example of this view in Chinese scholarship, see Cheng, *Tuoba Hong pingzhuan*, 250–79. Like others, Cheng praises the reforming emperor of the Northern Wei dynasty, who sought to compel his people to abandon their own language, clothing style, and traditions in order to replace them with a Chinese model. These "positive reforms," *jiji gaige* 积极改革, allowed him to "comprehensively break out of the intellectual level of all ethnic minority rulers of earlier ages": 多方面突破了前代各少数民族统治者所具有的思想水平. Ibid., 279.

by modern Chinese scholars would easily give the impression that his reforms of the 490s were one step prior to the reunification of China under the Sui.[2] Yet in the intervening near one hundred years, the Northern Wei was replaced by Särbi-Xianbei dynasties in the north, regimes whose elites continued to identify with their non-Chinese origins. Ethnic distinction and tension between Särbi-Xianbei and Chinese continued under the Northern Qi 北齊, and the Northern Zhou's 北周 founder reversed the Northern Wei edict requiring Särbi-Xianbei to abandon their traditional clan names in favor of Chinese equivalents; even Chinese subjects were awarded clan names in the Särbi-Xianbei language under the Northern Zhou.[3]

While this study has not entered into the debates over how the barbarians actually perceived themselves, it is interesting to observe that many scholars in either case continue to struggle with ideological burdens. In reaction to the Romantic and ethno-nationalistic scholarship of the pre–World War II era, some western scholars dismiss any suggestion that the various individual peoples identified as "Germanic" by modern philologists may have had any forms of political or cultural traditions that they themselves recognized as being distinct from those of the Romans.[4] It has been suggested that speakers of "dialects" that have been identified as Germanic were unaware of these similarities until the eighth or ninth century.[5] Accordingly, the "Germanic" peoples of Late Antiquity have lost the obviously fanciful

[2] The "obsession" with Sinification/Sinicization of the barbarians (see above, 272, n. 63) has led to some odd assertions. For example, Ho has noted while citing *Jin shu* fascicles 101–03 that he is surprised to find that "practically all of the leaders of various major non-Chinese ethnic groups of the early fourth century were not only well-versed in Chinese classics and history, but also took Chin Mi-ti [sc. Jin Midi 金日磾] as their model," citing *Jin shu* fascicle 101–03, *passim*. "In Defense of Sinicization," 131. Looking at the text cited by Ho, one may be surprised to find that Jin Midi is, *pace* Ho, never represented as such a model that non-Chinese were keen to emulate. The only context in which the name occurs in relation to a barbarian ruler is when, once each, the Xiongnu Liu Yuan and Liu Xuan are compared by someone else to Jin Midi.

[3] A thorough introduction in English to the Northern Qi and Northern Zhou dynasties is the dissertation of Lee, John, "Conquest, Division, Unification: A Social and Political History of Sixth-Century Northern China." Also see Dien, "The Bestowal of Surnames under the Western Wei-Northern Chou: A Case of Counter-Acculturation," 137–77.

[4] Representative studies of this vein of scholarship may be found in the volume *On Barbarian Identity: Critical Approaches to Ethnicity in the Early Middle Ages*, ed. Andrew Gillett.

[5] Goffart, *Barbarian Tides*, 5; Geary, *The Myth of Nations*, 75. I find it implausible that an Ostrogoth named Theoderic might not notice that a Frank could have the same name or that speakers of languages possessing such a large number of dithematic name elements in common (prefixes such as Theode-, Gund-, Sig-; suffixes such as –ric, –mund, -ulf, etc.) would be unaware of or wholly uninterested in this fact. That is of course not to say that such an awareness of shared aspects of culture would have determined political or other allegiances. But the suggestion that these peoples were the cultural blank slates that some modern scholars have made them out to be seems extreme. For a response to the arguments of Goffart and others, see Liebeschuetz, "The Debate about the Ethnogenesis of the Germanic Tribes," 341–55.

common consciousness ascribed to them by Romantic and ethno-nationalistic scholars of the nineteenth and early twentieth centuries, but these peoples are now no less remarkable for their absence of any sense of language or other form of culture that they may have recognized as distinct from the Romans and as the basis for an alternative identity.

By contrast, no one denies the valences of Xiongnu 匈奴 or Särbi-Xianbei political and cultural practices and symbolism, and it is clear from our sources that these expressions of non-Chinese identity could become points of contention under foreign regimes that sought to strike a balance between assuring the cooperation of Chinese literati on the one hand and not alienating native tribal elites on the other. Unlike many western scholars, Chinese scholars have been willing to accept that the peoples of the peripheries had their own notions of cultural and political life that were not simply emulations of Chinese models. Perhaps if crimes against humanity had been committed in the last century under an ideology that created and embraced a pan-Xiongnu or pan-Särbi consciousness, a ficti-tious ethnocultural essence inherited from antiquity analogous to that of the ancient "Germans," the case might be different. Yet the awkward fact remains that in the late or post-Roman case, it was the peoples without a meaningful ethnic, cultural, or political identity who ended up abandon-ing an identification with the political institutions of Rome and conferring their ethnonyms on what became the kingdoms of the early middle ages, names that persist today as names of regions and even nation states. In China, where the valence of such features of identity of barbarian peoples is taken for granted, the barbarians eventually disappeared. How does one account for such discrepancies? Hopefully, future studies of the degrees of acculturation and deculturation, as well as resistance to these processes, found among barbarian peoples as they entered and settled within the Roman and Chinese Empires in the early medieval period will contribute to our understanding of patterns of social change and transformation that occurred in either case.

Modern Chinese scholars, working within the prescribed parameters of the nationalistic propaganda of the Communist Party, have a different problem. A prominent trend in scholarship is to show that historical processes that operated during the Chinese equivalent to the "age of migrations" in the west illustrate a fundamental, and inexorable, pattern in Chinese history: foreign peoples will be drawn to superior Chinese civilization, be improved by it, and eventually shed their distinctive languages and cultural practices in order to become a part of the greater *Zhonghua minzu* 中華民族, the Chinese people. It is crucial to this narrative that the ultimately harmonious mixing of ethnicities that is said to have occurred in this period, the much talked-of *minzu ronghe* 民族融合 that marks the virtual disappearance of the Xiongnu, Särbi-Xianbei, and others from the historical record, be completed by the Tang. If this precedent is established, and uncontested, it makes clear that current Chinese control of peripheral regions such as Tibet and Xinjiang is a natural and necessary state of affairs whose justification is clear from the lessons of history. The Tang is, therefore, envisioned as a revitalized "Chinese people" that was characterized by its inclusiveness and cosmopolitanism.[6] More importantly, the territories inhabited by the disappeared "ethnic minorities" of China's past may be shown to have always been part of the motherland.[7] In both China and the west, it is clear that political realities and national mythologies have and continue to express themselves in historical scholarship.

The preceding chapter ended with the suggestion that modern scholarship on Roman Late Antiquity and Early Medieval China seems to have offered assessments of these periods that are both very much open to question. While such views may not be the majority, the later Roman Empire has been described as not only rife with anti-barbarian xenophobia but even, as some scholars would have it, possessing a worldview in which Romans and barbarians occupy wholly discrete and impermeable categories, irrespective of the fact that the latter could hold high military commands or political positions and that populations in frontier areas had been blending with outsiders for centuries. Chinese scholarship, on the other hand, has emphasized not only the breaking down of the barriers of China's own barbarian dichotomy in the historiography of the period but even, in some cases, its complete disappearance.

Both of these assessments are reasonable if one considers only certain aspects of the available historical evidence. In the Greco-Roman case, there

---

[6] While the Särbi Northern dynasties and the populations of other non-Chinese peoples are often hailed for their "contributions," *gongxian* 貢獻, the Tang itself, and the short-lived Sui that preceded it, are considered to be "Chinese" dynasties. This assumption can lead to curious claims, such as that of Ho, who has argued regarding the emperor Tang Taizong that "since his grandmother and mother were Hsien-pei [sc. Särbi], he was genetically 75 percent Hsien-pei, though legitimately Chinese." "In Defense of Sinicization," 131.

[7] Lin Gan has been quoted above in reference to the standoff between Han China and the Xiongnu Empire to the north as saying, "Within the national boundaries of a single country – China – the Han and Xiongnu ethnic groups respectively divided and defended their own territories in their original areas of habitation, and mutually refrained from transgressions": 在一个国家-中国-的国境内，汉匈两族彼此在原来生活的地区分疆自守，互不侵犯. *Xiongnu shi*, 46. The obvious understanding is that not only were the Xiongnu "Chinese," unbeknownst to themselves, but the lands they inhabited were, and therefore *are*, part of China.

is no shortage of ethnographic tropes and strategies of representing foreign peoples in Late Antiquity that exhibit not only a strong continuity with texts of earlier centuries but also a perpetuation of a binary schema that divides the world's human population into Greeks or Romans on the one hand and barbarians on the other. In the case of Procopius, the presence of this phenomenon has been considered at some length in Chapter 3. While several scholars have pointed out that the sixth-century Roman Empire had, in practice, seen the breakdown of any meaningful distinctions between Romans and barbarians along ethnic lines and that loyalty to the emperor was the defining characteristic of a "Roman" in this period,[8] the perpetuation of barbarian stereotypes and certain forms of ethnological thinking has, nevertheless, led others to conclude that the view of the barbarian in historiography had remained largely unchanged. After all, in Procopius' day, the Roman armies had been victorious: Vandal Africa and Ostrogothic Italy were a thing of the past, and Roman supremacy had been reasserted.

In China, there is no doubt that centuries of foreign rule in the north, the region that produced the unifying regimes of the Sui and the Tang, had seen a significant blurring of cultural or ethnic distinctions among the population.[9] It has therefore been argued that the worldview espoused by many of the literary elites of the period, and expressed in the historiography of the early Tang, likewise exhibits the famed inclusiveness and cosmopolitanism so often associated with the dynasty. Moreover, the royal family of the Tang itself was at least partly of non-Chinese ancestry, and the dynasty, at least in its earlier decades, traced its line of legitimacy through the Särbi-Xianbei Northern Zhou and Northern Wei.[10] It would

---

[8] Procopius himself laments that even the term *foederati*, which once referred only to barbarians in Roman service under treaty agreement with the empire, had lost any meaningful distinction and was applied to contingents irrespective of ethnic or political status (*Wars* 3.11.3–4).

[9] See, for example, Twitchett, "Introduction," 3–4; Hansen, "The Synthesis of the Tang Dynasty," 116; Elliot, "Hushuo: The Northern Other and the Naming of the Han Chinese," 180–81. The Sui founder himself had received the Särbi-Xianbei clan name Puliuru 普六茹 and, along with other members of his family and even of the Tang imperial house, shared the Central Asian practice of bearing a childhood nickname of non-Chinese origin. See Chen, Sanping, *Multicultural China in the Early Middle Ages*, 12.

[10] On the ethnic origins of the Tang royal family, see Chen, Sanping, "A-Gan Revisited: The Tuoba's Cultural and Political Heritage," 51–55; Chen Yinke (also written Yinque), *Chen Yinke xiansheng lunji*, 109 ff. Also see Hansen, "The Synthesis of the Tang Dynasty," 117. Tang-era debates on the dynasty's line of legitimate succession have been discussed in Chapter 5. Important to note is that even in the Tang period, the legitimacy of the preceding Northern Dynasties could be contested on ethnic grounds as evidenced by the statements of Tang scholars that "Northern Wei origins stem from mongrels who committed a theft and claimed to call themselves true lords" and that "the race of the Tabgach [Chinese *tuoba* 拓跋, the ruling clan of the Northern Wei] are actually Xiongnu." See above, 273.

seem natural to assume, then, that views on ethnic identity in the early Tang should have lost the exclusivity and rigidity often ascribed to the texts of the Han 漢 period.[11]

Yet the analysis of the two texts considered in this study indicates that both of these views require serious reconsideration in light of the conclusions reached in the preceding chapters. The *Wars* of Procopius, what has been called the "benchmark" historical work of the sixth-century Roman Empire, has been shown to exhibit a non-politicization of ethnic identity in its accounts of barbarian states. On the other hand, the *Jin shu*, an even more representative work for worldviews of the early Tang, shows a persistent interest in the delegitimization of barbarian states on ethnological grounds. The argument made by Heather that "individuals and groups were recategorised, or recatergorised themselves, for a variety of purposes" but "the actual categories, however, remained the same," in fact, applies much more accurately to the Chinese side of this comparison. While the Goths and Vandals of the *Wars* are represented as both legitimate rulers and barbarians simultaneously, the illegitimacy of the barbarian category is consistently and firmly reestablished in the *lun* colophons of the *Jin shu*.

Nor are the above features unique to these two texts. The Gothic history of Jordanes or *Getica*, a work contemporary with the *Wars* and also produced in Constantinople, presents a history of the Gothic peoples that extends back into a fictional antiquity, beginning with the Goths' emigration from the island of Scandza in the farthest northern regions. What Amory has deemed the "central paradox" of the *Getica* is "its praise for the Goths, even when they are in open revolt against the Empire, alongside its firm support for the central imperial system epitomized by the strong emperors Constantine, Theodosius, and Justinian."[12] The *Getica*, whose author claims to be a Goth himself, is a work dedicated to the history and political career of a people that is represented as an antagonist to the Roman Empire until the two "peoples'" happy unification is symbolized by the

---

[11] One of the most oft-cited pieces of evidence for this comes from a quotation from the emperor Taizong himself who is reported to have said, "Since ancient times, all have valued the Chinese and despised the Yi and Di; I alone love them both as one": 古皆貴中華，賤夷，狄，朕獨愛之如一 (*Zizhi tongjian* 198.6247). Unfortunately, this quotation does not date to his own reign, but is rather recorded in the *Zizhi tongjian* 資治通鑑, a text compiled some four hundred years later. It is also interesting to note, as Skaff has pointed out in consideration of the following quotation, that Taizong was not consistent in his views; he is also reported in the *Zizhi tongjian* to have said, "The Central Kingdom is like the roots and trunk; the Four Barbarians are like the branches and leaves ... had I not heeded Wei Zheng's advice, I might almost have been delivered over to the wolves and jackals!": 中國，根榦也；四夷，枝葉也 ... 朕不用魏徵言，幾致狼狽 (*Zizhi tongjian* 195.6148). Skaff, *Sui-Tang China and Its Turko-Mongol Neighbors*, 57–58.

[12] Amory, *People and Identity in Ostrogothic Italy*, 300–01.

actual marriage in 550 between Justinian's own cousin Germanus and the royal Gothic princess Matasuintha, granddaughter of Theoderic himself.[13]

If one accepts that the *Getica* represents a "Gothic" perspective, or at least one sympathetic to the Goths, we are also fortunate to have a history produced by Wei Shou 魏收 under the Särbi-Xianbei Northern Qi dynasty, which offers an account of the earliest origins of the Särbi-Xianbei people. The *Wei shu* 魏書 history of the Northern Wei dynasty, whose legitimate successor the Northern Qi claimed to be, begins by stating that the Yellow Emperor, the mythical progenitor of the Chinese people, had twenty-five sons, the youngest of whom lived in the northernmost regions where there was a certain "Xianbei" mountain from which the people took their name.[14] This origin myth ties the Särbi-Xianbei to one of the earliest figures in Chinese mythology, giving them an august pedigree that puts them on a par with the Chinese and distinguishes them from other barbarian peoples. The interesting contrast between the mythical origins of the Särbi-Xianbei people and those supplied for the Goths by Jordanes lies in the familiar element of ethnogenealogy. Both peoples had come from the far north, the direction from which many enemies of the empires had arisen over the centuries. Therefore, the Goths and Särbi-Xianbei are given origins in the extreme outer regions; in the case of the Särbi-Xianbei, the *Wei shu* explicitly states that while the Xiongnu and other northern barbarians had long plagued China over the centuries, the Särbi-Xianbei themselves had lived in even more distant lands and thus had not had contact with the Chinese.[15] Yet in these two histories that legitimize the Gothic and Särbi-Xianbei polities – some may argue that the *Getica* does not do this for the Goths, but the text certainly does not delegitimize Gothic rule on ethnological grounds – only the Särbi-Xianbei are incorporated into the larger Sinitic genealogical schema; the Goths are a people originally from outside the *oikoumenê*.

The purpose of mentioning these two other texts, the *Getica* of Jordanes and the *Wei shu* of Wei Shou, is to illustrate a principle that has been visible throughout the discussion of the two works that have been the focus of the preceding three chapters. While ethnic identity in general, and

---

[13] Cf. the ideological resistance of Chinese literati to the marrying off of imperial princesses to foreign potentates as observed by Skaff; however, practical expediency overrode such scruples in practice under the Sui and Tang. *Sui-Tang China and Its Turko-Mongol Neighbors*, 204.

[14] 昔黃帝有子二十五人，或內列諸華，或外分荒服，昌意少子，受封北土，國有大鮮卑山，因以為號 (*Wei shu* 1.1).

[15] 爰歷三代，以及秦漢，獯鬻，獫狁，山戎，匈奴之屬，累代殘暴，作害中州，而始均之裔，不交南夏 (*Wei shu* 1.1).

ethnogenealogy in particular, is minimally present in Procopius' representation of the Gothic and Vandal barbarian kingdoms, the *Jin shu* returns again and again to the barbarian origins of various states and the fact that a non-Chinese ethnogenealogy made political legitimacy to rule over China impossible. This correlation between ethnic identity, a primary component of which is a belief in shared kinship and descent, and political legitimacy is evidenced by the Särbi-Xianbei genealogy provided by Wei Shou, which virtually makes the Särbi-Xianbei Chinese, insofar as they are made a branch of the same genealogical line from which previous Chinese dynasties had claimed to descend. Nor was this fabrication of genealogies limited to royal houses. Luo has observed that lineages ultimately derived from the foreign peoples who had conquered and ruled northern China in the fourth to sixth centuries were, by the Sui and Tang periods, replaced by new family trees that tied families back either to the Han dynasty or even mythical times.[16] These new genealogies served to obscure barbarian origins, and Abramson has identified the "effacement of their non-Han ancestry and the abandonment or elision of practices and associations previously identified as barbarian" as a common phenomenon among Tang elites.[17]

Moreover, the *Wei shu*, when treating the Chinese dynasties ruling over southern China from the fourth to sixth centuries, refers to them as Dao Yi 島夷, "Island Barbarians," thus using the conventional barbarian designation Yi.[18] By use of such language, the *Wei shu* thus represents the Särbi of the northern dynasties as the true "Chinese," while the Chinese émigré dynasties of the south have become the barbarians, illegitimate by default. As Heather has argued in the case of Roman Late Antiquity, the categories, and the associations that went with them, stayed the same. Yet how different is the case of the barbarian states of the post-Roman west, even in texts written in Constantinople following the most powerful of those very states' destruction. As noted above, the assessments of ethnological thinking in Late Antiquity produced by some western scholars are actually far better suited to describe classical and early medieval Chinese ideologies than they are late Roman ones. A western barbarian equivalent to what we

---

[16] Luo, "Yiwang de jingzheng." For other examples during the Tang, see Yang, "Reinventing the Barbarian," 78–79.

[17] Abramson, *Ethnic Identity in Tang China*, 147.

[18] Li Peidong has argued that the *Wei shu* is also far more hostile toward other non-Chinese peoples than the *Jin shu*, that "the barbarians, i.e., the Tabgach Särbi-Xianbei, showing disdain for other barbarians, i.e., the Xiongnu, is far more extreme than anything witnessed in the Tang": 胡 (拓跋) 之賤胡 (匈奴)，竟大大超过唐朝. "*Jin shu* yanjiu xia," 88.

see happening in early medieval China would be if Theoderic changed his name to Theodorus, claimed descent from the fourth-century emperor Theodosius, and declared the Romans of the eastern empire to be barbarian usurpers. While the various barbarian kingdoms went to significant lengths in appropriating a wide range of Roman political and cultural practices, they did not find it necessary to disavow their barbarian ethnonyms or non-Roman names. While the short-lived son of Athaulf and Galla Placidia was in fact named Theodosius, Huneric gave his own scion of the Theodosian dynastic line the non-Roman name of Hilderic.

Perhaps the most salient illustration of this trend in China was in the choice of the early Tang emperors themselves to fabricate a genealogy that would link them not to their, at least partly, barbarian origins but to the Chinese Western Liang 西涼 dynasty of the fourth century and, ultimately, to a famous general of the Han dynasty, Li Guang 李廣.[19] While the barbarian kingdoms of the Roman west made no such efforts, at least not until the eighth century, even the Särbi-Xianbei Northern Qi had contrived to Sinicize its own ethnogenealogy for the sake of internal and perhaps external political consumption. The early Tang royal family's choice thus conforms with the view repeatedly expressed in the *Jin shu* that ethnogenealogy was a critical factor in the discourse of legitimacy. While the comparative approach to these ethnological traditions in general, and the *Wars* and the *Jin shu* in particular, has observed numerous points where similar strategies of rationalization and representation of foreign peoples were used, this point in particular is the one where the contrast stands out most markedly by virtue of the comparison. Barbarians could be stigmatized, feared, and even praised in both traditions; yet what they could not do in China is be represented in traditional historiography as legitimate political rulers. The stigma of a general barbarian identity as indicated by the markers of Yi 夷, Di 狄, Hu 胡, etc., or one of the specific ethnonyms of Xiongnu, Jie 羯, or Särbi-Xianbei, required that either the figure or people so identified be understood as illegitimate usurpers – unless of course a genealogy could be supplied that would construct a line of descent from exemplary Chinese of the historical or mythical past.

As discussed in Chapter 5, blood or marriage ties to an imperial dynasty, and the legitimacy they could confer, were clearly a factor in Roman politics. Roman emperors appointed as their heirs sons or relatives; otherwise a successor was adopted. Genealogy too was at times appealed to for legitimating purposes, as in the case of the Severans, who associated

[19] *Jin shu* 87.2257.

themselves with Marcus Aurelius and Commodus, or the fabricated genealogy linking Constantius I with Claudius Gothicus. Moreover, even ties through marriage to a royal dynasty were seen as legitimating factors: the emperors Marcian and Zeno both married either the sister or daughter of their predecessors. Marrying into the imperial family was desired by barbarians as well: the half-Vandal Stilicho married Serena, the niece and adopted daughter of Theodosius I; the Visigoth Athaulf married Galla Placidia, sister of Honorius; the Vandal Huneric married Eudocia, daughter of Valentinian III. While all of the above are ways in which "kinship" was a legitimating political factor, a Roman equivalent to Chinese practice would require the disavowel and suppression of any indicia of barbarian identity alongside some sort of genealogical claim linking an individual or dynasty to the Julio-Claudians.[20]

Yet the barbarians of the west did not deem it necessary to abandon their non-Latin names, surely a clear marker of, if not pride or prestige, then at least lack of stigma associated with them.[21] Also in the east one finds barbarian names borne by generals, consuls, and patricians over the course of as many as four or five generations of the same family, as in the case of the Ardaburii, whose naming practices give no indication of any political stigma attached to obviously foreign names such as Ardabur, Aspar, Hermineric, Godisthea, and Dagalaiphus. It is true that Aspar had the highest political hopes for his son Julius Patricius, whose Roman name stands in contrast to those of his brothers Hermineric and Ardabur; but there is no reason to assume that this choice of name at the boy's birth then determined the extent of his political career. This family intermarried with the imperial house, and one of its members, Areobindus, was even proclaimed emperor in a revolt against Anastasius in 512.[22] While Areobindus' candidacy was surely supported by his connection to the Theodosian line through his marriage to Anicia Juliana, the important point is that his well-known Gothic-Alan ancestry, not to mention his barbarian name, did not render him ineligible for the highest office of the state.

It has been argued that "The Confucian identity was open, inclusive, and universal, and unlike Western self-conceptions, supposedly not

---

[20] Indeed, Arnold has argued that the unapologetically foreign Amal genealogy of the Ostrogothic ruling family was itself actually a legitimating factor for the regime by virtue of its antiquity. *Theoderic and the Roman Imperial Restoration*, 174.

[21] On Germanic names in the empire, see Amory, *People and Identity in Ostrogothic Italy*, 86–91, 97–102. On the agnomen Flavius, see Ibid., 263.

[22] On the history of this family, see McEvoy's excellent study, "Becoming Roman?: The Not-So-Curious Case of Aspar and the Ardaburii," 483–511.

defined in terms of opposition to any 'Other'."[23] Indeed, the notion of inclusiveness of Chinese culture in a loosely defined "ancient time" is almost a truism in scholarship on early China.[24] It is of course the case that as the Chinese Zhou 周 community, and then the Qin 秦 and Han empires, expanded and took control of the territories of other peoples, many of the conquered assimilated and after generations became indistinguishable from other Chinese.[25] Yet what such talk of inclusiveness and universality leaves out is the fact that there was a strong current of xenophobia within Chinese historiography and political rhetoric that excluded, or recategorized as Others, those peoples who were identified under various contemporary or archaic ethnonyms indicating non-Chinese origins. While there was no single equivalent to the western term "barbarian," the Chinese civilizational identity was indeed constructed in opposition to an Other, who went by many names, which singly or in concert indicated an anthesis against which the Chinese community was defined. The usage of geographically correlated foreign ethnonyms in the first millennium BC, which was perpetuated by historians writing centuries later in reference to those "peoples'" imagined descendants, strongly argues against assertions that "the state of barbarity, in traditional Chinese conception, was not designated by race, religion, language, or national origin."[26] On the contrary, ethnicity and origin were of great significance in determining on which side of the internal/external divide an individual or people belonged. The ultimate result of this persistent division between Chinese and barbarians was the fabrication of ethnogenealogical links between mythical Chinese progenitors and would-be empire builders of foreign origin, such as the Särbi-Xianbei, or direct claims to Chinese lineages from the historical period in the case of the Tang.

The study of Procopius has shown, by contrast, that upon reaching a certain state of political prominence, the barbarian Vandals and Ostrogoths and their kings – not all of them, but even some of those who proved the most dogged enemies of the eastern empire – could be represented in not only a legitimate but even approving light by a

---

[23] Holcombe, "Re-imagining China: The Chinese Identity Crisis at the Start of the Southern Dynasties Period," 12–13.

[24] For other examples, see Poo, *Enemies of Civilization*, 124; Ling, "Borders of Our Minds: Territories, Boundaries, and Power in the Confucian Tradition," 88. Yang has suggested that such a notion was in fact not prominent until as late as the Qing dynasty (1644–1911). "Reinventing the Barbarian," xxvii.

[25] Holcombe, *The Genesis of East Asia*, 8–29.

[26] Hang Lin, "Political Reality and Cultural Superiority: Song China's Attitude toward the Khitan Liao," 388.

classicizing historian such as Procopius, who had served in imperial armies and wrote in the capital of Constantinople. While xenophobia and hostility toward barbarians are easy to find in the literature of Late Antiquity, and indeed they are hardly absent in Procopius, it is, nevertheless, remarkable that barbarian identities seem to have precluded neither sympathetic treatment by the historian nor even a significant degree of political recognition. Having entered the contest for political legitimacy in the Roman world, it is as if some barbarian peoples had become, if not Romans, recognized members of a greater political community.

It may well be objected that this study does not discuss a major facet of the two societies under consideration in this time period: the increasingly well-established faiths of Buddhism and Christianity. In the case of Buddhism, at least part of its appeal to a number of northern barbarian rulers was that it was a nonnative ideology, the patronage of which was especially useful for regimes of foreign origin, at times in direct opposition to the Confucian tradition.[27] The founder of the Later Zhao 後趙 state, Shi Le 石勒, associated himself with the miracle-working monk Fotudeng 佛圖澄 as part of his political program.[28] Tuoba Gui 拓跋珪, the founder of the Northern Wei dynasty, was "regarded as the personification of the Tathagata [sc. the Buddha]."[29] Lee has discussed not only the identification of barbarian rulers with the Tathagata but also the willingness of emperors to lecture on Buddhist texts and sponsor doctrinal debates.[30] Liu has argued that Buddhism was the only non-genealogical legitimating factor for barbarian states; otherwise, they had no option other than to appeal to either a Sinified barbarian ancestor or Chinese mythology.[31] The new faith, therefore, provided a rationalization for the exercise of political power by barbarians who themselves had their origins outside the empire.

A similar phenomenon has been discussed at great length regarding the impact of Christianity on ways of imagining community in the later Roman Empire. While a late-fourth–early-fifth century Christian writer

---

[27] Lewis, *China between Empires*, 205-07; Klein, "The Contributions of the Fourth Century Xianbei States," 123–24; Eberhard, *Conquerors and Rulers*, 127, 135; John Lee, "Conquest, Division, Unification," 16.

[28] Honey, "Sinification as Statecraft in Conquest Dynasties of China," 142–43. Indeed, Shi Le's successor Shi Hu 石虎 is said to have stated that not only were his own origins among the Rong barbarians of the frontier, but also that the Buddha was a god of the Rong: 朕出自邊戎 ... 佛是戎神 (*Jin shu* 95.2487–88).

[29] Klein, "The Contributions of the Fourth Century Xianbei States," 124.

[30] Lee, John, "Conquest, Division, Unification," 162–63. It is important to note that such imperial favor did not prevent the occasional persecution under the Northern dynasties. For a discussion of persecution of the Buddhist faith under the Northern Zhou, see ibid., 161–66.

[31] Liu Xueyao, *Wu Hu shilun*, 26–27.

such as Prudentius could express virulently anti-barbarian sentiment, authors in the following decades in the fifth century exhibited "the first signs of a synthesizing conception of that Roman-Germanic symbiosis under Christian auspices."[32] Considering works ranging from Salvian in the west to Procopius and Agathias in the east, Maas has argued that "in a Christian environment, barbarians could be seen as participants in a providential history that presumed the eventual salvation of humanity."[33] While noting that Augustine hardly had a favorable view of either barbarians or their Arian Christianity, Clark has suggested that "ethnicity did not matter in comparison with a citizenship that is not Roman but foreign, the *peregrina civitas* of the City of God."[34] The Christian historian Orosius represents the Gothic kings Alaric and Athaulf not as savage barbarians but as "Christian champions, reluctant to harm the Church and eager to do their part for the survival of Rome."[35] It has thus been argued that Christianity not only rendered earlier Roman–barbarian distinctions obsolete, but that it also provided a means of self-representation that allowed foreign conquerors to fashion themselves as defenders and sustainers of the Christian Roman order. More importantly for the purposes of this study, it must be noted that Christianity offered a new ideological framework for Romans of the east and west to include the barbarian world within a greater Christian community that was destined to extend beyond the frontiers of the empire and join all mankind in its embrace.[36]

That is not to say, however, that Christianity necessarily led to an abandonment of anti-barbarian and xenophobic thought in the Roman Empire. Kaldellis in particular has cautioned against overestimating the mitigating influence of Christianity on views of the barbarian Other; on the contrary, "it did not weaken the cultural chauvinism of the Romans, but rather gave it a new religious valence."[37] But more importantly, as has been pointed out by many scholars, there was already a strong basis for universal views of humanity in the pre-Christian tradition. A fourth-century AD example appears in an oration of the non-Christian orator

---

[32] Ladner, "On Roman Attitudes toward Barbarians in Late Antiquity," 23.

[33] Maas, "Barbarians: Problems and Approaches," 68. Also see Maas, "Ethnicity, Orthodoxy and Community in Salvian of Marseilles," 275–84; "'Delivered from Their Ancient Customs'," 152–88.

[34] Clark, "Augustine and the Merciful Barbarians," 42.

[35] Merrills, *History and Geography in Late Antiquity*, 43. Merrills notes that such a characterization omits the fact that the Goths were not orthodox. He elsewhere points to Orosius' conviction that even imperial weakness was a blessing in that it had allowed the barbarians to enter the greater Christian community and increase the numbers of the faithful. Ibid., 61.

[36] Garnsey and Humfress, *The Evolution of the Late Antique World*, 103–04.

[37] Kaldellis, *Ethnography after Antiquity*, 59. Also see Lechner, "Byzanz und die Barbaren," 300–01.

Themistius, where the subject is the peace concluded between the emperor Valens and the Gothic ruler Athanaric in 369:

καίτοι γε Ὅμηρος ὅταν αὐτὸς ὀνομάζῃ τὸν Δία πατέρα, οὐ τῶν Ἑλλήνων μὲν λέγει πατέρα, τοὺς βαρβάρους δὲ ἐξαιρεῖται, ἀλλ' ἁπλῶς φησι πατέρα θεῶν καὶ ἀνθρώπων. ὅστις οὖν καὶ τῶν ἐπὶ γῆς βασιλέων οὐ Ῥωμαίοις μόνον ὡς πατὴρ προσενήνεκται, ἀλλ' ἤδη καὶ Σκύθαις, οὖτός ἐστιν ὁ τοῦ Διὸς ζηλωτὴς καὶ οὖτος ὁ φιλάνθρωπος ἀτεχνῶς.[38]

When Homer himself names Zeus the "father," he does not say he is the father of the Greeks and omit the barbarians, but he simply refers to him as the "father of gods and men." Therefore, whoever of the kings of the earth has not only behaved as father of the Romans but also for the Scythians – this man is an emulator of Zeus and one who is completely humane.

Drawing on the earliest text of Greek literature, Themistius demonstrates what was at least a latent capacity for inclusion and ethnic relativism at the core of the Greco-Roman tradition.[39] While it is true that the adoption of Christianity by barbarian peoples would ultimately lead to the acceptance even of those beyond the former borders of the empire within an early, supranational Christendom, it is important to remember that universalist and inclusive views of humanity are already attested in the classical tradition, which continued to offer various ways of seeing virtue rather than vice in the Other.

Still, there is no doubt that Buddhism and Christianity allowed for a permeability of ideological barriers in this period that matched the breakdown in the physical frontiers of the empires. Moreover, rulers of barbarian origin had the option of styling themselves as patrons of the new faiths as part of their respective political programs, and such a strategy was surely a significant feature of some of their successes.[40] Yet this study has not sought to examine the introduction and impact of new modes of thought as a means of improving our understanding of continuity and change. Even if this were the goal, we would still be faced with the same problem: both Buddhism and Christianity broadened the range of factors that allowed inclusion in each society and offered new, alternative sources of political legitimation. But in the early Tang dynasty, pre-Buddhist

---

[38] *Oration* 10.132b. On this oration, see Vanderspoel, *Themistius and the Imperial Court*, 173–76.

[39] On the lack of Greek–barbarian distinction in Homer, see Edith Hall, *Inventing the Barbarian*, 21–47.

[40] See, for example, Daly, "Clovis: How Barbaric, How Pagan?," 619–64. Of course, other kingdoms used the Arian form of Christianity as a means of self-definition in opposition to the Nicene orthodoxy of the empire, the most marked example being that of the Vandals. See Conant, *Staying Roman*, 159–86.

classicizing ways of articulating identity and political orthodoxy redrew the
ideological frontiers of the empire, whereas the barbarians of the west ruled
as legitimate Christian kings over their domains. The purpose of this
study, then, has been to look for an explanation more deeply rooted in
the respective civilizational worldviews and hierarchies, i.e., by tracing the
later genealogies of ethnological thought as they appear in the works of
those who deliberately framed themselves as perpetuators of ancient literary, ethical, and political traditions. The fact that markedly different
conclusions as to Procopius' religious beliefs have been reached by modern
scholars is itself testament to his effort to work within the parameters of
pre-Christian imperial and ethnological worldviews. He wrote within a
literary and political tradition that asserted continuity with its imperial
past, not one seeking new and alternative modes of thought.

The contrast illustrated by this study raises the question of why this
should be the case: Why should a widely recognized classicizing and
conservative Roman historian of the sixth century have represented the
defeated enemies of Justinian in such a positive light? Even allowing for the
disillusionment he may have felt toward the Justinianic regime (a disillusionment expressed in virulent criticism in his *Anecdota*), how is it that
barbarians could be represented by a historian looking out from a victorious Constantinople as virtuous and legitimate figures? One might suggest
that the Roman victory over the Gothic and Vandal kingdoms allowed for
Procopius to be more generous in his representation of them. Yet the elites
of the Tang dynasty stood in a far more confident position: they were
rulers of a completely united empire that would soon turn to even greater
territorial conquests. The eastern Roman Empire, on the other hand, had
yet to recover other provinces in the west and was facing increasingly
immediate pressure from the north and the prospect of further, and
potentially disastrous, conflict with the east. By the 550s, the victories of
Justinian would have provided little confidence that imperial triumph over
the barbarians was assured in the years ahead.

One might also suggest that the distance of the barbarian kingdoms
from Constantinople attenuated anti-barbarian sentiment. But the Goths
and Vandals had conquered economically and symbolically critical parts of
the empire and claimed them as their own, a massive blow to Roman
imperial ideology. In contrast, the barbarian enemies in the *Jin shu* such as
the Xiongnu, Särbi-Xianbei, etc. of earlier centuries, peoples from whom
the Tang elites and imperial family were themselves largely and/or in part
descended, are judged with a hostility that clearly conflates foreign ethnic
identity with political illegitimacy and usurpation. We remain faced with

the counterintuitive fact that the possibility of barbarians becoming legitimate political figures is accepted in Procopius; in the *Jin shu*, barbarian rule is nothing more than a transgression, equivalent to tribal raiding and pillaging along the frontier believed to go back to even mythological times.

I propose two explanations, already touched on in the preceding chapters, which are rooted in the literary origins of the historiographical tradition within which Procopius wrote and in the political traditions of the empire. The first of these is the political nature of the Roman state itself. As Geary has characterized it, "Roman identity in the sense of *populus Romanus* was a constitutional one, ... based on a common cultural and intellectual tradition, a legal system, and a willingness to be part of a common economic and political tradition."[41] As a political entity, the Roman Empire did not simultaneously represent itself as an even mythically consanguineous community. The two Roman origin myths – the immigration of the Trojans into Italy and their fusion with the indigenous Latin peoples, and the story of Romulus and his asylum for runaway slaves and criminals – are both characterized by discontinuity, change, and the mingling of peoples. This narrative of dynamism and fluidity is recorded in the earliest extant historians of Rome, who chronicle or take for granted the incorporation of peoples who professed a variety of identities into the greater Roman state – Sabines, Latins, Volscians, Etruscans, Samnites, and many others – and who contributed to its growth from a city into an empire.

That the Roman community was conceived as an artificial and legal, rather than consanguineous and biological, community has its clearest expression from Cicero, whose notion of two *patriae*, two "fatherlands," is exemplified by Cato the elder who, "although he was born in Tusculum, was accepted as a citizen of the Roman people. And thus, as he was a Tusculan by birth, he was a Roman by citizenship; he had the one *patria* by virtue of place, the other by virtue of legal right."[42] As has been discussed by Farney at length, ethnic signifiers, or labels of identity based on ethnonyms, that had long since ceased to refer to politically or culturally distinct communities were still in use under the late Republic, and this practice continued under the empire. Nor was this simply a story the Romans told themselves. The Greek Aelius Aristides in the second century AD praised Rome for the fact that Roman citizens throughout the empire, legally joined to Rome though no less closely bound to their

---

[41] Geary, *The Myth of Nations*, 63.

[42] *cum est Tusculi natus, in populi Romani civitatem susceptus est. Ita cum ortu Tusculanus esset, civitate Romanus, habuit alteram loci patriam, alteram iuris* (*De Legibus* 2.5).

own kindred, τῶν ὁμοφύλων, continued to protect their own fatherlands, πατρίδας, on Rome's behalf.[43] It was this fundamental heterogeneity of what it meant to be "Roman" that allowed not only the "ever 'incomplete' identity of Roman Italy,"[44] but also the eventual extension of the franchise to all peoples living within the borders of the empire in the early third century AD. Yet even after the *Constitutio Antoniniana* in 212 granted citizenship to all free inhabitants of the empire, alternative identities persisted; it remained a convention in historiography to refer to Roman citizens of various parts of the empire as Gauls, Greeks, Syrians, Egyptians, Africans, etc. That there was space for such multiple, ethno-regional identities subsumed within the broader Roman category is also evidenced by the persistence of Celtic tribal names in the third and even fifth centuries.[45]

A clear example of this phenomenon appears in the case of the Galatians, a Celtic-speaking people who had invaded Anatolia from Europe in the earlier part of the third century BC and whose territory was annexed by the expanding Roman Empire some two hundred years later. The non-Christian orator Themistius in AD 383, only some four years after the catastrophic Gothic victory at Adrianople and following the ensuing years of violence in the Balkans, offered what turned out to be an overly optimistic assessment of Gothic assimilation into the Roman world. In a speech delivered in Constantiople, he points to the precedent of the Galatians as a people who had made the leap from *barbaria* to *Romanitas*:

καὶ νῦν οὐκέτι βαρβάρους Γαλάτας ἄν τις προσείποι, ἀλλὰ καὶ πάνυ Ῥωμαίους· τοὔνομα γὰρ αὐτοῖς τὸ πάλαι παραμεμένηκεν, ὁ βίος δὲ σύμφυλος ἤδη. καὶ εἰσφέρουσιν ἃς ἡμεῖς εἰσφοράς καὶ στρατεύονται ἃς ἡμεῖς στρατείας καὶ ἄρχοντας δέχονται ἐξ ἴσου τοῖς ἄλλοις καὶ νόμοις τοῖς αὐτοῖς ὑπακούουσιν. οὕτω καὶ Σκύθας ὀψόμεθα ὀλίγου χρόνου· νῦν μὲν γὰρ ἔτι τὰ προσκρούσματα αὐτῶν νέα, ληψόμεθα δ᾽ οὖν οὐκ εἰς μακρὰν ὁμοσπόν-δους, ὁμοτραπέζους, ὁμοῦ στρατευομένους, ὁμοῦ λειτουργοῦντας.[46]

---

[43] *Oration* 14.214–15.

[44] Farney, *Ethnic Identity and Aristocratic Competition in Republican Rome*, 232.

[45] Woolf has discussed the third-century orator Eumenius, who identified as a citizen of the Aedui, a people conquered by Rome centuries earlier but whose tribal name was still in use. *Becoming Roman: The Origins of Provincial Civilization in Gaul*, 1–4. On Gallic tribal names in the fifth century, see Geary, *The Myth of Nations*, 104–08. On regional identities in the later Roman Empire more generally, see Greatrex, "Procopius' Attitude towards Barbarians," 335–37, and the references provided there.

[46] *Oration* 16.211c–d. On the context for this oration, see Vanderspoel, *Themistius and the Imperial Court*, 205–08; Heather and Moncur, *Politics, Philosophy, and Empire in the Fourth Century*, 255–64.

And now one would no longer call the Galatians "barbarians," but would certainly call them Romans. For their ancient name has persisted, but their way of life is now the same as everyone else's. And they pay the taxes we pay, they fight in the same campaigns we do, they receive their governors on the basis of equality with others, and they submit to the same laws. We will see the same with the Scythians [sc. Goths] in a short time. For now, their offenses are still fresh; but before long we will receive them as allies and table companions, as those with whom we take the field and those with whom we perform our civic duties.

This passage indicates the conceptual possibility that individuals and communities, even if initially categorized as barbarians, were able to transcend that category through political allegiance to the empire alongside the adoption of Greco-Roman culture. An acknowledged fact of the Roman Empire was that barbarian enemies, after their defeat, had the capacity to adopt *humanitas*, a concept fusing Greek notions of *paideia* and *philanthropia*.[47] What is particularly noteworthy in the Roman case is that entering the civilized community did not require the negation of a previous ethnic identity. Though citizens of the empire, the Galatians retained an ethnonym linking them back to Celtic invaders of the third century BC. One does not need to turn to Christian ideology or the realities of Roman manpower needs to explain the observed *Ausgleich* between Romans and at least some of the barbarians in the *Wars*.[48] As noted in Chapter 5 in the discussion of political legitimacy, the Roman political system, in both east and west, was able to accept foreign peoples into its citizen body as well as to allow those professing provincial and sub-Roman identities to rule as heads of the state.

In the second case, we must also consider the strength of inherited literary traditions to condition the perception and representation of both the past and the present. Fornara has pointed out the "definitive" role of the Homeric tradition on the development of Greek historiography, claiming that "Homer's sympathies are dictated by the ordinary impulses of human nature and not by ethnic antipathy."[49] In describing the formation of Herodotus' methods of representing opposing sides of a conflict, Fornara goes on to argue that

[47] Woolf, *Becoming Roman: The Origins of Provincial Civilization in Gaul*, 54–55.
[48] Veh points to the latter factor to explain Procopius' use of "Roman" to designate Roman troops regardless of origin, and what he sees as Procopius' clear understanding that "Römer und Barbar kann also für des Reiches Beste Schulter an Schulter kämpfen." "Zur Geschichtsschreibung und Weltauffassung des Prokop von Caesarea," 24–25.
[49] Fornara, *The Nature of History in Ancient Greece and Rome*, 62.

> Herodotus assimilated from Homer the fundamental artistic (and histori-
> cal) rule that the participants on both sides of his great war must be
> sympathetically portrayed. Individuals were not necessarily good or bad
> because of the side they represented or because they were Greeks or
> barbarians. Even in a work intended for the winning side, there was no
> room for the caricature of an opponent simply because he was an opponent;
> rational or logical explanations – not the innate evil of one's antagonist –
> became necessary to account for major confrontations.[50]

In reading this assessment of Herodotus' methodology and the influence
exerted by Homer on Herodotus' pioneering work of history, it is remarkable how well this same characterization of the Herodotean historical
method remains visible in Procopius, whose representation of the enemies
of the Roman Empire is often articulated in sympathetic and even valorizing terms. Nor is such a strategy at all unique to Procopius, for it is
visible in other historians of the Greek classical age and is picked up by
Roman authors such as Caesar, Sallust, and Tacitus. He is thus not an
innovator by virtue of the fact that he does not "uniformly present
barbarians in typically classicizing terms."[51] While the preface to the *Wars*
has been cited as an example of the Greek/Roman–barbarian dichotomy,
one could just as well argue that Procopius, in allusion to the opening lines
of Herodotus' history written nearly one thousand years earlier, places the
Greeks/Romans and the barbarians on par with one another: together they
comprise the central actors of the work whose deeds will be recorded. The
barbarians are not a final appendage to the greater work, as is the case in
representations of barbarians in the Chinese historiographical tradition.
The fact that the Sui and Tang elites had grown out of conquest states
founded by these very peoples only underscores the strength of inherited
ethnographic paradigms and ethno-political categories in the latter case.
Seen in this light, Procopius does not represent a shift in ethnological
thinking brought on by new political realities that attended the crumbling
of Roman frontiers in Late Antiquity. On the contrary, he perpetuates
modes of conceiving and representing foreign peoples that are embedded
in the tradition within which he so carefully worked.

This book has argued for the power of classical texts and the ideologies
encoded within them to influence and shape the political and social
communities through which they were perpetuated. By all rights, the Tang
may well be expected to exhibit the very lack of interest in ethnic or non-
Chinese identities that so many modern scholars have wished to see in the

[50] Ibid.   [51] Sarantis, "Roman or Barbarian?" 233.

historiography of the period. Yet the influence of classical texts with their inherited categories of Chinese Self and barbarian Other continued to exert a significant force on conceptions of identity and legitimacy in the early Tang. In contrast, the beleaguered yet victorious empire of Justinian, whose historiography one might expect to exude the xenophobic and anti-barbarian hostility of earlier imperial panegyrics, nevertheless treats barbarian kings with equanimity and expresses little to no interest in their barbarian origins. Once some of the barbarians had made the leap from being tribal invaders to claimants of political rule over Roman provincials, these figures are no longer represented through the ethnographic lens, which remains in use for communities still beyond the borders or even fighting in the service of imperial armies. The fact that Procopius has been unanimously recognized as a self-consciously classicizing historian indicates that, while working firmly within the ideological parameters of earlier Greco-Roman historians, he was able to represent foreign political actors and even enemies as legitimate political figures whose ethnic backgrounds did not preclude their accession to power or delimit their claims to it. This observation thus has implications for our understanding of ethnological thought in earlier Greco-Roman texts as well. An argument that the ethnologically neutral representation of non-Roman rulers in the *Wars* should be read as a reflection of Procopius' individual disillusionment with the Justinianic regime, and thus a context-specific and rhetorical inversion of audience expectations, is based on the assumption of the absolute pervasiveness of a barbarian dichotomy, which this study argues has been overemphasized by modern scholars.

The fact that the populations of the western provinces of the Roman Empire were eventually willing to subscribe to the new identities of Frank, Visigoth, Lombard, etc., may now appear somewhat more explicable, at least in ideological terms. The objection may be raised as to how a close reading of an *eastern* Roman author sheds light on *western* Roman events, but such an objection assumes a significant divergence between west Roman and east Roman political and ethnological thought. Though their careers were spent in the service of the regimes of Roman Constantinople and Gothic Ravenna, Procopius and Cassiodorus shared the same intellectual and political tradition. Moreover, the provincials living under foreign conquerors doubtless had numerous incentives to make their peace with the new rulers' foreign origins; to analyze their rationalizations for the acceptance of barbarian rule would tell us less about the parameters of ethnological thought embedded in the classical tradition than it would about exigencies of preserving life and property in the face of newly settled

military elites. Far more instructive is to consider how an author free from
the pressures undoubtedly weighing upon western (post-)Roman elites
represented the new arrivals and the legitimacy of their political claims.
If barbarian ethnic identity was as delegitimizing a factor in late Roman
notions of political legitimacy as many scholars assume, it should certainly
be expected to appear in the writings of a popular Constantinopolitan
historian who narrated the wars of Roman reconquest. After all, despite the
centuries-long marginalization and Othering of Byzantium by modern
western scholarship (i.e., an entity that at an unspecified time ceased to
be the Roman Empire), the elites of both east and west in Late Antiquity
were alike heirs to the Greco-Roman political and literary tradition.

It is hypothesized here that former Roman provincials ruled over by
those barbarian kings, provincials whose political elites were fluent in the
same cultural and historical traditions that informed the worldviews of
Procopius, may have been able to look past the fact that their overlords
traced their lineage back to peoples who had come from either north of the
Danube or east of the Rhine – particularly once the barbarian kings had
proved willing to adopt many of the forms and conventions (titulary, legal,
iconographic, etc.) of Roman rule. Ethnic continuity with the Roman past,
and the genealogies through which such continuity might be articulated,
was simply not a central component of the political program in the post-
Roman west.

In China, the fact that the various ethnic groups who had conquered
imperial territory and set up their own polities would virtually vanish after
the political reunification under the Tang, along with any overt historical
representation of the perpetuation of northern cultural influence, demonstrates the great power that historiography can have in shaping political
realities and our perception of them. The Chinese political tradition
required an ethno-genealogical connection to Chinese of the mythical or
historical past, whereas ethnic identity was a weak, if not irrelevant,
component of Roman conceptions of political legitimacy. This comparative study, therefore, suggests that ideological conceptions of ethnic and
political identity help us understand the divergence in imperial trajectories,
which continues to shape political realities in our present day. Our
conventional understanding that "Rome" fell while "China" muddled
through is ultimately tied to as simple a question of whom those in power
chose to identify themselves with – or rather with whom the respective
political traditions did or did not require barbarian conquerors to identify.
Rome's *imperium sine fine* prophesied by Jupiter notwithstanding, Greeks
and Romans alike knew what Herodotus had known: "there are many

cities that were great in the past, but of these many have become small; those that were great in my time were formerly of little account."[52] Discontinuity, change, and a succession of empires characterized the Roman imagination of antiquity, an antiquity from which the Romans themselves had emerged on the civilizational periphery to become masters of the Mediterranean and beyond. In contrast, the Chinese historical imagination looked back to a single point in the mythical past and created an uninterrupted political genealogy to which each regime necessarily claimed its affinity. This contrast helps us understand how it could be that while in China the rhetoric of a barbarian Other as a figure antithetical to imperial civilization retained its strength through centuries of barbarian rule, the Greco-Roman historiographical tradition and even the inhabitants of Rome's western provinces may have been willing to accept – even if only from the safe vantage point of the reconquest – the political fact of a barbarian *basileus*.

---

[52] τὰ γὰρ τὸ πάλαι μεγάλα ἦν, τὰ πολλὰ αὐτῶν σμικρὰ γέγονε, τὰ δὲ ἐπ᾽ ἐμεῦ ἦν μεγάλα, πρότερον ἦν σμικρά (Hdt. 1.5.4).

Bibliography

Primary Sources

Aelius Aristides, AD 117–c. 181. *Aristides,* Vol. I. Edited by Wilhem Dindorf. Hildesheim: Olms, 1964.

Agathias, AD c. 532–c. 580. *Agathiae Myrinaei historiarum libri quinque.* Edited by Rudolf Keydell. Berlin: Walter De Gruyter, 1967.

Ammianus Marcellinus, AD c. 330–c. 395. *Ammiani Marcellini rerum gestarum libri qui supersunt.* Edited by Wolfgang Seyfarth. Stuttgart: Teubner, 1999.

Antiphon, fifth century BC. *Antiphon the Sophist: The Fragments.* Edited by Gerard J. Pendrick. Cambridge: Cambridge University Press, 2002.

Aristotle, 384–322 BC. *Aristotelis Politica.* Edited by William D. Ross. 1957. Oxford: Clarendon Press, 1988.

Arrian, AD c. 86–160. *Flavius Arrianus: Alexandri Anabasis.* Edited by A. G. Roos and Gerhard Wirth Teubner. Munich and Leipzig: Saur, 2002.

Aulus Gellius, AD c. 125–180. *Aulu-Gelle Les Nuits Attiques,* T. II. Edited by René Marache. Budé. Paris: Les Belles-Lettres, 1978.

Aurelius Victor, fourth century AD. *Sexti Aurelii Victoris liber de Caesaribus.* Edited by Franz Pichlmayr and Roland Gruendel. Leipzig: Teubner, 1970.

Ban Gu 班固, AD 32–92. *Han shu* 漢書. Edited by Zhonghua shuju bianjibu 中華書局編輯部. 1962. Beijing: Zhonghua shuju, 2002.

Caesar, 100–44 BC. *C. Iulii Caesaris comentarii rerum gestarum: bellum gallicum.* Edited by Wolfgang Hering. Leipzig: Teubner, 1987.

Cassiodorus, AD c. 490–585. *Cassiodori Senatoris variae.* Edited by Theodor Mommsen. Berlin: Weidmann, 1894.

Cassius Dio, AD c. 164–229. *Dio Cassius: Roman History, Books LXXI-LXXX.* Translated by Earnest Cary. Loeb Classical Library. 1927. Cambridge, MA: Harvard University Press, 2006.

Chen Shou 陳壽, AD 233–297. *Sanguo zhi* 三國志. Edited by Zhonghua shuju bianjibu 中華書局編輯部. 1982. Beijing: Zhonghua shuju, 2006.

Cicero, 106–43 BC. *M. Tulli Ciceronis de re publica, de legibus, Cato Maior de senectute, Laelius de amicitia.* Edited by Jonathan G. F. Powell. Oxford: Oxford University Press, 2006.

Claudian, AD c. 370–c. 404. *Claudii Claudiani Carmina.* Edited by John B. Hall. Leipzig: Teubner, 1985.

334

Confucius 孔丘, 557–479 BC. *Lunyu shizhu* 論語釋注. Edited by Yang Bojun 楊伯峻. Beijing: Zhonghuashuju, 2000.

Diodorus Siculus, first century BC. *Diodorus: Bibliotheca Historica.* Edited by Friedrich Vogel and Kurt T. Fischer. Stuttgart: Teubner, 1985.

Epitome de caesaribus. Sexti Aurelii Victoris liber de Caesaribus. Edited by Franz Pichlmayr and Roland Gruendel. Leipzig: Teubner, 1970.

Fan Ye 范曄, AD 398–445. *Hou Han shu* 後漢書. Edited by Zhonghua shuju bianjibu 中華書局編輯部. Beijing: Zhonghua shuju, 1973.

Fang Xuanling 房玄齡, AD 578–648. *Jin shu* 晉書. Edited by Zhonghua shuju bianjibu 中華書局編輯部. Beijing: Zhonghua shuju, 1974.

Guoyu 國語, c. fifth century BC. *Guoyu jijie* 國語集解. Edited by Xu Yuangao 徐元誥. Beijing: Zhonghua shuju, 2002.

Herodotus, c. 484–c. 425 BC. *Herodoti Historiae.* Edited by Nigel G. Wilson. Oxford: Oxford University Press, 2015.

Hippocrates, fifth century BC. *Hippocrate 2.2: Airs, Eaux, Lieux.* Edited by Jacques Jouanna. Budé. Paris: Les Belles-Lettres, 2003.

Homer, ninth–eighth century BC. *Homeri Ilias,* 2 Vols. Edited by Martin L. West. Leipzig: Teubner, 1998.

Homeri Odyssea. Edited by Peter von der Mühll. Stuttgart: Teubner, 1984.

Horace, 65–8 BC. *Q. Horati Flacci Opera.* Edited by Friedrich Klingner. Leipzig: Teubner, 1959.

Huainanzi, second century BC. *Huainanzi jishi* 淮南子集釋. Edited by He Ning 何寧. Beijing: Zhonghua shuju, 1998.

Isocrates, 436–338 BC. *Isocrates: Opera Omnia.* Edited by B. G. Mandilaras. Leipzig: Teubner, 2003.

Jordanes, sixth century AD. *Iordanis Romana et Getica: de origine actibusque Getarum.* Edited by Theodor Mommsen. Berlin: Weidmann, 1882.

Julian, AD 331–363. *L'Empereur Julien, Oeuvres Complètes, Tome II.ii.* Edited by Christian Lacombrade. Budé. Paris: Les Belles-Lettres, 1964.

Li Baiyao 李百藥, AD 565–648. *Bei Qi shu* 北齊書. Edited by Zhonghua shuju bianjibu 中華書局編輯部. 1972. Beijing: Zhonghua shuju, 1983.

Liji 禮記, c. fourth to fist century BC. *Shisanjing guzhu* 十三經古注, Vol. 5. Edited by Zhonghua shuju bianjibu中華書局編輯部. Beijing: Zhonghua shuju, 2014.

Livy, 59 BC–AD 17. *Titi Livi Ab urbe condita, Libri I–V.* Edited by Robert M. Ogilvie. Oxford: Oxford University Press, 1974.

T. Livius: Ab urbe condita, Libri XXIII–XXV. Edited by Thomas A. Dorey. Leipzig: Teubner, 1976.

T. Livius: Ab urbe condita, Libri XXVIII–XXX. Edited by Patrick G. Walsh. Leipzig: Teubner, 1986.

Lucian, AD c. 120–c. 180. *Luciani Opera,* Vol. II. Edited by M.D. Macleod. Oxford: Clarendon Press, 1974.

Lüshi Chunqiu, c. third century BC. *Lüshi Chunqiu jishi* 呂氏春秋集釋. Edited by Xu Weiyu 許維遹. Beijing: Zhonghuashuju, 2009.

Manilius, first century AD. *M. Manilii Astrnomica.* Edited by George P. Goold. Leipzig: Teubner, 1998.

Marcellinus Comes, AD c. 480–c. 540. *The Chronicle of Marcellinus: A Translation and Commentary (with a reproduction of Mommsen's edition of the text).* Edited and Translated by Brian Croke. Sydney: Australian Association for Byzantine Studies, 1995.

Mencius 孟子, 372–289 BC. *Mengzi yizhu* 孟子譯注. Edited by Yang Bojun 楊伯峻. Beijing: Zhonghuashuju, 2007.

Mozi 墨子, 468–376 BC. *Mozi jiangu* 墨子閒詁. Edited by Sun Yirang 孫詒讓 and Sun Qiqia 孫啟洽. Beijing: Zhonghua shuju, 2001.

Plato, c. 429–347 BC. *Platonis Opera*, Vol. I. Edited by E. A. Duke et al. Oxford: Oxford University Press, 1995.

   Platonis Respublica. Edited by Simon R. Slings. Oxford: Oxford University Press, 2003.

Pliny the Elder, AD 23–79. *C. Plinius Secundus: Naturalis historia.* Edited by Karl Mayhoff. Stuttgart: Teubner, 1967.

Polybius, c. 200–c. 118 BC. *Polybii Historiae.* Edited by Ludwig A. Dindorf and Theodor Büttner-Wobst. Stuttgart: Teubner, 1962-85.

Priscus, AD c. 401–c. 457. *Priscus Panita: Fragmenta et Excerpta.* Edited by Pia Carolla. Berlin: Walter de Gruyter, 2008.

Procopius, AD c. 500–c. 560. *Procopii Caesariensis Opera Omnia.* Edited by Jakob Haury and Gerhard Wirth. Leipzig: Teubner, 1964.

Ptolemy, second century AD. *Apotelesmatika.* Edited by Wolfgang Hübner. Stuttgart: Teubner, 1998.

Sallust, c. 86–35 BC. *C. Sallusti Crispi Catilina, Iugurtha, Historiarum fragmenta selecta, Appendix Sallustiana.* Edited by L. D. Reynolds. Oxford: Oxford University Press, 1991.

Seneca, c. 4 BC–AD 65. *L. Annaei Senecae Dialogorum Libri Duodecim.* Edited by L. D. Reynolds. Oxford: Clarendon Press, 1977.

Shangshu 尚書, c. sixth century BC. *Shisanjing guzhu* 十三經古注, Vol. 1. Edited by Zhonghua shuju bianjibu中華書局編輯部. Beijing: Zhonghua shuju, 2014.

Shen Yue 沈約, AD 441–513. *Song shu* 宋書. Edited by Zhonghua shuju bianjibu 中華書局編輯部. 1974. Beijing: Zhonghua shuju, 1996.

Shijing 詩經, c. 1000–600 BC. *Shijing zhuxi* 詩經注析. Edited by Cheng Junying 程俊英 and Jiang Jianyuan 蔣見元. Beijing: Zhonghua shuju chubanshe, 2008.

Sidonius Apollinaris, AD c. 430–c. 489. *Sidonius: Poems and Letters, Vols. I–II.* Edited and translated by W. B. Anderson. Loeb Classical Library. 1936. Cambridge, MA: Harvard University Press, 1980, 1984.

Sima Guang 司馬光, AD 1019–1086. *Zizhi tongjian erbai jiushisi juan* 資治通鑑二百九十四卷. Edited by Hu Sansheng 胡三省. Taipei: Minglun chubanshe, 1972.

Sima Qian 司馬遷, 145–c. 87 BC. *Shiji* 史記. Edited by Zhonghua shuju bianjibu 中華書局編輯部. 1982. Beijing: Zhonghua shuju, 2002.

Strabo, c. 64 BC–AD 24. *Strabonis Geographica*. Edited by August Meineke. Leipzig: Teubner, 1969.

Tacitus, AD c. 56–c. 120. *Cornelii Taciti Opera Minora*. Edited by Michael Winterbottom and Robert M. Ogilvie. Oxford: Oxford University Press, 1975.

    P. Cornelius Tacitus: Annales. Edited by Heinz Heubner. Stuttgart: Teubner, 1978.

    P. Cornelius Tacitus: Historiarum Libri. Edited by Heinz Heubner. Stuttgart: Teubner, 1978.

Themistius, AD c. 317–c. 389. *Themistii Orationes Quae Supersunt, Vol. I*. Edited by H. Schenkl. Leipzig: Teubner, 1965.

Virgil, 70–19 BC. *P. Vergilius Maro: Aeneis*. Edited by Gian B. Conte. Berlin: De Gruyter, 2005.

Wei Shou 魏收, AD 506–572. *Wei shu* 魏書. Edited by Zhonghua shuju bianjibu 中華書局編輯部. 1974. Beijing: Zhonghua shuju, 1997.

Xenophon, 430–c. 355 BC. *Xenophontis Expeditio Cyri: Anabasis*. Edited by Karl Hude and J. Peters. Leipzig: Teubner, 1972.

Xiao Zixian 蕭子顯, AD 489–537. *Nan Qi shu* 南齊書. Edited by Zhonghua shuju bianjibu 中華書局編輯部. 1972. Beijing: Zhonghua shuju, 1997.

Zhouli 周禮, c. third to second century BC. *Shisanjing guzhu* 十三經古注, Vol. 3. Edited by Zhonghua shuju bianjibu 中華書局編輯部. Beijing: Zhonghua shuju, 2014.

Zuozhuan 左轉, c. fifth to second century BC. *Chunqiu Zuozhuan zhu* 春秋左轉注. Edited by Yang bojun 楊伯峻. Beijing: Zhonghua shuju, 2008.

Secondary Sources

Abramson, Marc S. *Ethnic Identity in Tang China*. Philadelphia: University of Pennsylvania Press, 2008.

Adler, Eric. *Valorizing the Barbarians: Enemy Speeches in Roman Historiography*. Austin: University of Texas Press, 2011.

Adshead, Samuel. *T'ang China: The Rise of the East in World History*. New York: Palgrave Macmillan, 2004.

Alföldi, Andreas. *Studien zur Geschichte der Weltkrise des 3. Jahrhunderts nach Christus*. Darmstadt: Wissenschaftliche Buchgesellschaft, 1967.

Almagor, Eran. "Who Is a Barbarian? The Barbarians in the Ethnological and Cultural Taxonomies of Strabo." In *Strabo's Cultural Geography: The Making of a* Kolossourgia, edited by Daniela Dueck, Hugh Lindsay, and Sarah Pothecary, 42–55. Cambridge: Cambridge University Press, 2005.

Almagor, Eran, and Joseph Skinner, eds. *Ancient Ethnography: New Approaches*. New York: Bloomsbury, 2013.

Amitay, Ory. "Procopius of Caesarea and the Girgashite Diaspora." *Journal for the Study of the Pseudepigrapha* 20, No. 4 (2011): 257–76.

Amory, Patrick. *People and Identity in Ostrogothic Italy, 489–554*. Cambridge: Cambridge University Press, 1997.

Anastos, Milton V. "*Vox Populi Voluntas Dei* and the Election of the Byzantine Emperor." In *Christianity, Judaism and Other Greco-Roman Cults: Studies for Morton Smith at Sixty, Part 2*, edited by Jacob Neusner, 181–207. Leiden: Brill, 1975.

Ando, Clifford. *Imperial Ideology and Provincial Loyalty in the Roman Empire.* Berkeley: University of California Press, 2000.

Arnold, Jonathan J. *Theoderic and the Roman Imperial Restoration.* Cambridge: Cambridge University Press, 2014.

Bachrach, Bernard S. *A History of the Alans in the West: From Their First Appearance in the Sources of Classical Antiquity through the Early Middle Ages.* Minneapolis: University of Minnesota Press, 1973.

Barfield, Thomas J. *The Perilous Frontier: Nomadic Empires and China, 221 BC to AD 1757.* Cambridge, MA: Blackwell, 1989.

Basso, Franco, and Geoffrey Greatrex. "How to Interpret Procopius' Preface to the Wars." In *Procopius of Caesarea: Literary and Historical Interpretations*, edited by Christopher Lillington-Martin and Elodie Turquois, 59–72. London: Routledge, 2018.

Baxter, William H., and Laurent Sagart. *Old Chinese: A New Reconstruction.* Oxford: Oxford University Press, 2014.

Beecroft, Alexander. "Homer and the Shi Jing as Imperial Texts." In *Eurasian Empires in Antiquity and the Early Middle Ages: Contact and Exchange between the Greco-Roman World, Inner Asia and China*, edited by Hyun Jin Kim, Frederik J. Vervaet, and Selim F. Adali, 153–73. Cambridge: Cambridge University Press, 2017.

Bellen, Heinz. Metus Gallicus-Metus Punicus*: Zum Furchtmotiv in der römischen Republik*. Mainz: Akademie der Wissenschaften und der Literatur, 1985.

Benedicty, Robert. "Die Milieu-Theorie bei Prokop von Kaisareia." *Byzantinische Zeitschrift* 55 (1962): 1–10.

Bergeton, Uffe. "The Evolving Vocabulary of Otherness in Pre-Imperial China: From 'Belligerent Others' to 'Cultural Others.'" MA thesis, University of Southern California, 2006.

Bickerman, Elias J. "*Origines Gentium.*" *Classical Philology* 47, No. 2 (Apr. 1952): 65–81.

Bielenstein, Hans. "Wang Mang, the Restoration of the Han Dynasty, and Later Han." In *The Cambridge History of China, Vol. I: The Ch'in and Han Empires, 221 BC–AD 220*, edited by Denis Twitchett and Michael Loewe, 223–90. Cambridge: Cambridge University Press, 2006.

Birley, Anthony R. *Septimius Severus: The African Emperor.* Rev. ed. New Haven, CT: Yale University Press, 1988.

Blockley, R.C. *The Fragmentary Classicizing Historians of the Later Roman Empire: Eunapius, Olympiodorus, Priscus and Malchus.* Liverpool: Francis Cairns, 1981.

Bonfante, Larissa. "Classical and Barbarian." In *The Barbarians of Ancient Europe: Realities and Interactions*, edited by Larissa Bonfante, 1–36. Cambridge: Cambridge University Press, 2011.

Bonell, Victoria E. "The Uses of Theory, Concepts and Comparison in Historical Sociology." *Comparative Studies in Society and History* 22, No. 2 (Apr. 1980): 156–73.

Börm, Henning. *Prokop und die Perser: Untersuchungen zu den römisch-sasanidischen Kontakten in der ausgehenden Spätantike.* Stuttgart: Franz Steiner, 2007.

"Born to Be Emperor: The Principle of Succession and the Roman Monarchy." In *Contested Monarchy: Integrating the Roman Empire in the Fourth Century AD*, edited by Johannes Wienand, 239–64. Oxford: Oxford University Press, 2015.

Brindley, Erica. "Barbarians or Not? Ethnicity and Changing Conceptions of the Ancient Yue (Viet) Peoples." *Asia Major* 16, No. 1 (2003): 1–32.

Brodka, Dariusz. *Die Geschichtsphilosophie in der spätantiken Historiographie: Studien zu Prokopios von Kaisareia, Agathias von Myrina, und Theophylaktos Simokattes.* Frankfurt am Main: Peter Lang, 2004.

"Die Wanderung der Hunnen, Vandalen, West- und Ostgoten–Prokopios von Kaisereia und seine Quellen." *Millennium-Jahrbuch* 10 (2013): 13–37.

Browning, Robert. "Greeks and Others: From Antiquity to the Renaissance." In *Greeks and Barbarians*, edited by Thomas Harrison, 257–77. Edinburgh: Edinburgh University Press, 2002.

Brubaker, Rogers, and Frederick Cooper. "Beyond 'Identity'." *Theory and Society* 29 (2000): 1–47.

Burbank, Jane, and Frederick Cooper. *Empires in World History: Geographies of Power, Politics of Difference.* Princeton, NJ: Princeton University Press, 2010.

Bury, John B. *History of the Later Roman Empire from the Death of Theodosius I to the Death of Justinian, Vol. 1.* New York: Dover Publications, 1958.

Cai, Liang. *Witchcraft and the Rise of the First Confucian Empire.* Albany: State University of New York Press, 2014.

Cai, Zong-qi. *Configurations of Comparative Poetics: Three Perspectives on Western and Chinese Literary Criticism.* Honolulu: University of Hawai'i Press, 2002.

Cameron, Alan. "Theodosius the Great and the Regency of Stilico." *Harvard Studies in Classical Philology* 73 (1969): 247–80.

Cameron, Alan, and Jacqueline Long. *Barbarians and Politics at the Court of Arcadius.* Berkeley: University of California Press, 1993.

Cameron, Averil. *Procopius and the Sixth Century.* Berkeley: University of California Press, 1985.

"Writing about Procopius Then and Now." In *Procopius of Caesarea: Literary and Historical Interpretations*, edited by Christopher Lillington-Martin and Elodie Turquois, 13–25. London: Routledge, 2018.

Campbell, Gordon L. *Strange Creatures: Anthropology in Antiquity.* London: Duckworth, 2006.

Cao Meng 草萌. "*Jin shu* yanjiu shulüe" 晋书研究述略. *History Teaching* 历史教学 4 (1993): 55–56.

Carroll, Thomas D. *Account of the T'u-Yü-Hun in the History of the Chin Dynasty.* Berkeley: University of California Press, 1953.

Carson, Michael, and Michael Loewe. "Lü shih ch'un ch'iu." In *Early Chinese Texts: A Bibliographical Guide*, edited by Michael Loewe, 324–30. Berkeley: Society for the Study of Early China, 1993.

Cartledge, Paul. *The Greeks: A Portrait of Self and Others*. Oxford: Oxford University Press, 2002.

Cataudella, M. R. "Historiography in the East." In *Greek and Roman Historiography in Late Antiquity: Fourth to Sixth Century AD*, edited by Gabriele Marasco, 391–447. Leiden: Brill, 2003.

Cesa, Maria. "Etnografia e geografia nella visione storica di Procopio di Caesarea." *Studi classici e orientali* 32 (1982): 189–215.

Champion, Craige B. *Cultural Politics in Polybius' Histories*. Berkeley: University of California Press, 2004.

Chauvot, Alain. *Opinions romaines face aux barbares au IVe siècle apr. J.-C.* Paris: De Boccard, 1998.

Chen Qiyou 陳奇猷. *Lüshi chunqiu jiaoyi* 呂氏春秋校釋. Taibei: Huazheng, 1984.

Chen, Sanping. "A-Gan Revisited: The Tuoba's Cultural and Political Heritage." *Journal of Asian History* 30, No. 1 (1996): 46–78.

——— *Multicultural China in the Early Middle Ages*. Philadelphia: University of Pennsylvania Press, 2012.

Chen Yinke 陳寅恪. *Chen Yinke xiansheng lunji* 陳寅恪先生論集. Taibei: Zhonyang yanjiu yuan lishi yuyan yuanjiusuo, 1971.

——— *Wei Jin Nanbeichao shi jiangyan lu* 魏晋南北朝史讲演录. Hefei: Huangshan shushe, 1987.

Chen Yong 陈勇. *Hanzhao shilun gao: Xiongnu tuge jianguo de zhengzhi shi kaocha* 汉赵史论稿：匈奴屠各建国的政治史考察. Beijing: Shangwu yinshu guan, 2009.

Cheng Weirong 程维荣. *Tuoba Hong pingzhuan* 拓跋宏评传. Nanjing: Nanjing daxue chubanshe, 1998.

Chin, Tamara T. "Defamiliarizing the Foreigner: Sima Qian's Ethnography and Han-Xiongnu Marriage Diplomacy." *Harvard Journal of Asiatic Studies* 70, No. 2 (Dec. 2010): 311–54.

——— *Savage Exchange: Han Imperialism, Chinese Literary Style, and the Economic Imagination*. Cambridge, MA: Harvard University Asia Center, 2014.

Christensen, Arne Søby. *Cassiodorus, Jordanes, and the History of the Goths: Studies in a Migration Myth*. Copenhagen: Museum Tusculanum Press, 2002.

Chrysos, Evangelos K. "The Title Βασιλεύς in Early Byzantine International Relations." *Dumbarton Oaks Papers* 32 (1978): 29–75.

——— "Romans and Foreigners." In *Fifty Years of Prosopography: The Later Roman Empire, Byzantium, and Beyond*, edited by Averil Cameron, 119–36. Oxford: Oxford University Press, 2003.

Clark, Gillian. "Augustine and the Merciful Barbarians," In *Romans, Barbarians, and the Transformation of the Roman World: Cultural Interaction and the Creation of Identity in Late Antiquity*, edited by Ralph W. Mathisen and Danuta Shanzer, 33–42. Farnham: Ashgate, 2011.

Collins, John H. "Caesar as Political Propagandist." In *Aufstieg und Niedergang der römischen Welt: Geschichte und Kultur Roms im Spiegel der neueren Forschung*, edited by Hildegard Temporini, Wolfgang Haase, and Joseph Vogt, 922–66. Berlin: W. de Gruyter, 1972.

Conant, Jonathan. *Staying Roman: Conquest and Identity in Africa and the Mediterranean, 439–700*. Cambridge: Cambridge University Press, 2012.

Conterno, Maria. "Procopius and Non-Chalcedonian Christians: A Loud Silence?" In *Le monde de Procope / The World of Procopius*, edited by Geoffrey Greatrex and Sylvain Janniard, 95–111. Paris: Éditions de Boccard, 2018.

Cornell, Tim. *The Beginnings of Rome. Italy and Rome from the Bronze Age to the Punic Wars (c. 1000–264 BC)*. London: Routledge 1995.

Corradini, Piero. "The Barbarian States in North China." *Central Asiatic Journal* 50, No. 2 (2006): 163–232.

Creel, Herrlee G. *The Origins of Statecraft in China, Vol. One: The Western Chou Empire*. Chicago: University of Chicago Press, 1970.

Curta, Florin. *The Making of Slavs: History and Archaeology of the Lower Danube Region, c. 500–700*. Cambridge: Cambridge University Press, 2001.

Daly, William M. "Clovis: How Barbaric, How Pagan?" *Speculum* 69, No. 3 (Jul. 1994): 619–64.

Dauge, Yves A. *Le Barbare: Recherches sur la conception romaine de la barbarie et de la civilization*. Bruxelles: Latomus, 1981.

de Crespigny, Rafe. *Northern Frontier: The Policies and Strategy of the Later Han Empire*. Canberra: Faculty of Asian Studies, Australian National University, 1984.

Dench, Emma. *Romulus' Asylum: Roman Identities from the Age of Alexander to the Age of Hadrian*. Oxford: Oxford University Press, 2005.

"Ethnography and History." In *A Companion to Greek and Roman Historiography Vol. II*, edited by John Marincola, 493–503. Malden, MA: Blackwell, 2007.

Deng Lequn 邓乐群. "Shiliuguo huzu zhengquan de zhengtong yishi yu zhengtong zhi zheng" 十六国胡族政权的正统意识与正统之争. *Journal of Nantong Teachers College* 南通师范学院学报 (Social Sciences Edition 哲学社会科学版) 20, No. 4 (Nov. 2004): 84–87.

Dewing, Henry B., trans. *Procopius: History of the Wars*, edited by Jeffrey Henderson. 5 Vols. The Loeb Classical Library. Cambridge, MA: Harvard University Press, 1914.

Di Cosmo, Nicola. *Ancient China and Its Enemies: The Rise of Nomadic Power in East Asian History*. Cambridge: Cambridge University Press, 2002.

"The Northern Frontier in Pre-Imperial China." In *The Cambridge History of Ancient China: From the Origins of Civilization to 221 BC*, edited by Michael Loewe and Edward L. Shaughnessy, 885–966. Cambridge: Cambridge University Press, 2006.

"Ethnography of the Nomads and 'Barbarian' History in Han China." In *Intentional History: Spinning Time in Ancient Greece*, edited by Lin Foxhall, Hans-Joachim Gehrke, and Nino Luraghi, 299–325. Stuttgart: Franz Steiner Verlag, 2010.

Di Cosmo, Nicola, and Michael Maas, eds. *Empires and Exchanges in Eurasian Late Antiquity: Rome, China, Iran, and the Steppe, ca. 250–750.* Cambridge: Cambridge University Press, 2018.

Dien, Albert E. "The Bestowal of Surnames under the Western Wei-Northern Chou: A Case of Counter-Acculturation." *T'oung Pao*, Second Series, Vol. 63, Livr. 2/3 (1977): 137–77.

Six Dynasties Civilization. New Haven, CT: Yale University Press, 2007.

"Historiography of the Six Dynasties Period (220–581)." In *The Oxford History of Historical Writing Volume 1: Beginnings to AD 600*, edited by Andrew Feldherr and Grant Hardy, 509–34. Oxford: Oxford University Press, 2011.

"The Disputation at Pengcheng: Accounts from the *Wei shu* and the *Song shu*." In *Early Medieval China: A Sourcebook*, edited by Wendy Swartz, Robert Ford Campany, Yang Lu, and Jessey J. C. Choo, 32–59. New York: Columbia University Press, 2014.

Dihle, Albrecht. "Zur hellenistischen Ethnographie." *Entretiens sur l'Antiquité classique* 8 (1962): 207–39.

Dikötter, Frank. *The Discourse of Race in Modern China.* London: C. Hurst and Co., 1992.

Diller, Hans. "Die Hellenen-Barbaren-Antithese im Zeitalter der Perserkriege." *Entretiens sur l'Antiquite classique* 8 (1962): 39–68.

Dougherty, Carol. *The Raft of Odysseus: The Ethnographic Imagination of Homer's Odyssey.* Oxford: Oxford University Press, 2001.

Drijvers, Jan Willem. "A Roman Image of the 'Barbarian' Sasanians." In *Romans, Barbarians, and the Transformation of the Roman World: Cultural Interaction and the Creation of Identity in Late Antiquity*, edited by Ralph W. Mathisen and Danuta Shanzer, 67–76. Farnham: Ashgate, 2011.

Drompp, Michael R. "The Hsiung-nu Topos in the T'ang Response to the Collapse of the Uighur Steppe Empire." *Central and Inner Asian Studies* 1 (1987): 1–46.

Dué, Casey. "Tragic History and Barbarian Speech in Sallust's 'Jugurtha'." *Harvard Studies in Classical Philology* 100 (2000): 311–25.

Durrant, Stephen W. "The Literary Features of Historical Writing." In *The Columbia History of Chinese Literature*, edited by Victor H. Mair, 493–510. New York: Columbia University Press, 2001.

"The Han Histories." In *The Oxford History of Historical Writing, Vol. I: Beginnings to AD 600*, edited by Andrew Feldherr and Grant Hardy, 485–508. Oxford: Oxford University Press, 2011.

Eberhard, Wolfram. *Conquerors and Rulers: Social Forces in Medieval China.* Leiden: Brill, 1965.

China's Minorities: Yesterday and Today. Belmont, CA: Wadsworth, 1982.

Eck, Werner. *The Age of Augustus.* Translated by Deborah Lucas Schneider. Malden, MA: Blackwell, 2003.

Egan, Ronald C. "Narratives in *Tso Chuan*." *Harvard Journal of Asiatic Studies* 37, No. 2 (Dec. 1977): 323–52.

Elliot, Mark. "Hushuo: The Northern Other and the Naming of the Han Chinese." In *Critical Han Studies: The History, Representation, and Identity of China's Majority*, edited by Thomas S. Mullaney et al., 173–90. Berkeley: University of California Press, 2012.

Elton, Hugh. "The Nature of the Sixth-Century Isaurians." In *Ethnicity and Culture in Late Antiquity*, edited by Stephen Mitchell and Geoffrey Greatrex, 293–307. London: Duckworth, 2000.

Errington, R. Malcolm. *Roman Imperial Policy: From Julian to Theodosius*. Chapel Hill: University of North Carolina Press, 2006.

Evans, J. A. S., "The Attitudes of the Secular Historians of the Age of Justinian towards the Classical Past." *Traditio* 32 (1976): 353–58.

Falkenhausen, Lothar von. *Chinese Society in the Age of Confucius (1000–250 BC): The Archaeological Evidence*. Los Angeles: Cotsen Institute of Archaeology, University of California, 2006.

Farney, Gary D. *Ethnic Identity and Aristocratic Competition in Republican Rome*. Cambridge: Cambridge University Press, 2007.

Flaig, Egon. *Ritualisierte Politik: Zeichen, Gesten und Herrschaft im Alten Rom*. Göttingen: Vandenhoeck and Ruprecht, 2003.

Fornara, Charles William. *The Nature of History in Ancient Greece and Rome*. Berkeley: University of California Press, 1983.

Fracasso, Riccardo. *"Shan hai ching."* In *Early Chinese Texts: A Bibliographical Guide*, edited by Michael Loewe, 357–67. Berkeley: Society for the Study of Early China, 1993.

Garnsey, Peter, and Caroline Humfress. *The Evolution of the Late Antique World*. Cambridge: Orchard Academic, 2001.

Geary, Patrick. *The Myth of Nations: The Medieval Origins of Europe*. Princeton, NJ: Princeton University Press, 2002.

Gehrke, Hans-Joachim."Gegenbild und Selbstbild: Das europäische Iran-Bild zwischen Griechen und Mullahs." In *Gegenwelten: zu den Kulturen Griechenlands und Roms in der Antike*, edited by Tonio Hölscher , 85–109. Leipzig: Saur, 2000.

Gill, Christopher. "The Character-Personality Distinction." In *Character and Individuality in Greek Literature*, edited by Christopher Pelling, 1–31. Oxford: Oxford University Press, 1990.

Gillett, Andrew. "The Birth of Ricimer." *Historia: Zeitschrift für Alte Geschichte* 44, No. 3 (1995): 380–84.

"Was Ethnicity Politicized in the Earliest Medieval Kingdoms?" In *On Barbarian Identity: Critical Approaches to Ethnicity in the Early Middle Ages*, edited by Andrew Gillett, 85–121. Turnhout: Brepols, 2002.

Gillett, Andrew, ed. *On Barbarian Identity: Critical Approaches to Ethnicity in the Early Middle Ages*. Turnhout: Brepols, 2002.

"The Mirror of Jordanes: Concepts of the Barbarian, Then and Now." In *A Companion to Late Antiquity*, edited by Philip Rousseau, 392–408. Malden, MA: Blackwell, 2009.

"Barbarians, *barbaroi*." In *The Encyclopedia of Ancient History Vol. V*, edited by Roger Bagnall, Kai Brodersen, Craige B. Champion, Andrew Erskine, and Sabine R Huebner, 1043–45. Malden, MA: Blackwell, 2013.

Gizewski, Christian. "Römische und alte chinesische Geschichte im Vergleich. Zur Möglichkeit eines gemeinsamen Altertumsbegriffs." *Klio* 76 (1994): 271–302.

Goffart, Walter. *Barbarian Tides: The Migration Age and the Later Roman Empire*. Philadelphia: University of Pennsylvania Press, 2006.

Goldin, Paul R. "The Thirteen Classics." In *The Columbia History of Chinese Literature*, edited by Victor H. Mair, 86–96. New York: Columbia University Press, 2001.

"Steppe Nomads as a Philosophical Problem in Classical China." In *Mapping Mongolia: Situating Mongolia in the World from Geologic Time to the Present*, edited by Paula L. W. Sabloff, 220–46. Philadelphia: University of Pennsylvania Press, 2011.

Goldstone, Jack A. *Revolution and Rebellion in the Early Modern World*. Berkeley: University of California Press, 1991.

Goltz, Andreas. *Barbar-König-Tyrann: Das Bild Theoderichs des Großen in der Überlieferung des 5. bis 9. Jahrhunderts*. Berlin: De Gruyter, 2008.

"Anspruch und Wirklichkeit–Überlegungen zu Prokops Darstellung ostgotischer Herrscher und Herrscherinnen." In *Le monde de Procope / The World of Procopius*, edited by Geoffrey Greatrex and Sylvain Janniard, 285–310. Paris: Éditions de Boccard, 2018.

Goold, George P. *Manilius*: Astronomica. Loeb. Cambridge, MA: Harvard University Press, 1997.

Graff, David A. *Medieval Chinese Warfare, 300–900*. London: Routledge, 2002.

Greatrex, Geoffrey. "Roman Identity in the Sixth Century." In *Ethnicity and Culture in Late Antiquity*, edited by Stephen Mitchell and Geoffrey Greatrex, 267–92. London: Duckworth, 2000.

"Perceptions of Procopius in Recent Scholarship." *Histos* 8 (2014): 76–121.

Greatrex, Geoffrey, and Sylvain Janniard, eds. *Le monde de Procope / The World of Procopius*. Paris: Éditions de Boccard, 2018.

"Procopius' Attitude towards Barbarians." In *Le monde de Procope / The World of Procopius*, edited by Geoffrey Greatrex and Sylvain Janniard, 327–54. Paris: Éditions de Boccard, 2018.

Griffin, M. T. "The Lyons Tablet and Tacitean Hindsight." *Classical Quarterly* 32, No. 2 (1982): 404–18.

Griffiths, Devin. "The Comparative Method and the History of the Modern Humanities." *History of Humanities* 2, No. 2 (Fall 2017): 473–505.

Gruen, Erich S. "The Expansion of the Empire under Augustus." In *The Cambridge Ancient History: The Augustan Empire, 43 BC–AD 69*, edited by Alan K. Bowman, Edward Champlin, and Andrew Lintott, 147–97. Cambridge: Cambridge University Press, 2006.

Rethinking the Other in Antiquity. Princeton, NJ: Princeton University Press, 2012.

Hall, David L., and Roger T. Ames. *Anticipating China: Thinking through the Narratives of Chinese and Western Culture.* Albany: State University of New York Press, 1995.

Hall, Edith. *Inventing the Barbarian: Greek Self-Definition through Tragedy.* Oxford: Clarendon Press, 1989.

Hall, Johnathan M. *Ethnic Identity in Greek Antiquity.* Cambridge: Cambridge University Press, 1997.

  Hellenicity: Between Ethnicity and Culture. Chicago: University of Chicago Press, 2002.

Halsall, Guy. "Funny Foreigners: Laughing with the Barbarians in Late Antiquity." In *Humour, History and Politics in Late Antiquity and the Early Middle Ages,* edited by Guy Halsall, 89–113. Cambridge: Cambridge University Press, 2002.

Han Jie 韩杰. "Bei Wei shiqi 'Shiliu guo shi' zhuanshu de shixue chengjiu" 北魏时期十六国史的史学成就. *Sixiang zhanxian* 思想战线 4 (1993): 76–79.

Hansen, Valerie. "The Synthesis of the Tang Dynasty: The Culmination of China's Contacts and Communication with Eurasia, 310–755." In *Empires and Exchanges in Eurasian Late Antiquity: Rome, China, Iran, and the Steppe, ca. 250-750,* edited by Nicola Di Cosmo and Michael Maas, 108–22. Cambridge: Cambridge University Press, 2018.

Hartog, Francois. *The Mirror of Herodotus: The Representation of the Other in the Writing of History.* Translated by Janet Lloyd. Berkeley: University of California Press, 1988.

Heather, Peter J. "The Barbarian in Late Antiquity." In *Constructing Identities in Late Antiquity,* edited by Richard Miles, 234–58. New York: Routledge, 1999.

Heather, Peter J., and David Moncur. *Politics, Philosophy, and Empire in the Fourth Century: Select Orations of Themistius.* Liverpool: Liverpool University Press, 2001.

  The Fall of the Roman Empire: A New History of Rome and the Barbarians. Oxford: Oxford University Press, 2006.

  "The Western Empire, 425–76." In *The Cambridge Ancient History: Late Antiquity: Empire and Successors, AD 425–600,* edited by Averil Cameron, Bryan Ward-Perkins, and Michael Whitby, 1–32. Cambridge: Cambridge University Press, 2007.

  "State, Lordship and Community in the West (*c.* AD 400–600)." In *The Cambridge Ancient History: Late Antiquity: Empire and Successors, AD 425–600,* edited by Averil Cameron, Bryan Ward-Perkins, and Michael Whitby, 437–68. Cambridge: Cambridge University Press, 2007.

  The Restoration of Rome: Barbarian Popes and Imperial Pretenders. Oxford: Oxford University Press, 2013.

Hen, Yitzhak. *Roman Barbarians: The Royal Court and Culture in the Early Medieval West.* Basingstoke: Palgrave Macmillan, 2007.

Hinsch, Bret. "Myth and the Construction of Foreign Ethnic Identity in Early and Medieval China." *Asian Ethnicity* 5, No. 1 (Feb. 2004): 81–103.

Hirsch, Steven W. *The Friendship of the Barbarians: Xenophon and the Persian Empire*. Hanover, NH: University Press of New England, 1985.

Ho, Ping-Ti. "In Defense of Sinicization: A Rebuttal of Evelyn Rawski's 'Reenvisioning the Qing'." *The Journal of Asian Studies* 57, No. 1 (Feb. 1998): 123–55.

Holcombe, Charles. *In the Shadow of the Han: Literati Thought and Society at the Beginning of the Southern Dynasties*. Honolulu: University of Hawaii Press, 1994.

"Re-imagining China: The Chinese Identity Crisis at the Start of the Southern Dynasties Period." *JAOS* 115, No. 1 (1995): 1–14.

The Genesis of East Asia: 221 BC–AD 907. Honolulu: University of Hawaii Press, 2001.

"The Xianbei in Chinese History." *Early Medieval China* 19 (2013): 1–38.

Holmgren, Jennifer. *Annals of Tai: Early T'o-pa History According to the First Chapter of the* Wei-shu. Canberra: Australian National University Press, 1982.

"The Northern Wei as a Conquest Dynasty." *Papers on Far Eastern History* 40 (1989): 1–50.

Honey, David B. "Sinification and Legitimation: Liu Yüan, Shi Le, and the Founding of Han and Chao." PhD diss., University of California, Berkeley, 1988.

"History and Historiography on the Sixteen States: Some T'ang Topoi on the Nomads." *Journal of Asian History* 24, No. 2 (1990): 161–217.

The Rise of the Medieval Hsiung-nu: The Biography of Liu Yüan. Bloomington, IN: Research Institute for Inner Asian Studies, 1990.

"Sinification as Statecraft in Conquest Dynasties of China: Two Early Medieval Case Studies." *Journal of Asian History* 30, No. 2 (1996): 115–51.

Honigmann, Ernst. *Die sieben Klimata und die πόλεις ἐπίσημοι: eine Untersuchung zur Geschichte der Geographie und Astrologie im Altertum und Mittelalter*. Heidelberg: Carl Winter, 1929.

Hsu, Cho-yun. "The Spring and Autumn Period." In *The Cambridge History of Ancient China: From the Origins of Civilization to 221 BC*, edited by Michael Loewe and Edward L. Shaughnessy, 545–86. Cambridge: Cambridge University Press, 2006.

Hu Shaohua 胡绍华. "Puren" 濮人. In *Zhongguo gudai minzu zhi* 中国古代民族志, edited by Wenshi zhishi bianjibu 文史知识编辑部. Beijing: Zhonghua shuju, 1993.

Hulsewé, A. F. P. *China in Central Asia: The Early Stage: 125 BC–AD 23*. Leiden: Brill, 1979.

Humphries, Mark. "Late Antiquity and World History: Challenging Conventional Narratives and Analyses." *Studies in Late Antiquity* 1, No. 1 (2017): 8–37.

Isaac, Benjamin. *The Invention of Racism in Classical Antiquity*. Princeton, NJ: Princeton University Press, 2004.

James, Edward. *Europe's Barbarians, AD 200–600*. Harlow, NY: Pearson Longman, 2009.

Jones, Arnold H. M. *The Later Roman Empire, 284–602: A Social Economic, and Administrative Survey*. Baltimore: Johns Hopkins University Press, 1986.

Jouanna, Jaques. *Hippocrates*. Translated by M. B. DeBevoise. Baltimore: Johns Hopkins University Press, 1999.

Kaldellis, Anthony. *Procopius of Caesarea: Tyranny, History, and Philosophy at the End of Antiquity*. Philadelphia: University of Pennsylvania Press, 2004.

Hellenism in Byzantium: The Transformations of Greek Identity and the Reception of the Classical Tradition. Cambridge: Cambridge University Press, 2007.

Ethnography after Antiquity: Foreign Lands and Peoples in Byzantine Literature. Philadelphia: University of Pennsylvania Press, 2013.

The Byzantine Republic: People and Power in New Rome. Cambridge, MA: Harvard University Press, 2015.

Kelly, Christopher. *Ruling the Later Roman Empire*. Cambridge, MA: Belknap, 2004.

Kennedy, Rebecca F., C. Sydnor Roy, and Max L. Goldman, eds. *Race and Ethnicity in the Classical World: An Anthology of Primary Sources in Translation*. Indianapolis: Hackett Publishing Company, 2013.

Kim, Hyun Jin. *Ethnicity and Foreigners in Ancient Greece and China*. London: Duckworth, 2009.

"The Invention of the 'Barbarian' in Late Sixth-Century BC Ionia." In *Ancient Ethnography, New Approaches*, edited by Eran Almagor and Joseph Skinner, 25–48. London: Bloomsbury, 2013.

Klein, Kenneth D. "The Contributions of the Fourth Century Xianbei States to the Reunification of the Chinese Empire." PhD diss., University of California, Los Angeles, 1980.

Knechtges, David R. "The Rhetoric of Imperial Addiction and Accession in a Third-Century Chinese Court: The Case of Cao Pi's Accession as Emperor of the Wei Dynasty." In *Rhetoric and the Discourses of Power in Court Culture: China, Europe, and Japan*, edited by David Knechtges and Eugene Vance, 3–35. Seattle: University of Washington Press, 2005.

Kolb, Frank. *Diocletian und die Erste Tetrarchie: Improvisation oder Experiment in der Organisation monarchischer Herrschaft?* Berlin: De Gruyter, 1987.

Konstan, David. "*To Hellēnikon Ethnos:* Ethnicity and the Construction of Ancient Greek Identity." In *Ancient Perceptions of Greek Ethnicity*, edited by Irad Malkin, 29–50. Cambridge, MA: Harvard University Press, 2001.

"Cosmopolitan Traditions." In *A Companion to Greek and Roman Political Thought*, edited by Ryan Balot, 473–84. Malden, MA: Wiley-Blackwell, 2009.

Kulikowski, Michael. *The Triumph of Empire: The Roman World from Hadrian to Constantine*. Cambridge, MA: Harvard University Press, 2016.

Kuriyama, Shigehisa. *The Expressiveness of the Body and the Divergence of Greek and Chinese Medicine*. New York: Zone Books, 1999.

Ladner, Gerhart B. "On Roman Attitudes toward Barbarians in Late Antiquity." *Viator* 7 (1976): 1–26.

Laird, Andrew. *Powers of Expression, Expressions of Power: Speech Presentation and Latin Literature*. Oxford: Oxford University Press, 1999.

Lampinen, Antti. "Migrating Motifs of Northern Barbarism." In *The Faces of the Other: Religious Rivalry and Ethnic Encounters in the Later Roman World*, edited by Maijastina Kahlos, 199–235. Turnhout: Brepols, 2011.

Leban, Carl. "The Accession of Sima Yan, AD 265: Legitimation by Ritual Replication." *Early Medieval China* 16 (2010): 1–50.

Lechner, Kilian. "Byzanz und die Barbaren." *Saeculum* 6 (Dec. 1955): 292–306.

Lee, A. Doug. "The Eastern Empire: Theodosius to Anastasius." In *The Cambridge Ancient History: Late Antiquity: Empire and Successors, AD 425–600*, edited by Averil Cameron, Bryan Ward-Perkins, and Michael Whitby, 33–62. Cambridge: Cambridge University Press, 2007.

Lee, John. "Conquest, Division, Unification: A Social and Political History of Sixth-Century Northern China." PhD diss., University of Toronto, 1985.

Levene, David S. *Livy on the Hannibalic War*. Oxford: Oxford University Press, 2010.

Lewis, Mark Edward. *Sanctioned Violence in Early China*. Albany: State University of New York Press, 1990.

——. *Writing and Authority in Early China*. Albany: State University of New York Press, 1999.

——. *China between Empires: The Northern and Southern Dynasties*. Cambridge, MA: Harvard University Press, 2009.

Li Peidong 李培栋. "Jin shu yanjiu xia" 晋书研究下. *Journal of Shanghai Teachers University* 上海师范大学学报 3 (1984): 85–91.

Liebeschuetz, Wolf. "The Debate about the Ethnogenesis of the Germanic Tribes." In *From Rome to Constantinople: Studies in Honour of Averil Cameron*, edited by Hagit Amirav and Bas ter Haar Romeny, 341–55. Leuven: Peeters, 2007.

Lillington-Martin, Christopher, and Elodie Turquois, eds. *Procopius of Caesarea: Literary and Historical Interpretations*. London: Routledge, 2018.

Lin Gan 林幹. *Xiongnu shi* 匈奴史. Hohhot: Neimenggu renmin chubanshe, 2007.

Lin, Hang. "Political Reality and Cultural Superiority: Song China's Attitude toward the Khitan Liao." *Acta Orientalia Academiae Scientiarum Hung.* 71, No. 4 (2018): 385–406.

Ling, L. H. M. "Borders of Our Minds: Territories, Boundaries, and Power in the Confucian Tradition." In *States, Nations, and Border: The Ethics of Making Boundaries*, edited by Allen Buchanan and Margaret Moore, 86–100. Cambridge: Cambridge University Press, 2003.

Liu Pujiang 劉浦江. "Nanbeichao de lishi yichan yu Sui Tang shidai de zhengtong lun" 南北朝的歷史遺產與隋唐時代的正統論. *Wenshi* 文史 2 (2013): 127–51.

Liu Xueyao 劉學銚. *Xiongnu shilun* 匈奴史論. Taibei: Nantian shuju, 1987.

——. *Wu Hu shilun* 五胡史論. Taibei: Nantian shuju, 2001.

Lloyd, Geoffrey E. R. *Methods and Problems in Greek Science*. Cambridge: Cambridge University Press, 1991.

The Ambitions of Curiosity: Understanding the World in Ancient Greece and China. Cambridge: Cambridge University Press, 2003.

Ancient Worlds, Modern Reflections: Philosophical Perspectives on Greek and Chinese Science and Culture. Oxford: Oxford University Press, 2004.

Lloyd, Geoffrey E. R., and Nathan Sivin. *The Way and the Word: Science and Medicine in Early China and Greece*. New Haven, CT: Yale University Press, 2002.

Lloyd, Geoffrey E. R., and J. Zhao. *Ancient Greece and China Compared*. Cambridge: Cambridge University Press, 2018.

Lo Cascio, Elio. "The Emperor and His Administration: The Age of the Severans." In *The Cambridge Ancient History: The Crisis of Empire, AD 193–337*, edited by Alan K. Bowman, Peter Garnsey, and Averil Cameron, 28–66. Cambridge: Cambridge University Press, 2007.

Loewe, Michael, ed. *Early Chinese Texts: A Bibliographical Guide*. Berkeley, CA: Society for the Study of Early China, 1993.

"The Concept of Sovereignty." In *The Cambridge History of China Vol. I: The Ch'in and Han Empires, 221 BC–AD 220*, edited by Denis Twitchett and Michael Loewe, 726–46. Cambridge: Cambridge University Press, 2006.

"The Heritage Left to the Empires." In *The Cambridge History of Ancient China: From the Origins of Civilization to 221 BC*, edited by Michael Loewe and Edward L. Shaughnessy, 967–1032. Cambridge: Cambridge University Press, 2006.

Long, Timothy. *Barbarians in Greek Comedy*. Carbondale and Edwardsville: Southern Illinois University Press, 1986.

Lu, Xing. *Rhetoric in Ancient China: Fifth to Third Century BCE: A Comparison with Classical Greek Rhetoric*. Columbia: University of South Carolina Press, 1998.

Lu Xun 卢勋, Xiao Zhixing 萧之兴, and Zhu Qiyuan 祝启源, eds. *Series of Chinese Ethnic History in Past Dynasties: The Ethnic History of Sui and Tang Dynasties* 中国历代民族史：隋唐民族史. Beijing: Social Sciences Academic Press, 2007.

Luhmann, Niklas. "Deconstruction as Second-Order Observing." *New Literary History* 24, No. 4 (Autumn, 1993): 763–82.

Luo Xin 罗新. *Zhonggu beizu minghao yanjiu* 中古北族名号研究 (*Studies on the Titulary of Medieval Inner Asian Peoples*). Beijing: Beijing University Press, 2009.

"Yiwang de jingzheng" 遗忘的竞争. *Dongfang zaobao-Shanghai shuping* 东方早报-上海书评. March 8, 2015.

Ma Changshou 马长寿. *Di yu Qiang* 氐与羌. Shanghai: Shanghai renmin chubanshe, 1984.

Ma Tiehao 马铁浩. "*Jin shu* zaiji de zhengtongguan ji qi chengyin" 晋书载记的正统观及其成因. *Shixue shi yanjiu* 史学史研究 128, No. 4 (2007): 21–27.

Maas, Michael. "Ethnicity, Orthodoxy and Community in Salvian of Marseilles." In *Fifth-Century Gaul: A Crisis of Identity?*, edited by John Drinkwater and Hugh Elton, 275–84. Cambridge: Cambridge University Press, 1992.

———. "'Delivered from Their Ancient Customs': Christianity and the Question of Cultural Change in Byzantine Ethnography." In *Conversion in Late Antiquity and the Early Middle Ages: Seeing and Believing*, edited by Kenneth Mills and Anthony Grafton, 152–88. Rochester, NY: University of Rochester Press, 2003.

———. "Roman Questions, Byzantine Answers: Contours of the Age of Justinian." In *The Cambridge Companion to the Age of Justinian*, edited by Michael Maas, 3–27. Cambridge: Cambridge University Press, 2005.

———. "Barbarians: Problems and Approaches." In *The Oxford Handbook of Late Antiquity*, edited by Scott F. Johnson, 60–91. Oxford: Oxford University Press, 2012.

———. "The Equality of Empires: Procopius on Adoption and Guardianship across Imperial Borders." In *Motions of Late Antiquity: Essays on Religion, Politics, and Society in Honour of Peter Brown*, edited by Jamie Kreiner and Helmut Reimitz, 175–85. Turnhout: Brepols, 2016.

Maenchen-Helfen, Otto. "Archaistic Names of the Hsiung-nu." *Central Asiatic Journal* 6, No. 4 (Dec. 1961): 249–61.

Mair, Victor H. Review of *Written and Unwritten: A New History of the Buddhist Caves at Yungang*, by James O. Caswell. *Harvard Journal of Asiatic Studies* 52, No. 1 (Jun. 1992): 345–61.

Malkin, Irad, ed. *Ancient Perceptions of Greek Ethnicity*. Cambridge, MA: Harvard University Press, 2001.

Marincola, John. "Genre, Convention, and Innovation in Greco-Roman Historiography." In *The Limits of Historiography: Genre and Narrative in Ancient Historical Texts*, edited by Christina S. Kraus, 281–324. Leiden: Brill, 1999.

———. "Speeches in Classical Historiography." In *A Companion to Greek and Roman Historiography*, edited by John Marincola, 118–32. Malden, MA: Blackwell, 2007.

———. "Historiography." In *A Companion to Ancient History*, edited by Andrew Erskine, 13–22. Malden, MA; Blackwell, 2009.

———. "Romans and/as Barbarians." In *The Barbarians of Ancient Europe: Realities and Interactions*, edited by Larissa Bonfante, 347–57. Cambridge: Cambridge University Press, 2011.

———. "Introduction: A Past without Historians." In *Greek Notions of the Past in the Archaic and Classical Eras: History without Historians*, edited by John Marincola, Lloyd Llewellyn-Jones, and Calum Maciver, 1–13. Edinburgh: Edinburgh University Press, 2012.

Martin, Thomas. *Herodotus and Sima Qian: The First Great Historians of Greece and China: A Brief History with Documents*. Boston: Bedford/St. Martins, 2010.

Mathisen, Ralph W. "*Peregrini, Barbari*, and *Cives Romani*: Concepts of Citizenship and the Legal Identity of Barbarians in the Later Roman Empire." *American Historical Review* 111, No. 4 (Oct. 2006): 1011–40.

McCormick, Michael. "Emperor and Court." In *The Cambridge Ancient History: Late Antiquity: Empire and Successors, AD 425–600,* edited by Averil Cameron, Bryan Ward-Perkins, and Michael Whitby, 135–63. Cambridge: Cambridge University Press, 2007.

McEvoy, Meaghan. "Rome and the Transformation of the Imperial Office in the Late Forth-Mid Fifth Centuries." *Papers of the British School at Rome* 78 (2010): 151–92.

"Becoming Roman?: The Not-So-Curious Case of Aspar and the Ardaburii." *Journal of Late Antiquity* 9, No. 2 (Fall 2016): 483–511.

Merrills, Andrew H. *History and Geography in Late Antiquity.* Cambridge: Cambridge University Press, 2005.

Mi Wenping 米文平. "Gaxian dong beiwei shike zhuwen kaoshi" 嘎仙洞北魏石刻祝文考释. In *Wei Jin Nanbeichao shi yanjiu* 魏晋南北朝史研究, edited by Zhonguo weijin nanbeichao shi xuehui, 352–64. Chengdu: Sichuan sheng shehui kexueyuan chubanshe, 1986.

Miller, Bryan K. "Xiongnu 'Kings' and the Political Order of the Steppe Empire." *Journal of the Economic and Social History of the Orient* 57 (2014): 1–43.

Mittag, Achim, and Fritz-Heiner Mutschler. "Epilogue." In *Conceiving the Empire: China and Rome Compared,* edited by Fritz-Heiner Mutschler and Achim Mittag, 421–47. Oxford: Oxford University Press, 2008.

Moore, Jessica L. M. "Constructing 'Roman' in the Sixth Century." In *Le monde de Procope / The World of Procopius,* edited by Geoffrey Greatrex and Sylvain Janniard, 115–40. Paris: Éditions de Boccard, 2018.

Moorhead, John. "Totila the Revolutionary." *Historia: Zeitschrift für Alte Geschichte* 49, No. 3 (2000): 382–86.

Morley, Craig. "Beyond the Digression: Ammianus Marcellinus on the Persians." *Journal of Ancient History and Archaeology* 3, No. 4 (2016): 10–25.

Morris, Ian, and Walter Scheidel. *The Dynamics of Ancient Empires: State Power from Assyria to Byzantium.* Oxford: Oxford Unviersity Press, 2009.

Munson, Rosaria V. *Black Doves Speak: Herodotus and the Languages of the Barbarians.* Cambridge, MA: Harvard University Press, 2005.

Murray, James. "Procopius and Boethius: Christian Philosophy in the *Persian Wars.*" In *Procopius of Caesarea: Literary and Historical Interpretations,* edited by Christopher Lillington-Martin and Elodie Turquois, 104–19. London: Routledge, 2018.

Mutschler, Fritz-Heiner. "Vergleichende Beobachtungen zur griechish-römischen und altchinesischen Geschichtschreibung." *Saeculum* 48 (1997): 213–53.

"Zu Sinnhorizont und Funktion griechischer, römischer und altchinesischer Geschichtschreibung." In *Sinn (in) der Antike: Orientierungssysteme, Leitbilder und Wertkonzepte im Altertum,* edited by Karl-Joachim Hölkeskamp, 33–54. Mainz: Von Zabern, 2003.

Mutschler, Fritz-Heiner, and Achim Mittag, "Preface." In *Conceiving the Empire: China and Rome Compared,* edited by Fritz-Heiner Mutschler and Achim Mittag, xiii–xx. Oxford: Oxford University Press, 2008.

"The Problem of 'Imperial Historiography' in Rome." In *Conceiving the Empire: China and Rome Compared*, edited by Fritz-Heiner Mutschler and Achim Mittag, 119–41. Oxford: Oxford University Press, 2008.

Müller, Klaus E. *Geschichte der antiken Ethnographie und ethnologischen Theoriebildung: Von den Anfängen bis auf die byzantinischen Historiographen, Teil I.* Wiesbaden: Franz Steiner Verlag, 1972.

Geschichte der antiken Ethnographie und ethnologischen Theoriebildung: Von den Anfängen bis auf die byzantinischen Historiographen, Teil II. Wiesbaden: Franz Steiner Verlag, 1980.

Ng, On-cho, and Q. Edward Wang. *Mirroring the Past: The Writing and Use of History in Imperial China.* Honolulu: University of Hawai'i Press, 2005.

Nienhauser, William H. Jr., trans. *The Grand Scribe's Records: Volume IX, The Memoirs of Han China, Part II.* Bloomington: Indiana University Press, 2010.

"Sima Qian and the *Shiji.*" In *The Oxford History of Historical Writing, Vol. I: Beginnings to AD 600*, edited by Andrew Feldherr and Grant Hardy, 463–84. Oxford: Oxford University Press, 2011.

Nippel, Wilfried. "The Construction of the 'Other'." In *Greeks and Barbarians*, edited by Thomas Harrison, 278–310. Edinburgh: Edinburgh University Press, 2002.

Norena, Carlos F. *Imperial Ideals in the Roman West: Representation, Circulation, Power.* Cambridge: Cambridge University Press, 2011.

Nylan, Michael. "Classics without Canonization: Learning and Authority in Qin and Han." In *Early Chinese Religion, Part One: Shang through Han (1250 BC–220 AD)*, 2 Vols., edited by John Lagerwey and Marc Kalinowski, 721–76. Leiden: Brill, 2009.

O'Gorman, Ellen. "No Place Like Rome: Identity and Difference in the *Germania* of Tacitus." *Ramus* 21 (1992): 135–54.

Olberding, Garret P. S. *Dubious Facts: The Evidence of Early Chinese Historiography.* Albany: SUNY Press, 2012.

Oliver, James H. *The Ruling Power: A Study of the Roman Empire in the Second Century after Christ through the Roman Oration of Aelius Aristides.* Philadelphia: American Philosophical Society, 1953.

Pan, Yihong. *Son of Heaven and Heavenly Qaghan: Sui-Tang China and Its Neighbors.* Bellingham: Center for East Asian Studies, Western Washington University, 1997.

Parnell, David A. "Barbarians and Brothers-in-Arms: Byzantines on Barbarian Soldiers in the Sixth Century." *Byzantinische Zeitschrift* 108, No. 2 (2018): 809–25.

"Procopius on Romans, non-Romans, and Battle Casualties." In *Le monde de Procope / The World of Procopius*, edited by Geoffrey Greatrex and Sylvain Janniard, 249–62. Paris: Éditions de Boccard, 2018.

Pausch, Dennis, ed. *Stimmen der Geschichte: Funktionen von Reden in der antiken Historiographie.* Berlin: De Gruyter, 2010.

Pazdernik, Charles. "A Dangerous Liberty and a Servitude Free from Care: Political *Eleutheria* and *Douleia* in Procopius of Caesarea and Thucydides of Athens." PhD diss., Princeton University, 1997.

"Justinianic Ideology and the Power of the Past." In *The Cambridge Companion to the Age of Justinian*, edited by Michael Maas, 185–212. Cambridge: Cambridge University Press, 2005.

"Belisarius' Second Occupation of Rome and Pericles' Last Speech." In *Shifting Genres in Late Antiquity*, edited by Geoffrey Greatrex and Hugh Elton, 207–18. Farnham: Ashgate, 2015.

"Reinventing Theoderic in Procopius' *Gothic War*." In *Procopius of Caesarea: Literary and Historical Interpretations*, edited by Christopher Lillington-Martin and Elodie Turquois, 137–53. London and New York: Routledge, 2018.

Pendrick, Gerard J. *Antiphon the Sophist: The Fragments.* Cambridge: Cambridge University Press, 2002.

Pfeilschifter, Rene. *Der Kaiser und Konstantinopel: Kommunikation und Konfliktaustrag in einer spätantiken Metropole.* Berlin: De Gruyter, 2013.

Pines, Yuri. "Beasts or Humans: Pre-Imperial Origins of the 'Sino-Barbarian' Dichotomy." In *Mongols, Turks, and Others: Eurasian Nomads and the Sedentary World*, edited by Reuven Amitai and Michal Biran, 59–102. Boston: Brill, 2005.

The Everlasting Empire: The Political Culture of Ancient China and Its Imperial Legacy. Princeton, NJ: Princeton University Press, 2012.

Pohl, Walter. "Frontiers and Ethnic Identities: Some Final Considerations." In *Borders, Barriers, and Ethnogenesis: Frontiers in Late Antiquity and the Early Middle Ages*, edited by Florin Curta, 255–65. Turnhout: Brepols Publishers, 2005.

"Introduction – Strategies of Identification: A Methodological Profile." In *Strategies of Identification: Ethnicity and Religion in Medieval Europe*, edited by Walter Pohl and Gerda Heydemann, 1–64. Turnhout: Brepols Publishes, 2013.

Poo, Mu-chou. *Enemies of Civilization: Attitudes toward Foreigners in Ancient Mesopotamia, Egypt, and China.* Albany: State University of New York Press, 2005.

Poo, Mu-chou, H. A. Drake, and Lisa Raphals. *Old Society, New Belief: Religious Transformation of China and Rome, ca. 1st–6th Centuries.* Oxford: Oxford University Press, 2017.

Potter, David S. *The Roman Empire at Bay: AD 180–395.* New York: Routledge, 2004.

Prusek, Jaroslav. *Chinese History and Literature: Collection of Studies.* Dordrecht: D. Reidel Publishing Company, 1970.

Pulleyblank, E. G. "The Chinese and Their Neighbors in Prehistoric and Early Historic Times." In *The Origins of Chinese Civilization*, edited by David N. Keightly, 411–66. Berkeley and Los Angeles: University of California Press, 1983.

Purcell, Nicholas. "Rome and Italy." In *The Cambridge Ancient History Vol. XI: The High Empire, AD 70–192*, edited by Alan K. Bowman, Peter Garnsey, and Dominic Rathbone, 405–43. Cambridge: Cambridge University Press, 2007.

Qu Lindong 瞿林东. "Lun Wei Jin Sui Tang jian de shaoshu minzu shixue shang" 论魏晋隋唐间的少数民族史学 (上). *Heibei Academic Journal* 河北学刊 28, No. 3 (May 2008): 67–78.

Queen, Sarah A. *From Chronicle to Canon: The Hermeneutics of the* Spring and Autumn, *According to Tung Chung-shu*. Cambridge: Cambridge University Press, 1996.

Raaflaub, Kurt A., and Richard J. A. Talbert. *Geography and Ethnography: Perceptions of the World in Pre-modern Societies*. Malden, MA: Blackwell, 2010.

Raphals, Lisa A. *Knowing Words: Wisdom and Cunning in the Classical Tradition of China and Greece*. Ithaca, NY: Cornell University Press, 1992.

Rees, Roger. *Diocletian and the Tetrarchy*. Edinburgh: Edinburgh University Press, 2004.

Revanoglou, Aikaterine. *Γεωγραφικά και εθνογραφικά στοιχεία στο έργο του Προκοπίου Καισαρείας*. Thessaloniki: Κέντρο Βυζαντινών Ερευνών, 2005.

Riegel, Jeffrey K. "*Li chi*." In *Early Chinese Texts: A Bibliographical Guide*, edited by Michael Loewe, 293–97. Berkeley, CA: Society for the Study of Early China, 1993.

Riggsby, Andrew M. *Caesar in Gaul and Rome: War in Words*. Austin: University of Texas Press, 2006.

Rives, James B. *Tacitus Germania: Translated with Introduction and Commentary by J.B. Rives*. Oxford: Clarendon Press, 1999.

Rogers, Michael C. *The Chronicle of Fu-Chien: A Case of Exemplary History*. Chinese Dynastic History Translations 10. Berkeley: University of California Press, 1968.

Roller, Matthew. "The Exemplary Past in Roman Historiography and Culture." In *The Cambridge Companion to the Roman Historians*, edited by Andrew Feldherr, 214–30. Cambridge: Cambridge University Press, 2009.

Romm, James S. *Edges of the Earth in Ancient Thought: Geography, Explanation, and Fiction*. Princeton, NJ: Princeton University Press, 1992.

Rossabi, Morris. "Introduction." In *China among Equals: The Middle Kingdom and Its Neighbors, 10th–14th Centuries*, edited by Morris Rossabi, 1–13. Berkeley: University of California Press, 1983.

Saïd, Suzanne. "The Discourse of Identity in Greek Rhetoric from Isocrates to Aristides." In *Ancient Perceptions of Greek Ethnicity*, edited by Irad Malkin, 275–99. Cambridge, MA: Harvard University Press, 2001.

Sarantis, Alexander. "Roman or Barbarian?: Ethnic Identities and Political Loyalties in the Balkans According to Procopius." In *Procopius of Caesarea: Literary and Historical Interpretations*, edited by Christopher Lillington-Martin and Elodie Turquois, 217–37. London: Routledge, 2018.

"Procopius and the Different Types of Northern Barbarian." In *Le monde de Procope / The World of Procopius*, edited by Geoffrey Greatrex and Sylvain Janniard, 355–78. Paris: Éditions de Boccard, 2018.

Schaberg, David. "Travel, Geography, and the Imperial Imagination in Fifth-Century Athens and Han China." *Comparative Literature* 51, No. 2 (Spring 1999): 152–91.

A Patterned Past: Form and Thought in Early Chinese Historiography. Cambridge, MA: Harvard University Press, 2001.

"Chinese History and Philosophy." In *The Oxford History of Historical Writing, Vol. I: Beginnings to AD 600*, edited by Andrew Feldherr and Grant Hardy, 394–414. Oxford: Oxford University Press, 2011.

Scheidel, Walter, ed. *Rome and China: Comparative Perspectives on Ancient World Empires.* Oxford: Oxford University Press, 2009.

"From the 'Great Convergence' to the 'First Great Divergence': Rome and Qin-Han State Formation and Its Aftermath." In *Rome and China: Comparative Perspectives on Ancient World Empires*, edited by Walter Scheidel, 11–23. New York: Oxford University Press, 2009.

Schneider, Rolf Michael. "Image and Empire: the Shaping of Augustan Rome." In *Conceiving the Empire: China and Rome Compared*, edited by Fritz-Heiner Mutschler and Achim Mittag, 269–98. Oxford: Oxford University Press, 2008.

Schreiber, Gerhard. "History of the Former Yen Dynasty, Part I." *Monumenta Serica* 14 (1949–1955): 374–480.

"History of the Former Yen Dynasty, Part II." *Monumenta Serica* 15 (1956): 1–141.

Scullard, Howard H. "Carthage and Rome." In *The Cambridge Ancient History, Vol. VII, Part 2: The Rise of Rome to 220 BC*, edited by Frank Walbank, A. E. Astin, et al., 486–572. Cambridge: Cambridge University Press, 2006.

Seston, William. *Dioclétien et la tétrarchie.* Paris: E. de Boccard, 1946.

Skaff, Jonathan. *Sui-Tang China and Its Turko-Mongol Neighbors: Culture, Power, and Connections, 580–800.* Oxford: Oxford University Press, 2012.

Skinner, Joseph E. *The Invention of Greek Ethnography: From Homer to Herodotus.* Oxford: Oxford University Press, 2012.

Stein, Ernst. *Geschichte des spätrömischen Reiches von 284 bis 476 n. Chr.* Vienna: Seidel und Sohn, 1928.

Stuurman, Siep. "Herodotus and Sima Qian: History and the Anthropological Turn in Ancient Greece and Han China." *Journal of World History* 19, No. 1 (Mar. 2008): 1–40.

Suchman, Mark C. "Managing Legitimacy: Strategic and Institutional Approaches." *The Academy of Management Review* 20, No. 3 (July 1995): 571–610.

Tamvaki, Dionysia. "European Polity: Layers of Legitimacy." *International Social Science Journal* 60 (June 2009): 235–51.

Tanner, Jeremy. "Ancient Greece, Early China: Sino-Hellenic Studies and Comparative Approaches to the Classical World: A Review Article." *The Journal of Hellenic Studies*, 129 (2009): 89–109.

Taragna, Anna M. Logoi historias: *Discorsi e lettere nella prima storiografia retorica bizantina*. Alessandria: Edizioni dell'Orso, 2000.

Teng, S. Y. "Herodotus and Ssu-ma Ch'ien: Two Fathers of History." *East and West* 12, No. 4 (Dec. 1961): 233–40.

Thomas, Richard F. *Lands and Peoples in Roman Poetry: The Ethnographical Tradition*. Cambridge, MA: The Cambridge Philological Society, 1982.

Trüdinger, Karl. *Studien zur Geschichte der griechisch-römischen Ethnographie*. Basel: Emil Birkhäuser, 1918.

Twitchett, Denis. "Introduction." In *The Cambridge History of China Volume 3: Sui and T'ang China, 589–906, Part I*, edited by Denis Twitchett and John K. Fairbank, 1–47. Cambridge: Cambridge University Press, 1979.

Vanderspoel, John. *Themistius and the Imperial Court: Oratory, Civic Duty, and Paideia from Constantius to Theodosius*. Ann Arbor: University of Michigan Press, 1995.

Vankeerberghen, Griet. *The Huainanzi and Liu An's Claim to Moral Authority*. Albany: State University of New York Press, 2001.

Vasaly, Ann. "Characterization and Complexity: Caesar, Sallust, and Livy." In *The Cambridge Companion to Roman Historians*, edited by Andrew Feldherr, 245–60. Cambridge: Cambridge University Press, 2009.

Veh, Otto. "Zur Geschichtsschreibung und Weltauffassung des Prokop von Caesarea, Teil I." *Wissenschaftliche Beilage zum Jahresbericht 1950/51 des Gymnasiums Bayreuth*. Bayreuth: 1951.

Veyne, Paul. "*Humanitas*: Romans and Non-Romans." In *The Romans*, edited by Andrea Giardina, translated by Lydia G. Cochrane, 342–69. Chicago: University of Chicago Press, 1993.

Vlassopoulos, Kostas. *Greeks and Barbarians*. Cambridge: Cambridge University Press, 2013.

Von Rummel, Philipp. *Habitus barbarus: Kleidung und Repräsentation spätantiker Eliten im 4. und 5. Jahrhundert*. Berlin: De Gruyter, 2007.

Walbank, Frank W. "The Problem of Greek Nationality." In *Greeks and Barbarians*, edited by Thomas Harrison, 234–56. Edinburgh: Edinburgh University Press, 2002.

Wallace-Hadrill, Andrew. "*Civilis Princeps*: Between Citizen and King." *Journal of Roman Studies* 72 (1982): 32–48.

"*Mutatio morum*: The Idea of a Cultural Revolution." In *The Roman Cultural Revolution*, edited by Thomas Habinek and Alessandro Schiesaro, 3–22. Cambridge: Cambridge University Press, 1997.

Wang, Aihe. *Cosmology and Political Culture in Early China*. Cambridge: Cambridge University Press, 2000.

Wang, Ming-ke. "From the Qiang Barbarians to Qiang Nationality: The Making of a New Chinese Boundary." In *Imagining China: Regional Division and*

National Unity, edited by Shu-min Huang and Cheng-kuang Hsu, 43–80. Taipei: Institute of Ethnology, Academia Sinica, 1999.

Wang, Q. Edward. "History, Space, and Ethnicity: The Chinese Worldview." *Journal of World History* 10, No. 2 (Fall 1999): 285–305.

Wang Zhonghan 王钟翰. *Zhongguo minzu shi gaiyao* 中国民族史概要. Taiyuan: Shanxi jiaoyu chubanshe, 2006.

Wang Zhongluo 王仲荦. *Wei Jin Nanbeichao shi* 魏晋南北朝史. Shanghai: Renmin chubanshe, 2003.

Watson, Burton. "Some Remarks on Early Chinese Historical Works." In *The Translation of Things Past: Chinese History and Historiography*, edited by George Kao, 34–47. Hong Kong: The Chinese University Press, 1982.

Webster, Jane. "Ethnographic Barbarity: Colonial Discourse and Celtic 'Warrior Societies'." In *Roman Imperialism: Post-Colonial Perspectives*, Leicester Archaeology Monographs No. 3, edited by Jane Webster and Nicholas J. Cooper, 111–23. Leicester: School of Archaeological Studies, 1996.

Wechsler, Howard J. *Mirror to the Son of Heaven: Wei Cheng at the Court of T'ang T'ai-tsung*. New Haven, CT: Yale University Press, 1974.

Offerings of Jade and Silk: Ritual and Symbol in the Legitimation of the T'ang Dynasty. New Haven, CT: Yale University Press, 1985.

Wiedemann, Thomas E. J. "Between Men and Beasts: Barbarians in Ammianus Marcellinus." In *Past Perspectives: Studies in Greek and Roman Historical Writing*, edited by I. S. Moxon, J. D. Smart, and A. J. Woodman, 189–201. Cambridge: Cambridge University Press, 1986.

"Barbarian." In *The Oxford Classical Dictionary*, 4th ed., edited by Simon Hornblower, Antony Spawforth, and Esther Eidinow, 223. Oxford: Oxford University Press, 2012.

Wienand, Johannes, ed. *Contested Monarchy: Integrating the Roman Empire in the Fourth Century AD*. Oxford: Oxford University Press, 2015.

Wilkinson, Endymion. *Chinese History: A Manual, Revised and Enlarged*. Cambridge, MA: Harvard University Asia Center for the Harvard-Yenching Institute, 2000.

Wolfram, Herwig. *History of the Goths*. Translated by Thomas J. Dunlap. Berkeley: University of California Press, 1988.

Wood, Philip J. "Being Roman in Procopius' Vandal *Wars*." *Byzantion* 81 (2011): 424–47.

Woodman, Anthony J. *Rhetoric in Classical Historiography: Four Studies*. Portland, OR: Areopagitica Press, 1988.

Woods, David. "A Misunderstood Monogram: Ricimer or Severus?" *Hermathena* 172 (Summer 2002): 5–21.

Woolf, Greg. *Becoming Roman: The Origins of Provincial Civilization in Gaul*. Cambridge: Cambridge University Press 1998.

Tales of the Barbarians: Ethnography and Empire in the Roman West. Malden, MA, and Oxford: Wiley-Blackwell Publishers, 2011.

Yang, Shao-yun. "'What Do Barbarians Know of Gratitude' – The Stereotype of Barbarian Perfidy and Its Uses in Tang Foreign Policy Rhetoric." *Tang Studies* 31 (2013): 28–74.

"Reinventing the Barbarian: Rhetorical and Philosophical Uses of the *Yi-Di* in Mid-Imperial China, 600–1300." PhD diss., University of California, Berkeley, 2014.

"'Their Lands Are Peripheral and Their *Qi* Is Blocked up': The Uses of Environmental Determinism in Han and Tang Chinese Interpretations of the 'Barbarians'." In *The Routledge Handbook of Identity and the Environment in the Classical and Medieval Worlds*, edited by Rebecca Kennedy and Molly Jones-Lewis, 390–412. London: Routledge, 2016.

Ye Lang 叶朗. "Zhonghua wenming de kaifang xing he baorong xing" 中华文明的开放性和包容性. *Journal of Peking Unviersity* 北京大学学报 (Philosophy and Social Sciences 哲学社会科版) 51, No. 2 (Mar. 2014): 5–10.

Yu, Anthony C. "History, Fiction, and the Reading of Chinese Narrative." *Chinese Literature: Essays, Articles, Reviews (CLEAR)* 10, No. 1/2 (Jul. 1988): 1–19.

Yü, Ying-shih. "Han Foreign Relations." In *The Cambridge History of China, Vol. 1: The Ch'in and Han Empires, 221 BC–AD 220*, edited by Denis Twitchett and Michael Loewe, 377–462. Cambridge: Cambridge University Press, 2006.

"Reflections on Chinese Historical Thinking." In *Chinese History and Culture: Seventeenth Century through Twentieth Century*, edited by Ying-shih Yü et al., 294–316. New York: Columbia University Press, 2016.

Zhu Dawei 朱大渭. "*Jin shu* de pingjia yu yanjiu" 晋书的评价与研究. *Journal of Historiography* 史学史研究 100, No. 4 (2000): 44–52.

Index

Gunthamund, 215
Guoyu 國語, 48, 86, 92, 116

Han Anguo 韓安國, 54
Han shu 漢書. *See* Ban Gu
Han Wudi 漢武帝, 124, 128, 243, 280
Han Zhao 漢趙 dynasty. *See* Former Zhao
  dynasty
Han 漢 as ethnonym, 12, 18, 21, 98, 120,
    134–36, 211, 271, 315, 319
Han 漢 dynasty, 3, 5, 9–12, 16, 18, 22, 27, 48,
    59–60, 74, 89–90, 94, 116, 119–21,
    123, 127, 135, 137, 146, 150, 169, 190,
    206, 211, 247, 250–51, 269, 279–81,
    289–90, 315, 317, 319, 322
  Eastern Han, 53, 88, 123
  fall of, 9–10
  political legacy of, 12, 272–73, 279–81, 288
  political legitimacy during, 269–70
Hecataeus, 32, 57
Helian Bobo 赫連勃勃, 252, 288–90, 302
  characterization of, 252–53
Hellenistic period, 34, 111
Hephthalites, 156, 162, 173, 212
heqin 和親, 120, 135, 280
Heracles, 56–58, 159
Hercules, 262
Hermineric, 321
Herodian, historian, 265
Herodian, Roman commander, 143
Herodotus, 1–2, 5, 21, 31–32, 34–38, 44, 48,
    50, 56–60, 65–68, 78, 81, 92–93, 100,
    103, 106–12, 120, 126, 128, 139–40,
    142, 144, 146, 148, 155–56, 159,
    177–78, 191–92, 195, 205–6, 227–28,
    274, 306, 329–30, 332
  ethnography of Persia of, 37–38
  impact on later historiography of,
    329–30
Heruli, 132, 141–43, 155, 166–67, 183, 212,
    219–20, 233
Hilderic, 215–18, 290–92, 320
  characterization of, 216–17
Hippocrates, 33, 65, 67
  Airs, Waters, Places, 33, 65–66
Historia Augusta, 261, 265
historiography
  in ancient China. *See* dynastic history
  characterization in
    in Chinese historiography, 209–10
    in Greco-Roman historiography, 209–10
  classicizing historiography, 16, 21–22
    of Procopius. *See* Procopius
  comparative approaches to, 6
  under early Tang dynasty, 135–37, 211

as ideological expression, 25–26
in pre-imperial China, 48–50
shared features of in Greece/Rome and China,
    13–15
speeches in Greco-Roman and Chinese
    historiography, 274–77
as vehicle for ethnographic discourse,
    35–37
Homer, 29–31, 40–41, 92, 97, 103, 128, 140,
    146, 325, 329–30
  as early ethnography, 29–32
  Iliad, 30, 41–42, 57, 97, 149
  impact on later historiography of, 329–30
  Odyssey, 29–32
Honorius, 176, 179, 266, 321
Hou Han shu 後漢書. *See* Fan Ye
Hu 胡, 15, 76, 85, 320
  as collective term for non-Chinese, 26, 98,
    154, 164, 209, 283, 320
Huainanzi 淮南子, 75, 85, 122–23
Huang Fushi 皇甫湜, 273
huangdi 皇帝, 267
Huhanye 呼韓邪, 120, 278–79
humanitas, 81, 104, 107, 112, 329
Huneric, 215–16, 292, 320–21
  characterization of, 215
Huns, 46, 100, 141, 155–56, 159, 161, 177,
    207, 229, 233, 236, 295
Hyperboreans, 31

Iazyges, 124
identity
  definition of, 25
Ildibad, 234
Iliad. *See* Homer
India, 5, 7, 32, 70
Indians, 44, 66, 112
Indulf, 236
Isaurians, 263
Isocrates, 97, 109–11
Italians, 180, 205, 224, 232, 234, 296–98,
    301
Italy, 9–12, 78, 138, 295–302, 309, 316, 327
  as birthplace of Roman emperors, 264–67
  conclusion of wars in, 235–36
  East Roman reconquest of, 223
  Frankish invasion of, 183
  Gothic rule over, 299–303, 305–7
  Roman expansion beyond, 68
  Theoderic's rule over, 223–25
  Totila's rule over, 233–35
  Visigothic invasion of, 179

Jews, 35, 91, 159
Jiang Tong 江統, 149–51